GUMPTION

"Man Overboard!"

Aboard the destroyer John R. Craig en route to the Formosa Strait our division clashed with another typhoon. This one was severe with winds up to 90 knots and seas up to 55 feet. I had the 1200-1600 watch, and we had to "button down" the bridge because we were taking green water even up at that level. It was difficult standing on the bridge's wet and slippery deck. The inclinometer hit 55 degrees in one roll. We were all trying to right the ole' John R, and the skipper was on the bridge offering advice to "stay out of the trough."

The XO entered the bridge with a big smile proclaiming that "this is destroyer duty at its best" when we received a call that one of the life rafts on the 02 Deck was working loose and might go over the side if not secured. No one had been allowed on the open deck spaces. The captain ordered to get someone out on the 02 Deck to tie down the raft. A few minutes later we got the dreaded call, "Man Overboard! Starboard Side!"

My immediate reaction was to bring the ship back on its track to locate the crewman swept over the side. It was the standard procedure in the Navy that increased the probability of recovering a lost shipmate.

The ship came around and we miraculously found Roy Dunham, our First Lieutenant, but he was in trouble. He had bounced off the gunwale before hit-ting the water, and his back had been broken. He was obviously hurt and having difficulty. He clutched a life ring thrown at him by the man who accompanied him on deck. A petty officer tethered himself to the ship with a line, jumped into the water, swam to Dunham and maneuvered him toward the ship's side.

As I watched this life and death drama unfold, with the wind and waves lashing my ship, many thoughts ran through my mind, My concern was with the fate of my shipmate, and I pondered the risk of the decision to turn the ship around, exposing our broadside to the mountainous onslaught of the crushing waves. As heavy as those notions were, a thought flashed through my mind—I was sure a long way from Wabash College . . .

GUMPTION

MY LIFE - MY WORDS

WILLIAM THOMPSON

ISBN 145385357X
EAN-13 9781453853573
Manufactured in the United States of America

Dedicated to Zum (née Dorothy Elizabeth zum Buttel)
my stalwart partner for six decades and still counting.

She gave new meaning to the word Gumption.

Table of Contents

Acknowledgments

I am indebted to: Rear Admiral **Roberta (Bobbie) Louise Hazard**, USN (Retired) for astute guidance and editorship in reading the first drafts of all chapters and especially for exhibiting superb tack and patience with the author.

Dale Flanagan, a professional editor and journalist, for final editing and proofreading, Dale and I have become good friends in this process plus monitoring his son Ensign Tom's progress through flight training at Pensacola, FL.

Senior Chief **Don Dupuis**, USN (Retired), Director, Administration and Human Resources for the U. S. Navy Memorial Foundation, for his assistance in "bird dogging" various items incidental to these memoirs.

Senior Chief **Robert Carlisle**, USN (Retired) for his longtime friendship since my time as CHINFO and his expertise and quick response to my requests for photographic assistance.

Retired Captain **Brayton Harris**, author of scores of books and a publisher, who in my estimation was one of the Navy's best public affairs officers, for his counsel and advice on publishing this memoir.

Commander **Toby Marquez**, USN (Ret.) and his wife Carol Ann for work on photography and related design to the dust cover.

To my family, **Zum, Stevii** and husband **Randy, Craig,** and **Brian** for help throughout the entire project and especially for the nudges and prods.

Bravo Zulu!! (Well Done)

Introduction

This autobiography was written for my family and friends. Its pages welcome others who may turn them. I do not harbor an impression that my life has been any more significant than others. But I have had a propensity for getting into some interesting situations. My life was much more expansive than I ever expected or even imagined. I was a part of what has now come to be called the *Greatest Generation.* I am proud to be among those who brought our country and the world through World War II and helped to provide the sustaining leadership for our nation during the concluding years of the 20th Century. I was involved in, or on the periphery of, some of the pinnacle events of our time. What is important here is that I was there. I knew some of the key players by being associated with them professionally or socially. This manuscript may even ease the anxiety of some family members concerned about the strange mannerisms or faraway stares that I manifested at times.

This writing endeavor has provoked research into family background and genealogy that may prove helpful to others. It provided pleasurable excursions into the past and the opportunity to explore the sometimes arduous task my parents had with my development and maturing years. Perhaps it is too simplistic to ask, "What better way to stroke one's ego or find reasons to be humble, than to dwell on and delve into one's almost entire life?"

It was difficult at times to not be pedant in descriptions of events because this memoir was not written solely for my immediate family who shared with me our nautical and federal service environments. They are included in many of the experiences related here. Still I tried to focus on a distant but non-fictitious audience situated in Green Bay, Wisconsin, my hometown at the time of my enlistment in the Navy. Green Bay was also home to my deceased sister, Betty, and her husband, Lee LaHaye, and their relatively large, wonderful family (eight children) plus some friends of high school days. Amid my verbal wanderings, I hasten to add that I am proud of my heritage and the values that apparently continue to be instilled into youngsters in that area. Keeping this text in perspective, it must be said that I, like many others, *joined the Navy to see the world.* I was eager to deploy from Wisconsin's Fox River Valley for new adventures. Sixty-plus years later, I continue to enjoy those sojourns and the voyages offered by both the sea and my life.

Preface

When I was about 13 years old, my family was living with my grandfather who was a self-made man with a third-grade education and had been working since age 10, farming, driving teams of work horses, logging and finally a business man. He couldn't handle the situation of this teenager lounging around the house and one day lost patience, proclaiming, "Billy, you will never amount to anything unless you get some gumption and some business in your head" I didn't know the definition of "gumption" but got the general idea that I was to look occupied in the presence of Gramp. I never forgot his admonition and have perpetuated it through several generations. Besides, it is a nice word—unobtrusive and yet forceful.

Bill Thompson

First of Flights

As the old saying goes, "I was very young when I was born." The fact that I was born two months early attests to that. A second folksy saying, "I was just a small boy when I was born," applies as well. When my mother, Viola Ellen Woods Thompson, delivered me on September 16, 1922, I weighed in at four-and-a-quarter pounds.

My name was registered in the city of Escanaba, Michigan in Delta County as William Thompson—no middle name. I was obviously named for my father, Waino (Finnish for William) Alexander Thompson. With their firstborn asleep in an incubator, primary concerns surrounded my survival and my young mother's recovery from an infection following a difficult pregnancy. Choosing a middle name for me was a lesser priority. However, one or both had stated informally that my middle name should be John in honor of our family doctor who was thought to have performed well in handling my premature birth. If I had been consulted, I would have certainly accepted the name John.

As things go in tense situations, the name John was not entered on the birth certificate but did appear on a baptismal record. So I was known as William John until the day I enlisted in the Navy 20 years later and a birth certificate was required. Then I became William (no middle name) Thompson or William (nmn) Thompson. To the day she died—21 years after I entered the Navy—Mother was concerned about whatever happened to John. In fact, at mid-career, the officer register for the U.S. Navy contained 17 William Thompsons of varying ranks, but I was the only one without a middle initial. So I had some distinctive feelings about it all. Perhaps there was a lack of typical formal name appeal, but I wasn't mailed the wrong Navy orders or laundry bills.

First home of residence

Escanaba was a typical Upper Peninsula small town of about 10,000 situated on Little Bay de Noc, an extremity of Green Bay that is a land carving of Lake Michigan. Escanaba existed because of its docks; long iron ore boats were loaded there daily fed by seemingly endless railroad trains. They carried ore pulled out of the Upper Peninsula mining sectors stretching as far west as Minnesota. It was rugged country inhabited by people who knew about survival.

Escanaba, an Indian name, had two main thoroughfares. The most important was Ludington Avenue, which was "Main Street." All the important businesses were housed there such as the Fair Store, the city's department store, the Ford dealer, the Escanaba Daily Press, the Escanaba First National Bank, a few drug stores, a Woolworth's, some pool halls and 20 or so saloons. It was a wide street, more typical of western locales, which led into a broad scenic view of the harbor, Little Bay de Noc, and Ludington Park, a community picnic and recreation area. My father played tennis at Ludington Park where I remember swings and slides for the town's children. There were several slides of varying heights. The big one captivated me. I managed to fall off of it one day when fooling around, probably showing off for some blue eyed cutie who was romping around in ruffled bloomers. My parents were concerned about a possible head injury, and it probably caused my youthful forgetfulness, short retention span and some of those "Cs" and "Ds" on later report cards.

Ludington Park also had a swimming beach that was popular for a couple of months during the summer. During the dog days of late August folks voluntarily stayed away. After Labor Day, fall was upon us and winter was not too distant, so Escanaba had a short swimming season. I remember the beach as one of my "Waterloos." I once witnessed a person being hauled onto the beach where futile attempts were made to revive him. The trauma of that event was indelibly inscribed in my mind. It was magnified by another "Waterloo" incident which occurred during a swimming class when I was seized by fear of jumping into water about nose deep. Afterward, I was a non-swimmer until age 20. I missed a lot of fun in my adolescent days because many of my friends enjoyed swimming. They kindly referred to me as a "heck of a wader." Then the Navy insisted that I get acquainted with water as part of survival training. I can't say that I ever developed an affinity for water except for baths, showers or occasionally as a mix with Scotch Whiskey.

Delta County's Poor Farm

The other primary street in Escanaba was Stevenson Avenue which ran north and south, perpendicular to Ludington and heading up to the County Poor Farm, where my father's friend Scotty was the cook. A little farther up the road was the township of Wells and still farther—a total of five miles—was Gladstone, a little town of about 5,000. Gladstone's high school was the arch rival of Escanaba High School, and the annual football battle was staged on November 11, Armistice Day. We lived on Stevenson Avenue for a few years in a three-bedroom flat. It was nice for my father because his office at a branch of Swift & Company was only seven or eight blocks away on that same avenue. He was manager of the office that distributed Swift's products, primarily meats, to the eastern half of upper Michigan. Across the street and a block to the south of our nest were the city's car barns that housed the streetcars that traversed Ludington and Stevenson Avenues.

Throughout the years I have had some fond reflections about the Delta County Poor Farm, but I didn't fully realize the social implications of its purpose. It was a place where my brother Don and I were greeted with warmth and enthusiasm by the resident caretakers and Scotty, the cook. On our visits we were fed well and had the opportunity to see farm life in living color: slopping the pigs, milking the cows, petting the soft noses of the big plow horses and watching the rooster chase the hens around the barnyard. We had almost free roam of the facilities but didn't stray far from the kitchen and Scotty, a short, peg legged Scotsman with the brogue from "Shanty Shannon." The residents of the county project were mostly elderly men, obviously unemployed, down on their luck (I wonder where the poor women went), and who slept on cots in a dormitory. These folks would attempt to talk with us, but we were instructed to keep our distance. That was probably good advice despite those poor elderly souls cherishing the opportunity to talk with youngsters. They worked the farm during the day helping to sustain its existence. All in all, the Delta County Poor Farm was a good place to visit but not a nice place to live. And it was probably a good customer of Swift's.

Fortified by pictures in the family album, my earliest recollection is that we lived on 11th Street in a stucco house set relatively far back from the street. There 21 months after my initial appearance¬, my one and only brother, Donald Adolph, stepped onto center stage on June 20, 1924, crowding me from that favored position. It wasn't until 15 or so years later I finally realized he was a pretty good fellow and a good friend. I am fortunate to have had such a fine person for a brother. Our respective careers brought us to the same areas so we could always communicate, visit and stay in touch.

I don't know the rationale or derivation of Don's first name, but his second moniker, Adolph, honored my father's brother, Adolph Tomberg. My father's mother died at age 23 in 1904 shortly after giving birth to her third son Rudolph, who died two months later. Adolph was subsequently adopted by his mother's sister, Anna Besonen Tomberg, and her husband, Isaac Tomberg. I never learned of the circumstances, but Dad lived with his father for some time until the latter disappeared. He was believed to have been lost in a mine fire where he was employed. Dad then lived with his maternal grandparents until they became too old to care for a youngster. He then moved in with the Tombergs before he departed for college at Lansing, Michigan. Anna Tomberg was a wonderful, large Finnish woman whom we always referred to as "Auntie." But Dad remained a Thompson.

My father was born on Memorial Day May 30, 1900, in Ishpeming, Michigan, a Finnish settlement in mining country near Lake Superior and the major port city Marquette, Michigan. I remember a wintertime trip with Dad and Don to Ishpeming when I was 5 or 6 years old. The snowdrifts were up to the top of the telephone poles, and pathways to the houses were like narrow caverns. Among other things I remember about Auntie was her baking. The breads and coffeecakes were delicious, as were her pasties, meat and potato pies and a Finnish specialty. I later learned that pasties originated in Cornwall, England, and are known in some areas as Cornish Pasties. Auntie always had a big pot of coffee on the stove. The Finns seemed to spend most of their time at the table, eating a meal or dunking coffeecake into very sweet coffee between meals. Auntie apparently smoked a pipe until her dying day. I was told that it "kept her regular." I recall that after breakfast each day she would disappear into the basement and light up. She loved us so, showing affection at every opportunity with hugs and gushes. In between she was always kind, even in her twilight years, when I was in my twenties, and she was living out the last of her life with Adolph (Tom) and his wife Esther Tomberg in Chicago. She lived to be 84, dying in 1957.

Brother Don and I have done some cursory genealogy on our paternal side but have been stymied, principally because Thompson is not a Finnish name. If we were named in true Finnish fashion, we and everyone else would undoubtedly have had a difficult time pronouncing it. Finnish is a strange and intricate language. Thompson is basically of English or Scottish origin, but a clue to our puzzle is that the name was also common in Sweden. My wife Dorothy and I have visited Helsinki, the capital of Finland, several times. Our investigations with the locals reveal that Sweden dominated Finland for at least a century. To this day the street signs in Helsinki are displayed in both languages. So our background is definitely Finnish, but the name is obviously Swedish borne.

Don was born in a house on Ashland Avenue in Green Bay, Wisconsin, that was the home of my maternal grandparents. Mother— fearing another calamitous birth—chose to return to her parents' home and the family physician, Dr. Knox, for the delivery. In those days the great majority of deliveries were done at the home. In our 11 years in Escanaba, we lived in five different houses. I suppose a growing family needing more room necessitated some of the moves, but the last was probably to escape the outstretched palm of the landlord and mounting bills. We started out in a small bungalow on 11th Street, then to a first floor flat with a basement on 17th Street where the third sibling, Elizabeth Charmain Thompson, took over the household on June 28, 1928. She became her Daddy's favorite. In my early years of fatherhood, I learned that was part of the package; embracing a baby girl was a supreme delight. We moved to a bigger flat on Stevenson Avenue and then to our first single family dwelling on Third Street across from Washington Elementary

School where I made my acting debut.

I hastily add that it was a short-lived career during the fifth grade. I was selected to be an End Man in a minstrel show, complete with burnt-cork cosmetics, white gloves and a top hat. The show was a huge success! We opened in the school basement, and it was so well received, we next appeared before the Parent-Teachers Association (PTA). This must have been a joint venture between the teachers and parents because Mother helped make costumes for the participants. Our whole household became involved with top hats and tails littering the living and dining rooms, and all our daily schedules oriented to the minstrel show. The reviews must have been fantastic, even making the Escanaba Daily Press. We moved on to the ultimate in Escanaba stage productions: we played before the Escanaba Post of the American Legion at the ODD Fellows Auditorium. This pinnacle of amateur theatrics was probably arranged by my mother prevailing upon my father who was a Legionnaire. He had considerable clout in town because he was the coach and general manager of the Escanaba Rangers, a semi-pro football team.

I can't remember the joke the interlocutor set me up for, but I do remember that I had to do my "shtick" and sing a song. Unfortunately, the teacher-director-stage manager-playwright didn't want me to sing. She was my fifth grade teacher and had heard me sing before. So it was arranged that the son of the coach and general manager of the Escanaba Rangers would deliver a monologue of *A Shanty in Old Shanty Town* ... "and the roof was so slanty, it touches the ground." I can deliver it as well today as I did in 1932. I haven't lost a beat or a step, and it continues as a ... monologue.

As things go in show business—probably because I couldn't handle success at such a young age, and as I was casting about for other fields to conquer—I fell in love. My mother probably warned me, but I couldn't resist the charms of one of our dancers, Lila Jean Funk, a third grader. She was extremely attractive in her tutus and had me chalking her name on the sidewalks of Escanaba. It was a short-lived romance because her father, who ran the White Tavern diner on Ludington Avenue, thought I was too old for Lila Jean. I always thought she would have had a great career on Broadway, and I imagine to this day that she has probably been a Rockette at Rockefeller Center.

I recall my first foray into politics was in the 1928 presidential election when I campaigned in the alleys of Escanaba where we played "Kick the Can," proclaiming, "Herbert Hoover will live in the White House, and Al Smith will live in a garbage can." I doubt if I swung any votes to Mr. Hoover, the candidate from California, but he did defeat Mr. Smith, the governor of New York. My proclamations usually ended in a fight, and I would go home with a bloody nose, or the other kid would suffer the same consequence. My next realization of political force was after the 1932 presidential election in which Franklin D. Roosevelt was elected to his first of four terms. The immediate result was the repeal of the Prohibition Act fulfilling one of Mr. Roosevelt's campaign promises. That meant the sale of alcoholic beverages was legal, and the saloons in Escanaba were legalized. It didn't make much sense to me, but I can remember there was joy in Escanaba's streets. It had the endorsement of my father and many of his friends. I feel sure that several of them toasted the event.

As Swift's branch manager, my father was well paid and respected in Escanaba. One of the bonuses of the job was a company car: a cherry red Ford coupe with the company's logo on each door. We always knew his whereabouts because the red coupe was parked nearby. When we were 5 or 6, he would take Don and me for rides before or after dinner. He would let me "drive" or at least steer the car when I reached age 6 or 7. As a father he tried to instill a sense of independence in us. That trait reflected his childhood when he obviously spent much time alone or at least did not have parental dominance. While his father was supposedly killed in a mining fire in Ishpeming, that belief evaporated 15 to 20 years later when his father, Alexander, showed up in Escanaba. He told his eldest son that he had taken the opportunity provided by the fire to escape from Ishpeming and prospect for gold in Alaska. I don't know the details because my parents did not communicate with their children about family problems. I do know that Dad was extremely upset about the resurrection of his father. He apparently told him that he could not accept him nor forgive his selfishness and irresponsibility. Alexander went away the same day he appeared in Escanaba. He later died in Philadelphia in 1928 at age 50. His father's reappearance must have been a shocking event in my dad's life. I don't know if I would have handled it in the

same manner. But Dad was tough-minded and personified the traits of absolute stubbornness and high principles often characterized by Finnish people.

About my Dad

Dad was also an intelligent man, graduating from high school at age 15. He
was an accountant, well-read, breezed through crossword puzzles and devoured the Chicago Tribune that was picked up each day at the Chicago and
North Western rail depot. He spent about three months in the Army in World
War I but did not get off the Michigan State University campus. Michigan
State in those days was a state agricultural school. One of his first jobs was as
a bookkeeper for Swift in Escanaba. His boss was Leon Woods who had an
attractive daughter, Viola Ellen. Waino and Viola became acquainted much to
the distraction of her father. Leon must have thought the situation was rectified when he was dispatched by Swift headquarters to head the Green Bay
office, a large plum in the Swift operating structure. Dad was "fleeted up" to
be in charge of the Escanaba branch at the very young age of 20. Although
Viola departed the Escanaba environs with her family, she soon returned
alone to wed Waino on February 25, 1922. Leon was not pleased with this
turn of events citing only the normal fatherly protective stance that "no man
is good enough for my daughter."

Dad was a good athlete, even though not a big man, only about 5' 9". He
was interested in all types of athletics and could recite statistics and records
across the broad spectrum of sports. He played football in high school and
at Michigan State which at that time was Michigan State A&M. He told me he
had played against The Gipper, George Gipp, of Notre Dame. When Knute
Rockne, Notre Dame's immortal football coach, was killed in an airplane
crash in 1931, I could tell Dad was upset, and Mom said he cried "very hard."
Rockney was an institution, and I think Dad tried to emulate him. He directed
me toward an interest in athletics and participation in sports. He was proud
of what he saw me accomplish which was not much. He showed up at some
of my freshman high school games and was vociferous about coaching me
during and after the games. It's unfortunate he didn't live to see his youngest
son Don perform because Don was a better athlete than I.

Dad had Don and I scrimmaging together on our front lawns, and he drilled us. I recall our lawns were not the greenest, particularly in the fall months when they were mostly mud. He bought season tickets for the high school football and basketball games for me, and I regularly attended games with him or alone at a very young age. In 1932 I saw Ralph Metcalf, a sprinter from Marquette University and an Olympic star, run an exhibition 100 yard dash during an Escanaba High School track meet. Many years later when I was a Navy Flag Officer, I met Metcalf, a U.S. Congressman, and recalled the incident. He remembered "going to Escanaba." My first success in sports was in the sixth grade when I entered my first track meet and placed second in a citywide meet in the hop, step and jump event. Although Dad was proud of me, he didn't overplay it. I remember his comment that if I had tried a little harder, "jumped another inch or so," I would have gotten the blue ribbon.

The Great Depression that engulfed the United States and spread throughout the entire world took its toll on the young Thompson family. Nationwide unemployment reached devastating proportions (33%), and we were victims of that onslaught. Swift & Company decided to close the Escanaba office, and Dad was out of a job. He worked for awhile in the program setting up the new Michigan state sales tax, but that job was phased out. We moved into a duplex on 14th Street, living there for about a year and a half. The family was broke and in desperation "broke camp." Aunt Dodi, Mother's sister, drove to Escanaba in her Essex coupe with a rumble seat and transported Mother and her three kids to Green Bay in June 1934 to live with her parents. Dad closed up the house, stored the furniture and went to Chicago where he worked with Adolph as an accountant.

Unfortunately closing this chapter, I cannot ignore one of the primary reasons for the demise of a once happy, prosperous Bill Thompson family. Dad had a problem with alcohol. I don't know if he was an alcoholic, or if he became one later. I don't have any knowledge of his being treated for alcoholism. Only once did I see him in a condition of drunkenness. It upset me considerably; that was the only time I ever saw him in an unstable state. I learned later that Mother was distraught over his situation, and it precipitated our move to Green Bay. Alcoholism may be a disease and hereditary, but looking back 55 to 70 years, I think Waino Alexander's childhood background contributed to his frailties. His mother dying when he was 5-years old, being abandoned by his father and being reared by grandparents and Auntie, who, I imagine, did their best. Everything together had a telling impact.

I know that the culture existing in Michigan's Upper Peninsula and in Wisconsin was centered around churches and social clubs. Especially for men, alcohol was characteristic of groups such as the Moose, Elks, ODD Fellows, and then there were the saloons, bars and taverns. Most men were blue-collar laborers who worked long hours in unpleasant situations especially in the mines of the Upper Peninsula. Many men stopped in the local pub on their way home from work for a couple of beers or a few shots of whiskey. Often they brought home a bucket of beer to share with their spouses. There was no television, and radio was in its infancy as was the motion picture industry. Human beings are social animals, and for many, the local bars were the focal point of their society.

I doubt if Waino was addicted to alcohol, but he was apparently attracted to it and enjoyed the male camaraderie afforded by the local pub. For many years I remained confused by his deportment and could not understand the situation. I was 11-years old when those events overtook us. I know I missed him, or at least his presence, and am convinced that I would have benefited from his guidance, counsel and authority.

Life by the Bay

For a few months in the summer of 1934, we lived on Clay Street on the East Side of Green Bay until Gramp and Gram (my mother's parents, Leon and Elizabeth Johnson Wood) moved to 425 North Ashland Avenue. Coincidentally, it was across the street from where they had previously lived and where Don, my brother, was born. On our arrival in Green Bay, my grandparents probably had a few anxious moments with a house full of family and questions about the future. Uncle Neil, their youngest son, was still at home and seeking employment. Aunt Dodi, Mom's younger sister, and her husband, Fred Carlson, had also been living under their roof. When we visited Green Bay the previous summer, Dodi gave birth to Cousin Ronnie, a cute towhead, in the front bedroom of the Clay Street flat. Dr. Knox was again the attending physician. Fred, who had emigrated from Sweden, worked on boats—yachts, ore boats, whatever floated, particularly on the Great Lakes. In 1934 he found a job as a deck hand on an ore boat that plied the Great Lakes. He, Dodi and Ronnie left Green Bay to reestablish housekeeping in Manitowoc.

For sure, the Wood family was feeling the effects of the Great Depression. Many other families were going through the same situation, somewhat reminiscent of the American classic *The Grapes of Wrath* written by John Steinbeck and the subsequent movie. The Wood family was not about to be identified as "Okies" or drifters. They continued to exhibit a great sense of family pride and cohesiveness and were not lured to go west to California. Both Gramp and Gram were native to Wisconsin. Gramp Leon was born in Oshkosh and Gram Elizabeth in Winnieconnie, a short distance away.

President Roosevelt had started his *Alphabet Soup* depression recovery programs, so named because of their acronyms—National Recovery Act (NRA), Works Progress Administration (WPA), Public Works Administration (PWA) ,Civilian Conservation Corps (CCC), and Social Security. Many federal and public buildings constructed then and standing today are evidence of the partial success of the President's programs. Unemployment rates in the late 1930s were over 17%, which gave substance to the argument that President Roosevelt's pump priming programs were not as effective as predicted. In fact, there is a strong argument that they contributed to the outlook lingering 80 years later that *"big government will take care of you"* in its well-established welfare state. Some believed that Roosevelt did not bring the country out of the Great Depression as other pundits averred. The country largely rose from those economic depths because of World War II and its demand for goods and high productivity.

My grandparents left Green Bay after Don's birth in 1924 to live in Manitowoc where Gramp oversaw Swift & Company's operations. Mom and we kids spent a good part of the summers there with our grandparents. We had fond memories of their home at 8 River Drive, overlooking a valley where the Manitowoc River flowed and the site for the city's primary industry, shipbuilding. Our frequent visits with the grandparents were always pleasant. I recall spending a number of Christmas vacations with them. Our grandparents were the storybook type—loving, caring and kind. They spoiled us rotten.

Mom was obviously close to her parents and the entire family. She was the eldest of four children. Her brother Lee was the next oldest, and he was an excellent mechanic. Gramp financed a couple of business ventures for him. A service garage was one of them, but they all failed because Lee was not an efficient businessman. He too had a problem with alcohol. He had several children we knew during our pre-teens, but they became lost in life's ensuing shuffle. I later learned that Lee ultimately lived and died in Chicago. His marriage broke up, and the children remained primarily in the Manitowoc area.

Neil was Mom's second sibling, and I knew him well. Neil worked most of his life as a sausage maker for Reimers Meat Market in Green Bay. He was kind to us kids. He managed to give me an allowance of 10 or 15 cents a week from his meager income providing me with movie money. He also took me to old City Stadium for my first glimpses of the Green Bay Packers. He fell in love with and married a girl named Pearl who became afflicted with a disease that had a catatonic effect. They had two children, a boy Wally and a girl. Neil died of a cardiac arrest when I was stationed at the Navy Pre-Flight School in Ottumwa, Iowa, in 1946. I was able to get home for his funeral flying to Green Bay in a Navy T-6/SNJ. Pearl was institutionalized and died a few years later.

Dorothy, or "Dodie," was the youngest of the Woods' children. Born on Valentine's Day in 1911 in Escanaba, she was the closest relative I had, and we were friends over those long years. She was always kind and considerate of Don, Betty and me. I guess the nicest thing I can say is that she was a "real aunt" and one of my favorite people. She and her husband, Fred Carlson, reared their son Ronnie in Manitowoc. When he later headed west to settle in San Diego, they followed. Fred did maintenance work on yachts in San Diego harbors and provided a comfortable living. They lived in nearby Santee until their deaths. Dodie died in 1998 and Fred in 2002.

Home of the Green Bay Packers

Compared to Escanaba, Green Bay was a sprawling industrial metropolis with its 40,000 population, two high schools, the Fox River, a "real" professional football team, a few cheese factories and two or three paper mills. It has been said that Green Bay exports three products: professional football, cheese and toilet paper. During bad Packer seasons their brand of play was said to support the city's third industry. But the "Pack" has brought worldwide attention and fame to Green Bay by far the smallest city represented in the National Football League (NFL). Being one of the first teams to play in the then fledgling professional football organization, the team is synonymous with the NFL that today is recognized as the most outstanding success in professional sports.

Naturally, the well-being of the Packers monopolized about 90% of the conversation in town, and its youngsters idolized the players. As a lad, I delivered newspapers. The distribution headquarters, Bosses' News Stand, was next to the Astor Hotel, the domicile of the manly Packers during the season. That gave me the opportunity to get a good look at the heroes. The days of

Don Hutson, Arnie Herber and Cecil Isbell still have instant replay in my mind, and I wasn't different than other town worshippers. It wasn't until I was in the Navy, more worldly, with broader horizons, that I realized God didn't wear a Green and Gold sweat suit. I had learned there were a few other interesting things in life besides the Packers' league standing and the gossip about the players' private lives which was almost always gross exaggeration.

My seven years in Green Bay were formative, fulfilling, exhilarating and yet somewhat disappointing. There were flashes of success and failure, anxiety, sadness and uncertainty. Those were adolescent growing up years, not any tougher than those faced by the average teenager. I was aware that we were more fortunate than some and credit my mother for keeping the family together and struggling through extremely difficult times. For me it was a difficult adjustment to be without a father with his guidance and discipline. Transitioning to living with a loving but domineering grandfather in a new town and new neighborhood and attending a new school was much more intense than I anticipated. The house was a duplex with three bedrooms and an attic. Gram and Gramp had the master bedroom; Uncle Neil, still a bachelor living at home, had the second bedroom, and my mother occupied the third. Betty roomed with Mom, and Don and I slept in the attic on a fold-down sofa bed. It wasn't bad, except for freezing in the winter and steaming in the summer! However, once in a while when it was considered too cold, we could sleep on a cot in Mom's room. In the summer the front porch was our haven.

Gram was one of the great ladies in my young lifetime. She had an endless supply of love, hugs and time for her grandchildren. She was also sickly. Gramp was something else, a self-made man who was relatively un-educated, leaving school after the third grade. I've been told that my mother helped tutor him in reading, writing and arithmetic. He was born in 1890 and had worked since age 10 on farms, logging camps or in other physically demanding jobs. He was gruff but a cream puff under his rough exterior. He tried to keep Don and me busy washing and polishing his cars and doing odd jobs. I can still hear him say to me, "Billy, you never will amount to anything unless you get some gumption." At the time, I didn't check the dictionary, but I had a pretty good idea of what he meant. I understood that he was telling me to get off my butt and do things. "Gumption" has obviously remained with me since those now glorious days of washing Gramp's cars even finding its way into the title of this book.

When Gramp wasn't working on his cars or tinkering with something, he was in his leather rocking chair reading the *Green Bay Press-Gazette* or listening to the radio. In every season he had his slippers and a cardigan sweater on and his beloved dog Spot at his feet. I remember the smell of his favorite cigars permeating almost all the rooms. Gabriel Heater's voice brought us the evening news; Jack Benny, Fred Allen, Joe Penner and Eddy Cantor entertained us on the radio. Once in a while we kids got to listen to *Jack Armstrong, The All American Boy*, *Buck Rogers in the 25th Century* and *Little Orphan Annie*. As long as we lived with Gramp, it was a ritual for me, as well as Don and Betty, to kiss him good night. He was the patriarch of the family, and as long as he was paying the bills he demanded respect for his position. In fairness to him and his background, he well fulfilled his multiple roles. I will be forever grateful and fond of him.

Dad returned from Chicago disappointed. Times were tough, and he could make only enough to lodge and feed himself. He lived with us for a while but left because he couldn't get along with Gramp. I believe Gramp thought Dad could get some kind of a job, menial labor or the like, so he wouldn't be underfoot at home and could contribute to the family income. Dad lived with a friend of the family for a while and found only intermittent work. He tried Milwaukee and Chicago again, but it didn't go well. On May 26, 1937, Mom gave birth to another daughter, Viola Jeanne. It was great to have her in the household, and I often held and helped care for her. Tragically she died at only seven weeks old from Whooping Cough.

That was my first experience with death, but more soon intently followed. Gram died later that year of cancer, and on Thanksgiving Day, November 24, 1938, Dad died in the Fort Leonard Wood Veterans Hospital in Milwaukee. He had found employment in Manitowoc with a sausage works, and we planned to move there at the beginning of my sophomore year in high school. That didn't come about because he lost the job and became ill. He was hospitalized in Green Bay with carbuncles on his neck. By the time it was discovered that he had colon cancer, it was too late for treatment.

Mother made a big decision to leave the immediate protection provided by her father and move into the duplex next door at 423 North Ashland Avenue. Part of her rationale for moving was so Dad would have a place to recuperate when he left the hospital. Another important factor in the decision was that we had a roomer. Leona was a long time friend of Mom's, and she had a good, steady job as a clerk-secretary. Doubtless, her rental fee was a good part of the monthly payment to the Platten family, the landlords. Mom had been doing seamstress work to bring in a little money. She was good at it, making most of her clothing as well as Betty's and some for her sons as well. She also did some part-time clerking at Prange's Department Store that must have given her confidence things were going to get better.

Franklin Junior High School was formerly West High School. It was adjacent and connected to the new high school building, so additional shared space was available making a relatively large complex. I developed and cultivated an interest in journalism, starting in the seventh grade when I became a reporter for a column about junior high happenings. It appeared about ever week or so in the local *Green Bay Press-Gazette*. In my freshman year I started writing for the "Purple Parakeet," the fourth page of the West High School *Purple Parrot*, the school's bi-weekly. The name was undoubtedly derived from the school's purple and white colors. It didn't seem to jibe with the athletic team nickname, Wildcats, but then, why should it?

My experience with the *Purple Parrot* may reveal a side not normally attributed to my character. I continued to write for the paper, penned a sports column, became the sports editor, and in my senior year, the managing editor. Our faculty advisor, Miss Seaverson, and I had basic differences in the approach to the *Parrot*. I wanted it to relate solely to its student readership. She was inclined toward balance, so that it provided coverage and communication for the faculty as well. We had a heated disagreement, and I quit resigning with a bold statement that I would start my own paper. Which I did! With the help of a couple of other recalcitrants, we formed the *Verbal Burp*, a play on the *Purple Parrot*. Our motto was, "Why burp, when you can buy one?" It seemed funny at the time but doesn't do much for me as I write this. Our first issue was mimeographed on 8 X 14 inch yellow paper, believing that we exemplified true "yellow" journalism and that sounded very dramatic at the time. We sold it for 2 cents a copy at a school basketball game. It was widely read as witnessed by a sea of yellow paper in the stands even when the game was in progress. We were a journalistic success!

The content was pure nonsense, student gossip, sports (my column—"Shower Room Steam") and jokes. We had a net profit on Vol. I, No. 1. The next issue was even more successful because we had advertising. We enlisted the help of Larry Kitchen, the school athletic hero, who had the personality to go with the title of Director of Advertising. Some of the ads came from the *Purple Parrot* advertisers, and that worried the faculty advisor who was on a tight budget. We were officially warned to discontinue the "foolishness" or suffer the consequences. We continued to publish and were expelled. Aaah ... Freedom of the Press.

The forced recess was not prolonged, only half a day. We were summoned to appear before the super potentate headmaster, the Superintendent of Schools himself, in his downtown office. The message was to definitely desist, or we would not be recommended for college. Our last hurrah was bestowed by a columnist in the *Green Bay Press-Gazette* who stated, "With little fanfare, the *Verbal Burp* has died." He continued, lamenting that journalistic initiative was being stifled at good ole West High and so on.

Looking back on that episode indicates several things. If my father had been with the family, he undoubtedly would have advised or counseled me differently. My reactions were typical of me at that young age. If things got messed up, or the play action broke down, my philosophy was, "Put thine head down and plow straight ahead." Bullheadedness and stubbornness were innate. Because of responsibilities I have had in my Navy career, I learned to replace those two lesser traits with perseverance and persistence, tempered with a little tact and discretion—or, I hope so. And finally, the case is made for good teachers and leaders to direct and channel the energies and strong motivations of the young toward more beneficial goals and objectives. So be it.

Mr. Lee Delforge was my West High School history teacher and one whom I got to know much better while we served together in the Green Bay Summer Recreation Program in 1941. I grew to deeply respect him as a person who was concerned about the situation in Europe and the Far

East. His classes became more centered on current events than U.S. history. Because of the kind of man he was, I'm sure Mr. Delforge's major concern was that his students would soon be thrown into a war that our country would be compelled to enter. His trepidation was not only for the boys who would fight the war but also for other students who would bear the brunt of the war in other ways at home. He wanted us to know and understand what was happening, so we could better cope with it. In 1939 Germany invaded Poland igniting a conflict that would flame into World War II. Japan's militarist government had already leaped into an expansion mode and invaded China in 1936. The United States responded to Japan's attack on Pearl Harbor by declaring war on the Axis Powers—Japan, Germany and Italy—making the existing conflicts truly a world war. How prophetic was Mr. Delforge.

West High School

My high school experience was rewarding with lasting positive memories. I doubt if my children took as much with them from high school. My daughter "Stevie" probably would have because she was gregarious and an active participant in school activities. But she was in three schools in different cities for her high school years. It may have been that Green Bay West's graduating class of 1940 was such an outstanding group of youngsters who experienced many successes. The class did well academically and seemed to have more than its share of achievers. Athletically, West High was the Fox River Valley champion in football, basketball and track, plus runner-up in the state track meet and had an excellent wrestling team.

One of my great disappointments occurred at the state track meet in Madison when I faulted three times in the broad jump and was eliminated. I should have easily placed in the top five and could have won. Even a fifth place would have been good enough to carry the team to the championship. We finished second by 1/2 a point. I had won the Fox River Valley Conference broad jump the week before and the next week set the City Stadium record in Green Bay in our season finale against cross-city rival East High.

I had continued my hop, step and jump (now triple jump), and it developed into an interesting story. Green Bay had an extensive summer park (playground) program and among many things, it featured a Northeastern Wisconsin track meet. In my first year in Green Bay, I won the triple jump event and broke the record. The next year, I moved up an age level and repeated the previous year's performance breaking that record. Brother Don, following me, won the event and broke my previous year's record. A couple years later, he again broke my record. But at age 15, I put the record out of reach, jumping a couple inches short of 40 feet. Being aware of track and field minutiae, I knew that the number three man on the 1936 U.S. Olympic Team was a 43-foot jumper and that the 1940 Olympic trials were to be held in Milwaukee. I was confident that I could do 43 feet and even more with some coaching. My goal was to compete as an Olympian, and I had interested some in sponsoring my trip to Milwaukee. Unfortunately, Herr Hitler was pushing German machismo throughout Europe, and the 1940 Olympiad was canceled as well as the U.S. trials in Milwaukee. So much for athletic fame and glory.

By 1940 the world was chaotic and heading into a full blown war. Congress passed the Selective Service Act by one vote, and the draft started. Those of us who did not go to college were visiting recruiting offices and looking to enlist in order to get ahead of the draft. That option provided more choices such as aviation or some other exciting activity. Three chums, Bob "Strecky" Streckenbach and Don "Berky" Berkstrum (who were partners with me in the *Verbal Burp* venture) and Don Davidson joined the Army Air Corps. But I decided at the last moment not to go. Berky and Don became pilots, and Strecky, a navigator who was lost flying over Papua, New Guinea. Berkstrum was the only one of the trio to survive the war, and he continued flying as a career corporate pilot. I understand that Don was killed in a training accident.

With no financial resources available and no full scholarship (athletic) on the line, I did not go to college the first year after graduation from high school. I was destined to become a member of the workforce. Armed with a social security number, I knocked around at several menial tasks provided by the local employment office. My first job was at the Green Bay Drop Forge unloading steel from boxcars at the minimum wage of 35 cents an hour. That lasted until I latched onto the delivery/maintenance job at Golden's

Women's Apparel for $14.00 per week. I cleaned and vacuumed the place every morning, kept the windows shining and sparkling and delivered packages by bicycle. The deliveries went mainly to the affluent East Side of Green Bay. Golden's was an upscale dress shop, and its clientele came from as far away as northeastern Wisconsin and Michigan's Upper Peninsula. I next tried the Fairmont Creamery where I was a $15.00 a week employee working primarily in the ice cream making department. I didn't eat my way through the department, but being an ice cream freak, I'm sure I had my share.

Carl Zoll was a benefactor to me in my young days. He was a friend of the family and a product of early Green Bay and Wisconsin. Carl, like his brother Martin, was one of the original Green Bay Packers. Another brother, who was much younger, had gone to the University of Indiana as a football player and matriculated to the Packers in the late 1930s. Carl was also a professional wrestler until rock fell on his legs at his stone cutting plant. That ended his football and wrestling career. He was a physically strong man who believed the basics of life were survival, competition and giving an employer a day's work for a day's wages. He was kind to Don and me, providing some work at his plant, but it never really interested me. Stone cutting was dirty, dusty and heavy-duty work.

Carl had a hunting shack in northern Michigan where we enjoyed many days with him. Nearby was a tavern where "Rule, the World's Homeliest Man" hung out. We met Rule, a rather nice humble man with a small face, ruddy complexion, large nose, deep sunken eyes and no teeth. He had shaggy eyebrows and scraggly hair. Our impression was that Rule's face was just worn out. But he probably would have been a finalist in any "Homeliest Man" competition.

Like the stone he worked, Carl Zoll was a rock. He may not have had much influence on me and my character because when we first met, the die had been already cast for me. However, I appreciated him then and even more so in later life. He died of cancer during my last tour of duty in the Navy.

A Titan

When visiting with Larry Kitchen at the University of Wisconsin in Madison, he introduced me to Guy Sundt, the track coach. Coach Sundt agreed to accept me on a track scholarship, get my tuition paid —which wasn't much—and most importantly get me a job on campus. Larry was on a basketball scholarship and playing freshman ball. In those days freshmen were not permitted to play on varsity teams at least in the larger Division I schools. I was pleased at the prospect of going to THE University where there was an excellent journalism school and having a chance to compete for a spot on a Big Ten team. Plus, I would get some more advanced coaching that I didn't get in high school. I had a similar offer from the University of Minnesota the previous year, but things were not firm, and I did not feel comfortable about it.

A year at home working at assorted jobs convinced me that I should go to college; at least, I should get started before going into the Armed Services. The Selective Service had the draft underway, Herr Hitler had already begun his conquest of Europe, and President Roosevelt was having difficulty educating the American public about the dangers of isolationism. In retrospect, it was inevitable that the U.S. would get involved. It was fortunate for the world that this country did take up arms against Adolph Hitler's tyranny because Der Fuhrer almost succeeded in his conquest of Europe and beyond. President Roosevelt foresaw the German goals and possible results. He sensed the need of coming to the aid of England and Russia in order to save the world and the U.S. from domination by the Axis powers: Germany and Italy—Japan was to come but after December 7, 1941. If it hadn't been for President Roosevelt's vision, leadership and tenacity, we and our children might have been *goose-stepping* down our boulevards on Memorial Day. (Goose-stepping was marching with an exaggerated high stepping motion adopted by the German military and popularized by Hitler.)

In the course of saying farewell to some of the faculty and coaches at West High, the assistant track coach, Ed Boguski, told me to stop in at Oshkosh State Teachers College on the way Madison and talk to his old friend, Bob Kolf, the athletic director and coach of everything at OSTC. I didn't think much about it until I was on my way to Madison, hitchhiking, of course. The first ride I got was to Oshkosh, and I was dropped near the school. By chance, I thought I should call on Bob Kolf. Within an hour after meeting him, I was enrolled in the school, had taken a required IQ test and had football gear issued to me. West High was true to its word and had not recommended me for college because of my *Verbal Burp* publishing episode. Therefore, in addition to the IQ exam, I had to pay my tuition, a full $26.00. I was given a job in a rooming house to help cover the cost. Bob Kolf proved to be a persuasive fellow, but part of his initiative was that freshmen were allowed to play on varsity teams at the teachers college level. I could play football there and not get killed which might have happened at the "University" if they had even given me a practice uniform.

So I was in school at Oshkosh instead of Madison. I have often wondered what would have happened if the kind soul who picked me up as I departed Green Bay would have been going beyond Oshkosh, perhaps on to Fon du Lac or even all the way to Madison? I may have been completely intimidated by the size of UW and perhaps fallen in with the radical crowds for which the university was famous. All things considered, fate probably helped me make the correct decision. Besides, I was interested in a girl who was going to Lawrence College in Appleton about 15 miles from Oshkosh.

That romantic interest lasted only about two months until the local OSTC coeds seemed to develop an interest in the freshman starting right end for the *Titan* football team. On the football field, I was enjoying myself because of instant success. There was a pretty good team nucleus with several seniors being deferred from the draft so they could graduate. The main problem was overall lack of depth and the low number of athletes on the squad. Our season's opener was against Northern Michigan University at Marquette, Michigan, on Lake Superior. It was a beautiful day, and I caught a couple of passes and generally played a good game. Coincidentally, two of the officials were from Escanaba. One had played for Dad on the *Rangers,* and the other was the high school principal who also knew Dad. They were at the restaurant where the team had a post game dinner before returning to Wisconsin, and we talked. They both said I had played well, and that my dad would have been proud of me.

I especially remember that game because the tackle I lined up against on offense was a big Finn. He outweighed me about 50 pounds, had a black patch over one eye and no front teeth. He was a mighty intimidating character and probably the toughest guy I ever played against—at least, I thought so at the time. I kept hoping our quarterback would call more pass plays, or that the running plays would go where I had to block someone in the defensive secondary. It was fun, but we lost by a touchdown.

On the trip home, I got off at our front door in Green Bay because the bus route traversed Ashland Avenue where we lived. My mother was impressed. "Billy was playing first team, and the team bus took him right to our front door," she told everyone. It had been about three weeks since I left home, and I was eager to tell Mom and Don about my good fortune.

On Monday morning Coach Kolf put out the word that he wanted to see me. He complimented me on the game I had played the previous Saturday. He had decided to move me from end to halfback because Eddie Kiddie, our All Conference halfback, who had been injured before the first game, was a doubtful starter. Kolf remained persuasive. He stated that I was the fastest man on the team, and he was trying to put together a good offense. I was flattered, but I had always played end and wasn't keen about shifting positions. Still he was the coach, and I said I would do my best anywhere he put me. So during the week I was learning the plays of right halfback in the single wing. That meant I would be blocking most of the time. As the week progressed, I wasn't a happy halfback, especially in our last scrimmage before the next game. I got hit hard and bruised the quadriceps muscle in my left leg so badly I could hardly walk let alone run. Coach suited me up for the game with Stevens Point State Teachers College. Since I wasn't mobile, I sat it out watching their fullback, Teddy Fitch, chew up our line and entire defense. I had heard of Fitch and wanted to play against him. After graduating he played with the Packers and became an All Pro NFL fullback.

Practice the following week wasn't much better; I could only walk through the plays. The weekend game was at Milwaukee against its State Teachers College. It was a much larger school that drew heavily on the Milwaukee area for its athletes. Coach told me to come along on the trip, but that I wouldn't play. On Friday he told me to bring my gear but reiterated that I definitely would not play. Like any freshman, I was anxious to make the trip and be a part of the team. So I brought the football togs along as my trip ticket. Before the game warm-up, Coach taped my leg with me standing on a table in the locker room. I thought it was useless, especially when the team left the locker room for the pre-game warm-up. The tape was as tight as my sore muscle, and I was left standing on the table unable to bend my leg or get down off the table. Coach came back to the locker room about five minutes later looking for me. He was naturally uptight as coaches get before a game. He grumbled, cut the tape a bit, helped me off the table, swatted me on the fanny and said, "Get out there and try to loosen up. Eddie Kiddie will start, and I hope he holds up. However, we may need you."

Egad, I thought, he wants me to die for *Dear Old OSTC* and at such a young age. I was only a freshman. I wondered if he had a shield on which to carry home his Titans. I did my best to loosen up but didn't relish the idea of playing, not against all those big *Milwaukee Polacks*: Polish boys from the large sector of Milwaukee's population. The *Big Green Wave* of MSTC kicked off. Eddie Kiddie received the ball and ran it back about 15 yards on what was the last football play of his career for OSTC. Coach came to me and said, "Tommy, go in there and do the best you can." For me it was a big change from two weeks ago when I was on Cloud Nine and a triumphant warrior. Now I was a wounded Titan in a new position against the best team in the conference. On the first play, I received a pass in the flat which was short. By the time I got turned around to run up field, I was creamed by a couple of real big guys. I looked to the bench for some relief. The coach clapped his hands and shouted, "That a way to go, Tommy!" I played the rest of the game, not doing badly on defense but not worth much on offense. We lost again.

My leg got better and I was a starter for the rest of the season, but it was a winless one. My teammates thought I was destined for great things as a Titan. However, I knew that I would have to work hard at being a halfback reminding myself that football was fun, and I would be contributing to my team.

This day of infamy

On a lark my roommate, a football teammate and former track teammate from West High, Ray Stazak and I hitchhiked to Wheaton, Illinois, to visit my high school best friend, Garfield "Curly" Crawford. He was a student at Wheaton College near Chicago. We talked to the coach there about transferring for the next semester. He was receptive, but Wheaton was a church school and naturally heavy on religion. Ray was a devout Catholic, and the Wheaton ambiance wasn't to his liking except that it presented a new batch of coeds. We hitchhiked back through Chicago and finally home to Oshkosh where we were deposited on the far side of town. We took a bus back to the campus. It was on that bus on December 7, 1941, that we learned Pearl Harbor had been attacked on the *"Day of Infamy."* That sobering event precluded any transfer or even any further thoughts about it.

I was 19 years old and advised by faculty members and city fathers in Green Bay not to volunteer for the draft or enlist. The word was to get as much schooling as possible before going into the Army or Navy. *"Go Naval Aviation"* were the words I kept hearing, and I was determined to do it. Although I became more serious about studying, I was never good at it probably because I seemed to find other more interesting things to do.

One of my observations about OSTC and other teachers colleges was that more and more fellows were leaving for the draft or enlistment. The classrooms indicated that there would be a paucity of male teachers for a long time in our elementary and secondary schools.

OSTC was an enjoyable experience. I didn't break any records for grade points but was strong in extracurricular activities. I worked on the school paper, was president of my fraternity and the International Club, and I was involved in campus politics. I played football, ran track and had a job to support myself. The job was sweeping and cleaning up a tavern each morning for which I was paid $15.00 per week. By the third semester, I was a Big Man on Campus, but that was largely because the male population had diminished and was fast continuing in its decline. I suppose under normal circumstances, I would have been a mediocre man on campus. In retrospect, it was a good experience and a part of the maturing process for young Willie Thompson. To say the least, my time at Oshkosh did boost my confidence.

Becoming Institutionalized

An interesting event occurred during the summer of 1942 between my freshman and sophomore years. I always had an interest in psychology and thought it would give me a better understanding of the people around me and myself. An opportunity to work at the state institution at nearby Winnebago popped up, and Carl Engles, a fellow trackman and West High graduate, and I sought employment there. Carl was going to summer school, and I was in the process of buying a car—a Ford Model A we called the "Little Jewel." We were successful in our quest and roomed together at the State Asylum for the Insane. It was said there were two institutions in Oshkosh and in one of them you had to show improvement to leave. I had now been enrolled in both of them. My first assignment was Wards 7 & 8—the "Untidy Wards." In these wards many of the patients were not capable of caring for their basic needs and had to be helped and cleaned. This was not the most appealing job I ever had, but I endured. One afternoon, I had a group of 20 or so patients outside enjoying the fresh air and sun on the institution's campus. I had them situated in a circle to keep an eye on them. I was sitting under a tree about 10 yards away. My white coat was neatly folded on the ground next to me, my sleeves were rolled up and I was smoking a cigarette. The institution's superintendent chose that time to check up on his recent hires. He came up to me and started a conversation. I told him work on that ward was a little boring. He then informed me that I had broken several attendant regulations by being removed from my charges, sitting, smoking, sans white coat and shirtsleeves rolled up. "What if one of your patients bolted for a gate and freedom?" he asked. "Not all of them want to stay here, you know." I responded that I was fast enough to catch any of the patients if they chose to bolt. He told me I should read the Regulations for Attendants and check the Attendants' Bulletin Board at the end of the day.

I checked the bulletin board and was surprised to see the freshly typed notice that William Thompson was to be assigned to Wards 4 & 5. I did a quick check that verified Wards 4 & 5 were for patients who had a history of being *violent*. I said to myself, "Hey, Willie. That should teach you about being so cocky. You'd better keep your coat on and be ready to run. Some of those guys in the Violence Ward have super strength and might be as fast as you think you are. You won't be chasing them. They'll be coming after you."

On my first day in my new assignment, the other two attendants departed together for lunch leaving me alone on the ward. I was sure this was a setup or ordered by the superintendent. I didn't appreciate it but survived the longest hour of my life to that point by making sure that my back was against the wall, and I could see everyone on the ward. I developed a definite defensive attitude as well as friendships with some of the patients. I started to learn about their maladies. That was the underlying purpose in my being there. Some of the attendants were informative and would discuss things with me. Others were just doing a job and glad to have one. Some were caring and demonstrated a degree of expertise when working with patients, even during the times when the patients were *disturbed*. Some of the others were rather brusque and harsh with the patients.

I was doing all right and didn't get into any more trouble. I even got to chuckle with the "Sup" about my new life, where I wasn't bored. However, the stress of living and working at the institution was more than I wanted. After about three more weeks, I quit to go back to Green Bay and put in time on the night shift at Kraft Cheese Company.

One of the things I remember about OSTC was a man whom I truly respected and admired. He was Professor Nevin S. James who taught English I, II and other things. He was also the school's debating coach. To me the most impressive thing about Professor James was his teaching method. He was capable of spellbinding his students into thoughts of great things and universal problem solutions. Then he would burst the bubble he had created by disproving his initial teaching stratagem. The suds from the bubbles would crash down on the heads of his unwashed students and thoroughly douse them. It was an effective learning process. During one instance in my freshman year, he had convinced the entire class, including gullible me, that capitalism had failed, and that socialism was the only recourse. He intimated that a strong cadre was standing by to unite and save the world from the robber barons and other wealthy industrialists They were ready to oppose those who were enslaving all and playing *Monopoly* with the world's wealth.

Our class met three times a week, and he let us fester with rage against the world as it was and feeling the great need to save it until the next class. Then after goading us into extemporaneous expressions of vile hatred for the system that was enslaving us, he dismantled our arguments. It was an exhausting experience. I resented it until I realized what he had done. After considerable thought, I concluded, "What a learning experience he has put us through." I admired him greatly for it. He enforced the concept that there were at least two sides to almost every issue great or small. He demonstrated that unstructured, emotional and passionate debate wasn't the answer and usually contributed little to the solution. Examining all aspects of an issue and avoiding hasty, emotional decisions were pertinent. I have tried to respect and live by those lessons. However, at times, I have caught myself being tantalized by the "Save the World from the Robber Barons" syndrome.

I corresponded with Professor James during my early years in naval service and saw him in 1962 when I scheduled my boss, Rear Admiral (RADM) Ira Nunn, to be a speaker at the University of Wisconsin (Oshkosh). As I recall at that time, the draft was the biggest thing on college kids' minds and probably the faculty's as well. Professor James was not as impressed at seeing me in a commander's uniform as I thought he would or should be. Perhaps he would have been more impressed if he had seen me as a journalist or a high school teacher. But I continue to think of him of as one of the great men I have encountered in my life.

Another person in that category was Don Hutson, the "All Everything," pass catching end for the Green Bay Packers. I had spoken with him only once before when Gar "Curly" Crawford, a roommate and my best friend in high school, and I humbly called on him to ask for recommendations to attend his alma mater, the University of Alabama. He agreed. Curly spent a couple of weeks during a first semester at Chattanooga before leaving with a bad case of homesickness. I did not venture forth to Alabama.

Hello Navy

Prior to my 20th birthday, the magic date for the draft, I consulted some people about returning to school for the 1942 fall semester. School started only a week before my birthday. Our neighbor, John Howland, was the head of the Brown County Draft Board, and he indicated I would not be called for several months after my birth date. So I enrolled in school with the thought that I would slowly move toward Naval Aviation or the Army Air Corps. Two weeks after my birthday, I received an ominous letter from the Selective Service Commission that started, "Greetings." It further instructed me to report to the draft board for examination and possible induction into the Army. I immediately went to the Navy recruiting office in Oshkosh and talked with a chief petty officer (CPO). Fortunately, I wore my letter sweater. He said that as long as I had received notice from the draft board, I could not enlist in any of the services. However, there was a push to get young-sters into the V-5 (Naval Aviation Cadet) Program because of the expected high attrition rate of pilots in the Pacific Theater. The Navy was the primary operational service there and was expanding its carrier forces. Further, the program was centered on athletically inclined young men. Being that I was a college jock, the chief said he would try to get me enrolled provided I didn't tell anyone I had received my draft notice. After a few minor physical and mental tests, he sent me to Chicago for major examinations.

I was tense when I departed Oshkosh for Chicago on the Chicago North Western Streamliner 400. (It was called "The 400" because it was 400 miles between Chicago and Minneapolis, the two terminals of the run.) During the previous week, I had become much more conscious of the military and what I wanted to do in the war. I was told that if drafted, I would have little chance of getting into the Army Air Corps because the pressure was on to get ground troops not flyboys. I had never considered myself to be cut out for the military, but the Navy seemed to be the way to go—even though I couldn't swim. In the Midwest the Navy was considered to be the elite corps, probably because little was known about it except through Hollywood movies. The reality of Army life was clearer because Army personnel were more evident in the area, and more Army facilities were located in Wisconsin. The idea of clean sheets on a bed was much more appealing than living in a tent or foxhole. Also, the Navy officer's uniform was much more romantically appealing than the brown Army duds. Time was of the essence. If I was lucky, I'd go Navy rather than being a GI Joe.

It was my first trip as an adult to the "Windy City." The big city of Chicago was the country's second largest. I had been there with my mother when I was about six or seven, but all I could remember was the zoo and that we had stayed at Adolph and Esther Tomberg's apartment. What I got into at the Navy's headquarters in Chicago's Board of Trade Building was another zoo. The walls—or bulkheads as I soon learned to identify them—were emblazoned with posters to "*Avenge The LEX!*" That was the rallying cry for the *USS Lexington*, an aircraft carrier sunk at the Battle of the Coral Sea. The place was a flurry of activity, and a little unsettling for a country boy.

I phoned the Tombergs to ask about visiting them for a day or two and was cordially welcomed. On the first day at the Trade Center, I took the mental test and passed with no strain. At least, they did not send me back to Oshkosh. I was told to report back the next morning for the physical exam. I thought that should be routine because I had taken many physicals and never had a problem. One of the first things that happened the next morning was that I had my teeth examined by a lieutenant named Dr. Toothaker. I couldn't wait to get back to the OSTC campus to tell about that experience. What happened as I progressed further into the morning was bewildering because I flunked the physical. Me, the perfect specimen whom I admired every morning in the bathroom mirror had failed. My blood pressure was too high! Egad, in most previous exams, the doctors or nurses wondered if I was alive because my pulse and pressure were so low. The Navy doctor told me to go relax someplace and return in a few hours for another try at the blood pressure test. I did and flunked again. By this time I was really up tight and could see a banner headline in the *Chicago Tribune*: "THOMPSON FLUNKS PHYSICAL, ENDS UP IN ARMY."

I was told that I could have another try the next day, but in my mind time was running out. With my head bowed and spirits low, I went to the Tombergs' home in Norwood Park and worried some more. Esther did her best to soothe me and put me to bed with a glass of warm milk, so that I would sleep—an old Upper Michigan practice. There was compassion and encouragement on the part of both Tom and Esther. The warm milk did the trick, and I slept well. In fact, Tom and Esther were nervous about my boarding the commuter train into Chicago's Loop because I was taking so much time getting organized and ready to leave. We got to the depot on time, and the ride into town was inconsequential. My thoughts were about getting out of Chicago that day, Friday, October 9, 1942, to get back to Oshkosh. We had a football game the next day at home against Pulaski State Teachers College. I had missed a whole week of practice and classes. I took my usual fatalistic stance and was ready for the Army, if that was what was going to happen. But I still preferred to be a Naval Aviation Cadet.

My musings were of no consequence. My blood pressure was normal, and so was the pulse. I breezed through the rest of the procedure including an interview consisting of more football talk than anything else. The interviewer was a Reserve Officer from Chicago who had just recently reported to active duty. He knew of Wisconsin's teachers colleges and their rivalries. When the interview was completed, he walked me to the yeoman who was to process my record. He gave him instructions to move my papers expeditiously. He wanted to get me on The 400 to return to Oshkosh because I was OSTC's starting halfback, and there was a big game the next day.

If it hadn't been for Esther and Tom and the glass of warm milk, I might have ended up in the Army. At least, that is the story we have been telling ever since that trying week in Chicago and my eventual accession into the ranks of the Naval Aviation Cadet Corps. I believed it then and still do.

"Avenge the LEX!"

Prior to leaving the Chicago Board of Trade Building, I was sworn into the U. S. Naval Reserve as an Aviation Cadet in what was called the Navy V-5 Program. Naval officers there encouraged me to stay in college and told me that I would be called to active duty when a vacancy occurred in the program in another two or three months.

I am reluctant to put in writing what the chief petty officer, who was putting my papers together, said to tell the draft board in Green Bay. I did not consider what the chief said to be an order and thought I should exercise better discretion. Eventually, I was admonished by the draft board, but there was nothing they nor I could do or undo. My body and soul already belonged to the U.S. Navy. I rationalized that the Selective Service Administration's purpose was to ensure that able bodied men were positioned in one of the Armed Forces. But another way to look at it was that some other guy had to fill my spot, so the board could make its monthly quota. I decided not to get emotionally involved in that aspect because Uncle Sam was only interested in numbers at the time—big numbers.

I was *taken aboard* by the Navy figuratively and literally. I was impressed by the statements made by the officers during interviews and the swearing-in ceremony. By the mere fact we had been enlisted in the V-5 Program, we were in a select group. At that point my goal in life was to gain those coveted *Wings of Gold*. To be a Naval Aviator was to be a member of America's military elite corps. I had already become obsessed by the posters that were omnipresent in the Navy spaces at the Chicago Board of Trade. They aggressively incited us to "*Avenge The LEX!*" I even became a little anxious about learning how to swim.

Afterward I arrived at Oshkosh about 8 p.m. and walked (Walking in those days was the primary means of getting around.) the mile and a half from the railroad station to the "House of Earl," our rooming house. The house was named for Mr. and Mrs. Earl, senior citizens of Oshkosh who owned and maintained it. The house was nearby the campus, and that made it convenient to rent the topside (upstairs) to students. Two of the three rooms featured cooking privileges that proved to be an advantage for the students but not the neighborhood. We were only two blocks from the main campus buildings and conveniently located near the restaurants and bars. Being only a few blocks off the main thoroughfare, we were also close to our favored means of transportation— traffic for hitchhiking.

I seemed to enjoy the new experience that was taking hold of my conscience. I was no longer a civilian but part of the "military," whatever that was. The military was still a vague concept. All I knew about it was what I had seen in the movies or read in the newspapers, *Time* and *Life* magazines or novels. That feeling was manifested throughout the country as the nation mobilized from a standing military of a few hundred thousand to 10-15 million. This was not just a bump in the road of life; it was a major adjustment encountered by young men and women from 1941-1945. They were the embodiment of what was later identified as the *Greatest Generation*: those American youngsters who bore arms, separations and new working roles during World War II.

When I arrived at the House of Earl, I was given the message that Coach Kolf wanted to see me first thing in the morning. I was to be the new starting fullback, another new position for me. Football had taken on a different dimension during my sophomore year. I wasn't as enthusiastic about it as I was previously and wasn't enjoying it as much. The team was very thin in numbers and had little overall depth of talent. We were continually being beaten. The only excitement for me was that brother Don was now on campus and rooming with me as well as playing right end. Ivor Henig and Bob Patzke, two other Green Bay West football players, were with us playing first team. They also roomed with us at the house. Another roommate was Gar "Curly" Crawford, my best friend in high school and the one who had gone to Alabama and Wheaton. Curly was already in the Army Air Corps but was being *stashed*, awaiting orders to active duty. His military status was essentially the same as mine. He was taking some math and physics courses in preparation for his *call to service*.

The next football game was inconsequential except that we were defeated again, and I was ejected from the game in the last couple of minutes for fighting. It was uncharacteristic of me but probably symptomatic of frustration. I had reported to the Field House and Coach Kolf in the morning. I spent the time until kickoff studying the playbook from the fullback position and walking through the plays in the gym. Playing fullback was fun because I carried the ball more. However, I could not excel running on the inside where there were no holes. Playing defensive linebacker was also a new experience, and I quickly resolved that the best defensive position was halfback or in today's vernacular, cornerback.

I really enjoyed playing defensive halfback and felt I was more valuable to the team than just being an offensive halfback. Linebackers, bless 'em, were in the middle of five to 10 clashing bodies and sometimes more. I didn't like the idea of exposing my knees to errant blocks, clips or the piling on that most often occurs in the middle of the line. The defensive halfback slot was wide ranging, wide open. There were cleaner tackling opportunities whether it was stopping a receiver in the open field or coming up to the line of scrimmage to stop the run. But I've always been aware that football is a team sport relying on all 11 players to do their job.

What I learned from football and team sports helped me in later life. Beyond the immediate results of winning, exercise and recreation, team sports are supposed to instill teamwork. It definitely disciplined me for what I was to encounter in the Navy. Teamwork in the Navy often was the means of survival as well as the means to accomplish objectives. Loners don't survive in the Navy environment. I have grown to accept the exceptions to all rules and dogmatic statements. To better state it, few loners make it in the Navy, but if they do, bless those associated with them and those who depend on them.

Our winless season ended none too soon. It produced another seven losses making it 14 straight losses in my two years as a Titan. I tried to look at that record philosophically. Loosing was distasteful, but I was confident I had done my best and contributed to the team. Loosing wasn't easy for me to digest because we seldom lost at West High School. I thought I was perhaps playing my last football games, not knowing when, if ever, I would be back on a college campus. That didn't seem to distress me much. I was looking forward to my time in the Navy and the excitement that was anticipated.

However, loosing 14 consecutive games was tucked away in my mind as an experience I didn't want to repeat.

Good-Bye OSTC

Christmas vacation came and so did the end of the semester. With no orders in sight, I enrolled for the next semester because OSTC was the best place for me. Things were different, however. Don was drafted into the Army, and Gar Crawford went off to fly airplanes for the Army. Ivor Henig also went into the Army, and Bob Patzke followed me into the V-5 Program. My orders finally were cut in February 1943, and I was directed to report for active duty at Northwestern University in Evanston, Illinois for Civil Pilot Training (CPT).

It didn't take long to get myself disassociated from OSTC. I got my $26.00 tuition refunded and said my good-byes. I got things organized at home readying to make the break to join the Navy. Mom, of course, was worried about her two sons leaving home territory. I'm sure she felt uneasy about the situation and was already starting to get lonely. She was realizing her two boys wouldn't be just 50 miles away at Oshkosh and knew we were *"going in harm's way."*

I took another ride on the Chicago North Western Streamliner 400, but this time I got off at Evanston, the last stop before the Chicago terminal. I joined about 50 other NavCads who formed the first group to be assigned to Northwestern for CPT and ground school. We were one of the first groups assembled for this type of naval aviation experience. So it was understandable that there were some glitches in the arrangements. It wasn't the impressive introduction to the Navy I had imagined. A CPO headed the group, although there was a Navy doctor on board at least part-time. The CPO was Tommy Boyle, a Chicago native and former Tulane All-America football player. He wasn't very salty, but he got the job done. None of us was going to disagree with what he wanted us to do or the direction he wanted us to go. We were formed into platoons and squads with assigned leaders.

At ground school, we studied meteorology, aircraft engines and the basics of aviation. There was some marching, physical training and we were gradually moved into a military situation with both personnel and room inspections. From a flashback situation, it was akin to the amateur night at the Bijou Theater. But we didn't know any better and were eager participants. Student dormitories were our domiciles on campus, and we were fed in the regular student dining hall. The best part was done at Sky Harbor's airport north of Chicago and at the Naval Air Station in Glenview near a town called Northbrook.

We flew Piper Cubs with all the 40 horsepower they had. These early Pipers had room for the instructor and the student in tandem. I really enjoyed it. It was an exhilarating experience. (I said the same thing about skiing more than 30 years later.) It was particularly profound after I soloed. I was pleased to solo on schedule while many others were delayed for additional instruction. I logged about 40 hours of flying before we left Northwestern. I was confident I had gotten off to a good start and was on a true course. To be in the air all by yourself, in control of your aircraft, looking down on mere earthlings and viewing the splendor of creation from above was sublime. I was oblivious to the problems and stress of pedestrian earth dwellers.

World War II was in progress, and Navy uniforms were apparently difficult to procure. The Navy was expanding rapidly, and the textile industry was severely taxed to keep up with the demand. The NavCad uniform was the same as that for a Midshipman—blues in the winter and khakis and whites in the summer. However, at Northwestern, blues were not available for issue. As a stopgap measure, we were garbed in green Civilian Conservation Corps (CCC) uniforms with garrison type hats. The CCC had been dissolved by that time because of the war. The issue was heavy wool that boded well for Chicago's Lake Michigan winter. We left Northwestern in late April to go home and await orders for Pre-Flight School.

While at Northwestern, I spent almost every weekend with the Tombergs. Tom was a little fellow, not more than 5'6," and a nice, intelligent man of many interests. He was kind to me being patient and always helpful. Esther was a fine, poised lady whom I admired, respected and appreciated. They were most hospitable to me, and their house became my second home. Their two daughters, Mary Ann and Gloria, were in grade school. We became good friends and have remained so throughout the years.

Northwestern also provided me the opportunity to see almost every stage play, most of the museums and other cultural things Chicago had to offer. That included the Rialto Theater on State Street which had the last of the great vaudeville shows. I learned to consider Chicago as a wonderful Toddlin' Town.

Pre-Flight—Jock Heaven

As opposed to Civil Pilot Training (CPT) at Northwestern, the Navy's Pre-Flight program at Iowa City, Iowa, was organized and smooth running. It was objective and had established its place in the NavCad educational process. We could feel the freshness of the organization, and the staff exuded a welcoming attitude in this new environment. Called Iowa Pre-Flight School, it was located on the University of Iowa campus in Iowa's capital city. It comprised a quadrangle of dorms and had a lock on all the university's adjacent athletic facilities.

The V-5 Program was under the direction of Capt. Tommy Hamilton, a former Naval Academy star athlete, who was working in the Bureau of Naval Personnel in Washington, D.C. The program emphasized athletic prowess and physical fitness; a concept I later considered flawed. One didn't need to be a "jock" to fly an airplane. Many pilots I have known were not athletes. A few were even classic examples of the *"98-pound weakling"* of the Charles Atlas muscle building advertisements. But they proved to be good, proficient naval aviators. Physical fitness was important, and it was understood that war, at least combat, is not for the weak. To be physically fit means being ready to withstand the rigors of battle and all other war-related activities. During the war our administrators and leaders along with training and medical technicians gained knowledge and experience regarding aviation requirements and sustained operations. By the war's end the heavy concentration on athleticism had diminished. More emphasis was put on other requirements for being a naval aviator such as eye-hand coordination and mental agility. At the start of World War II, our country's leaders jumped to many conclusions and made snap decisions that needed to be rectified over time. The steep learning curve revealed, among other things, that one did not need to be an All-American athlete to qualify as an aviator.

The Navy strategically positioned several pre-flight schools, around the country. North Carolina's school was located on the University of North Carolina campus. It became a major factor in the flight program as was St. Mary's at Moraga, California. Both had excellent football teams that clobbered opponents, usually college teams, each fall. Some of the athletes were aviation cadets, but most were young officers. They were All-Americas in various sports, who were recruited for the Navy and performed as instructors at the pre-flight schools and on other bases. Other sports team members were enlisted personnel who dispensed towels and athletic equipment except during their own varsity sport seasons.

When we arrived at Iowa Pre-Flight, accomplished athletes were everywhere. One of the first individuals I saw was Bernie Berman, an all-time great football coach at the University of Minnesota. My platoon commander was Ensign Bud Wilkinson, an All-America at Minnesota and later one of the most successful collegiate coaches who won several national championships as coach of the Oklahoma University Sooners. My Company Commander was Lt. Cmdr. Lou Cordell, an All-America at Notre Dame and afterward a coach at the University of Georgia. My company's soccer and football coach was Lt. (JG) Forrest Evashevski, a Michigan All-America and the blocking back for standout running back Tommy Harmon. He later became the head football coach at the University of Iowa. Jim Turner of University of Maryland and North Carolina coaching fame coached our company football team.

I thoroughly enjoyed myself at Iowa Pre-Flight. Our leaders constantly pumped us up to fit the mold of the proverbial super guys who were destined to save the world. Better yet, "If we couldn't do it, nobody could." It wasn't difficult to let that philosophy take hold and inspire us. Who could argue? We had no one to contend with but ourselves. We challenged each other in all types of sports—football, soccer, track and field, boxing, wrestling, judo and swimming. Our days were split between ground school and physical training. Ground school comprised basic subjects: aircraft recognition, Morse code, semaphore and general Navy background and folklore. I will always remember Lou Cordell conducting a daily lesson on aviation ordnance. To introduce the subject and give us a general idea of his knowledge of the subject, he started with, "Boys, this mornin' I'm gonna talk to y'all about the casteristics of torpeeders." It went down hill from there.

The inevitable happened. My illusions about swimming—my *Waterloo*—returned rather dramatically in Iowa University's swimming pool. During the first week, we were all herded by squads and companies, into the pool area and told there would be swimming tests. To pass, we had to swim using the breast, side and back strokes for 25 yards each. Then we had to jump fully clothed into the deep end, take off our trousers, tie the legs at the cuffs and fill them with air in order to use them as a life preserver. We also had to do the same with our shirt. The initial test started with a climb to a platform about 15 feet above the deep end of the pool. From there we were to jump and start swimming. When my turn came, I thought better of it and backed off to reconsider. To my surprise I was pushed into the water and a couple minutes later was dangling at the end of a long bamboo pole that seemed to be the only thing saving me from drowning. On extricating myself from the pool—coughing, embarrassed and angry—I was told by a gruff, snarling commander, the Officer-in-Charge of Swimming, to report to the other end of the pool to join the aptly named "Sub Squad." I was advised I had better *walk* there. My fear and disdain for the man quickly turned to pure hatred. My disdain lasted for 99 hours in the pool, until I was relieved of the burden of being a sub swimmer. Each day before the evening meal, we spent an hour in the pool learning to swim. At first a large can was strapped to our backs. Then, Voila! I could swim! While I first detested the chore, I got to like swimming practice. I actually delayed leaving for a couple weeks because Iowa's hot summers are great for growing corn but tough on humans. Being able to swim in a relatively cool pool after class or athletics became a pleasure and a relief. Those of us on the Sub Squad were actually envied by other cadets. To show I was a good guy and didn't hold grudges, I thanked the commander for helping me overcome my fear of water and pass his swimming tests. Passing the swimming tests was a major milestone, and I felt good about it as another step in building my naval career. Nothing would deter me!

I had some other good moments at Iowa City. About a month into the program, the staff came up with the brilliant idea to have a giant track meet. It was compulsory for all 2,000 cadets to participate, but it wasn't spectacular. Most of the cadets were on a breather because they became spectators, doing nothing, while the ultimate champions competed. They should have been compelled to do push-ups while observing. My varsity sport was football, chosen primarily because Evashevski was the coach. I enjoyed playing the sport again. Many on the team had played college ball, and many more had done so at the high school level. It was tough football, much more so than at Oshkosh, but fun because the coach had a great sense of humor. He would come around to our company spaces on the nights he had the duty to shoot the bull with us, telling stories about Tommy Harmon and other luminaries. Man, we were really living! We couldn't have had it any better.

For the battalion track meet, each cadet had to compete in at least one event. I chose the triple jump and placed second. It was the first time I had done it since I was 15. We weren't enthused about the contest because we wanted to get back to our varsity sport. However, it was a weeklong contest and sort of a respite from a grueling schedule. Our company, the Kingfishers, named for a ship-based seaplane, got itself into contention for the Battalion Championship. The last event, the 880 yard relay, was crucial to the outcome. I can't remember how I got into the situation, but I was chosen to be a member of the Kingfisher 880 yard relay team, and in fact ran as the anchorman. I didn't considered myself a sprinter, although I had competed in dashes and run many relays usually as the number three man. When we took our positions to receive the baton for the final leg, I realized that one of my opponents was a cadet who had won the 220 yard dash and set a Pre-Flight record doing it. My attitude was, "Here goes nothing." He was in the outside lane next to mine and got the baton about a yard ahead of me. He naturally tried to get to the inside immediately, so that he would have a clear shot when we came out of the curve and hit the straightaway. He never got there. Somehow I picked up the yard immediately and didn't let him get to the inside; in fact, by the time we came into the straightaway, I had forced him into the third or fourth lane which he didn't expect or like. He almost got me at the finish but didn't. I got there first. Our company won the relay, the track meet and all the glory by one point, and I was the momentary hero. Among those who gathered around me at the finish line was the commanding officer of the school, Capt.Hanrahan, a Naval Reserve Aviator, who was portly, elderly and sported a handlebar mustache. In his dress khaki splendor, he embraced me and shouted, "That was a hell of a race, son! You are going to be one hell of a Naval Aviator."

In our platoon was a fellow from the Tennessee hills named Robins. A good, solid person and strong as an ox. He showed us a clipping of himself in the Robert L. Ripley feature *"Believe it or Not"* stating he had lifted 225 or so pounds with one arm. He used to do a hundred or so push-ups for us in the evening as we sat around shooting the breeze. One evening we let him know that we had heard about a cadet in the next dorm who had done 50 push-ups with his roommate sitting on his shoulders. "Robbie" shrugged as if he didn't care, and after a period of silence he left. About 20 minutes later he returned glistening with perspiration and proudly stood before us in his sweat stained under shorts. He announced that he had just done "60." At his side was his roommate ready to attest to the statement.

Robbie was indeed strong. I wrestled him for the company heavyweight championship. I was faster than him and put a hold on him that I thought was almost impossible to break. But all he had to do was flex his muscles, and I snapped liked a broken rubber band. I was eligible for the heavyweight class weighing in at 178 pounds, but Robbie was 220 plus. I got some consolation from the fact that while he did win the decision, he didn't pin me. I got even when we played football. If I didn't let him get his hands on me, he was pretty easy to move around.

Pre-Flight was one of the best three months of my life. I had never been in such good physical shape acquiring great stamina and muscle tone. The food was excellent, and the life quality was good but somewhat Spartan. I recall that we had only one weekend off campus. One last story to illustrate the shape we were in has to do with track. After the Kingfisher relay incident, I was moved to the Kingfisher track team. We had about three meets each week against other companies. I ran dashes, relays and broad jumped. We didn't have some of the field events like hurdles, shot put, discus, high jump and pole vault. We had gotten into a groove within the team, planning who would win and pretty much paced ourselves. However, the coaches had developed a little rivalry amongst themselves. Toward the end of our stay at Iowa City, our coach must have had a bet with an opposing coach because he really got on my case before the meet accusing me of loafing. He succeeded in raising my hackles, and I told my teammates that all deals were off. It was going to be every man for himself for this particular contest. I won the 100 yard dash, 440-yard run, broad jump and shared the 880-yard relay victory. Even though I had never run it before, I probably would have won the mile run if we had the event. About three years later when I was teaching air navigation at the Iowa Pre-Flight School (which had moved to Ottumwa, Iowa), I encountered our track coach who was then a lieutenant commander. We laughed about the meet even though he was rather vague about recalling the incident. He allowed as to how he was practicing "motivation skills" in preparation for coaching in civilian life.

Off Into The Wild Blue

I left Iowa City by train for my next duty station, the Naval Air Station in Minneapolis, where I was to undergo basic flight training. The Naval Air Station was adjacent to Wold-Chamberlain Airport, the Minneapolis air terminal. We did the usual half day ground school, and the other half was devoted to flight training. The aircraft was the famed N2S *Stearman*, better known as the "Yellow Peril." It was a yellow biplane with an air-cooled engine and two tandem cockpits.

My instructor was a Marine captain with the surname of Thompson. I had confidence in him as a competent pilot with a cool demeanor, and he was a good instructor. Flying was fun and I was ready to solo on schedule. So I was turned over to another instructor for a final check and got a thumbs down. I was in a state of shock! The check pilot said I had used prohibited cross controls to get into a small field when he gave me an emergency flight scenario. I cut the engine and had to pick out a field to either land on or to simulate the procedure. I told him I thought I was coming in a little high, so I slipped the plane to lose altitude. His position was that I should have used S turns saying slipping wasn't in the flight syllabus until C Stage. I argued that I had logged 40 hours in aircraft at Navy expense before coming there and didn't consider slipping to be an advanced procedure. My protest was still rebutted with a "down" decision. So I was sent back to Captain Thompson for another hour of instruction and then another pilot check and solo. I was tense but got through the B Stage but still received another down because the check pilot said I wasn't aware of another aircraft near us when doing turns to a circle. The pressure was on me. I didn't do well in C Stage and was *boarded* (an appearance before a Board of Instructors) and dismissed from the flight program.

I later learned that things were going extremely well for U.S. Navy carrier aviation, and battle attrition was much lower than anticipated. The supply of cadets in the training program far exceeded the demand, and an order was issued to cull 50% of the student aviators. Pilots and instructors I talked with later in my career verified they were forced to look for any excuse to reach their 50% reduction quota. If I had been in flight training three or four months earlier or later, I probably would have completed it. However, I had a depth perception problem that was discovered later, and it may have eventually curtailed my quest for Navy Wings of Gold or even my life. Although distasteful at the time, washing out of the V-5 Program was a stroke of luck for me and undoubtedly saved the Navy some money for the repair or loss of aircraft and possibly some lives, particularly mine.

I also soon learned that I wasn't alone in my plight. When arriving at Great Lakes Naval Training Center, about 40 miles north of Chicago, there were several barracks filled with ex-cadets awaiting decisions as to their future in the Navy. I waited about six weeks being interviewed by various officers, wandering about Great Lakes and having "open gangway" for liberty and very little supervision. While there I was privileged to see one of the great football games of all time. The Great Lakes team defeated the Fighting Irish of Notre Dame using a last minute pass from a former Duke All-American quarterback named Perry Moss to a fellow named Anderson. Notre Dame had been undefeated and was named the National Collegiate Champion. Johnny Lujack, who later starred with the Chicago Bears, was the ND quarterback. I arrived at Great Lakes in November, too late to join the football team, but I did get to play with some of those winning team members the following year.

Those in charge of my destiny informed me that I was being considered as a candidate for a direct commission and Communications Officers School. But I flunked my last code test at Minneapolis and was disqualified. My defense that I didn't even take the test because I had been discontinued prior to the exam which was actually only a weekly quiz did not prevail. I was finally told that I was to attend Recruit Training meaning boot camp. It was to be a specialized course for washed-out cadets lasting only four weeks instead of the usual eight or nine.

Boot Camp

The ignominy of turning in my NavCad (Midshipmen) uniforms and being issued a sea bag and enlisted uniforms was a disquieting event. The hype and inspirational military line I had embraced for the past year evaporated. I was to become an enlisted man, one of the masses, no longer one of the chosen few. I was definitely in a funk and a little confused as to which way to exert my efforts. While I was more of a fatalist and not inclined to lash out at systems or life in general, there were several in our 120-man boot company who did. There was a rebellious attitude and a definite, outward feeling on the part of some to screw the stupid regulations. On the first or second night we were in our barracks, the duty CPO was given an unexpected welcome to our midst. On his arrival after lights out, he stumbled over some miscellaneous gear that was strewn about. We had been instructed to have all gear off the "deck" with our sea bags and ditty bags lashed to a 4 X 4 that ran the length of the barracks. Shoes were to be tied together and slung over the bunk post. The chief was doing his duty and boisterously turned on the lights and tried to rouse the entire company to dress and go out on the grinder for some midnight marching in the below zero weather. The response was that three or four of our leaders boldly picked up the CPO, ceremoniously carried him to the door and threw him into a snowbank. Everyone cheered and applauded and then turned out the lights to resume or feign sleep.

It hit the fan the next morning. The entire company was restricted to the barracks for the remaining time in boot camp. We could not leave the barracks during what little free time we had to visit the ships store or the *gedunk* (a precursor to fast food places). The tone of the company, battalion and regimental officers and CPOs was not pleasant. Eddie Arnold, the famed country musician and vocalist was the one exception. He was a commander assigned to the Welfare and Recreation Department at Great Lakes. When he heard we were restricted to the barracks, he made a special appearance in our barracks on Christmas Day to cheer us up. He and his two accompanists also passed out bags of hard Christmas candies. Arnold was big in show business then, and they tried hard to rouse us. No one in our group so much as clapped their hands in appreciation. He finally gave up in disgust and stomped out of the barracks. That sparked a free-for-all with the Christmas candy.

To break up the four-week internment, I applied for and got a week of leave to go home. Don was there prior to shipping out with the Army 77th Division. Our CPO company commander (not the one who got the snow-bank treatment) helped me get the leave. But he grumbled I would probably have to drop back to another class on return. I remember that Don's moral was high. He was enthused about his unit and its role as a combat construction outfit. I thought he was riding the enthusiastic emotional wave like I experienced in the V-5 Program. I was thankful to have had some time with him, even though he spent most of his leave with his "bird," Mary Jane Koerner. Five years later she became his bride.

At about this time, I thought I would like to go to Quartermaster School. Quartermasters are enlisted personnel who generally man the bridge most of the time while assisting the navigator, keeping charts current and doing celestial navigation. When I returned to Great Lakes, I was assigned to my old company, awaited graduation and requested assignment to the Naval Station, Bainbridge, Maryland, site of the Quartermaster School. While enduring the boredom of the remaining two weeks of boots, I was excused to go to officer procurement for another interview. There was a relatively new program on the bulletin boards called V-12, a college program prepping Officer Candidate School designated as V-7. To prolong my absence from the rigors of the daily routine, I interviewed for the V-12 Program. The officer who conducted the interview thought it would be beneficial for the Navy to send me to college for a semester or two and then on to Midshipman's School and commissioning. However, I didn't hear anything about his recommendation and after graduating from boot camp, I went home again for another week's leave. When I bid good-bye to my mother to return to Great Lakes, I remember telling her I would write from Bainbridge. On reporting to Great Lakes Naval Training Center, I was assigned to the Outgoing Unit (OGU) barracks. Later I was told I would go to V-12 and subsequently that it would be Wabash College. My first reaction was, "Where is Wabash College?" I soon learned that it was in Crawfordsville, Indiana about 45 miles west of Indianapolis and not on the Wabash River.

I spent about six interesting weeks in the OGU barracks before being sent to Crawfordsville. I volunteered to work in the Great Lakes Naval Training Center Library and enjoyed the duties of checking in and out books and helping research information and periodicals for individuals. At other times I picked up a little pocket money by volunteering to work at places like Campbell's Soup where I wheeled around produce and products like cans of tomato soup. Naturally, the war brought about a labor shortage. The Navy provided manpower in various numbers for some local businesses that qualified as essential wartime industries. Transportation was provided to plants like Campbell's and Oscar Mayer in Chicago and Abbott Laboratories in Waukegan. Those were three places I worked. There were working parties dispatched to many other places in the early mornings. These groups were organized from OGU barracks men who were awaiting assignment or openings at schools. Their labor was put to good use in the private sector. The work was normally manual labor, and minimum wage was the stipend.

Chicago, my favorite town

When I went into Chicago, I would usually blow the day's wages on a show in town before returning to the Lakes. I saw most of the legitimate theater productions in Chicago and some of the better vaudeville shows on State Street. I became familiar with Chicago's Loop and its entertainment spots. I loved to spend time in some of the better watering holes listening to some of the great and budding musicians. Chicago became my favorite town because there was never a lack of something to do. The people were kind and generous to men in the military services. I felt a strong Midwestern quality of homeliness and kindred spirit I didn't sense in other areas. During those few months at Great Lakes I also spent time with the Tombergs in Norwood Park. They remained encouraging and kind.

The enlisted personnel with whom I had contact were not much different in character than the V-5 Aviation Cadets. There were more youngsters in the V-5 Program with some college background, but in my new community there were many 18 to 20-year-old youngsters who were just as eager to succeed and were just as intelligent. What did surprise me was the old timers who en-listed. They were the 30 to 40-year-old men, some with previous naval service and others just as "fresh caught" as the average recruit. They added a great degree of maturity to the group and leveled off the adolescent anxiety and impatience that was omnipresent in the enlisted branch. I came to respect sailors who were rated Third Class Petty Officers and above, especially those who showed some *salt* (fleet experience). My respect for them continued to grow and mature over the years.

I remember sitting next to a rated man on a bus in Chicago. I learned he was home on leave and was soon to return to his ship. He was in the Armed Guard in the Merchant Marine. Those men were U.S. Navy personnel assigned to merchant ships to man the guns. It was an unglamorous assign-ment, and depending on the area could be extremely dangerous. The young man had been on the Murmansk Run delivering supplies to Russian ports above the Arctic Circle and cruising the rough North Atlantic. They were relatively easy prey for German *Stuka* dive-bombers flying out of Norway and the U-Boats. The underwater hunters traveled in *Wolf packs* and were responsible for sending many U.S. and Allied ships to the bottom.. He de-scribed seeing ships in his convoy going down and lamenting how little could be done to save the merchant crews and Armed Guardsmen from the frigid North Atlantic waters. I told him where I was stationed and how I felt guilty by comparison just hearing about his experiences. Without bitterness, he said not to feel guilt-ridden, that my time to see action might come. He advised not to be foolish and volunteer for Armed Guard duty in the Atlantic. He left the bus at his stop, shaking my hand and wishing me luck. I've never forgotten that encounter.

I learned to like the Navy Bluejacket uniform. It was sharp and prac-tical and had survived and developed over a couple hundred years. I learned it was and should be a respected uniform. Previously I didn't have much experience with enlisted personnel. There were a few at Pre-Flight and at Minneapolis. But not many were found in those officer candidate training environments. Naturally, Great Lakes presented a different setting with about 100,000 sailors in recruit training, attending service schools or in transit to other places and assignments.

A Little Giant

On February 12, 1944, I boarded a Monon Railway train in Chicago for Crawfordsville, Indiana, marking the beginning of a new adventure for me in the Navy's V-12 Program. The Monon was undoubtedly the best and cheapest way the government could get me to Crawfordsville. Its aged coaches indicated the imminent end of its passenger service. It was definitely destined not to be one of the survivors of World War II. Still it did embody some of the region's background and charm. The last football game I played had the Monon Bell as the prize trophy. The Bell was a polished relic lifted from an authentic Monon Railway locomotive that chugged between Chicago and Louisville, Kentucky. The Monon Bell Game pitted arch rivals Wabash College and DePauw University. The Bell became the prized possession of the winner until the next fall contest. It added credibility and tradition to a time-honored local event recognized as the oldest football rivalry west of the Allegheny Mountains.

Founded by a church, Wabash College was then a small, all male, private school of about 500 students. Even in 1944 there was still a weekly chapel meeting. The chapel was the focal point of the campus, and as I recall one of the major degree programs was theology. It was evident the Navy was a guest on campus, and it acquiesced to most of the school's wishes. I'm sure that the school wasn't overly demanding because Wabash would have succumbed financially if the Navy hadn't supported it. At one time during my year at Wabash there were only five civilian students.

The Navy V-12 Program originated for three reasons: (1) the Navy and Marine Corps were expanding rapidly, and existing programs were not supplying enough manpower into the officer structure; (2) Washington was concerned that most small private schools would close because of dwindling student enrollment and saw the solution as some form of government subsidization; and (3) President Roosevelt was apprehensive that World War

II could become prolonged leaving the United States facing an educational drought. Britain had suffered that circumstance in World War I when a decade went by with few young men enrolled in college.

On July 1, 1943, 125,000 youngsters, all male, entered the V-12 Program at 131American universities and colleges. Some 70,000 were ultimately commissioned as ensigns in the Navy or as second lieutenants in the Marine Corps. Eventually 40 of them became admirals or generals, and many more went on to national leadership positions in various sectors. It was a program that definitely contributed to the health and wealth of the nation on both a short and long-term basis.

The program was so successful that in 1946, when there was no longer a need, it was curtailed. One reason it flourished was the Navy's reliance on the local academicians to run the program. Academics were the primary focus of the curriculum. Military subjects and training were often secondary to academics. True, there were formations, V-12ers marched to meals and participated in concentrated physical training. But significantly, academia was largely, in control, and many unit commanding officers were commissioned right off the campuses.

"A Sig I Am, A Sig I Be ..."

The only living quarters available at Wabash were the fraternity houses. I was assigned to live in the Sigma Chi House and had four roommates, all from Illinois. There were seven national fraternities on campus, and I was rushed by all of them. I had been in fraternities at Oshkosh that were local oriented organizations, but they made me aware of the rushing and pledging system. Two of my roommates were "Sigs" and Steve Canyon, a comic strip hero done by Milton Canniff, a Sigma Chi from Ohio State, influenced me. On one of my weekend trips to Chicago to visit the Tombergs, Tom (my uncle) replied to my questions about fraternities by saying he hadn't been a fraternity man in college. But he believed the important factor was camaraderie within a group. He added his opinion that beyond the undergraduate level, the only fraternity of significance was Sigma Chi. That cinched it for me. I pledged Sigma Chi and was initiated in the spring of 1944. It was a wise choice because I have been proud of being a Sigma Chi and have met some fine men through the association. I adapted readily to the fraternity's creed involving fellowship, integrity and good citizenship. At Wabash I was still suffering from the shock of being washed-out of the V-5 Program. I credit my fraternity brothers, particularly my pledge brothers, with helping me regain confidence and readjust. The song, "The Sweetheart of Sigma Chi" stirs good memories whenever I hear it.

Meeting Zum

For a small school, Wabash had ample tradition. When we arrived on campus, we were told that per number of graduates Wabash had the highest rate listed in *Who's Who*. West Point was second. The nickname for the student body and athletic teams was the *Little Giants* or *Cavemen*. The saying was that Wabash Cavemen had to go Purdue University, 18 miles up the road or to DePauw University, 18 miles down the road to drag coeds by their locks back to the dens at Crawfordsville. To be sure, the pickings in "C'ville" were slim. For a semester, I dated a girl from Indiana State at Terre Haute. That cooled when I went home on leave between the second and third semester and met Dorothy Elizabeth zum Buttel who was teaching at West High School. She was from Sheboygan, a German settlement about 70 miles from Green Bay. I was not only smitten, but I fell like a totem pole. We were in the rumble seat of a car cruising around Green Bay. I thought we had to be the perfect match. She was a pretty, spirited, perky girl and a GYM TEACHER! What more could I ask?

Actually, I had met Dorothy, whom I dubbed "Zum," about eight months earlier when I was home on Christmas leave prior to going to Wabash. Zum had just reported to West High School and was visiting at the home of a college classmate, Marge Loos. I had dated Marge for nearly three years in high school and then sporadically a couple years thereafter. Mrs. Loos, Marge's mother, was to be Zum's assistant. However, our first meeting was just a quick "Howdy," as I picked up Marge for a date. Unfortunately, our getting reacquainted some eight months later was on the last evening before I returned to Wabash for the fall semester. I recall that Zum and I were crammed into the rumble seat of our borrowed car along with a couple of others and I was forced to put my arm around Zum's shoulders and that led to a little hug. From that I developed a new pen pal, and in less than a year we were married.

Back at Wabash, math and physics were required subjects as directed by the Navy. We were allowed to cluster electives around those two core subjects. I got along in math but had trouble in physics because the final grade was based on a national physics standardized test. I flunked the first semester along with three-quarters of the football team. The second time around I studied hard, aced the weekly tests and still ended up with a "D." That reestablished my strong belief that I was strictly a liberal arts student. I enjoyed Wabash, got by scholastically and was the editor of the school biweekly newspaper, *The Bachelor*. I also took a journalism course from the Dean of Admissions, Bob Harvey, who in his earlier days worked for one of the Indianapolis newspapers. He became my friend and mentor, and he was a Sigma Chi.

Little Giant football

With me from Great Lakes came a couple of football players from the successful team of 1943 that had defeated National Champion Notre Dame. Our coach was Pete Vaughn, a legend in his time in football and basketball as a player and later as a coach. I enjoyed playing for Pete, had some good moments and played a couple of good games. I was the starting right end and finished strong in the last game when we won the coveted Monon Bell in the 50th game of the Wabash-DePauw series. Some fifty years later, I watched the 100th game of that rivalry on national TV.

Next on my training agenda was the Midshipman School or V-7 at Notre Dame University in South Bend, Indiana near the Michigan border. It was invigorating to be on the campus of Notre Dame, the home of the Fighting Irish, formerly coached by Knute Rockne, my father's idol. At the time, I considered Notre Dame to be just a football factory. I was impressed by the Golden Dome atop the chapel. The focal point of the campus, it reminded everyone of Notre Dame's strong spiritual roots. When I heard the Notre

Dame Fight Song, I got a tingling sensation throughout my body and was ready to hit somebody really hard with a body block or a tackle. I doubt if there is any football player who wouldn't feel the same way hearing that song in that place. It certainly got the adrenalin moving through my system. I learned about and came to appreciate Notre Dame as an outstanding university in addition to its success in sports programs. Midshipman School was a four-month course of instruction in difficult Navy classes such as navigation, gunnery and seamanship. I held my own and was in the middle of the class of about 800.

Most weekends, I spent with Zum either in Sheboygan or Chicago. I introduced her to the Tombergs one weekend and got their approval. We were planning to marry after I was commissioned. That didn't set too well with Zum's Father, Frank zum Buttel. Being a conservative and practical man, he thought we should wait. He felt Dorothy should continue teaching, so she could receive her teaching certificate. It could be awarded after two years of classroom experience. He saw the certification as a pathway toward employment for her, if that need arose. It was important to him. The certificate would be solid, earned value for his investment in her college education. However, Zum and I had other ideas. We would be married; I would go off to fulfill my Navy responsibility while she continued teaching to get her certificate. When I got out of the Navy, we would settle someplace where I could get a college degree. Then I could get a good job, we could raise a big family and live happily ever after. "No problems, Frank," we thought. "You must understand. We're in love!"

Graduation and commissioning were on July 9, 1945, and mother, Betty and Zum were in South Bend for the event. There I was— almost two and one-half years since I started— a commissioned officer in the United States Navy. Little did we know that it would result in a 32-year career ending as a flag officer. I had never even seen an admiral except on Commissioning Day when the Commandant of the Ninth Naval District appeared. The event was somewhat anticlimactic although I rejoiced with the other Midshipmen and shared a sense of accomplishment in the obtained goal. Many times I had felt sheepish about my quest for a Navy commission. I thought primarily of my brother Don who spent most of the war in the Pacific Theater groveling around in the mud with the 77th Division. They had gone through several campaigns in the heaviest fighting of the war—Guam, Leyte Gulf and Okinawa. I definitely wanted to be an active participant in the war, but that was not to be. World War II was winding down. Germany had fallen, and within a couple of months Japan would surrender following the atomic bomb drops on Hiroshima and Nagasaki.

While I was at Notre Dame, President Roosevelt died from a cerebral hemorrhage on April 12, 1944. He had been weakened by a long struggle with poliomyelitis, generally deteriorating health, the intense pressures of war and the demands of his presidential administration that began in 1932 and stretched into four terms. He was perhaps the most imaginative American president firmly believing in a liberal, progressive democracy. He led his country well when faced with potential loss of its freedoms and possible financial collapse of our capitalistic system. The country survived World War II and brought the world from the darkness of a broad global economic depression. The country continues to suffer from the expense wrought by some of his liberal welfare programs created to combat the Great Depression. A malaise remains instilled in the minds of many who think the government will always provide for them. President Roosevelt's public programs were largely "pump primers." Their effect did not succeed in restoring a productive industrial base alleviating the drag huge unemployment rates had on our society. World War II's demands helped to catapult the full industrial potential of the country. Those who were not serving their country in a uniform of the Armed Services became gainfully employed in the strengthened industrial sector. Before his death, Roosevelt signed into law the GI Bill of Rights, officially known as the Servicemen's Readjustment Act of 1944. For the next five decades it made available billions to educate and train millions of veterans. The act contributed immensely to the wealth and health of the country and is recognized as one of the most important pieces of legislation ever enacted.

President Roosevelt was a charismatic, inspirational leader. He maintained a strong feeling towards the U.S. Navy shaped by sailing experiences during his younger days and his successful tenure as Assistant Secretary of the Navy during World War I. He was unashamedly proud of the response and development of the Navy, especially in the Pacific Ocean theatre. The Navy grew to be history's most significant sea power, controlling the sea, the air above it and the depths below. That precedent would continue well into the next century.

A short time after his death, Germany surrendered unconditionally, and Hitler died by his own hand. The country was uneasy with new president Harry S. Truman, a former haberdashery co-owner and U.S. Senator. Truman lacked FDR's aplomb and presence but went on to become a good president, hailed by some historians as a great president.

My four months at Notre Dame became both wearisome and stressful. Being involved with Zum added significant pressure because of our impending marriage. The academics were not difficult, but there was the constant cramming, testing and the excitement of being issued Midshipmen uniforms again. It was tough on the nerves and stomach. However, a good breakfast usually settled my queasiness.

Wedding Bells

Our wedding was a small affair with Zum's sister, Frannie, as the Maid of Honor, and a classmate from Notre Dame, Warren Tempas, was my Best Man. Warren was from a small town near Sheboygan. It was convenient for him to be with us because he was on leave following commissioning. I have seen Warren only once since the wedding. The pastor from Zum's Lutheran Church married us in the living room of the zum Buttel residence at 521 Euclid Avenue. From my family we had Mom, Betty, Dodie, Ronnie and Gramp as guests. Zum's attending family included relatives from Manitowoc and Sheboygan plus some neighbors. It was a nice family gathering. There was a reception in the evening, and then Zum and I broke away and drove the family's Hudson Terraplane to Manitowoc. We traveled to a cottage in the Door County peninsula which was bounded by Lake Michigan and Green Bay. It was a practical, quiet and economical wedding. As I came to know repeatedly in later years, Zum had things well planned and carried out.

We spent three or four days at the cottage and then returned to Sheboygan to get me prepared to go to the Naval Air Station, Clinton, Oklahoma. There I was to undergo training to become an Air Navigator. On returning to Sheboygan, I realized that I wasn't the most popular guy in town. There were no outward comments or overt feelings exhibited. But her dad Frank was still disturbed about Zum's teaching credentials. Being the new kid in the house, I tried to get along. Shortly after our arrival, Frank was weeding in the garden, and I cheerfully asked if I could help. He replied that I could weed next to the fence. I managed to pull up all his tomato plants. I was dispatched to the house to see if there was something I could do there. Within a short time, I burned a hole in two of Olga's (Zum's mother) best tablecloths. That's when I quit smoking cigarettes for good.

Oklahoma Here I Come

I left Sheboygan and my beautiful bride, so I could become a Naval Air Navigator, and she continued teaching school. The train ride to Clinton was long and hot, and I only stayed a couple days at the air station located about 20 miles out of town. Clinton's population was around 5,000, and approximately half were Native Americans. There seemed to be about 500 dogs around. I called Zum to say our being apart wasn't going to work and she should come to Oklahoma—I might need some help fighting off an Indian attack. Zum arrived in Clinton a few days later. After a night in Clinton's prime hotel, she found a room with cooking privileges in the home of Mrs. Williams, a widow who worked at the post office. She had a daughter Lou living with her while her daughter's husband was fighting in the war with the Army. We got along well with Mrs. Williams and exchanged Christmas cards with her for many years after our departure from Clinton.

Earlier in the war, the Navy's base at Clinton was doing highly classified work involving remote controlled aircraft that were actually flying bombs. The airplanes were loaded with explosives and controlled by radio signals from the ground or another aircraft. Lt. Joe Kennedy, eldest of the four famous Kennedy boys, trained there and was later killed while attempting to execute one of those missions in Europe. The base was phased out of the special warfare operations at the end of the war and temporarily used as a training base for air navigation. Most of our class was comprised of pilots transitioning from flying lighter-than-air craft (blimps) to become Air Navigators. Blimps were used primarily for anti-submarine work, and there was no need for them because the U-Boat threat had disappeared when

Germany surrendered in April.

I worked hard at Clinton, especially after we were told the war had ended. Only a select few would be joining air squadrons to serve as Air Navigators (and receive flight pay). We flew missions in Navy R4Ds, the Navy version of the Douglas DC-3. I did well in the course work and in flight except for once when I became very airsick. I was so sick I couldn't navigate and flunked the flight but made up for it on the remaining flights. When orders were written, five of us were sent to be air navigation instructors at Iowa Pre-Flight School. The school had been moved to Naval Air Station, Ottumwa, Iowa. All the rest went to squadrons or sea. At first I was agitated about not being assigned to an operating squadron and missing out on flight pay. But staying in the Midwest near home wasn't bad. At that time I didn't intend to remain in the Navy, and by then Zum was pregnant.

One thing I remember about Clinton was the football season. Oklahoma A&M had a great back named Bob Fennimore, an All-America and later a star with the Chicago Bears. I read about him frequently because the Aggies were the only sports news in the state. I wanted to attend the last game of the year, the Oklahoma Classic, featuring Oklahoma University against A&M. Zum said she didn't, probably because she had gone to a couple of high school games with me and considered my body action as a spectator to be dangerous to her health. My arms and legs would flail around, and my hip movement would have been the envy of an Egyptian belly dancer. I considered it to be simply a pseudo jock's reaction to what was going on down on the field. At one game she said I bruised her ribcage with a flying elbow when a kid missed a tackle. So I went to Oklahoma City to see the game alone, hitchhiking the 150 miles. Zum was crushed; she didn't think I would ever leave her for a football game. On my return about midnight, she tried to give me the silent treatment but finally gave in because I was babbling at length about having seen the great Bob "Feenimint" play and destroy the Sooners.

Preflight School again

When we left Clinton, we had to hitchhike to Oklahoma City or Tulsa. I can't remember why but we did. We shipped most of our stuff in a "cruise box" and carried a suitcase or two. After a week or so in Sheboygan, we departed

for Ottumwa, Iowa, an old railroad city. Obviously the best thing to happen
to it economically was the Naval Air Station built on the town's outskirts. It
was an "E-Base" used for basic (elementary) flight training of Naval Aviation
Cadets. It was the same as Minneapolis, except now it was the Navy's Pre-
Flight School. At first we lived in a couple of one-room places but eventually
found a farmhouse about a mile from the base. Naturally, we had a garden
and even raised chickens. I became a pretty good chicken farmer working
under the philosophy that give anything tender loving care, and it, or they,
will prosper. The chickens prospered until our daughter, Stephanie "Stevie"
Jo, arrived. My daughter's birth has to be the second most significant event of
my life. The first, of course, was being married to Zum. Stephanie was born
in the Ottumwa civilian hospital on June 1, 1946, with a Navy flight surgeon
attending. When we brought her to the farmhouse, the chickens were forgotten. They thrived anyway being pretty well grown by then.

My career as an instructor was brief but interesting. My first class comprised cadets from the V-12 college level. Three or four of them were from
Wabash and were occasional visitors to the farm. I was firm that in the presence of other officers, they would give me the courtesy of my rank and not
call me "Bill." Those guys were sharp and did not need to have anything
explained to them twice. Navigation was a snap for them, and the class compiled one of the highest averages in pre-flight history. My superiors, as well
as I, concluded that I was a hot instructor. So as a further test of my abilities,
the next class I had was filled with enlisted pilot trainees. The Navy referred
to them as Aviation Pilots (APs). Most of these men were veterans of the
war. Some had applied for the flight program only to "get off that damn
ship." Most were looking to accumulate service points leading to a systematic
discharge and going home. Their interest in navigation was less than their
desire for physical training or close-order drill in the snow. The first weekly
test was not much more than measuring distances, setting courses and plot-
ting relative winds. I assured myself the class would pass the test by looking
over their shoulders. If they had a wrong answer, I'd point to it and shake my
head. I wouldn't have done that on succeeding tests, but I wanted those prospective Aviation Pilots to get off to a decent start. They definitely needed
a little encouragement. The class average for the test was 2.7. On the Navy's
4.0 system, 2.5 was the cut off for failure.

That first week with the AP students gave me pause to consider my role as an instructor. As a coincidence, there was an opening for a junior officer in the Naval Air Station Public Information Office (PIO). I applied with no second thoughts, was accepted immediately and transferred within a few days. My career as an instructor came to an abrupt but happy ending. It indicated I was learning to survive in the Navy bureaucracy.

Lt. Larry Frawley was my boss at the PIO. He was an aviator and fine naval officer. His wife Alice was also outstanding, and our two families became good friends. About three months into the job, a notice was received from the Navy Department requesting applicants to attend a summer semester at the University of Missouri School of Journalism to do postgraduate level work. I applied and was accepted. For 10 weeks I commuted from Ottumwa to Columbia, Missouri, by Navy SNJ aircraft courtesy of aviators getting in their flight time. It was about a two-hour flight. I enjoyed Missouri's J-School and had good courses in photography, editing and freelance writing. In fact, I sold my first magazine piece as a result of an article I wrote for speculation. It was a class requirement, and I was the only one of the 10 Navy men in the class who sold a story. I recall the payment was $20.00. We also met frequently for discussions on journalism and public relations subjects and shared field trips to St. Louis and Kansas City. I was impressed by the quality of instruction as well as the University of Missouri's School of Journalism that was then considered the best in the country.

It was evident that I was not going back to Ottumwa for duty, and I was almost knocked off my feet in surprise when I received orders to proceed to Guam in the Western Pacific's Marianas Islands. I was to work there on the island newspaper, Navy News, Guam Edition. That brought a new dimension to our lives. Separation was certainly a major concern, but the excitement of going to the Western Pacific and working on a newspaper that was the equivalent of the Army's Stars and Stripes was awesome. The Navy was at last going to show me some of the world other than the Midwest of the United States.

Columbia to Agana

I was excited about going to Guam, but it was difficult leaving Zum and Stephanie who was only three months old and had completely captivated both my time and me. She constantly received attention, and the more she got; the more she demanded. She was a beautiful, happy child, who jabbered continuously and ultimately became like her mother—never at a loss for the right words.

So I was off to the Navy, at least to a part of the Navy new to me. En route to Guam I was fortunate to get space on an airplane as far as Hawaii. I was delayed at Pearl Harbor for a week awaiting a flight further west. I eagerly took advantage of every available minute to explore Oahu and a few of the other islands. I recall visiting the Moana Hotel, the original first class tourist hotel on Waikiki Beach. In the 1930s it hosted the popular radio broadcast, *Hawaii Calls*. The hotel had a large courtyard overlooking the beach and a huge banyan tree covered the entire space. Featured at the bar was the famous Mai Tai, a sweet drink with rum and other liquors. I had my first Mai Tai in that fabulous setting on Waikiki Beach overlooking the blue Pacific Ocean with soft Hawaiian music playing in the background. I thought I had reached another major milestone in my life. Subsequently, I have visited Hawaii perhaps 30 times or more. On each trip I made an effort to sit under that same banyan tree at the same hotel, drink a Mai Tai and peer out at the same blue Pacific Ocean with its long curling waves. Those seemingly same combers have offered endless activity for seemingly the same surfboarders. As the saying goes, "Life's a beach, ain't it?"

I met and associated with some U.S. Air Force pilots who were flying out of Hickam Field, and got myself included on flights to the island of Molokai and the Big Island, Hawaii. Later on the flight to Guam, I penned a letter to Zum trying to describe beautiful Hawaii and my adventures there, but I couldn't do it adequately. I did conclude, however, by saying that the U.S.

should consider making Hawaii an American state..

To me Guam was an exotic, exciting place steeped in the romance of the South Pacific and World War II. Ferdinand Magellan, the Portuguese explorer serving Spain, discovered it for the Western World in 1521. It came under Spanish rule in the late 17th century and under U.S. governance in 1898—as as a result of the abbreviated Spanish-American War. The U.S. Navy governed the island from 1917 until 1950 except for the three years of Japanese occupation during World War II. In 1950 it became an unincorporated U.S. territory under the Department of the Interior. It was a forward U.S. outpost when I arrived in September 1946. Guam was scaling down from major base status for the Navy, Army, Air Force and Marine Corps. At that time, there were more than 125,000 military and naval personnel on the island's 203 square miles. It was about 30 miles north to south and 8 to 10 miles laterally. There were also about 30,000 native islanders. They were descendents of the Chamorro, ancient Polynesians who migrated from mainland Asia to the Pacific islands. They were pleasant, accommodating Pacific Island people, and by U.S. standards were not viewed as overly ambitious or industrious.

Guam has one of the world's best deep-water harbors at Apra. For the 60 years since World War II, Guam was considered to be the logical backup support base in the event the two major U.S. bases in the Philippines, Clark Air Force Base and the Navy complex at Subic Bay were lost. Guam came to the fore in 1993 when the U.S. pulled out of the Philippines, closing the Subic Bay Naval Base and not reconstructing Clark Air Force Base when it was destroyed by the volcanic eruptions of Mt. Pinatubo in 1991and 1992.

I was accompanied to Guam by a Missouri classmate who was a journalism buff. He had all the necessary characteristics to succeed including innate curiosity, a flair for writing, a good personality and a penchant for asking, "Why?" After about three months, he was dispatched to Saipan about a 100 miles north of Guam to be our stringer—our man in Saipan— and the Public Information Officer for the Navy base. Our newspaper was the only one on the island. A sister publication in the Philippines had closed by the time I got to Guam. We were able to cannibalize their identical offset printing equipment and salvage their newsprint stock. Copy was set on a Linotype, composed, then photographed and transferred to a zinc plate for offset printing. The process was called lithography. We had one Navy petty officer trained to operate the Linotype and one assistant, a Guamanian named Pedro, who was capable but only worked when he felt like it.

Since 1944, Naval Reservists who were former newsmen or had experience on the production side staffed the paper. The paper's editor was a Naval Reserve lieutenant commander who was the last vestige of the abundant wartime contingent. I was an ensign, fresh out of graduate level training, trying to fill in for the wise old professional. I was sure I would yearn for a few tutorials and some rudder instructions along the way, but we were eager to get started.

Guam and Saipan were scenes of heavy fighting against the Japanese. Guam was lost to the Japanese on December 9, 1941 and not retaken until July 1944. On my frequent tours around the island and when I visited Saipan, the remnants of war, particularly rusting ship hulks and field equipment, were visible everywhere. Brother Don landed with the 77th Army Division at Agat in Guam, about half a mile below the site of our printing plant, and was a part of the heavy fighting. There were still several Japanese soldiers living in caves, foraging for food and evading the patrols sporadically searching for them. They refused to surrender and apparently did not know the war was over. Gradually they were captured and sent home. In the 1970s the last one was brought out of his hermit like existence after some 30 years of isolation.

First priority—build a house.

My first and foremost priority was to get my family to the island. Needless to say, I was in good company in that quest. Many dependents were already on the island, but many more were awaiting notification to board a Navy transport ship in San Francisco for transit to Guam. In order to energize that notification, the local command had to certify that quarters were available. There were not many houses available. The name of the game was, "Build your own." The great majority of us used our spare time to build shelters out of Quonset Huts. The Quonsets had been barracks or support sheds and were anchored to platforms raised on stilts to provide air circulation beneath the flooring. Heavy cables were strung over the top of the huts to hold them down in the event of high winds or a typhoon. This home building was a major experience for me. Despite almost flunking breadboard making in junior high school manual training, now my motivation was strong. I dutifully attacked the job, laying out plans, sawing dearly rationed lumber and pounding nails.

A humorous, exciting and memorable experience occurred in October. I had become acquainted with the Fleet Weather Central officers who had offices in the Commander, Naval Forces, Marianas (COMNAVMAR) headquarters complex. It stood atop the appropriately named COMMAR Hill, one of the highest elevations on the island. I was informed one day that a typhoon was heading our way. Typhoons—the high velocity, powerful storms originating in the equatorial waters of the Pacific Ocean—are the scourge of mariners, airmen and residents of the islands and coastal regions. In the Atlantic the same cyclonic conditions are called hurricanes. I immediately went to their office to gather more information. The head of the office, Cdr. Best, said it looked like the typhoon would pass between Guam and Rota, an island to the north. We were to get heavy winds and rain, but there appeared nothing to worry about. I returned to the news desk, wrote the lead story for the next morning's paper with the headline, "TYPHOON PASSES NORTH OF GUAM." I checked back with Cdr. Best at 10 o'clock that night. He affirmed his previous position and bluntly said, "Go with it."

It was already raining and the winds were gusting. By midnight it was "lights out" because of power outages, and it became flashlight time. A miserable night ensued. I decided to stay with our troops because they were at the publishing plant. The security patrols and police had orders to direct all personnel to shelters and stopped all vehicular traffic. We had a Marine Corps corporal assigned to our staff, who was not only a good journalist but also a good, savvy Marine. He led our group to a covered concrete blockhouse near the newspaper plant that had been a Japanese gun emplacement. We huddled in that relatively safe spot for several hours. En route to the shelter, we could see 2 x 6 feet sheets of the corrugated metal sheathing for Quonset Huts flying around like leaves. By mid-morning the winds had abated, and the rain was intermittent. Traffic was moving on the roads, and a major effort was underway to clear uprooted palm trees and debris. I returned to my Bachelor Officers Quarters (BOQ) to change into a clean, dry uniform. The siding had blown away from my Quonset, and almost everything inside was wet. I managed to get together a decent uniform and went to the Fleet Weather Central office to find it in a mess too.

I learned that just before the typhoon reached Guam, it veered south passing over the northern part of the island with winds up to 120 knots. Our newspaper had been delivered with the headline, "TYPHOON PASSES NORTH OF GUAM." I was tempted to ask Cdr. Best if it would be a good idea for me to fly up to Rota to see how things were there, but thought better of it. He was such a nice man and fine officer; it would really have tested his patience to have a smart-assed ensign questioning his original decision. He continued to be a good news source for our newspaper. Years later our career paths crossed again in Washington, D.C. where we reminisced and chuckled about the Guam typhoon story.

Later we remembered it humorously, but the typhoon was alarming then. The storm leveled my partially completed quarters, the entire housing project and my morale by delaying my family's arrival. I would have to start building over again. There would be an additional time lag for the local command to clear another housing area, find the excess Quonset Huts and move them to the site. So another three months was added to my wait for Zum and Stevie to join me on Guam.

About that time one of the personnel officers reminded me I had a bonus 30 days leave coming because I had transferred to the Regular Navy. I had completely forgotten about that incentive designed to encourage Naval Reservists to transfer to the Regular Navy. It seemed like a good idea to exercise the leave option and visit my family in Sheboygan while the housing crisis was being solved. The typhoon had also destroyed one of the two elephant sized Quonsets that housed the *Navy News*. Fortunately the damaged hut contained the editorial offices and storage spaces and not the production facilities. We missed only one day of publication before we were back on a daily schedule. Our circulation was reduced because water and debris damaged much of our newsprint.

I returned to Guam in mid-January, having had a wonderful month's shore leave in Sheboygan. My return to Guam was delayed when I had to have an appendectomy in San Francisco's Treasure Island Naval Hospital. Slowing things down more, I had to travel by surface ship because of my leave status. Return air travel was not part of the incentive plan. Zum and I had a serious conversation about me resigning my commission and not going back to Guam. She won. I returned to Guam.

Upon my arrival in Guam I was pleasantly surprised to discover the Navy had gotten serious about the newspaper and added two "Mustangs" (officers promoted from the enlisted ranks) to the effort. Assigned were Lt. (JG) Ernest "Ernie" Twiss as officer-in-charge and Lt. (JG) Edward "Ed" Loud as Production Officer. Loud, an enlisted printer, clearly knew production. Chief Warrant Officer (CWO) Charlie Hatcher was doing the editing. Hatcher had written frequently for *Our Navy* magazine and was actively assigned to the Commander-in-Chief, Pacific Fleet (CINCPACFLT) Public Information Office at Pearl Harbor. He was a prolific writer and seemingly devoted 24 hours a day to his job. He stayed with us for about three months before returning to his primary duty at Pearl Harbor. He was a big help in stabilizing the newspaper operation.

Editor Guam News

With Hatcher gone, I took over as editor and continued to search for qualified youngsters who could help us on the editorial side. We worked hard to improve the quality of news content and make the newspaper an integral part of intra-island communication. We were the only newspaper on the island and the primary news media. There was an Armed Forces Radio station that featured music and some news read off the Associated Press (AP) wire. Any local news via radio was paraphrased from our writings. We had an obligation and took it seriously. I was a tough taskmaster at reminding our crew of its responsibility.

Twiss was a former enlisted Electricians Mate and developed into a good manager and fine friend. It was evident that neither the Army nor the Air

Force was going to help finance the *Navy News*. Discouragingly, the Navy was looking for ways to cut overhead and always considered the paper an aberration to naval operations. A solid solution to some of our problems occurred when the newspaper was transferred to Island Government. Our leader, Rear Adm. Charles A. Pownall had two titles: (1) Commander, Naval Forces, Marianas and (2) Governor of Guam. He had two different staffs to assist him with these tasks.

Under the Island Government umbrella, our little enterprise made a major move. We went commercial. We started charging a nickel for the paper. The token fee enabled us to reduce circulation from 75,000 to 25,000. We doubled the size of the Sunday paper to eight pages and occasionally went to 12. Next, we started accepting and publishing advertisements, including classified ads. The name of the newspaper was changed to *Guam News*. It kept that title until 1970 when the Gannett newspaper chain bought it for $1.3 million and changed the name to *Pacific Daily News*. It carries that masthead today and continues to be the only newspaper on the island.

Our ultimate objective was to sell the newspaper to a Guamanian, so the Navy could get out of a commercial business and encourage the locals to seek opportunities to rehabilitate their island. It was seen as a step toward helping economic recovery. The paper and similar business starts could provide stability and move the island toward self-government. Privatization of the paper was accomplished a few months after I left, when a native, Jose Flores, bought the paper for $12,500. He later sold it to the Gannett Company. Flores became Governor of Guam, an elected post by that time.

As for my housing situation, the local command assigned an unfinished Quonset Hut to me in a much better location than the previous one. I spent most of my free time at the hut and got a lot of advice from Twiss and Loud. They were handy at building and were finishing their own huts, so their wives could join them. The COMMAR Headquarters Command, to which we were assigned, assisted us as much as possible. Tools were provided as was one package of 24 sheets of 1/2-inch plywood. Before signing off on the completed hut, which authorized requesting passage for dependents, there was a strict inspection for safety, sanitary conditions, fire prevention measures, electricity and plumbing. I had my plumbing done by professional plumbers who were civilians employed by contractors working on various large projects on the island. The job consisted of completely plumbing the house, tying into the water source and providing a sewage system. My cost was a case of whiskey that officers could get for a dollar a bottle at the package store. Liquor was difficult for civilians to obtain, and many of them depended on it. My plumbers resold the whiskey for up to $50.00 a bottle. Twiss did the electrical work at no charge for the Thompson Hut, but beer was available.

Suddenly they were just off shore! Zum and Stevie sailed into Apra Harbor in the troop transport USS *Breckenridge*. I cumshawed myself aboard the pilot boat, so I was able to board the *Breckenridge* before it entered the harbor. It was a great moment. Sadly Stevie didn't recognize me and was reluctant to get mixed up with a strange man, even if her mother didn't exhibit any constraints. In my jeep, a new experience for them, I hauled them to their new home on COMMAR Hill. On entering the hut, the first thing I did was go to the refrigerator to get a drink of water. As a convenience, I had stored drinking water in liquor bottles, and I took a long swig. When I offered it to Zum, she started crying. She thought it was booze and that I had succumbed to the island's No. 1 disease—alcoholism. After that little crisis, she almost went into hysterics with laughter. I had built everything inside to my height, and Zum, being 10 inches shorter at 5'2" could only see half of her head in the bathroom's medicine cabinet mirror. The kitchen counters caught her a little bit above amidships. I could lower the medicine cabinet, but the kitchen counters were permanent. We could only hope the officer following us as a resident would have a tall wife.

Life on Guam

Island life was generally rather prosaic, straightforward, often dull, and time consuming, but not for Ensign William Thompson, editor, *Guam News*. Being an ensign placed our family at the lower end of the Navy social structure. However, in my role as "Editor, *Guam News*," we were circulating within the island's elite social structure. We didn't crack the military social sphere, but we were highly visible almost every evening and weekend representing the newspaper. In retrospect, being on the inside provided opportunities to help the newspaper and Island Government. I was attuned to the Island Government's agenda, the Governor's objectives and the desires of many Guamanian leaders. Conversely, the main questions of the ne'er-do-wells assigned to Guam were, "What's new at the commissary?" and "What are those Package Store (booze locker) hours again?" And there was always the continual dribble about the immediately past, present or future bridge game.

Of course not everyone assigned to Guam was a ne'er-do-well. Rear Adm. Pownall, Commander, Naval Forces, Marianas and Governor of Guam was a carrier leader in World War II at the Makin Island engagement. He was the first admiral I grew close with. His eyes probably glazed over when I talked to him about Island Government policy from the perspective of the editor of the *Guam News*. Still he always exercised considerable patience and control. His Chief of Staff was Edward N. "Butch" Parker, a tough World War II surface warfare Navy captain. Parker became a vice admiral as the Navy's Strategic Targeting Agency (STA) representative at the Strategic Air Command (SAC) Headquarters in Omaha, Nebraska. I remember him as being extremely fair to me as an ensign who was trying to maintain independence while editing the island's only newspaper and working to do a good job for the Navy at the same time. Perhaps his attitude would have changed had I misspelled his name, but that didn't happen. It was a difficult situation, which I didn't fully comprehend at the time. Many decisions made by the governor slowly began an evolution toward Guamanian self-government. Programs were set up that positively affected the island's economic well-being. I was allowed to sit in on some of those decision making processes because the Island Government was an important news source. It would have been better, if I had been about 20 years older with a few gray hairs to back up maturity and judgment. However, I appreciated being in that position. I rate highly the way the Navy—and I'm sure the other Armed Forces as well—give responsibility to young officers and enlisted personnel. Putting a youngster into a difficult situation is one thing, but having more experienced, patient, senior staff standing by to give direction and counsel is another. That's a Navy practice I learned throughout my Navy career. There aren't any sectors of our society I know of where youngsters are given such heavy responsibilities and patiently allowed to develop and mature under intense circumstances, considering the encumbrances often involving the safety of others, such as ship and aircraft operations.

Staffing the newspaper

One of the difficult tasks I faced with the newspaper was finding and training an editorial staff. The Navy had a "Specialist X" rating during the war that covered a multitude of "odds and ends" activities including journalism. With the end of the war, most of the journalists went home. It wasn't until about 1948 that a rating for journalists was adopted. In the meantime, we had several jobs for journalists, but there were few in the Navy's personnel pipe-line, and none were assigned from Pacific Fleet Headquarters. I quickly established a relationship with the personnel officer at the Naval Operating Base at Apra Harbor. All enlisted personnel assigned to Guam passed through his control. If any of the youngsters had previous writing experience in high school or college, he notified me, and we interviewed them. Our editorial staff was formed that way. It was up to us officers to train the kids how to write for a daily newspaper. It was laborious, and patience was the key. I insisted, regardless of their writing experience, I wanted no dummies. And we got few. I needed an alert, bright staff who would respond intelligently to editorial demands for covering any story or reacting to any crisis affecting our mission. For the most part, they were good men, some better or more motivated than others. They recognized COMMAR Hill duty was preferable to the Apra Harbor Naval Operating Base or a stevedore assignment, and they responded in a positive manner. We tried to make their stay on Guam and their two years in the Navy productive; something they could look back on with satisfaction and pride. The newspaper participated in many sporting events by sponsoring a Golden Gloves boxing tournament and a Marinas Tennis Tournament. We got involved in cultural activities, fostered exhibitions, photo competitions and health campaigns. We focused on being the primary news provider on the island. I think it paid off for those young men and helped our mission succeed.

The experience sparked some long lasting careers and created enduring friendships. Our best writer was George Wilbur, a young man from upstate New York, who was one of the most prolific writers I have ever known. Even while working for us, he became a stringer for the Associated Press (AP) and was highly regarded by AP managers in Honolulu and New York. After his two-year stint in the Navy, George returned home, completed a college program and went to work for AP in Richmond, Virginia. He had a successful career there. We have maintained contact through visits, weekends together and correspondence. He remains a good friend.

Another notable was my sports editor, Bob Crosley, who returned to Knoxville, Tennessee, and became a Sigma Chi at the University of Tennessee. He got a law degree and had a successful practice in Knoxville where he and his family reside. He also once served as Knoxville's mayor. We have kept in touch. George Dissinger was another sports editor on the island. He returned to his native Pennsylvania but then moved to San Diego where he too became a Sigma Chi. He graduated from San Diego State with a degree in journalism and went to work for the *Evening Tribune* (San Diego). Later he retired from there as managing editor. Through the years we saw a lot of George and his family, both in Pennsylvania and San Diego. I was pleased to serve as his Best Man when he and Lois Large, a promising columnist for the *Tribune*, married back in the mid 50s.

Bill Jury was another sports writer on Guam. Afterwards he returned to Seattle and received a degree in journalism from the University of Washington. He had a successful career in newspapering and became the director of public relations for Boeing's Aerospace Division. We have spent vacation time together with Bill and his wife Jo visiting them several times in Seattle. Bill made frequent trips back east to Washington, D.C. stopping by frequently to see us. We even got George Wilbur and his wife Vi to join us during one of Bill's visits.

To say the least, we had some good young men working for the island paper. Zum and I have had the pleasure of continuing a dialogue with the above four. Stevie knows them too, although they know her better because all of them babysat her. They adored her and relished the opportunity to get out of their barracks and lounge in a house with a full 'fridge and well-stocked bar.

War Crimes trials

Naturally, we had some interesting projects and stories develop on Guam. A long continuing major story was the war crimes trials in 1947. Internationally reported, the trials were primarily held for Japanese Army personnel who were charged with committing atrocities. Six were found guilty of murder—some even cannibalism—and sentenced to be executed. After the normal appeals failed, utmost secrecy cloaked the executions. We were given the authority to publish the story in the *Guam News*. However, we could not release the paper or its contents until our normal morning delivery time which coincided with release times in Washington and Honolulu. Having been assured we had done our job properly protecting secrecy, I got to bed at my usual time at midnight. I was awakened an hour later by a jeep driving into the housing area and stopping in front of our hut. Our managing editor called out, "Hey, Mr. Thompson. We have a problem. Should that headline go 'SIX JAPS HANGED' or 'SIX JAPS HUNG'?" I quietly told him we were only interested in the execution, so the word to use was "hanged." Then I worried the rest of the night if any of the neighbors had heard the question or the secrecy was blown.

During my tour on Guam, I didn't draw any Navy pay for the last 15 months. At the time the Navy had a program for unclaimed money to draw interest at about 3%. So I just let it accrue. The reason for this affluence came about because I got involved in promoting professional boxing. I did it before Zum and Stevie arrived when there wasn't much to do except cobble together our Quonset Hut and attend biweekly boxing matches. Most of the fighters were military kids with high aspirations or eager to pick up a few extra bucks. I was appalled at the conditions of Guam's professional boxing. The dressing rooms were almost nothing, doctors were not at ringside and the fighters were paid paltry prizes in relation to the gate receipts.

The promoter was Bill Lujan, a Guamanian, who claimed to have promoted fights before the war. I wrote a couple of columns about the lousy situation Lujan was promoting and recommended that the Island Government do something about it. I didn't particularly like boxing and didn't know much about it, My only motive was to show that *Guam News* was a gutsy newspaper with the community and particularly the enlisted personnel at heart.

Resulting from our crusade, the Island Government established a Boxing Commission that required promoters, judges and fighters to be licensed, and the boxers had to have proper physical examinations. I was asked to be the commissioner but declined. I became a judge and scored every boxing match on the island until we left Guam. Judges were paid about $25.00 per night, and that supported the Bill Thompson family during its stay on Guam. Lujan continued to promote but was not as flamboyant. In fact, he became the *Guam News'* deliveryman, distributing the paper to all sectors of the island. Eventually, we even became friends.

Guam News had its prestige enhanced by the Boxing Commission stories, and I carried it even farther. The paper's first annual Golden Gloves Tournament was a successful series of boxing nights. To cap that I took our team of eight champions to China for the Western Pacific Golden Glove Championships. We fought the team from the U.S. Marine Corps in Tsingtao, China, and won six of the eight fights. I brought Bob Crosley along to cover the event. It was an interesting trip, and most importantly I got to visit China for the first time. That was in 1948, just a few months before the Communists sealed up China for 30 years. We could see the communist encampments surrounding Tsingtao probably waiting for the Marines to leave China. Shanghai was a fascinating place, and there was a marked contrast when I returned to China in 1993. There was no inflation like I saw on my first visit when an exchange of a few U.S. dollars would get a wad of several thousand Chinese bills.

In 1948 poverty was everywhere. Early one morning, I saw a truck crew gathering up bodies of those who died on the streets during the previous night. In 1993 there was no poverty. Everyone worked and got paid. There were lots of street cleaners, but the people seemed content. The Communists had also ended the birth control problem. The government decreed that urban families could have only one child and those living in rural areas could have two. Those children were unbelievably spoiled in 1993!

Photography brought me into a friendship with one of the world's unusual characters. Frank Kasukaitis was a Third Class Photographers Mate working for me as the paper's one-man photo shop. He was a Polish kid out of St. Louis who was a diamond in the rough. To say Frank was the best photographer the Navy ever had is an understatement. His only rival would have been Captain Edward Steichen, who headed up Navy Combat Photography in World War II. Frank could really nail a picture and got himself into several excellent tours of duty to fulfill his work. He was in Korea at the time of the armistice. For the signing of the cease-fire papers at Panmunjom, in the Demilitarized Zone (DMZ), the Communists insisted the United Nations have only one photographer present. All the photographers accredited to the United Nations in Korea selected "Kaz." He later spent a couple tours in Antarctica, married an Australian girl, retired and lived in New Zealand doing freelance photo work. He was a free-spirited man and a great talent. Some of the pictures he gave me of our days together on Guam are treasures.

In June 1948, we left Guam following a series of farewell parties and receptions not normally accorded an ensign. I was thoroughly satisfied with what I had accomplished during my 22 months and thought I could not have accomplished much more if we had been extended for several years. Incidentally, one of the wealthier Guamanians, a Mr. Bordello, was considering buying the Guam News. He contacted me about resigning my Navy commission and remaining on the island to run the newspaper. His offer was $10,000 per year, an astronomical figure, more than four times my Navy pay. At that time there was a dearth of housing for anyone other than military, and we would have had to move out of Navy housing. In retrospect, a housing situation could have been negotiated, and the prospects for business investments on the Guam frontier were plentiful. Many former and retired Navy personnel flourished financially by staying on Guam. However, I couldn't see putting Zum and Stevie in a grass hut until I could build an island paradise. For many years the Guam deal lingeringly looked good, but the Navy offered me the opportunity to travel and mature with increased responsibilities.

We departed Guam in a Navy transport ship. We left with fond memories. Especially cherished were the many good Navy and civilian friends we had made. I and my family were considerably more knowledgeable and mature than when we arrived.

Guam to Washington

We had shipped our new 1948 Ford four-door sedan from Guam to San Francisco, and it was awaiting our arrival. I doubt if many automobiles had as much sea duty as our Ford—it had more than I did. Our voyage was uneventful and pleasant for me as an ensign. I had to stand a few watches, but they were nothing of consequence, just enough to remind me that I was in the Navy and aboard a Navy ship. Actually, I felt honored to be a watch stander and enjoyed it.

Upon arriving we stayed in a San Francisco hotel before picking up the Ford at the Navy's supply depot in Oakland and heading east. Reno was the initial stop for us fledgling "Wagoneers" crossing the country for the first time, and that was only to get the 1,000 mile check on the car. From there we drove straight through to Sheboygan. We did so mainly because it wasn't convenient to stop when we should have, or we weren't tired when it was. The excitement of being back in the United States, going home after a long overseas tour and heading toward Gramma Zum—who was widowed during my absence—also helped stretch the driving stints. Zum and I swapped driving responsibilities frequently. Stevie was wonderful and not a problem as long as we interacted with her when she was awake.

Using Sheboygan as headquarters, we visited family in Green Bay, Manitowoc and Chicago. We arrived in Green Bay in time to hear Don and Mary Jane Koerner recite their marriage vows in St. Patrick's church near our old neighborhood. Don had converted to Catholicism, and his church wouldn't allow me to be his Best Man. Allowances were made for me to be a part of the official wedding party, so I was something like a "Second Best Man." Church rules then required a Catholic to sign the wedding certificate as Best Man. Mary Jane's brother Greg inked the pact. I didn't mind; I was just happy to be there. In Manitowoc we became reacquainted with Aunt Dodie and Uncle Fred Carlson and cousin Ronnie as well as Zum's relatives from the maternal side of her family. We also spent time in Chicago's Norwood Park with the Tombergs. We picked up a new Nash sedan off its assembly line in Kenosha, Wisconsin, and sold the Ford in Chicago for a little more than it cost in Guam. Of course, Stevie was the center of attraction during our entire stay, and she enjoyed the attention. Zum and I didn't mind a bit. We enjoyed showing her off.

Return to Great Lakes

On detachment from Guam, my orders read to report to the U.S. Army Carlisle Barracks in Carlisle, Pennsylvania, to attend the first class of the Armed Forces Information School (AFIS). While at home, I received a modification to those orders, sending me to the Ninth Naval District Public Information Office at Great Lakes for six weeks. My reporting to AFIS was delayed because its opening date was postponed. While at Great Lakes I was assigned to help do some planning for a Veterans Day celebration in Chicago. I had the opportunity to meet people who would remain our acquaintances for 40 years or more. They included the boss, Lt. Cdr. Bob Hart, Lt. Bob Rogers and Ensign Ed Castillo.

While I was at Great Lakes, the Navy's Bureau of Naval Personnel (BUPERS) came after me, telling Hart and me through the Director of Information in Washington that Ensign Thompson had better get to sea, or he would be far behind his contemporaries. In other words, they wanted to cancel my orders to Carlisle and send me to sea. I told Bob I would prefer to go Carlisle and then take my chances on being selected for a change of designation to the Public Information Officer (PIO) program. I added that I would seriously consider resigning my commission if I wasn't sent to Carlisle. Hart wrangled for me and won. I was allowed to go to Carlisle. I felt indebted to Bob acting on my behalf. I knew then—and it was repeatedly confirmed during my career—that ensigns have little leverage and should not be obstinate. Clearly the officer in the Bureau of Naval Personnel was doing his job and was correct in his evaluation. I needed to go to sea and learn how to be a naval officer. However, I thought I was destined for other things. For that term, I lucked out. For sure I had much to learn about many things if I wanted to continue to serve as a naval officer.

Secretary of Defense, the Honorable James F. Forrestal (formerly Under Secretary of the Navy and later Secretary of the Navy during a good part of World War II) was the principal speaker at the opening convocation for the first class of the Armed Forces Information School. Communications with the public, specifically telling the Navy's intent to ensure safe, free use of the seas carrying 97% of the commercial cargo to and from the United States had been a primary focus for Forrestal. He personally originated the concept for the AFIS. The Navy had a relatively good public information effort during World War II, but there was room for improvement. Symptomatically, Admiral Ernest King, the Chief of Naval Operations, is reputed to have said about the news media's interest in World War II, "Tell them nothing until the end of the war, and then tell them who won." I'm sure that wasn't a true statement because Admiral King was an astute naval officer.

AFIS

Being impressionable at the age of 25 and having demonstrated an eager, aggressive attitude, I became engrossed with my first formal educational experience involving mass communications fundamentals. I was by far the most junior officer in the class but not when measured by experience. Up to that time I thought journalism was the basis for the business of mass communications. I kept that premise throughout my career. However, I learned that other disciplines were equally important such as public speaking, community relations, problem solving, radio and then television broadcasting. My experience with high school and college newspapering and particularly my two years with the Guam newspaper put me in good stead within our student body. My assessment of the faculty was that it was uneven in quality. Some obvious leaders were "old pros." Their professionalism was immediately evident. It clearly eclipsed those looking for a graceful exit from the military and others with limited knowledge and experience. The deeper we got into some subjects, the more fragility and lack of professional experience began to show among some. I quickly gravitated toward the old pros and sought their advice and counsel at every opportunity. Fortunately, two of them were naval officers who allowed me to slip under their wings; a place I appreciated.

Zum, Stevie and I enjoyed the Pennsylvania countryside for my 14 weeks at AFIS. Pennsylvania is a big, beautiful state filled with colonial, ethnic, civil war and industrial history. We visited Philadelphia, the birthplace of our government, Hershey, the Mecca for chocolate lovers and Lebanon where George Dissinger, the sports editor on Guam, lived with his parents. We picked apples one weekend, and Zum got a bad infection from poison ivy. That convinced us to leave that activity to those who knew what they were doing. Even Carlisle Barracks was interesting as once having been Carlisle Indian School where the legendary Jim Thorpe began his athletic career. Thorpe, a Sac-and-Fox Indian from Oklahoma, excelled as an amateur and professional in three sports: track and field, football and baseball. In 1950 he was voted "Athlete of the First Half of the Century" by the Associated Press.

I left Carlisle Barracks, fortified with a new knowledge of basic principals of public relations. However, AFIS inoculated me with another related concept that I kept throughout my entire career. I embraced the concise statement made by George Washington that shapes the basis for the Army's Internal Information Program. Simply put, "An informed troop is a good troop." What General Washington essentially conveyed was, *if your officers inform their troops of why they are where they are and the general objectives, they will perform much better.* The Army's internal information program was superior to the other services. Air Force was No.2 because it had recently been weaned from the Army. The Marine Corps was third since it was a much smaller, more manageable service. I carried George Washington's statement throughout my career until I was able to do something about it for the Navy.

Duty In Our Nation's Capital

My orders from Carlisle Barracks assigned me to my first Washington, D.C. duty in the Office of Information, Department of the Navy. I was delighted because I was going to the "Head Shed," the top of the mountain, the fountain of all Navy information. Zum and I decided she would return to Sheboygan with Stevie while I reported to work and looked for housing. On arrival in Washington, I stayed in the Bachelor Officers Quarters that were marginal at best. I wasn't happy there. Fortunately, within a few days, an officer from the Photo Section offered me a room in his home and was even agreeable to including Zum and Stevie. I accepted immediately and called Zum.

Zum spent most of her first D.C. days looking for housing. We (considering our status and age) had accumulated a pretty good size nest egg and could afford a decent house. Zum found a house in Alexandria, not far from the Pentagon and Main Navy Headquarters. It was a new development, and the price was $10,300. We didn't cash out all our savings but made a substantial down payment and qualified for a Veteran's Administration loan. The house was in a sea of red clay Virginia mud caused by continual rains for two or three months. So we became members of Virginia's landed gentry and settled in after reclaiming our sparse furniture that survived transit from Guam and a few months storage stateside.

The Office of Information was in the Zero Wing of the old Main Navy Building on Constitution Avenue. Main Navy (the federal nomenclature designating the buildings that housed the Navy Department) was a historic eyesore dating back to World War I. These temporary buildings gave credence to the adage, "There is nothing more permanent than a Federal temporary building." The structures stood for 50 years as the domicile of the Navy's hierarchy and were so Spartan they could be nothing but a deterrent to morale, career development and recruitment. President Nixon ordered them razed in 1968. Not many bureaucrats or veteran Washingtonians believed they would ever be destroyed. Notable among the disbelievers was Adm. Hyman Rickover, Father of the Nuclear Submarine, and whose offices were in Main Navy. At that time, Rickover was emerging as an arrogant, petulant, S.O.B. He announced to the world he was not going to move from his offices. A memorable cartoon in one of the Washington newspapers showed him standing in his office window staring at a wrecking ball as it swung down upon him and the empire he had created on Constitution Avenue. He thought he was impervious to everything, including a presidential edict. However, he did move. He was the last to vacate the "Ghost Offices" of Main Navy.

The Zero Wing of the enclave was the eastern most segment cornered on Constitution Avenue and 17th Street NW. That meant the next wing was First Wing, followed by Wing Two and on to Seventh Wing. I was delighted to be assigned to the Press Section comprising nine or 10 officers, an enlisted Chief Journalist and two or three civilian secretarial types. United States Naval Reserve (USNR) Cdr. Bob Jackson headed the Press Section, and his deputy was Cdr. Jack Pillsbury, another Naval reservist. Both were holdovers from World War II as was No. 3 in the structure, USNR Lt. Cdr. Marshall Baggett. He was followed by a couple of lieutenants and on down to me and a couple of other ensigns.

Our job was to answer queries from newsmen and to publish four or five news releases—most originated by the ensigns—each day. We young folks were assigned to a beat covering the important offices in the Navy Department. They were considered news sources, and we maintained a liaison with them. One office on my beat was the Navy's first "Missile Office." It provided my first encounter with Rear Adm. Dan Gallery who was not only an unusual character but also a legend. He was a naval aviator whose greatest claim to fame at that time was the capture of the German submarine U-505. The capture happened while he was a Task Group Commander of a Hunter-Killer Group during World War II. It was the first submarine captured and became a prize, as well as a symbolic manifestation of the U.S. Navy's success against the German U-Boat menace. In my mind, the U-505 also served as a reminder of Germany's success against U.S. shipping during the war and the near capitulation of the Allied effort against Adolph Hitler's aggression. The submarine ended up at the Museum of Science and Industry in Chicago. Adm. Gallery was from Chicago and that meant the possession of the U-505 was a must for the City of Chicago. As the Navy's first Missile Czar, Gallery didn't have much time for me, but his office staff collaborated feeding me information it wanted to promulgate. Gallery went on to other things, including starting the Navy's Steel Drum Band in San Juan, Puerto Rico, which became a big attraction in Navy entertainment. After retirement, he authored several popular books featuring Navy enlisted shenanigans. He spent a few hours in my Chief of Information Office (CHINFO) and other offices under my domain researching material for his books. He died in Oakton, Virginia, as an esteemed, legendary flag officer.

I learned so much in the less than the year I had in the Press Section. I relied on that experience even when I became the Navy's Chief of Information some 20 years later. The responsibility of handling queries from news people, ferreting out the answers from within the Navy Department, meeting deadlines and working with tough, intractable reporters was daunting. Interacting with obstinate naval officers and civilians was equally a challenge. Together, those experiences blended into an outstanding primer for a career public information officer.

Cdr. Jack Pillsbury was my boss on the Press Desk and the only Public Information Officer (PIO) I ever worked for. I am proud to say that because he was a class person. The reason I never worked for another PIO thereafter was because I was always the boss and usually the only officer in the office. There was a downside because there were no more opportunities to learn and develop skills under the tutelage of an experienced senior officer. I compensated for this void in my education by spending time with respected senior officers and corresponding with them. I sought their guidance on general public relations philosophy, procedures and, at times on specific actions.

Annie Urban

One of the civilian secretarial types was Miss Annie Urban, Bob Jackson's secretary. Annie was still in the CHINFO when I became the Chief of Information. In 1990 it was my pleasure to host a luncheon to honor her departure from Navy Federal service after 50 years. Annie and I have been friends for more than 50 years. Another civilian secretarial lady was a youngster from Minneapolis who was seeking her fortune in the nation's capital. Jerri Anderson was an attractive Swedish girl, who when strolling through the office had a dozen pair of eyes following every movement. Jerri took great delight in teasing me as well as the other men in the office. One day she stopped in front of my desk and leaned over to say something nice to me. I reacted by biting the stem off my pipe that was forever in my mouth. That incident accelerated my notoriety as well as Jerri's in the entire Office of Information and seemingly the Main Navy complex and the entire Navy.

forty some years later when Annie Urban retired, she presented me with a new pipe.

Black Media

When things slowed in the office, or I was eating my lunch packed by Zum, I occupied my time by reading newspapers published for black communities, such as the *Chicago Defender,* the *Baltimore Afro-American,* and the *Norfolk Journal and Guide.* I would pick up the papers from the desk behind me occupied by Lt. Dennis Nelson. The Navy was severely segregated at that time, and although there were a few black officers in World War II, all of them were reservists. Dennis was one of the "Golden 13," the first black officers commissioned in the Naval Reserve during World War II. The Navy civilian leadership was under pressure to doing something to support the integration program announced by President Harry Truman in 1948. So Dennis became the only black, recalled to active duty and given a commission in the Regular Navy. It was a hasty move and not well planned. Nelson was at least 35 years old. Because of his age, the Bureau of Naval Personnel commissioned him as a lieutenant. He had little or no sea experience, so he couldn't be assigned to a ship to compete with seagoing officers of his grade. Navy leadership acting in good faith, decided to make him a Special Duty Only Officer in Public Information. Although previously a professor at Fiske University in Tennessee, Dennis had no background in journalism or public relations. To make matters worse, the powers-that-were put him in the Press Section. Bob Jackson and Jack Pillsbury didn't know what to do with him. Everyone handled Dennis with the proverbial kid gloves because he could—and did—get to see Secretary of the Navy John L. Sullivan on a regular basis. Secretary Sullivan was interested in how Nelson was getting along in the Navy. With 20-20 hindsight, Dennis should have been assigned to Community Relations where he could have worked with the NAACP and other black-oriented organizations. Being a gregarious, outgoing, articulate person, he would have been an asset there to the Navy's public information effort.

Dennis Nelson was a compassionate, personable and engaging man who found himself in a tough position. He was normally cheerful, fastidious about his uniform and presented himself well. I was one of his favorites because I read his newspapers—which was more than he did—and I talked with him. I became the office expert on Afro-American newspapers because I was the only one who took the time to scan them. Being a self-confessed news junkie, my primary interest in the papers was to study their style, interests and focus. Naturally racism was the key issue throughout them. Initially I thought the papers were journalistically rather sophomoric but that was in comparison to the *The New York Times, Chicago Tribune, The (Baltimore) Sun* and the Washington newspapers we read constantly. My conclusion was the black newspapers communicated well with their audiences, and that is a basic element of journalism.

Going to sea at last

The annual summer Midshipmen Training Cruise, wherein Naval Academy and Naval Reserve Officer Training Corps Midshipmen spend about six weeks in fleet ships learning the trade, is an excellent time to embark civilian guests. The Secretary of the Navy had—and still has—a "cruise program" in which influential civilians were invited to cruise with the Navy to learn more about the sea service and the people who run it. Dennis recommended that the Secretary include three black guests in the 1949 Midshipmen Training Cruise that had a manifest of 12 civilian guests to be embarked in the battleship USS *Missouri*. The three black guests were newspaper editors Lucius Harper, *Chicago Defender*, Bernard Young of the *Norfolk Journal and Guide* and the Deputy Assistant Secretary of Defense for Minority Affairs James C. Evans. This caused a delicate decision when Dennis was not designated to be the escort officer because the other nine guests were white. He understood the situation and accepted it. He recommended me for the duty, and I was directed to do so.

Not aware of the racial dilemma until after I was told I was the escort designee, I was thrilled by the adventure of going aboard the *Missouri* and cruising to France and Guantanamo Bay (Gitmo), Cuba. The *Missouri* was the site of the peace agreement signing with Japan bringing World War II to an end. It was a famous ship, primarily because of the formal surrender conducted in Tokyo Bay on September 2, 1945. Named for President Truman's home state, the ship was christened by Mrs. Truman. I was particularly excited about being aboard the *Missouri* on the fourth anniversary of the signing ceremony. I was already thinking of an appropriate way to observe the special event.

My introduction to Rear Adm. Allen E. Smith, Commander Battleship-Cruiser Command, Atlantic Fleet and Commander of the Task Group for the Midshipman Training Cruise, was an extraordinary moment for me as a young officer. It was a precursor for an eventful cruise and introduction into the *real* Navy. Setting the tone, Rear Adm. Smith was not pleased with having an ensign assigned as escort officer and PIO for the cruise. At our first meeting he stated his view that he deserved at least a lieutenant commander. That widened the eyes of this ensign, already selected to be a lieutenant junior grade. As one ready to serve diligently, I had envisioned many things that should be done on the cruise in the interest of national defense and the U.S. Navy. Smith was also keenly aware of having blacks guests aboard for the cruise. He lectured us about the possibility of a mutiny or revolt in the ship's wardroom because the ship was carrying three blacks, even though the threesome included two newspaper editors and a Defense Department official. Rear Adm. Smith's chief of staff, Capt. Ferdenall "Goat" Mendenhall, had been adamant that a mutiny would occur if blacks were allowed on the cruise and assigned quarters in the same spaces as Navy officers. Adm. Smith and Capt. Mendenhall thought those in Washington's ivory towers weren't in sync with the real world. They felt the fleet was being forced to solve the nation's social problems.

Needless to say, the cruise PIO was not positioned to carry the Washington viewpoint to the fleet, nor was I briefed to do so. Besides, there was work to be done with all the Midshipmen and the cruise events. I strongly believed that the biggest advantage I had going for me as the PIO was working with people. There were numerous interesting Midshipmen aboard from the Academy and Naval Reserve Officer Training Corps (NROTC) universities and colleges. Each individual presented a unique story. The work assigned to the PIO and enlisted journalists was to search out that information. One of the basics of journalism is to understand everyone is a potential story and some are better stories than others.

As it turned out, we could not have asked for three better Secretary of the Navy (SECNAV) guests than the three African-Americans. They were gentlemen befitting their professional positions, knowledgeable in their fields and intelligent. Julius Harper was an excellent raconteur and had a story or joke to tell for any and all occasions. By the time the cruise was over, he was regaling the wardroom at each evening meal with his stories. There was no mutiny.

Other guests whom I escorted on that cruise included Melvin Payne who was with *National Geographic* and did a picture story about the Midshipmen Cruise. He later became Chairman of the Board of *National Geographic*. Other editors on board were James Kerney of Trenton, New Jersey's *The Times*, Joseph Roberts of Galligin, Missouri with the *Missouri Herald* and Mack Sauer of the *Leesburg Citizen* in Ohio. Dr. Phil B. Narmore of Georgia Tech and Dr. Henry Mills, Dean, University of Rochester (New York) rounded out the group of 12. I was the Den Mother, constantly serving and striving to meet their needs.

Rear Adm. Smith scheduled several meetings with the guests in his cabin and enjoyed lecturing to them or telling sea stories. He proved to be sort of a showboat and a little off course. Early in the cruise he went to great lengths to tell the civilian guests the Navy was the only service that conversed in English, did not use acronyms and how everyone could understand Navy people. One of the guests volunteered that he had just written to his wife saying that he was having a great time, and the Navy had fine people who talked a funny language. That was true. All Washington government employees profusely use abbreviations and acronyms. Pentagon personnel, unfortunately including Navy people, are the worst offenders.

Viva La France

We moored alongside a dock in Cherbourg, France, and I took care of the news media representatives who met our arrival. I then headed for Paris to see if there was media interest in our "Mids." There was. *The France Soir*, the country's largest newspaper, indicated it was interested and intimated its Sunday paper, *The France DiManche*, might do a full page spread for the following week. The daily paper had a picture of some Mids being tourists, but their Sunday supplement had a full page of photos most of them showing the Mids with girls. The center picture was of a couple of Mids with some bare breasted chorus girls from the *Follies Beregre*. I dutifully took a couple copies back to the ship and showed them to the admiral. If I hadn't done that, he probably would never have seen them. He was horrified. I'm sure he feared that the papers would get to Washington, and he would have to answer for them. He blamed me for letting them print such terrible pictures. There wasn't much I could do to dissuade his distorted concept of how newspapers were run. I was fast losing enthusiasm for my job and for Rear Adm. Smith, and I was sure the feeling was reciprocal. I became impatient for the cruise to end, but there were still about two weeks to go. Cuba was the next stop.

Before we got to Cuba, we were to hold the fourth anniversary of the signing of the Japanese surrender instrument aboard "Big Mo." I recommended to the admiral that we should do something to commemorate the occasion like laying a wreath at the appropriate time. The best idea I had was to get a picture of sailors and Midshipmen in dress whites covering almost every available space. They would stretch across the ship's forward end from the bow and gun turrets up to the superstructure and yardarms. The admiral bought the idea. The photo taken from a helicopter proved so good, it was used for several years. *National Geographic* published it as well as other periodicals. We also sent a message describing the event to General MacArthur who was then in Japan heading the occupation forces. MacArthur returned a message which ended with, "... there will always be a Navy as the world goes round and round and round ..." Rear Adm. Smith was pleased with the whole event, and I was slightly relieved of the blight from Paris.

Gitmo

At Guantanamo Bay the ships did some shooting. It was a new and fabulous experience for me to see and hear the *Missouri* fire her 16-inch guns. We fired the 5-inch 38 cal. guns from the battleship as well as from the eight destroyers cruising with us. The base at Gitmo was part of a 99-year lease dating from the Spanish-American War. It was used as an underway-training base with a gunnery range for surface and air targets. It remains an active base today. There I was introduced to Anejo Rum Punches. A large amount of rum is made in Cuba, and I observed a significant quantity consumed at the Officer's Club in Gitmo.

I left Rear Adm. Smith's staff at Annapolis where the *Missouri* transited to disembark the Naval Academy Midshipmen. His last words to me were that I had much to learn about the Navy and I should stay at sea if I really wanted to make the Navy a career. He also said he thought I had done well for a junior officer in the public information game. I thanked him for the compliment and agreed with him about the career advice. I knew I was still largely unaware about the seagoing Navy. Years later when I was the Navy's Chief of Information (CHINFO), I met Rear Adm, Mendenhall, then retired, at a reception. I identified myself as the Lt. (JG) who upset his staff back in 1949. He immediately recalled the time and said, "What an ignoramus Hoke Smith was."

The best part of the cruise was the homecoming. Zum and Stevie met me at Annapolis, and we went to our house in Alexandria for a wonderful reunion. The next day at the Pentagon, (The bulk of Navy's information business had moved there during my absence.) I settled into a new job on the Press Desk in the Navy Section at the Office of the Assistant Secretary of Defense for Public Affairs. Cmdr. Jack Pillsbury was still my boss. I was only there a couple of weeks when I received a phone call from a captain in BUPERS who detailed junior officers. He said I was an unrestricted line officer not a public information specialist, and I would be ordered to sea. BUPERS had struck again. Only this time, I agreed and asked for a carrier or battleship assignment. The captain advised I would learn more in a destroyer, but I said I would take my chances in a big ship.

Within a couple of weeks after leaving the *Missouri*, she had a change of command, and Capt. Page Smith was relieved by a Capt. Brown. The *Missouri* was to be a principal participant in a fleet exercise. When transiting from Norfolk Naval Base to the Atlantic Ocean for training exercises, she went hard aground near Hampton Roads, Virginia. Except for the new skipper, the *Missouri* had an experienced crew and an outstanding group of officers, most of whom I knew well. The *Missouri* became a monument to Naval stupidity for several weeks as it was high out of the water during low tides providing many negative photographic opportunities in her helpless situation. Probably the most beautiful ship (an *Iowa* Class battleship) ever built and by far the most powerful surface warfare ship with its 16-inch guns was stranded immobile, stuck in the mud, for the entire world to see. For two weeks the Navy struggled to free the ship. Each failing effort and futile plan was documented by the media. It was reported (and denied, of course) that when my old friend Rear Adm. Allen E. Smith, Commander, Battleship-Cruiser Force, Atlantic Fleet, was informed the Missouri was hard aground in Hampton Roads, he reputedly said, "For God's sake, don't let the Press see it." Being the ship Type Commander, Rear Adm. Smith took charge of getting the *Missouri* out of the mud. One of the best although not flattering statements came from Smith's mother in Detroit. She said she had, "... utmost confidence that Allen would get the ship out of the mud because even as a child, what he lacked in intelligence, he made up for in perseverance." Only a mother could …

The *Big Mo* was refloated, replenished with all the ammunition that had been removed to lighten her and sent back to sea. Capt. Page Smith was recalled as skipper to once again take command of the proud ship. Capt. Brown, who would have been a shoo-in to make flag rank if he had kept his nose and that of the *Missouri* out of the mud, was retired. He went to Florida to live out his remaining years. I understand he was a fine person and an outstanding naval officer, but he became a case study for the officer corps on how not to end your naval career. I most certainly learned from that episode, as well as from association with Rear Adm. Smith and others in *Missouri*. Capt. Page Smith later became the Chief of Navy Information and wound up his superb career as a four-star admiral, serving as Commander-in-Chief, Atlantic Fleet.

In the single year since returning from Guam, I had experienced a short stay at Great Lakes, 14 weeks at AFIS, duty with the Main Navy, the Midshipmen Cruise in Missouri and an introduction to the Pentagon. The learning curve the Navy had put me on was packed with interesting exploits and tracking like a steep rollercoaster. I was enjoying the ride and looking forward to more Navy adventures.

Midway 1949-1951

I received with anticipation and delight orders detaching me from the Director of Public Relations, Navy Department, to report for duty in USS *Midway* (CVB-41). *Midway* would become the name for the Navy's most durable class of carriers. She was commissioned in 1945 being named for the Battle of Midway which many historians claim to be the most significant battle in history or World War II. Three football fields long, she was the largest warship in the world at that time weighing in at 45,000 tons (easily 60,000 tons fully loaded as usual when she was underway). She had heavyweight champion designed into her as a result of the wartime experience of the Navy's ship architects and builders. Equipped with the latest technology designers could find, she was highly compartmentalized to prevent sinking from damage to a single section. She was retired in 1992 and is now a museum ship in San Diego, California.

"CV" was the designation for an aircraft carrier, and "B" was for Battle—or was it BIG? As a junior officer, I was proud to be a part of *Midway*—in my humble, unbiased opinion the most beautiful, most powerful ship in the U.S. Navy. My enthusiasm for the ship was tempered somewhat by some more calculating, mature officers who referred to her as a "Pig Iron Monster." I learned that some considered her a temporary way station in their progression to higher rank and status in the Navy or as a checkoff for another tour of sea duty. Despite having six years in the Navy, I was naïve, and my imagination and fantasies told me that I was in "Hog Heaven." Where else would a kid from the sticks of Green Bay have the opportunity to be in one of America's first and foremost defensive and offensive units? I had found a professional home and was comfortable in it. In port, when I strode down the pier to board her, I marveled at her size and strength. Each day I couldn't wait to get on board.

After reporting aboard, I was assigned to the Operations Department's

Communications Section for the first six months of the tour. I became proficient in encoding and decoding classified messages, handling the watch, routing all messages and delivering highly classified communications to the captain and department heads. The Communications Officer, my boss, was Lt. Cmdr. *"Mac"* McClure. Cmdr. Tom Moorer was the Operations (Ops) Officer and would later become the Chief of Naval Operations and eventually the Chairman of the Joint Chiefs of Staff.

I intently wanted to succeed but was conscious of lacking sea experience and was competing with Naval Academy and Naval Reserve Officer Training Corps (NROTC) graduates. Cmdr. Bill Woods, the Executive Officer (XO), interviewed me upon my arrival on board. He sympathized with my career pattern and understood my desires. He said the Communications Section would give me the opportunity to learn the ship, and in six months I would be ready to transfer to another division to acquire more experience. Bill Woods became a good friend and mentor. He must have accepted me because within six months he assigned me as the ship's Administrative Officer and Aide to the XO. That job really got me acquainted with all the ship's departments. Working with all the department heads and serving as the X Division Officer, meant I was in charge of seventy-five yeomen and other personnel. Additionally, I made the Shore Patrol Officer assignments at all ports of call. I learned that some of the junior officers wanted the first day or night Shore Patrol Officer duties. They were interested in quickly finding out the good spots to visit and what "dens of iniquity" to avoid when they went on liberty for a day or two. I also coordinated the Senior Shore Patrol Officer assignments meaning I had lieutenants, lieutenant commanders and commanders looking over my shoulder and sometimes smiling at me.

It was no surprise that I was also assigned initially as the Assistant Public Information Officer (APIO). I wasn't eager to get involved in public information because I wanted to concentrate on finding my way about the ship and learning my job. Besides, there was a commander who had the title as Public Information Officer (PIO). It was evident immediately that his primary responsibility was as official host (meeter and greeter) for guests, and I had observed that he was good at handling that part of the PIO tasks. I thought if I became actively involved, I would become his legman doing menial chores.

Once he confronted me with a "threat" saying I would not become the ship's PIO, a position he assumed I wanted, if I didn't show more interest in being his assistant. I flatly stated I didn't aspire to be the ship's PIO and explained I was trying to catch up with my contemporaries and learn more about the seagoing Navy. He was not pleased, but I think he understood my situation since I was allowed to proceed as before.

Introduction to wardoom dining

My first breakfast in the *Midway* wardroom was preceded by great expectations. There I was being served by Navy stewards in the wardroom of the world's largest warship. I even had a choice of entrée from a printed menu. I selected an old favorite—hot cakes. Served to me properly from my left side, the hot cakes looked delectable. Betty Crocker's best food promotion photos never looked better. The stack was three high and covered almost the entire plate. I put a pat of butter on top and was just about to smother the gourmet presentation with syrup. But then I thought I should go all the way and put another pat of butter between the first and second hot cakes. In the process of doing the same thing between the second and third cakes, I was forced to change my mind. There before me, stretched out in all its museum-style magnificence, was a large fried cockroach, face down in the bottom hot cake. Lesson learned—When dining in the wardroom, proceed cautiously. Welcome aboard, Lt (JG) Thompson!

Operation Bluenose

Within a week of reporting aboard, *Midway* deployed on an exercise entitled, "Operation Bluenose." We were to maneuver in North Atlantic waters above the Arctic Circle. The United States and the rest of the world had discovered the "Big Bear" in the Soviet Union was not friendly, and Josef Stalin was really not a nice man. Some exercises were scheduled in waters near the USSR, and the "aggressor nation" in all exercises was identified by a "hammer and sickle." Bluenose was an excellent training exercise of about three weeks' duration. We were training and learning about cold weather operations. Our primary concern was the possibility of losing an aircraft and the pilot having to survive in the icy arctic waters..

Operation Bluenose was my introduction to two memorable people—one a real character. He was Rear Adm. Joseph James "Jocko" Clark, who was at least part Indian from Oklahoma and skipper of the World War II carrier USS *Enterprise*. The "Big E" was the star of a Hollywood movie about the heroism of its crew and Air Group. Embarked in *Midway*, Jocko's current assignment was Commander, Carrier Division Four. He compelled everyone to sit through a showing of his treasured movie reel. He sat transfixed during the viewings always riveted to the screen. Jocko was a legend and enjoyed adding to his celebrity characterization.

The other and even more memorable person was Cmdr. Tom Moorer, *Midway's* Ops Officer. Communications was within the Operations Department, so he was one of my super bosses. A task of the Communications Watch officer was to ensure that appropriate officers were informed of message traffic affecting their departments or offices. Many times I had to awaken Moorer in the wee morning hours to have him "chop" or sign for a message. He never complained. *Midway* was like a city of about 4,000 - 4,500 except that everyone aboard had a job to do to make the city function. It was definitely a team effort. Moorer was the "third man in charge." He had a unique quality. A natural leader, he knew all the personnel (senior and junior). Those of lesser rank he called by their first name or nickname. He always made me feel good about myself, the ship and the Navy when he called out, "Good Morning, Tommy!"

Even frigid Bluenose was not without humor, I well recall one event. Jocko Clark became acquainted with a Naval Reserve aviator during World War II in the *Enterprise*. After the war, the aviator returned to civilian life, became a successful businessman in New York City and remained close to Admiral Clark. He died unexpectedly before Bluenose, and Jocko knew of his friend's desire to have his ashes strewn at sea. Jocko thought Operation Bluenose was the ideal time to do this. He conjured up an elaborate plan to have a full launch of all aircraft from *Midway* to commemorate the burial at sea of his friend. Cmdr. Moorer, another close friend of Jocko, persuaded him to tone down the plan. He made the argument that because of rough seas and low temperatures, if by chance a plane or any of its crew were lost during the ceremonial flight, it might be difficult to explain. Jocko finally agreed, and it was decided to launch one aircraft, a TBM *Avenger*. Riding along, Clark's Flag Secretary (Flagsec) was to be responsible for scattering the ashes from the bombbay. At the prescribed time, the Flagsec, properly attired in his Service Dress Blue uniform, climbed into the plane and was launched from *Midway's* flight deck. The pilot said the task should be done expeditiously, so they could return to *Midway* while the seas were relatively calm. The solo pallbearer agreed, realizing he wasn't dressed for an extended flight in a bomb bay. When the *Avenger* reached a couple thousand feet altitude, the bomb bay doors opened, and the flagsec attempted to empty the ashes from the urn, only to have some of the urn's contents blow back into his face and throughout the bomb bay. The aircraft returned successfully, and Admiral Clark told Commander Moorer to have the flagsec come to the bridge immediately to report. Moorer greeted the flag secretary and was amazed to see a gray uniform, gray eyebrows and gray everything else. The urn bearer quickly described the circumstances. Moorer told him to take a quick shower, get into another uniform and report to the Flag Bridge to give the admiral a report on the mission. He added that it wasn't in the best interest of the day to reveal anything but a successful burial at sea. Tom then went to the Flag Bridge to inform Jocko that the flag secretary was so touched by the event, he needed a few moments to compose himself, and then he would report to the bridge in a few minutes. The flag secretary dutifully reported, and a well-pleased Jocko was gratified he had taken care of his old friend.

After Bluenose we returned to home base in Norfolk, where the ship was readied for a five-month deployment to the Mediterranean Sea. This effort was another manifestation of teamwork, only this time it involved the unglamorous but essential area of logistics. The Supply Corps personnel were responsible for the steady progression of semi-trailer trucks unloading pallets of every imaginable thing—paperclips, bombs, potatoes, airplane propellers, bullets and shaving cream. Going on board was everything needed to keep a city of 4,500 and its large airport functioning for several months in a possibly hostile environment. It was amazing to see this evolution, to realize the ship would consume all these supplies and to watch the receiving personnel keep finding places to store them. And the ship remained afloat. Despite all the forklift trucks and elevators available, extensive "tote that barge, lift that bale" work was necessary. The sailors in the working parties got a good workout. Even though the workdays were long and hard, the excitement of deploying to *Mare Nostrum*, the Mediterranean Sea, kept their spirits high. Morale was good, and I witnessed strong leadership during those few weeks before deployment.

Since World War II the U.S. had kept at least one carrier and usually two in the Mediterranean to protect U.S. interests and provide a balance of power. History reveals that Stalin and some of his successors would have been more aggressive in the Balkans, overrunning Greece and Turkey to get to Middle Eastern oil, if it had not been for the U.S. Sixth Fleet in the Mediterranean. Whenever the Sixth Fleet was reduced to one carrier or it was even discussed as a possibility, the North Atlantic Treaty Organization (NATO) countries became uneasy and vocal.

Zum, Stevie and I squirreled our way into the Pinecrest Hotel in Norfolk where they would live for the next year. I was excited about the deployment but not delighted to leave behind my two favorite ladies. Stevie was becoming such a precocious young girl, completely devouring anyone's time and being such a love. As a father, I knew I was being had at every encounter. I conceded and loved it.

Mare Nostrum

Deploying in January, the first stop was Gibraltar, "The Rock." I was intrigued, but there wasn't much to do or see after the first 30 minutes or so. The monkeys living near the top of the rock were entertaining but almost too friendly. The British had The Rock essentially under control with the civilian denizens organized and disciplined. They seemed to share the excitement and novelty of having *Midway* visit their shores. We were warned the ship's personnel were not permitted to cross the border into Spain and the city of Algeciras, but scuttlebutt on the mess decks had it that some did cross the border. It wasn't true, but it made conversations a little more exciting. The next ports of call were more interesting to me but were gruffly set aside by the Sixth Fleet veterans who were awaiting Southern France, Italy and Greece. We visited Sfax, Tunisia; Taromina and Palermo, Sicily; Istanbul, Turkey; Athens, Greece; Cyprus; Naples and Livorno, Italy; the French Riveria in southern France; and Oran, Algeria. I remember walking from the pier to the city of Taromina. Women were hawking from open windows, "Hey, Chief, you want a pizza pie? Hey, Chief, I've got something you have never had before." Everyone was called "Chief" regardless of their rank or rate. I overheard a legitimate chief petty officer comment in regard to the last invitation, "Let's get out of here. She's got leprosy." Generally, it was apparent the ports we visited were still recovering from the ravages of the war that had ended less than five years previously. The local lifestyle was strained and difficult, a reflection of the economy that was still suffering but improving. The benefits of the U.S. sponsored Marshall Plan had not yet taken effect, but prospects of better days lay ahead.

With each port we visited, I got more involved in the public informa- tion aspects—informing the crew of local restrictions and what to do and see in the various ports and working with the United States Information Service (USIS) offices ashore. I gravitated to the internal information effort, and before long I was hooked. Halfway through the cruise, Commander Bill Woods decided it would be nice to publish a cruise book. I was designated to be the editor, much to the distress of my boss, Mac McClure. It was a lot of work but fun. Supposedly, everyone aboard was to have his picture in the book, and there was plenty of writing required about the ports we visited. Sales were crisp; the book sold out, and was profitable for the publisher.

One day during our deployment, there was a little consternation in the wardroom. One of the two 10-gallon coffee urns had started to leak and had to be taken to the Pipe Fitters Shop for repairs. There they discovered that the urn's bottom contained a cleaning rag, a watch cap and a black sock. A little more discouraging was the report that there was also about six inches of cockroach remains in the bottom of the urn where the coffee was filtered. After the urn was soldered, returned to its position in the wardroom galley and restored to duty, wardroom members complained about the different taste of the coffee. Nonetheless, new, somewhat basic instructions were issued about operation and maintenance for coffee urns.

Being an advocate of Wisconsin's favorite product, milk, I had never drunk coffee. In the ship's wardroom, coffee was the main fare at all times of the day and night with meals or just relaxing in the lounge. Somehow, it didn't seem right to sit there with a glass of milk and what was served for milk was reconstituted and passable only for cereal at breakfast. I tried drinking cocoa, but it was loaded with calories. I got a few looks from the "Wardroom Cowboys" with imagined questions of, "What gives with this guy who hasn't been to sea and drinks cocoa. What's happening to the Navy?" So I tried coffee, first British style with half milk and lots of sugar. By the time the cruise was over, I was drinking Navy coffee that was pretty strong, neat, straight and black. It became a habit I've faithfully continued.

The Aga and Ali Kahn and Rita

At the time of our cruise, Ali Kahn and movie star Rita Hayworth were romancing and married. They spent lots of time aboard *Midway*. We in the wardroom had the impression that Jocko Clark had fallen in love with Rita or was at least infatuated with the beautiful lady. Clark hosted a reception in the ship when it anchored off Cannes, France, honoring the Ali and Princess Rita. The Aga Kahn, Ali's father, was also a feted guest. However, he was so obese he couldn't climb the ship's accommodation ladder. Ever so resourceful, *Midway's* crew maneuvered the visitor's boat under a hoist and lifted the boat, the Aga Kahn and his entourage to the flight deck. Then, using a forklift, they transferred the Aga Kahn from the boat to the flight deck. His chair and its attached skid were well decked out in Navy bunting. When he left, the procedure was simply reversed. We got a great picture of him sitting in his entire regal splendor on the draped chair and pallet. It was rumored that his supporters paid the Aga Kahn in gold equal to his weight. It was readily apparent he wasn't conforming to any diet program.

Capt. Wallace M. Beakley was the *Midway's* commanding officer. He was an attractive, brilliant, strong willed and hard driving man. His life was tragic as his wife became an invalid and later died. He went on to become the Seventh Fleet Commander and retired as a vice admiral. After his wife's death, he married a lovely widow. I would see them occasionally at the Army Navy Country Club in Arlington, Virginia, and he seemed so happy. He was always pleased to see me, and we would chat about the "good old days in *Midway*." Regrettably, his new wife died suddenly. The admiral was so grief-struck that he shot and killed himself. I felt badly because he was a man who served so well, but missed the familial happiness he so needed and treasured. He had found that comfort and happiness briefly, but it ended suddenly and cruelly.

We returned to Norfolk as scheduled, and it was my first homecoming witnessed from the shipboard side. It was impressive. Emotions pent up for five months burst loose on the pier and aboard ship. Most all were elated with the homecoming experience. But some remarked, "I'll never do this again," while sinking into the arms of their loved ones and vowing they would leave the Navy at the first opportunity. I was elated and glad to be home with my two gals. I was looking forward to a job change in the ship and new responsibilities. I learned over the years that was the Navy's way of sinking the career hook deeper.

A story Zum related almost brought me to my knees. After *Midway* deployed from Norfolk to start our Med Cruise, Stevie took it upon herself to come see me in the Mediterranean. Living near the beach, Zum took her to the salty waters each day, pointed to the vast expanse of the Atlantic Ocean and explained, "Daddy was out that way in his ship." Stevie, a determined, adventurous child of four, wrapped herself into an inner tube and set sail for Gibraltar or parts thereby. Zum, usually relaxed on the beach, discovered the vacuum created by Stevie's absence and had to swim out eastward to get Stevie back to the calm waters of Virginia Beach. My dilemma—Was the Navy worth disrupting the tight family the three of us had? The answer was that *Midway* was scheduled for about six months of East Coast operations and then a four-month overhaul at the Norfolk Naval Shipyard at Portsmouth, Virginia. The next 10 months would be a breeze followed by refresher training in Cuba and possibly a deployment to the Med again. So let's try it!

Along with the new job as Ship's Administrative Officer was the opportunity to get "up on the bridge" and to qualify as Officer Of the Deck
(OOD) Underway. With Bill Woods' help, I was assigned as a Junior Officer
of the Deck (JOOD). His help got me there, but I had the responsibility of
proving myself. My immediate goal was to become qualified as OOD in the
Navy's biggest warship. The OOD is the officer who usually has the "conn"
(control of the ship), and although the commanding officer is never relieved
of his total responsibility for the ship, he trains, qualifies and maintains trust
and confidence in the OOD. In turn the OOD is in charge of ship operations and its safety. It's an excellent example of the responsibility given to
young officers and enlisted personnel at an early age in the Navy.

A turn of events

One of the first things we were scheduled to do after returning to Norfolk
and taking time for leave to get reacquainted with our families was to host a
Defense Orientation Cruise for 65 guests of the Secretary of Defense. Later
that week these same people would be hosted by contingents of the Army,
Air Force and Marine Corps at their respective bases of operations. It so
happened that the guests' embarkation coincided with the invasion of South
Korea by North Korean communist forces on June 6, 1950. It was a Sunday,
and the Secretary of Defense Louis Johnson came aboard to address the
group and a throng of news representatives. He said the United States would
respond to help South Korea. Ironically, Secretary Johnson had zealously
led a program to reduce all forces in the Defense Department, especially the
Navy and particularly aircraft carriers. The country's defenses were perilously
thin after World War II, and the U.S. was relatively weak in its military structure. Louie Johnson was a cigar chewing West Virginian who was a friend and
cohort of President Truman. His style was not popular in Washington, especially with the media, and he was heavily criticized for the ineptness of U.S.
military forces. So intense was the criticism that he resigned soon after the
start of the Korean conflict (Officially, the "war" could not be called a war
because of legal definitions, yet almost 37,000 Americans were killed during

the conflict.) and disappeared ignominiously into the wilds of West Virginia.

With the southward movement of North Korean troops across the 38th Parallel came a United Nations resolution that resulted in U.S., British and Australian forces deploying to help the South Koreans. This action revived the Navy to a great extent. Its numbers and vitality grew primarily by the infusion of funding that hadn't been available since the end of World War II. Many Naval Reservists were recalled to active duty, and many ships were recommissioned and restored to active service. I noticed the difference in the wardroom where the majority of the officers (most Naval Academy graduates) had been Regular Navy, some ex-reservists like me and a few "Mustangs" (former enlisted men). Because of the camaraderie of the majority, conversation was rather stilted with continual talk about "classmates" and questions like, "What class was he in?" There didn't seem to be much substance to ordinary conversation. When the reservists reported aboard—being recalled to active duty from a variety of venues, occupations and cultures—I noticed a difference in the dialogue. It seemed to be broader and on a variety of subjects. I developed many good friendships with Naval Academy graduates and harbored no grudge against them. In fact, I respected them and expected more of them. As I matured in the Navy, I perceived the difference between Naval Academy officers and others was more apparent at the low junior officer level. The difference gradually disappeared at the senior lieutenant grade. Academy grads had four years of training in Navy ways and customs in a rigorous, disciplined environment. They reported aboard ship as new ensigns ready and eager to take over the world. Their NROTC or Officer Candidate School (OCS) counterparts were still struggling with the fundamentals. I observed the spirit and integrity engendered into graduates of the Academy goes a long way in providing the substance, resolve, cohesion and "gumption" that is endemic in naval services. Go Navy!

The most startling news of that day was that *Midway* had three weeks to prepare for redeployment to the Mediterranean. We were dispatched to the Eastern Med where we were positioned in the event the Soviet Union used the war situation in Korea, to which the U.S. was heavily committed, as an opportunity to launch an offensive through the Balkans to take Greece and

Turkey. We had a different Air Group on board, the same flag, Commander, Carrier Division Four (COMCARDIV FOUR), but a different rear admiral. Commander Tom Moorer had moved from the ship to the CARDIV staff, and we had a new skipper, Capt. Frederick N. "Nappy" Kivette. Capt. Kivette was different than Beakley. He was more aggressive on the bridge and extremely tough on the Air Group. We lost some pilots and had a few more accidents, so the skipper was under pressure to react to the situation. He had to toughen up. At one time he had at least a dozen Air Group pilots in "hack" (confined to their rooms), mostly because he didn't like the way they approached the ship from the landing pattern. But I liked him and got along with him well, being his PIO and also on the bridge with him as a JOOD.

For the next four months *Midway* was deployed in the eastern Mediterranean, and we got well acquainted with Athens, Istanbul, Crete and Cyprus as our ports of call. Finally returning from the Med, on the last watch (a mid-watch) coming into Norfolk, I rated "qualified," was given the OOD watch and survived. This was one of the great thrills of my life. I thought now I could stand with my contemporaries and be considered a professional. I had the formal OOD designation as part of my official record.

On arrival at the Norfolk Naval Base, I was the In-Port OOD. That meant I would be extremely busy on the quarterdeck and miss out on an immediate homecoming with Zum and Stevie. They would have to wait until I got the ship settled down at pier side in Norfolk. The task involved moving the customs officials on and off the ship, securing all lines, bringing the welcoming party aboard, fending off the custom jewelry and used car merchants, and getting the leave parties ashore. I had already had an exciting day, starting at midnight, assuming the OOD watch on the bridge, qualifying, zipping down to the wardroom for a cup of coffee and assuming the in-port watch on the quarterdeck. As another deployment was concluding, Zum and Stevie were already waiting for me in the wardroom. My adrenaline was moving fast. Wow! What a great time to be alive, and what a great Navy I was in.

After being relieved of the In-Port OOD watch, I was able to properly and happily welcome Zum and Stevie aboard. Naturally, I had seen them on the pier but could not participate in the normal reunion rituals because the quarterdeck was the center of activity. Another deployment was behind us.

Hello Portsmouth

The ship was going into a six-month overhaul at Portsmouth Naval Shipyard. We thought it would be better to get out of the one-bedroom place at the Pinecrest Hotel and take a cheaper two-bedroom unit in Portsmouth. Zum was pregnant with our second child, so we certainly had a few things to do. Living in Portsmouth was not sumptuous, but it was closer to the shipyard and saved commuting time.

A shipyard tour is an experience every naval officer should have. It is not attractive, inspiring duty, but instead a period to endure. The ship is a mess, torn apart with cables and air hoses winding throughout all its open spaces. Noise levels are high during working hours, and the ship's complement is almost decimated with about 75% of its crew and officers assigned to other duties. New faces show up gradually, so the numbers are at manning levels when the ship leaves the yard. For those who remain with the ship, it's the time for shore leave and advanced schooling. One of the important events was Cdr. Woods being detached for other duties, and we received a new executive officer, Cdr. Dick Ashworth. I came to like, admire and respect him most highly. Dick was a naval aviator who served as a part of the Manhattan Project during World War II. He was the bombardier for the war's second atomic bomb drop that fell on Nagasaki. Obviously bright, he had commanded a squadron before coming to *Midway*, but had not been aboard a ship since his days as an ensign, fresh out of the Naval Academy before going to flight school.

Enter Craig Donald Thompson

The most important thing that happened to our family during the yard period was on March 30, 1951, when Craig Donald Thompson was born into the Thompson clan. Zum did well being the strong, Midwestern woman she was. Craig was born at the Portsmouth Naval Hospital. The day he was born, I brought a close friend and shipmate, Lt. (JG) Doug Cummins, to the hospital to see Zum and to show off our newborn. After we visited the new mother, she advised we should go down the hall to see the future presidential candidate. We went to the nursery window and asked through the 1/2-inch glass pane to see the Thompson child. The nurse dutifully inspected all the cribs and selected a child to display to the new father and his friend. My initial impression was that she got the wrong baby. "It" had a beet-red head that looked like it had been put into a pencil sharpener and actually coming to a point. I thought that all the sins of the father had descended on the child, and poor Zum didn't even realize what we had wrought. On returning to Zum's room, I expressed a mild concern. She brushed it off saying, "He's only a couple of hours old," and adding that in a few more, he would look okay. And he did! By the next day, Craig immediately became the All-American Boy. I devoted plenty of time to him. Surprisingly, Stevie, who was not quite five, was a great help to Zum in caring for the baby. She loved him and mothered him until he grew to be a "pest." Little brother was not appreciated again until they both matured. That may be an overstatement because Craig grew into a handsome, tall, articulate man. His great sense of humor drew him into becoming the family's court jester.

I took two weeks leave from the ship when Craig was born. When I returned, we were immediately underway for sea trials. On the bridge, Capt. Kenneth Craig acknowledged my return and asked perfunctorily about "Dorothy" (Zum) and the new baby's gender. He courteously inquired what we had named the boy, not that he cared nor would he even remember long enough to tell his wife who was more interested in personal things. Enjoying the attention, I replied, "We've named him ... Craig." Standing beside the captain I almost didn't get the name out. I didn't realize until that moment my new son's name was the same as the skipper's last name. Failing to make the connection, Capt. Craig passed it off as if we had named our son Jack or Joe.

When I got off watch and went to the wardroom for a cup of coffee, the word had already reached the lounge vultures. I was greeted with, "Hey Tommy, I understand your new son is named Craig. What's his middle name, Ashworth?" Ashworth, of course, was the last name of the executive officer. Actually, Zum and I never thought about the skipper in this regard. She had heard the name Craig while watching TV shortly before he was born and thought that it would be appropriate. I deferred to her on the name choice.

She didn't have an easy time during the pregnancy, so I would have probably agreed to any moniker. Craig turned out to be a popular name for boys in those days. In retrospect, naming him Craig wasn't a bad idea because I did cherish the time I had in *Midway* with Capt. Craig. Even if we had given our son the middle name "Ashworth," that would have been fine. The two names recall a pair of outstanding officers. Actually, Craig's middle name is Donald, honoring another great fellow in my life, my brother.

Before returning to sea, *Midway* was given a major facelift including installation of steam catapults for launching aircraft, a British innovation that was considerably enhanced by the U.S. Navy. The "Steam Cats" contributed significantly to the modern day success of carrier aviation. There had been serious doubts about the general utility of carrier aviation even after enormous success (primarily in the Pacific) in World War II. The Air Force had always tried to debunk the need for carrier aviation claiming it was unrealistic and wouldn't work. I suspect a major contributing factor was the stark fear of trying to land on a moving postage stamp in the ocean. It was much better to have 10,000-foot runways and be able to make a commercial airline like approaches on the final leg. The Air Force usually performed well when it had airfield rights near ongoing actions or over flight authority from countries on the route to military objectives. However, the Navy carriers were always first on the scene. Whenever a crisis occurred during the latter half of the 20th Century, every American President, Secretary of Defense and Secretary of State would ask, "Where are the carriers?"

When we left the shipyard, I was the only qualified OOD on board; all others had been detached for other duties. Overall there was inexperience on the bridge. Cdr. Dick Ashworth was the Executive Officer. He had not had a sea-billet since he was an ensign. The ship's new navigator was Cdr. Jack Grayson, a multi-engine pilot, who had never been to sea. Capt. Craig, the new skipper, was a naval aviator, had not been "to sea" since he commanded a stern-wheel ferryboat that had been converted to a practice platform aircraft carrier plying Lake Michigan. That vessel was used to train young aviators flying SNJ training planes out of Naval Air Station, Glenview, Illinois, just north of Chicago. We had to move *Midway* about 10 miles from Portsmouth Naval Shipyard to an anchorage off the Naval Operating Base, Norfolk. I had only qualified as OOD Underway just prior to entering the shipyard on the last watch when we returned from the second Med cruise in1950. I hadn't been on the bridge for six months, so the "pucker factor" was up considerably. But we made it and eventually tied up to Pier Seven at Naval Operating Base (NOB), Norfolk . We were provisioned and outfitted for sea trials and a six-week cruise to the Caribbean for refresher training. All ships emerging from an extensive overhaul with a new crew aboard were required to go to the Guantanamo Bay area for intensive training and qualification before deploying as a "Ship of the Line."

Teamwork

The backbone of successful military operations is teamwork. The epitome of that "spine" is the crew working the flight deck of an aircraft carrier. It is continuous, dangerous work carried out around the clock in all kinds of weather. Aircraft and other heavy equipment cover the deck, and 1,000 or more people, each with a specific job are in motion. Flight deck personnel are broken down into groups or "gangs." Their group specific colored shirts designate their respective tasks such as aircraft handlers, catapult crew, arresting gear team or fueling group. It was precision, dictated by the "Air Boss," officially known as Head of the Air Department. Housed in an "Air Plot," a little shack hanging from the ship's island superstructure providing a view of all his domain, the Air Boss continually monitors the flight deck and the 1,000 plus colored shirts scurrying around it. Additionally, he is responsible for the hangar deck and a few other incidental areas supporting flight operations.

I spent hours observing the evolutions on the flight deck. I witnessed the training, labor, sweat and exertion that transformed 1,000 inexperienced individuals into an efficient flight deck team. The average age of a flight deck crewmember was about 19. They were good examples of boys maturing quickly into men. Their shoulders carried the responsibility for expensive equipment, aircraft and human lives.

During normal operations the flight deck kids work 15 hours a day. Sea exercises or combat operations keep them on the flight deck continuously except for chow time and brief rest periods. Staying near the action, they often tucked themselves away for naps right on the flight deck or in the catwalks that paralleled it. I feel fortunate to have seen their transformation into professionals staffing the driving work demands. My respect for those youngsters, the chief petty officers and other officers who supervised them, became ingrained. I have often thought that the movement and drama on a carrier's flight deck should be set to music, a symphony surrounded by a choreography of men in motion on deck as dancers. In my work much later with the Navy Memorial Foundation, I continued to think about it and hope that someday it might some how come about.

After leaving the shipyard, I changed jobs again and became a Gunnery Division Officer. My responsibilities included directing 120 men, and half of the ship's 5-inch, 54 cal. guns. It was probably the toughest job I ever had in the Navy. Being in charge of 120 rough cut men, each with his own problems and distinct personality, was challenging. Trying to get to know each man personally was too much to accomplish during the six months I had remaining in the ship. I have always thought I should have done better in that aspect of my tour in *Midway*. But the division did well, and we passed all of our tests. I largely credit my chief petty officer for the division's success.

Personally, I thought I achieved new heights by being designated *Midway*'s General Quarters Officer of the Deck (GQ OOD). When the ship was in its premiere combat situation, the role made me the OOD, the only person on the bridge with the captain. It was an honor because the job always went to the most experienced OOD, the one in whom the captain had the most confidence. Dominating the skipper's mind was getting the ship through the tough refresher training program and passing all the required tests. Capt. Kenny Craig was a superb leader who forced responsibility on his subordinates. He was fair, considerate, somewhat passive but discerning. He knew what he was doing and generated calm on the bridge in all actions. He differed completely from the two previous skippers who brought tension to the bridge. I now know internal tensions don't belong on the bridge of a 60,000-ton warship with 4,500 people on board. That responsibility defines leadership. In deference to the three commanding officers I served under in *Midway*, their leadership styles differed. All three of my *Midway* skippers made flag rank; two of them wore three stars.

Obviously, friendships and relationships are established in all Navy sectors, but it seems especially so at sea. Some are professional and others social, but both are important to someone in a career status. Of the three *Midway* skippers I knew, the two with three stars both commanded the U.S. Seventh Fleet in the Western Pacific. Dick Ashworth also wore three stars at time of his retirement having commanded the U.S. Sixth Fleet in the Mediterranean. Tom Moorer went all the way to the top as Chief of Naval Operations and finally Chairman, Joint Chiefs of Staff. At the time of this writing he remains a good friend. Jocko Clark served as a three-star Commander of the Seventh Fleet in the Korean War. Several Air Group officers went on to big things. The most impressive was Alan Shepard, a lieutenant (junior grade) who became the first man in space and later walked on the moon, He and I were selected for flag rank at the same time. Al was one of the first men I put on the Navy Memorial Foundation's Board of Directors. Lt. (JG) Wally Schirra was in the Air Group and also became an astronaut. Lt. (JG) Robert "Dutch" Schoultz was a Combat Information Center (CIC) officer in *Midway*. We have remained friends and Dutch, an aviator, had a fine career. He became Commander of the Sixth Fleet; Commander Naval Air Forces, Pacific Fleet; and Deputy Chief of Naval Operations for Air Warfare. Little did I know when Lt. George Selfridge was working on my teeth in *Midway,* that he would become the Chief of the Navy's Dental Corps, the top job for Navy dentists. As should be expected, alumni of a ship with the complement size of *Midway* would have an impact on the future Navy. Naturally, the camaraderie developed in early careers has a lasting benefit.

Midwatch

Things were quiet and boring one night on a mid-watch as we were steaming along independently off the East Coast. I decided we should have some coffee for the watch, if nothing else, it would provide activity and perhaps keep people alert. I instructed the JOOD to send a messenger down to the wardroom galley to get some cups and a jug of coffee from one of the two big 10-gallon urns. I heard him instruct a messenger to do so. I was anticipating a cup of black coffee, no matter how old it was—perhaps left over from the evening meal. A half hour went by, and I started to ask questions about the missing messenger. I learned he was a new seaman just out of boot camp and may have become lost. About the time I was ready to launch a search, the befuddled messenger returned to the bridge and was told to report to me. "Lieutenant Thompson, sir," he blurted out. "I couldn't find no coffee in any of those urinals." I told him not to worry and said I appreciated the fact he had reported. I made a mental note to have us be more explicit in our directions the next time.

Another event in *Midway* has stuck with me over the years. We were returning from Guantanamo Bay having successfully completed refresher training. I had the morning (0800-1200) OOD watch. We were off the coast of northern Florida and about to launch part of the Air Group that had been with us for the past six weeks to their home base in Jacksonville, Florida. We were on a northerly course bound for Norfolk and home. It was a calm day. Only a couple of knots of wind blew from the south. The sea was like a pane of glass. We had a destroyer, probably out of Mayport, Florida, assigned to us as a "plane guard" rolling off the carrier's starboard quarter. Positioned there it could assist in picking up any downed aviators, who might have the misfortune of colliding with the water on takeoff or landing. Normally, we turned into the wind to increase wind over-the-deck (a sum of the wind velocity and speed being made by the ship). At the direction of the captain, I ordered the Signal Bridge to hoist the signal flag, *Turn 18* (turn 180 degrees) and to put "Fox at the Dip." The second signal was to alert the destroyer and any other ships in the vicinity that we were about to conduct flight opera-tions. Translating into laymen's language, it means the "F" signal flag is run halfway up to the yardarm on the signal halyard. When the Signal Bridge gets the order to "Two-block Fox," the F flag is run all the way up to the yardarm, against the stops. It signals everyone to stand clear—flight operations are in progress. When the bridge orders "Execute," it means the turn evolution is to commence. Normally, we would *Execute, Turn 18* and come about into the wind and then *Two-block Fox* to start flight operations. However, before Capt. Craig gave me the order to come about into the wind, he and the Air Boss decided to try something different. With little or no wind, they decided to deck launch some of the propeller driven aircraft on the northerly course. We did just that, after two-blocking the Fox flag. There was little risk because there was scarcely any wind, the ship was cranked up near 30 knots, and the aircraft were light being without armament and probably not even topped off with fuel. We launched aircraft for about 20 minutes until the skipper finally said, "O.K., that proves it can be done. Tommy, execute your turn signal, come about and see if we can find any wind."

We executed the turn signal, reversed course and continued to launch the remaining planes with the "Small Boy" (what carrier people call destroyers and ships smaller in size) maintaining station in a proper manner. On completion of flight ops, we returned to a northerly course. I released the destroyer "to duties as previously assigned," meaning it could leave our company and return to its homeport. On the Primary Tactical Network (PRITAC), I also thanked the Small Boy for the assistance it rendered. The destroyer's skipper came back immediately on the PRITAC saying they enjoyed the opportunity to be in company with *Midway* and adding it was "always a pleasure to work with someone who knows what they are doing." On receipt of the message, I looked askance at the captain wondering if he wanted to reply. Capt. Craig smiled and shook his head. "I think we had better leave that one alone," he said. I "Rogered" receipt for the message, thanked the skipper and ended the dialogue with "Out."

The accompanying destroyer was USS *Hobson*. It sank in the North Atlantic about six months later after a night time collision with the aircraft carrier USS *Wasp*. Almost all hands in Hobson were lost. A turn signal from the *Wasp* had been misinterpreted.

Before I departed Midway, Zum and I thought it would be significant and memorable to have Craig baptized aboard the ship. We did that following the ship's regular Sunday Protestant church services with Cdr. Herb Sears, the senior chaplain, officiating. We looked on the ceremony as one of the intimate Navy family things to do. In retrospect, those special events have become more and more important to us.

My 26 months in Midway *served as an important introduction to the "Real Navy." Being on the ocean with mariners dedicated to the Navy's sea control mission to protect our country's interests was invaluable. That collection of experiences contributed to making me a better person and more proficient naval officer. Those I served with in Midway, the vicissitudes of assignments, observations about the value of training and the esprit extant in a ship with good personnel and good leadership were all etched in my mind. I have appreciated the experience throughout my career and lifetime.*

Being in Midway *was a great adventure. And I was looking forward to more of the same. In early December 1951, we left* Midway *and the Tidewater area bound for the Naval Air Station, Glenview, Illinois. A six-month course of instruction at the Combat Information Center Officers School awaited me there.*

Destroyer's Wake

About the only significant event for me over the six months at the Naval Air Station in Glenview, Illinois happened in April 1952 when I was selected for and promoted to lieutenant. That provided a pay raise and put another half stripe on my sleeve. Lieutenant is a good rank. It marks the individual as more knowledgeable and mature than is true of most ensigns and JGs while youthful energy, drive and ambition still burn. As they say in the wardroom, a lieutenant is still a young *stud*. But he's somewhat reined-in by experience and is usually more dependable.

Zum, Stevie and Craig resided at Gramma Zum's in Sheboygan where Stevie could get into a school and perhaps stay for a year. My destination after Combat Information Center (CIC) School was undetermined, but I requested assignment to destroyers, preferably active in the Korean War. It would have caused wear and tear on the family to set up residence in or near Glenview and then uproot them to resettle on the East or West Coast. My request was approved, and I was assigned to the San Diego based USS *John R. Craig* (DD-885) after completing the CIC track. The *Craig* was en route to WestPac (Navy acronym for the Western Pacific or anything west of Pearl Harbor) to report for duty with the Commander Seventh Fleet for a six-month tour in the Korean conflict.

While at Glenview I commuted, arriving on Monday and departing on Friday to spend the weekend in Sheboygan. I went frequently to the nearby Chicago suburb of Norwood Park to see the Tombergs. As for the school, we spent considerable time running intercepts which was vectoring *friendlies* to engage *boggies*. (Using radar and radio, we talked to pilots who were on our side—*friendlies*—about enemy aircraft—the bad guys or *boggies*—by directing them by course, speed and altitude to intercept the boggies.) The not so modern aircraft we "controlled" were flown by our aviator classmates. The altitude radar didn't work most of the time, so we were often without that dimension. But we learned the basics, terminology and technology, and it readied us for the next assignment. I assumed that I would be the CIC officer in *Craig*.

My roommate, who was going to another destroyer in WestPac, and I drove a car from Chicago to Los Angeles. It was a new 1952 Ford sedan that we were to deliver to a dealer in Los Angeles. There was no cost to us other than lodging and meals. The best part was getting to see the Grand Canyon. We didn't have time to make the trek to the bottom of the canyon, but we were impressed with its beauty and enormity.

I boarded *Craig* in Sasebo, Japan, where she had just arrived from her homeport of San Diego. Sasebo is a seaport on the western side of Kyushu Island, the southernmost part of the Japan chain. It was near Nagasaki the target for the second nuclear bomb dropped in World War II. Getting to Sasebo was not easy. When traveling Navy Air, one needed plenty of time to spare, but usually made it. I deplaned from the extended flight to Japan at Naval Air Station, Atsugi near Tokyo and was then flown to Sasebo in a Grumman *Duck*, a small seaplane. But the ever cheerful, *gung ho* aviation Navy delivered me pier side to the fightin' *John R. Craig* at about 2200 (10:00 p.m.) on a dark, rainy and dreary night. After dutifully logging in, I decided I wasn't the least interested in hearing tales about the voyage from San Diego, but I respectfully met the few officers who were aboard. After changing into dry clothes, all I wanted was a sack, some privacy and a place to put my head. Most of the officers were ashore on liberty, and I thought it would be best to "turn in." We would all be in better condition to handle the introductions in the morning.

Come the morning I met the skipper, Cdr. Jim Robertson, U.S. Naval Academy's (USNA) Class of 1939. The Executive Officer (XO) was Lt. Cdr. Les Adkins (USNA '43). The Operations Officer was an old acquaintance, Lt. Bruce Flory, who with his wife and son, lived in the Pinecrest Hotel in Norfolk while we were there. Bruce was deployed to the Mediterranean at the time I was in *Midway*. He was a flag lieutenant and aide to a rear admiral, embarked in the cruiser *Newport News*. Bruce was one of the most senior lieutenants in the Navy and was promoted to lieutenant commander when he left *Craig* some six months later. There was one ensign, just out of the Naval

Academy, and two or three recently commissioned from Naval Reserve Officer Training Corps (NROTC) schools such as Auburn and Alabama. Most of the others were recalled reservists, not happy about being recalled and not pleased about being in a destroyer, especially one starting a six-month deployment in a shooting war. Most of these reservists were World War II veterans who had started their careers, were married and had young children. They were bright, educated and would do their job and not let their inner feelings dominate their presence or conversations. The ship had a good mix of officers for a destroyer in a wartime situation. Shades of World War II, half of the officers were career types, Regular Navy, and the other half were recalled reservists and ensigns out of the Naval Academy, Officer Candidate School (OCS) or NROTC.

Instant certification as OOD

I stood one watch on the bridge under the instruction of Bruce Flory, the designated Senior Watch Officer, and was immediately moved to the Officer Of The Deck Underway (OOD) Watch List. We had been underway for 30 days on the firing line off the West Coast of Korea screening a British carrier at night along with our destroyer division. The Officer in Tactical Command (OTC) was on the carrier. On my first watch, the mid-watch (0000 – 0400 or midnight to 4:00 a.m.) we were tooling along screening the Brit carrier and zigzagging in true World War II anti-submarine tactics. Stunningly out of the blue, the Brit signaled to reverse course and reorient the screen using "Method Rum," the most complicated maneuver in the book, at least for destroyers. Of course, the carrier sitting in the middle to the screen was relatively safe. But the destroyers (DD(X)s) had to dodge the other DD(X)s and the carrier while crossing the formation to take a new position in the screen. This was absolutely unnecessary and foolhardy. The Brits would do anything to complicate a situation, tweak an embarrassment or amazement out of the U.S. Navy, or at least give us a good workout. Fortunately, we had done this maneuver at CIC School in simulators. We had laughed about the "group grope" affect of this maneuver because there was inevitably a collision. It wasn't too catastrophic in a school simulator, but in real life, it could ruin your whole day if not more. This was definitely a maneuver that should be done only in a simulator or at least in daylight.

Ens. Sid Eddinger was my Junior Officer Of The Deck (JOOD) and had control of the ship or "conn" at the time of the order to reorient the screen and reverse course. I told him to keep the conn while I masterminded us through the maneuver. I jumped into the Advanced Tactical Publication (ATP) and tore through to the pages about the Rum Reorientation Method. I worked out the maneuvering board solution and checked with the Combat Information Center (CIC) to see if they were on top of the problem. They were. We made it, but the "pucker factor" was up considerably. Sid, being in the Navy only a few months, was amazed that I had him keep the conn. When joshing about it in the wardroom, he would say that it was too tough to handle, so the lieutenant let the ensign do it, and if anything went wrong, he would swing from the gallows. My usual retort was that ensigns were expendable, and I was too busy looking for a life jacket. I did let him know I was still in charge on the bridge, and even if he had the conn, he was following my orders. I could have taken the conn, and the situation would not have changed. But the JOOD would not have been part of it, and he would have shrugged the incident off as a blip on a dull watch. As it was, he never forgot it because he reminded me of it 25 years later at a *John R. Craig* reunion.

Training and educating subordinates

A senior officer in the *Midway* told me that the greatest contribution an officer can make to the Navy is to train and educate subordinates. Ultimately, the junior officers are going to perpetuate the Navy and will be responsible to maintain its high standards and efficient operating procedures. I also learned that one doesn't have to wait until he or she is a captain to pass down the experience and lore gained during a career. It is a constant procedure that should, and usually does, occur throughout one's career at all levels of rank. The same philosophy goes for enlisted personnel. It helps to solidify loyalty up and down and unite the trust, confidence and knowledge that should imbue the entire structure of a successful naval (or military) organization. I tried to do that throughout my Navy career and in my work in the private sector. I know I worked my JOODs and junior officers harder than many others did, and I only hope it paid off.

In *Midway* there was a procedure for shifting the steering of the ship to After Steering, a compartment in the engineering spaces near the rudders manned by a group of sailors whenever the ship was underway. This was supposed to be done in the case of an emergency on the bridge, a bomb hit or fire. Aboard the *Midway* it was tested during refresher training at Guantanamo Bay, Cuba. I tried it at least once each watch when I was on the bridge. There were men who had stood the After Steering watch for months who had not heard the frightening alarm and orders to "Shift control to Steering Aft." The word got out among the "Snipes," the Engineering Department personnel, that there was a nut on the bridge by the name of Lt. (JG) Thompson, who was disturbing the tranquility of the After Steering watch by cutting into nap or reading time. I saw it as an emergency procedure that wasn't to be tested only at Guantanamo Bay. I knew some day, it might be necessary to execute it punctuated with the statement, "This is not a drill," words that always gets an officer's or Bluejacket's attention.

Maurice "Mo" Hayes was an ensign out of Auburn University's NROTC program. He was a serious youngster who worked hard at all his assignments and frequently was my JOOD on the bridge. Aviation was his desire, and we talked about it often during slow watches. After his second deployment to Korea, he was accepted for flight training and became a successful naval aviator. We kept in touch, mainly through Christmas cards, and were together at the Naval War College. Mo had a tour of duty in Washington which brought him, his wife June and family together with us. He retired as a captain and used to josh that I had a great influence on him as a junior officer. Having stood watches with me in a destroyer convinced him to apply for flight training. I interpreted that to mean that he heeded my good counsel to *Fly Navy*.

In *Craig* I learned from Skipper Jim Robertson's experience. He was a good teacher and was not reluctant to pass on his knowledge to juniors. Our communication was usually on the bridge. When evolutions (tasks and assignments) were routine, we had long conversations. His naval officer dedication was obvious. He was all "Blue and Gold," and I gleaned much from him about destroyers and the Navy, principles I would carry with me throughout my life and adapt to new situations. One thing I remember discussing extensively with him was relative motion, how our ship was reacting in regard to other ships going at different speeds and on different course headings. I was pretty good at maneuvering board work because I liked doing it. It was akin to what I had learned and taught in air navigation and Midshipman's School. Relative motion, whether it is relative to wind, drift, the seas or the course and speed of other ships as well as aircraft, could be solved easily on maneuvering boards. However, there can be a problem relating those maneuvering board solutions to actual scenes when you are on the bridge and have binoculars on the other moving ships, many of them potential collisions.

Another thing that Captain Robertson dwelled on and has been indelibly imprinted on my mind is to continually *THINK AHEAD*—somewhat akin to defensive driving in an automobile. Have a plan in your head for circumstances that might occur especially when in close proximity to other ships. Accidents are not planned events. To save lives and ships, action must be taken immediately. Forethought about emergency procedures saves time in actual emergency actions. To emphasize that point, I recall Admiral Arleigh Burke, a legendary naval leader and an excellent destroyer skipper, replying to a question about the difference between a good commanding officer and a mediocre one, "About two seconds."

Life in a destroyer was much different than in *Midway*. The mission of other types of ship differs, but also has a great deal to do with the nautical experience and expertise. Going to sea in an aircraft carrier, especially one the size of the *Midway* was akin to going to sea in a hotel, a big one capable of sleeping about 5,000. Heavy seas don't deter the big ships unless the length of the swells is long enough to match the size of their hulls. However, it was a much different situation in "small boys," as aviators refer to destroyers. Almost any kind of sea will have some effect on a destroyer. I had a motion sickness problem as a youngster, and it carried over into my adult life. Thankfully, I had no problems with it during the 26 months in *Midway*. In *Craig* I was nauseated each time we got underway. I learned to control it by eating some soda crackers and busying myself so I wouldn't think about it. In an hour or two, I was functioning normally and got my *sea legs*. Even the rough seas of a typhoon didn't bother me. Oddly, when debarking after a month's deployment, it took a short time to regain my *land legs* when swaggering down the pier.

There was a lot of action and experience crammed into my tour in *Craig*. I learned about handling a destroyer but regrettably didn't get an opportunity to bring the ship alongside a pier or to get it underway. The skipper was good at it, and Lt. (JG) George Eidson, who became my best friend in the ship's company, was next in line. He was the ship's navigator, gQ (General Quarters) OOD as well as OOD for Special Sea Detail. He logged extensive bridge time and gained valuable experience. (George went on to a successful career as a surface warfare officer, retiring as a captain.)

I did, however, get to handle the ship in restricted waters and in all phases of Replenishment at Sea. I did well at making the approaches, conning while alongside a tanker or supply ship and doing the breakaway. George and I had a little friendly competition in this regard, to see who would make the fewest engine changes while alongside in an Unrep (Underway replenishing) situation. The supplying ship was always the station ship, which meant we were to keep station on it, usually at about 15 knots and about 95 feet apart. I had previous experience in *Midway*, but we were so big and stable that it wasn't difficult, and the captain was usually so intense that he had the conn. A destroyer is much smaller than the tanker or carrier (at times we replenished from a carrier), and we were subjected to the bow wave coming off the bigger ship, forcing the smaller ship away. That action caused the lines between the two ships to extend. It was important to keep the transfer gear— the hoses—out of the water. My objective was to settle in at the proper speed and distance, judge the wind and direction of the seas, and stay there with a minimum jockeying of speed and course.

It was distressing to see ships and some of our own OODs seesawing up and down the side of the tanker and yawing from 75 to 150 feet. The best I can remember doing was being alongside for 25 minutes with one change in speed, and that was only one "turn" (one RPM). This was the way an officer got the opportunity to demonstrate some skill and show off a little. But the best compliment I got was from the Snipes in the engineering spaces, who more than once said, "We knew you were on the bridge, so we all took a nap."

The firing line

One day on the firing line, off the east coast of Korea, I had the noon to 1600 watch on the bridge. We had been working all afternoon with a Marine forward controller who was ashore directing our fire at enemy targets. At about 1530, the Marine called to say we could secure for the day and paid a compliment to the accurate gunfire support from our 5-inch, 38 cal. guns. While we were in the process of securing the mission and congratulating ourselves, Ens. Art Gotshalk (who later became a career Civil Engineer Officer for the Navy, retiring as a captain) called down from his director post atop the bridge, saying he had just spotted a group of troops moving in and out of a bunker. He said the bearing and coordinates were on the north side of the Demarcation Zone (DMZ). I put the bearing on our chart on the bridge and told the captain that the position was very close to the DMZ, but I had it on our (South) side and the troops were probably "friendlies." The captain asked "Combat" which was the shortened version of Combat Information Center, for their assessment of the target. Combat came back with, "It looks like it's on the North Side."

The captain then said to inform the Forward Observer and ask for permission to open fire if he concurs. The Marine came back with, "I don't see it but sounds O.K. to me. Shoot."

Gotshalk screamed through his sound-powered phones that the first shots went right into the door of the bunker, a direct hit! The next voice was that of the Marine Forward Observer, shouting that we were firing right over his head and that we had hit a Republic of Korea (ROK) bunker. "Cease fire!" the captain ordered. We were devastated. Within about four minutes the mood had changed dramatically, about 180 degrees if one could measure moods in degrees. An investigation ensued, and it was revealed that six to nine South Korean Army troops were killed by our gunfire. The captain was not held accountable for any neglect or poor judgment. It was one of the *mistakes of war.*

Another short sea story occurred when we were on Korea's West Coast, operating with a British carrier. We had completed firing on targets north of the DMZ, and the skipper decided that we needed to refuel. Fuel is the constant worry of a commanding officer. Unlike nuclear powered ships that can go for several years before being "recorded" (nuclear reactor core replaced), fossil-fueled ships need and should have frequent refueling to ensure sufficient fuel is aboard to enable them to respond to any directive. We were directed to refuel from the British cruiser *Belfast* that was anchored in a cove off North Korea. We proceeded to the rendezvous point steaming at "General Quarters." All hands were at their battle stations. There was another British ship in the cove, and all seemed serene.

We nested with *Belfast* and were amazed that its officers were in their whites, having cocktails on the fantail before dinner. During the fueling process that lasted about 30 minutes, Capt. Robertson had been invited aboard the *Belfast* and joined the Brits to "splice the mainbrace" on the fantail. Several times he looked over at the *Craig* and acknowledged our presence with a big grin, tipping his glass in our direction. (Consumption of alcoholic beverages is not permitted in U.S. Navy ships, and the Navy has been "dry" since July 1, 1914.) When refueling was completed, Capt. Robertson made his manners to the *Belfast's* captain and returned to the *Craig*. Slightly aglow, he smiled at us and announced, "War is Hell."

"These Brits are nuts," he said to the XO, "Let's get the hell out of here." That we did—at General Quarters.

Getting shot at was another war experience we absorbed on that WestPac duty tour. The first time we received counter battery was a shock to me, because I had always thought I would act like "Mr. Cool" in that situation. I wasn't. I was in CIC when the word came down from the bridge that we were under fire. The captain ordered an increase in speed and a few turns, and we returned fire. It was over in a minute or two, and my reaction was a bit strange because I had never before experienced any symptoms of claustrophobia. I definitely wanted to get out of CIC. I wanted to see what was going on. I don't think it was an act of cowardice, just a lack of confidence in the equipment we had in CIC. The North Koreans fired at us on two later occasions, and I was much calmer. Again, the pucker factor was up, but not to any degree like that experienced during our first time "in the barrel." *Craig* was one of few destroyers to participate in the Korean "engagement" and to be fired on three times during a Korean War deployment. I was confident I had tested well except for the first counter battery. The lesson learned—do what you have been trained to do and fight the ship the best you can from your assigned position. And keep your head down!

Like most destroyers operating with the Seventh Fleet, our division was given a respite from the rigors of Korean War operations. We were assigned to the Formosa Patrol followed by liberty in Hong Kong. Wow! The Navy sure was taking me to the exotic places of the world. The Formosa Patrol was established to help prevent Red China from invading Taiwan where Chaing Kai-shek, the premiere of the Republic of China, had fled in 1949 with his family and remnants of his government. Since that time Communist China had threatened to reclaim Formosa or Taiwan (today) and return it under China's regime on into the 21st Century. Without the United States' presence and its declared intention to assist Taiwan, there is no doubt China would have succeeded in fulfilling its boasts.

A tough lesson

En route to the Formosa Strait our division encountered another typhoon aboard the *John R.* This one was most severe with winds up to 90 knots and seas up to 55 feet. I had the 1200 -1600 watch, and we even had to "button down" the bridge spaces because we were taking green water up at that level. The inclinometer on the bridge hit 55 degrees in one roll. We were all helping the ole' *John R.* to right itself, because it would have been uncomfortable if it didn't. The skipper was also on the bridge and offering advice to "stay out of the trough." That was like my mother saying we could go swimming but not get wet. It was difficult standing on the bridge's wet and slippery deck, but we managed. No one gave evidence of *mal de mere* probably because we were too busy trying not to fall and to keep out of the trough.

The XO Les Adkins entered the bridge with a big smile proclaiming that "this is destroyer duty at its best." He was also smoking a big black cigar. I immediately sensed what was going to happen because I began to feel the jumbling effects of the cigar and the ship's jarring motion. I approached Adkins and said, "XO, you are going to regret it if you don't douse and get rid of that cigar or leave the bridge." Just then the lee helmsman grabbed a metal helmet off the bulkhead and lost his lunch in it. Others were looking for receptacles, including me. The XO quickly exited the bridge, saying that he could take a hint.

We received a call on the bridge that one of the life rafts on the 02 Deck was working loose and might go over the side if not secured. No one was allowed on the open deck spaces. The captain called the First Lieutenant, Lt. (JG) Roy Dunham, telling him of the situation and saying he should get someone out on the 02 Deck to tie down the life raft. Dunham shot back that he would do it himself because it was too dangerous to detail one of his men for the job. The skipper agreed with Roy but advised to take someone with him. A few minutes later we got the dreaded call, "Man Overboard! Starboard Side!" Dunham was in the water!

My immediate reaction was to execute the Williamson Turn maneuver to bring the ship back on its track and hopefully to locate the lost person. I had not been trained in the Williamson Turn in a destroyer but had read about it. I was well trained in the procedure in *Midway*. The difference was that the carrier was so large and long that the initial helm order would be to get the stern away from the person in the water because he might get sucked into the screws. I hesitated about two seconds during which time I decided that it didn't matter with a small ship such as a destroyer. Just Do It! Good thought but the skipper interceded by calling out an order to the helmsman. He then announced that he had the conn. And by that time George Eidson, the Special Sea Detail OOD showed up and relieved me of the watch. The skipper was upset and invited me to my stateroom saying he would call for me later.

The ship came around on its track and miraculously found Roy, but he was in trouble. He had a life ring in his grasp thrown at him by the man who accompanied him on deck. He was obviously hurt and having difficulty. His leading petty officer, Boatswain's Mate (BM) First Class Robbie Robinson, tethered himself to the ship with a line and jumped into the water, swam to Dunham and maneuvered him to the ship's side. We later learned that Roy had bounced off the gunwale before hitting the water, and his back had been broken. The *Craig* was dispatched to Keelung, Taiwan, to offload Roy, and he was soon on his way to the U.S. Naval Hospital in Yokosuka, Japan. Roy's naval career was over. He returned to Kentucky where he worked with Ashland Oil Company, becoming its top executive.

I met with Capt. Robertson a couple hours later in his stateroom where I recited my situational response and admitted that within the dictum of planning ahead, I should have rehearsed in my mind the exact scenario that transpired and been ready to act immediately. The skipper realized that a good ream job was not necessary and that I had pretty well chastised myself and thought through the situation. He spent most of our discussion trying to bolster my morale and assure me that he was pleased with the development I had shown since coming aboard. On leaving his company, I facetiously remarked, "Incidentally, Captain, all the time we were fishing Roy out of the water, we were in the trough." He laughed and retorted, "I was well aware of that." Is that a great captain or what?

The ensuing five days in Hong Kong constituted the first of my many subsequent visits to that unique former British colony. Hong Kong was then a financial center of the Far East and fast becoming an industrial and manufacturing power. It was packed with refugees from Red China, many living on sampans, others stuffed into apartment buildings which were being rapidly constructed. We saw a proliferation of amazing bamboo scaffolding, essentially a graphic description of how to build a "House of Cards."

One of the items I purchased in Hong Kong was a pair of brown boots to wear with either khaki uniforms or civvies. Hong Kong was famous for making shoes overnight, measuring one day and returning the next for final fitting or delivery. The boots were comfortable and warm in cool weather. Shopping for Zum, Stevie and Craig was always on the agenda, and I remember buying a jade ring and earrings for Zum. The merchants came aboard ship to sell their wares. After sensing my interest in jade, one seller demonstrated that the jade was authentic by rubbing it vigorously on the steel deck and proudly showing the piece had no scratches. I picked out a setting for that specific piece of jade and had it delivered the next day. When I presented the ring to Zum for Christmas, she actually scratched the surface of the jade when doing dishes. The crook had given me a different piece of jade than what I had selected. An expensive lesson learned.

Another unusual event in Hong Kong was the ship getting its sides painted. Mary Soo Wong bargained with the ship to do the paint job using the *Craig's* paint. The remuneration was the collection of our garbage for the duration of the visit. This was a tradition, and she had a good reputation. Her painters were all women, and they did a good job. Over the years many U.S. Navy ships used Mary Soo's services. She then sold the garbage to hog farmers on the Kowloon side of Hong Kong and became a wealthy lady. At least, that is what we were told.

Back aboard ship we returned to the war and operated with Task Force 77, the carriers, for about a month. We were then given a port of call at Ominato, a small city in the northern Japanese island of Hokkaido. It had only about 5,000 people and two or three restaurants. The first day ashore was my birthday, September 16, 1952, and I thought it a good idea to celebrate. After all, I would never be 30 again. Wearing my new Hong Kong boots, I went ashore with all the officers in the off-watch sections joining me. We found one of the restaurants and took over the place from about 1500 in the afternoon to about 2100 that night. In accordance with Japanese customs, we had to doff our shoes on entering the establishment and don Japanese sandals. We drank Asahi beer, ate Japanese sushi and sang all the old songs we could recall. We finally got tired and prepared to leave. To my dismay, my boots were missing.

The proprietor was upset and called the police. I think there was one policeman in the town, and he arrived in the "paddy wagon" which was a tricycle, or a pedicab, with an open box in the rear with seats. I was assisted by the Chief of Police who didn't want me to walk the three or four blocks to the pier in stocking feet. He kindly "gave me a lift" in his only official means of transportation. My friend, George Eidson, joined me in this open-air paddy wagon for the short ride. Along the way we were hailed by enlisted men who exclaimed delightfully, "Hey, Look! They got some officers! Look at that. The cops got Lieutenant Thompson." I was rather enjoying my birthday and waved to them but with no comment. At the pier I was greeted with more guffaws as I sheepishly strode down the dock in my stocking feet to board our boat to return to the ship. I dutifully reported my presence on board to the Officer of the Deck, an ensign, who did a poor job of keeping a straight, serious face. On entering my stateroom, I was surprised and pleasantly relieved to see my new Hong Kong boots on my desk awaiting my arrival.

In the wardroom the next morning there were the expected jibes and banter about my boots and the birthday party. At Quarters for Muster at 0800, I reported to my position and department to be greeted by the entire Operations Department, at attention honoring my arrival, with all personnel standing in their stocking feet sans shoes or boots.

It wasn't until February of 1953 at a ship's party in San Francisco, that I learned from one of the Snipes that it was he who removed my boots from the Ominato restaurant for "safe-keeping" and delivered them to my stateroom. I thanked him for being so thoughtful and for providing me with a memorable experience. We toasted the event that, by this time, had been institutionalized in *Craig* sea stories.

Craig was scheduled to return to San Diego in mid-December, but the presidential elections in November 1952 provoked a different scenario. During his campaign General Dwight D. Eisenhower, USA (Retired) stated that one of his first priorities as the president-elect would be to go to Korea to shorten the war. In early December our destroyer division received high priority orders for its ships to be strung out between Japan and Guam spaced about 200 miles apart. Each ship was to continuously broadcast a two-letter signal to serve as a beacon for the Presidential airplane. We were also poised to provide sea rescue assistance in the event the aircraft was forced to land at sea with its prized passenger manifest.

Craig was to broadcast "M O," Mike Oboe—dah dah -- dah dah dah. Cdr. Robertson was the junior commanding officer in the division, so we were positioned closest to Korea somewhere off Okinawa. Other ships in the division were further down the chain, all closer to home. We were told when to commence broadcasting Mike Oboe, but no time for terminating the ordeal. All of us in communications took our turn at manually sending out the signal Mike Oboe—dah dah -- dah dah dah. I had it going through my mind continuously. My guys intercepted the news broadcasts, so we knew General Eisenhower had been to Korea and was back in Hawaii, but we were still pounding out Mike Oboes.

Two days later, a routine message addressed to us appeared on the Fox Schedules (Fleet Broadcast). Because of the large volume of communications in the Western Pacific war zone, very little message traffic was transmitted less than priority. Our message was classified "Confidential" and coded, so I had to "break it," that is decipher the coded text. By this time the captain had heard there was a message for us on the Fox Skeds and was sticking his head into the crypto shack, a 3 x 4 foot cubicle next to the radio room. I admit I was a little disturbed with him looking over my shoulder as I was typing out the coded text because I was trying to expedite the deciphering. That meant I was more prone to errors. However, I knew the skipper was most concerned about our situation. When I finally got the plain language text printed out on a tape, I handed it to him and said, "Thank, God. No more Mike Oboes. We can go home!" The captain immediately got on the 1MC, the ship's public address system, to announce the news to the crew. They responded with a cheer so loud that it probably rattled the windows on Okinawa a hundred or so miles away. The message releasing us from this important, but perfunctory task was dated two days prior to its appearance on the Fleet Broadcast. I remember Dick Ashworth growling to me in anguish one time in *Midway,* "The Navy was conceived and designed by genius and run by idiots!" In the *Craig's* wardroom, we all agreed, especially about those idiots who handled communications concerning our mission.

Our orders were to "proceed on duty assigned ..." which meant to head for San Diego. We had burned up some fuel being on station two days longer than necessary, so the captain opted to head for Guam to top off and then set course for Pearl Harbor. We didn't waste any time at Guam, just enough to fill the fuel tanks and depart from Apra Harbor. I didn't get to see my old haunts on the island but wasn't much concerned. We were headed for home. We had been gone six months and had other more interesting thoughts. A call at Pearl Harbor was a little longer, to top off again and to take on provisions. During our four-hour stay, I got to see Cdr. Jack Pillsbury, then the Commander-in-Chief, Pacific Fleet, Public Information Officer (CINCPACFLT PIO).

The cruise from Guam to San Diego was a lazy one. The seas were calm and placid, and morale was good with the decrease in pressure and the advent of homecoming and Christmas. Almost everyone was feeling benevolent and in good spirits. Quartermaster Len Martin came up with an idea that we should collect a fund to be presented upon our return to San Diego to some child who might have a better Christmas than he or she was anticipating. The captain thought it was a good idea, and we aptly called it "Operation REJOICE," *Rejoice* being *Craig's* call sign. In voice communications a ship or unit name or number is seldom, if ever, used. Every ship, squadron, unit, or commander has a call sign published in a classified document. The Seventh Fleet Commander's (COMSEVENTHFLT) call sign was *Jehova*. It was on this deployment that I actually heard Vice Adm. Joseph James "Jocko" Clark, then fleet commander, address the Seventh Fleet in the Sea of Japan saying, "This is Jehovah himself..."

Operation REJOICE was a success. More than $3,700 was raised and given to a young lad who was a hemophiliac, and whose parents were having a difficult time financing his blood program. I have always been impressed by the generosity of Navy enlisted personnel, and Operation REJOICE gave further testimony of their kindness and thoughtfulness. It seemed the officers were not as forthcoming, at least not as generous, to the notions that "they were going to make some kid's Christmas happier." The generosity of Navy personnel is legendary, and I became increasingly aware and appreciative of it when I was trying to finance the U.S. Navy Memorial 35 years later.

We arrived in San Diego on December 23rd with band music and flourishes. To meet us was Lt. Jim Jenkins who was the Commander, Cruisers Destroyers, Pacific (COMCRUDESPAC) Public Information Officer (PIO). Jim had relieved me in Washington when I was detached to join *Midway*. He confided that he had tried to get me as his relief, but the Bureau of Navy Personnel (BUPERS) said, "Not only NO, but Hell NO. Thompson had just started a tour of duty in *Craig.*" As far as I was concerned, that was the end of the story, and I thought no more of it. I was pleased to be in *Craig.*

I also saw George Dissinger who was finishing up his college program at San Diego State College (later San Diego State University) and was to embark on a successful career with *The San Diego Union-Tribune.* My plane reservation was for a next day departure bound for Chicago, and I was to take the train to Milwaukee where Zum would pick me up. It happened to be Christmas Eve. Stevie was with Zum. What a joy it was to be with them, and we were looking forward to the next day, Christmas 1952. It proved to be a downer!

Merry Christmas!

After a morning of Christmas in Sheboygan, we packed the car for a visit to Green Bay and our extended family. We had Zum, Stevie and Craig in the front seat with me. Gramma Zum (Olga) was in the back. Outside of Denmark, Wisconsin almost half way to Green Bay, Craig got carsick. I tried to get a blanket stuffed under his nose, so he could throw up into it. In the meantime with my eyes off the road, I didn't negotiate a turn and left the highway at about 55 miles per hour hitting a snow covered concrete abutment, hidden in a field, totaling the car. Result: Olga broke a leg, Zum had a broken ankle, my face was cut up from impacting the steering wheel, and Stevie's head broke the windshield. We were concerned about skull fractures, but Stevie didn't suffer any. Craig was unscathed, but it scared the heck out of him. He was probably afraid to ever get carsick again. I was really distressed and couldn't understand why after just completing an adventurous six months in a war, getting shot at three times, and going through five typhoons, I had to be so stupid as to put the whole family in the hospital. Merry Christmas!

We purchased a new Nash Ambassador sedan in Green Bay and returned to Sheboygan. I got a two-week extension on my two week's leave from the ship, After taking time to heal from our wounds, we departed for San Francisco where the *Craig* was undergoing a six-month overhaul at the Navy shipyard. We lived in half a Quonset Hut at the shipyard. I had to reflect that when I was an ensign on Guam, we had a whole Quonset Hut. By the time I got to the ship, Bruce Flory was gone as was George Eidson, and I became the operations officer and navigator and, in fact, the acting executive officer. Lt. Cdr. Les Adkins, the XO, was on leave and telegraphed that he (like me) needed two more weeks to recover from a car accident.

Shipyard time is as dreadful to a destroyer ship's company as to a carrier's crew. The ship is a dirty mess. But it is a time to take care of lots of details:

get your men assembled, trained and schooled, and even grab a couple weeks of school yourself to better prepare for the future. I took the occasion to get myself into the Command Anti-Submarine Warfare course at San Diego. It was a two-week course, and I busied myself that first week, studying at night, except for one when I got in touch with George Eidson, who was assigned to the Fleet Training Command in San Diego.

George and I duplicated some of the "liberties" we had in WestPac, imbibed a bit, had a meal and somehow ended up in Tijuana. A merchant accosted us on the street, vending some "authentic jade." This vendor picked the wrong guy to barter about jade, one with Hong Kong experience. He swore that a large piece was true jade and would withstand any abuse. I challenged him to let me scrape it on the sidewalk. Naturally, he had to permit me to test it, and when I returned the piece to him marred and scarred, he shouted for the police and demanded that I pay for it. George and I escaped back to San Diego post haste. At my own expense, I returned to San Francisco for the weekend and was informed that the skipper wanted to see me "immediately."

Jim Robertson was waiting for me with a speech prepared and rehearsed for at least three days. He had in his hand a letter written to me from Jim Jenkins, the COMCRUDESPAC PIO, in San Diego stating that I was to receive orders detaching me from *Craig* to report to the COMCRUDESPAC staff as Jenkins' relief. The letter was addressed to me, but the envelope was addressed to the Commanding Officer, USS *John R. Craig*. Jenkins' yeoman had goofed!

"Why did you go to San Diego? To try to get off my ship?" Robertson yelled. I told him I had not seen Jenkins since we arrived in San Diego from WestPac when he told me that he had recommended me as his relief but had failed. I had totally forgotten about the situation. I tried to tell the captain that I was not unhappy in *Craig* and that I had nothing to do with the impending orders.

I later learned that Rear Adm. Hopwood, COMCRUDESPAC, didn't take kindly to a BUPERS detailer turning down a request for an officer in his force to report for duty on his staff. It was one of the items he had on his list of "things to do in Washington." Rear Adm, Hopwood had no knowledge of me as a person, but he told me later he wanted a PIO who knew something about his ships and fleet operations as well as having public information skills. The "Admiral network" prevailed in the situation when "Hoppy" mentioned to one of his flag officer friends in BUPERS he very much wanted Lt. Thompson on his staff.

I doubt that Jim Robertson ever believed me, and my fitness report from him was not the greatest. However, orders arrived and a relief for me reported aboard. I left *Craig* with some remorse because I had matured Navy-wise in the nine months I was aboard. I would have been happy to stay with my then current status in the ship. But being the idealist, I thought I had a good couple years ahead of me as a PIO for the Cruisers Destroyers Force in the Pacific Fleet. I loved destroyers, liked sea duty and with my strong penchant for public information, I honestly believed I could do a better job for the Navy on the admiral's staff than as a lieutenant in a destroyer.

As I have looked back on my career, I enjoyed all my assignments after Craig, but I learned so much and matured in that too short a tour in a destroyer. I thought I was destined to remain with the Craig because my son's name was Craig and my last Commanding Officer with the Midway was Kenny Craig, a great skipper. It was not to be.

Many years later I became friends with the British artist, John Hamilton, who asked me one evening over a brandy about my most memorable time in the Navy. After considerable thought I replied, "My time in the destroyer John R. Craig (DD-885)." He asked why, and I shared with him some of the unforgettable episodes including going through five typhoons in the six months during the Korean War. A few months later, John sent me a beautiful oil painting of the Craig in very heavy seas. It is the centerpiece of my Navy treasures at home, and its waves still roil the memories of the people, places and oceans I knew then.

A New Career A-Borning

The second week of Anti-Submarine Warfare (ASW) School was different. I had been dedicated to learning more about the anti-submarine warfare business from the position of a shipboard officer—the nitty-gritty, hands on tactics as a destroyer lieutenant operations officer. My perspective had changed somewhat to an overall observer, looking at a bigger picture of anti-submarine warfare and how the destroyer force was deployed on that mission. This slight shift was precipitated by receipt of orders to the Commander, Cruiser Destroyer Force, Pacific (CCDP) staff. CCDP was a "type" commander, meaning he had administrative control of all cruisers and destroyers (including destroyer escorts) in the Pacific Fleet. He had little operational control of his ships, which would normally be under the control of an operational commander such as Commander Seventh Fleet in the Western Pacific. The CCDP's job was to keep his ships in a high state of personnel and material readiness. He handled all the funds for training both tasks. At times he would schedule training exercises in which he would participate as an operational commander, utilizing and exercising his staff. He was responsible to the Commander in Chief, Pacific Fleet headquartered at Pearl Harbor.

Also, during that second week of ASW School high on my priority list was to find a place for our family to reside in San Diego. George Eidson and George Dissinger drove me to some of the advertised real estate. By the end of the week with nothing to show for my efforts, I was getting a little concerned. On a Thursday evening, the day before I was to return to San Francisco Naval Shipyard, we came upon a new house built on speculation by Mr. Carol Worden. It was just outside the San Diego city limits in LaMesa, one of the fast growing suburbs. It was on a corner lot and had three bedrooms, two-car garage, cream stucco finish and beautiful hardwood floors. The cost was about $16,000. Mr. Worden questioned whether a lieutenant in the Navy could afford such a house. I told him that I didn't know about all Navy lieutenants, but "this one could!" We consummated the deal with a handshake, me signing a piece of paper and giving him a check for earnest money.

When I got back to home base the next evening, Zum and the kids were excited and asked a lot of questions about their new home in LaMesa. My recollection of the house was vague, seeing it for only a half hour in the dark. I thought it had three bedrooms, and yes, there was a large living room, we were on a corner lot and there was a school not too far away. Zum sort of rolled her eyes, and I responded by trying to resurrect the proceedings of the previous evening. I assured her that we were going to be happy in our new house, but I admit to sounding rather vague. I decided, with Zum's full concurrence, that I would not buy a house by myself again because she had many more criteria to check off.

On the drive down to San Diego, I was surrounded by a bunch—well, three anyway—of skeptics including Craig who was just a little more than two years old but had gotten the message from his mother and sister. When we arrived at Camellia Avenue—Voila, there was a pretty house and a comfortable home. All was forgiven; the three of them liked it! Even Craig liked it! We had 30 satisfactory months there. It was a good neighborhood, and Stevie's school was excellent. The Sunday school nearby was pleasant for both Stevie and Craig and commuting to the Fleet Landing at San Diego Harbor was not ponderous.

I carpooled with my immediate boss, Cdr. Everett "Easy" Glenn, who was the staff's Administrative Officer (ADMINO) as well as Force Personnel Officer (FPO). Our across-the-street neighbors, George and Doris Randall, became good friends, and we maintained a quality relationship for more than 50 years. We socialized on the weekends and did a lot of camping in the Cuyamaca Mountains about 60 miles to the east of San Diego. Camping was a deliberate family recreation choice. It was not expensive and gave us the opportunity to spend time with the children in a healthy environment. I always liked the outdoors—hiking, winter sports and camping—having participated in those activities while growing up. Now I had the chance to participate in a second childhood but with maturity. I found that one is never too old to get into second childhood activities. Zum didn't mind, although I doubt if she ever became an ardent fan of camping. She did like the Sunday morning breakfasts we always prepared—fried potatoes mixed with eggs and onions with a couple of rashers of bacon on the side, all with lots of black coffee boiled over an open fire. If she served something like that at home, I would have probably said something to ruin the entire day, but it sure was good early in the morning in the forests amidst Mother Nature's critters.

The CCDP and his staff were embarked in a destroyer tender, either the *Dixie, Prairie* or *Piedmont* rotating between San Diego and the Western Pacific. A tender in Navy terms means a repair ship; one that tends a flock of small ships. They are not combatant ships per se but rather support ships for combatants. They are essentially floating machine shops or miniature shipyards, a valuable asset for ships deployed to forward areas. There are tenders for destroyers and submarines, and when the Navy had seaplanes, there were tenders especially equipped to maintain them when deployed to forward areas.

When in San Diego, they serviced destroyers home ported there and were moored in the middle of San Diego's magnificent harbor at Buoy #23. Occasionally, Rear Adm. Herbert G. Hopwood, the commander, would get the tender underway, so it could go to sea like all good Navy ships, and smokers could buy "sea store" cigarettes and cigars at about five cents a pack for cigarettes and about the same for a good cigar. Sea stores, as they were called, were sold outside the U.S. territorial waters or three-mile limit where no federal or local tax was imposed on the product. To smokers, buying sea store cigarettes was like finding gold, they were so cheap. The tender would clear the harbor, cruise around Catalina Island and return to Buoy #23 in one day. It was figured in just that one day, the currents and flushing action of the ocean's tides would clear away the coffee grounds which had accumulated under the ship while it was moored to Buoy #23 during the previous months. The quarterly cruise served other purposes too and let the seagoing personnel exercise and train.

Small boats including admirals' barges, captains' gigs, officers' motor boats and enlisted liberty launches operated from the ship to the San Diego Fleet Landing or the Coronado Landing transporting personnel to their work place and then returning. Duty in CCDP staff was not considered sea duty. Whatever it was called, it didn't bother me. I was happy to be a part of the Pacific Fleet and active with the operating forces.

When I came aboard the CCDP staff, I was not comfortable with the organization chart that had me reporting to Easy Glenn before I could see the chief of staff and then the admiral. I soon learned that Easy was no problem, because he was pretty much laid back (therefore his nickname) and up to his armpits in personnel work. He didn't understand the basics of public information skills and wasn't about to get involved in trying to deter or filter my interfaces with the chief of staff or the admiral. I made a point to always keep him informed and cut him in on the reactions to my proposals by the CoS and admiral. Riding with him each day to and from work was a benefit. Easy was helpful to me, and we became good friends. His wife Mary and Zum became well acquainted. We partied and got into square dancing together.

Rear Admiral Herbert Hopwood

The only negative aspect of my relationship with Rear Adm. Hopwood was that it didn't last long. He was promoted to three stars and left within six months for the Op-04 (Deputy Chief of Naval Operations for Logistics) job on the Chief of Naval Operations (CNO) staff in Washington. He was a gregarious little man and like his wife Jean was originally from Shamokin, Pennsylvania. She was a lady of German background and sort of mothered me for a period during my career. "Hoppy," as he was called, was eager to do something in the public relations area and was receptive to occasionally sending our ships into other-than-home ports following training exercises. He was also pleased with my recommendation to expand our civilian guest cruise program. This was a successful program administered Navy-wide by the Secretary of the Navy, through the Chief of Information (CHINFO). Civilian guests were invited to cruise in Navy ships to learn more about Navy operations, ships and personnel. Invited guests made their way to and from the port of embarkation at their own expense and usually paid for their meals aboard ship. I significantly increased CCDP nominations for embarkations, and occasionally I would be the guests' escort.

Hoppy said he had asked Jim Jenkins to investigate the possibility of producing a radio show about some of the 200 or so ships in the force. He was disappointed that Jim had several reasons why it could not be done. That sort of stuck in his craw, or otherwise he probably would not have said anything to me about it. I tried to get something started in that area before Hoppy left, but it didn't take shape until later when I found a friend in the Navy Electronics Laboratory (NEL) who said he could help. The friend was Charlie Hatcher who served with me on the *Guam News* staff and after retiring from the naval service, became the PIO for NEL. We produced a weekly 15-minute radio show, taped and distributed to 27 radio stations on the West Coast. Format for the show was music from the CCDP band wrapped around a seven to eight minute-dramatization of an incident in the history of one of our ships. We also produced a half hour TV show for a 13-week series on one of the San Diego stations. We discontinued the TV series because it involved extensive work for a show that aired in the middle of the afternoon competing with the soap operas. Hoppy was impressed when I told him about these enterprises when visiting with him on one of my trips to Washington.

I wanted to use the band for more public relations programs because even at that stage in my career, I thought music was an important medium of communication. That personal concept has grown with me over the years. One of the youngsters in our band was Jack Imel from Indiana who was superb on the xylophone and could tap dance. He later spent some time with the Navy Concert Band in Washington. After leaving the Navy, he was part of Lawrence Welk's organization and had a long career with him. I was one of his fans for more than 40 years.

What impressed Rear Adm.Hopwood most was a fleet visit to San Francisco following a large training exercise. We brought about 15 ships into the San Francisco Bay area for a three-day weekend visit. Hopwood was the star of the show with interviews, a news conference, receptions and dinners. He enjoyed it and played it well. He was so pleased about the occasion, he recommended to higher authority that we, the Navy, do more "... to let the

American public see our ships and personnel." I initiated and wrote the letter, and the admiral enthusiastically signed it.

Whenever our ships were involved in other than routine training exercises, I tried to make a hometown news release on all their personnel. This was an excellent way to get word out about the Navy in local papers and radio stations, and have a youngster's name and possibly a picture published in his hometown paper. It was a method that already existed but had not been fully utilized. It was beneficial to the morale of the sailors and for those of their family and friends who read about them. It really was a "win-win-win" situation. The ships had to cooperate by sending their rosters of personnel and hometown addresses to the Fleet Home Town News Center (FHTNC) at Great Lakes, Illinois, that processed the stories. It was an excellent system, and I was successful in having the CCDP energize it by insisting that all of his ships have up-to-date rosters on file with FHTNC. Each ship had an officer designated as its PIO, and it was his responsibility to ensure, especially when they were deployed, the roster was current. I followed up on this procedure by inquiring of the FHTNC Officer-In-Charge (OIC) about ships of the CCDP. Those ships that were delinquent got a letter from the CCDP telling them to get with the program. News of the Pacific Fleet's cruisers and destroyers increased significantly.

Rear Admiral "Germany" Curts

Rear Adm. Hopwood was relieved by Rear Adm. Maurice "Germany" Curts, another wonderful man with whom I worked well. We started the annual fleet visit to Seattle for its Sea Fair in August of the early 1950s and to Portland, Oregon, for its annual Portland Rose Festival in June. These were fun occasions for ship personnel because the locals made them feel welcome and appreciated as well as inviting them to most of the festivities. In turn, ship commanding officers welcomed local citizens to visit their ships, and thousands did so. Those visits continue to be scheduled each year.

I was particularly proud of the excellent relationship with the media in San Diego that Jim Jenkins had started, and I nurtured. I also extended our reach to Los Angeles, Phoenix, San Francisco and Seattle. Rembert James was the military writer for *The San Diego Union* and later worked with Copley Press Service. He was replaced by Lester Bell at the *Union*. John Bunker was the San Diego *Evening Tribune* military writer. The four of us had a good business relationship, and we got along well socially. Coverage of the Cruisers-Destroyers Force, Pacific (CRUDESPAC) ships was greatly improved because of that good relationship. I kept them advised of news developments and potential stories and maintained a steady stream of releases to them as well as other outlets. One release I remember was a short squib about a lieutenant commander taking command of one of our destroyer escorts. He reported to this new duty from the NROTC unit at the University of Idaho at Moscow, Idaho. I slugged the story: "Man from Moscow takes command of San Diego based ship. (Moscow, Idaho, that is.)" It played well in San Diego and was picked up by the wire services appearing in many newspapers across the country. It was a good story for a slow news day.

When Thomas S. Gates, Secretary of the Navy and later Secretary of Defense, visited San Diego, Rear Adm. Curts had a large cocktail reception for him and introduced me to Gates saying, "This is Lieutenant Bill Thompson, the best damned Public Information Officer in the whole Navy."

Gates smiled and dressed me down with his cold, steely eyes, patted me on the shoulder and said, "Those are nice words for a lieutenant, but I have to say, I don't trust any of you guys."

"Oh, you can trust Thompson," Curts interjected. "He's a naval officer. He's not one of those specialists."

That was the only time I had seen Gates, who was regarded to have been one of the better secretaries of the Navy and Defense. But I never forgot the introduction or his few cryptic words. Curts' label and amplification elated me, but Gates' evaluation of the business was disquieting.

It was unsettling because I was contemplating applying for a change of designator to that of public information specialist. After two years in the job, it was time for me to move on to another assignment. I had a strong desire to go back to destroyers and as an executive officer. When I had left the *Craig*, I was acting XO and confident I could handle the job. However, the Korean War was over, forces were being reduced and most all, if not all, destroyer executive officer jobs were being filled by lieutenant commanders. I let my desires be known to Admiral Curts, and he reported back to me that BUPERS would not budge on destroyer XO jobs. I was concerned that if I was going to stay in the Navy, I could be assigned to some nondescript job and lose interest in it and the Navy. I knew I had done a credible job at CCDP and was confident I could compete as a public information specialist. Zum liked the idea primarily because there weren't many PIO jobs that would compare with ship driving deployments, meaning I would be home more.

So I submitted an application for change of designator to that of a Special Duty Only Officer, Public Information, Code 1650. That got the attention of staff. First, "Easy" Glenn's successor tried to talk me out of it to no avail. Next, the Chief of Staff, Capt. Joshua W. "Josh" Cooper, tried to counsel me not to make a rash decision or a "foolish move." I had grown to appreciate and admire Josh Cooper as a wise, experienced naval officer, probably the best administrator I had ever worked with or for (up to that time and in fact, throughout my remaining days in the Navy). I persisted, and he shrugged me off by saying, "The admiral wants to see you." (Thirty-seven years later when visiting the Navy Memorial, Josh asked for me and after learning I was not on the premises, said, "Tell him that the guy who tried to talk him out of transferring to PIO many years ago was in to see him. He'll know who I am!")

After being announced by the flag lieutenant, I entered the admiral's cabin to find him pacing the deck. He turned on me blurting, "You don't want to be one of those, do you?" This was heavy pressure, coming from Rear Adm. Curts, whom I admired and with whom I felt extremely fortunate to be associated. I was flattered to be told that I should remain an unrestricted line officer by Cooper and Curts. But somehow I hung in there. I explained my rationale and finally said to that wonderful "Old Man" that I thought by transferring from the unrestricted line community to that of the specialist PIO would raise the competence level of both entities.

He laughed, sat down for a few moments to think and finally wrote on the bottom of the endorsement to my application, "Lt. Thompson is a good all-around naval officer." To this day, I consider that to be the best recommendation I ever received.

Anyone for Tennis?

Orders detaching me from the CCDP staff had me going to Monterey, California, for "duty under instruction" at the U.S. Navy Post Graduate School to attend six months of courses at the General Line School. I had requested a change of designator, but a board had not yet been convened in Washington to consider my request and those of other aspirants for special duty only. So I was considered an unrestricted line officer. The detailers in the Navy's Bureau of Naval Personnel (BUPERS) made the decision I should be included in the second half of a program designed for former reservists who transferred to the Regular Navy. The first part of that program, called The Five Term Program, was to place these officers in colleges around the country and let them garner up to five semesters of credits. In many cases that amounted to a bachelor's degree. They were then sent to the second part, the School of the General Line, intended to "bring them up to speed," so they could compete with Naval Academy graduates. The school was actually designed to give the great number of former Naval Reserve aviators who transferred to the Regular Navy a more rounded knowledge of the Navy, especially the seagoing Navy. The program was significant because many of those officers entered the Navy as aviation cadets with little or no college work. If successful in the flight training program, they flew airplanes for the remainder of the war. The Navy's objective was to have all its officers with at least a college degree. The Navy always stressed education, and I knew to survive on the promotion ladder, I would need a degree. I continually sought ways to obtain that degree.

In retrospect, neither the Navy nor I gained much from my attending the General Line course. Having spent the previous six years at sea, except for the six months at Glenview at the Combat Information Center Officers School (a school with fleet applications), I didn't really need six months at the beautiful Monterey institution. I learned little other than I was not a good tennis player. That wasn't difficult to discern because tennis was on the agenda almost every day. The school was situated at the former Del Monte Hotel, a resort complex that was taken over by the Navy during World War II as a Pre-Flight School in the aviation V-5 Program. The Navy has retained custody of the facility, and to this day it is the Navy's Post Graduate School. Fortunately, the time was not lost or wasted because I made many lasting friendships there. Bob Close, the helicopter pilot who was a shipmate and friend in *Missouri* and *Midway*, was an "across the hall" resident. He was a student in a different course—a year long postgraduate course in Operational Analysis. Bob and I frequently played tennis and spent free time together although his curriculum was more strenuous and demanding.

Bill "Sam" Houston was there on the faculty of the Navy's Aerology Postgraduate School. Aerology was Navy's way of saying meteorology, making him a "weather guesser." It was Bill's second tour at Monterey, and he was well schooled in the local geography and eateries. Bill and his wife Jean had been our next door neighbors on Guam. We were in Norfolk at the same time; he was on another aircraft carrier when I was in *Midway*. We had played a lot of bridge together on Guam and in Norfolk, and Bob substituted for Zum in Monterey. He was probably a better bridge player but not nearly as pretty.

Zum and I had deferred moving to Monterey because it would mean more wear and tear on the family and furniture. There was a good possibility we would find ourselves back in San Diego after the Monterey stint. We thought it best not to move Stevie out of her La Mesa school where she was happy and doing well. This meant I was a commuter and employed Navy aircraft traffic between Monterey and San Diego. Most of our students were aviators, and at that time aviators were required to maintain flight proficiency, flying twin-engine Beechcraft Navy SNB planes for at least four hours a month. Almost every weekend I was able to be home.

Because of the poor weather conditions in the Monterey area—mostly fog, emanating from the gorgeous Monterey Bay—we had some anxious moments while aviating with the Navy. The SNB was a pre-World War II airplane, and the aviators flying them were barely proficient, just putting four hours in the pilot or co-pilot seat each month. However, I was eager to get home; I had time to spare and the cost was right.

Even though Monterey wasn't important to my career, the timeframe was pivotal. Shortly after arriving at Monterey, the selection board in Washington reported out, and Lt. William Thompson was on the list of transferees to the Special Duty Only designations. So, I was a 1650, Public Information Specialist, another factor militating against my staying at Monterey. I didn't need Line School as an unrestricted line officer and certainly didn't need it as a public information officer. However, I made the best of it, tried to learn something and spent some time contemplating my new career as a PIO specialist.

I fired off a letter to Capt. Dick Lane, whom I had known at Carlisle, and who was currently in the Office of Information coordinating assignments for the PIO community. The Navy term for that type of work is "detailing," and the "detailer" is the person who performs those chores. The detailer matches personnel to assignments and works, directly or indirectly, for the Bureau of Naval Personnel. BUPERS is the only authority that can issue Permanent Change of Station (PCS) orders. Capt. Lane advised me the one thing I could be sure of was that I would *not* be going back to San Diego for duty. There were no lieutenant billets open in that area. Knowing that my family had remained in San Diego, he was helpful and, almost immediately, followed up with a telephone call and official orders detailing me to Fourth Naval District Headquarters in Philadelphia.

Philadelphia sounded exciting—The City of Brotherly Love, Ben Franklin's home and the site of the Liberty Bell—with plenty of history and being a thriving city mixed with heavy industry, famous financial institutions and outstanding colleges and universities. It was also a great professional sports center with the Phillies and Athletics of major league baseball and the NFL's Eagles. It was also not far from "Gotham" where the Yankees, Dodgers and Giants played baseball and home to professional football's Giants who bowed regularly to the Packers. We went through the usual excitement about a change of duty and new environments, reading about it and contacting friends who were familiar with the area. Where should we live? Should we buy into the real estate market? What about the schools? And the job? Who would be my boss? What's the admiral like there? All Navy folks knew the feelings. A change of duty set the scene for interesting and exciting times. The unknown always provided enthusiasm, anxiety, conjecture and conversation.

With the Commandant, Fourth Naval District (COMFOUR) orders a reality, Zum and I decided to sell the La Mesa property and move to Monterey. If the house sold readily, we would have three months in Monterey. It would be a nice change for the kids providing a different environment and the beautiful scenery at Big Sur and the surrounding area. Besides, I was getting tired of bumping around in a Beechcraft on weekends. Zum sold the house herself, not using a real estate agent. It was a quick sale, and we profited about $1,000 on the transaction. She made arrangements to move the furniture, and the move was falling in place. Zum was always good at that. In fact, it was best that I was not involved. Meanwhile back at Monterey, I succeeded in getting accommodations for our three-month stay in off base Wherry Housing. It was called Wherry Housing after Nebraska Sen. Kenneth Wherry who started the legislation to sponsor that type of government housing. The quarters were adequate, comfortable and convenient.

Course change

The movers packed us out on a Friday, and our household goods were immediately on the way to Monterey. I arrived in La Mesa that night. We spent Saturday cleaning the house and making it spotless; otherwise, Zum would have been embarrassed. Early Sunday morning we said good-bye to Camellia Drive and La Mesa. With the Nash Ambassador loaded including a car top carrier, we headed North for different climes and new adventures. Ten hours later we started unloading again in our abode in Foster Village at Monterey. The next morning the moving van appeared, and by the end of the day we were fairly comfortably situated. Of course, I was in school, and Zum did all the work including enrolling Stevie in a school and getting the telephone, water and other utility services installed. All was well, except I had sudden news for her. I came home from school with an official piece of paper in hand canceling my orders to Philadelphia and sending me to San Diego for duty in Commander First Fleet (COMFIRSTFLEET) staff. Wow! All that work for naught, and we had sold a perfectly good house in the process!

What had happened was that Vice Adm. Hopwood had been assigned to the job as Commander First Fleet headquartered on North Island Naval Air Station. Adm. Hopwood, my first boss at COMCRUDESPAC, had gone to Washington to be the Deputy Chief of Naval Operations for Logistics, then on to First Fleet. One of the first things he did was to go on record that he wanted and needed a public information officer and proceeded to swap one of his other officer billets for that of a lieutenant commander PIO. Next he needed to find a lieutenant commander to fill the billet. He learned I had left COMCRUDESPAC for duty under instruction at Monterey and was destined to go to COMFOUR in Philadelphia. The fact I was still a lieutenant didn't deter him. He had pulled me off of a destroyer previously, so getting my orders changed to COMFIRSTFLEET was a cinch. All he had to do was call his ole' buddy, Rear Adm. E.B. "Whitey" Taylor who was the Chief of Information to make it so. Needless to say, I was pleased. It was an odd turn of events for the family. But I thought I was going to do better professionally by staying with the fleet than by going to a Naval District, especially moving into a lieutenant commander billet. We, the family, were pleased to return to San Diego.

We left Monterey in mid-December and worked our way south from whence we came only three months previously. We immediately decided we wanted to live in Coronado adjacent to the naval air station, if we could afford it. Coronado was expensive because there was a great demand for housing, but few houses were available. I definitely did not want to live in La Mesa again and have either a long commute around San Diego Bay or ferry across it. We tested the real estate market and found it over our heads financially. At least that was our initial perception. A new development was being constructed on the former city golf course next to the fence surrounding the base. The cheapest—there were only a couple models—was $23,000, about 45% higher than the house we left in La Mesa. Zum agonized about it. I was convinced it was the place to live, and she could make it go financially. One argument was it would cost more to commute and live in La Mesa. Depression-oriented folks like Zum and I had a difficult time risking money or letting it work for us by going into debt. However, the decision was made, and we bought the house. The agents were a little skeptical of a lieutenant being in a neighborhood designed for commanders with flight pay. We made a large down payment and got on with the transaction. Zum has recited many times how she lay awake for several nights worrying about making mortgage payments of about $68.00 a month.

Our house wasn't to be completed until April, so we were temporarily quartered in Navy transient housing in Pacific Beach, a suburb of San Diego. We had our Christmas there, welcomed the New Year 1956 and celebrated Craig's fifth birthday on March 30th by gifting him with his first airplane ride. The little guy was greatly impressed and excited about the half hour ride in a Piper Cub.

In Coronado Stevie entered her fourth school as a fourth grader, and it was a memorable year for her. Apparently the fourth grade was the time when California children studied the genesis and development of the religious missions in California and the work of the Catholic priests in the early days. In each of the schools (La Mesa, Monterey, Pacific Beach and Coronado) she entered, her class embarked upon the study of the California missions. Stevie became an expert on California Missions, a historian if you will, and was always good for a response when questioned about them. She was especially helpful to workers of crossword puzzles concocted by Californians. In later life, she wowed her peers at cocktail parties. And that's not bad for a young lady reared as a Protestant.

I was beginning to understand that the Navy was an exciting place to be, even with the inconvenience accompanying the assignment of new duties. Our six months at Monterey proved beneficial in many respects. It was a beautiful area. My mother visited us when we camped out at Big Sur on a weekend. Craig and I appreciated that opportunity although Mom and the rest of the family didn't seem to enjoy it as much. Maybe it was just a guy thing. I linked up again with Bob Close, the helicopter pilot extraordinaire, and met other officers with whom I worked later in my career. Monterey was a big plus and served as a strong launching platform toward the new adventure of being a public information specialist and returning to the Pacific Fleet.

The First Fleet

The three and a half years at First Fleet were most pleasant for the development of our family and my career. Coronado was an ideal place to rear young children. The weather was nearly perfect with few days the kids were forced to be in the house. Many civic activities were planned for youngsters. Coronado had some local cultural, entertainment and educational events, and there was a large variety of happenings in San Diego and Los Angeles. Additionally, the beaches were good, and the mountains were not far away. The educational level of Coronado's inhabitants was high. Most residents were senior active duty naval officers, retirees or people who had or were experiencing success in other endeavors. Coronado measured only one square mile, bordered by the Naval Air Station, San Diego Bay and the Pacific Ocean. To reach the island, one had to ferry from San Diego or drive the length, about nine miles, of "The Strand," from Imperial Beach that was close to Tijuana, Mexico. Sailing was and remains one of the principal recreation activities in the area. Boaters can enjoy the sheltered and spacious San Diego Bay plus Mission Bay and the Pacific Ocean. Golfing and surfing are other prime recreational activities, and of course, the San Diego Zoo is world famous.

Our house was adequate. There were three bedrooms, two bathrooms, a large living room, dining room, foyer, atrium entrance, fenced yard, large patio and two-car garage. Stevie and Craig developed handsomely, and Brian was born on August 6, 1958. Zum was active with the staff wives, and we entertained continuously. She was a substitute teacher in the local system but quit during the last months of her pregnancy with Brian. The First Fleet staff was a close, active social group, and we kept up with our previously established friends.

Professionally, duty in First Fleet staff was outstanding. I prospered and thoroughly enjoyed being with "fleet" people and the operating forces. It was a continuing adventure, and I particularly enjoyed the opportunity of being proactive, helping to make things interesting and even making events happen. Making things happen was not expected of a lieutenant. A numbered fleet (there were four in the Navy's operating structure: First with its counterpart in the Atlantic Fleet, the Second and the operating fleets, the Sixth in European waters and Seventh in the Western Pacific) staff had a preponderance of senior officers. This was an excellent opportunity to learn from officers who had experienced World War II and the Korean War, most in command assignments. Although I would never think of being subdued, I initially thought it was a good time to be quiet, not brag about my sea duty, keep my eyes and ears open and voice box muted. That has remained my philosophy and *modus operandi*.

Vice Adm. Hopwood and I immediately picked up the good relationship we had at COMCRUDESPAC. He provided an "open door" for me because he, being an outgoing person, liked the business of public relations and wanted the Navy to take advantage of opportunities to communicate more with the public. However, he was a solid Navy professional, and I knew I had to produce and have the answers, or that door might close or only be slightly ajar. Although the admiral spoke to me about his open door, I did not abuse that privilege and handled it judicially. Most of the time he sent for me. Everyone in the staff knew the admiral had handpicked me and that strengthened my position. However, like most fleet staffs, it was loaded with experienced senior officers. There were seven or eight captains, twice that number of commanders, four or five lieutenant commanders, a couple of lieutenants and about 10 junior grade lieutenants and ensigns. Most of the lieutenants and ensigns were assigned to the communications division. My relatively junior rank didn't add much stature to our public information effort. There were a few jibes expressing the opinion that the billet or the effort was unnecessary. To be sure, the Navy in 1956 had not yet accepted the value of public information/relations activities.

There was also evidence of some jealousy and envy within the staff. Some were ready to test this young "hotshot." The tests were amateurish and subjective, and I was accustomed to that type of trivia. I tried to dispel any negatives by working through the staff on all our public information initiatives. I believed that was the best approach and worked hard at it. Soon, the Chief of Staff, Capt. Frank Albin "Buck" Brandley, was a supporter. He was a gruff, blunt and candid naval aviator. He was a fine naval officer who had the respect and devotion of all in the staff.

He delivered a great endorsement of me and what I was trying to do at one of the daily staff meetings. In the session he instructed everyone saying, "Keep Lieutenant Thompson informed of what is going on in the First Fleet. With the increased interest in the First Fleet on the West Coast, it is expected that the admiral will be queried or interviewed by media representatives. Lieutenant Thompson will be responsible for providing words and guidance to the commander." He added that the staff had not before considered or bothered about public information aspects, but from now on, it would. The admiral wanted it; the chief of staff wanted it and the staff would soon realize the benefits. As he was talking, I felt uneasy and my body language probably showed it, as I tried to screw myself into my chair. I was amazed at this abrupt thrust as well as being uncomfortable in an unusual and unwanted spotlight. I had only been aboard about a month and felt privileged to be a part of the staff meetings. I was the only lieutenant present, and there was only one lieutenant commander, the flag secretary, who attended these meetings. Many commanders were not included; only their bosses were in the staff meetings.

My leader

In one of the frequent discussions I had with Admiral Hopwood, we were talking about the Navy's overall public relations efforts. I voiced the opinion that it seemed disjointed. I followed by saying "about 22 PIOs" were in the San Diego area representing the various commands, and there was no central thrust. PIOs did not get together except by happenstance, meeting at a cocktail party or as guests at a luncheon. As soon as I said it, I thought to myself, "Stupid, you have enough to do. You don't have to take on the entire universe." Hopwood's chin jutted from his cherubic face, and he said, "Tommy, why don't you call a meeting of the area PIOs? The purpose would be to get acquainted and to put some focus on the Pacific Fleet. I am not the SOPA (Senior Officer Present Afloat) here, but I do represent the Commander in Chief Pacific Fleet in the Eastern Pacific, which includes the West Coast of the U.S. Handle it diplomatically, and we will see what happens."

Alas, PIOs generally mimicked their peers and commanders when it came to fencing their turf. It traditionally went with the command and tasks assigned. Admiral Hopwood's assessment of the situation was proper and on target. He was Commander In Chief U.S. Pacific Fleet's (CINCPACFLT) West Coast representative. Commander, First Fleet (COMFIRSTFLT) operated east of Hawaii. It did not have an integral operating force like Commander, Seventh Fleet (COMSEVENTHFLT) in the Western Pacific or Commander, Sixth Fleet (COMSIXTHFLT) in the Mediterranean. Ships were assigned or chopped (change of operational control) to First Fleet (FIRSTFLT) for training exercises by their type commanders, three of which were headquartered in San Diego—Naval Air Force, Pacific Fleet (AIRPAC); Amphibious Forces, Pacific Fleet (PHIBPAC) and Cruisers-Destroyers Force, Pacific Fleet (CRUDESPAC). The AIRPAC and PHIBPAC had vice admirals as their commanders, both senior to Admiral Hopwood. When one wasn't the SOPA, the other one was.

Another wrinkle in Admiral Hopwood's venture into public information leadership was the Naval District Commandant. In San Diego, it was Commandant, Eleventh Naval District, who, per U.S. Naval Regulations, was responsible for all public information within the confines of the district. Naval district commandants were normally two-star rear admirals and, at that time in their twilight tours, were all pushing mandatory retirement age of 62. The regulation was well-placed and had full meaning. The district commandants had relatively large public information staffs to go with the responsibility and were there to support the operating forces. As residents, they had the continuity for community and media relations. An operating fleet commander was transitory and when making a visit to a port would and should rely on the district commandant for public information support. With those parameters in mind, I set the agenda for this Hopwood initiative in the public information business. The intent was to enhance camaraderie within the San Diego area PIO community, give the combined efforts a Navy direction, acquaint the PIOs with the objectives of the First Fleet and to definitely work within the existing system.

The first meeting was a breakfast in the COMFIRSTFLT wardroom attended by about 12 PIOs. Some there out of curiosity, a couple were a little agitated and suspect and then some thought it was a good idea. I had to allay the suspicions of the District, AIRPAC and PHIBPAC PIOs. However, I accomplished the tasks of having a get-acquainted meeting, described COMFIRSTFLT's agenda in the Eastern Pacific and discussed problems of mutual concern. Cdr. Merle Macbain of Commander, Eleventh Fleet (COMELEVENFLT) was the most perturbed. In later years, even 15 years or so later when I was the Chief of Navy Information, he would needle me about being "That aggressive, young lieutenant from First Fleet trying to conquer the world." Professionally, Merle Macbain was a good PIO. He knew the basics, had the prerequisite writing skills and Navy background. I respected him and liked many things about him. After getting through his crusty continence, we became good friends and remained so for the next 20 years until his death.

The breakfast meetings continued about once a quarter, and I even had the group meet in the First Fleet wardroom for a discussion with Admiral Hopwood. The boss was satisfied and pleased we were making progress. He told me as much and instructed me to stick with it and not to lose momentum.

Going Hollywood

One new aspect in Pacific Fleet administration was that CINCPACFLT assigned the scheduling of fleet assets (ships, aircraft, etc.) for Hollywood motion picture and television productions to COMFIRSTFLT. This action occurred shortly after I reported aboard. Although it was a surprise to me, it made sense because of our proximity to Hollywood. I was tasked to coordinate fleet activities and have local interface with industry representatives. I had done some work with Hollywood industries at COMCRUDESPAC, primarily with Bob Hope who did some of his weekly TV shows on the decks of our Long Beach based cruisers. There was also some minor work

I had done for the motion picture, *The Cain Mutiny*. Initially, I absorbed the Hollywood tasks as routine and enjoyed working with the planners and producers. Most were solid, hard working people.

For various reasons, primarily the increased popularity of military-related motion pictures and televisions productions, the Hollywood part of my job grew larger. With the advent of the *Navy Log* TV series, I became extremely busy. *Navy Log* was a syndicated 39-week series produced by Sam Galleau in Hollywood. It proved to be a good venture for the Navy because it was well-done and broadcast by many outlets nationwide. Each weekly segment was an individual story, mostly based on fact, and an episodic link to Navy life or history. Work essentially entailed being the technical advisor. It meant meeting with Galleau's location staff and planners to review the script and appraise their desires for shooting sites. Selecting shooting sites involved determining what part of a ship or land-based location was feasible. Then arrangements had to be made with the various commands in the area. I worked the first 13 weeks before urging the Chief of Information (CHINFO), "Get someone out here permanently to handle those details." It was time consuming and almost a full-time job. Realizing the importance of the *Log* series, CHINFO ordered Cdr. John Thom, a newly designated PIO, to the First Fleet Staff to coordinate the *Navy Log* business. John was a naval aviator who developed serious cataracts and was grounded permanently as an aviator. I worked on the Hollywood picture *Run Silent, Run Deep* starring Clark Gable and Burt Lancaster. And I met then Senator John F. Kennedy and Cliff Robertson at the filming of *PT 109*.

Admiral Hopwood left about six months after I arrived and gained his fourth star as Commander-in-Chief, Pacific Fleet with headquarters at Pearl Harbor. Naturally, I was sorry to see him go, but we did get in one fleet visit to San Francisco that was a huge success. Initially, I received considerable static from the Operations Department officers who scheduled fleet operations (training exercises) in the Eastern Pacific. They had the usual argument that crews of the ships should return to their homeports, so they could be with their families. They were adamant that ships' crews would prefer to return home instead of making a port visit elsewhere, and COMFIRSTFLT should not ignore that fact. I offered to conduct a survey of personnel in

ships visiting San Francisco and worked with the Ops Officer, so he could
scrutinize the procedure. Admiral Hopwood understood what I was doing,
approved the survey and was not the least bit surprised by the results. The
results were conclusive. About 97% of the unmarried men said they would
prefer to visit a port like San Francisco, and 99% of the married personnel
said they would prefer the same. I was a little surprised by the almost unanimous endorsement of the fleet visit program. There was no more guff from
the operators; in fact, they often came to me with the same "great idea."
They would have a small fleet exercise going on up north and think it would
be good for the crews, if the ships could visit Seattle, Portland or the like.
I always tried to help, complimenting them on their "innovative idea" and
establishing contact with city leaders. Regardless of the infighting and the
byplay, the results were always good for the Navy's public image and for Navy
personnel. The recruiting slogan "Join the Navy to See the World" was and
still is valid.

One small incident, indicative of my position in the staff, occurred with
Capt. Buck Brandley, who had just been selected for promotion to rear
admiral and was leaving the First Fleet staff. I had arranged for the Mayor
of San Francisco to host a reception at the Sir Francis Drake Hotel for our
senior officers. We had a discussion about getting a proper distribution of
senior officers from all of our visiting ships. When we finished, he summarized our meeting by counting the list and announcing we had so many flag
officers, so many captains and some commanders. I smilingly added, "And
one lieutenant (meaning me)." He looked at me, being a little disturbed at
my getting involved in such decisions and thinking it wouldn't be right to
not include me. He threw his pencil on his desk and growled, "God damn
it, Tommy. You don't know what it is to be a junior officer." I took that as a
compliment, and I am sure that was the way he meant it. After thinking about
it, I did try to act more like a lieutenant.

Vice Adm. Robert L. Dennison replaced Hopwood, and it didn't take
long for us to establish a good rapport. I had been told he was bright, and
I soon learned he was very bright. Almost immediately he had a handle on
getting the most out of me. Even though he was basically a reserved person,
he would josh with me and delighted in needling me. He seemed to enjoy

having me in his office where he was a virtual captive.

It didn't take long for this land-based Pacific Fleet Commander to develop a local social mobility and network for the entire West Coast, our domain. Some of his successful endeavors in this regard were with my help but largely drawing on his impressive background and personal contacts made during his career. He developed a cadre of "lieutenants" in the public sector who were available to assist him. We got into a few situations where I helped make him look good, and he appreciated it. "Robert L." had been President Harry Truman's Naval Aide and was savvy about Washington and the workings of that capital city. He had a good understanding of public relations and was willing to be a player as long as it benefited the Navy. He definitely was not a "showboat," nor did he overplay his role. I had the feeling that he was in control and was keeping me on a long leash. I was comfortable with the situation. I also felt he would be tolerant if I screwed up, as long as it wasn't serious or didn't embarrass him.

One of the first events to occur with Vice Adm. Dennison aboard was the "Mrs. US Navy Fleet Review." Long Beach harbor was the site. With its two entrances to a spacious outer harbor, it proved to be a natural for a fleet review. The "Flag" ship with the reviewing dignitaries aboard was anchored in the outer harbor. The "fleet" of ships entered the harbor from the south and passed in review to exit from the north gate. Of course, Mrs. U.S. Navy, wife of a chief petty officer, was one of the dignitaries aboard the flagship, along with Secretary of the Navy Charles Thomas and Vice Adm. Dennison.. It was a great day for her and the Navy as attested by the Secretary in many laudatory letters and messages. We did draw a crowd. The entire spectacle resulted in considerable publicity for the Navy. Fleet reviews were something you read about or saw in reruns of *Pathe Newsreels* because in reality they were news—something that occurred infrequently, maybe once every 20 to 25 years.

The focus of the program was to recognize the value of the Navy wife and the part she played in the life of the seagoing Navy man. It was a good program—at least a good idea—for the Navy. Unfortunately, the event was localized to Southern California. I learned later that the Chief of Information in Washington did not unite his forces to make it a national event. One reason was because the program was initiated in the Bureau of Naval Personnel (BUPERS) and became a vested activity. BUPERS was led by a small group of relative amateurs in creating special events. They were officers, who though well-meaning, were clawing for recognition from the dungeons of the Arlington Annex, home of BUPERS. They thought the program could be handled by dealing solely with COMFIRSTFLEET. Wrong! We needed help to extend the event beyond the reaches of Southern California. Another reason, on speculation, was that the Chief of Information didn't grasp the significance of the event, or his staff didn't tell him it was something "we should get behind." Probably, the staff didn't know because BUPERS did not let it be known in Washington this was an event with possible national implications.

I, for one, was bewildered about things like that, especially working in the far reaches of Southern California away from the Washington swirl. Vice Adm. Dennison's immediate reaction was positive. He was pleased that the event was a spectacle of precision. The ships performed well, the weather was beautiful, Mrs. US Navy was superb in her role and the Secretary of the Navy was elated. We didn't know of the publicity reach shortcomings until a few days later. I am sure in his quiet way, Vice Adm. Dennison let the Washington group know we were working hard out in the hinterlands, and they might consider giving us a little help.

An officer's career is pretty much controlled by three factors: (1) How the officer is judged by superiors who control his/her destiny through the power and influence of the periodic reports of fitness, the primary medium affecting promotion in rank; (2) How he/she is judged by peers (reputation); and (3) How the officer performs—to a great extent, that depends directly on the support derived from subordinates. Performance relates to the trust and confidence developed by how the officer leads and trains subordinates. An officer has to be cognizant of all three factors because they are interrelated, but he or she has better control over the third criterion. In my career, I had been fortunate to have a succession of outstanding chief petty officers working for me. Starting at COMCRUDESPAC, Chief Journalist Jeff Jeffreys was my senior enlisted man. Jeff was an older man (in his 50s), an experienced civilian and Navy journalist, and was a principal member of the

Navy's *All Hands Magazine* staff for several years. He had a keen sense for news and was an excellent writer. He was a respected leader and managed our young journalists superbly.

Chief Journalist Don Collett

At First Fleet, I was able to get Chief Journalist Don Collett assigned to my office. Don was not a stranger to me because while on Guam, I would read about his athletic feats when he was a young journalist on duty at Pearl Harbor. I remembered him as a member on the Pacific Fleet's basketball championship team, the softball championship team, and as a runner up to the top tennis player. He later won the All Navy Golf Championship, and golf became his primary sport. While I was at COMCRUDESPAC, Don Collett was the "Chief" in Jim Lloyd's Air Forces Pacific Fleet Public Information Office. I worked a deal with Jim Lloyd, who was about to lose Don anyway because he was completing his tour at Commander, Naval Air Force, US Pacific Fleet (COMNAVAIRPAC). With Vice Adm. Dennison's muscle and the help of Capt. Walter Bright, who headed a BUPERS's data processing office in San Diego and was an avid golfer, Don was assigned to COMFIRSTFLT staff. He was an excellent writer and in his off duty hours edited a magazine on junior golf. By editing, I mean he wrote the entire magazine and even did some of the photography. If he persuaded a recognized personality to author an article, he normally had to write the piece anyway. He also had an easy, laid back demeanor, but he was an individual who wasted little time. He was always busy, usually doing something associated with golf.

Don Collett was a golf professional even though he was on active duty in the Navy. He would play in tournaments and collect prize money not forfeiting it like amateurs had to do. He was also an excellent golf instructor and conducted clinics for all ages, especially for junior golfers, kids who were learning how to swing. Vice Adm. Dennison liked to play golf and would call Don into his office to talk about swing techniques. They would go off together to the driving range only a couple blocks from the headquarters building. At other times, they would play a round of golf together. I wasn't

about to get annoyed because the boss had an association with my office
that I thought was good as well as enterprising. However, I felt I might be
losing control of my chief, so I started to play golf. Don was my instructor
and mentor. Golf was the prime topic of conversation in the office when we
weren't working on a project. Over the years, I developed a strong interest
in golf, but it became another of my disappointments. I have never done
well at it. My best was a 15 handicap when at I was at Great Lakes. For me
it has been a great social game. I didn't abuse myself or family by devoting
an excessive amount of time to golf, and that's probably one reason I didn't
do better. Many times, after a bad game, I would lament about that chief of
mine who got me into golf.

Don got itchy feet and wanted to leave the Navy. He and his wife Verla
had five children, all boys, and he thought he could do much better as a provider by being a golf pro in the civilian sector. He had 13 years in the Navy.
Vice Adm. Dennison let it be known, "Collett should stay in the Navy for
seven more years and retire on 20 and then venture off into golfdom." He
would at least have a Navy retirement check to fall back on. I think Dennison
had the idea that Don had aspirations of playing the circuit as a professional.

Don did play in some local tournaments and in Utah, his home state, but
knew there were other avenues for making money in the golf world. He was
offered the job as head golf professional and manager of the new Coronado
Golf Course, if he could be released from the Navy. He asked for a "hardship discharge" that meant, if granted, he could break his enlistment contract
and leave the Navy. With the help of Captain Bright, Cdr. Bob Watkins, a
golfer in our staff, and Vice Adm. Dennison, who finally came around to our
conviction, Don was released from the Navy and took the Coronado job. He
was a success because of his hard work and imagination. He stayed at the
Coronado Golf Course for a few years, and then took a job as head pro at
exclusive Brae Burn Country Club in Houston. That led him into developing
golf course resorts and communities eventually lining his pockets with something other than golf tees and ball markers.

He became restless again and developed a concept for a World Golf Hall
of Fame. He even selected a spot to build it and then tried to market the idea.
He succeeded, but the backers said it was mandatory for him to be a part of

the package. He was asked to fulfill his vision—take the concept to the site and build it. The site was Pinehurst, North Carolina, the Mecca of golf in the United States. He succeeded in completing the project. Demonstrating once again his innate grasp of public relations, he had President Jerry Ford as the principal guest for the dedication,

Don then returned to his roots in Provo, Utah, where he developed and built golf courses. Eventually, he went to San Diego to build a few golf courses and lives there today. He has remained a close friend since our days at First Fleet. Some of his boys work with him. All five became golfers. All of them went to Brigham Young University on golf scholarships, and at least two of them tried the PGA circuit. One went into journalism and functioned in the business until his death at a relatively young age. The other brothers have been in and out of golf and its many aspects.

When Collett left the Navy and First Fleet, I had a big hole to fill in my office. He and I had been successful in several projects, and I knew I couldn't continue the momentum by myself. The solution was to get another outstanding Chief Journalist, and I focused my attention on doing just that. On my scope came Chief Phil Russell who had taken Collett's place at AIRPAC. We hit it off immediately because I had a few projects on the front and back burners. Phil slipped into Collett's seat like he had always been there, and we were off. I soon identified him as the most prolific person I had ever known in the public relations business. He still has that title in my book. A 6'4" figure, he was not that imposing to anyone needing help. He developed a reputation for assisting young Navy enlisted journalists professionally and personally. He did the same for photographers and even young public information officers. He was also in the vanguard of the equal opportunity movement, especially for women in the labor force. Phil was a savior of the underdog, at least to anyone who legitimately needed help. Woe be it to anyone who was a malingerer or a "sluff off" who faked his way to a level of pity or welfare. He ate them alive!

The son of a preacher in Wheaton, Illinois, (home to church supported Wheaton College in suburban Chicago) he ventured out into the world and made a success of himself. Apparently he did this without the help of his religious background, but that heritage bestowed on him a high sense of moral right and direction. For the next 18 months, he and I went through many projects that we left behind as models and standards for excellence of purpose and objectives. As for productivity and high standards, Phil and I left a legacy for other public information offices to emulate.

Phil Russell and I have remained good friends. He retired from the Navy and Civil Service Navy. He and his wife Betty settled in Waldport, Oregon, where he took up desktop publishing on an Apple Macintosh computer. He became a syndicated columnist and critic in the computer business. Macintosh introduced the mouse to computing, and in Corvallis, Oregon, Phil started a Macintosh User Group (MUG) magazine called *Mouse Droppings*. It has become one of the best MUG magazines or newsletters in existence. I subscribed to it, even though I was 2,500 miles from Corvallis.

While poking around in a Navy history book, a fact popped up that monopolized much of our time for a year. The 50th anniversary of the Great White Fleet was approaching. A secondary fact became evident: nobody was doing anything about it. About the only thing one could expect from the Navy's large bureaucratic organization was an event note in *All Hands Magazine*. Presumably, that would take care of it for another 25 to 50 years. To do much more than that would require expending energy not only to plan and execute an observance but also to fight the inertia of the organization. Unfortunately, there is little creative thought put into motion in a large organization, especially the Navy or other military organizations. Bureaucracy often kills initiative.

The Great White Fleet was a major story in the development of our country and particularly our Navy. President Theodore Roosevelt sent battleships around the world to establish the USA as a world power. The U.S. Navy was his "Big Stick," in the context of his proclaimed motto, "Speak softly, but carry a big stick." Those tenets were enough to energize us.

Still basking in the success of the fleet review at Long Beach, my staff, Chief Journalist Russell and I brainstormed the idea. We envisioned having a fleet review in San Francisco under the Golden Gate Bridge to commemorate the 50th anniversary of the Great White Fleet's visit. To us, a fleet review was a spectacular, a unique opportunity to display the Navy's power and its personnel. Because this would be a rare assemblage of ships for an official event, it would attract the media amplifying the impressive occasion beyond its immediate audience. We researched further and learned the fleet had visited San Francisco in early July 1908 before heading westward to Hawaii and Japan. We put together a plan for a fleet visit to San Francisco to coincide with that anniversary. We were thinking of a formal fleet review as it passed under the Golden Gate Bridge with perhaps Fleet Adm. Chester W. Nimitz as the reviewing officer. Nimitz was a revered man of the 20th Century Navy and lived in the Bay Area. Ships could be open for general visiting over the weekend, and there would be entertainment and parties for the officers and enlisted men. Another important aspect was San Francisco's reputation as being a great Navy town in World War II and before. Navy activities had been concentrated in Oakland and Alameda, across the Bay and at Hunters Point Naval Shipyard in the southern far reaches of the city. Politically, the city had drifted to the left seeing only dollar signs in relation to Navy. It had not exhibited the kindred spirit and hospitality of previous years. The First Fleet visit to the Bay area with Rear. Adm. Hopwood a year earlier was successful but relatively small, and the leading hosts were the cities of Oakland and Alameda. We would need to take some soundings to learn about the reaction from San Francisco.

I sold the idea within the staff with the only admonition coming from the boss, Vice Adm. Dennison. He cautioned us to get the concurrence of the CHINFO, Rear Adm. E.B. "Whitey" Taylor and ask if he would take it on as a project. I was going to Washington for a conference, and the reaction I got from the Chief of All Navy Information and his staff was, "Sounds like a good idea. Let us know how you make out." So Lt. Thompson and Chief Russell had bitten off a huge chunk of work, but we managed not to choke on it, even enjoyed it and to this day savor reminiscence of the "San Francisco Caper."

A personal phone call was made from Dennison to Rear Adm. Taylor. Then an aviator lieutenant commander from CHINFO was assigned for Temporary Additional Duty (TAD) for three months to the 12th Naval District Headquarters in San Francisco. It was immediately obvious that he was inexperienced in public affairs. He presented a good appearance, had all the good bars and restaurants staked out and was good to be with on liberty. Without much help from Washington, we received the support of other West Coast Fleet commands that provided public affairs personnel for two weeks TAD in San Francisco. We established a Command Information Bureau (CIB) in San Fran with all of us reporting to the 12th Naval District PIO, Cdr. Harry Holton.

We were on the scene two weeks in advance of the event and had the situation in hand except for the weather. We did sun dances hoping the usual summer fog would lift, so the ships could enter port. They were headed by the COMFIRSTFLT flagship, USS *Helena*, a heavy cruiser. The *Helena* arrived early and anchored at a vantage position inside the Golden Gate Bridge. Fleet Adm. Nimitz was taken aboard with other guests including some veterans of the Great White Fleet whom we managed to locate. About 50 media representatives were also received aboard. However, the fog was playing games with the ships, and at one time a delay of arrival was considered by COMFIRSTFLT. He consulted his aerologist, Cdr. Max Jack (our good friend and across-the-street neighbor in Coronado), who stated bluntly, "Admiral, we will break out of the fog at 1230 and will be able to meet our schedule." At 1230, *Helena* poked her nose out of thick fog and into a beautiful day in San Francisco Bay. When I got aboard with the media reps, the entire staff was talking about how Max had saved the day.

The day progressed successfully with Fleet Adm. Nimitz enjoying himself thoroughly. Even Vice Adm. Dennison was smiling. There were 27 ships of all types involved. The second to last ship in column was a tanker, the USS *Chemung*. Although not a pretty thing, she was to become famous on that day. She ran aground on Alcatraz Island! In front of 50 newsmen, Admiral Nimitz and God, himself! I was one of the first to know the *Chemung* was in trouble because I sensed something was wrong and studied the situation with binoculars. Before Admiral Dennison was officially notified, I whispered to him as he was being seated at a table in his stateroom. He was surrounded by newsmen and guests, who had retired there having completed the review. I told him I understood one of the ships had gone aground. His response was an icy glare and a "If you are kidding, it's not funny." I assured him I wasn't kidding and would verify things adding that we would have a bigger problem with the newsmen aboard. If it was true, he must announce it to them. His reply was, "Get me the Operations Officer." Capt. Harry Cook arrived and also whispered the situation to Admiral Dennison.

I thought Admiral Dennison exhibited himself as an outstanding naval officer by putting things in proper perspective. He got up and approached Admiral Nimitz, informed him and then made a brief statement to the newsmen. He said that it was apparent that one of the last ships in line had encountered difficulty and was apparently aground on Alcatraz Island. He added we were trying to get additional information and at this time there were no reported injuries. This announcement caused a stir with the newsmen who clamored to get aboard the tanker. Admiral Nimitz, who had the respect of everyone in the Bay area, including the newsmen, settled them somewhat by relating how he would have been a part of the original Great White Fleet except that he was undergoing a General Courts-Martial at the time for running a destroyer aground!

I hastened the departure of the newsmen in a motor launch and instructed Lt. Fred Snyder, the COMCRUDESPAC PIO and a member of the Combined Information Bureau (CIB), to take the launch and make a pass by the *Chemung* but not to board and then to discharge the newsmen back at the morning depature point. The reason was obvious. Everyone aboard *Chemung* had a job to do to take care of the ship, free it and not allow oil to pollute the Bay. Admiral Nimitz disembarked with full honors and was sent off in a barge to his home on Treasure Island. Admiral Dennison and I went to the beach, heading for the St. Francis Hotel where he had a suite awaiting him. He growled that he hoped I told those newsmen they couldn't go on board the tanker. He had been informed that *Chemung*'s captain had just reported on board. He was an aviator who was the first to get a deep draft command before taking command of an aircraft carrier. This was a new Navy program designed to let aviators get their "water wings" before taking command of one of the big "bird farms" or aircraft carriers. Dennison was really upset about the whole incident. It had ruined a beautiful day and event. He blamed the captain and the dumb program of giving aviators a deep draft command before "they knew the sharp end from the blunt end of a ship."

On arrival at the St. Francis, he ordered, "Let's go to the bar!" Naturally, we did. He ordered a "double scotch on the rocks with not much ice." The waiter looked at me. I thought for a moment and then said, "There's a new drink in town. See if your bartender can mix a *'Chemung* on the Rocks'." I cracked up over that funny only to be chilled by a glare from Dennison.

"A couple months from now that will be funny, but not now, please," he said with some chagrin. But he didn't throw me in hack or even out of the barroom, so he must have deep down thought it had some merit.

I begged my departure, saying I had to get to the District Headquarters to learn about the *Chemung*. He said I could call from his suite, but I insisted I had to leave. His parting shot was, "Don't let those newsmen get on that ship." As I left the hotel, I saw a street sale "extra" published by the *San Francisco Call-Bulletin* with the top half of the front page blaring, "TANKER RAMS ALCATRAZ." What a terrible headline! The admiral was right. That S.O.B. captain DID ruin the day and event. In the cab going to the District HQ, I lamented about, "What a way to crash and burn while trying to pull off a spectacular." And it was a lousy way for the press to handle the incident overriding the beautiful spectacle of a Fleet Review. It was the first one since the end of World War II. Of course, that was from my myopic perception.

On arrival at the HQ, I learned that *Chemung* had been pulled off Alcatraz with no damage to the ship because she had fortunately settled into mud or sand. She was being moved to the Navy Supply Depot piers at Oakland. Knowing what Dennison had ordered, I asked Cdr. Harry Holton a rhetorical question about who had the authority for public information about First Fleet ships once they were in port. Everyone in the Navy information business knew the answer. Harry became fully responsive declaring it was the District Commandant's responsibility, and that he acted for the District Commandant.

I retorted that we had a tough situation on hand. I iterated that Admiral Dennison had instructed me not to let newsmen on board *Chemung*, and there was a group of newsmen who were clamoring to do so. Harry blanched and asked the whereabouts of the newsmen. I allowed that Fred Snyder had them in tow possibly at Oakland. Harry ordered someone to get Fred Snyder on the phone, and said he would call his boss, the District Commandant, and have him call Admiral Dennison. Soon Fred was on the phone. He was encouraged to talk with the captain of *Chemung* and have him talk with the newsmen. It was done. The captain played it straight, explaining that he was second to last in line of 26 ships, and those ahead had slowed to approach their piers. He had to slow so as not to run up the stern of the ship ahead of him. Before he knew it, he had lost steerageway, and the current took him softly onto the beach at Alcatraz. He was sincere. He was a nice guy. The newsmen believed him and sympathized with him. And the story died quickly. The "Ramming of Alcatraz" was buried in all follow-on stories if used at all. This was a classic lesson in handling bad news.

I met the *Chemung* captain that night at a reception and concluded he was indeed a nice man, obviously a top-notch naval officer. I sympathized with him for a situation that almost ruined a great day for the Navy but then thanked him for saving it.

The next morning I visited with Admiral Dennison aboard *Helena*. He was still upset about the *Chemung* and asked, "Who in the hell authorized those newspaper guys to talk with the captain?" I gave him the full story and said I understood that the District Commandant was to call him. Concluding, I added that the press conversations with the captain appeared to be a good thing because it essentially killed the "Tanker Rams Alcatraz" story. I had to amplify that statement, but a newspaper editor, E. Robert Anderson of the *The San Diego Union* and friend of the admiral, came aboard and commented that the Navy handled the tanker story right by letting the reporters to talk with the *Chemung* captain. I think Admiral Dennison was convinced the right thing happened. My next report of fitness didn't reveal he had any lack of confidence in me, nor did it reflect any doubt about my integrity.

The Great White Fleet celebration in San Francisco was a great success. Records were set for ships' visitation and for hometown news stories distributed nationwide about the event. Everyone seemed to enjoy the visit; the sailors were happy. San Francisco loved the Navy again, and we gained a considerable amount of good publicity. It was also a tribute to Phil Russell. The activity also proved to be my forte—the ability to plan for a special event project and execute it. My relief at First Fleet, Cdr. Hardy Glenn, said I was a great planner. "Whenever I thought about doing something, all I had to do was go into the files," he said. "Usually there was something you had already done, and all I needed to do was dust it off." Special events are fun to plan and execute. As long as the resources were available and I had the support of my boss, there was an assurance of a relatively high degree of success.

Before I was scheduled to leave First Fleet, Admiral Hopwood requested CHINFO to detail me for duty in his staff at CINCPACFLT at Pearl Harbor. The Chief of Information, Rear Adm. Charlie Kirkpatrick, replied that CINCPACFLT PIO staff was at 100%. He stated he couldn't afford to send Lt. Cdr. Thompson there because he did not have sufficient officers to fill all his PIO billets. I remember Admiral Dennison calling me in and sharing a copy of a letter Hopwood had sent to Kirkpatrick requesting that I be moved to his staff. It included some flattering words about my profession-alism. Handing me the letter, Dennison said quizzically, "After reading this fiction, my first reaction was to stuff it back into its envelope and mark it, 'Return to Sender, Opened by Mistake.'" Dennison had essentially extended me for another year on his staff. I didn't mind because I was thoroughly en-joying myself. We were accomplishing things, setting records and establishing standards. My family was doing well, and it was a good break for us to have another year in Coronado. It was a great locale to get newborn Brian started. And Stevie and Craig were happy with Coronado and their new brother.

Introducing Brian William Thompson

Brian's arrival was typical of a Navy launching in Coronado. At that time, the Navy's only maternity ward was at the Naval Hospital in Balboa Park at San Diego. Expectant mothers and fathers were well briefed on procedures for the life changing event. About 2300 (11:00 p.m.) on the night of August 5th, Zum nudged me and said, "I think it is time to go." I awakened Stevie and Craig, telling them to get dressed because we were going to take a midnight ferry ride to the hospital in San Diego. I then called the Coronado Ferry to inform them we would be there in a couple of minutes and to hold the ferry for an expectant mother. I was told they would as it was the last ferryboat to San Diego that night. We were in only one of two or three cars aboard. As soon as we got embarked and I identified myself as the one who called, the ferry started moving.

The crew was cordial, hospitable and offered help. But Zum only wanted to get across the Bay and to Balboa Hospital. Once there, the "Thompson

Labor Movement" slowed considerably, and the doctor told us that it might be several more hours. I told Zum it would be best if I went back to Coronado with the kids. They could get some sleep, and we would return in the morning. We left, and Zum called about 0600 with word the baby had arrived. He was a boy named Brian. She added that everything was in good order. Zum remained in the hospital for two days. Stevie, Craig and I had a ball. Our meals were introduced with, "Well, what are we going to have with our ice cream for this meal—pizza, hotdogs, hamburgers?" Craig said that he liked the way I *cooked*. It was certainly "Not all that stuff Mom makes us eat."

From 1948 to 1953 Captain Bob Dennison served as the Naval Aide to the President of the United States Harry S. Truman. During this period his Naval Academy classmate and close friend Captain Arleigh A. Burke or 31-knot Burke fame had been given the ominous task of heading Op-23, an ad hoc office created to present the Navy's story aimed at combating cuts in naval forces. Louis Johnson, Secretary of Defense was levying these reductions, with the full support of the Air Force. The latter was show casing its B-36, a propeller driven bomber, as the end-all for the thrust of US power projection. It was the B-36 vs. carrier aviation and the Air Force was conducting Madison Avenue public relations and it was rumored that they had the backing of some Madison Avenue agencies headed by Air Force Reserve officers. Captain Burke was in a no-win situation. He would be blamed for all successes or defeats in the controversy. He would make enemies in the White House, Defense Department, Army, and Air Force and on Capitol Hill. And he did!

When Burke's name came to the White House as one of those selected for flag rank in 1949, his name was removed by Truman himself or a trustee in his office, thinking the boss would want it to be. Captain Dennison is credited with persuading President Truman to restore Burke's name to the list. Arleigh Burke went on to become the Chief of Naval Operations in 1955, being selected over 92 more senior flag officers and served an unprecedented three two-year terms. He was heralded as the living legend of the Navy, a legitimate WWII hero and one who guided the Navy through six perilous years in Washington, bringing into being the Polaris Fleet Ballistic Missile

System and continuing carrier aviation. He was placed on a pedestal, idolized and loved by all in the Navy. He was a solid, down-to-earth naval leader with a wonderful, dedicated, faithful wife, Roberta—Bobbie— as we all knew her.

Admiral Dennison moved along, leaving COMFIRSTFLT to be Commander-in-Chief Atlantic Fleet, Atlantic Ocean Areas and Supreme Allied Commander, Atlantic in the NATO structure. I was happy to see him move up the ladder and considered myself fortunate to have experienced a good relationship and accomplishments with him. He departed San Diego with a strong, quality image as a naval leader and fleet commander. The admiral and I remained friends until his death.

Dennison's relief was Vice Adm. Ruthven E. Libby. I was leery about him because of his reputation. When I was serving in USS *Midway*, CHINFO had tried to entice me to be a PIO for Libby when he was a cruiser division commander in the Korean War. He had just fired his PIO, and he was known to be a tyrant. I declined at the time because I thought I wanted to be a surface warfare officer and didn't want to expose myself to the likes of the reputed Ruthven Libby. Admiral Dennison counseled me to "just continue to do the good job you are doing, and you will get along with "Libs." Whatever you do, don't show any fear."

Dennison departed before Libby arrived, so for about two weeks "the billet was gapped" as they say in the Navy. Libby descended on the Coronado scene on a Sunday evening and was to take command in a ceremony aboard an aircraft carrier at 1000 (10:00 a.m.) the next morning. I scheduled a news interview with him at 0900 and met and briefed him five minutes prior to meeting the newsmen. The interview went well. It was a short, get acquainted meeting with no pronouncements. Fortunately, we had to break off the interview, so he could get to his Assumption of Command ceremony. I took care of an inquisitive news corps who wanted to meet the new admiral in town but were not interested in a hard news story.

I assumed the chief of staff had briefed Libby about the interview because he had agreed with me it was a good way to introduce the new boss to the newsmen. It would be a start toward continuing the excellent relations we had with the media in Southern California. When the dust had settled on the primary activities of the day, Libby sent for me and asked, "What is this press conference (to be) all about?" I replied by apologizing for not being able to thoroughly brief him before, but I presumed he had the information. Then I gave him a dose of our status in Southern California and concluded by saying I hoped he would continue to be cordial and receptive to the local media reps as his predecessors had been. He paused, grumbled that he wasn't accustomed to it, but said I should carry on.

Libby was a thin, wiry man—alert, quick, caustic and cryptic. Without too much difficulty one could easily realize why he had the reputation as a S.O.B. He ripped through *The New York Times* crossword puzzle each morning and had a crossword puzzle book in his desk drawer. He took great delight filling in all the blanks. By reputation he also took great delight in ripping people. He had been an aide to Adm. Earnest King, CNO during World War II, and he apparently learned from him. However, it wasn't long before he became comfortable with me and vice versa. Perhaps he mellowed or was mellowing. I soon learned to like him.

One of the first things I did was to take him to his hometown of Spokane, Washington. That's something I had always wanted to do with my boss, and Libby went along with it. He hadn't been *home* for many years, having no living family members in the area. I gave this project considerable attention because: (1) I hadn't done it before; (2) the admiral became enchanted with the idea; and (3) it was fun. I advanced the event, spending a weekend in Spokane prior to Libby's appearance on a Monday morning. I arrived at the Spokane airport in a Navy S2 *Tracker* combatant aircraft. By advancing, I got to meet the volunteer group who were to host the admiral and to attend the Washington State versus University of Southern California football game on Saturday.

I had a great time, but by Monday morning I was ready for the admiral to take center stage and the spotlight. The Spokane people were wonderful home folks, outgoing and excited about "their boy who made good." They were pleased to have a chance to be affiliated with the Navy. They normally had to go across the state to Seattle to see a sailor suit or a ship. The host group comprised the remnants of an almost defunct Navy League Council. Having Admiral Libby come home rejuvenated the council.

I scheduled the admiral to speak at his former high school. He had a little difficulty at first but loosened up, got into the spirit of the event and enjoyed the students. The rest of the stay involved a banquet in his honor, a speech and visits with the local newspaper and radio stations. And, of course, there was a tour of the city.

We later brought the Spokane contingent to San Diego for four days of naval indoctrination and a little infusion of "Blue and Gold." They had a couple of days in an aircraft carrier and a submarine, witnessed amphibious training and had another day with the Marines at Camp Pendelton. They finished up the week with one of them being the guest of honor and "taking the Recruit Review" at the Recruit Training Command. I kept a correspondence going with a few of the Spokane people over the years.

One of the nice things we did before I departed FIRSTFLT was host 15 high school students whom the Navy had recognized for excellence in the study of science. We conferred an award of getting to spend a week with the Navy. We called them "Science Cruisers," and Phil Russell and I came up with a program to treat them like VIPs. They spent a day in a carrier at sea, a day in a submarine and a day with the Marines. Then we gave them a dose of science as it applied to Navy and its environment with a day at the Navy Electronics Laboratory. It was a little different and more fun than working with an adult group or newsmen. Even Admiral Libby joined us in welcoming the youngsters. Each youngster was the subject of a news story going to his or her hometown media. This was another example of our attitude towards public relations. With a little effort and the employment of some imagination to use readily available, we could and did make a difference.

It would be interesting to learn what each of those 15 youngsters did in later life and if the week they spent with the Navy made any impression on them or led to careers in science or the Navy. We definitely provided a launching pad for them. The same wonder applies to all those who followed in the Science Cruiser Program. It means "following through," and we didn't always do well at that. It is a pity when that slips, because much time, energy and funds were expended in those type of projects. It's just good management to learn if those efforts were worthwhile.

For us San Diego was a quiet, Southern California retirement town until we started having guests in La Mesa and Coronado. First, Vince Muzzo, a second lieutenant in the Marine Corps, was assigned to Camp Pendelton, fresh out of Northern Illinois at DeKalb, Illinois. He was engaged to Mary Ann Tomberg my cousin from Chicago. Vince became a regular at our La

Mesa home during his training at Pendelton. He left briefly to return to Chicago to marry Mary Ann, then they set up housekeeping in La Mesa and stayed. Vince left the Marine Corps and became a teacher at Lames High School. Their two children, Mark and Karen, were born there. In 1994, their entire family moved to Idaho, but they left their mark on La Mesa.

As mentioned previously, another cousin, Ronnie Carlson, (Dodi and Fred Carlson's son) came to Coronado to visit. Being a quality machinist, he was hired at Convair Corporation in San Diego. He returned to Manitowoc, Wisconsin, to gather up his wife, four children and Labrador retriever for permanent settlement in San Diego. They are still there.

With San Diego such a lure, it had to be explored by Dodi and Fred. They visited us and, of course, Ronnie. They returned to Manitowoc, sold their house, quit their jobs and moved to San Diego in 1960. They remained there until their deaths, Dodi passing in 1999 and Fred in 2002.

We thought it best to depart the San Diego area for fear that Wisconsin would be depleted. Our departure from FIRSTFLT and Coronado was triumphal in a way. The family had thrived on the Coronado environment and was happy. We had an enormous amount of enjoyment there. We made many friends with both senior and junior officers and peers in the public information community as well as the broader Navy spectrum. The same could be said about acquaintances established outside the Navy perimeters. We had accomplished much, contributed to the good name of the Navy and FIRSTFLT and developed a good reputation.

The development of a good reputation may have contributed to a dilemma I faced concerning my next tour of duty. The Chief of Information, Rear Adm. Charlie Kirkpatrick, apparently received several letters from other flag officers asking for me to be assigned to their staffs. Their PIOs, who thought it would be nice to have Lt. Cdr. Thompson as their assistant, initiated those letters flag officers signed. I wasn't impressed by the aggressiveness of some of those PIOs I met and worked with on the West Coast. It figures that they wanted a "horse" to be their assistant or deputy.

A couple of the West Coast Naval District PIOs had asked me in passing if I'd like to go to Seattle or San Francisco. They alluded to asking for me or getting their bosses to do so. I replied I wanted a good place for my family, quality schools and a pleasant locale. I knew a Naval District was somewhere on the horizon in my professional development. But I would have preferred to have my own shop—that is be the senior PIO. With what I considered to be a noncommittal answer, I forgot about it.

I would have much rather stayed with the fleet and gone to Pearl Harbor, Norfolk or overseas to Japan, Taiwan, the Philippines or London. However, I did not campaign for those locations. Charlie Kirkpatrick was a bombastic sort and took me to task when I was in Washington for a PIO conference in the spring of 1959. He accused me of negotiating those letters, in fact, embarrassed me in a plenary session of all the PIOs when he announced defiantly that *HE* did the detailing and *HE* didn't appreciate PIOs like Thompson big dealing their next assignments. I got a lot of kidding from the other PIOs, such as "Looks like you are on the short list for assignment to McMurdo Sound (Antarctica), Bill."

I doubt if Kirkpatrick ever believed I wasn't behind those letters. A classmate of his, Rear Adm. Harold Thomas "Dutch" Deuterman, dropped by his office to make a plea for a PIO. He indicated he had a billet for a commander PIO, and it was vacant. Charlie's eyes lit up and said, "I've got just the guy for you, a hot shot LCDR from the Pacific Fleet." Without any counseling or forewarning, I received orders to Omaha, Nebraska, to the Headquarters for the Naval Reserve Training Command. Yipes! I had the urge to call Washington and ask if that job in McMurdo Sound was open. Omaha had only the Missouri River for "wetness," but it could prove interesting. I resolved that perhaps the Omaha staff had problems, and I could help them. Like the good naval officer I tried hard to be, we packed out and left the balmy climes of Coronado for a new adventure.

A note closing out my First Fleet Staff tour—I was the first PIO assigned to the staff. The last was Brent Baker. During his watch, First Fleet became the Third Fleet. In between Brent and myself were Jack Garrow, Bob Sims and Jimmy Finkelstein. All of the them except Bob Sims became Chief of Information (CHINFO). Sims later did a tour as Assistant Secretary of Defense for Public Affairs (OASD(PA)), the top job in the Department of Defense for public affairs. No other fleet or assignment can match that record. Could it have been the water?

Was This Trip Necessary?

Our trip east from San Diego to Omaha offered the opportunity for a leisurely journey while camping along the way. At least, that was our intent and how we started our trek to the Great Midwest. Our Nash Ambassador, an excellent road car with ample space, was again fully loaded including the car top carrier. Taking an easterly heading, we stopped overnight at a Lake Tahoe campsite. I can still see one-year-old Brian bravely trundling into the waters of Lake Tahoe and suddenly realizing, "Hey, Folks, this is cold!" and then scurrying out. That scene was recorded on our 8mm-movie camera. We have experienced the chill of Lake Tahoe many times since.

After a pleasant and cool night at Tahoe, we headed for Salt Lake City and, of course, the Great Salt Lake with the intention to camp out that night. After a respite at the Lake, where we all tried unsuccessfully to sink in its salty brine, we searched for a camping area. It was raining, and Zum was driving with me as the Forward Lookout. Camping sites were nonexistent; at least on the roads we traveled. We couldn't find a site, so we kept driving all night and the next day. Fortunately, the big Nash had front seats that folded down to make some stretching out possible. The kids weren't happy campers, but the anticipation of getting to "Zummy's" (Zum's mother's nickname) house in Sheboygan quieted their anxieties to a small extent, which only means it could have been worse. We stopped in Omaha overnight. I checked into the command, unloaded my uniforms and gear not needed in Sheboygan and in the morning we got an early start for Sheboygan and Zummy's house at 521 Euclid Avenue.

I hadn't been in Sheboygan for five years or more, and it looked just as I had left it. It was—and probably continues to be—one of the cleanest towns in America. It has also had the same population size for the last 50 years or so and lacked new industry. In fact, there was nothing new in this German/ Dutch settlement. It gave evidence that it was an old town without much leadership. Many taverns remained, and bratwurst was King. A smoke pall hung over the city at noon on Sundays because most of the citizens were frying "brats" on charcoal cookers in their backyards. The smoke was probably not good for the environment, but the brats, a delicious treat, more than compensated.

Despite some of its obvious faults, Sheboygan was a good place for children. There were many parks, and Vollrath Park, only three blocks from Zummy's house, had a small zoo. Another block away was Lake Michigan with some good beaches. However, the lake was too cold for recreational swimming, and only a few members of the Polar Bear Club ventured into the water. Our main reason for visiting Sheboygan was to provide Zummy with a little needed attention. She had made several trips to California to be with us, and we wanted to reciprocate. Zummy was a wonderful person, a kind, thoughtful and loving grandmother who devoted much time to Stevie and Craig—reading to them, playing "Dirty Eights" and other card games. She loved my teasing her, and we had a good relationship. I facetiously stated on occasion that I had fallen in love with Zummy, so I married her daughter. An old adage says, "If you want to know how a girl will mature, physically and mentally, look at her mother." In this case, it was a truism.

We enjoyed the stay in Sheboygan and, of course, trekked to Green Bay to see my mother Betty and her family. Important, too, were visits to Manitowoc to see Dodi and Fred Carlson. My brother Don and Mary Jane were rearing a family in Manitowoc at the time. Don was working as the comptroller for the Aluminum Specialty Company.

My allotted leave eroded quickly requiring my return to Omaha. I left the family to enjoy Sheboygan for a couple more weeks. Our priorities at the time were to find housing and get the kids enrolled in school. We reunited and stayed in the Omaha's Broadway Hotel. Living in two hotel rooms with a wife and three kids was not like Coronado, but in later years we joked about the travail and how we survived.

Snow, Beautiful Snow

Ultimately, we purchased a house on beautiful Fontenelle Boulevard. We busied ourselves with the new house, got to know some of the neighbors and played bridge several nights a week with a newfound friend from the staff, Cdr. Joe Peak and his wife Vi. A short, beautiful Midwestern fall ushered in "Jack Frost" followed by an avalanche of snow. Craig, then an 8-year-old, and I seemed to spend the next five months shoveling snow. The biggest deterrent to our efforts was lacking a place to deposit the snow we tried to shovel. As our story goes, the first snows were fun because we hadn't experienced those conditions for six years. One lesson we learned in this process: When buying a house in the Midwest, don't buy one with a 120-foot driveway unless you also want to invest in a snowplow.

Omaha was a sprawling metropolis supporting the state's agriculture. As a former railhead, it had several industries, the primary one being the cattle stockyards. "If you ain't never had an Omaha Steak, you ain't never had a steak," was something we often heard in our new town. I endorsed the statement because good beef was plentiful in Omaha, and most restaurants featured steak on their menus.

The Missouri River flowed south through the city and at Kansas City turned east to St. Louis where it joined the Mississippi River. Omaha was an Army base for many years and boasted several forts within the city. Fort Omaha had once been commanded by legendary Lt. Col.George Armstrong Custer. He ventured westward from Fort Omaha to the Little Big Horn out into Sioux Country in Montana, where he and his troops made their famous "last stand." When I arrived, Fort Omaha was the headquarters for the U.S. Naval Reserve Training Command. My boss, Rear Adm. Dutch Deutermann, inhabited the house occupied by Custer in the early 1870s. There was a plaque attesting to that fact in the foyer of the house. It provided an instant conversation piece for callers.

I wasn't the first PIO to be assigned to the Naval Reserve Training Command in Omaha. Cdr. Bart Jackson was part of the original staff when it was structured and placed at Fort Omaha. Bart did a tour and departed, leaving the billet vacant. CHINFO, not having a sufficient number of officers to fill all the billets, left it vacant. Apparently the commander didn't ask for a replacement or make any noise about it. The billet was vacant for more than three years.

Not having had an immediate predecessor, I had time in the first few weeks to determine what my job should be and to learn about the command, its history, structure and plans for the future. As for defining my billet description, no one had a clue, including Admiral Deutermann. He sort of dismissed it by telling me, "Just go do your public relatin' thing, and if you get into trouble, let me know." Not desiring to get started on a wrong course, I hesitated and delayed delivering my oration on command responsibilities regarding public relations. However, he agreed I should compose a plan and present it to him for approval.

Naval Reserve (Other Than Air)

Prior to the restructuring, the Naval District commandants were the principal functionaries of the Naval Reserve (Other than Air). "Other than Air" was a term used in Naval Reserve vernacular. The Naval Air Reserve was headquartered at Naval Air Station Glenview, Illinois. The focus of the reorganization was to remove the "surface" reserves from the command of the 13 or 14 Naval district commandants and centralize them under a single commander similar to the Chief of Naval Air Reserve. District commandants were part of the Navy's structure for years. But as time went on, changes occurred that diminished their territorial usefulness. Administering Naval Reservists, Other than Air, who resided within the confines of their districts, had become the primary function of the district commandants. However, the Navy kept postponing the inevitable funeral of the Naval District structure. At least it was delayed for about a decade by the reorganization of the surface Naval Reserve. A Commander, Naval Reserve Training Command (CNRTC) was established to administer the Naval Reserve (Other than Air) through the Naval District commandants.

The Surface Naval Reserve was a cumbersome structure and an expensive apparatus. Each Naval District had it own Naval Reserve staff to administer its reservists. Eventually, in 1970 the death knell was sounded for the Naval District structure, when it was removed from the Navy's realm of command and territorial responsibilities. Some were replaced by Naval Base Commanders such as Commander, Great Lakes Training Command; Commander Naval Base, San Diego; and Commander, Naval Base, Norfolk. The Naval District of Washington substituted for the Patuxent River Naval Command and continues to perform the high profile, extremely busy task of representing the Navy in the nation's capital. The Naval Reserve, including the Naval Air Reserve, was consolidated under one commander, a three-star admiral who had as a deputy, a rear admiral. They—one was a surface warrior and the other was a naval aviator—were headquartered in New Orleans. The headquarters at Glenview and Omaha were closed, and no middlemen were in evidence in maintaining and training the Naval Reserve.

Meanwhile, back in the 1959 timeframe, other than working with the various Naval District commandants, Admiral Deutermann's job was to energize the newly enacted Selected Reserve, foster a vigorous recruiting program and promote the concept within the Naval establishment and the public at large. Most of those objectives had to be accomplished by working with and through the existing Naval Districts. Dutch Deutermann was an interesting person with long, bushy eyebrows, an old face and even though he was in his mid-fifties looked like an older man. His appearance was deceiving because he was an energetic, gregarious man. He had the facade of a "down home" country boy from White Plains, New York. He had cultivated a few homey expressions that amplified his country boy style. He was a devout vegetable gardener, so Zum got along well with him. He said he always had the "ole iron kettle on the back of the stove" and each day added something to the "soup." He said he loved to have company. It was never an inconvenience, because all they would need to do was add some water to the soup kettle. Of course, his vivacious wife Sally denied all that soup talk. They were excellent hosts and enjoyed people and socializing. It was always a pleasure to be in their company.

Dutch was a surface warrior and ideal for the CNRTC job. He could easily get along with the district commandants. If they desired to play games with him, he ensured it was on his field where they played. If someone tried to tilt the field, they would soon be brought in line, either from Dutch or from a loud voice from the Pentagon or the Bureau of Naval Personnel. Admiral Deutermann had the backing and the clout if they were needed. The Navy leadership in Washington was serious about the Naval Reserve and communicated constantly with our staff. When situations became strained (usually when someone didn't agree with what Dutch was trying to do or promulgate on behalf of the program), Dutch would frown and pull out one of his back home farm expressions like, "It's time to get out the nuttin' knife."

The Selected Reserve was the first major overhaul of the Reserve program since World War II. Prior to and during the war, there was a Naval Reserve, but it lacked the magnitude of the current peacetime edition. During World War II, the great majority of personnel were Naval Reservists, and the only new Regular Navy personnel were commissioned from the Naval Academy. All new enlistees and officer accessions were in the Naval Reserve. Following World War II demobilization, many veterans decided they would like to affiliate with the Naval Reserve. Some were paid for attending drills; others garnered points for retirement purposes. In the Korean War, it was the reserve forces that again carried the brunt of rapid remobilization. President Truman acted promptly and intelligently by calling up National Guard units and reserve forces. Most of the reservists were rusty, not having hands-on training or experience for the past five to seven years. The exception was those who trained as a part of a unit, an air squadron, a ship's company or a detachment that worked and trained together as a team. The Selected Reserve was intended to cure those ills. It was to become the Naval Reserve's elite corps and was paid for it. Selected Reservists were eligible for immediate recall to active duty and would be able to fill in alongside their Regular Navy sisters and brethren. The Naval Air Reserve performed well in this regard, and squadrons deployed for duty assigned throughout the world operating with Regular Navy elements.

Omaha was selected as the headquarters for the CNRTC because it was centrally located in the continental U.S. The commander had at his disposal an aircraft, a two-engine Convair R4Y, and an aircrew to give him mobility around the country. Precipitating such movement, the program called for an annual inspection of Naval District reserve staffs and some of their components. Each month a Naval District was flagged for inspection. An "Omaha" team was dispatched to inspect Reserve units within the district during the week from Monday through Thursday. Friday morning was the "Day of Reckoning" when the Omaha staff descended upon the Naval District Headquarters with the results of its inspections. As most inspections go, there was little in a positive nature to be discussed. Within a short time, Omaha took on a cloak of peril and negativism. The Naval District staffs were irritated by the procedure. That attitude proved futile because Dutch Deutermann would roll up his sleeves and "get out the nuttin' knife." He personally participated in most of the inspection trips and was an extraordinary communicator.

Selling Sheep In Omaha

On the community relations aspects of my job, trying to sell the Naval Reserve Training Command in Omaha was like trying to sell sheep in the "City of Beef." With Dutch Deutermann's help, I instigated the formation of a Navy League Council in Omaha with a nucleus of Navy World War II veterans. However, Omaha was definitely an Air Force town with the Strategic Air Command headquartered there, and Offutt Air Force Base was a principal economic element. I counseled Admiral Deutermann saying we had established our small footprint in Omaha and should maintain that presence. But Omaha should not be our primary public information objective. Creating a metaphor, we would keep Omaha in our tidy little backyard, but our front yard was the entire United States. The whole country should be our field of activity, and we should exploit the considerable resources embodied in the Naval Reserve to help us. Our efforts should be to inform about the Naval Reserve, particularly the Selected Reserve, and design the program to create an environment to assist Naval Reserve recruiting. The admiral pondered a short time and agreed. I doubt if he really comprehended my rational, but his "hot button" was Naval Reserve recruiting.

I was urged to accompany the inspection teams deploying monthly from Omaha, and it was rare that I did not. It gave me an excellent opportunity to meet and talk with news media representatives throughout the country. Most had not heard about the Selected Reserve. There were many newsmen, both print and electronic, who were affiliated with the Naval Reserve or were Navy veterans. That helped me significantly to have doors opened to media outlets. The Naval Reserve also had a sizable contingent of public relations people in its Standby Public Relations Companies including practicing news media personnel. I regularly met with their units when visiting their communities.

I convinced my boss that the large community of PR Reservists should be informed about the Selected Reserve and scheduled a weekend meeting in Omaha in January 1960. It turned out to be the coldest day of the year, in fact, setting some records for the below zero weather. But we gathered these Reservists (more than 100 of them) from all over the country for a weekend of Selected Reserve and CNRTC saturation because, again, many didn't know the Omaha command existed. Additionally, they didn't even know I was the program manager for the Naval Reserve Public Relations program. A successful event resulted and paid dividends for many years. Even 30 years later, I received comments about that meeting "someplace above the Arctic Circle" at a place called Omaha. Zum and I hosted at home about 20 of my closest friends in the visiting group. As PIOs are wont to do, it became a long and fun-filled evening with many sea stories and other kinds as well. Stevie, who was 13 going on 33, helped us as co-hostess. The next morning she said, "Dad, you sure have a lot of funny friends. Some of them are a little weird." I thought that was a fair assessment.

Dutch Deutermann departed Omaha and CNRTC to a three-star assignment in Norfolk. Rear Adm. Don Eller relieved him and brought another dimension to the job. He liked to play golf, and we got along just fine immediately. When we traveled, our golf clubs were usually included with the baggage. He was a proper, gentlemanly man of average height, slim build and wore a pencil-thin mustache. He had a good sense of humor when we were playing golf or relaxing at the "19th hole" or at a restaurant. He was a pragmatist and tried hard to help solve Naval Reserve problems. However, I had a feeling that Dutch Deutermann didn't leave his "nuttin' knife" for him to use.

Our deputy commander was a Reserve rear admiral who was brought on active duty as a showpiece. Rear Adm. John William McElroy was a merchant mariner and had been "around the horn" a few times. He was also pure

"Irish." He loved a good tory. His laughter was often heard above the usual din in the office, and I was usually laughing with him. On one occasion, he headed the inspection team doing Southern California. After visiting Naval Reserve Training Centers in Compton and other places, Admiral McElroy and I were having a nightcap when I teased him with a provocative thought.

"Why don't you and I take off and do our own inspection of the Naval Reserve in Palm Desert?" I asked. He gave me a quizzical look and stated he didn't know we had a training center there. My reply was that I didn't know either, but there should be one because Capt. Horace Brown lived there. I explained who Horace Brown was—a former Merchant Marine skipper who became the bodyguard for William Randolph Hearst and was married to Marion Davies whom Hearst had tried to make a movie star. After Hearst's death, Brown married Davies, and in Palm Desert they owned, lived in and ran the Desert Inn among other things.

McElroy became serious and said to me, "Bill, why don't you see about you and me inspecting the Naval Reserve at Palm Desert?" Then he added he had already met Horace Brown but sure would like to meet Marion Davies.

America's Sweetheart, Mary Pickford

The Navy had a public relations office in Hollywood to primarily interface with the motion picture industry. It was run by a contemporary, Lt. Cdr. Joe Williams, and the No. 2 was a good friend, Lt. Herb Hetu. I contacted them, and within a few hours a plan was put together. On a Thursday at noon, we took off in two Navy cars to inspect the Naval Reserve at Palm Springs. Admiral McElroy was told that neither Brown nor his wife was in Palm Springs, but they welcomed the admiral and his staff to be their guests at the Desert Inn.

The admiral's disappointment didn't last long. Joe Williams had arranged to have us invited to a cocktail party at the home of Mary Pickford and her husband, Buddy Rogers, famed for being Pickford's husband as well as the leader of a dance band. After checking into our suites at the Desert Inn, we made our way in uniform to the Rogers' residence. The admiral made the mistake of bringing his hat into the house. After an hour the party warmed up and was buzzing with chatter and laughter. The decibels were increasing. Our hostess got a little "buzz on" and paraded around her house with the admiral's hat on her still pretty head. I warned her that girls shouldn't get under a sailor's hat because that would lead to a kiss. "Is that all?" she came back with. The admiral did get a kiss but that was all.

About that time, Buddy Rogers' mistress made an appearance, uninvited of course, at least by Pickford. But this was Hollywood or the Hollywood crowd, and kinky things do happen and did. Pickford started yelling, fighting and throwing things. Someone called the police. We, the Navy, thought it was time to deploy and were going out the back door when we spotted a police car. We retreated to a first floor bathroom and exited through a window pushing the corpulent admiral through the tight space. The fact the admiral had taken more than his ration of grog and didn't want to leave such nice people certainly didn't help. We made our getaway with Joe driving the admiral in one car, and Herb and I following in the other. Somehow the two cars became separated. Herb and I soon realized there weren't any lights around. We were in the middle of the desert, and it was dark. The only solution was to reverse course and drive towards some lights. That worked.

We returned to Palm Springs and our rendezvous point, Jack Dempsey's Restaurant. Joe and the admiral were already there. Joe was eating, and the admiral, sort of snoozing, was using his forearms as supports to hold his head up from a table in a subdued area nearby. The restaurant's namesake was present, and we talked for about five minutes. I asked if he would like to meet my boss, Admiral McElroy. He replied to the affirmative, and we went to the table of the "Contemplating Admiral." I put my hand on his shoulder and said, "Admiral, how would like to meet Jack Dempsey?"

He groggily raised his head and said, "Sure, how many rounds do I get with him?" When he saw Dempsey standing in front of him, he sheepishly stood and held out his hand. The admiral was no slouch, and within a few seconds. the two of them were laughing and enjoying each other.

After getting something to eat, we talked a while longer with the former Heavyweight Champion of the World before returning to the Desert Inn.

The party was over. Bidding adieu to Williams and Hetu, the admiral and I returned to our suite about midnight. McElroy was a bit unsteady but got himself into bed. We had to be on the road no later that 0430 (4:30 a.m.) in order to be in San Diego by 0800 to meet our inspecting party and begin the debrief for the Eleventh Naval District staff. I figured I couldn't go to bed for the three hours or so and still be sure of awakening to get the admiral dressed and into the car for passage to San Diego. So I stayed up and read, walked, paced and yawned. Packed and ready to go at 0400, I awakened Admiral McElroy and helped dress him because he refused to fully respond. We were in the car and moving at 0430. The first stop was an all night truck stop where I got us some coffee and a couple of doughnuts. The admiral cooperated and dozed off again. We were on the straightaway Highway 15 booming across the desert. There was no traffic, so I let the black Navy Chevrolet get up to max speed—about 85 mph. The admiral, sitting next to me in the front seat, bobbed his head, opened his left eye, looked at the speedometer and muttered, "You're going a little fast, aren't you?"

I let up slightly on the accelerator, looked over at him and said, "Oh, I'm sorry, Admiral. I thought you were driving." He jerked his head up, looked around and said, "You're kidding me again. Just take it easy." He didn't go to sleep for another 15 minutes, and once during that time, he smiled and averred, "Great inspection, wasn't it!"

We made it to San Diego on time, and it was a successful week on the road. Many times in the ensuing year, he would open the day with me, even at staff meetings, with a sly grin asking, "Who's driving?" He often remarked when we socialized how he was sorry he missed seeing Marion Davies but sure enjoyed talking with Jack Dempsey on one of the best field trips he had been on while at Omaha.

Publicizing the Selected Reserve continued, and I was paid for an article featured in the *Naval Institute Proceedings*. I was once given almost an entire edition of Navy League's *Seapower* monthly magazine with two long pieces on the Navy's Selected Reserve. It was overkill, but it was the editor's call. The articles should have been split and run six to 12 month apart.

Itchy Feet

I was not the Navy's happiest PIO at Omaha, but I did a credible job. It was a definite contrast going from a Pacific Fleet staff to a Naval Reserve staff. About 75% of the Omaha staff officers were reservists. They were good folks, easy to work with and experts in their specific fields. I got along well socially and professionally with the staff officers and came away with some long lasting friendships. I had a small staff (a secretary) but was satisfied with the arrangement. I kept busy, had an excellent relationship with the admiral—golf on weekends and sometimes during the week—and a relatively busy social life. I admit to having difficulty adjusting to a slower pace and less pressure (usually brought upon myself). I made up for it by spending more time with the family and got interested in tape recording as a hobby. I continued my interest in still and motion picture photography. Craig was my assistant with the stereo tape projects, and by the time he was 10, he surpassed my technological capabilities. He was good at it.

It became known to Zum and me that my mother had cancer. I thought if the Ninth Naval District job was open, it would be convenient for us to be near Green Bay—the closest place the Navy could send a PIO. My tour at Omaha would be normally completed in August, and an assignment change then would work out well for the kids' schooling. I called Cdr. Dick McCool, the Commandant, Ninth Naval District (COMNINE) PIO, learned he had orders and CHINFO was looking for a relief for him. I then called Capt. Jim Dowdell, the Deputy Chief of Information, and explained my situation. He responded that if my boss could spring me, I would be ordered to COMNINE in January. It was then October. I immediately went to Adm. Eller and was most pleased with his reaction. He said it was most "fortuitous" (one of his favorite words) I could be placed in a more challenging assignment close to my mother. He added his thought I was spinning my wheels at Omaha, and I should have greater responsibilities. He said he would be delighted to have me stay on his staff, but he would endorse my leaving on an obvious hardship case.

My good Navy wife was there again. Even without the orders, she sold the house on Fontenelle Boulevard and found a rental home for temporary lodging. Zum knew that I wasn't happy at Omaha and would find a way to leave soon. She rationalized we could wait if necessary until August in the rental house. Orders were cut, and I was to leave in early January after a year and a half at Omaha. Zum was happy thinking about not only being close to Green Bay but even closer to Sheboygan. And besides, she didn't like me being grumpy most of the time.

Again, I had learned and profited this time by assignment to Omaha. I developed a working knowledge of the Naval Reserve, an increasingly important element of the Navy. My acquaintanceship with news media outlets, writers, columnists, commentators and executives was vastly increased and had grown on a nationwide basis. My Rolodex and business card files were crammed with names of Naval Reservists who were employed in mass communications, media and public relations in all sectors of the country. All of these dimensions assisted me in future assignments as a Navy Public Information Officer. Fortuitously, I gained from the relationship with the three flag officers I worked with—I learned from them and developed allies and friendships. And you can't beat those Omaha Steaks!

Great Lakes—Now So Beautiful

It was my third time at Great Lakes. The first was when I "washed out" of flight training and was ordered to participate in recruit training during the middle of winter 1943-44. That experience was not a favorite time in my life. The second tour was in 1948 when I was "stashed" for six weeks awaiting the Armed Forces Information School to open at Carlisle Barracks in Pennsylvania. That scenically lovely place became the battleground over my body with the Bureau of Naval Personnel demanding Ens. William Thompson, having been a commissioned officer for three years, go to sea. My thoughts at the time were, "Nuts! I'm going to do public information work or go home." That resulted in a reprieve for a year, but much had happened since 1948. In those 13 years I had spent almost 10 either at sea in ships or in a fleet staff while considering myself to be a happy sailor.

The third time at Great Lakes was the proverbial charm. I was aboard the Navy's largest training center located about 45 miles north of Chicago and 90 miles south of Milwaukee. There I was near two of my favorite cities and on Lake Michigan all known to me during childhood. The Ninth Naval District was by far the largest in the Navy's shore establishment. It covered one-fourth of the continental U.S. and was the residence for one-quarter of the country's population. As a further challenge, there were few naval activities in the district. The Great Lakes Naval Training Center district was the largest followed by the Naval Air Station at nearby Glenview, Illinois. There was a small avionics activity operated by the Navy in Indianapolis, and except for the Naval Reserve training centers scattered throughout the District, that was about it. The Naval Reserve Training Command at Omaha, my last duty station, was significant, but it was not near the magnitude of personnel or budget.

I was eager to take on a large assignment with the logical progression of increased responsibilities for a PIO in a big shore establishment position.

Great Lakes was a natural place for me presenting unusual opportunities. My domain was America's Great Midwest. I had a few friends in Chicago, a city where I was eager to work, to learn more about and to associate with those who molded its personality and character. I admired Chicago's ebullience, its energy and its ample work ethic as mirrored in the character of its people. Throughout our lives and travels together, Zum and I were attracted to Midwesterners and shortly after being reintroduced to them, we felt we could identify well with their background. So in a broad sense, as Zum and I had discussed and agreed, we were "at home," in familiar territory. I now had an excellent job with unlimited potential for enjoyment and success.

I arrived alone at Great Lakes in January 1961. I was fully charged to get into a new job. It would require using different skills and operating in different areas. Venues such as community relations, working with local governments, civic organizations and various Navy interest groups were all involved. My previous experience had been based on strong media relations, planning and positive success in staging special events. Internal relations was a strong focus in my background, and I looked forward to shaping it in some new dimension. Like all good sailors, I wanted to hit the deck running. However, on reporting aboard to relieve Cdr. Dick McCool, I was slowed to a walk by the news that Dick's orders had been canceled. More dismaying, there was no prospect of another job opening for him in the near future.

Dick was a Naval Academy graduate. In the Leyte Gulf action late in World War II, he commanded a Landing Craft, Infantry (LCI) and earned the country's highest award, the Medal of Honor. Although seriously wounded, he courageously fought to save his ship and his crew. He became a PIO primarily because he was limited in the type of duty he could perform. Shipboard duty was definitely not to be in his future. He was a large man at 6-0 and 220 pounds. He was laid back, gentlemanly, serious when necessary and also enjoyed a good story or a laugh. As a PIO, he was a "status quo" type—efficient, dedicated, loyal and reactive but not proactive.

He worked for a proper, dignified, handsome rear admiral who was in the last few months of his naval career. At this stage in his career and life, Rear Adm. John M. Higgins was not about to rock the boat or muddy the waters with anything out of the ordinary in the area of public information. After a couple of months working alongside Dick McCool and picking up the routine of a Naval District, Dick decided to unofficially turn over the helm to me and shifted to the background. He was sensitive to the heat of having me sitting with him with not much to do. He was also frustrated. CHINFO had not produced orders for him to another assignment. In the face of the situation, our relationship remained good and continued that way long after we both retired. We became good friends. During the course of business, I had a conversation with Capt. Jim Dowdell, the Deputy CHINFO. He intimated he needed Cdr. Hardy Glenn in the office of information to head the press section and was considering sending McCool to First Fleet. He asked what I thought.

My reply was stifled a bit and discreet. "A great move," I said, "Captain. Hardy would do well running the press desk, and Dick McCool would do well out there in San Diego." Orders were eventually received, sending Dick to First Fleet and Hardy Glenn to CHINFO. Dick didn't actually leave until May after we had been together for about five months.

In the meantime, Zum and the kids and all their trappings moved from Omaha to Great Lakes. We had to take temporary quarters in what was called "Little Brick Row" and designated for junior officers. These quarters were adequate but smaller than McCool's which we later inherited in "The Gulch" area. Although I was a lieutenant commander, I was filling a commander's billet. Because we would be doing more than average entertaining, we were designated for The Gulch. Fortunately, Quarters N, next to the McCool's became vacant and we were assigned there.

Originally designed for mid-ranked officers but inhabited by captains and a few commanders, the backyards of these quarters overlooked a gulch that separated the Great Lakes Training Center from the Great Lakes Naval Hospital. The gulch was about 40 to 50 feet deep. It served as a drainage trough for the plains of the training center and emptied into the Great Lakes harbor on Lake Michigan. It was the site of the boathouse that sheltered the admiral's barge and other craft. Some handsome, large sailing yachts there had been donated to the Navy and were used by Navy personnel for recreation. Adjacent to the harbor was a large recreational area with a beach. The harbor included a fleet of smaller sailboats available to naval personnel and their dependents. Stevie and I joined the sailing instruction program and used the boats on Lake Michigan.

Life in The Gulch was a new and exceptional experience for us. Except for the Quonset Huts on Guam and the San Francisco Naval Shipyard, The Gulch was our first experience with "adequate" Naval Housing. It was two blocks from the office. The yards were mowed, snow removed and there was a semblance of proper maintenance. If something went wrong with the appliances or the structure, the public works people eventually took care of it. A few phone calls to the right people usually helped expedite proper care and maintenance. Most importantly, Zum was pleased. She enjoyed the Great Lakes environs. On request, she was assigned a plot in the nearby officers' communal garden space. She loved the therapeutic values of gardening, the social interfaces and most certainly the fresh produce. Stevie and Craig did well, especially Stevie who was in high school at the 10th and 11th grade. She flourished in school and was involved in declamatory and oratory competitions winning some awards. She became adept at standing before a group and thinking on her feet. She developed a good stage presence and poise that helped in later life. Craig became active in Boy Scout programs and developed a few good friends on the base.

Brian Alert!

Brian was different. The three to 4-year-old lad was a wanderer giving us some concern. The gulch and the harbor were only about two blocks from our back door. On occasion he caused what became known as a "Brian Alert." The base police would declare, "The Thompson kid is on the loose again!" One time he was found at the Naval Hospital where he was obviously checking out the Navy nurses. To get there, he had to traverse a narrow bridge spanning the gulch. On another occasion, he was found at the boathouse talking with the boatswain mates who manned the facility. They took good care of him, not letting him wander far. The base police were always cooperative and became well acquainted with Brian. Another time he showed up in my office to visit with Lois Merkel, my secretary. A set of dog tags was in order identifying him, his parents, our quarters and phone numbers. We used positive persuasion to get him to wear them. I wore mine for a while to show him, "If it's good enough for Dad, it's good enough for you." It was usually at nap time when he decided to take off to see the Great Lakes spread. Zum would be trying to get some things done during her respite from constantly watching over him, and he would slip out of the house forgoing his nap.

Meeting Harry Truman

Even before Dick McCool left the headquarters, I was doing the interface with Admiral Higgins and didn't load him up with much public relations work. We did go to Kansas City, Missouri. There he spoke to a group headed by Maj. Gen. Harry H. Vaughan, the military aide and personal friend of former President Truman. General Vaughn was close to the President—a card-playing buddy—and was active in the National Guard. We had a good time, and Admiral Higgins seemed to enjoy it, even the speech making.

Coupled with the Kansas City trip, I made arrangements for a visit with President Truman at his library in Independence, Missouri. My entrée for this occasion was to have Admiral Higgins present two large lithograph reproductions of the USS *Independence*, both the sailing ship and the newly commissioned aircraft carrier. Comprising our party was the admiral, Lt. Paul Leighton (his aide), the local naval reserve public information officer, who coordinated the itinerary, and me. We arrived on time and were informed the President was speaking to a group of Russian students and a few Russian newsmen in the auditorium across the hall from his office.

After about another five minutes when the President had not appeared, his secretary said he was really getting involved in his discussions with his guests. She invited us to view some of the interaction through a peephole in the door leading to the auditorium. We observed the President being very animated including some finger pointing punctuating his statements. He finally emerged, graciously received us in his office and apologized for being late.

He was a little flushed and irritated. I said we had been allowed to watch him for a short time through the peephole and saw him making what appeared to be some forceful statements.

President Truman chuckled saying he was making a few points in reply to a stupid question asking if there was any validity to the stories of America's Lend Lease Program. He told them they wouldn't be in the auditorium or even alive, if it hadn't been for the United States' generosity extended to Russia through Lend Lease and saving Russia from being over run by the Nazis. He turned aside that business and expressed pleasure in receiving the lithographs. He then escorted us on a half hour tour of the library. At one stop, he showed us an icon that had been a gift from General Dwight Eisenhower at the end of World War II. The note from "Ike" was sort of gushy. Harry S. smiled at us and said, "That's what Ike thought of me then."

A few days after we returned to Great Lakes, Admiral Higgins' secretary confided in me, "The admiral said to me the other day that Lieutenant Commander Thompson seems to have a good handle on the PIO business. He has an agenda, and it might be fun to stay around here to see what it is." Naturally, I felt good about that bit of intelligence, but thought that I had better solidify and define my agenda just in case someone would ask.

Protocol

In those days, it was proper and expected that junior officers would call on their seniors leaving calling cards behind. This part of the "Old Navy" has been phased out for many reasons including waging World War II. There was some good to be realized by the tradition, but most of it was a boring ordeal. Zum and I had experienced both ennui as well as enjoyable social events in the process. However, it seemed to belong in a different era. This type of social action left the scene in the late 1960s and isn't in the books of today's Navy. Many naval officers today have business cards, but calling cards seemed to have been phased out.

We made our call on Admiral and Mrs. Higgins as we were expected to do. His aide briefed me on how the admiral preferred to have this event carried out. Under no circumstances were we to be there more than 20 minutes and definitely not more than one drink. And BE ON TIME! I was also told the admiral's previous tour of duty was as Commander, Naval Forces Japan with headquarters in Yokosuka. His current home, Quarters A, had an oriental theme extensively featuring Japanese decor and artifacts. I was told Mrs. Higgins would probably appear in a beautiful Japanese robe or kimono, and she would most likely have applied a heavy white makeup to her face.

The aide had adequately briefed me because there were no surprises. We arrived on time and were greeted by a steward waiting at the door. Mrs. Higgins, garbed in a beautiful Japanese garment and pasty white facial makeup was waiting a few steps up from the entrance. She led us to Admiral Higgins. We sat properly and rather stiffly and had one drink. At about the 18-minute mark, I made a move for our exit. The admiral asked if we would like to have another drink. I declined, not wanting to fall into some trap and possibly get chewed out in the morning. He got up and walked me toward the bar with a large, heavy hand on my elbow and said in a muffled voice, "I'd like to have another drink, and I'd like for you to join me."

Being an accommodating soul, my reply was "Well, Sir, I would not want you to have to drink alone." We had a second drink and left 20 minutes later. I had the impression that Mrs. Higgins frowned on the admiral having a second drink but did not seem to worry about having broken a barrier. She even lightened up and smiled. I was amazed the white chalky stuff didn't crack, shatter or crumble. The next morning the aide and secretary shrugged and said it didn't happen very often even with the captains who call. I guess we were just lucky to catch the admiral when he wanted to relax and enjoy himself, his callers and a second drink.

Admiral Higgins retired in May, ending 44 years of service to his country. The significant ceremony was held on Ross Field with the historic Great Lakes Tower in the background. The retirement ceremony's central element was a Recruit Review. Normally the weekly spectacle featured the traditional graduation from boot camp. However, that week it was a little more special. Admiral Higgins was superb in appearance and the delivery of his farewell address. He was resplendent in his Service Dress Blues with medals and sword. He kept his speech short and pithy. No one doubted that before them was a fine naval officer who had given his best for many years and was hanging up his sword (to fade away). It was a somber but inspiring event with recruits marching, many flags cracking in the breeze, the Great Lakes Navy band playing martial music and a few speeches. The Recruit Review was and remains a colorful, exciting and thrilling spectacle. It gives evidence of what the Navy does with 17 and 18-year-old kids in just two months at boot camp. At these events, the graduates are literally pushed out of the Navy's nest to find themselves in the fleet or going to A-School for specialized training. Wherever they go from Great Lakes, they step into the real world and the real Navy. And they are most pleased to do so.

The Nunn Era

Higgins' successor was Rear Adm. Ira Hudson Nunn from Arkansas. He was of the Naval Academy Class of 1924 and was a ship driver. He was a surface warfare officer with a superb war record in destroyers. He was also a lawyer and had been the Judge Advocate General of the Navy. His immediate previous duty was as head of the Military Assistance Group (MAG) in Norway.

There was a gap in the presence of a flag officer in the Great Lakes Tower office. The Chief of Naval Air Reserve Training at Glenview had additional duty as COMNINE for the few weeks until Admiral Nunn arrived. He was to get there on a Sunday evening. I told the chief of staff that I needed the admiral all day on Monday to tour the media and meet some distinguished people in Chicago. This was awkward for the chief of staff because he didn't know our new boss any better than I did. He had no feeling for the admiral's reaction to being sent to Chicago with the PIO even before putting a foot inside his office. I argued it would probably be another month before I could set up a similar welcoming tour in Chicago. This venture was being done with the assistance of the Chicago-based Naval Reserve Public Relations Unit 9-2 (NRPAC 9-2). It was comprised of several middle management influence reservists as well as some potent news media personnel. They included the managing editor of *The Chicago Examiner*, marketing vice president of ABC

Chicago, the head of the McCann Erickson Advertising Agency, financial editor of the *Chicago Sun-Times*, and several public relations and businesses activists in Chicago agencies.

Most naval officers, especially superiors, would voice concern I was taking a chance by coming on too strong and demanding all the admiral's time on his first day. I thought I wouldn't be too far off the mark even if he passed on the offer. He would at least know he had inherited a proactive public information office. Through our PIO network, I learned Admiral Nunn had been exposed to public information activities and was rather active in Norfolk when he had an Atlantic Fleet command there. When he saw the schedule of events I provided the chief of staff, he shrugged and said, "O.K. Let's go."

The admiral's driver picked me up at Quarters N; we gathered the admiral at Quarters A and were off for Chicago and a great adventure. The first stop was on the near North Side of Chicago at WGN, radio and television—the largest in Chicago and the Midwest although it was an independent, non-affiliated station. WGN's staff was ushered into a reception room to meet the admiral. We had an interesting half hour, listening to WGN's status, ambitious plans and kind remarks about the Navy and WGN's association with the Navy at Great Lakes. Next was a call on Bill Wrigley of chewing gum fame. Bill had been in the Navy and had participated in meetings with NRPAC 9-2. Then we were off to a reception hosted by Mayor Richard Daley in City Hall in Chicago's downtown "Loop" where I observed a phenomenon. Whenever it came time for us to depart, Admiral Nunn spoke to each person he had previously met by name, and there were no name tags in sight. Wow! What a talent! A luncheon with more dignitaries was followed by meetings with *The Chicago Tribune*, *Chicago Sun-Times* and network affiliate executives. Each time Nunn did the same thing. He flattered all the individuals by remembering their names. He made a good first impression, and it proved to be a lasting one.

We completed the scheduled activities with a dinner at the private Tavern Club before heading north to Great Lakes. It was an hour's drive that turned out to be significant. It had been a successful day, and as I learned later in my career, few admirals had ever experienced such a warm welcome. Essentially, it was a day-long salute to the new commandant of the Ninth Naval District. He obviously felt good about it as did I. We were happily jovial in our comments about the day. Although it had been on my mind for several months, I almost surprised myself when I asked the good admiral if he had time to draw any conclusions about the next 18 months (the last of his Navy career). I was relieved when he replied, "Well, I don't know. Why do you ask?"

This gave me the opportunity to put the subject in a more expansive light and not so abruptly. I explained what he had witnessed that day was probably only the tip of an iceberg. The people were big city urbanites, rather blasé about dignitaries and celebrities, but I thought the reception for him was genuine. Chicago had a reputation of being a "great Navy town," and he could perceive that many of the people we met had served in the Navy in World War II. Even those who didn't normally seem to like and appreciate the Navy appeared receptive. This could have been a residual feeling from World War II when the Navy had two aircraft carriers operating out of Chicago, Great Lakes and Glenview. Things were big and busy then contributing extensively to our success in World War II. Perhaps an enigma shrouds the Navy, because its people board their ships and sail over the horizon. Intrigue and romance are entwined in that image. People are curious. What do Navy people do when they pass over the horizon? I further explained his Naval District covered one-quarter of the contiguous United States. We had more than 60 ongoing naval activities, mostly Naval Reserve training centers, within the district in cities where an admiral had never been seen.

I closed my impromptu presentation saying, "I propose that you consider a well-planned program. Try to visit each of those cities, speak at a Rotary, Lions Club and Navy League or make an appearance at the Reserve Training Center. You will evince your support and interest in the Naval Reserve and the Navy League. Publicity will be a large part of it, but I will worry about that. At the end of 18 months, you will have a bag full of keys to the cities of the Midwest and will have accomplished a lot of good will for the Navy. Among your responsibilities out here in this vast district is public relations, and you are obviously good at it. Naturally, I think it's your primary responsibility, and I am here to help you. It's a big undertaking. There will be some nights when you will be very tired, but I think it is worth the investment. I have a lot of energy, and I will work hard to conserve yours."

Admiral Nunn kept a half smile and a partial twinkle in his eyes as he stared at me quizzically. I didn't know if he was testing me or himself. I half expected him to blurt out something about being questioned by half-assed lieutenant commanders in today's Navy who have more gall than brains. His face didn't change. It was more or less frozen for what seemed to be an eternity but actually lasted only about a minute or so. Finally his head started moving up and down, affirmative to be sure. Finally he said in his stentorian admiral's voice, "O.K., Bill, let's go!"

The rest of the trip back to Great Lakes was a trail of gibberish. I kept cautioning myself to slow down, don't overkill but still show enthusiasm for the project. Returning to the gates of Great Lakes with Admiral Nunn was a great relief. The scene was repeated more than a hundred times in the next 18 months. As I look back on them, I loved them all. It was the time of day when I could check off another event in our great saga. I was really livin'!

There's that adage in the Navy about "hitting the deck in full stride." That's what I did on the Tuesday morning after our full-day excursion to Chicago. I actually slept well after our Monday long escapade and the strong message I asked for and received on the return ride to Great Lakes. We were launching a program that would tax the admiral's energies and demand much from my imagination, ingenuity and time. Was I ready? You could bet your life I was. I was feeling cooped up in the District Headquarters building after six months or so and was ready to explode or implode. I saw so much potential. So many acres of land were available to sow seeds of salt (the Navy brand) and yield so much good for the Navy. I sensed those seeds would continue to grow and proliferate many years into the future.

Yes, I was ready. At the same time, I was cognizant I had little experience with community relations, but felt confidant I could rub elbows with people in all areas. I delighted in being the behind-the-scene maestro sitting behind a typewriter or planning and scheming what others (usually my boss or other superiors) should do. I envisioned myself wielding an electronic prodding rod to ensure my charges responded on cue. Our goal of visiting each locale with a naval activity was extensive and would require considerable planning, scheduling, research and funding. Of course, we were to get well acquainted with O'Hare International Airport and to use all other transportation resources available. I realized much of the effort could not just be delegated within my small office. I foresaw using the commanding officers of the various naval activities as primary assistants for each visit. I impressed on them how they were integral to the visit and direct beneficiaries of the program. They would profit in many ways—community relations, increased stature within the city, recruiting and the resulting publicity.

I enlisted their support for the visits to their local activities, and they responded enthusiastically. They were excited about having their boss, Commandant, Ninth Naval District, visit their environs. I let the local skippers have almost complete control of the local itinerary but provided guidance about judicious time use when we were in their cities. The program's onus within our office fell to my secretary, Lois Merkel, who fortunately was bright and efficient.

I soon learned that Admiral Nunn was an excellent speaker with great stage presence and a good sense of humor. If we could hold him to two martinis, we could escape on the plus side of the spreadsheet. The admiral liked his martinis and having a few with him in the evening was a ritual. He always seemed to enjoy the circumstances and the company. Basically, he liked people and had that extraordinary retention for names and ensuing conversations. He was the rare type of individual who when talking with someone concentrated on just them and wasn't looking around the room seeking out someone more interesting. He enjoyed most of our exhausting project and appreciated the achieved results as we progressed through our schedule. In the cold, calculating way of looking at my job and available resources, I saw the admiral as a rare commodity. His talent could and should be used to the benefit of the Navy.

Two Speeches

Over the years, he had essentially developed two speeches. One was on the Navy, its history and accomplishments, and the other was about leadership. He used about six jokes that were appropriate not only for his speeches but to the audiences. One of my ancillary jobs was to track which speech he delivered to what audience in what city and what jokes he told. I did this to ensure when we returned to a site, which we frequently did, he didn't repeat his limited repertoire. He was always a proper gentleman and well organized. But if he got too much into the martini sauce, he might (and did) deliver half of each speech and tell all the jokes. The audience didn't know the difference, but it sure screwed up my bookkeeping.

Admiral Nunn also had a low tolerance for people, especially subordinates in his staff, who evinced weaknesses. This trait was particularly evident, if the person was male (99% of the time) and had no guts. I relate this behavior to his experience as a commanding officer for a ship, division or being a squadron commander for destroyers in World War II. Those were arduous times, and there was no tolerance for temerity, reticence, confusion or even slight evidence of cowardice. A high level of training, readiness and resolve were at hand. Any weakness was seen as the faulty link in a chain. As mentioned previously, I had heard Rear Adm. Arleigh Burke say that the difference between a good commanding officer and a mediocre one was about two seconds. There simply could be no tolerance. Ira Nunn was a lawyer and proud he had been the Judge Advocate General of the Navy. First and foremost he was a naval officer, and he was until the day he retired. Whenever he took on the cloak of being a lawyer and a counsel for whom or whatever he represented, he was one of the most impressive but most difficult people I had ever worked for.

I easily surmised that he was "old school" with the strong opinion that there was no need for "specialists" in the Navy. I know I became one of his closest allies and one of the best of friends he developed in the Navy. I know he liked, championed and trusted me. I also knew he wouldn't hesitate to give me a spectacular ream job. When he did, perhaps over some obscure or miscellaneous detail, he threw around words that were near fatal or homicidal. However, he would soon forget them, as if they were never emitted. I began to realize how close we were. But I didn't fully comprehend it until after he retired when I could view him at arm's length and from a different perspective. We remained good friends. I reveled in his tutorship and mentorship until the day he died in Arlington, Virginia, in 1990. I was able to help his daughter Frances bury him at the Arlington National Cemetery with full military honors. I served as a pallbearer, wrote his obituary and handled many aspects of the last respects for a great naval officer, warrior, lawyer and friend.

During those 20 months we were together, we managed to achieve our objectives set for his first forays into Chicago. We visited every city in the Ninth Naval District with a naval activity. Most were triumphal. Only a few were not what I had planned and expected. Success was directly proportional to local Navy support. In most cities we visited there was a Naval Reserve Training Center with a lieutenant commander or commander serving as commanding officer. All of them were excited about having the commandant visiting their domain.

It was heart warming to go into a town in Montana or North Dakota where the local Navy representative was a petty officer first class running a Navy branch recruiting office. He was recognized as "Mr. Navy" in that environment. There was never a need to enhance my appreciation for the Navy's "White Hats," but it was fortified and boosted on some of our excursions into the heartlands of the United States. Since my days on Guam and at sea, I had learned to respect and appreciate the vitality and dedication of enlisted personnel. To be sure, those young men in the environs of the Ninth Naval District "carried the flag" and comported themselves professionally. They were able to relate to the local populace and achieve their mission of recruiting young people into the U.S. Navy.

At some time in my life, I should have ceased to be surprised at the resourcefulness and dedication of the Navy's "Bluejackets." We cast the responsibility, leadership and confidence on those enlisted personnel to do jobs many would have considered unlikely to accomplish. We officers were not imbued with the stereotype happy-go-lucky sailor who was out for a good time at all times. (Throughout most of my career, I have clung to the image that the U.S. Navy sailor was a happy person, satisfied with his job, his environment, his Navy, his supervisors and doing his tasks to the best of his abilities. I later tried to imbue that spirit into the Lone Sailor statue at the Navy Memorial in Washington.) I subsequently learned that ours is the only navy where enlisted personnel have played such a dominant role. In others, particularly that of the former Soviet Union, enlisted personnel were not trusted, being short timers who were partially trained and not likely to satisfactorily perform assigned duties.

Admiral Nunn was not a morning person; he definitely was a nocturnal type. That fact complicated my life. Two or three times a week we left Great Lakes at an early hour bound for O'Hare to fly someplace in pursuit of our program. The admiral's driver and I would arrive sharply at Quarters A, to "fetch the Admiral" as the chief (the driver) would say. Admiral Nunn was always on time; punctual as a military person should be, but usually without a smile. I had determined if I could get him smiling or, better yet, laughing before we got the half mile to the main gate, it boded well for a good day. Otherwise, he would be grumpy at least until he had a martini fix for lunch. I would save jokes or possible funny comments about the news—anything to lighten him up a bit.

One morning, I didn't do well. He announced to me as he got into the car, "The paper wasn't there this morning." He always made a point of telling me, because my son Craig was the paperboy. Even though it was 0600 (6:00 a.m.), or as we would say, "Oh Dark Hundred," it was a manner he employed to evince disgruntlement with the world. I had just about given up hope for the day as the chief glided up to the sentry and surprisingly stopped. Normally, we would breeze through the gate with everyone in sight in a brace, saluting the admiral and wishing him a good day. The chief stopped the two-star car because the sentry—obviously a youngster who had just graduated from recruit training—had stepped out to block the egress. I thought it was strange, but it became much more so when the chief lowered his window. The sentry stuck his head inside and shouted to the admiral, "Render a right-hand salute!"

Instantaneously, I could see the day being elongated. To my surprise, the admiral complied. The chief, bewildered like me, was about ready to exit the car and give the sentry a few groups about recognizing the two stars on the license plates and the flags on the front fenders. The admiral began to laugh (He had a wonderful, infectious laugh.) and told the chief to drive on. He continued laughing and stopped only when he saw my puzzled expression. Explaining his merriment, he said, "I know what that youngster did. It reminds me of a similar situation I was in when I reported right out of the Naval Academy aboard my gunboat on the Yangtze River in China. I had the in-port OOD watch, and we had a Japanese counselor come aboard to make an official visit. I stood there with my long glass as the gentleman strode aboard, stopped in front of me, bowed and said, 'Good Morning, Sir, or Madam, whatever the case may be.' He had read the boarding instructions and repeated them verbatim. To say the least, he was not very discerning."

I laughed, and then the chief laughed. And the admiral further explained the sentry had obviously interpreted the instructions incorrectly. It was the sailor who should have rendered a salute. I told the admiral that when we got back, I'd call Capt.Hank Ford, the base commander and inform him about the sentry. The boss smiled and said, "The young man should be corrected, but tell Hank about my version of the story. Maybe he will see the humor in it, too. Anyway, it provided a good laugh so early in the morning."

"Yes, sir!" I smiled and replied.

That evening we returned to Great Lakes after midnight. As we approached the main gate, I saw the same young sentry at the entrance. It had been a long, arduous day with the admiral in relatively good humor. We were tired because of the busy schedule and long plane rides. As we slowed to enter the gate, I commented to the admiral that the same sentry was on duty. He didn't change expression, which could have been interpreted to be a little on the negative after a long day. To my dismay, the sentry did the same shtick. He demanded a right-hand salute, which the admiral rendered. Once beyond the ignominy, the admiral said to me, "Tomorrow morning you should call on Captain Ford to report about his sentries."

My reply was, "Yes, Sir. You have a leisurely morning tomorrow. A group from the Lake County Navy League will be in to see you. There's nothing pressing. I'll lead the conversation. You just be your gracious self. And your paper will be delivered on time."

The admiral had a half smile on his tired face when he exited the car. Was he thinking of having breakfast with the *Chicago Tribune*? Or was the day's end blurred by thoughts of being the young ensign back on the Yangtze?

Enter RADM John Sidney McCain, Jr.

Adm. Robert L. Dennison, Commander in Chief, Atlantic Fleet, phoned me from Norfolk asking a favor to help one of his subordinates, Rear Adm. John Sydney McCain, Jr. McCain had the assignment as Commander, Amphibious Training Command, Atlantic Fleet. Admiral McCain was coming to Chicago to speak to the prestigious Executives Club. "Jack said he had a problem but did not elaborate," Admiral Dennison related. I responded saying I knew the Executives Club and its managers and would be pleased to help. Arrangements were made. I contacted the club and was invited to join the speaker as a guest. I was to meet McCain at Naval Air Station Glenview and accompany him to the luncheon. Admiral McCain arrived on time in a Navy aircraft, and we immediately embarked into a Navy automobile to be driven to the Loop area about 35 minutes away. After the usual pleasantries, the admiral led the conversation touching on several subjects and not mentioning a problem area. I finally said, "Admiral Dennison set me up to help you with a problem you have in connection with your speech to the Executives Club. Would you mind telling me what it is?"

"Oh, yeah," he responded. "I didn't get my speech cleared."

I was amazed but didn't manifest such. "Well, that's interesting," I said. "We don't submit Admiral Nunn's speeches for DOD clearance because they are pretty much the canned speeches he has been delivering for years about leadership and basic Navy things. Are you going to say something controversial? Are you worried about it?"

He replied he wasn't worried, but there was always a possibility someone might misinterpret or misunderstand. I hurriedly said it was too late to get a clearance stamp on it, and there would be news media people at the luncheon. I added I would be in the audience, probably with the media folks. If I detected anything controversial or picked up any special semblance of interest by the reporters, we would have time to talk with them after the luncheon. He agreed.

Admiral McCain's speech was harmless. In fact, it was one of the seapower slide presentations produced by his former office in the Pentagon, Op 09-D. That office was commissioned to prepare presentations to educate naval personnel and the public. Admiral McCain was an excellent presenter.

He was a rather self-effacing man whose physical stature was small and slight, but he had a salty, voice. He was considered colorful because he waved a long cigar around using it as a pointer. More importantly, people liked him.

On our return trip to Glenview, he finally asked me how his speech went. I said it was fine, and there wasn't anything to worry about. He pushed me by demanding my real thoughts about it. "Well, Admiral, in answer to your question, I will give you my candid thoughts," I replied. "You are an excellent presenter. You have stage presence, and you communicate. People like you and trust you.

"Even though your slides were outstanding, the audience couldn't see you. You were in the dark, and there should have been a light on you. The presenter is still the main part of a presentation. The slides are merely a visual aid. The message was good, the slides were good, but the presenter wasn't visible. You could have sent a tape recording and saved a lot of time."

I didn't need to say that last sentence and almost regretted it. "Well," he laughed, "that's the first time anyone has said I could be replaced by a tape recording." Jack McCain needled me about that gratuitous remark for the next 15 years. We became good friends, and I was able to assist him several times in his career. He became the Chief of Information, Commander, Naval Forces, Europe and finally Commander in Chief, Pacific during the Vietnam War. He retired with a four-star rank.

Navy League boost

One of the amazing accomplishments of the 20-month program was the chartering of 27 Navy League councils in the district. This was done to support the Naval Reserve Training Centers. The first step was having the skippers rally support for chartering the councils. I helped with guidance and the promise Admiral Nunn would show up for the chartering event. I also worked on bringing one or more Navy League national officers to the occasion.

Another important adjunct to our program was inviting leading citizens of our communities to "go to sea" with the Navy. They learned first hand about the taxpayer's investment in the ships of their Navy. It proved to be an excellent public relations program aimed at supporting the NRTC commanding officers. I set up the cruise program, so the local commanding officers issued the invitations in whatever way they wanted. We followed with a letter from the admiral making it official but giving the commanding officer credit for the invitations. CHINFO coordinated the cruise program for the fleet commanders by allocating billets in ship on a quarterly basis. Some districts didn't utilize their quotas, and it became automatic for those billets to go to COMNINE. We used them all, and I kept constant pressure on CHINFO saying we could use more cruises. It was a good program. The ships' personnel liked having civilians aboard, and it was a not-to-interfere-basis for the ships. Guests paid for own their travel to and from ports of embarkation and debarkation.

The cruise program and the chartering of the Navy League councils helped to get the skippers into community relations and to establish a strong presence in the city. If a skipper positioned the right people in the right jobs, the council would be of great value to him. Several times in our chartering business, I was able to get Robert Crown, then national president of the Navy League, to participate in the ceremonies. Another person I was able to call on was Leo Poret, a local businessman in Waukegan and then the Navy League's national vice president. Naturally, I became involved with the Navy League and got to know both Bob Crown and Leo Poret well.

Crown was a Naval Reserve commander and attended drills at Great Lakes, as did Poret who was a captain. I was initially attracted to them because they were community leaders and proved to be helpful in my ambitious public relations program. Bob was the eldest son of "Colonel" Henry Crown who rose from being a small concrete contractor to owning Material Service Corporation in Chicago. Material Service bought the Empire State Building in New York, administered it for a few years (with Bob as the manager) and sold it at a profit. He later became one of the largest stockholders of General Dynamics and helped steer that corporation into being one of the largest defense contractors. He held other interests such as 10% of the Hilton Hotel enterprise and land developments in Arizona, California and Florida. He became a powerful man and a Chicago legend. Bob was his able understudy and heir apparent. The second son Lester was also involved in the Crown enterprises. The youngest son John chose a career as an attorney and became a judge.

A classic story to describe Bob's interest and modus operandi concerns the German U-505 Submarine. The sub has been a principal display at the Chicago Museum of Science and Industry since the latter half of the 20th Century. A Chicago native, Rear Adm. Daniel Gallery, commanded a Hunter-Killer Anti-Submarine Warfare task force in the Atlantic and succeeded in capturing the U-505. It was towed to the East Coast and sat there for a few years until Gallery, an activist, sold the City of Chicago on the idea to bring the submarine to its lakefront for permanent display. Bob Crown was a principal in making it happen. He was not only involved in fundraising aspects but also in helping solve engineering problems associated with the project. Challenging project issues arose such as how to get a 1,000 ton, 100-foot long submarine across Michigan Avenue and deposit it alongside the museum. I first met Bob when he was about to take over as national president of the Navy League, succeeding the free spirited, aggressive and flamboyant Frank Gard Jamison, who was the president of Douglas Aircraft Company.

Bob became a close friend. He helped get things done. Many of them were on my wish list such as donating an office in his Mercantile Exchange Building in Chicago for a branch of my office. I stationed Lt. Jim McCain in Chicago for about six months until we got Lt. Cdr. Stan Williams, an aviator, to be there permanently. It certainly saved wear and tear on my body and others in the office by not having to trek to Chicago whenever we frequently had something to do there. The office there was successful. It proved to be the forerunner of the Chief of Information Branch Office, Midwest which I was responsible for instituting a few years later when assigned to the Secretary of the Navy's office.

Chicago Mafia

Our social life was active at Great Lakes, and much of it centered on some of the Naval Reservists and Navy Leaguers such as Bob and Joanne Crown, Leo and Charlotte Poret, Morgan and Helen Fitch, Carl and Margaret Stockholm, Randy and Pearl Cooper and George and Lorett Wendt. We often referred to our group as the "Chicago Mafia." Leo was a newspaper distributor in the Waukegan/North Chicago area. Morgan was a patent lawyer, banker and later became the national president of the Navy League. Carl had an interesting background as a six-day bicycle racer in his young days. In fact, he was on the U.S. Olympic team in 1920. He served as a national president of the Navy League and was successful as owner of a chain of laundries and dry cleaning shops in Chicago. Randy was the executive director of a Chicago Loop development association that had authority over all urban development in downtown Chicago. George Wendt was big in real estate development in the southern environs of Chicago. He was the father of George Wendt who became better known as "Norm" of the television series *Cheers*. It was a pretty hefty group. We enjoyed being together, and those who are still living continue to relate.

Bob Crown died in 1967 from a cardiac arrest or embolism at the early age of 48. He left behind Joanne, a vivacious wife of about the same age, three children and a legacy. I profited from our relationship through the wisdom he imparted to me. He was a role model possessing a high degree of ethics while surviving in a tough business and political world. Morgan Fitch and I were the only two non-Jewish pallbearers at Bob's funeral. I have privately treasured that honor ever since. Zum and I have remained close with Joanne, a delightful lady. Had he lived longer, I am sure Bob would have been a flag officer in the Naval Reserve. When working for the Secretary of the Navy, I arranged for him to have some active duty for training with the Office of Navy Material. He got along well with the then commander, Adm. Ignatius Joseph "Pete" Galatin, who gave Bob a strong fitness report. I figured after a couple more tours, Bob would have been able to bring to bear his business acumen for the good use of the Navy. Even though he has been gone more than 40 years, I still miss him, his counsel and friendship.

Carl Stockholm had a close friend and contemporary in George Halas, the venerable owner and coach of the Chicago Bears football team. I met George at Stockholm's home when Carl had a reception in his honor. While waiting in line to shake the hand of the National Football League great, I reflected back to the Packer-Bear rivalry that is second to none in any sport. When I arrived at the appointed moment facing this legendary giant of the sport I loved, I said to him, "I am pleased to meet you, Captain Halas.

(George had been called to active duty during World War II and served as the Special Services Officer for Admiral Nimitz, the Commander in Chief, Pacific.) I am pleased to see you don't have horns on the top of your head or fangs for teeth."

Halas looked at me with some mild indignation, not wanting to waste too much time with the smart-assed lieutenant commander confronting him. He replied, "I don't know what you mean, son."

I came back with a smile saying, "Captain Halas, I'm Bill Thompson, from Green Bay. I'm sure you must know what I mean."

He smiled, and grasped my other arm while chuckling, "I sure do. We have a great rivalry, don't we?"

"Sir, I was brought up on that rivalry, and I saw some great Packer-Bear games. It's a great thrill to meet you."

He responded by warmly telling me to advise my friends in Green Bay he didn't have horns or fangs. I developed a relationship with Coach Halas over the years. It was kindled to an extent by his assistant, Rudy Custer. He was a Naval Reserve PIO, who had been George's assistant in the Pacific War, and at that time was business manager of the Chicago Bears.

Randall and Pearl Cooper became good friends. Randy, the Chicago Loop association's executive director, was well acquainted and connected in Chicago because his association was involved in most developments in that area. His board of directors was a force. Naturally, he and the Crown family aligned themselves accordingly making Randy and Bob Crown steadfast friends. Their mutual respect was always evident. Randy was brought along as an active Navy League member. His activities centered on the local or state level and were not national in scope like those of Bob Crown and Morgan Fitch who served as national presidents. Randy and Pearl were kind to the Thompson family, and they were great fans of Zum.

Morgan Fitch was a rising patent lawyer in Chicago and was roped into the Navy League conclave by Bob Crown. It was he and Bob Crown who masterminded the Navy League Sea Cadet program and succeeded in getting it chartered by the U.S. Congress. It was a big event in their lives when they returned to Chicago triumphant with the Federal Charter in hand. Morgan was a bright chemical engineer and lawyer, but tolerated no frills or nonsense.

He progressed to the top of the Navy League, and to this day continues to be one of the most respected former national presidents. He headed his law firm and made it the best and most successful patent law office in Chicago and the Midwest. He became progressively involved in his father's bank on the South Side of Chicago. When his father died, Morgan and his brother took over. Morgan became a banker on the evenings and weekends. He was one of the first I knew to have a personal computer. The machine combined well with his work or "workaholic" ethic permitting him to take on all those responsibilities. His wife Helen was as bright as he was. She trooped along with him on all the chores for the Navy League, the bank and the law firm. They had two boys and two girls. All four were well educated and attended either the University of Michigan or the Illinois Institute of Technology, Morgan's two schools.

Chicago abounded in interesting, successful people, and we were exposed to many of them. Through my relationship with the Naval Reserve Public Relations Group, I got to know Bill Wrigley of the chewing gum company and currently head of that firm; Pat Rastall, a sales vice president for ABC (Pat had been a young Army officer and later became a lieutenant in the Naval Reserve. He took great delight in wearing his Combat Infantryman Badge on his Navy uniform. It turned a few heads and was an immediate conversation item. He had lots of fun with it.); Warren Purcell, a real professional in the public relations business, who was a kingpin in the Illinois State Saving and Loan Association (It was Warren whom I sought for advice and counsel on public relations problems.); Rudy Custer, business manager of the Chicago Bears; George B. Wendt, a Chicago banker; George R. Wendt, a successful Chicago real estate developer; Sam Sax, a banker; Tom Denton, Chicago office manager for large international advertising and public relations firms; Augie Cisco, financial editor for , the *Chicago Sun-Times*; and many more.

We worked with and became well acquainted with other media types such as Ward Quall, head of WGN, one of country's largest free channel radio and television stations and others in the community and throughout the Naval District. For many years later, Chicago and the surrounding areas were identified in Navy PIO circles as "Bill Thompson's Stomping Grounds," and we have maintained many friendships there.

Scrambled Eggs On The Hat

A nice thing happened to me during our second year at Great Lakes. I was promoted to commander. It was the first time any ceremony accompanied the act of renewing my vow to "honor and obey all the laws of the Constitution." Admiral Nunn invited Zum and the kids to his office where he officially promoted me. Stevie and Zum bracketed me with a kiss on the cheeks. Craig was much more impressed than Brian. I thought it was gracious of the admiral to have the family participate. I had time to reflect on donning another half stripe and having "scrambled eggs" on the visor of my "cover" (hat). A few months prior to my promotion, while I was attending a convention of public information officers at the Naval Air Station, Pensacola, Florida, the promotion list to commander was released from Washington. Bob Brett was there and on the promotion list, and I had the pleasure of informing him. Needless to say, the "Happy Hour" that evening was a real happy event. I had the feeling I was getting older and more serious. Definitely, the brash ensign of the Guam days wasn't present, nor was he any longer part of my character.

Do We Have Public Affairs or Public Relations?

During one of our many airplane or car rides, Admiral Nunn and I were on the subject of public information and its applications. I stated the title was a misnomer because our office did more than distributing information to the public by news releases or answering queries. We were involved in community relations, working with a diverse group of associations as well as government offices at all levels. We were also responsible for internal relations, communicating with our Navy personnel and dependents as well as staging special events. I doubted we would ever be permitted to use the common "public relations" title used in the private sector. We were bound by government ethics only to inform not to persuade public opinion.

I thought the term "public affairs" was more appropriate. Obviously, this was not the most engrossing subject we had ever discussed, so the admiral sort of set it aside by agreeing with me. He added he could endorse the

latitude of activity in our office as judged by the number of letters we originated for his signature. He then surprised me by saying, "If you feel strongly
about it, draft a letter for me to the Chief of Information recommending a
change in title."

I tried to assure him I wasn't interested to that extent. He came back
with, "The more I think about it, the better I like it. In your vernacular, public
affairs is more 'sexy' than public information. Go ahead with the letter." He
was teasing me about a colloquial expression I used. Sexy meant good or
"cool" in latter day slang. Another one he laughed about was when I took
leave from him, saying I was going to "bug off." That one I probably got
from Stevie or Craig.

The public affairs issue was actually introduced to me by Capt. E. Robert
Anderson, USNR, who had been the Eleventh Naval District PIO in San
Diego and later was an executive with Copley News Service. Copley published the *San Diego Union* as well as the *Evening Tribune* and eight other newspapers around the country. It seemed like a good idea. I had thought about it
at times but didn't advocate any changes previously. Before writing the letter
for Admiral Nunn, I checked with the Deputy CHINFO who said they had
been thinking about it, but it wasn't a hot issue. He added it was probably at
the bottom of someone's "too hard basket." He wasn't enthusiastic about
my discussion with Admiral Nunn but agreed the letter was appropriate and
might initiate some action. Three months later I called again to learn they
had received the letter. In six months or so when the new manual for Public
Affairs Regulations was distributed, it would become official. We would be
public affairs because the Defense Department used that title. Admiral Nunn
was delighted. He ordered me not to wait, change the title on my office door
and make the change officially within the staff. Six months later it became the
official title throughout the Navy. I'm not taking credit for the change, but
I was the first Navy Public Affairs Officer, and the sign on my office door
proved it.

My staff size was limited but by far the largest I had ever had. Don
Collett followed by Phil Russell and I were the entire PIO staff at First Fleet.
At COMCRUDESPAC, I had a chief journalist and two other journalists.
At Omaha, I was "it" with the help of a civilian secretary. Now I had the

"executive" worries with four officers, a secretary, a chief journalist and four or five other enlisted journalists. An initial concern involved keeping them busy. As it turned out, they were all gainfully employed and morale was high. So I assumed they liked what they were doing and enjoyed the successes we experienced. Shortly after I arrived, Lt. Cdr. Sid Moore left to become the Naval Training Center PIO about two blocks down the street.

I wanted a "live wire" young officer, and I wangled a deal with CHINFO to get Lt. Jim McCain out of Washington. There was nothing devious about it. I was the disadvantaged party having to take a four or five-month gap in the billet, so he could complete his tour in CHINFO. I thought it would be worth it. I had known him since he was a First Class Journalist at AIRPAC when I was at CRUDESPAC. When Jim was commissioned at Officer Candidate School (OCS), his first assignment was to the aircraft carrier USS *Shangri-La*, home ported in San Diego. While at First Fleet, I got myself assigned as an escort officer for a group of 15 civilian guests of the Secretary of the Navy who embarked in *Shangri-La* for a cruise to Pearl Harbor. Jim and I became reacquainted. I was impressed by the job he was doing in the ship being qualified as OOD on the bridge. He was also the ship's administrative officer; the same job I had in *Midway*. A good argument for the job at Great Lakes was his wife being from Waukegan, the Navy Training Center, Great Lakes' home port city. Jim worked well with me although he was not too receptive to all the ideas I kept throwing out. He thought most them were too labor intensive, especially when it was his labor.

Hal Swanson was a lieutenant commander in the Naval Reserve and was retained on active duty as a Training and Administration of Reserves (TAR) officer specialty. He was assigned to the Reserve Supplement at District Headquarters. I had made arrangements to have him work in my office, unlike his predecessor, because I had many thoughts and program ideas that would involve the Naval Reserve training centers. It obviously would be better if he was physically in my office. I didn't surface this issue with the admiral but had discussed it with the Deputy Chief of Staff for Reserve who was in agreement. I had a reputation from Omaha that the reserves respected, and they wanted me on their side. Besides, moving Swanson into my office was not difficult for them. My first directive to him was to be the constant, direct liaison between my office and the Deputy Chief of Staff (DepCoS), Naval Reserve.

Hal was a Norwegian from Minnesota. He was a Merchant Marine Academy graduate who was injured in the Korea War when the minesweeper he was assigned to collided with a mine. He had been standing on deck, and the explosion shattered his knees. He spent a long time recuperating in hospitals in Japan and on the West Coast. His wife Clarice had been a Navy nurse. Hal was conscientious, dedicated and still had a little of the "gee whiz" factor about being in the Navy.

In our first meeting I was explaining what I saw us doing in the next few years and how the office would be structured. He balked and said he had been told having a public information job in his background would not be good for his career. That lit my fuse. I lectured that he wasn't a career PIO, and I didn't intend to even attempt to make him one. Further, my experience indicated one tour would not be of harm, and he would be working with the Reserves. As a "slam dunk," I said the final result of his time in the staff would be measured by how he performed, and that performance would be described in his Report of Fitness. I concluded by saying the programs I had in mind would greatly benefit the Navy, the Naval District, the Naval Reserve and its recruiting programs. If he didn't want to be a part of it, he should go see the captain, the DepCoS, Naval Reserve, and tell him I wanted someone who was better motivated toward the job and the Navy. That ended the meeting. I called the Deputy Chief of Staff and explained the situation. I said I didn't know if Swanson would talk to him, or if he did, what he would say. I requested he consider nominating someone else for the job. Some of my actions were posturing. But I thought he had spoken foolishly, and I didn't want to be bagged with a loser.

Within a few hours Lt. Cdr. Swanson requested to see me, and I said the door was open as always. He said he had talked with the captain and now had a better concept of his position in the staff. He wanted to work for me and would do the best he could. That was all I asked of him. He did not have nor need any public information skills. I needed someone to administratively handle the programs relating to the Reserves. Because of rank, I treated him as my deputy, my alter ego, who would act in my stead when I wasn't present.

This didn't set well with Jim McCain, but Hal turned out to be a team player, and we all got along well. He gained confidence, earned respect and made commander in due course. We became good friends working and playing well together. Clarice and Zum were in sync and got along well, too.

Next was Lt. Cdr. Stan Williams, a classic naval aviator, who handled our Chicago branch office. He was married to Dorothy, a pediatrician. They lived in a suburb near where he worked in the Loop. Stan came up through the Flying Midshipmen program and was a fighter pilot who served in the Korean War. Being an outgoing, laid back, jolly and positive guy, he had a natural bent for "PR." He rapidly picked up on the details and scale of his job, and he was a positive professional and social addition to the group.

I had been blessed in the past with a good stream of chief journalists. This time out I had a real jewel in Richard H."Rock" Rothrock. He was creative, diligent, dedicated and had a good sense of humor. He loved tennis and participated in many citywide programs including working extensively with youngsters. His wife Margie was equally talented and helpful to Rock. They had two boys who made their parents proud; both did well in school at the upper levels of education. He worked in the famous Great Lakes Tower atop the District Headquarters building. It housed some of our public affairs offices, and it was from there a monthly newsletter for the district was published.

After a few faulty starts, I finally got a good secretary, Lois Merkel. She was a native of Gurney, Illinois, grew up as one of nine children and was superbly competent. When I was later assigned to the Secretary of the Navy's office, I recruited her move to Washington. She became an office mainstay and retired in the mid-1980s.

The tour at Great Lakes was going so well, I didn't spend much, if any, time thinking about my next assignment. However, a couple of things happened. Rear Adm. Charles C. "Charley" Kirkpatrick, the former CHINFO who shanghaied me to Omaha, was assigned as the Superintendent of the Naval Academy. He wrote to ask if I would join him at the academy because he had many irons in the fire and needed help. In translation his message was, "Come be my PIO." I thought it to be pleasantly ironic. He knew all the officers of my vintage in the public affairs business and recruited me. His offer was tempting because there was a challenging job there. Kirkpatrick would be a boss who understood most aspects of public affairs. Additionally, the Naval Academy would be a great place to raise kids. I thought with 4,000 Midshipmen, there wouldn't be many dull periods. Each "Mid" was a potential story. Stevie thought it would be fantastic saying, "With all that talent there, Dad ... please!" But I did not and could not pick up on the Naval Academy. Jim Jenkins had been talking to me about relieving him as the PIO for the Secretary of the Navy (SECNAV). I thought it might be a little over my head, but I didn't say "no." At the time of Kirkpatrick's letter, the SECNAV scenario was in play.

I was also called by Admiral Dennison, my old boss at First Fleet who was the Commander in Chief, U.S, Atlantic Fleet, Atlantic Command and the Supreme Allied Commander, Atlantic in NATO, headquartered in Norfolk. Capt. Bob Mereness was his public affairs officer and about to move to the Pentagon. Bob had arranged for Capt. Barney Solomon to relieve him. On the phone I told Dennison I was probably too junior for the job. He curtly replied he had all the rank we would need. He thought it was a great opportunity for me and was confident I could do the job. Again, I couldn't say anything about the SECNAV proposal. I had to turn down the admiral, and it didn't please him. I regretted my response because I really relished going to a fleet job again.

Capt. Jenkins had me ordered to Washington to be interviewed by Secretary of the Navy Fred Korth. The secretary greeted me in his gracious Texan style, and I was seated alone with him in his office. He then proceeded to talk to me about loyalty; it being the strongest characteristic he was seeking. I began to reflect on what I had done in my past that could be considered disloyal. He concluded the interview with, "Well, we will miss old Jim Jenkins, but I will be pleased to have you in the staff." I was asked not to talk about moving to Washington. About a week later, Jim Jenkins called me to relate things had gone awry. He had agreed to spend an additional year in the Secretary's office. He affirmed it was not a negative on me. Instead, I was being sent to the Naval War College for a year and from there to be ordered to the Secretary's office. He assured me I had not "Flunked the Korth."

By that time I thought I was ready to leave Great Lakes. My two and a half years (1961-63) had been a happy, productive and tremendously successful tour of duty. There wasn't much more I could do professionally beyond maintaining our established programs. I felt it was time to move on. I looked forward to going to the Naval War College at Newport, Rhode Island, as a change of venue and relief from a busy schedule. However, there was some hesitation and reticence because Stevie was finishing up her junior year in high school. She would be leaving behind a most enjoyable two years in North Chicago High School and many friends and associates.

Berlin Crisis

Two special significant events affected me in the early 1960s. The first began when the Berlin Crisis erupted in August 1961. President Kennedy mobilized many of the country's Reserve and National Guard forces. Included in this mobilization were 6,400 Naval Reservists, 40 Naval Reserve destroyers and destroyer escorts and 18 anti-submarine warfare air squadrons. The move was precautionary and in reaction to the Soviets building the Berlin Wall isolating East Germany. Chicago was the homeport for the Reserve Destroyer Escort USS *Daniel Joy*. It had a Selected Reserve crew assigned meaning those personnel were eligible to be put on immediate active duty. They could be sailing off in their ship to "protect the best interests of the United States." It happened, and suddenly Chicago was going to war! The *Joy* was a fixture on the Chicago waterfront for many years. It plied the waters of the Great Lakes during the summers training Naval Reservists. The Chicago media featured the *Joy* story for several days, even though only about 125 Naval Reserve personnel were involved. Meanwhile, hundreds of National Guard units were being mobilized. The group included some prominent citizens and celebrities like Paul Hornung, star halfback of the Green Bay Packers. As in past mobilizations, a few reservists called, "Foul! You are ruining my career and family!" They didn't elicit much sympathy. They had declared themselves for the program and received money for the time they spent in training—usually one weekend a month and two weeks a year. Nevertheless, there were some hardship cases, and the media naturally featured them prominently.

The situation became exacerbated. The National Guard units were not prepared for the mobilization and had done little, if any, planning for the transition to active duty. I was instrumental in getting Admiral Nunn to move fast in setting up a program to take care of the *Joy* personnel. The *Joy's* Selected Reservists and their dependents were gathered for briefings on their new status. New identification cards were issued. They were told about the facilities available to them such as the commissaries, Naval Exchanges, legal services and medical and dental care. They received decals for their automobiles, acquainted with hours of operation for the facilities and generally brought into the "Navy Family." Most dependents had never considered themselves a part of that family. All they knew was the husband did something in uniform once a month.

Our program was going well in sharp contrast with the beating the Army and Air Force were taking about their problems. The media was on a negative kick digging up instances where people were foundering and uninformed about the immediate future. Every day brought a new story of families in tears, bewilderment and fear attributed to the National Guard or Air Guard. However, the Midwest media reported the Navy and by extension the USS *Daniel Joy* as being on top of this contingency. While there were hardships envisioned for their people, the issues were being handled expeditiously. The Navy was perceived as in control of the situation. The sailing of *Joy* from its berth at the Naval Reserve Armory in Chicago was almost anticlimactic. Nonetheless it was heralded by the media as visible evidence of Chicago being brought into the world crisis.

While the Pentagon training program, call up and support arrangements for the Reserve and Guard Forces took a heavy beating, the Navy at Great Lakes was identified as a bright spot amid dire circumstances. I had routinely kept CHINFO apprised of what we were doing out in the heartland. Other telephone traffic occurred within the Reserve staffs and involved the admiral. I was surprised to receive an official letter of commendation from the Secretary of the Navy and another one from the CHINFO himself. Admiral Nunn was pleased and smiled most of the time although professing to be perplexed about the media and its modus operandi.

Silver Anvil

The second event was winning the Public Relations Society of America's (PRSA) coveted Silver Anvil Award in 1963. It was in the category of Best Press Relations in 1962. I had run several tours for Midwest media representatives to both coasts for cruises in Navy ships. I had personally taken a group as far as Honolulu in a carrier deploying to the Western Pacific and then flying them back to the West Coast. I had Lt. Jim McCain escort one group to Pearl Harbor, setting up the airlift and assigning activities in Hawaii. Jim submitted his tour for the PRSA annual competition. The office also submitted one for the return of the *Joy* to Chicago. I was told by a PRSA staffer that both of our presentations were judged winners in different categories including Community Relations. However, a decision was made that only one award should go to a single command. It appeared they didn't want the military hogging all the awards. As I recall a major corporation received the Silver Anvil in the Community Relations category. I purchased a duplicate of the Silver Anvil, so Jim McCain and I could each have one. We shared the award and looked at it as a big win for the office. There was enough credit available, so everyone could relish the distinction. I had a small metal plate listing all personnel in the office attached to the award.

The PRSA awards were presented in New York at the Waldorf Astoria Hotel. I was invited to receive the prize, but I had orders written for Jim to accompany me. To save money on commercial air travel, I got Stan Williams to get an airplane from Naval Air Station (NAS) Glenview, and we flew to New York landing at NAS Mitchell Field. Rear Adm. Jack McCain, who had become CHINFO, was present and sat at our table because "the Navy" had won an award. The wiry little man with the voice still liked to have a drink or two and loved to smoke big cigars. He enjoyed himself immensely throughout the evening. After Jim McCain and I received our award, Admiral McCain announced he had to return to Washington. I escorted him out of the banquet room, each with an arm around the other's shoulders. As he stepped into the elevator and the doors were closing, he growled, "Well, God damn it, Bill. God bless you!" I have never forgotten that send off.

The triumphant return of the *Joy* was a significant event in Chicago land,

and a superb public relations effort ensued. It was recognized as such by those in the inner circle of our "Mafia" and others close to naval milieu in the Midwest. The *Joy* had departed Chicago to enhance the Navy's presence at sea and to back President Kennedy's resolve to stand up to the Soviet Union. She left Chicago with much fanfare and made it through the Great Lakes, the St. Lawrence Seaway and down the coast of Nova Scotia. She glided past Halifax, Nova Scotia; Portland, Maine; Portsmouth, New Hampshire; Boston; and finally snuggled up to a pier in Newport. There she was detained for almost a year until released to return home to Chicago. It was determined by Navy material inspectors that the *Joy* was not fit to go to sea or "in Harm's Way" unless it received an extensive overhaul of most of its engineering and weapons systems.

That reality crimped our planning for the *Joy*'s return to Chicago. We decided to stay with the human aspects and concentrate on the personnel who were uprooted from jobs, schools and homes to answer the President's call to arms. The people of the Chicago area considered the *Joy* to be their ship. It was clearly evident they would participate in welcoming home the ship and its crew. Naturally, I kept Admiral Nunn fully apprised of the planning for the return of *Joy*. By that time, I had his full confidence and could move with a large degree of certainty and assurance. It was evident because the public affairs officer was the point man on planning for the return. My objective clearly concentrated on community and media aspects. I was concerned about ensuring preferential treatment for the dependents of crewmembers. There were no intra-staff problems. I knew my parameters and got other COMNINE people involved in logistics and ancillary parts of the action. Interfaces with city officials, dignitaries, celebrities and others kept us busy.

I decided early on it would be nice to have a tickertape parade down State Street with our crewmembers and families riding in convertibles to meet a welcoming Mayor Daley. There were scoffs and attempts to talk me out of that concept. Randy Cooper, the executive director of the Loop Authority and by that time a good friend, asked me if it was essential to the success of the event to parade down State Street. Did I really want it? He cautioned he would have to use up a bandoleer of silver bullets because the noon hour, when we wanted to do this deed, was the busiest time for retailers. His association members did not like the idea and threw out dollar figures in the thousands about how much business would be lost if there was a parade on State Street. I replied it was not totally necessary. But what better way was there for Chicago, which prides itself on being a "Big Navy Town," to recognize the sacrifices of its own. Keep in mind those who were called up for a year's active duty to help President Kennedy stabilize a festering communist action in Europe. My parochialism aside, Randy agreed and a street parade was scheduled for State Street on "J-Day" (*Joy* Day) in Chicago. Plans jelled for the event. Car dealers donated convertibles for the parade. Mayor Daley's office cooperated extensively with a key to the city for "All Hands." There was a welcome home luncheon in the Loop with assorted speeches and entertainment by *Peter, Paul and Mary*, Chicago's famed singing trio.

One of the more interesting aspects of the event, at least for me, was the attention the naval aviators at Glenview showed in our event. At that time, Glenview was the headquarters for the Chief of Naval Air Training, Rear Adm. Bill Martin. I had been keeping Lt. Cdr. Byron "Jug" Varner apprised of our project. He, being a 1650 (Public Affairs designator) in Martin's staff, would properly inform his superiors. I was asked if it would be convenient for me to drop by Glenview and brief Rear Adm. Martin about the homecoming plans for the *Joy*. I had met Admiral Martin previously and was impressed by his back home, "Ozark" approach to things. He claimed to be from "Bugger County" in the Missouri Ozarks. He had a shtick that entertained almost anyone who had the time to listen. He was a legitimate Navy Air hero being one of the pioneers in carrier night flight operations that eventually branched out into all-weather carrier operations.

The admiral was concerned about the hype given to the Naval Reserve Ship *Joy* on its return to Chicago after a year's absence while the public was being told nothing about the Naval Air Reserve Squadron from Glenview. Those flyers had performed well too during that same timeframe. My reply was contrite but positive. I said our objective was to give credit to the Naval Reserve crew of *Joy*. Despite the ignominious fact the ship did not deploy from Newport, it was beyond the crew's control. They had been torn away from their roots for over a year. I assured the admiral we were not competing with the Naval Air Reserve. If he would want to participate in our plan, we would welcome Navy Air Reserve input and assistance at the working level. I told the admiral there should be ample opportunity for the Naval Air Reserve to gain some recognition. My statement presented an easy out for Admiral Martin. He responded favorably and assured me of his support. I still felt a little uneasy on my departure, but knew I could withstand the wrath of his staff, especially his public information people. They probably had to endure Admiral Martin's ire by letting some non-aviation type steal their thunder. However, if it hadn't been for what we at COMNINE were doing for the forces returning from the Berlin Crisis deployments, there would probably not have been any thunder.

I had always had an "All Navy" approach to public affairs work and was always dismayed at the "unionism" that existed within the Navy. I thought it to be self- defeating and not only in public relations work. It was a negative in many efforts to present an argument for the Navy and sea services, particularly to Congress. Perhaps it was because of my background, having been in naval aviation and having served aboard the carrier *Midway* and also with surface Navy units. I looked at various elements of the Navy as a total force. However, I knew I was personally competitive and wasn't going to be outdone by the opposition, no matter which side I was on. That may be the root of the unionization problem—competitiveness resulting in parochialism.

The results were gratifying. Especially seeing the parade down State Street at noon with almost every family associated with the *Joy* represented. The Glenview squadron was assigned several automobiles loaned by car dealers for use in the parade. It was an event that surely must retain prime space in the memory of the crewmembers and their families. Admiral Nunn was pleased as was Admiral Martin, Randy Cooper and Bob Crown. So was I. I told Zum that night at "pillow talk time," "Check off another one!"

Good Bye, Uncle Tom

A downer occurred in the fall of 1961 when Uncle Tom Tomberg died of a cardiac arrest while on a trip to Washington, D.C. The Tombergs had moved to Columbus, Ohio, from Norwood Park, a suburb of Chicago. Tom had been working for the U.S. Air Force and enjoyed a successful career as an auditor. He retired from government service, and he and Esther were sharing their first trip together following his retirement. He died in the Harrington Hotel on 12th Street Northwest in D.C. (Since 1964 when we settled in the Washington area, I have frequently passed by that hotel and always saluted Tom, either physically or mentally while reflecting on the good relationship we had.)

I was informed of Tom's death and the time of the funeral in Columbus. Admiral Nunn was scheduled for a trip to Michigan at the time. I had secured an airplane for us from Commander, Naval Reserve Training Command in Omaha. I informed Admiral Nunn I would like to peel off after our commitment and fly commercially to Columbus for the funeral. Arranging commercial air connections to Columbus was difficult. The admiral kindly said that he would divert our military airplane's return to the Chicago area to make a stop at Columbus. We arrived in time for me to attend the funeral. I returned shortly afterward to the airport and a commercial flight to Chicago. I deeply appreciated the admiral's help. It made it possible for me to be present to pay my last respects to a man I respected. Tom provided good counsel and guidance in times when I needed it. It was a good lesson to me. I had never found it convenient to express my appreciative thoughts personally to Tom. Since then I have tried to not duplicate that faux pas. One doesn't need a special occasion or platform to directly express appreciation or give thanks for favors large or small.

A previous visit to Columbus was much more positive when we attended the wedding of Gloria Tomberg to Jim Steckel. Jim was a local boy who joined the Navy V-5 Program. He was successful in winning his "Wings of Gold," designating him a naval aviator. He was a Sigma Chi at Denison University not far from Columbus. We have been good friends since that occasion and continue our relationship. Jim has been a successful businessman in the pest control sector as well as other entrepreneurial enterprises. He and Gloria reared two fine youngsters, Scott and Kathy, who continue to reside in the Columbus area. I had the pleasure of swearing Scott into the U.S. Air Force as a second lieutenant upon his graduation from the U.S. Air Force Academy at Colorado Springs, Colorado.

One other event places highly on our family's memories of Great Lakes. It was a going away gift, a black poodle puppy, from Admiral Nunn. We immediately named her "Dubonnet," because it was French and invoked the only thing of alcoholic content (Dubonnet on the rocks), other than a little beer on occasion, I drank. Ira Nunn, the martini drinker, was always intrigued by my choice of alcoholic beverage, but lived with it for the 18 months we had together. I think he was pleased with the name. We hung it on to the puppy, and she brought joy, entertainment and love to the family. The admiral was a poodle fancier and had a friend in Oregon who bred poodles. Somehow, he thought that we should have one. He made it happen, going out to O'Hare International Airport to take receipt when the pup was flown into to Chicago. "Dubbie" was a miniature poodle and as sassy and lovable as any poodle could be. She learned quickly and was obedient. We entertained Admiral Nunn frequently during the three months we had at Great Lakes after he retired and took up residence in Lake Forest, an adjoining town. He was pleased to observe the dog's development. One trick we taught Dubbie almost immediately was to put a treat or dish of food in front of her and announce it was "Army Grub!" Although she wanted it, she would stand and stare at the morsels. We would then reconsider telling her it was "Navy Chow!" and she would devour it. Admiral Nunn thought that was an outstanding stunt. Stevie, Craig and even little Brian took great delight in showing off Dubbie's culinary preferences.

I end this chapter on Great Lakes coinciding with Admiral Nunn's retirement because that event marked the end of a great adventure. It provided memories he and I shared for many years when we would get together and inevitably reminisce. We accomplished most of our goals and definitely surpassed many of them. Indeed, we struck a new standard for Naval District public affairs programs measured by verifying success. He said several times he had enjoyed the ride and voiced the possibility I would have succeeded in doing the same thing with whomever had been assigned to Great Lakes. I doubted that. After I had become a flag officer, I could say, "We made a good team, and it was fun doing what we did because we knew what we were doing."

Three Long Months

Normally, when concluding a successful tour of duty as we had at COMNINE, the last three months should have been much more relaxed with me on "cruise control," tidying up a few loose ends and ensuring my relief had a good handle on the job before I departed. Such was not to be the case.

I learned that one of the worst things that can happen to an officer is to be turned over by a superior to his or her successor with a statement like, "Red, Commander Bill Thompson is the best Public Affairs Officer (PAO) in the Navy bar none." Admiral Ira Nunn said just that in my presence to his successor, Rear Adm. Howard "Red" Yeager. It instigated a not so harmonious situation. Initially, it was evident Yeager did not hold Ira Nunn in the highest regard, as he iterated to me during the next three months. He chaffed at the oft-repeated statements to him about having "big shoes to fill." I soon learned Red Yeager was an egoist, dependent on personal attention, recognition and praise. I had difficulty in fulfilling related requirements.

I had not met Admiral Yeager until the introductory incident when I was summoned to the admiral's office. Nunn thought he was doing me a favor, but as it turned out, I didn't need that type of favor. However, I doubt if there was any other circumstance where I could have fit into Yeager's equation, unless he had discovered me under a rock and created his own competent PAO. One of the first things he said to me after Ira Nunn's departure was that I would probably be in a state of shock transferring from a "candy ass" like Nunn to him; meaning he was an aggressive, salty, proactive flag officer. On many occasions he shared glimpses from his background about being an orphan and how growing up was not an enjoyable adventure. He had been taken under the wing of a schoolteacher who helped him mature and go to the Naval Academy. Yeager said he was a football player, but he had no size, and I never bothered to check out his athletic career at the Naval Academy.

His wife Jean was a talented woman, and he was devoted to her. At the time she was bedridden with a terminal illness. I was brought to the admiral's quarters to meet her early on, and although it wasn't a pleasant sight, I was impressed. She was involved in the book publishing field and was an editor. That alone was enough to convince me that she was a cut above the average. Yeager would normally have retired as a vice admiral, but with her malady, he chose to hang on as an active duty flag officer as long as possible—until he reached age 62—so his wife could be near a naval hospital. Great Lakes excellently answered that need. Quarters A was ample for them, and the naval hospital was only a driver and a five iron away.

Leo Poret was a close friend for two years at Great Lakes. But we had worked together on so many projects; it seemed we had eons of friendship and partnership. We remained close, and as we grew older, we relished our mutual accomplishments. Leo was immediately clutched to the bosom of Red Yeager, who proceeded to milk him for everything he could get—meeting the right local people, getting into the local country clubs and being introduced at social and fraternal events. There was nothing wrong with that approach, except Yeager was blatantly aggressive about it.

I felt uncomfortable with Yeager at first considering him to be a show-boat-type character who wasn't taken seriously except by those who had to work for him. He was an aberration in the continuum of flag officers with whom I had been associated. (In years to come, I would meet many more flag officers. In reflection, I realized Yeager wasn't unusual, being one of a broad assortment of personalities.) I thought he had many good qualities that could be useful in our public affairs program. But my departure was imminent, and I didn't want to start something my successor wouldn't be comfortable with.

"I imagine you're having a little trouble adjusting to Red Yeager," Leo confided one day. "Judging from what I have observed and heard, I guess he is jealous of you, your acceptance in the Chicago area and the friends you have made over the past couple of years." I argued that admirals weren't jealous of commanders. I said Admiral Yeager would settle down, adjust to the local environment and become an asset to the naval community in the Chicago area.

Yeager rode me hard, goading me about my anointment as the "Navy's best

PAO." I detested the impromptu title and knew I didn't deserve it. However, he seemed to sense when he was getting under my skin. Occasionally, he would call for me and suggest "we get out of the office and play golf." That meant I was to set up the event with one of my friends who was a member of a country club. At times I had only a couple of hours notice. However, it wasn't difficult because most of my friends didn't get to play golf every day with an admiral. Yeager was a better than average golfer. He was about a 12-handicap player, but he carried a card indicating he was a 16. He called it his "traveling handicap." Red was a gambler and a tough competitor. He would bet on anything and used his traveling handicap to good advantage. He seldom lost on the golf course. Normally, he would be liberal with his winnings, buying drinks and several times gifting me with a golf hat carrying the logo of the course he had just conquered. The hats went to Stevie, Craig, Brian or folks in the office.

One of the leftovers from the Nunn days was a speaking engagement in southern Illinois. I should have canceled it, but the admiral's secretary had it on her books, and Yeager insisted we fulfill the request. We flew down to the city and were greeted by a good representation. We visited the Naval Reserve Training Center, went to a cocktail party at a private home and then on to a country club dinner with about 40 of the city's finest. Much heavy drinking ensued prior to dinner, and Yeager was showing the effects. His speech was done without the script I had given him. He spent most of the time, glorifying himself and seeking pity for the sacrifices he was making for his wife. After dinner there was more drinking and some gambling games.

About midnight I was exhausted. My attempts at conversation with the locals were trite and trying. I told the admiral I was turning into a pumpkin. If it was all right with him, I would take a cab back to our motel and turn in. The driver in the Naval Reserve car would await the admiral's desires about returning to the motel. He belligerently told me, "Hell, no! You're staying here with me. Enjoy yourself." About 0400 (4:00 a.m.), he announced to the crowd, "Commander Thompson and I appreciate your kindness, but it seems we will not be getting laid tonight, so we will retire. Thank you."

Riding back to the motel, he said something about my probably not having experienced an evening like that with Ira Nunn. I agreed. I didn't say,

"Thank God. I only have one life and one liver to give to my country."

At times I may have thought the three months I had with Red Yeager were the worst of my life. In reality, the worst similar trying timeframe was at the same place in 1943 after washing out of the Aviation Cadet program. Awaiting my next assignment then was far worse. At least in this three-month window, I got to play golf, relax at times and "laugh and scratch" with the admiral. I even learned to play a good game of Gin Rummy. Proficiency in cards was necessary to keep up with Red Yeager, who seemed determined to send me to the Poor Farm without the clothes I was wearing.

My next duty was to be the Naval War College at Newport, Rhode Island. Classes started in mid-August, and I thought it would be nice to take at least two weeks leave and visit some of our family before departing the area. Admiral Yeager insisted that I stay until the last day, departing Great Lakes with no leave, only travel time. That largely resulted from my relief reporting late, and the admiral wanting me to thoroughly brief my replacement on the area and personalities.

Sadly, my mother died on July 22, 1963. I was given the normal bereavement leave to attend the funeral and family business. The previous week, we had spent a weekend in Sheboygan and Green Bay. Mom was bedridden at the time. It was certain she would not live long, but we soon had to depart Great Lakes for Newport. So without saying so, it was our last good-bye. It was a difficult situation. Being sedated, she was not in any pain from the uterine cancer but was obviously failing. We had several conversations. Mother said many times she was proud that I was a commander in the Navy although she never really understood much about it. She would rather have had me at home working for the *Green Bay Press-Gazette*. She had been moved to live with my sister Betty, Betty's husband, Lee LaHaye and their eight children. They did a superb job of caring for Mother. Fortunately, my brother Don and his family were visiting in Green Bay at the time. They lived in Battle Creek, Michigan, where Don was the comptroller for the Civil Defense Agency.

The funeral was like most, only it had an ironic twist. The funeral home handling the arrangements had a new Cadillac hearse. Mom was the first deceased person to be transported in it to the cemetery. Halfway to Fort Howard Cemetery, the hearse stalled, and the driver could not get it restarted.

The procession was waved on to the cemetery. After we were assembled in the chapel, Mom arrived. I thought it was a typical end to a life continually marred by mishaps and unhappiness. She could not even experience an uneventful final ride to the cemetery. As I recall, there was no graveside internment ceremony. It was many years later when I had the opportunity to visit the gravesite where she was laid beside the man she loved, my father, who had been waiting for her for some 25 years. I remember having a difficult time seeing them there together. Next to them was my infant sister Jeanne, who died of whooping cough at the tender age of two months.

My Aunt Esther, widow of Uncle Tom Tomberg, had flown to Chicago to join us for the trip to Green Bay and the funeral. We were delighted she could be with us. We returned her to Chicago to be with friends and family while we returned to Great Lakes to pack out for the move to Newport. Within a few days we bid adieu to Great Lakes and picked up Esther. Thus ended an extremely productive, successful tour of duty. I appreciated the Navy assigning me there, so I could be near my ailing mother.

Admiral Red Yeager was a factor, although small, in the magnificent maturing process I experienced in my two and one-half years at COMNINE. I grew there immensely professionally and personally. It was indeed a fun-filled, exciting tour of duty.

Back to College

Our trip to Columbus with Aunt Esther was uneventful except for our Pontiac "Green Hornet" developing fuel line problems. We finally stalled out about five miles outside Columbus. The Green Hornet was towed to a garage in the city, and we awaited its repair. The wait gave us a couple days to visit with Esther, Jim and Gloria Steckel who by this time had a son Scott. It was a typically hot, humid Ohio August, but we survived and had an enjoyable time.

Our family departed Columbus thinking of a few additional days of relaxation. The first stop was Niagara Falls where we walked in the mist around the spectacle's perimeter on the American side. Dubbie behaved well for a puppy but kept all of us busy attempting to react to her inquisitive, aggressive and playful demeanor.

After a night in a motel room with three kids and a dog, Zum and I were rather pleased to get into the car again and move on toward Massachusetts and Connecticut. We scouted the trail for an interesting place to spend the night and decided on Uxbridge, Massachusetts, a town of 3,400. The name itself sounded historic, and we thought that would be interesting for the kids. At the first place we inquired, we were rebuffed by a no dogs allowed rule. The next place was an inn of obvious historic distinction, and Dubbie was allowed to be with us. We had three large rooms and enough beds for all. The best thing was the price of only about $10.00. We were pleased, proceeded to freshen up, changed clothes and set out to find a suitable restaurant for dinner leaving Dubbie in the room.

A short walk down the main street revealed nothing attractive in the way of sustaining two adults and three children. We came to our negative conclusion by pricing menus on restaurant doors, viewing exterior appearances and noting the wafting ambiance. The "Diner," an aluminum clad structure, gave the appearance it could be rolled away on short notice and parked in another vacant lot. It offered no confidence for an enjoyable meal.

Zum and I had noted our inn's dinning room but had nixed it because of the coat and tie requirement. However, we decided the inn presented the best menu and atmosphere, so I rummaged through the luggage in the car's trunk to find a shirt, tie and coat. And so we settled in for a great meal in a place where our forefathers, certainly the Pilgrims or revolutionary patriots, had dined. We tried to impress on the kids what a momentous occasion this was and certainly one they would reflect on later in their lives. However, Stevie was more concerned about the boy friend she had left behind at Great Lakes, and Brian, who had just turned five didn't grasp the significance. Craig was more interested in the wild game mounts adorning the walls and how many pieces of chicken would be entrusted to him. So it remained for Zum and me to be entranced by the name Uxbridge and its historic significance, fact or fiction. When we got the bill for the dinner, we momentarily lost all perspective for the inn's charm and lineage. The bill was more than $25.00, a hefty fee for us in those days. Needless to say, we appreciated the meal and the surroundings more as we retired to the rooms and Dubbie.

On the next day we made it to Newport, our home for the next 10 months. Newport and the surrounding towns of Providence, Fall River and Tiverton had the history we were seeking. We didn't have to venture far to see other sights. We scurried to Boston on one of the early weekends to walk the Freedom Trail, get acquainted with Paul Revere and trod the decks of the USS *Constitution*, "Old Ironsides." On that excursion, we visited Plymouth to gaze down upon the Plymouth Rock where the Pilgrims were supposed to have first set foot in North America. Like many tourists, we were disappointed by Plymouth Rock because it was so small that the Pilgrims had to be nimble to step on it. Certainly, they had to do it in single file. (Many years later, I became well acquainted with the Pilgrims' departure point in Plymouth, England. It was a much more imposing granite quay from which the Pilgrims left the shores of "Jolly Old England" aboard the *Mayflower*.)

I had an attraction to seafood, and we were in the right place for lobsters, clams, mussels, crabs and fish of all types. Zum was not keen about the denizens of the sea but was a good sport about it. One of our favorite "night out" spots was the Viking Hotel. On Friday evenings they served a lobster for a ridiculous price of $1.25. They weren't large lobsters but were tasty. We didn't dare to order two of them because the extravagance didn't fit our budget. It was a treat to visit surrounding towns such as Bristol on the weekends to feast on their lobsters and other sea morsels.

Brian got started in kindergarten, and Craig was in the seventh grade at Thompson Junior High School. It wasn't every kid who had a school named for him. Stevie became a student, studying her last year in high school and not getting as involved in extracurricular activities as she had been in North Chicago. Craig was active in the thriving Boy Scout program in Newport. Almost every merit badge had at least one Navy or Marine officer or a Navy War College (NWC) student as the counselor. There were many boys of his age in the area, and Fort Adams was an interesting place for youngsters to roam. There were gun emplacements to climb on and relics of a fort built to defend Newport's harbor.

One of the families we interacted with was Bill and Chris Hurst's. They were good friends from Coronado days with the First Fleet staff. Bill was a captain heading the Operations Department of the NWC Senior Course. Chris was a former Navy nurse and a good trooper. They had four children, two of each gender, and lived in the Captain's Staff Quarters. Those residences were large houses, grossly large compared with ours. Although our quarters were much smaller, we did not complain—it would not have done any good. There were many advantages to living at Fort Adams considering the economy in the surrounding area. Most of the students lived in Navy housing at Fort Adams with its wall-to-wall furniture, three bedrooms and spin-around kitchen meaning you could stand in the middle and spin around to touch everything. Things were cohesive and convivial. We took the attitude, "It's only for a year, so let's relax and enjoy it," knowing we were there to study, not to luxuriate.

Fort Adams sat at the entrance to Newport harbor and had water on three sides including of course the Atlantic Ocean. It afforded a breezy condition being pleasant in the spring and summer, but not so welcoming in the late fall and winter. With the dampness and winds, Newport seemed to be one of the coldest places I had ever been during the winter months. On most days the Atlantic Ocean provided interesting sound effects with waves crashing on the surrounding shores and cliffs. There were spectacular water shows of sprays and occasional rainbows, too, provided on those few days blessed with sunshine. After first being cursed for all its negatives, the environment blessed by the beautiful days we experienced grew on us. Taken as a whole, it was an attractive area in which to live—or at least spend a year—and certainly a superb place to revisit. It had ample charm, even in our situation as cloistered students who managed to enjoy what little free time the school afforded. The weekends were always an adventure.

First piece of business

I was initially assigned to the Naval Staff College (the Junior Course) primarily for up-and-coming lieutenant commanders and "fresh-caught" commanders. The Chief of Information had only one billet for the War College, and it was for the Junior Course. It was the proper billet alignment because most PAOs of my vintage did not have the benefit of fleet staff assignments or know much about the Navy. The Staff College was an excellent forum for a person with that background. Those students learned about staff structures, how to move papers and ideas through a staff and all the necessary basics after serving an apprenticeship afloat and ashore.

I had been apprised of the curriculum at the two schools—the Junior Course and the Senior Course at thè Naval War College—and what I should be getting out of that year's "sabbatical." After being designated to go to Newport, I decided early on it would do me more good to attend the Senior Course. First, I had served in two fleet staffs and didn't need to learn the staff work basics. Secondly, being a graduate of the Senior Course would look better in my record. Further, as was the case for many officers, I probably would not have the opportunity to return to Newport. Senior naval officers could be assigned to either the Newport Naval War College, the National War College or the Industrial War College, both of the latter two being at Fort McNair in Washington. Finally, the officers I would affiliate with in the Senior Course would be those I would be interacting with later in Washington when we departed the academic life and returned to defending our country. In one of my conversations with Admiral Nunn before departing Great

Lakes, he said I should give his regards to his old friend, Vice Adm. Bernard L. "Count" Austin who was the president of the Naval War College. They had been in destroyers together during World War II. Indeed, Count Austin had been in Arleigh Burke's "Little Beaver Squadron," being a destroyer commanding officer and later as a division commander. On my first full day at Newport, I made an appointment to call on Admiral Austin. He received me most graciously. I was surprised at the ease of getting in to see him. I surmised Ira Nunn had sent him a note saying I was going to be in one of his classes.

I not only got in to see him to pay my respects but spent about half an hour with him. He did most of the talking. Naturally, I led off with Admiral Nunn's compliments and described what a great job he had done in the Ninth Naval District. Austin was a gracious man, but I sensed immediately he was on the downside of his career. In fact, the War College was his twilight tour of duty. He wanted to reminisce and gave freely of his advice on most aspects of the Navy and career planning. I had always been a good listener and paid heed to what he said.

He delighted in talking to me about his exploits in Navy public relations. He considered himself to be the Navy's first Chief of Information when he was a lieutenant in the Navy's Intelligence Division. Public information at that time was the responsibility of the Director of Naval Intelligence, and Count Austin was the staff fellow who inherited that collateral duty. He said it was not a demanding job, but once in a while he did get to issue a "press release." I offered my assistance to him in the event there was a need for public affairs support at the War College. I also presented my argument for being elevated to the Senior Course. He agreed replying he didn't know what the numbers situation was for the Senior Course but would look into it. The next morning, I was notified I was assigned to the Senior Warfare Course.

An intriguing aspect of the Senior Course was its relatively large student composition from other branches of the service, the State Department and other federal agencies. The Army, Air Force, Marine Corps and Coast Guard were well represented. Naturally, the officers were part of the anointed "chosen few" from those services. Some naval officers were sent to other war colleges of the Armed Forces. I'm sure the Navy did not send lesser lights to those establishments, and it was the same for the federal agencies. The great majority were good officers. Some were inspiring, some were questioning and some were provocative. It was a good mix and contributed to interesting discussions and presentations. I had anticipated the stimulation. In retrospect, it was said our class rated well and had more than the average number continuing on to perform duties as flag and general officers.

As historians report, the Pacific campaign of World War II was planned at the Naval War College in war-gaming sessions where wooden blocks representing ships and fleets were moved about on gigantic grids housed in the school's main building. These "simulations" modeled multiple levels of engagements and confrontations were teams of individuals executed tactical plans. Admiral Nimitz was one of the participants and planners. Today computers now do such evolutions.

Us and Them

The thread weaving the fabric for the year's course at Newport was the confrontation of the Soviet Union and the United States in the best dictates of the Cold War. The student body was divided into two equal groups; one representing the Soviet Union and the other the United States. The primary emphasis was to develop a top level, National Strategy Paper for each country. The strategic statement began with a national mission, cascaded to plans for the military establishment (Defense Department) and each of the services and then down to the individual fleets and commands. Armed with this document, we marched over to the War Gaming Building and had at it. A scenario had been developed. I don't remember who won. I believe we were at a standoff when we got to the stage of deploying nuclear weapons and good sense prevailed. We uniformed types were amazed how trigger-happy the civilians were. In the end, most of them threw up their hands and cried out, "Nuke the Sons of Bitches!" It was the military comrades and compatriots who wanted to negotiate.

The school was further broken down into groups of about 15. Our group was Number Six, and we were part of the Soviet Union team. It was a good mental exercise to develop a national strategy for the Soviet Union. We had to learn more about the Soviets and their political, economic and military structures. It would have been easier for us to develop a U.S. strategy, but we were all bewildered when we were told a National Strategy Paper didn't exist for the United States. The rationale was that one existed in the minds of those in the White House meaning the National Security Council (NSC) and, of course, the President. The NSC was undoubtedly the repository for several documents relating to national strategy, but there was no book per se. This may have all been a matter of semantics. The nation had to have a national strategy although it wasn't put together in a formal publication.

Another obviously important player in the nation's capital is Congress. The Legislative Branch is justifiably concerned and vociferous at times and has increasingly exerted itself into the area of national security. To be sure, the White House is the keeper of the keys to the "National Security Locker." With each new administration, the nation's strategy is altered, nudged or tweaked. Much depends on the personalities and ideologies of the incumbents, the country's economy, allies and potential threats. Other crucial factors include the status of forces and the existing international environment or how it is perceived to be. It was all encompassing, and the learning process we followed was engrossing, interesting and at times exciting. Several associates have assured me that since my time at the War College, a National Strategy Document does exist. I think I have slept better each night since learning that.

Navy people are not only dedicated and hard working but also socially-oriented. Those traits are especially true when put under the pressure of a confining, academic environment. Circumstances are considerably different than a naval officer's normal habitat of being at sea, a situation with obvious constraints. So starting Friday evenings through the weekend, the student body devoted time and effort to relaxing from the rigors of academic physical inertia. Our Group Six was especially active. Each of its 15 officers entertained the group in his homes during the first five months of the course. At the five-month mark, the groups were then reconstituted and provided a different and broader mix of the officers. We then started the weekly entertainment cycle again. It helped to enhance and accelerate the level of camaraderie existing at the school, and the wives were involved. Partying was only a small part of our relaxation sessions. We used the weekends to visit numerous historic sites in the area, enjoy walking trails and spend quality time with the family.

To save wear and tear on the automobiles and to maximize limited parking spaces, carpooling was encouraged. Four of us initially in the same group lived near each other. It was a good mix—an aviator, a surface warrior, Sam Gravely and myself. Sam was a ship driver. He was a surface warfare officer and an African American who had compiled an impressive and interesting career in his Navy tenure. He had been in the V-12 Program and spent extensive time at sea having several commands. In fact, he was the first black naval officer to command a Navy ship. He had a lovely wife Alma and three children. They lived about three doors from us, and Stevie baby-sat for them throughout our stay at Fort Adams. Seven years later, Sam was the first black naval officer to be selected for flag rank, and I was in the same selection group. Thereafter we boasted to each other that 50 percent of our carpool made flag rank, and no other carpool could make that claim!

Getting a bit ahead of my story, I should note that in spite of his continuing success in the Navy, Sam was media-averse. In 1965, a couple of years after our Naval War College experience, *Ebony* (the African-American version of *Life* magazine) wanted to do a cover feature; Sam responded that he preferred to be known as a Naval officer, not as a *black* Naval officer. However, once he was selected for flag rank, the game had changed, and Sam knew that he now had a responsibility to step up and show the world that the *Navy* had changed.

With Sam's concurrence, I asked the head of our New York office, Cdr. Brayton Harris, to "get Gravely on the TV show 'What's My Line?'" This was a very popular game show, along the lines of "20 Questions," where a three-person celebrity panel had twenty tries to guess what the guest did for a living. Brayton came through, and escorted Sam to the studio. As Brayton later told me, "When the studio audience was privately told that the guest was an 'Admiral in the U.S. Navy," they went wild, applauding, cheering." Twenty questions. Some of them were "Do you work for the government?" "Do you wear a uniform?" The nearest the panel came the right answer was, "Post office?" I couldn't have asked for a better outcome. They made my point, that the Navy, indeed, had changed. (A small bit of irony: Sam had once, indeed, worked for the Post Office).

Enter Jack and Jackie

Across a small inlet from Fort Adams was the Hammersmith Farm, the summer home of the Auchincloss family who reared Jacqueline Bouvier Kennedy, the President's wife. The Kennedys were regular visitors in the area in the summer. They were seen at Fort Adams because the Secret Service, charged with providing security for the President, berthed the small presidential yachts, the *Patrick J.* and the *Honey Fitz* at the fort. President Kennedy was a skilled sailor and had three crafts designated as Presidential yachts including the *Sequoia*, The Presidential Yacht, used for official and pleasure boating by the White House. He grew up with boats at the Kennedy's compound at Hyannis Port on Cape Cod, Massachusetts. And, of course, he became a Navy hero during World War II as the skipper of PT Boat 109 in the South Pacific.

When the *Patrick J.* or *Honey Fitz* would put into or out of Fort Adams' ample docks, it drew a crowd. If the President was aboard, word would seemingly pass electronically throughout the Fort Adams complex, and wives and children would congregate. Jack Kennedy was charismatic and a down to earth person. He was a great attraction to the kids and seemed to enjoy the interaction making the most of each occasion. Wherever he went, it was an event. We at Fort Adams professed to be rather blasé about it, but Jack and Jackie always drew attention. They were considerate of the children, mingling and being photographed with them.

The Assassination

It was at noon on Friday, November 22, 1963, that the student body, faculty and support people at the Naval War College were shocked by the news quickly racing throughout the campus and naval base that President Kennedy had been assassinated in Dallas. He had been in Texas, purportedly to mend a few political fences or to harmonize warring factions in the Texas Democratic Party. He was obviously looking forward to his reelection campaign in 1964. He was in a motorcade along with Jackie and Texas Governor John Connolly and his wife Nellie. Connolly was also shot and narrowly escaped death. The President, shot in the head and throat, was dead.

I was in the student wardroom we used as a lounge to congregate for coffee and snacks. We were all silent, listening to the radio and trying to assimilate the sketchy, repetitious reports as news personnel scrambled for facts and statements. Things were particularly sensitive at Newport because of the frequent Kennedy presence and the Auchincloss estate's proximity. Certainly, the President's personality and charisma magnified the stupefying news of the assassination, particularly for us at Fort Adams.

An additional factor normally affecting the mindset of military personnel was the gap created by the President's death and the swearing-in of the Vice President Lyndon Baines Johnson. There was a brief but definite void in the continuum of the country's leadership. It was potentially a time to let down your guard and perhaps become vulnerable to a surprise punch or attack. Civility would dictate that the Soviets wouldn't press the advantage at such a time. Or would they? I doubt if history would reveal potential enemies had previously taken advantage of a nationally stressful situation such as Kennedy's assassination presented, especially to start a war. However, it was a technically logical approach to warfare and caused a cautious edge to be exhibited by military personnel. As we said in the wardroom when at sea, "It raised the pucker factor!"

The weekend was a somber one for the entire country. Naturally, the media saturated its forums with the Kennedy tragedy. Lyndon Johnson had been sworn in as President as soon as possible after Kennedy was pronounced dead. Lee Harvey Oswald, a 24-year old former Marine, was arrested as the principal assassin suspect. Then he was shot and killed by Jack Ruby, an operator of a Dallas nightclub, as Oswald was being moved to a jail. President Kennedy's body lay in state in the Rotunda of the U.S. Capitol. Thousands of dignitaries, celebrities and others paid their last respects to the fallen President who had shed the political biases and the prevailing skepticism of his ability to lead the United States, let alone the Free World.

He was not only the President and a World War II naval hero; he was the father who had left behind an attractive, faithful, loyal and resilient wife and two lovely children. Not many will ever forget the image of young "John John," the intrepid three-year-old son, who saluted his father's casket. JFK was given a full military funeral with caisson and symbolic riderless horse. A parade of bands and marching units escorted the President's cortege from the Capitol to Arlington Cemetery. An indelible image persists of Jacqueline Kennedy walking the full length of the route to Arlington, dressed in black—a strong woman with extraordinary poise. We were proud of her and the manner in which she handled the situation. The sympathy of the nation was extended to her and the two children, as they poignantly captured the hearts of their countrymen.

In the late afternoon of the funeral day, Zum and I left the confines of the television set and took Dubbie for a walk along the golf course at Fort Adams near the water's edge. The sun was setting, and we observed across the water at the Hammersmith Farm where, by chance, the flag in the spacious back yard was being lowered. It is another vivid visual memory of this poignant historic event—the death of President Kennedy—that we treasure.

Research Paper

Each student in the Senior Course was required to do a research paper with a subject and title approved by the faculty. The research was to relate to a military matter and preferably to one woven into the tapestry of the Class of 1964 course of instruction, the national strategy effort. Being interested in research, I thought of many areas that could be studied along those intended lines. But I chose instead a subject area much more within my professional parameters and certainly needing to be researched. I wanted to put together a study on the effectiveness of the Navy League of the United States and decided to entitled it, *"The Navy League of the United States—A Status of Forces."* The title helped quell some of the skepticism that it was not a legitimate project.

There was a little static from some of the "hard core" unrestricted line officers on the faculty. They perceived the subject matter as out of the ballpark, but they more or less shrugged their shoulders and said that PAOs were a little out of the ballpark, too. I saw Admiral Austin at a social function and talked with him about it. He provided an enthusiastic reaction saying, "Great idea and I want to see the results." The Chief of Information in Washington, Rear Adm. Bill Mack, was interested and supportive, too. Through Bob Crown, I got the support of the Navy League's national headquarters and its president, Robert Barnum, an executive with U.S. Steel.

The basic rationale for the research program was to impress upon the students some of the vicissitudes and mechanics of doing research. There is no doubt in my mind that my project demanded more research than normally required for the effort. I did three surveys, conducted interviews with the Navy League's national president, immediate past president, a future national president, two regional presidents, several council presidents and two executive directors and supplemented the effort by sending out 160 pieces of correspondence.

Additionally, I read extensively about volunteer associations, an ancillary subject I found to be interesting and beneficial in later endeavors. Zum helped where she could with the coding of source material, developing statistics and typing. At times response cards covered the living room floor and practically every available horizontal space in the house. The Navy League financed a mailing to 5,000 of its members selected at random from its 36,000 membership. We had an astounding 49% response. From all this information, I was able to develop a membership profile, the first time it had been done for the League. It proved the Navy League was justified in calling itself "The Civilian Arm of the Navy."

For its assistance in the research, the Navy League gained the right to use any and all of the final document. There was much ado about it, clearly evidenced by how it was appreciated in many areas. I was further pleased with a secondary benefit of the study. It became my thesis for a master's degree program I had started under the auspices of The George Washington University (GWU) in Washington, D.C. This program was endorsed and encouraged by the Naval War College as an extracurricular activity.

Classes were held on campus following the War College routine each day. I had not held a bachelor's degree because I had not established a residence (four semesters) at a school anywhere. I had three semesters of work at Wisconsin University at Oshkosh and Wabash College. But I had no opportunity to return to either of those campuses to gain another semester to qualify for a residence and graduate. So when I was offered the opportunity to get a master's degree bypassing the bachelor's program, I grabbed it. Midway through the process, I was informed GWU would not allow me to achieve a master's degree for several reasons. Even though I had considerably more than the required number of hours or semesters, I lacked concentration in subject areas and was one semester short in a foreign language—French. The result was I took a master's program, so I could qualify for an undergraduate degree. I had strong convictions that a degree would help get me promoted to captain.

The thesis was worth nine semester hours, and the advisor assigned to work with me by GWU was Mrs. Carol Hills from Boston University's School of Communications. She was well known to the many Navy PAOs who attended BU for postgraduate work. Carol and I worked together well. She turned out to be a good resource and academic guide, and we developed respect for each other and remained friends for several years. I was able to help her work around the Pentagon when she aspired to be on the Defense Advisory Council on Women in the Services (DACOWITS) Board. I was helpful in getting her appointed to the board and later assisted on some of the projects on which she toiled.

Dubbie's Demise

Our dog Dubbie was happily an integral part of the family and many times the center of family fun. She was spirited and playful, and we all loved her. The boys were fond of her and spent much of their free time playing with her and orchestrating her routine of tricks for their friends. Of course, Stevie thought Dubbie was her dog, and it was true there was a strong bond between them. All three fought to have Dubbie as a bed partner. She obliged by trying to please all of them, making her rounds to all their beds during the night.

Zum learned early on that animals were nice to pet and play with but were a pain to house and care for. In many ways there were more concerns for our pet than raising a child. She was taken by Dubbie's exuberance and vitality but not as enthusiastic about the situation as other family members. They frequently regaled at the scene when Zum was fluffed off by the 10-pound doggie dynamo. The kids and I would sneak a chuckle or two when Dubbie completely ignored commands or demands by the "Queen Bee." At times, she actually stopped to give Zum a look as if to say, "Who are you to talk to me that way?" and then continue independently on her way to her intended mischief. Our reactions could have resulted from the secret envy we harbored because we knew we couldn't get away with any such arrogance.

On a very dark winter night with rain, gusting winds and temperatures around 40 degrees, Dubbie was let out for her evening stretch. She chose that night to do the neighborhood. I spent an hour or so searching for her and calling to her in the pitch black. The thought occurred to me that it would have been nice if Admiral Nunn had selected a white poodle. Finding a black poodle in that dismal milieu was like chasing a raven through a tar pit. Such thoughts were running through my mind when I gave up in despair and returned to the warmth of our abode. Try as I may, I could not sleep and was alerted by a whimper and scratch at the front door at roughly Oh Dark Hundred about 0230 (2:30 a.m.).

It was Dubbie. She was shivering and wet from head to what there was of her short poodle tail. She knew she had erred and aware I was upset with her. I scolded her and tried to give her a swipe across her behind. The smack was deflected by her quick dodge as she scampered for shelter behind a chair. I tried to reach for her, and she growled bringing me to my senses. I realized she needed more than a roughing. She was cold and drenched. I finally coaxed her out of her retreat and held her while drying her fur with a towel and speaking to her softly. She responded, relaxing and apparently regaining confidence that I was her friend and that she was "my dog."

Not getting much sleep, I was grumpy the next morning and stumbled into the back seat of the pool's car and slouched into the corner. I thought there might be a chance for a few minutes of shut eye before bumping around the War College campus. "What's wrong with you?" One of our group asked bluntly. "Get thrown out of the house without breakfast?"

"Naw," I growled back. "I just spent most of the lousy night prowling the neighborhood trying to find a black bitch." I then realized sitting next to me was Sam Gravely, our black compatriot. I gather myself up and offered Sam an apology,

"I'm sorry, Sam," I said. "My black poodle got out last night in this rain and ..."

"That's all right, Bill," he interrupted. "I have been in a similar situation in the past. But I usually had a smile on my face in the morning."

I have recalled that conversation many times since, and Sam and I have laughed about it when our paths have crossed and we had time to reminisce.

Dubbie didn't fare so well. Resulting from that terrible night, she contracted distemper. She had shots as a puppy to ward off the dreaded and potentially fatal disease, but within two or three months, she was lifeless and listless. She wanted to be the lively, peppy center of attraction, but her body wouldn't respond. I took her to the veterinarian several times where she was given shots and pills to no avail. Finally on a Saturday morning, I couldn't see her suffer any more. I told Zum it was time for us to recognize she was not going to recover, and we shouldn't let her dwindle away. It was a pall over the family. Alone, I took her to the vet and asked bluntly if there was any chance she would recover. The answer was a shake of the head and a muted "no." I then asked if he thought it best to have her put away, and he nodded in accent. With Dubbie lying on the table between the doctor and me, I said, "Well, OK, What will it cost to have her taken out of her misery?"

"Well, you have already made a large investment in this dog, particularly in the past couple months," the doctor replied. "Just give me five bucks, and we'll end it."

As I was removing the five dollar bill from my wallet, the doctor said, "It's sure tough on the kids, isn't it." I nodded in agreement, knowing if I tried to talk, I wouldn't be able to make a dignified exit. I patted Dubbie for the last time and turned to hurriedly depart. I sat in my car unable to function for about 10 minutes before I corralled my emotions and trusted myself to drive safely on the narrow streets of Newport back to Fort Adams. A situation like that is truly "tough on the kids." I acknowledged in that moment that some of us never grow up.

The lesson we learned from that small but heart rendering episode was that dogs are nice pets, but we humans can become too attached to them. We have witnessed several similar circumstances with friends. Zum and I have shunned the responsibility of ever owning another dog. We have welcomed our children's' dogs, but have been thankful we have not had to go through the emotional trauma of their pets' last months or years. Dubbie remains a warm memory in our family history. The pictures we have of her in many situations recall happier times "when we had a dog."

An Important Decision

There comes a time in most high school seniors' lives to make a decision about what they want to do with the rest of their lives or at least for the next few years. Discussions with Stevie about college never reached a traumatic level. She knew a decision was needed, and her perspectives were basically narrowed to schools within a reasonable distance from our future home in the Washington, D.C. area. I doubt if I was much of a factor in her decision, but I made my thoughts known mostly through Zum's filter. I considered how Zum had been through the same process not long ago and could communicate better on the subject than I could. My thoughts were primarily on the costs, but I was prepared to spend according to Stevie's decision. I did interject that if she chose a school nearby within commuting distance, she could live at home, and I would buy her a car. It was a minor consideration, but may have carried some weight. I offered perhaps a new Volkswagen Beetle, or in street nomenclature, a "Bug."

Her decision was a good one. She chose Marjorie Webster Junior College, a two-year all girls' school in the District of Columbia. It had the reputation of being a girl's "finishing school," was accredited and popular as a jumping off platform for transfer to four-year programs at other colleges or universities. With the decision made, she pulled me by the arm (with a mean twist included) to the VW dealership in Newport. About a month before she graduated from high school, she became the proud owner of a cherry red VW

Bug. She learned to drive a stick shift in a minute or two, and I doubt if she ever returned to sit behind the wheel of the family's Pontiac Green Hornet.

We were to graduate from the Naval War College in mid-June, and by March I was still without orders to our next duty assignment. I realized I had been stashed at the War College and was satisfied with that evolution. I knew Secretary of the Navy Fred Korth had asked Jim Jenkins to remain on as his special assistant for public affairs for another year because of some pressing problems confronting the Navy in those areas. I continued to believe I was destined for the Secretary's office, but I had learned long before not to "assume a damned thing in this man's Navy." Shortly before his assassination, President Kennedy had fired Fred Korth as Secretary of the Navy and nominated Paul H. Nitze to the post.

It was no secret Korth had been slipped into the SECNAV job by Vice President Johnson. Fred was a big, "good ole boy" Texas banker who almost anyone would like immediately, unless he didn't like you, and then it didn't matter. He loved being the Navy's Secretary and did a good job administering the Navy and Marine Corps. When it came to light he had conducted some Texas banking correspondence on Secretary of the Navy letterhead, the White House axed the Johnson crony.

I felt if the job with the Secretary of the Navy fell through, I would end up in Washington anyway. It was time for me to do my penance and pay for the good duty I had in San Diego and Great Lakes. Besides, I had burned my bridge to the Atlantic Fleet job with Admiral Dennison.

In mid-February Jim Jenkins wrote a long letter thanking me for not pressuring him about the job over the past six months. He had been busy and appreciated my patience. He said he was definitely leaving Washington in June, and if I was still interested, he saw no reason to go in any other direction for a relief. Of course, I would have to come to Washington to be interviewed and approved by Secretary Nitze, but Jenkins thought that would only be a formality. He would make the arrangements including getting BUPERS to issue travel orders to the War College for me to officially visit Washington. I nonchalantly replied, "But, of course. I could probably wrench myself away from the rigors of the War College." It was done by return mail followed with a phone call the same day.

Jim and I concocted an extended weekend for us in Washington, coinciding with the Good Friday and Easter Sunday holiday granted by the War College. The purpose of our visit was to acquaint us with the area, check out the real estate and hopefully make a choice on a house. Naturally, Jim wanted to sell his house in Alexandria and thought it would be a good idea if we bought it. We were to stay with him over the weekend and try out his digs. He, Verona and their three boys readily provided courtesies and hospitality making us welcome. They had obviously worked hard on fixing up the place for the occasion. I liked the house and found it comfortable. It was only about five miles from the Pentagon. Sagacious Zum saw flaws, especially with the neighborhood and the schools. We contacted Joe Peak (from Omaha days) and his wife Juanita. They devoted an entire Saturday to showing us other available real estate. Clearly there were better places than Alexandria. If we were willing to up our price to the mid-$30,000 range we could do well in North Arlington or McLean.

A fortunate coincidence was that CHINFO was having a social event on Friday evening. We got to see the Washington contingent of the Public Affairs community. Many of them Zum hadn't met or not seen for several years. It became clear to me that evening that Capt. Jim Dowdell, Deputy CHINFO, wasn't enthralled with me being detailed to the Secretary's office. Jim Jenkins explained that was only because Dowdell didn't control the effort and wasn't a part of the move. I later learned Dowdell was one of the best professionals in our business. He had become a dour, grumpy old man but had no particular negative thoughts about me. In fact, he admitted, after I was in the job a few months, he had me tentatively slated for the CNO's PAO job. However, that was a minor item in the everyday politics of the CHINFO. I wasn't familiar with the arena, but I was to become a central figure in its midst for the next 11 years.

We visited my brother Don and his family in Fairfax. They lived only about a mile from Joe Peak's home. Don had left Battle Creek, Michigan, the previous year when Civil Defense moved its headquarters to the Pentagon with him as its fiscal director.

Easter that year was in early April, and everyone was surprised when the day brought about eight inches of snow. We departed the Jenkins' abode and thought we should make a pass at a house in McLean that was advertised for sale by its owner. We managed to get into the unplowed road and were welcomed by an Air Force colonel and his wife at 6529 Divine Street. We liked what we saw and although impressed with all their answers, we decided to consider the matter further and informed them we would call back in a few days. The house was not far from the Beltway (Interstate 495) encircling Washington. We learned soon after reaching it that the "Loop" was not yet completed. We had to go north on Interstate 270 and cut across Maryland to Baltimore on Interstate 70.

Despite the weather, we managed to talk about the house and decided early on it was what we wanted. The price was $34,500. We could handle it with a good down payment provided by our past real estate ventures. We had been in Navy government quarters for the past three years, so the equity we had gleaned from Coronado and Omaha realty was building into a sizable nest egg. We got a 25-year, 5 1/4 % mortgage rate from the Carey Winston Company in Washington. When we paid off the loan in 1989, our monthly taxes were higher than the mortgage payments. The house could have sold for $350,000 that year. We had added a two-car garage, but otherwise we just rode the real estate boom in Northern Virginia.

Bud Zumwalt

In early June, I made an overnight trip to Washington to meet Secretary Nitze. It was a five-minute formality, and I must admit I was initially underwhelmed. He was a passive individual who had been briefed on my background and didn't attempt to have me elaborate. However, I was keenly interested in his Executive Assistant and Senior Naval Aide, Capt. Elmo R. Zumwalt, Jr. who identified himself as "Bud."

He had an exciting career, and I first heard of him at COMCRUDESPAC in San Diego when he commanded the destroyer USS *Isbell*. He had taken command of that ship when it was ranked lowest in the Pacific Fleet. In two years it had all the pennants and honors flying from its superstructure. I remember being part of a COMCRUDESPAC staff inspection group that boarded *Isbell* primarily to learn just what the young skipper had done and how. I wasn't normally a part of readiness inspection parties, but had volunteered because I wanted to see this modern day "King Neptune." I got to see him but can't remember if I shook his hand then. I was a lieutenant, and there were so many captains and commanders in the group; I was relegated to the background. I do remember a young officer with a sort of bashful, but engaging smile being totally alert and in control of the situation.

Now, nine years later, there he was eyeing me. In the two or three minutes we had together, he kept up the chatter. He asked questions about me and my family while doing three or four other unrelated tasks and taking two or three phone calls. His telephone manner was as concise as you could possibly get. There was no fluff, no flowery hellos, no baloney, just straight terse instructions or requests for information. The interactions were done politely and with a degree of finality. He summarized his perspective on my position with the office concisely. "We have an outstanding Secretary of the Navy in Mr. Nitze," Zumwalt said. "He deserves much more credit than he gets internally within the Navy and with the public. We are looking to you helping in this regard. Enjoy your last few days at the War College, and I want to talk with you in detail when you report for duty."

As I exited his office, he had a phone to his ear and two or three people around his desk. I didn't notice, but they all must have been clad in track shoes. I thought, "Cripes! What am I getting into here? This must be a new Navy!" I did have a question, "Is this guy for real?"

Departing from the War College and Newport was an interesting and an unusual sight. Relying on good management and organization by Newport Naval Station personnel, several hundred officers and families moved out of Fort Adams simultaneously—well almost. Because of the large number of personnel involved and the high volume of moving vans in the restricted area at the fort, pack-out and moving days had to be staggered over a week's time. It might have seemed chaotic to a casual observer, but it was never out of control. It was like a busy symphony orchestra with instruments working away in all sectors, and Navy wives taking turns conducting. Fortunately, the husbands were at the college, winding down their 10-month curriculum and not adding to the chaos at home. Most Navy husbands caught in a situation

like moving, soon realize their wives are in charge. To eventually do the un-
packing, they needed to know what stuff was packed in what box. We all
praised the logistics people at the naval station for handling the annual mass
exodus so well. We knew how much our wives contributed to the success
as well.

Our household effects (navalese for furniture and other personal gear
needed to make a household function) were packed out and on the road the
day before graduation. Then we roughed it, sleeping in camping gear in the
house. After graduation we were on our way to new adventures in our nation's capital.

Graduation was a formality. We had to dig out our service dress white
uniforms for the occasion and appear as squared away naval officers after 10
months of wearing civilian clothes. Secretary of the Navy Nitze was the principal speaker for the event, and Bud Zumwalt accompanied him as the aide. I
was surprised to see Zumwalt. We managed only a brief conversation because
of all the jostling going on among the graduates. There were many "good-
byes" and "great to have been with you" farewells. Naturally, I was interested
in the Secretary's speech, keying in on its content as well as his delivery. It
was a mild disappointment because it was a so-so speech and Nitze's delivery
was academic. He read the presentation with his head down, without eye
contact and in a monotone. I was to learn that Secretary Nitze was a scholar
and believed speeches were synonymous with the "reading of papers" with
the content being of greatest importance. We students could not help but
compare his presentation with the parade of outstanding speakers we had at
the college. However, any concerns I might have had about the speech were
immediately dispelled by the backslapping, hand shaking and sincere adieus
of the students as we departed.

Zum, Stevie and Brian were in the vanguard departing early that morning
for Washington in Stevie's new VW. They even stopped at the commissary store before entering our new home, so the pantry would not be bare.
Washington's heat and humidity greeted their arrival, but fortunately the
house had central air conditioning. The household effects arrived the next
day, the same day Craig and I headed south in the Green Hornet. By nightfall,

we were all united again in our new home.

I had two weeks shore leave before reporting for duty. It was ample time to get situated in our new house and neighborhood. We found our home to be ideally located for our next tour of duty. It was only eight miles to the Pentagon, and I could reach it in about 15 minutes. We were about a mile and a half from the Beltway that eventually would completely loop the District of Columbia, Arlington, Alexandria, parts of Maryland and pass through McLean.

We were also only a mile from beautiful downtown McLean, the crossroads of Old Dominion Drive and Old Chain Bridge Road. McLean was fast developing into an upper level bedroom suburb for Washington. It possessed little manufacturing industry but office buildings were sprouting throughout the landscape. They were to be occupied by "Beltway Bandits," staffing consulting and service firms. Those groups provided support for the rapidly expanding federal government. The federal sector was growing quickly and needed help especially in technical fields, administrative services, research and analysis. Only three miles from our home, Tyson's Corner Mall was in its early construction stages, and at that time would soon become the world's largest shopping mall. Hechinger's super hardware store was also nearby, facilitating weekend shopping to care for those endless "Honey-Do chores."

Our tour at Newport was successful for our family. It was exciting to me as a learning venture. The college's lecture program seemingly offered unlimited introductions to new vistas. The experience alone was memorable for the interaction with officers of the other services and departments as well as for creating new friends and associates in the Navy. It was a most valuable experience, and I arrived in Washington with the great satisfaction of being a member of the Naval War College's Class of 1964.

Back to Work

Reporting for duty in the Office of the Secretary of the Navy on July 1, 1964, I was eager to get into the job and return to the active Navy instead of being in its academic forum. Except for dialogue, the Navy didn't have much immediate visibility in the Pentagon nor did the other services. Here again, we wore civilian clothes. The rationale, elicited by the Defense Department, was that uniforms were intimidating and stifled a free exchange of ideas during conferences. A few years later, the Armed Services requested uniforms be worn on Wednesdays to remind the personnel they were a part of the uniformed services.

My predecessor, Jim Jenkins, had departed for San Diego but had given me a good briefing when I was in Washington in May. He was only a phone call away, if I had questions. In my younger years, three to five days were about normal to accomplish a proper "turnover." However, as time moved on and the business of public affairs became routine in my mind, turnover time was greatly reduced. Once a briefing on the local situation, personalities involved and the office routine was absorbed, it was best to take charge of your new desk and become engrossed in the new assignment. Under the circumstances, Jenkins and I had an ideal turnover—he was not there when I arrived.

Jim Jenkins had a unique political sense among his accomplished public affairs skills. He was the proverbial "political animal" with the ability to quickly discern the political nuances involving a situation or solution to a problem. He was more perceptive about political aspects than most other PAOs with whom I had been associated. The political arena was not strange territory to me, but I realized I had to ratchet up to the Washington level from the mayor's offices in Chicago, Waukegan and even North Chicago. It might take some time, but I looked forward to the challenge.

As a special assistant to the Secretary, he would expect my input to his decision making. My basic input would be advising on the immediate media reaction and how they would report a story, if there was one. Much would be based on intuition, punditry, guessing and crystal balling. I knew a good PAO could make a valuable contribution by predicting "how the story would be played," what questions would be asked and prepare the boss for any ensuing action. My goal in these situations for all questions was to have at least 95% of them carefully predicted, itemized and thoroughly staffed for response, so the boss could react fluently and with confidence.

Despite all the resources the Secretary had at his disposal, he relied heavily on four people in his immediate staff. They were: (1) the Senior Naval Aide and Executive Assistant, a Navy captain; (2) the Marine Corps Aide, a colonel; (3) the Special Assistant for Legal Counsel, a commander; and (4) the Special Assistant for Public Affairs, another commander. A fifth officer, a commander, was the Administrative Aide who was the Secretary's office manager and an integral member of the immediate staff. However, normally the Administrative Aide had interfaced little with the Secretary other than working closely with the Executive Assistant.

Initially, I perceived my position would be the personal "flak" or the Secretary's publicist or public relations agent. In reality, that was true; I would be concerned about the image and operating welfare of the Secretary. However, I soon learned he relied on his special assistants for professional counsel on a variety of subjects. Their input covered almost the entire spectrum of matters concerning his leadership role for the Navy and Marine Corps.

To be sure, the Secretary had other public affairs assistance available to him. For matters involving the Defense Department, there was the Assistant Secretary of Defense for Public Affairs. For Navy business, he had the Navy's CHINFO. I maintained constant contact with the CHINFO, his deputy and staff in my effort to keep continuity intact. There may have been more than one voice involved in advising the Secretary on Navy public affairs matters, but we wanted the direction to be of "one voice." Despite other sources for guidance, the proximity of being in the office and accompanying the Secretary on most of his travels made it convenient for him to discuss public affairs matters with his special assistant.

My office staff comprised Chief Yeoman Muriel Hansen and Chief Journalist Al France. Both were stellar, loyal, supportive coworkers who were Navy professionals. Chief Hansen retired about a year later, and Al stayed on for a couple more years before retiring. I remember Chief Hansen was so dedicated and professional. One day the Secretary called me directly on the phone. She, knowing I had gone to the head (lavatory, rest room), barged in and announced, "Commander Thompson, the Secretary wants to see you right away."

The Secretariat

The Navy's Secretariat, another title for the Office of the Secretary of the Navy, represented a solid, talented group of individuals, who united with their staffs, manifested formidable support for the Secretary and strong, dedicated leadership for the civilian side of the Navy's hierarchy.

My office in the Pentagon was on the E-Ring across the corridor from the Secretary and next to that of the Special Assistant for Legal Counsel, Cdr. Horace B. Robertson. "Robbie" was a Judge Advocate General (JAG) officer, a Naval Academy graduate and a solid naval officer who had commanded a Landing Ship Tank (LST) before becoming a JAG officer. The Executive Assistant was Capt. Bud Zumwalt who was a surface warfare officer. Col. Douglas "Chuck" Haberly was the Marine Corps Aide. The Administrative Aide was Cdr. Richard "Dick" Nicholson, a surface warfare officer.

Across the corridor was the Under Secretary of the Navy Paul Fay who served with President Jack Kennedy in PT Boats during World War II and remained a close friend of the President. Fay had handled the Kennedy campaign affairs in California and helped Kennedy carry the state in the election.

Nearby was the Assistant Secretary for Research and Development, Robert Morse, and next was the Assistant Secretary for Financial Management Victor "Vic" Longstreet. In the old Main Navy Building on Constitution Avenue resided the Assistant Secretary for Installations and Logistics Graeme Bannerman, a career civil servant. John Dixon, the Navy's General Counsel was also in the Main Navy Building.

To further manifest solidarity of Navy leadership, proximate to the secretariat and immediately next to the Secretary was the Chief of Naval Operations, Admiral David Lamar McDonald. Next to him was the Vice Chief, Admiral Claude Ricketts with his cordon of Deputy CNOs, three-star flag officers, and their support personnel who constituted the OPNAV Staff, numbering about 500 officers. Secretary Nitze had encouraged Admiral McDonald to move the CNO office adjacent to his. A few years later the Marine Corps Commandant moved into the Pentagon from the Arlington Annex, so the Secretary was and continues to be bracketed by his two uniformed service chiefs.

It didn't take long to realize that the facilities, tools and channels at my disposal provided some leverage. However, with this advantage in my back pocket, I continued operating as in the past, working within and with the staff, with CHINFO, with the CNO's office and the Secretary of Defense Public Affairs Office. It was a superb job. I was pleased to be a part of the team and was determined to make the most of all opportunities and enjoy the process. Keeping in mind a few long-term objectives, I developed the perspective of setting short-term goals. It was an appropriate tact because I was cast into a wide spectrum of tasks and projects with several ongoing simultaneously.

Having always been an observer of people and their characteristics, I was enjoying this new environment. It provided an unprecedented number of quality individuals to observe. Their intelligence and professional levels were top grade. The pace of activities and events was quicker than I had experienced before, but I surprised myself by how I could keep up and contribute.

The most interesting person I encountered and studied was Capt. Elmo Russell Zumwalt, Jr. It was intriguing to watch him operate in his relatively small office (small in relation to the job he was doing) and observe him in his normal activities. It wasn't an exhibition he gave occasionally; it was his normal behavior. The telephone at his ear was omnipresent. It seemed he was always talking into a phone cradled between the side of his head and his shoulder. Locked there it freed his hands enabling him to shuffle the innumerable stacks of papers on his desk or to write. He was undoubtedly a juggler, keeping more balls in the air than anyone I had ever been with and constantly maintaining a level head. His demeanor was extraordinary. He never wasted a minute nor forgot anything, and he was always conscious of those working with him.

Once he determined an associate or a subordinate had sufficient experience, background and integrity to handle a task, he brought him or her into his confidence. He then shared tasks working with his subordinates until project fruition and then gave them all the credit. I also learned he was a delegator. He didn't harbor many tasks to himself. He remembered all the cards he had dealt and didn't forget all those who were involved in his projects and issues. He seemed to get more out of his small staff than even they thought they were capable of performing. Essentially, that is the basis of leadership—getting others to do things, some they don't think they are capable of doing or don't care about doing. With all the other interesting things going on about me, I was participating in a Leadership 101 lab course and enjoying it!

Prioritizing The Job

On my first day in the office, I received marching orders from Captain Zumwalt. He immediately took the time to brief me on what he thought should be my objectives and tasks. As I recall, he didn't stop everything he was doing in his office, but without much distraction, he proceeded to give me 98% of his attention. It was also apparent he had given some thought to this presentation. He told me of Secretary Nitze's background and how the Navy was fortunate to have the likes of Paul Nitze as its Secretary.

He described how Nitze was concentrating on a few selected programs. He was positioning himself as the Anti-Submarine Warfare (ASW) czar and wanted to move the Navy into a better position to combat the Soviet Union's submarine threat. He helped develop a Forward Deployed Logistics Ship (FDLS) concept seeking to reduce costs for building Navy ships. He also wanted to modernize U.S. shipyard capabilities to further reduce ship building costs. He then averred Nitze was not conscious of publicity or its benefits and wasn't a person to seek publicity or acclaim. He was totally dedicated to gaining results from his programs and interests and thought those results would speak for themselves.

Zumwalt concluded that Nitze was not being recognized for what he was doing. He sought a program to ensure the American public knew about the Secretary's efforts and objectives and kept Navy personnel aware of what the leadership was trying to do for them. He warned that Nitze would probably not be supportive of my efforts. But he promised his backing and said he would encourage "The Boss" to be patient and understanding.

Other than literally giving him a cheery "Aye, Aye," saluting and marching off, I commented that "our" program would commence immediately, but success would take a little more time. The toughest part would be if Nitze chose to be a reluctant player. I would need Bud's help to convince Nitze to sit still for interviews in the office and when in the field. I recommended that at times we should have media reps accompany us on trips starting with the domestic ones for the time being.

I cautioned this little project of ours should be done in a subtle, dignified manner befitting the man we wanted to recognize. I clearly added we shouldn't label it a "Publicity Program." In fact, it should not be referred to as a program at all but as normal operating procedure. Our success would not be measured by one story or one event but from an aggregate of activities over a year or two. I knew it would take time for me to learn about the Secretary's initiatives, so I could talk intelligently with newsmen and incite their interest. I was ready to start the process immediately.

Bud's 15-minute briefing was probably the longest time we had together in his office for one session, although we socialized and got well acquainted in other venues. I reported regularly but briefly to him on various things, and he would act or react immediately. He comprehended what I was saying without me to going into detail. Most importantly to me, Bud and I communicated, albeit in a somewhat concise, abbreviated form. I was pleased with our relationship and developed increasing respect for him.

More About Nitze And Zumwalt

Bud Zumwalt and Paul Nitze had a profound influence on the Navy Department over the next 10 years. Zumwalt had become a protégé´ of Paul

Nitze, and in later life they were closest of friends. An interesting story about how they met and became associated was related to me. I witnessed its re-telling several times during my tenure with Paul Nitze and afterward. Nitze was the Assistant Secretary of Defense for International Security Affairs when he delivered a speech at the National War College at Fort McNair in Washington. The procedure for such events was a cordial affair where the speaker spent some time with faculty members prior to the speech.

Immediately after the presentation, they gathered again, sometimes for lunch. Nitze observed during this routine that the conversation focused several times to an "amazing" speech on the succession of command in the Soviet Union delivered by one of the students the previous day. This was obviously a matter of pride for the faculty, and apparently the speech had "staying power" not normally associated with student presentations. To em-bellish his story, Nitze usually indicated that he was disturbed because the student "stole his thunder" with a speech given 24 hours prior to his, even though there was no duplication or overlap in content.

I personally doubt if Nitze was disturbed. That was not his nature. But being intellectually inquisitive, he asked about the substance of the speech and finally the name of the student. When Nitze returned to the Pentagon, he asked for background information on Captain Zumwalt and without in-terviewing him, requested he be assigned to his office. Upon graduation, Zumwalt reported for duty to work for Nitze. Initially, he was assigned to the Strategic Arms Limitations desk and later became a principal assistant to Secretary Nitze during the Cuban Missile Crisis. Nitze was a major advisor to President Kennedy during that event.

When he became Secretary of the Navy, Zumwalt went with him to be his Executive Assistant and Senior Naval Aide. Bud was counseled by the captain "detailer" in BUPERS not to go to International Security Affairs (ISA) with Nitze because the job would not be career enhancing. Instead, he was going to assign him to Op-06 (Plans and Policies) or to the Joint Chiefs of Staff in J-5 (Plans). Playing averages, the detailer was probably correct in his assessment. However, Bud Zumwalt wasn't an average guy.

It had been rumored, and later personally verified to me several times by Paul Nitze that he was not particularly pleased to be nominated as the Secretary of the Navy. He was one of the most capable men in Washington having been "the man" behind the scenes to conceive, negotiate and prosecute more policies and programs at the federal level than anyone else. However, despite his achievements, Paul Nitze seemed to be left "holding the bag" or the coat of a colleague who was named to a high government post. Perhaps because of his demeanor as a reserved intellectual, who was a thinker and silent achiever, the quiet, never pushy man may have missed out on some visibility and the accompanying appointments.

After serving on Jack Kennedy's campaign for the presidency as his advisor on international affairs, Nitze wasn't nominated to be the Secretary of State, a job for which he was eminently qualified. Neither was he selected as Secretary of Defense, a job many thought he had locked up. Robert McNamara, the Ford Motor Company whiz kid, was named instead. Further, it was speculated that he would be named as Deputy Secretary of Defense, but McNamara chose Roswell L.Gilpatrick. Nitze was then offered the position as Assistant Secretary of Defense for International Security Affairs. He accepted and buried himself into that milieu for which he had no master.

In November 1963 when Fred Korth, the Secretary of the Navy, was asked to resign, Paul Nitze was called. He wasn't impressed. In fact, he rebelled and asked for an audience with the President. It was granted, and Nitze recited how he thought the SECNAV job was not a promotion. Instead, he saw it as a lateral assignment or demotion. He was not pleased to be nominated. Kennedy assured him that heading the Navy and Marine Corps was a very good job in Washington and urged him to accept. Out of loyalty to the President, Paul agreed. Fortunately, he had Bud Zumwalt to guide him through the Navy bureaucracy, translating some of its idiosyncrasies as well as providing a good "saltwater" approach to problem solving. In the process, Nitze put together a strong, effective Navy secretariat team.

A developing Nitze fan

My reaction to my new boss changed over time as I adjusted to his brilliant, calm, self-assured, poised and confident self. We in the office learned that his quietude did not mean he was a "cold fish" as some outside the office, especially the Pentagon press corps, thought. We tried and were successful in helping him grow and become recognized as a more forthcoming and humane leader. That process also helped me retain my usual persona of candor and realism, and I learned a great deal from him.

Early on, after sitting in many conferences with Secretary Nitze, I was fascinated by how he analyzed situations, came to conclusions and made decisions. He was a pragmatist but had a degree of surgeon-like precision for analysis and definition. A few years later after retiring, he authored a book entitled, *Tension Between Opposites*. In it he described in detail how he devised a framework for decision making in international politics. He had one of the keenest minds I have ever observed.

Along with all of that, he wasn't much interested in what I was trying to do for him, the office and the Navy. He didn't object, but it was evident he did not enjoy being an active participant in my game. I was sure Bud Zumwalt had spoken to him about our plan or at least our intentions, but he was uncomfortable with the process.

One day I had something to discuss with Nitze and went into his office as I was accustomed to doing. I walked up to his desk and stood there waiting for him to acknowledge my presence. He was presumably concentrating on reading something, but his body language indicated he knew I was standing there. I saw his eyes sneak a glance at my feet. He had apparently decided to ignore me. I thought it would be stupid to exit the office, and give him a victory in this little game. I decided to continue standing there waiting for him to eyeball me. I even cleared my throat a few times. It seemed like a long time, but he finally put down his paper and addressed me with a sigh. "And now what?" he asked with an expression of resignation. I always thought that was a great opener for a discussion.

Having worked in the Pentagon for a short time prior to this tour of duty, I was not enamored with the romance of being part of the power exuded from that five-sided building. I also harbored no great feeling about the Pentagon as a nice place to work. It was enormous, the world's largest office building, housing more than 27,000 folks employed by the defense establishment. It has 17 miles of corridors, 25,000 telephones and 1,200 toilets, which some cynics say are the most functional parts of the building. Its stark architecture presented a cold product obviously built in great haste during the early stages of World War II to house the War Department (the Army and its Air Corps).

Its interior was no better being cold and dungeon-like with its drab, unimaginative colors. People were crammed into any available working space or cubicles. Navy captains and commanders returning from command at sea had more space in their at-sea cabins aboard ship than in their working spaces at the Pentagon. It was cavernous and confusing to navigate the spoke-like halls. From "Ground Zero," as we labeled the center of the structure, they emanated outward toward the high prestige E-Ring where offices had windows revealing the outside world.

Another thing unknown or unappreciated by the public was that people in the Pentagon worked hard and put in exceptionally long hours. Uniformed personnel were salaried and didn't punch a time card; therefore, the first 24 hours of each day rightfully belonged to Uncle Sam. Charges of dilatory performance and abbreviated work hours could be attributed to some Civil Service employees. Yet many personnel, including political appointees and top civil servants in management positions, were visibly dedicated to their work and extended themselves, working equally long hours alongside their military counterparts.

I doubted that all that effort was necessary because there was much duplicative work caused by the system and usually generated by Congress or the White House. Adm. Hyman Rickover, the great iconoclast, stated several times to the media and the Congress how the Pentagon was overstaffed. He claimed one way to cure it would be to lop off the fifth deck of the building along with all of its people and no one would miss them. Those seeking to remedy the situation could then proceed from there to the fourth deck and so on.

Our hours in the SECNAV office were usually from 0715 in the morning to whenever the Secretary departed the office in the evening—about 1900 (7:00 p.m.). He usually arrived in the office about 0800. We were prepared to greet him with up-to-speed information about problems pertaining to our areas of concern. We had read the Pentagon *Early Bird*, perused all the overnight message traffic and energized some of the offices that might be "close to the fire" or the interest of the day. The Pentagon *Early Bird* was a daily publication of news clippings from the wire services, major newspapers and periodicals. Compiled and distributed by the Assistant Secretary of Defense for Public Affairs (ASDPA), it was beneficial and a time saver. We didn't have to duplicate the ASDPA effort. It had its shortcomings, however. It didn't reproduce the comics or scores of athletic contests.

Hello Vietnam

Six weeks into the job, one of the more interesting events of my life occurred. It was my first extended trip with the Secretary, and we went to the Western Pacific. It was planned as a routine, periodic orientation trip for the Secretary. It was his first and designed for him to see and be seen in that part of his domain. The Marine Aide, Col. Doug Haberle, and I were to be the accompanying aides. Bud Zumwalt stayed behind to run the shop.

Trip planning wasn't a new experience for me, and I assisted Doug who was in charge. There was a considerably different load factor in planning a two-week trip throughout the Western Pacific for the Secretary of the Navy. It contrasted sharply with setting up an overnighter to Denver for a two-star Naval District commandant. Still the objectives and considerations were similar. There were time factors, comfort and safety conditions, and works with local commanders to ensure the trip would be successful. We wanted a win-win situation for the Secretary and the locals, so we needed to provide briefing data on all commands, problem areas and personalities.

Additionally, we worked with the Air Force, utilizing their C-135 VIP aircraft and abiding by the rules prescribed for the utilization of their crews. It was a good exercise with an extensive detailed work. The "Fear of Failure Factor" always dangled over the planner's desk. If things go wrong on a trip, it usually results from the planner failing to do a good job. Missing one or more contingencies can derail the success formula normally designed by experienced trip planners.

A contingency we could hardly be held responsible for came on the scopes throughout the world while we were en route to Tokyo. The Tonkin Gulf incident flared up, and on arrival in a rainy, dreary Japan, we were besieged by Japanese news personnel. The news flash of the moment was Tonkin Gulf. However, the information provided by the local Navy commanders was sketchy. (History has revealed that at that time, few if any, knew what was transpiring in the Tonkin Gulf.) Secretary Nitze was encouraged to meet with the media reps, and what ensued was ridiculous and onerous for him. Japanese newsmen, who made up the bulk of the group, took time to laboriously phrase their lengthy questions properly. They did so first in Japanese, then were followed by an equally discreet interpreter. During this ordeal, his answers became monotonously "No" more discreetly, "No, I have no comment on that," or as a last resort, "No, we have no information on that." Fifteen minutes of this interaction signaled Secretary Nitze was no longer the story. His visit in the Western Pacific was coincidental to what was going on in the Gulf and in Washington. There were no regrets when I terminated the interview.

After a brief stay in Yokosuka, we made our way to the Seventh Fleet in the South China Sea and the Gulf of Tonkin landing aboard the aircraft carrier USS *Bonhomme Richard*. The "Bonnie Dick" and the USS *Constellation* were involved in the initial air strikes against North Vietnam. Some of them were carried out while we were aboard. The incident developed into a major event—perhaps better described as a tragedy—in U.S. history. Within a few weeks after I reported for duty in Washington, the Vietnam situation had escalated. Eleven years later at the time of my retirement, we were fleeing those Asian premises having lost a war. During those 11 years, I saw the development of this strange conflict from the vantage position of the Secretary's office and later from my own office as CHINFO. I was witness to some sadly "unglorifying" leadership on the part of our government and the waste of more than 58,000 lives of our country's best and finest youngsters. It became a depressing memory.

Back in Washington, the job took on additional concerns. We were now at war, one which almost all naval and military leaders I have known and read about did not want. We had been ingrained with the philosophy of not getting into a land war in Asia. As time went on, we could add that we should not get into a war without our country having the desire to win or wanting to provide the necessary resources.

Leadership demonstration

However, I had the pleasure to observe a fascinating demonstration of leadership, diplomacy and maneuvering. It was a privilege to be on the periphery of this daily saga. The two principals were Capt. Bud Zumwalt and Capt. Isaac "Ike" Campbell Kidd, Jr. Kidd had the position with the Chief of Naval Operations (CNO) equivalent to Bud's with the SECNAV as Executive Assistant and Senior Aide. Ike was the son of Rear Adm. Isaac C. Kidd, who was killed at Pearl Harbor in the battleship USS *Arizona* and was awarded the Medal of Honor. Bud and Ike wielded considerable clout, much more than normally ascribed to captains, and both used the leverage of their bosses judiciously and subtly. It would be fair to say those two executive assistants orchestrated the Navy Department, making it work and hum. Both were conscious of turf and dedicated to protecting their prescribed domains. But they were also devoted to the common objective of contributing to making the right decisions to project and protect the Navy's interests.

Their mental and physical demeanors were completely different. Bud was slender and always in good physical shape. Precise and always concise, he wanted things done yesterday. He sometimes gave you the feeling you were only one of several persons standing in line awaiting his dictates. He was forever impatiently trying to get to the next guy. He did it with dignity, polish and a great deal of intellect.

In the other corner of this macramé ring, Ike was a portly, "old shoe" type. He was just as intelligent and cleaver, but not obviously so. He was often seen huddled with Bud, arm around his shoulder and talking in a low voice. "Well, Bud, old friend, we've got to take a good hard look at this issue and think it through." he would say.

I got to know Ike well and tried to work both camps in the name of "duumviratism." It was a term the Secretary and the CNO used to describe equally shared authority and leadership of the Navy. I tried to keep him apprised of things the Secretary was doing in the area of public affairs. I even attempted to share some of the Secretary's limelight, because it had become evident to me that Nitze was getting far ahead of Admiral McDonald in the image business. We got together occasionally in the SECNAV/CNO staff mess for late lunches. I would be returning from an hour playing racquetball in the Pentagon Officers Athletic Club (POAC), and Ike would just be getting away from his besieged desk. A good deal of our conversation seemed to center on me getting him on the popular TV show, *I've Got a Secret*. Ike's secret was that he was a direct descendant of Captain Kidd, the pirate. I didn't warm to the concept of revealing this heritage (or baggage) of a future Navy leader. He was a strong, deliberate leader with a good sense of humor, and I went along with his quest because I had the feeling he was also a great Kidd(er).

While it is common knowledge that the United States Constitution dictates the military be controlled by civilians, at least in the Navy there is a natural rivalry as to how to conduct daily business. The uniformed side, though respectful, has an innate distrust of the civilian side. The "Feather Merchants" or political appointees, most of whom had no sea experience, lacked the instincts or background knowledge to manage personnel or ships at sea. It was always exasperating and time consuming to explain the basics of procedures, strategies and tactics, but it was a constant necessity. Distrust emanated from concern over the civilians establishing policies that would not work.

The civilian side was equally anxious about the perceived intransigence of the senior uniformed personnel who were thought to be dogmatic, resistant to change and slow to accept suggestions. However, in the aggregate, the system survived and produced teams working together under pressure and coming up with good solutions. Beneath the surface tensions, mutual respect developed as well as the realization that each contingent brought something to the table to benefit the ultimate solutions.

One example from the early days on my SECNAV watch fortified the uniformed group's constant fear that changes would come about without their knowledge or be at the whim of one of the civilian keepers. Reenlistment rates were down, and morale in the fleet was not considered adequate to perform our missions. So everyone in the Navy and Marine Corps was looking for solutions and as usual seeking a panacea to make us well again. An Under Secretary of the Navy had just the solution—get rid of the sailors' bell-bottom trousers and blouse and give them a "real uniform." He didn't coin the phrase, the "Cracker Jack" uniform, but used it extensively. This "solution" was moving along and gaining support when Admiral Dave

McDonald, the CNO, heard about it and became irritated. He was so upset; he raised the issue with Secretary Nitze. McDonald said the sailor's uniform was universally recognized, respected and accepted. For that and many other reasons, any substitute would not meet the unique requirements aboard ship. He argued the research into this matter had no depth. He wanted it put to death immediately, and it was.

Another example that caused great consternation within the Navy was the fabled story of the TFX airplane. Defense Secretary McNamara decided, along with his systems analysis whiz kids, there should be one fighter aircraft universally adaptable to the Air Force, Navy and Marine Corps. It would be more "cost effective," a key phrase in the lexicon of the McNamara team. Naval aviators objected because what the Air Force wanted was too big and too heavy to operate from aircraft carriers. It became a long difficult fight.

Much interest was exhibited on Capital Hill with the ensuing investigations, inquiries, testimony and resulting publicity. The media likes nothing better than a controversy, so they can thrash both sides and pit them against each. They became the conduit, expediter and initiator of inquisitions, barbs and subjective quotations. The Navy rationale finally won, The F-111 became the Air Force fighter/bomber of little success. The Navy's recommended substitute, the F-14, went into service as a successful interceptor with its Phoenix missile system and remained effectively in the active inventory into the next century.

At the encouragement of Bud Zumwalt, Paul Nitze initiated a weekly meeting each Friday. Comprising the session were the Secretaries, CNO, Marine Corps Commandant, Vice Chief of Naval Operation (VCNO) and deputies. Essentially, the Navy Department's leadership was crammed into the SECNAV office where they awaited Nitze's debrief of his weekly meeting with Secretary McNamara. Then in turn, each participant was asked to show and tell the major concerns of his area. It proved to be a successful venture, unifying the leadership and serving as a forum to air complicated problems. Paul Nitze reveled in this medium. He could recite policy, discuss, communicate and be heard! He also listened. No support officers were allowed in the meeting. I was privileged to read a few short hours later the transcripts classified as Top Secret. My interest concerned the important trends. I focused on the direction the Navy Department was going and what specific programs might be approaching that would need the Secretary's attention in the public affairs arena.

Duumvirate leadership

Paul Nitze and Bud Zumwalt espoused the duumvirate leadership philosophy for the Navy. They wanted the SECNAV and CNO both reading from the same page and acting in concert when and wherever possible. In reality, it should have been called a triumvirate because the Commandant of the Marine Corps was always included. The concept made for better harmony, a feeling of teamwork and accomplishment. The smiles and exhibited confidence of the upper level leadership always permeated throughout the entire Navy Department. To a large degree, the success of this style of leadership depended on the personalities of the incumbent leaders. They had to be independently assured of their own position and maintain an understanding and appreciation of the position and responsibilities of the other. They needed to be amenable to discussing and negotiating decisions.

Basically, the SECNAV is responsible for establishing policy, and the CNO and Commandant are charged with the implementation and execution of those policies. Nitze and McDonald evinced one of the better examples of this leadership effort in modern times. Unlike most CNOs, McDonald was open and communicative with Nitze, having a dialogue with him three or four times a day, either face-to-face or by telephone. I recall the pro forma routine Admiral McDonald used stopping by to report or chat with Nitze after his meetings with the Joint Chiefs of Staff. Neither was a grandstander, and each seemed content to get the job done in a harmonious manner. The Secretary had the same relationship with Gen. Walter Greene, the Marine Corps Commandant.

Bud Zumwalt used the duumvirate term and philosophy in talking with the SECNAV staff and others when describing the relationship between his boss and the CNO. In fact, when listening to Bud addressing convocation of Naval District commandants in Washington, I learned of the term for the first time. After struggling with a dictionary, I learned how to spell it, too.

In the normal rotation of senior officers, Bud Zumwalt was getting to the point where he had to go to sea. Because he was an obvious front runner, it would mark him up for a major command. It would be a cruiser because we had no battleships in commission at the time. Word came that BUPERS was ordering Bud to sea as commanding officer of the cruiser USS *Chicago*.

I jumped on that news immediately, offering to get Bud to Chicago for a few days. It would provide the prospective commanding officer of Chicago's namesake ship time to do the rounds with the media and city leaders and end up with a big send-off luncheon or dinner. I knew the people who could stage this type of event. My initial thoughts were to get the Naval Reserve Public Relations Company 9-2 involved as well as my friends, Bob Crown and Morgan Fitch. It was a natural! The idea was not new, but few prospective commanding officers ever got to do it, probably because of the lack of funds or an interested PAO. Over the years, the Navy had tried to establish a close relationship between such a ship and its namesake city. However, there was no program to make it routine.

A new admiral

One day in April of 1965, I was getting ready to present a full plan to Bud about the Chicago visit. There was the usual organized chaos about the office that morning, but something was a little out of character. I couldn't identify it, but I knew that the Flag Section Board List was in the building. I didn't know of any reason to be concerned about it. There would be a few E-Ring captains who would be happy to learn they were on the list. I approached Bud at his desk. He seemed to be having a difficult time in his usual realm of activity. I started the conversation with, "Bud, about taking you to the Windy City. We have to come to grips with some firm dates and when we can make the announcement that you will be in Chicago. As you realize, I can't do this thing right by making last minute arrangements. We have to get down to details."

Bud gave me a sheepish grin looking around nervously. "Looks like we will have to postpone Chicago for a while," he said in a low voice.

Before I could utter a dismayed, "Why?" I realized I had walked into something. The son-of-a-gun was on the list! I stuck out my congratulatory hand. He grabbed it and said, "We can't say anything yet."

Bud thought I knew about his selection and felt I was pulling his leg with my talk about Chicago. He had asked me several times in the past about how I knew of things being held close. I always feigned ignorance saying I couldn't reveal my sources. Most of the time it was just luck or happenstance. But I did develop a knack for putting miscellaneous pieces of data together to reveal the fabric of something being "held close." This time I just let it pass.

Standard procedure was for the list to be delivered to the Secretary for approval and then forwarded to the Secretary of Defense. In turn he would send it to the White House where, when approved by the President, it was released to the public and passed on to the Senate for passage into law. Supposedly, the list was "scrubbed" at all junctures, scrutinizing individuals on the list for possible discrepancies. Within the SECNAV office, the list was held tightly. Only the Secretary, the Executive Assistant and the Legal Assistant saw its contents, with the Legal Assistant initiating the scrubbing.

This was my first experience with the flag list in the Secretary's office. I could see no reason for the Special Assistant for Public Affairs to be privy to its contents. My view on such matters was that I didn't need to know its contents; therefore, I couldn't be held accountable for any leaks. The process took a minimum of two or three weeks and even longer in later years when the "Tailhook" scandals wrought havoc with the selection lists. The time-frame allowed advance planning and contingency thoughts in the event there was an unusual or controversial individual on the list. Naturally, the selection process was serious business and an important part of the Navy's personnel structure at all levels.

Of special significance, the selection list contained the names of a few in-dividuals who were "deep selected" or designated for promotion before their normal time. Deep selections were rare in those days and almost unheard of prior to that. Bud Zumwalt was selected two years before his class would normally come before a selection board in the "Zone for Selection." Navy records revealed that at 43 he was the youngest officer ever promoted to flag rank in the history of the U.S. Navy. And wow, I was there for the landmark event.

That evening, by coincidence, Rear Adm .Bill Mack, Chief of Information, and his wife Ruth were hosting a cocktail party at their home. Of course, invitations were extended and accepted previously by Paul and Phyllis Nitze, Bud and Mouza Zumwalt, Robbie and Trish Robertson, and Zum and I. The men in the group knew of Bud's achievement. To this day, Bud says he did not tell Mousa, but "she suspected something."

The party was a success as evidenced by the noise level. Bud, Robbie and I gravitated to the lower level of the Mack home. We found a niche under a staircase where we gathered to slap Bud's back, laugh and scratch. At some point, Bud said, "Well, when I get to be CNO, Robbie, you are going to be the Judge Advocate General and Bill, you are going to be the Chief of Information." He punctuated the statement by respectively poking each of us in the chest. We laughed at the ludicrous statement. Here was a captain, early selected, not even in an admiral's suit and already predicting he would one day be the CNO. Normally, the CNO was in his late 50s, about five or six years before the maximum retirement age of 62.

After a few more guffaws, I countered Bud with, "Hey, Captain, I can't wait around very long for that to happen. How long do you think it will be before you are knighted as CNO?"

He scrunched up his face, pursed his lips, tilted his head and after a few seconds came out with, "Give me five years." After a few more laughs, we thought we should get serious and find our wives.

Amazingly, it was almost five years to the day when Bud Zumwalt called me from Washington—I was at the Harvard Business School— to say he was nominated by the President to be the Navy's Chief of Naval Operations. Another initial absurdity in his remarks at the party was that there was no provision for a Special Duty Only (Public Affairs) Officer to even be considered for flag rank. No PAO even aspired to reach flag rank because of that limitation. Most PAO captains retired after serving their obligatory time in rank, so they could get into the civilian job market at a mature, but not critical, age. Others served out their 30 years to "retire to the ranch" and obscurity

Rear Admiral Bud Zumwalt's departure to take command of Cruiser Division Seven in San Diego is a good time to end my reflections on my time in the SECNAV office. Though it was only one short year, it was an unusual chapter in my career and life. Professionally, life was good! I gained confidence working at that level, participating in the office and contributing to its effectiveness. Secretary Nitze was being recognized as a tour de force in the Pentagon, at least with the Pentagon press corps, and the Navy was becoming comfortable and confident with his leadership. Strangely, and ancillary to our daily objectives, I began to develop the feeling that Paul Nitze was even liking the job as SECNAV.

On the home front, while I was traveling extensively and spending long hours in the Pentagon, Zum was doing her usual efficient job of keeping things running and holding the family together. Our social life was a little different, but not too demanding. Stevie was in her first year at Marjorie Webster College and doing well academically and socially. It seemed the only time I saw her was arriving or departing in her red Volkswagen. Craig was in his eighth grade year at Cooper Middle School and going through the tough teenage era. I regret I did not get to spend more time with him, but I tried to do so on the weekends. Brian was in the first grade and doing well. Zum had dinner for the boys at six o'clock. By the time I got home at 7:30 or 8:00 p.m., they would be into homework. Zum usually had them return to the table for dessert, and then it was bedtime for Brian. Normally, I was beat when I got home and usually hit the sack by 10:00 p.m., so I could be back at it the next day. Arising at Oh Dark Hundred (about 6:00 a.m.), I could be in the office no later than 7:30. We were happy with our house, the neighborhood, neighbors and location. We were beginning to appreciate the advantages of being in the Washington area. From almost every aspect, it was a plus.

SECNAV OFFICE A-Z
(After Zumwalt)

It would be folly to say that Bud Zumwalt would not be missed. Any stellar performer departure from a key position creates a void. In the year and a half Zumwalt was in SECNAV's front office, he definitely made his mark. His dynamic, focused personality and vitality were central to the functioning pace of the office. Any follow-up change would be abrupt, regardless of the personality, background and potential of the new person taking over that hot seat. However, in Navy life the process moves on. Ships continued to operate in most seas of the world, a half million Navy personnel were completely absorbed in their work, and 300,000 civilian employees were at their tasks. At the time we were involved in a hot war in Vietnam and the long standing Cold War to prevent Communist world domination.

When the remaining staff refocuses to solve the day's problems, the departed are usually soon forgotten. Normally, it was expected there wouldn't be any glitches, a qualified person would quickly fill the vacancy, and the office would continue to function as before. The Executive Assistant (EA) to the SECNAV was one of the top captain jobs in the Navy. It was a wellspring of power and influence on things Navy. Historically, only the best were considered for the position. Mounted on the bulkhead of the EA's small office was an impressive photo gallery of past Executive Assistants to the Secretary. It served as a reminder to visitors and staff alike of the impressive parade of the Navy's top talent who had occupied the job. Of those pictured, only one had not gone on to serve as a flag officer, and that was because of health problems. Several had been fleet commanders at the vice admiral (three-star) level, and some had achieved four-star rank. They all had distinguished careers.

Bud Zumwalt's successor was an exception and an aberration to that procession of outstanding senior officers. He proved that systems dealing with people are not infallible, no matter how foolproof or fail safe they are intended to be. In spite of his clumsy manner of handling people and setting staff objectives, he tried hard to measure up to the job. But he was sent packing within a year in the office. He took out his frustrations on the staff with vindictive, subjective beratings. The tribulations were aptly summed up by Cdr. Harry Train, the Administrative Assistant, who along with me felt much of the heat. "Patience, Bill," Harry advised me. "This too shall pass, and we can count it as a valuable experience." It did pass, and it was indeed a valuable experience.

Moving with the secretary

Serving in the SECNAV office continued to be an exciting adventure. There were always events of national and sometimes international consequence, some good and some bad. New projects surfaced, and new priorities took shape again either perennially or unanticipated. I looked on each day as a challenge and was eager to get to the Pentagon each morning to learn what awaited us. I was seldom denied that prophetic pleasure. Becoming involved in interesting projects that were not reactionary particularly pleased me. As a Navy PAO, it bothered me that most of our time, especially at the Washington level, was expended being reactionary. We were often putting out fires or being on the defensive, instead of planning for events to focus on some positive aspects of the Navy. To be sure, "reacting" properly and with imagination, verve and sometimes panache was commendable. Still there was always a lingering thought about how it would be nice to get out ahead of the eight ball instead of being behind it.

Once after a subject briefing, Secretary Nitze became interested in the Navy's program for deep submergence vehicles to be used for exploring the oceans depths. They would be valuable in searching for sunken ships or submarines, lost missiles or bombs and aircraft lost at sea. To give this project more emphasis and visibility, he participated as the principal speaker at the launching of a deep-sea submersible called the *Aluminaut*, (aptly named because it was made of aluminum). On another occasion, he spoke about humankind's quest for knowledge of "inner space" in addition to outer space.

I liked one of the quotes from a speech he made on Navy Day, October 27, 1965 in Long Beach, California. "The sea is an unnatural environment for man, and it takes something extra for men to live with it," he said. I was with him when he made that speech. Twenty-five years later I had those words included with other famous Navy quotations etched in granite at the Navy Memorial. It captures what the Navy is all about—learning how to use the seas for the benefit of our country and its people. Up to that time, our Navy had done almost all the United States' exploration and research on oceanography. The oceans' depths were being probed during the mid-1960s in a program called *Sea Lab*. Experiments were being carried out with Navy divers actually living in habitats at various depths in the ocean.

Some of our excursions were exotic as well as adventurous. One memorable moment was the rollout of the C2-A *Greyhound*, the Carrier-Onboard-Delivery (COD) aircraft at Grumman's Bethpage assembly plant on Long Island. The *Greyhound* was, and still is, a transport aircraft to move personnel and key logistic items like mail (always important to sailors at sea) between underway or deployed carriers and shore bases. It was the first airplane designed and built as a COD aircraft. Its predecessors were all adaptations of other carrier-qualified aircraft.

Following the traditional ceremonies and speeches for the introduction and unveiling of a new aircraft, Secretary Nitze was offered a ride, the ceremonial "First Flight." In talking with the test pilots, I learned there were only three seats in the aircraft—two for the pilots and a jump seat just aft but between them. If I were to accompany Nitze, I would have literally been a straphanger. That wasn't appealing to me nor encouraged by the pilots. Nitze agreed to the ride, but I was skeptical. I told him it wasn't necessary nor a part of the scripted ceremony. However, the Secretary, always the adventurer, cheerfully said, "Let's go!" With some fanfare the aircraft took off. I watched it circle the field a couple of times and land safely. Mission accomplished! We were informed that the aircraft flew again the next day but crashed killing the two test pilots.

Aviation was a major Navy asset. Both the hardware and personnel naturally were in the forefront of tactics, strategy, planning and budgeting. One area that caught Nitze's interest was the need for a replacement for the AD

Sky Raider, a propeller-driven dive bomber that came along immediately after World War II. It was the fleet's mainstay for several decades as a heavy lift, reliable airplane. It performed well in the Korean War but was becoming "long in the tooth" (obsolescent) when the Vietnam War began. Further, the Air Force lacked an aircraft to fulfill troop support and flak suppression missions. It was also employing the AD *Sky Raider.*

To develop a new aircraft would take five to 10 years and be costly. Nitze became intrigued by a proposal from Pat Parker, a civilian with the Naval Air Systems Command, that literally chopped about four feet off the fuselage of the F-8 *Crusader*, a fighter aircraft, and would expeditiously fill the attack airplane void. Nitze picked up on the idea, started asking questions and instigated further study and development of the concept. When it was determined to be feasible, Nitze personally moved the project through the Defense Department and got it funded.

Within the confines of the Secretariat, the new A-7 *Corsair II* became Paul Nitze's airplane, although the naval aviation community usually had vested interests in its manifestations. He was especially pleased and obviously proud to participate in the rollout ceremonies of the aircraft at the Chance-Vought plant in Dallas. (The Secretary was not aboard the A-7's "First Flight.") Albeit a stopgap project, the A-7 went on to be a successful attack bomber for the next 10 to 15 years. The Air Force had several squadrons of A-7s operating in Vietnam.

Another project the Secretary developed started out with Lt. Cdr. Charles Di Bona in the Under Secretary's office. The concept involved building or buying large cargo or tanker ships and properly adapting them as storage facilities for emergency deployments. They were to be fully mobile, ready to be deployed in war zones and capable of cruising to ports to unload their assorted cargos of tanks, trucks, guns, ammunition and sundry supplies and stores,. The concept was called the Forward Deployed Logistics Ship (FDLS). The idea was applauded but not funded. However, it proved to be the precursor for the successful and large Afloat Pre-Positioning Ship Program started in the early 1980s and deployed in the 1990 Gulf War and the War on Terror in Afghanistan and Iraq.

Another program, also initiated by Charlie Di Bona, was to insist on

modernizing American shipyards building Navy ships and their incorpora-
tion of modularized construction processes. Some foreign ship builders were
already constructing commercial ships that way, and there were obvious benefits for the U.S. Navy's ship construction programs. Modular construction
held the dual promise of reducing building time and cost savings. Basically,
it involved simultaneously constructing ship sections (modules) in different
parts of the shipyard. When the separate sections were ready, they were
welded into place.

This project became a major endeavor for Secretary Nitze, and he
devoted considerable energies to it. We visited several foreign shipyards
to learn about their progress with modular construction. He enlisted
the assistance of Senator John Stennis of Mississippi, a member of the
Appropriations and Armed Forces committees (Stennis later chaired the
Armed Forces Committee.) This liaison resulted in a new, modern shipyard
built in Pascagoula, Mississippi and owned by Litton Industries. That yard
has been building warships for the Navy ever since and features modular
construction. To be competitive, other U.S. ship builders adopted modular
construction and modernized their yards.

Nitze had an innate quality of effective leadership. He was skilled at
focusing his attention and that of others and directing resources to solve
problems. He never put himself in the position of brandishing a saber and
calling out, "Follow me, boys!" He was more subtle and considerate of those
working with him, especially if he was getting onto their turf or areas of
responsibility. He brought with him to the SECNAV position his keen interest in submarine warfare knowing how effective it was for the Germans
in both world wars, particularly World War II. For a while Germany essentially controlled the Atlantic Ocean with only about 50 to 60 U-Boats.
A determined effort on the part of the Allied Forces—the U.S. and Great
Britain—in the arena of Anti-Submarine Warfare (ASW) quelled the Nazis'
devastating U-Boat threat and made it almost totally ineffective in the latter
part of the war.

He felt a major, continuing effort in anti-submarine warfare was needed
and should include forces operating above, on and below the seas. The Soviet
Navy obtained several German submarines, as did the United States, at the

end of World War II hostilities. From that acquisition sprung concentrated, major programs in submarine development. An attentive U.S. Navy reacted by planning countermeasures and forces. Secretary Nitze discussed the situation with the CNO, Admiral McDonald, and they decided to focus more of their energies in that area.

They developed a consortium of Navy flag officers and civilian technicians along with industry representatives involved with anti-submarine warfare. There was a constant flow of information with a major focus on periodic presentations attended by the consortium members. All were cleared for Top Secret work. This initiative helped to develop a phenomenally successful deterrent to the potent Soviet submarine threat. It involved significantly better facilities, improved equipment, specialized training for aviation, surface, subsurface personnel and task forces and even utilized satellites. Several people working with ASW told me, "By the end of the Cold War, we knew where all of their submarines were most of the time." I am also advised that similar programs involving industry continue to be utilized.

New Marine Aide

The Marine Aide, Col. Douglas "Doug" Haberle, was replaced by Col. Ross Dryer. He was an imposing character, over six feet tall, in good physical shape but without any hair on his head. The first time I saw him, I thought, "My God! It's Mr. Clean!" (a contemporary TV commercial character with no hair to interrupt the sun's radiation). Ross had long ago accepted the designation, "Mr. Clean" with a shoulder shrug and a so-be-it, quizzical grin. He was a stereotypical Marine—serious, dedicated, rather rigid in decorum and thought and always referring to superiors in the third person. He also was very thorough, precise and well organized. After my first trip with him, I surmised, "Gad, this guy rehearses everything, including reveille each morning." I realized he was a class guy, and we were lucky to have him on our side. He was fun to work with, and I learned from him. I would have followed him anywhere.

One evening at a naval social event at the Decatur House, a block away from the White House, Ross was in his full Marine Corps formal regalia, including the resplendent red and blue Marine Corps cape. I was wearing my relatively conservative Navy formal wear. As we were leaving, he flung his cape around with a flourish to properly align it on his back. He looked around expecting approval of the maneuver. I said, "OK, Zorro, where bound?" I was forever endeared to Mrs. Nitze, who was rather impatient with military protocol and circumstance, and with Paul Nitze himself, who was always intrigued with the byplay among naval professionals. Even Ross could never be accused of being thin skinned, acceding graciously to the barb from a junior. But I knew within the next few days a harpoon would be coming my way.

Capt. Worth Bagley was next to take on the SECNAV EA responsibilities. He was a favorite of Bud Zumwalt and the brother of Dave Bagley who had been the EA to the Under Secretary and an academy classmate of Bud's. Worth was a surface warfare officer, as was Dave, but they seemed opposite in personality. Dave at least gave the impression of being a convivial extrovert. Worth was quiet, reserved, serious and enjoyed deep strategic discussions. Worth fit in well with Secretary Nitze, and we seemed to be back on track as a team and productive office. The Bagley boys were close brothers, referred to humorously as "Worth" and "Worthless." When confronted with that moniker, it usually brought guffaws from Dave followed by a joke or anecdote and more laughs. Both Bagleys rose to the rank of four-star admirals.

The Bagleys had an interesting background. Their father had been a three-star flag officer, and an uncle was Ens. Worth Bagley who was the only U.S. naval officer killed in the Spanish American War. The Bagleys were also related to the North Carolina Daniels family who comprised a journalistic dynasty. They controlled the Raleigh, North Carolina newspapers, and Josephus Daniels was the Secretary of the Navy (1913-21) and Ambassador to Mexico (1933-42). Worth had the burning ambition to be a journalist, but such a vocation became a "back burner" while he pursued the career of a naval officer.

After about a year in the job, my secretary, assistant and loyal compatriot, Chief Campbell decided to retire. It became a chore to find someone to replace her. The requisites for the position were the ability to keep me organized and pointed in the right direction, excellent typist skills and an outstanding telephone demeanor. I called Lois Merkel at the Ninth Naval District Public Affairs Office to inquire if she would be interested in making a break from living in Gurnee, Illinois for 30 years and come to her nation's capital. After a few conversations, Lois was successfully recruited to move to Washington to work for me again. She was a great fit in our office and had the patience to put up with my propensity of keeping too many different things going at one time. I relied on her extensively. She became a significant contributor to the success of our public affairs efforts and was also an immediate plus for the SECNAV office. In later years she was a renowned and recognized able assistant to my successors. When she retired, it was said, "Bill Thompson's greatest claim to fame was to encourage Lois to move to Washington."

CHINFO conceived the idea of having branch offices in various major cities, and Capt. Pickett Lumpkin asked for my assistance to sell the idea to the Secretary. I had experienced the success of a branch office in Chicago, which I established at COMNINE, and I had done extensive work with the CHINFO branch office in Hollywood. Although it wasn't a new concept, I was convinced it could be valuable. The barb was that along with getting the idea approved, it would take money to establish and operate the offices. Additional funding was always difficult to acquire. However, Nitze bought off on the idea, and money was made available to open the first office in New York.

The Assistant Secretary of Defense for Public Affairs, Arthur Sylvester, didn't like the concept. He and he and his deputy, Philip Goulding, called on Secretary Nitze to protest. Nitze sent for me and said I had to defend the case. It was an impromptu presentation that didn't impress Sylvester and Goulding, but Nitze backed me, and the program went forward. I was surprised because I didn't think that Nitze was particularly impressed with the concept. He wasn't against it, but I felt he had no enthusiasm for it. I learned he was a strong proponent of backing his people, so he supported me and CHINFO in the matter. The New York office was opened and exists today some 35 years later. When I became CHINFO, we enlarged the program to include Atlanta, Dallas, Boston and San Francisco. All those offices have been closed for various reasons.

In the meantime back at the Thompson household, Zum continued in charge, but no one ever imagined that would not be the case. She was her bouncy, energetic, perpetual motion self and the children were maturing much faster than we would have ever imagined. We were all on a fast track, but mine was in the office. I didn't get to share much of the day-to-day family experiences, but I tried to make up for it on weekends when I wasn't traveling.

Stevie was enjoying college at Marjorie Webster and doing well grade-wise. Her college hang out was the 1789 Restaurant in Washington. I learned later it was a place where singles got together, or at least where the young ladies put themselves on display to the lecherous eyes of Washington's young Lochinvars and Romeos.

Craig was in high school and suffering from the usual teen problems young fellas have. He was a little behind in physical development keeping him out of football. I didn't concern myself with it because I had seen too many incidents of injuries to kids not ready for contact sports. He tried wrestling for a while and learned much about being a grappler. I saw a good pair of hands on Craig. He could catch a football. He wasn't especially fast but not slow, and given another year he might have developed into a wide receiver. When he went on to college, he grew another three inches and bulked up to good size, comfortably carrying over 200 pounds on his 6-2 frame.

Brian had an experience that undoubtedly happens to many youngsters. His eyesight was poor. It was unknown to us and wasn't discovered until a doctor put an eye chart in front of him. Eyeglasses changed his life. He could see things in their unblurred, proper perspective. We wished the condition could have been discovered earlier. Maybe that was why he kept getting lost at Great Lakes, and we had continual Brian Alerts!

Our Family's First Wedding

About this time, Stevie was becoming a little more sophisticated. She demanded that her name, which she liked, should be spelled S-T-E-V-I-I. That was easy, no argument. Being a myopic father, I always thought Stevii was the most beautiful, brilliant child ever to grace this earth. I knew the natural progression was that some day another man would replace me in her life. So I tried to help along the process by scheduling her for "Tea Dances" at the Naval Academy.

There she could meet a Midshipman who would at least become the Chief of Naval Operations. Of course, it was preferable for him to be the starting quarterback or wide receiver on the football team. Or perhaps he would shine as one of the Naval Academy's greats on the track and field team. My applied psychology didn't work, and those Mids who did show an interest, I crossed off the list, but of course with deference to Stevii, who seemed to agree. In one of our talks, she shared she could never marry a civilian because, "They stay in the same place all the time, and I am used to moving every two or three years," she said. I felt pretty secure in her philosophic expression.

Stevii had a pal at Marjorie Webster named Marilyn Wiltshire. They commuted to school together and spent extended time in each other's company studying, cramming for tests, jabbering and visiting the 1789 Restaurant. Stevii got to know Marilyn's family, and for several months she was the evening companion for Marilyn's grandmother, "Ma Ball." The lady lived in the oldest house in Arlington, called "The Glebe." Stevii stayed at The Glebe many nights providing security and companionship for Ma Ball. The Ball family members were early settlers in Arlington. Mrs. Ball's husband was a prominent lawyer and would be politician, who served one term in the Virginia State Assembly. At one time he was a candidate for the U.S. Senate from Virginia.

In the early summer of 1966 Stevii had Marilyn's cousin as a suitor. He showed up occasionally at our domain driving a 1964 Corvette. He lived in Virginia Beach and was employed with the National Aviation and Space Agency (NASA) at Langley Air Force Base near Hampton, Virginia. I didn't pay much attention to him because he was sort of nerdy looking, skinny and probably couldn't play linebacker for a kiddy league football team. However, I thought his Corvette was impressive, especially parked in front of our house. It was equally impressive alongside my 1965 Ford Mustang, one of the originals but very basic. The best thing to say about my Mustang was that it was bright red. However, not to be outdone by this fellow, who had been impressed upon me by Stevii, I referred to him as the "Chevrolet Driver."

On the Fourth of July 1966, we were preparing for a family gathering with brother Don and family and a few others. It was a good old Wisconsin Fourth of July celebration with beer, hot dogs, beer, bratwurst, beer, potato salad, beer, hamburgers and more beer. I was busying myself in our utility room getting things arranged and ready for the festivities. Randy, as I had recently learned was the name of the driver of the Chevrolet, had arrived rather early. He and Stevii were going to do their own thing—watch the fireworks from the Mall or something different than a mundane family affair. At about 0830 or 0900 (early in the morning), Randy came into the utility room. It was soon obvious there wasn't room for the two of us, especially with me working and him standing around with his hands in his pockets. I finally said as diplomatically as I could, "Hey Randy, have you had breakfast yet? If not, why don't you go up to the kitchen where Dorothy or Stevii will be glad to feed you?"

Randy's rather impetuous response was, "Thank you, Commander, I have had breakfast, but I have an important question to ask of you." I whirled around, looking wide-eyed at this interloper. The bottom had just fallen out of my world, and he was in charge. I knew what he was going to ask, but I couldn't believe it! He followed saying, "Stevii and I want to get married, and I want to ask your permission."

"Well, have you talked with Stevii about this?" I defenselessly blurted out,

"Oh, yes!" he eagerly replied.

"Well, er, Randy, that's your name, isn't it?" I asked. "I hope you have thought about this. You know, Stevii is strong willed and has an independent mind. I have always thought she would be hard to get along with."

I realized I had no chance of turning this thing around and knew it was a setup from the beginning. Why didn't she at least give me a hint about this romance, so I could have been better prepared? Despite any mental scrambling I could do, it was a lost cause. So I gathered myself up in the best available Commander, U.S. Navy presentation stance and stated perfunctorily, "Well, it looks like you two have decided this is what you want to do with your lives. So I guess we should go talk with Stevii's mother."

I felt I had not handled this situation well and sensed my last statement was a weak, ungenerous thing to say. I realized I was being rather unkind to my future son-in-law as I ushered him into the rec room to meet a grinning Dorothy and Stevii. "They want to get married," I said.

Zum smiled, approvingly, and said, "That's nice. When?" while thinking perhaps about near Christmas or Easter of next year.

"August 20th," Stevii said assuredly. "Randy starts grad school at VPI on the first of September, and we want a short honeymoon before settling in at Blacksburg."

Zum dropped a load! All circuits went out!

"I can't do a wedding in just six weeks," she strongly retorted. "Don't you realized what all has to be done?"

We then simultaneously concluded we weren't getting this twosome off to a good start. So we shrugged, gave our blessings and welcomed Randy into the family. They seemed triumphant and departed saying they had to "Go tell Ma Ball!" As they zoomed off in the Chevrolet, I put an arm around Zum and said, "Are you ready for the rest of this Fourth of July—fireworks and all that kind of stuff? Incidentally, what's his last name?"

Zum kept busy around the house for the next six weeks with wedding planning and associated things. Dresses had to be made, and naturally, Zum did all the sewing. Locations were selected for the wedding and the reception. The invitations were selected and ordered along with another list for the rehearsal dinner. It was all a piece of (wedding) cake, and I was going off to the office anyway. In crisis situations like a wedding, not everything went according to plan or at least not in our domain. The invitations did not arrive on time, so Zum got us together, and we made copies of the invitation with a note that the desired ones had not arrived from the printer as promised. Still we got an invitation of sorts in the mail on schedule.

My friend Rear Adm. Jim Kelly, former Chief of Navy Chaplains, who had retired and lived in southern Virginia, conducted the wedding. It was done at one of our favorite sites, the Navy Chapel on Nebraska Avenue in the District of Columbia. It was a part of the Navy Security Agency complex. Our reception was held at the Officers Club at the National Naval Medical Center in Bethesda, Maryland. Craig and Brian participated. Craig borrowed tuxedo trousers, but forgot to tell Zum they were a few sizes too large in the waist until they were at the church. Safety pins saved the day, and nobody noticed his fly was unzipped for the entire ceremony. After a nice reception, we again witnessed the bride and groom roaring off in the Chevrolet, this time to Nova Scotia for their honeymoon.

Together they did one year at VPI. It concluded with Randy getting his master's degree in mechanical engineering. They then returned to NASA at Langley where he was successful in some of the space program projects including working on the heat shielding tiles for the Apollo capsule and later the Space Shuttle. He was easily assimilated into the family and became a good husband, father and son-in-law.

At the time of the wedding, I had been selected for promotion to captain but didn't officially add the stripe until a ceremony in Secretary Nitze's office later in the fall. To go along with my seniority, Zum convinced me to let my hair grow and stop trying to look like a high school football coach. I had been content with a crew cut since college. It was easy to care for, and it wasn't necessary to carry a comb. One thing about having longer hair was the ease to detect the graying on the roof. It was suggested I should try some Grecian Formula, popular on the market, to restore hair to its original color. I was given the remains of a bottle for trial but quit after the first application and an exclamation by Christine Coon, Harry Train's assistant of, "My God! Your hair is turning green!" I cast aside the remains of the Grecian Formula and let nature take its course. Everyone on my mother's side of the family was prematurely gray, and I was no exception.

More on the War in Vietnam

The war in Vietnam was taking on larger proportions. Secretary McNamara continued adding additional numbers of forces and inventing ways to fight a war. His concept of "body count" of enemy killed as a quantitative measure of success proved to be a fallacy. It provoked an unreal aspect of the war. Commanders at all levels were exaggerating body counts to protect their positions and logistic support. The fighting was driven by the Pentagon and being run by the Joint Chiefs of Staff controlling targeting, movements and support much to the consternation of the field commanders.

The morning news briefs in the Pentagon were like the "5 O' Clock Follies." These daily news conferences in Saigon were supposedly the hot scoop from the field for the news personnel who were accredited to the United States Military Advisory Command, Vietnam (USMACV). Additionally, President Johnson refused to "fish or cut bait." He wanted to have "butter" as well as "bullets" and refused to mobilize reserve units of the various services. Such a mobilization would have placed too much emphasis on the war in Southeast Asia and would have interfered with his "Great Society" crusade he wanted to be his legacy. The decision contributed directly to inflation and an economic crisis for the country. There was also severe racial unrest, and anti-Vietnam War demonstrations proliferated. Everything together brought President Johnson to the realization he could not win reelection in 1968, and he dropped out of politics to retire to his ranch in Texas. He died on January 22, 1973, just five days before the conclusion of the treaty marking the withdrawal of U.S. troops from Vietnam.

I accompanied three Secretaries of the Navy on inspection tours of the war in Vietnam each year since it had started. I wish I had kept a journal of those visits as well as noting the progress of the war as it developed in the Pentagon. It might have provided the background for a different approach to a Vietnam War manuscript unlike the multitude published and continually showing up in the bookstores. But that is hindsight. I had reaffirmed a strong feeling that it was futile to be in a land war in Vietnam. But it was a war U.S. forces could have won, if the politicians had not intervened. Additionally, the U.S. media turned the American public against the war. The media had lost confidence in the war and particularly in the way the Pentagon's conduct of the war was being deceitfully presented to them. The military establishment and the U.S. government lost considerable credibility which it has not recovered. It widened the abyss of distrust between the government and the Fourth Estate.

One of the many sobering effects of the war, even in our Ivory Towered bunkers in the Pentagon, was the too frequent, Medal of Honor posthumous presentations in the Secretary's office. It usually involved parents and siblings of the honoree, but at other times a widow and children were assembled for the presentation of our nation's highest military award. Most were "down home folks." They were often a little awed by the attention, hospitality and gratitude that were demonstrated. They appreciated what was being done for them and what was being said in remarks by the Chief of Naval Operations, Commandant of the Marine Corps or the Secretary. They held dear the brief, concise words describing the bravery, courage, heroics and sacrifice written in the citation accompanying the award. It was evident the ultimate sacrifice was not only made by the honoree, but shared by the survivors.

Another series of incidents in the Secretariat brought the war painfully closer. A succession of three Marine Corps Aides to the Under Secretary departed the office to personally fight in Vietnam. The first, Col. Bill Smith, was badly wounded but survived. Next was Lt. Colonel Bill Leftwich who was killed, and then Lt. Colonel Mike Sparks, also killed in action in Vietnam. They were real troopers and outstanding Marine officers with whom we had worked side-by-side through the years. All had families. It was said Bill Leftwich had "Commandant" written all over him, meaning he was destined for high rank in the Marine Corps. A destroyer was named in his honor.

One of the first items I researched in the message traffic each morning was the casualty list. One Saturday morning I learned that Cdr. Jim LaHaye had been shot down over Vietnam and was presumed killed. Jim was a high school classmate, and we were at Oshkosh together before he left to enter the Naval Academy. We were also shipmates in *Midway*. Another casualty that brought the war closer was Lt. Cdr. Dick Rich who had lived one door away from us in McLean. We had partied together, and our kids were friends. Dick was assigned to the BUPERS as an aviation officer detailer and gave me his commuting car, a mid-fifties Buick Roadmaster "Four-Holer," nicknamed for the four cosmetic portholes on each side of the hood. Dick was flying F-8 *Crusader* fighters and was listed as Missing in Action (MIA), but his wing mates said they were certain he was Killed In Action (KIA). Later, his widow Susie married a future business associate whom I worked with on some Navy Memorial tasks.

Cruisin' with Bud Zumwalt

Bud Zumwalt had gone to his first flag billet, Commander, Cruiser Destroyer Flotilla Seven, home ported in San Diego. The task awaiting him was typical of the "Old Navy." The word was out in the Pacific Fleet contingent on the West Coast to closely scrutinize this young deep-selectee Zumwalt. His being selected for flag rank two years early had caused many eyebrows to be raised, especially with the old timers who were awaiting their time for selection. Early selection was not a part of the main menu in those days. Vice Adm. Lawson P. "Red" Ramage, a Medal of Honor submariner and Commander First Fleet in San Diego, was a member of the Army Navy Country Club in Arlington, Virginia. In retirement, we played golf together, and he once related, "We were ready for Zumwalt and were waiting for him to make his first mistake, so we could teach him a few things. I must say, as his boss, he was good, damn good. Everything we piled on him, he made look easy. He usually came up with ways to do it easier and better.

"Communications has always been a problem in fleet operations. We had an exercise featuring that (communications), and I put him in charge. The exercise was done so well, and the results were so good and revealing, that I sent him back to Washington to brief the rest of the Navy on how it should be done. I was convinced. He was a winner!"

Bud was gone from Washington for only a year when the CNO, Admiral Dave McDonald, with Paul Nitze's urging, opened a new Division of Systems Analysis within the Naval Operations (OPNAV) staff devised to keep up with Secretary McNamara's whiz kids. He assigned Bud Zumwalt to head this new office. Bud's first job was to put the F-111B in proper systems analysis language to convince McNamara the airplane was too heavy for carrier aviation and wouldn't be effective as a Navy fighter/interceptor.

Even though the new System Analysis office was structured on paper, it was not staffed when Zumwalt arrived. He was it. He prevailed upon Admiral McDonald and Secretary Nitze for help, so he could meet their deadline of six weeks to finalize the F-111B study. One naval officer he wanted was Lt. Cdr. Charles DiBona in Under Secretary Robert H.B. "Bob" Baldwin's office. DiBona was involved in many projects for Baldwin, and the chances of getting him were slim. However, with loud protestations Baldwin agreed with Nitze to release his star player to join Bud as the nucleus of the new office and the F-111B study.

Bud gathered others into his fold and within three weeks made a presentation of their interim findings. Charlie DiBona accompanied Rear Adm. Zumwalt who made the presentation. At the conclusion, DiBona piped up with the comment the admiral had forgotten to mention one fact and proceeded to relate the forgotten fact. When they retired to their Pentagon office, DiBona asked, "How do you think it went?"

"I think it went well, Charlie, and it was well received," Bud replied. "But, Charlie, next time, instead of saying I screwed up, why don't you just say something like, 'in addition to what the Admiral said, I would like to add ...'." They teased each other about that incident for many years.

On a Saturday morning the study was finalized, and a jubilant Bud Zumwalt searched out the new CNO, Adm. Tom Moorer. He found him at the Army Navy Country Club diligently working at one of his passions, the game of golf. Moorer was in the process of relieving his host, Rear Adm. Jerry Miller, of a few leafs from his wallet. Bud had commandeered a golf cart to intercept the foursome they were playing in. He hastily explained the study had been completed, citing high ratings for the AUG 9 (radar) and AIM 51 (missile) systems but said the aircraft, the F-111B, could not operate from a carrier. Admiral Moorer caught the significance of the conclusion. But Miller, an aviator involved in the controversial F-111B, beat the turf with his driver, said the conclusion was too subtle and the bird should be killed ... dead.

The study praised the F-111B because of its effective AUG 9 and AIM 51 systems. The AUG 9 radar was unique being able to simultaneously track 24 targets and attack six while continuing to scan the airspace. The "Phoenix" or AIM 51 missile could be deployed out to 100 miles. However, the airplane could not operate on an aircraft carrier because it was too heavy. Eventually, the CNO, Secretary of the Navy Paul Ignatius (who later replaced Paul Nitze) and the DOD Systems Analysis group all bought the idea. Nitze, then Deputy Secretary of Defense, convinced McNamara the F-111B was not suitable for the Navy.

The Grumman Aircraft Company, a co-producer of the F-111B and a major manufacturer of naval aircraft, had the right response. They thought the weapon systems could be integrated into an aircraft that would encompass many of the F-111B attributes and could include additional adaptations such as variable swept wings to make it lighter and aircraft carrier operational. The Grumman built F-14 incorporating those features became a mainstay of fleet aviation for more than 30 years and into the 21st Century.

To close out the F-111B saga in the Division of Systems Analysis, the naval aviators in the staff presented their boss with a plaque inscribed:

To Rear Admiral E. R. Zumwalt, Jr., USN
Naval ACE
Credited with shooting down 270 F-111B aircraft.

Once again Bud Zumwalt was riding high. He had impressively established Navy's Systems Analysis and ensured its prominence in the decision making process. Perhaps to cool him off, he was nominated to go to Vietnam to relieve Rear Adm. Kenneth Veth as Commander, Naval Forces Vietnam. When Secretary Ignatius was presented that slate of Flag Officer movements, he insisted the job be bumped up to three stars, and off Bud went to fight the war in Southeast Asia. There, he again did an exceptional job, clearing out the Mekong River Delta, interdicting troop and supply movement from North to South Vietnam and utilizing riverine warfare assets—Brown Water Navy—like never before in history.

When Secretary of Defense Melvin Laird went to Vietnam to talk about a Vietnamization program (turning over assets and responsibility to the South Vietnamese), Zumwalt was prepared with his already implemented Accelerated Turn Over to Vietnam (ACTOV) plan. Laird was impressed. The same story had repeated itself. Bud Zumwalt's innate charisma, backed by professionalism and hard work, brought him to the fore. However, he was still a team player, this time under the leadership of Gen. Creighton Abrams, Commander US Military Assistance Group, Vietnam. Abrams let it be known that for the first time, the U.S. Navy had contributed to the war in-country. When Admiral Tom Moorer, the CNO, visited Saigon, he asked General Abrams how Zumwalt was doing.

"He's doing such a great job," Abrams replied with a chuckle. "I think he must want my job."

"That's good," Moorer responded with a smile. "I thought he wanted mine."

Bud had asked me to go to Vietnam with him as his PAO. After considerable thought, I graciously declined for several reasons. First, there wasn't a billet in his staff for a captain PAO (although it wouldn't have been a big deal to change it). After the normal, one-year tour in Vietnam, I would be coming home to retire from naval service. To start looking for a another job after having been out of circulation for 12 months would have made job hunting more difficult. In addition, I was comfortable in my job with Secretary Nitze and had agreed to stay on active duty to work for Secretary Ignatius.

It would have been exciting to work for Bud in a war situation. I was confident he would bring new zest, enthusiasm and ideas to the effort. However, I was nearing the end of my naval career, while his was continuing to climb, in fact, just getting into "boost" phase. Also, Zum reminded me that as a PAO, I had spent more than my share of time away from home. Bud accepted my apologies and decision but made me promise that before I "did any more stupid things like retiring," he was to be consulted.

Speech Writing for SECNAV

Within the SECNAV staff there was a billet for a civilian speechwriter. When I arrived, it was occupied by Dave Clinger, a young lawyer who aspired to a career in foreign affairs. Being ideally allied with Paul Nitze, who had been integral to U.S. foreign affairs since World War II, wasn't at all shabby. Dave moved on after a year and enjoyed a successful career in the environs of the State Department. He was replaced by a contemporary and friend of Paul Nitze, Edward Hidalgo, a lawyer who was returning to the United States from a successful law career in Mexico City. He thought he would be taking on major legal responsibilities but ended up being the replacement for

Dave Clinger as speechwriter. As a youngster—a lieutenant—near the end of World War II, Hidalgo was an aide or assistant to James Forrestal, the Secretary of the Navy.

His return to the Navy secretariat was not ingratiating. He had sought employment from his old acquaintance Paul Nitze, who acquiesced and thought Hidalgo could be used somewhere in the office. For Hidalgo, being a speechwriter was beneath him. His office was a 9 x 9 cubbyhole adjacent to mine. I sympathized with him and was impressed with his background, at least from his description. I offered as to how his being the speechwriter was a "foot in the door." He could work into another position as the powers-that-be got to know him and became cognizant of his potential. He feigned graciousness at my suggestion. As I got to know him better, I realized he was a proud, self-serving fellow, who wanted immediate, not eventual, status and position upon his return to Washington. After all he had been a professional and social success in Mexico City as a powerful, influential and wealthy lawyer.

Complicating the picture was the fact he couldn't write, at least not speeches. His law practice had taken him far from the skills of communicating with an audience. Another problem was that Nitze was reluctant to see him or spend time with him relative to the Secretary's forthcoming speeches. I was told Nitze did not hold much respect or admiration for his "old friend." I didn't push the subject and dealt with the situation on a prima facie basis.

In reality, I became involved in writing the Secretary's speeches, ghost-writing for Hidalgo. Speech writing was something I had vowed not to do. I didn't mind being involved in planning, scheduling, selecting subject matter and accompanying the speaker to do the public relations chores. But I did not want to write the speeches. It is a grinding, time consuming, laborious task. And it would take me away from fulfilling my assigned job. Fortunately, Ed Hidalgo did not last long in the secretariat. He succeeded in taking on a few tasks for the Under Secretary, came to see he was not needed and then departed for Paris to do legal work. I have facetiously said Hidalgo worked for me as the speechwriter. What makes it even more outrageous, if not ironic, is that about 15 years later, Ed Hidalgo became the Secretary of the Navy.

He was replaced as speechwriter by another lawyer, this time the bright, young John Rhinehart. He was impatient to progress rapidly in the fast moving Washington milieu to things other than being a speechwriter for a sub-cabinet member. He was successful in taking on other responsibilities for the Under Secretary, Bob Baldwin, and undertook some tasks involved in the workings of the Navy Department. But at the same time, he filled the needs of being Nitze's speechwriter. Rhinehart moved on to have a successful career as a lawyer and government bureaucrat. He alternated tours of duty with the government and affiliation with a law firm, usually doing business with the government.

His career path was common in Washington and provides some fiber and strength to the function of our democratic process. Most Washingtonian workers are bright, talented people with a dedication to making government perform, but usually from the perspective of the Republican or Democratic Party. When their political affiliation goes dormant or is voted out of office, often those individuals are hired by a law or consulting firm at healthy salaries. Frequently those earnings are recouped by fees from clients the new hire brings into the firm's fold. They regularly become lobbyists and perform an important function in the governmental process, bringing experience and background to whatever side of an issue they represent. A few years in that endeavor makes it possible for them to return to government at a lower pay scale. Government, although not a good source of income, provides more latitude of issues and participation in a diversity of projects and programs. Rhinehart was a classic example of character in federal government. He justified the respect I developed for him during his short tenure in the SECNAV office.

Enter the Executive Ensign

The next speechwriter was Craig Whitney, one of the most delightful individuals I encountered during my naval career. After Craig graduated from Harvard, he spent a year on a fellowship working as an intern with James R. Reston, the well-known columnist based in Washington for *The New York Times*. After his one-year position terminated, Reston brokered his protégé' to help him find gainful employment. Reston's next door neighbor was Paul Nitze. With Scotty Reston's encouragement, Nitze thought Craig could be a reasonable speechwriter and a good addition to the office.

Craig was to be hired as a GS-7 mid-level Civil Servant. However, Uncle Sam's Selective Service Commission (draft board) had other thoughts. Craig's number was up! Not to be outdone, arrangements were made to take Craig into the Navy Officer Candidate program at Newport. Thereafter, Ens. Whitney was ordered to duty in the Secretary of the Navy's office. He overlapped with Rhinehart a couple months but emerged as the speechwriter. Craig was a rarity in Washington because the ensign contingency of the U.S. Navy officer corps had little visibility in Washington. Naturally, ensigns were supposed to be at sea in ships, learning port from starboard and bow from stern. It has been said there were more admirals in Washington than ensigns, and that was probably a truism.

I was put in charge of "The Ensign," and it became a delightful task. Tall, blonde, bright, articulate and somewhat precocious, Craig possessed a strong, subtle character and easily exhibited a sort of bashful smile. He liked to laugh and was genuinely modest. We got along well together. One nice thing was that he handled the speechwriting in a superb manner and had no problem gaining an audience with the "Boss." Nitze liked him and enjoyed discussing subject matter for forthcoming speeches. Of course, politics and international affairs always seemed to creep into the conversations. Young Craig was able to hold his own with the old master and could keep a discussion going with good questions or provocative assertions that would move the Secretary to the front edge of his chair. Nitze enjoyed the process and thought Craig was a great find. Additionally, he and Mrs. Nitze thought Craig would be a great match for their youngest daughter Nina. That combination was given ample opportunity to flourish, but nothing became of it.

Naval officers normally don't need formal courses in assertiveness, but not many would voluntarily engage Paul Nitze in a discussion on foreign affairs, even if they had the opportunity to do so. Craig's relationship with Nitze was amazing and amusing to most of us in the office. Word soon passed along the E-Ring that there was "an Ivy League ensign who was arguing foreign affairs with the Secretary." One day Adm. Bernard A. "Chick" Clarey, the Vice Chief of Naval Operations, stopped me in the corridor. "Bill, I understand you have an ensign from some Ivy League school who is doing some writing for the Secretary and persists in arguing foreign affairs with him, sometimes getting him upset," he said. "Is this true? And should we (meaning me) counsel the kid about whom Paul Nitze is? We don't want the kid to embarrass the Navy, and we don't want the Secretary be to upset."

I assured Admiral Clarey that the "Ensign" was doing well, and that he would be proud of him. Secretary Nitze was certainly not upset with or about him, but liked him. He especially liked the discussions they had on foreign affairs as well as the speeches he produced. Admiral Clarey was pleased with my response but cautioned me to keep an eye on the youngster.

Lois Merkel put the label of "Executive Ensign" on Craig. Others in the staff picked it up, and to this day reference to the Executive Ensign brings smiles and good memories. Craig declared to me one day he enjoyed his job. But someday in the future he did not want to respond to his children's or grandchildren's question, "What did you do in the Navy?" by saying he was once the Secretary of the Navy's speechwriter.

I replied he was welcome to stay, but I understood his concern. Being in the midst of a war, if I released him, there was only one place for him to go. That was to Vietnam or to a ship deployed near there. His response was in the affirmative, and he added he would not want anything different. I said I could try to get him assigned to a public affairs billet in Saigon but could not assure it. He agreed, and I found out CHINFO had a billet open in Commander, Seventh Fleet, Detachment Charlie in Saigon. They were willing to try to slip Craig into it. It worked! Craig finished his Navy career in Saigon, doing good things for the Navy.

He left naval service and spent a year in New York with *The New York Times* and then returned to Saigon as the *Times* bureau chief. After that he worked again in their home office and then in Bonn, West Germany and Moscow. He became the Washington Bureau Chief, London Bureau Chief and in 1998-99 was a foreign correspondent in Europe working out of Paris. Later he served as the paper's assistant managing editor in New York. His has been a great career, including authoring a book on espionage in East Germany entitled, "*Spy Trader.*" We have remained in touch and visited many times always snickering about his being the Executive Ensign. While in Bonn, Craig married a lovely German lady named Heidi. They have two children who have done well in college and are productive young adults.

Paul Nitze Assigned to be Deputy SECDEF

Paul Nitze was finally beckoned to assume the duties of Deputy Secretary of Defense, and he accepted. Having started in the Secretary of the Navy role he earlier was hesitant to accept, I think he liked holding the post. He came to fully realize he had done well during his 42-month tenure. I have heard him say many times since the "SECNAV job was the best in Washington." Navy personnel worldwide appreciated him and his accomplishments.

In his last fitness report on me, he wrote, "Captain Thompson has done a superb job as my Special Assistant for Public Affairs for the past three years but without much cooperation or assistance from me." That was a truism. Nitze never felt comfortable with newsmen, nor liked to be showcased or participate in public events. However, he usually went along with my recommendations, realizing that as Secretary of the Navy he was a public figure.

There was a lot of hand shaking to be done, and visibility was necessary especially with Navy and Marine Corps personnel. I really felt sorry for him the first time we visited a hospital in Vietnam. He toured the wards, talking primarily with enlisted men who were dismembered, banged up and not in good shape. It was awkward for him at first, but he accepted the responsibility and did the best he could. I put him in several situations which were not comfortable and perhaps, in hindsight, not necessary. But he always did well adding dignity and poise to the occasions. We were proud of him. He was one of the most impressive individuals I ever had the honor and pleasure to know and to serve with in my lifetime. As a Navy history buff, I rate him as the finest and most productive Secretary of the Navy. The fact that I can, and will, vigorously defend that assertion, verifies it.

John McNaughton, an Assistant Secretary of Defense, was nominated by the Johnson Administration to the Congress as Nitze's replacement. I contacted him concerning details of his swearing-in ceremony, subject of course to his nomination being approved by the Congress. He had been invited to his hometown, Peoria, Illinois to speak prior to taking over as SECNAV. I offered to help him with his speech. It was agreed. I would fly to Asheville, North Carolina where he and his family were vacationing. We would work on the speech together there and on the return flight to Washington. The day before we were to meet, he called to say it would not be necessary for me to come to Asheville. He conveyed the thought the speech was already in "pretty good shape."

The next day, we were saddened to learn the Allegheny Airlines plane carrying McNaughton and his family had crashed shortly after take off, and all the passengers were killed. Pentagon personnel were shocked because McNaughton was well known and liked. The entire family, except for one son, had been swept away. My only contact with him was by telephone, and I was looking forward to working for him. Personally, if thoughts about the circumstances entered my head, I had to shake it to clear away the intense feelings and get on to a new subject or task. I am essentially a fatalist, and negative life circumstances don't bother me or linger. I have thought much more about passes I dropped or blocks I made or didn't make.

Paul Ignatius, another Assistant Secretary of Defense (for Installations and Logistics), was next nominated as Secretary of the Navy. He was approved expeditiously by the Congress probably because of the McNaughton tragedy. Ignatius was a World War II naval officer and on the faculty at the Harvard Business School. He was another of Secretary of Defense McNamara's brain trust and highly respected in the Pentagon.

I considered him as one of the most outstanding bosses I have ever had. He was a straight shooter, tough, a decision maker and not overly impressed by the ranks of admirals surrounding him. Additionally, he was cordial and communicative. His loyalties were to McNamara and the DOD structure. For him being Secretary of the Navy was not much different than being an Assistant Secretary of Defense. In fact, I have been told that McNamara looked on the service Secretaries as department heads in his DOD structure.

Early in his SECNAV stint, there was a strike against US Steel virtually paralyzing the country's economy and delighting the United Steel Workers of America in their quest for increased wages and benefits. In exasperation, President Johnson sent the steel combatants to the Pentagon to meet with Paul Ignatius in his SECNAV office. The president was trying to conduct a war without price controls, especially on commodities and products used to produce munitions.

In his earlier days in the Pentagon as Assistant Secretary of Defense for Installations and Logistics, Secretary Ignatius had been successful in hammering out an agreement with striking copper and aluminum workers. Their products, too, were considered vital to the war effort. President Johnson had a good idea of whom to turn to for support. The day after the steel combatants met with the Secretary, it was announced the strike was settled. What went on behind those closed doors we will probably never know, but Paul Ignatius' stock spiraled upward within the secretariat.

Col. Harvey Spielman became the next Marine Corps Aide to the SECNAV, and we developed a good relationship and friendship. He was a solid trooper, a former V-12 from Dennison University in Ohio and eventually went on to serve as a General Officer. Naturally, we traveled with the Secretary on long trips and worked well together. Paul Ignatius seemed to be comfortable with us.

In fact, the Secretary was not much for protocol. On trips he preferred to get together with his wife Nancy, Harvey and me and have a drink and a hamburger or do something relaxing. On one occasion he was the principal speaker for the Navy League annual meeting in Honolulu. After a full day of briefings and visitations at Pearl Harbor and the Marine Base at Kaneoe, we squeezed in a short session to relax on Waikiki Beach and later attended a reception in the evening. The chairman of a Navy League committee made some remarks including a jest that soon after being designated as chairman, he found himself "... up to his ass not in alligators but admirals." When we closed the day with a nightcap in his suite, Ignatius quizzed me about being responsible for the Navy League and being a friend of the committee chairman.

"Where does he get off saying he found himself up to his behind in admirals?" Ignatius asked. "He has no idea what it is to be 'up to his ass in admirals'." We chuckled that the guy was in the minor leagues compared to the Secretary of the Navy.

Keep Him Out Of Trouble

During his 18-month tenure as Navy's Secretary, there was a spate of accidents, unfortunate events that hit the Navy's worldwide operations. Several times when introducing me, Ignatius would relate how on his first day in office, he called together his immediate staff to get acquainted and to inquire about the duties of each person. He would say when he got to Captain Thompson, he was told, "Well, Sir, I help to keep you out of trouble. I'm your Special Assistant for Public Affairs." He would then go on to say since he had been SECNAV, there had been a major fire in an aircraft carrier, the Lt. Cdr. Arnheiter removal case broke open, the USS *Pueblo* with its entire crew was captured by the North Koreans and a destroyer floundered and broke up off the Isle of Rhodes. All of these incidents brought much negative publicity to the Navy and naturally demanded his attention.

"I lay awake at night, trying to imagine what kind of trouble he (Thompson) is keeping me out of," he would sigh.

One of the aberrations to smooth sailing during Paul Ignatius' tenure was the "Arnheiter Affair." It "shivered the Navy's timbers" and provided the media with the opportunity to criticize the Navy for curtailing the career of an obvious Navy hero, or at least one whom the media was trying to promote. Lt.Cdr. Marcus Aurelius Arnheiter had command of the destroyer escort USS *Vance* in the Western Pacific including in combatant situations in Vietnam. He was in command for 99 days before being summarily relieved of command and banished with the label, "Never to command again." Arnheiter had hit the deck of the *Vance* at full speed when he assumed command. It was almost immediately evident he was consumed with the vision he was at last going to be a recognized hero as a just reward. His vivid imagination helped to put his ship and crew in unnecessarily awkward situations, at times creating the illusion of danger when none existed.

He sent a speedboat (he bought with the crew's recreation funds) loaded with a machine gun to terrorize the Viet Cong (VC) on the beach. No VC was found, only refugees, but the skipper's report to his operational superiors was more in line with his fantasies. At another time he towed the ship's motor whaleboat astern loaded with enlisted personnel at high speeds swamping it and endangering their lives. He nosed into other ships' (destroyers with 5-inch guns) gunfire support situations and fired at imaginary targets (at least not targets reported by spotters, forward controllers or other ships) and fouled the gunnery of some ships. He dictated a citation awarding himself a Silver Star for gallantry and heroism and had junior officers sign it for forwarding on to higher command. He also composed and released news stories that were not factual. He depleted the ship's recreation fund using some of it for personal expenses. Morale in the ship was extremely low, and it was evident the officers and the crew had lost confidence and trust in their commanding officer. They awakened each day wondering what new adventure he was going to lead them into.

[The statements in the preceding paragraph were taken from sworn testimony in the investigative report of the Arnheiter case.]

The Arnheiter affair became a cause celebre. Of the extensive publicity resulting, none was favorable to the Navy and most championed Lt. Cdr .Arnheiter. Congressman Joseph Y. Resnick from upstate New York glommed onto the situation as a means to gain easy public exposure because he planned to challenge Senator Jacob K. Javitz in the next election. The congressman's actions only enflamed the absurdity of the situation. Next to the Washington Monument, Senator Javitz was probably the most solid fixture in Washington. But in the ways of getting things done in Washington, a common procedure was to hold a public hearing to force an issue, champion an underdog and whip one of the federal agencies. Resnick conducted his own hearing on the matter even though his only connection with the Armed Forces was an indirect link as a member of the Veterans Affairs Committee. His quest was to force the Navy to convene a formal court of inquiry.

Some in the media picked up on his action as a means to attack the staid, conservative, stogy Navy which was in the process of ruining the career of a potential national hero. Arnheiter himself had gone public and referred to his situation as the "Vance Mutiny." He had corralled support, not only from the media but also from some prominent individuals in the Navy. Following the relief of Arnheiter, the Navy sent a senior captain (Coincidentally, it was Capt. Bill Hurst, my old friend from First Fleet Staff days.) to conduct an investigation into the conduct of Marcus Aurelius. He concluded there was strong evidence that Arnheiter should not command anything.

The Navy's chain of command plodded away at its approval process, agreeing with the punitive action. Reacting to the heat of Arnheiter's blustering, the House Armed Services Committee looked into the matter, concluded the Navy had handled the situation properly and refused to hold hearings. The Secretary became involved because the investigation documents from Bill Hurst had finally arrived and were being "staffed" (reviewed) by the Navy's JAG. JAG instructed there should be no comment from the Secretary of the Navy's Office on an action under official judicial review. When the JAG completed its deliberations, recommendations would be made for the Secretary's approval. At that time the Secretary could release his final judgment, the findings and whatever background information considered appropriate.

I had a copy of the Hurst investigation and naturally knew the Navy's decision to summarily relive Arnheiter was solid. It was frustrating that we could not show the document or even quote from it with newsmen because of the JAG word embargo. (This was a "Thou shalt not converse publicly about an ongoing investigation, inquiry or court proceeding," and a normal procedure throughout the governmental related to judicial functions.)

Neil Sheehan of *The New York Times* had written several articles, leaning progressively in favor of Arnheiter. James J. Kilpatrick, a nationally syndicated columnist, joined the pro-Arnheiter group, referring to the errant former skipper of the *Vance* as a potential John Paul Jones or Lord Nelson. Pertinent to Kilpatrick's thinking was his own wayward son, who as a youth, had a difficult time staying out of harm's way until he enlisted in the Navy. He got "direction" starting in boot camp, then serving at sea and becoming a petty officer. Kilpatrick credited the Navy with "saving" his son and making a man of him. When I sought out Kilpatrick, he recited his son's scenario and tried to put the Arnheiter story in a more proper perspective. Of course, anything I said was limited because I was under the JAG's wraps and also discredited by Arnheiter with whom Kilpatrick had a constant dialogue.

Because of the Secretary's involvement, I became the Navy's spokesman for the Arnheiter Affair and worked closely with CHINFO, especially the Deputy, Capt. Pickett Lumpkin. Ignatius was getting weary of the adverse publicity and in an expression of the swirl of futility asked me, "Isn't there something we can do about this?"

"Yes," I replied. "You can release the Hurst investigation report that JAG has for review. That is the true document of the affair, and it will blunt most of the accusations made against the Navy. Our hands are tied until that happens."

Within minutes for a few phone calls, it was done. I made sure the document was released to CHINFO to put it in proper channels. Capt. Lumpkin and I each had a copy and were busy for the next couple days talking with news representatives. The story was concluded quickly after the newsmen read the document, and they went on to other interests. Neil Sheehan, however, had been so consumed with the story that he went to San Francisco to spend about two weeks with Arnheiter and interview members of the *Vance's* crew. He concluded that Arnheiter possessed a great imagination and in actual life tried to live with those imaginary figures.

When things didn't go as Arnheiter imagined, he lied blatantly. To characterize him as a zealot would have been an oversimplification. It is difficult to simply label an individual. Amid the complex situation there was a demand for an all too elusive, comprehensive and preventative summary for such behavior. The documentation revealed a complicated psychotic. He presented obvious dangers to a long honored, established service institution, to those assigned to serve under and with him and to himself. The personnel structure of the Navy is designed to weed out such individuals. Fortunately, Arnheiter was stopped before he caused greater damage or killed someone. Unfortunately, it took 14 years of commissioned service before it was discovered he should be relieved of command. He lost command of the USS *Vance* and never commanded again at sea or ashore. He did cause extensive collateral damage because many people in the public sector and some within the Navy thought Arnheiter was a true patriot who was shafted by the Navy hierarchy.

Being a Special Duty Only officer precluded me from being eligible to command at sea. I fully realized that restriction when I applied to be a specialist. That barrier became more personally poignant as the years went by. In my mind, command at sea was the ultimate in responsibility, authority and the exercise of all one's skills. I could not comprehend Arnheiter's disregard for those responsibilities and his abuse of authority. He completely demeaned his training and education for a few moments of fanatical illusions of grandeur.

To me, losing the trust and confidence of his officers and crew was not only an indictment of his character but a life-long punishment. Experience has taught me to avoid getting emotionally involved in projects and cases. However, I must confess that after reading Bill Hurst's investigation of the Arnheiter Affair, I was compelled to try harder. In whatever way I could, I wanted to strive as a man in uniform to help undo the harm Arnheiter's dishonorable actions and deceit had done to the reputation of the service I and so many others sought to uphold.

Commissioning USS John F. Kennedy (CVA-67)

A piece of unfinished business left behind by Paul Nitze was the commissioning of the aircraft carrier USS *John F. Kennedy* (CVA-67). The ship had been launched during Nitze's tenure but took nearly two years to be outfitted and readied for sea. Because of President Johnson's edge of disquiet concerning the Kennedy family, there were intense, scrutinizing eyes watching the progress of the ship and plans for its commissioning, always a major focus in the Navy's chronology of events. In the federal bureaucratic chain of command, the White House's concern about the *JFK* commissioning was passed to Secretary of Defense McNamara who in turn handed it on down to Secretary of the Navy Ignatius. The task stayed within the Secretary's office, and a *JFK* team was formed.

Capt.Bob Long, Executive Assistant and Naval Aide to the Under Secretary, and I were to report on all aspects of the commissioning plans to Ignatius. I was to keep Bob Long informed of any conversations I had with the Secretary on the subject. One advantage we had was Capt. Earl P. "Buddy" Yates, the prospective commanding officer of the *JFK* and former Administrative Aide to SECNAV. He knew our style and the exigencies of the relationships with the Secretary of Defense and the White House.

Commissioning a U.S. Navy ship is a celebration and an enjoyable occasion when a ship is brought to life. The first watch is established; the crew dashes aboard double timing to man their stations; the national ensign is hoisted; and the captain officially informs his superior the ship is reporting for duty. Perhaps evident to only a few of us, there was extra tension not normally experienced in the commissioning of a capital ship. However, everything worked according to schedule, and there were no untoward incidents.

Secretary Ignatius was a master at organization as evidenced by his flying to Newport News the day before the commissioning to personally check out details and talk with the right people. I accompanied him and made it a point to talk to whom I considered the "right person" that day—the ship's doctor. Stevii, our precocious, determined "Navy Brat," was fixed on attending the ceremony. It was a big Navy moment, and she was getting a little lonesome for something Blue and Gold. She was also very pregnant and "due anytime." I sought out and explained to the doctor, a captain, my situation and advised him, "You might have another commissioning aboard—my first grandchild. That will make a great story!"

"We will be ready," he said while nodding and smiling. "Thanks for the heads up."

Zum and I drove early the next morning to Hampton to pick up Stevii and Randy. On the door of their apartment was a note saying, "Someone else is knocking at the door. Randy has taken me to the hospital. Enjoy the commissioning." Grandson William Alexander Graves was born on that good day, September 27, 1968 coinciding with the great ship, the USS *John F. Kennedy* officially joining the United States Navy. Capt. Buddy Yates, the skipper, signed a picture of the ship to our new grandson "Willie," certifying the two significant births occurred on "27 September 1968." When Zum and I reached the ship, I informed the ship's doctor who appreciated the news, but seemed a little crestfallen on missing out on the moment. There's nothing like that great Navy family spirit!

Secretary of Defense McNamara was known as an unemotional, cold, numbers-crunching man. Prior to the formal ceremonies on the platform, he told Ignatius to stand by, because he might have to deliver the speech McNamara had crafted so diligently. Most of speech referenced the former president with whom he was so close. However, McNamara gutted it out even though it was clearly difficult for him. He got to the end of his address before breaking down into uncontrollable emotion. It was a poignant, masterful speech that won him some converts. Perhaps after all, he too was a human being with feelings and obviously a deep caring regard for the late President Kennedy. That dramatic revelation was in itself a significant event.

The Capture of USS Pueblo

Another infamous international incident that occurred during Secretary Ignatius' watch was the capture off the coast of North Korea of the USS *Pueblo*, one of our intelligence gathering ships. Six North Korean Navy ships assaulted the *Pueblo* in international waters on January 23, 1968. The *Pueblo* had little, if any, armament except for two 50-caliber machineguns mounted on the open deck and a few rifles and handguns aboard. One U.S. Navy enlisted man was killed and others wounded, including the captain. Eighty Navy personnel and two civilian technicians survived the capture and were imprisoned, beaten, tortured, starved and forced to sign false confessions before being surprisingly released 11 months later.

The decision confronting the *Pueblo*'s commanding officer, Cdr. Lloyd Bucher, was whether or not to fight the ship with small arms against six relatively heavy armed North Korean ships and MIG aircraft. A full engagement would have almost certainly guaranteed loss of the ship and many, if not all lives of those aboard, or to surrender and hope for the best. His decision was arguable and provided a topic discussed by many in the Navy, the military, the American public and even the international community.

Bucher and his crew were released by the North Koreans just before Christmas 1968. A Court of Inquiry commenced with worldwide media coverage on January 20 in Coronado, California. Capt. Vince Thomas, the

CINCPACFLT PAO, held the position as Public Affairs Advisor to Vice Adm. Harold Bowen, president of the Court of Inquiry. Because of the intense interest by the media, Thomas remained on the scene as long as the court was in session. Vince did an outstanding job with the media, being as open with media representatives as is appropriate in a legal procedure. Newsmen respected Vince and trusted him, knowing that he was doing the best that could be done in this situation.

Most of the media representatives appeared to be in Lloyd Bucher's corner. They thought, wrote and broadcast how the Navy admirals were too moralistic regarding the Code of Conduct designed to guide the conduct of any Prisoner of War (POW). POWs were instructed not to divulge any information beyond their name, rank or rate and serial number. They are to resist as long as possible the torture and cruelties administered by the enemy. The "Code" was written and endorsed by nations (essentially Western countries) subscribing to the Geneva Convention, and certainly not accepted universally by many other nations. Another complication regarding the *Pueblo* was North Korea's contention that because there was no war in progress, the captured American personnel were not POWs. North Korea contended that the incident was a "civil case."

There was constant evidence the Code was misunderstood and criticized by many in the public, but at the same time it was admired and respected by others. Studies initiated after wars have questioned or asked for changes or verifications about the Code of Conduct. Generally, it has been concluded that it may be impossible for individuals to abide by the Code, especially when prisoners fall into the hands of non-Geneva Convention countries. Still it was a must to have a structure in place regarding captured prisoner conduct. Vietnam War POWs have testified the Code was a binding force keeping their groups alive and functioning even though the tortures they experienced were almost beyond belief.

Our military court's other primary interest focused on the divisive issue running throughout the Navy concerning Commander Bucher's conduct. Without putting up much of a fight, Bucher surrendered to the North Koreans resulting in the loss of the ship, its crew and a large quantity of classified material. In the early stages of the shocking realization of losing the ship and not having full information, I thought Bucher should "have gone down with the ship," or at least put up a "John Paul Jones style" fight.

However, I later learned he had overwhelming odds against him. It wasn't one ship of superior size and firepower confronting him. There were six ships backed by air support converging on him in a planned and well orchestrated maneuver. He did try to escape, but his Auxiliary General Environmental Research (AGER) intelligence-gathering ship was no match for the aggressors in speed, armor or armament. It was soon evident there would be great loss of life and eventual capture. By moving farther out to sea, he gave his crew additional time to destroy and burn classified material, but the delaying tactic was not adequate.

It was difficult for an American to stomach the capture of one of its ships on the high seas by a third-level adversary. After all, our citizens know our Navy personnel have been instilled with a strong fighting philosophy. The classic expression "Don't give up the ship," voiced by Capt. James Lawrence, or Father of the American Navy Captain John Paul Jones' battle cry, "I have not yet begun to fight," are not words for the timid or the weak.

Commander Bucher was neither timid nor weak. He was a gutsy man who faced adversity throughout his younger life. He was an orphan reared in Boys Town, Nebraska and became a rugged halfback who always looked for ways to win. A testament to his leadership and courage was the adoration his crew had for him. They would have followed him anywhere. It was not easy to put oneself in his position. I was amused to observe the breast-beating and macho proclamations of many of my contemporaries and superiors. I am sure in ships' wardrooms and officers clubs around the world the scene was repeated about how "they" would have responded. Perhaps they knew as little about the situation as I initially did.

The court recommended that Commander Bucher and several others be tried by a Courts Martial. The recommendation was passed up the line to the Secretary of the Navy moving much faster than the Arnheiter case. Governor John Chafee had become Secretary of the Navy. In May Capt. Merlin Staring, the Secretary's Special Assistant for Legal Affairs, and I were called into Chafee's office. Chafee stated the time had come to make a decision on the *Pueblo* case. After a lengthy discussion—both Staring and I had been forewarned and had readied ourselves by studying the case and the court's recommendation—I believe it was Staring who said, "They have suffered enough." I agreed. Secretary Chafee nodded his accent. We then got down to the details of clarifying his conclusion, readying his statement and preparing to issue it at a news conference to be held the next day.

It was not a popular decision within the Navy, and Chafee was also criticized by the media. It drew their ire not so much for his decision but for not recommending that Bucher, several officers and other members of the crew be commended and awarded appropriate medals. Still many in the media considered a Unit Citation, even a Presidential Unit Citation, appropriate.

Generally, the media took the Navy to task for allowing ships like the *Pueblo* to deploy (on what proved to be a dangerous mission) without consideration to support by other ships or aircraft. *Pueblo* personnel had no survival training like that given to aviators and others who were going into harm's way. Neither did they receive any indoctrination about the Code of Conduct. The *Pueblo* incident taught the Navy some tough lessons. "Most lessons and regulations thereof have had to be written in blood," an old Navy sage once told me, "We hope we learn from them. I wouldn't be surprised if some anonymous gent had said, 'War is hell, and its prosecutors are often presented with tough, untenable situations that require unpopular decisions'."

"Request permission to leave the ship, sir."

I was enjoying myself professionally and socially in the Secretary's office. However, my PAO contemporaries and I realized the milestone of being a permanent captain (at that time, two years in grade) was the signal to say "Good-bye," leave the Navy, "*go home*" and get on with life. When I was notified I had reached that plateau, I became consumed by thoughts of venturing out into the civilian world. Underlying the rush of this decision was the knowledge there was no opportunity for progression to flag rank in the public affairs community. It simply had to be accepted as a *fait d'accompli*.

Some of my contemporaries had done well in the civilian domain. I knew I was going to have to work for a living, if for no other reason than to educate two more of my offspring. I had to retire at a relatively young age to compete in the work place. So without much thought beyond my own situation, I submitted my request for retirement two or three months later up the chain of command to the Bureau of Personnel. I had talked informally about retiring around the office and on trips with the Secretary, but apparently it wasn't taken seriously.

When I notified the Executive Assistant, Capt. Stansfield Turner, who had just come aboard, he was surprised but understood my situation. Naturally, he brought this action item to the attention of Secretary Ignatius who immediately sent for me. Our discussion began with one of the most perfectly executed ream jobs I had experienced or ever heard about. "Why in the hell didn't you discuss this with me before taking such drastic action?" Ignatius growled starting the level voiced one-way discussion. "This is a team we have here, and we work together."

After he finished I gave him my rational outlining the lack of opportunity for advancement to flag rank in our community (something I had talked about to him previously), the obligation of putting two more kids through college and the need to take advantage of my relatively young age to get my name out to potential employers.

"That's a crummy concept," he said obviously zeroing in on the dearth of continuing opportunity in the Navy. "You people should have a chance at making admiral. I'll talk to the CNO about that."

He then shifted to the second phase of our interaction and surprisingly encouraged me to withdraw my request for retirement until after he talked with Admiral Moorer. "Bill, the grass is always greener on the other side of the fence," he continued. "I want to tell you with the highest degree of confidence there is nothing you can do in civilian life to match the experience, excitement, drama and the demands that you face in the job you are in today.

"Just look at what has happened in the short time I have been here and before that with Paul Nitze. You are in the middle of what goes on in the Navy, and you are helping me make decisions. We have confidence in you, and the media people trust you. Think it over."

I thought it over for about five seconds and apologized for being precipitous. However, I thought there were several other PAOs who could serve in my billet. I then said that I would appreciate his talking with Admiral Moorer, but I doubted if the Navy bureaucracy would change the flag selection precepts at the time. I told him I would withdraw my request for retirement, if it could be done cleanly and with no evidence of it in my record or official documents. I knew if by chance there was a selection, evidence of a request for retirement would not look good. There would be little opportunity to explain the circumstances to a selection board.

"I'll make it so," Ignatius said.

I thought perhaps with the coming elections, there was the possibility a new administration would be taking charge, and I could remain with Secretary Ignatius throughout the remainder of his Navy tenure, delaying my retirement by six months. He did talk with the CNO about the flag selection possibilities and reported back to me that the PAO community lacked the numbers to justify a flag billet. That static answer was exactly what I expected.

Brainstorming on the Potomac

Indeed, there was a new administration headed by Richard Nixon. John Chafee was nominated as Secretary of the Navy. He had been the governor of Rhode Island and was a Marine officer during World War II. In the Korean War he distinguished himself as a company commander in action at the Choisin Reservoir. Subsequent to his SECNAV tour, he became a U.S. Senator from Rhode Island. He was also one of the nicest men I had ever encountered. Kind, considerate, honest, diligent and conservative, he could be firm when necessary. It was a pleasure to work with and for him.

The Naval Aide then was Stansfield Turner who became a four-star admiral and later the Director of the Central Intelligence Agency in the Carter Administration. Stan was a bright (a Rhodes Scholar), energetic Naval Academy graduate who was fun to work with. He liked a good laugh and took time to do so. But he had some Zumwalt characteristics. He wasted little time and moved fast.

One of the memorable items about the Chafee era was Captain Turner's idea to do some brainstorming with the Secretary and his inner circle. The first session was in the Presidential Yacht, the *Sequoia* which rested comfortably in the custody of the Navy, but the White House, of course, had first call on its usage. We had no trouble scheduling it for two days. Things began with lunch on the first day, and we relaxed before our first brainstorming session as we cruised past Alexandria and Mount Vernon. The brainstorming crew comprised Rear Adm. Ray Peete, Director of Program Analysis; Joseph "Joe" Grimes, a civilian member of the Secretary's staff; Capt. Merlin Staring; Capt. Stansfield Turner; Col. Harvey Spielman, Marine Aide; and me.

We met with Secretary Chafee on the 01 Deck, grabbing a few rays of sunshine while beginning the attempt to solve some of the Navy and Marine Corps issues. The thrust of this first meeting was to get away from the telephones and delve into personnel problems. We realized Chafee was a people person and not particularly interested in technology per se or weapons systems.

The first of two things taking shape in that session was more and better parking for deployed enlisted personnel. The areas needed to be secure, lighted spaces and expanded. The second consideration was a worldwide program to provide transient quarters for Navy and Marine Corps personnel in the process of departing from duty stations or arriving at new locales. A safe place was needed for them to reside temporarily while looking for housing. These dwellings were envisioned to be self-sustaining and usually located on public land, on bases or stations. We all agreed on those two proposals, especially about the need for temporary living accommodations.

We jokingly dubbed the transient quarters proposal as "Chafee's Cottages." Not surprising, it was not viewed with zest and enthusiasm back in the Pentagon. But Stan Turner persisted and monitored the development; the resulting Navy Lodge program grew to become well managed and utilized. Forty years later, it is a well-established benefit to naval personnel, and almost every naval base has its own Navy Lodge.

After a good dinner, we anchored off Mount Vernon for the night. After breakfast the next day, we had another meeting before returning to the Pentagon. It was an effective way to get something done, stimulate thought and generate ideas. I liked the way that fellow Turner operated.

Life with John Chafee was as fast moving and eventful as with the two previous Secretaries. We did not have any negative incidents except for his rendered judgment on the *Pueblo* case. I got reacquainted with Newport because we spent time in Rhode Island where the Navy was reducing its presence. It was considered best for Secretary Chafee to personally appear on the scene to defend the government's position. Traveling with the former governor of Rhode Island made me wonder how he ever lost an election there. (Chafee ran against the incumbent Senator Clayton Pell in 1972 and lost. But he won in 1974 and remained a Rhode Island senator through the turn of the century.) He was a popular man and genuinely liked. However, he was a Republican in a heavily pro-Democrat state. It was largely a blue collar, strongly unionized region.

After about a year with Secretary Chafee, I began to get restless again about retiring and getting on with the rest of my life outside the familiar cocoon provided by the Navy. Jim Jenkins had been successfully employed by the City of San Diego as its Washington representative. He had the opportunity to move to Sacramento to work for Governor Ronald Reagan and asked if I would like the San Diego job. I was interested because it paid more than the public relations jobs that I was exploring.

In the meantime, Stan Turner had been talking to Chafee about my intention to retire. He countered with the proposition of the Navy sending me to the Advanced Management Program (AMP) at the Harvard Business School for 14 weeks. Afterwards, I would return to Washington to be the Deputy CHINFO for two years. I was intrigued with attending Harvard and thought it would be a bonus on my resume. We inked our pact with me going to Harvard and then returning to serve as the Deputy CHINFO for a guaranteed one year. Rear Adm. Larry Geis, the Chief of Information, agreed with Chafee's charted proposal, and I was to relieve Capt. Kenneth Wade as his Deputy in June 1970.

Prior to leaving the SECNAV office, I traveled to the Western Pacific and Vietnam with Secretary Chafee and once again visited Bud Zumwalt in his Naval Forces, South Vietnam headquarters in Saigon. Chafee was impressed with the briefings and tours while in Admiral Zumwalt's domain. It was his first opportunity to see Zumwalt in action and learn of his accomplishments and plans.

As we continued on to Subic Bay in the Philippines and up to Okinawa and Japan, we learned more about Chafee. He was not one to sit and listen to the local flag officer brief him. He wanted to see things and talk with the troops. Of course, he was always delighted to meet anyone from Rhode Island and would contact the parents or wives of those he met from there upon his return to Washington. In some instances, he knew the parents. It may have been good politics, but it was an innate desire in John Chafee.

Dinner in Yokosuka

On the trip, I contacted Rear Adm. Daniel F. "Dog" Smith, Commander, U. S. Naval Forces, Japan (CNFJ) who was a former CHINFO. I told him the Secretary would like to have dinner with some of the locals. Afterwards he wanted to walk around the famous "flea market" outside the gate at the Yokosuka naval base and then visit a couple bars frequented by Navy personnel.

Dog barked about the bar tour, because he couldn't provide the security he thought was needed. I assured him I had a big Marine colonel with me, and we could take up the security slack. Naval Intelligence personnel staked out the bars offered, and there wasn't much "action" in them. We had a drink in one bar and talked with the owner and then just walked through another. That satisfied Chafee. He wanted to learn more about the environment naval personnel confronted when on shore leave or liberty there. At the flea market he even bargained hard for a few souvenirs and came away happy. Things weren't much different than when he was a Marine on active duty during World War II and in the Korean War.

Admiral Smith went all out and hosted an outstanding dinner complete with an impressive group of Japanese businessmen to honor the Navy's Secretary. I sat next to a kindly gentleman named Toyoda who explained to me his product line of Toyota cars and how he was invading the market in the United States. I remarked to him that he had to be a very ambitious, courageous man to think that he could slip into the U.S. car market and compete with General Motors, Ford and Chrysler. I wished him well. Since it was 1969, I should have asked him where I could buy a few share of Toyota stock, too.

On a trip to Chicago as the guest of George Halas to see the Chicago Bears play the St. Louis Cardinals in the annual pre-season game (the proceeds went to the Navy Relief Society), I spent a couple of hours with Secretary Chafee in the Hilton Hotel before the game. He asked me who I thought should be the next Chief of Naval Operations, if Admiral Moorer was selected to be the next Chairman of the Joint Chiefs of Staff. Without mentioning any other names, because I didn't want to be critical of others, I told him that in spite of his young age, Vice Adm. Zumwalt was what the Navy needed at that time.

Because of the war, reenlistment rates were down. Budgets were low, spare parts were scarce and the high tempo of operations schedules was driving people out of the Navy. Zumwalt was a natural leader, charismatic, bright, imaginative, fearless and an extremely hard worker. If he were to be the CNO, he would be proactive, not merely reactively sitting in his Pentagon office presiding over the Navy. I also cited his evident success in Vietnam as an inventive leader who used every asset available to him to achieve unprecedented success in an area unfortunately almost forfeited as an assumed loss. Further, I stressed how I had never known another flag officer with such a grasp of historic and current geopolitics. He knew international relations as it affected the military and had the benefit of a background in dealing with arms control at the highest level. The Secretary remarked I must have rehearsed the answer to his question. I denied it and added that Bud Zumwalt was the most inspirational and remarkable guy I had met in my lifetime, and I knew the Navy was fortunate to have him.

I selected Cdr. Herb Hetu as my relief, and he was certainly pleased. His selection got him out of Vietnam at least two months early in time for Christmas 1969. Previously, Herb had been the PAO for the CNO Adm. David McDonald and then went to London to the Commander- in-Chief, U.S. Naval Forces, Europe (CINCUSNAVEUR) and then to Vietnam to head up the Seventh Fleet Detachment Charlie in Saigon. He was eminently qualified as a professional PAO and as an old friend.

Extricating myself from the Secretary's Office after five and one-half years was not difficult, perhaps because I was to return to the same arena. There was no precipitous cut-off or termination of affiliation. Secretary Chafee cited my departure in his office where he presented me with a Legion of Merit medal and invited the Pentagon press corps and others including Secretary Nitze, Admiral Tom Moorer and my family. What I remember most about the event was that our grandchild Willie was being held by *The Washington Post*'s George Wilson, and Willie dutifully dribbled all over his shoulder. Willie was a little more than two years old, but George should have known better. He was at least 45 and had kids of his own.

To sum up my time in the Secretary of the Navy's staff, I can succinctly say it was invigorating, stimulating, and educational. I had the privilege to work with bright, focused people, not only in the staff but across the broad spectrum of military and governmental units and agencies. I worked for three superb Secretaries, leaders of divergent strengths, who contributed significantly to the benefit of the Navy and Marine Corps and their missions. Now in reflection, I know I was indeed fortunate to have been in their company. My professional growth and development on this fast track at times presented a steep learning curve. I matured and gained confidence learning to feel assured I could contribute at that level. I held good feelings about our family and myself. The Navy had been good to us, especially by providing me the opportunity to serve in the SECNAV staff.

Next Stop: Harvard

One of the prerequisites for acceptance to the Harvard Business School Advance Management Program (AMP) was to provide three letters of recommendation. I chose Paul Nitze, a Harvard graduate and former trustee at the university; Paul Ignatius, formerly on the Harvard Business School faculty; and John Chafee, a Harvard graduate, former Governor of the State of Rhode Island and then the current Secretary of the Navy. Stan Turner, who attended the AMP a few years previously and who set up my appointment, chuckled and said I had a formidable posse of supporters. He thought it was probably recommendation overkill. Turner doubted if Harvard ever turned down someone from the Armed Services. I'll never know the reaction at Harvard, but I was accepted.

The next 14 weeks—from February 8 to May 7, 1970—were to unfold as unusual but pleasant experiences. First, there was the anticipation of being on the Harvard campus. Harvard was a long way, figuratively and literally, from Oshkosh State Teachers College. Although it was a far piece down the road from Crawfordsville, Indiana, it wasn't totally unlike Wabash College except in magnitude. Harvard University in Cambridge, Massachusetts, nurtures its mystiques of tradition—Harvard Square and Harvard Yard and the red brick, ivy covered walls are really there—as the leader of the elite Ivy League schools. Across the Charles River in Boston proper, the Business School was aggressive and more modern in appearance. Wabash College is much smaller (even in the 1990s it had only 800, all male students) but it should not yield to any other college or university when considering traditions, values, quality of education and productive graduates.

To survive as one of our country's and the world's preeminent business schools, Harvard has had to be the leader in understanding the history of business, keeping up with current developments and preparing its graduates. Clutching their new MBAs, their graduates will be venturing out into the various sectors of business and industry with the intent to lead the development of new business products, procedures and concepts.

The AMP was housed in a new building on the Graduate Business School campus. Members of our class, AMP-58, were the first to use the new structure. It was a state of the art, self-contained educational facility. The building included living quarters, conference rooms and auditoriums. Eight students were assigned to a group called a "Can." It was a throwback to the former AMP building where a group's living quarters surrounded a bathroom (Can). Each group carried the number designation of its assigned bathroom. My group was "Can Six."

Our living arrangements were not as dated as those in the former building. The eight-person groups had two students sharing one bathroom facility, and all eight using a common lounge, dining room and kitchenette. All the facilities were well appointed and comfortable. Our lounge had a large floor-to-ceiling window that afforded a view of the Charles River with Harvard Yard as the backdrop. Dining facilities were in an adjacent building, Kressge Hall. It could be easily reached during inclement weather by an underground walkway. The passageway was especially beneficial during our term at AMP, because that winter was typical of Boston's nasty ones.

There were 160 men in our class. Fifteen were military captains or colonels. Forty participants were from foreign lands representing foreign corporations. In our Harvard conducted indoctrination session, we were told the new facility permitted larger classes and there was pressure to increase the foreign student contingent. With the exception of the military and government executives, the other students were corporation presidents or would soon take positions of high authority and responsibility.

In our Can was Richard T. "Dick" Kramer who was to be Eastman Kodak's production chief when he returned to Rochester, New York; Morris A. "Morrie" Steinberg who became Lockheed's chief scientist; William L. "Bill" Anderson who had a manufacturing company in Erie, Pennsylvania; Francis P. "Paul" Kendall, who was top man in Continental Oil (CONOCO) headquarters in London; Wilson F. "Wils" Barnes, who headed Kraftco's Metro Glass Division; Thomas C. "Tom" Pitney, a partner in the Arthur

Young accounting firm's New York office; and Daniel J. "Dan" Crowley who became president of Southern Union Gas Company in Austin. It was a diverse group. They were congenial, fun, serious and cooperative.

The course was designed to provide mature, experienced personnel with a curriculum to encourage brainstorming and concentration on business concepts. At the same time, participants were being updated on the latest developments in infrastructure and decision making processes, and some delved into the introduction of new technologies. At that time, computers were blossoming and their usage was expanding fast. Those industries that could afford computers benefited. The business school had computer capability.

We used it in a four-day simulation exercise during which 40 companies were born, each with four students serving as the CEO, CFO, Marketing VP or Production VP. The task was to produce a "widget," while handling a gauntlet of all the problems of production, marketing and employment while avoiding bankruptcy. It was fun, exciting and a great learning experience. Our company was one of the last to go under, giving us reason to celebrate. The course was heavy on financial aspects, and it was assumed that all students had a good grasp on the elements of accounting. I didn't have the accounting background but had worked with a correspondence course provided as a pre-school courtesy. I learned a lot and by graduation day completely understood the importance of the always important "bottom line." But I was still vague about how to get from the top line to that all-important bottom line.

Stanford, Wharton, MIT and others emulated the Harvard Business School's AMP program. None of them had the success of the Harvard program. A former naval officer, H.B. Van Gorder was the AMP dean and obviously did a great job. AMP graduates were considered to be Harvard alumni and received all the privileges associated with university's fundraising efforts. We were encouraged to affiliate with the HBS chapters throughout the country as well as the Harvard Club, the prestigious alumni club with chapters in most major cities. I affiliated with the HBS Washington club for many years and enjoyed its programs.

Case Method of study

AMP was also unique, at least for me, because its entire curriculum was done by using the Case Method of presentation. Actual "cases" or real situations in a company's operating history were studied, dissected and critiqued. These practical reviews made the work much more interesting than listening to tedious lectures. There was considerable background information available for each case study. As students we benefited significantly by reviewing and analyzing the materials prior to classroom case presentations. At times we had as a guest the CEO of the company being studied adding drama and realism to the case review.

The faculty comprised a team of "All Pros." They were outstanding in their fields; some were excellent speakers and facilitators. Experts at leading classes, they were teaching without us being conscious of being in a traditional classroom environment. We became totally involved in the cases almost as if we were the real world participants. It was an enjoyable method of learning, and we gained considerable knowledge and background information. It was a busy schedule from 0800 (8:00 a.m.) in the morning until 1630 (4:30 p.m.) in the afternoon with an hour off for lunch. Saturdays were only half days. We had three breaks during the course. They were long weekends that began with us being released at noon on Friday. On those weekends most of us traveled back to our homes. For me it was about an eight-hour drive to McLean, Virginia.

We had an active social life in the evenings. The faculty encouraged the American students to interact with their foreign counterparts. The interaction proved beneficial to everyone. We learned from each other, and fast friendships were established. Most of the students were seasoned, corporate world performers and family separation for travel was not a new experience. However, time hung heavy for some of the foreign students whose families and friends were 4,000 to 10,000 thousand miles away. We "locals" made an effort to include them in our evening cocktail parties, dinners and weekend activities.

Many of our colleagues invited their bosses to visit the school and to attend a class or two. When this happened in Can Six, we would have a cocktail party in our lounge area and then go to dinner at Kressge Hall or a local restaurant. I found it interesting and entertaining to meet the corporate world leaders and to realize how much respect they had for military people. Not to be outdone in this area, I invited John Chafee, Secretary of the Navy and my boss, to visit. I arranged with Dean Van Gorder to have Chafee speak to the class. I had the privilege of introducing him, and it turned out to be an interesting event and a pleasant change from the normal introduction routine. Chafee was a Harvard graduate, so he was enthused about returning to the school, especially while he was serving as the Secretary of the Navy. I also asked Capt. Ken Wade, Deputy Chief of Navy Information, to stop by for an overnight, and I introduced him to class the following morning.

Most of the corporate students were well paid, and some had the additional benefit of having an expense account. Naturally, the government did not take care of its contingent in that manner; we had no expense accounts. Can Six decided early on that each of us would host an event or an evening. I explained to my Can Mates I felt a little constrained, but I wanted to be the first host and quickly relieve myself of the obligation. On the first weekend we were together, we went to the Charlestown Navy Base in Boston to see the USS Constitution and had cocktails and dinner at the adjacent Officers Club.

It turned out to be an unusual and enjoyable evening for them. There was the added attraction of having most of the officers of a U.S. Navy frigate (undergoing an overhaul in the shipyard) join us. The frigate officers were enjoying a Saturday night together. I observed them having a good time at a large table and invited them to join us for after dinner drinks. The ship had returned from Vietnam prior to entering the yard for overhaul. The skipper, Lt. Cdr. Steve Edwards, and his young officers engaged my Can Mates by just being their natural, congenial selves. We visited the ship again later after its overhaul was complete and it had returned to its homeport in Newport. At graduation, all the member of Can Six agreed our first Saturday night together was on top of their AMP memory list.

About 25 years later, a gentleman stopped me at a Navy Memorial reception. "You don't know who I am, but I know you, Bill Thompson," he (Steve Edwards) said. "I was the commanding officer of a frigate in the shipyard at Boston. We met you and some of your classmates from the Harvard Business School at the Officers Club one Saturday night, and you visited our ship in Newport. My officers thought it was a great night and talked about it for a long time. I've followed your career, and I'm pleased to finally meet you again." What a nice remembrance that was. I didn't have total recall of the evening, but everyone obviously had a good time. Maybe it was the good food or something in the water we drank.

VADM Zumwalt calls

On an April morning I got a call in my room from Vice Adm. Zumwalt. He was calling from Washington, and the conversation went like this.

"Hi, Bill," he said. "This is Bud Zumwalt. Have you heard the word?"

"What word?" I asked.

"I've been nominated to be the CNO!"

"Oh, yeah. I know about that. Congratulations."

"How could you know about it? I didn't even know about it until this morning. It's just being announced now. What's your source?"

"You know I never reveal my sources, Bud." (I had received a call the previous day from the SECNAV office advising me of the nomination.)

"Well, I'll be damned. The second thing I called you about is that I want you to get down here immediately and return to Saigon with me. I'm going to call in Robbie (Robertson) now in the Philippines and Worth Bagley who has a cruiser division operating off Vietnam. We're going to plan what we will do in the next four years. And then when I am relieved, you will accompany me around the world, returning to Washington just before I am to relieve Tom Moorer. Okay?"

"Yes, I hear you, Bud. But you know the Navy has spent about $5,000 to send me to this school. I'm real pleased with the way it is going, and I'm learning something. I'd hate to leave it."

"Apparently you didn't understand me, Bill. I want you to return with me to Saigon to work with Worth, Robbie and me on a plan for what we want to accomplish while I am CNO. Think about it!"

Then there was a click as he hung up the phone.

I immediately began to think about it. I didn't want to leave the AMP course to go to dirty, hot, humid Saigon, but if he thinks I can contribute to his plan, I guess I have no other bona fide option. "Hey, Willie, that was the CNO-to-be who called," I reminded myself.

Two minutes later, I called Bud Zumwalt in the Visiting Flag Officer office and he answered. "Bud, I've thought about it," I said, with a laugh. "When is your plane leaving for Saigon?"

"The day after tomorrow," he said. "See you then." This time before I heard another click, he said, "Thanks, Bill.'"

I called Herb Hetu in the SECNAV office to inform him of my situation and how some logistic support might be required. I was still assigned to the Secretary's Office, and orders would have to be written for me to accompany Zumwalt to Saigon. I asked for the orders be open-ended, because I wanted to get back to Boston at least to graduate.

And that is what happened. My stay in Saigon was productive. I worked with Worth Bagley, who didn't stay long because he was then a rear admiral and task group commander embarked in a cruiser in the Tonkin Gulf. He had to return to his flagship for operational matters. Robbie Robertson joined us, but he too didn't stay long. My role evolved into interjecting some general ideas about communications, primarily within the Navy, but some involved the public sector. I also "scrubbed" the plan after it was completed to determine where public affairs could assist in its implementation. The plan basically involved strategic use of sea power. There were details on the scrapping of older ships and proposals for getting on with new construction and logistical support of Navy worldwide operations.

While in Saigon I got to visit with Ross Dwyer, the former SECNAV Marine Aide, who was a brigadier general by this time and was assigned to Vietnam. I also made some helicopter trips with Bud Zumwalt visiting some of his commands in the Mekong Delta region and others on the East Coast of Vietnam. En route to Saigon, we stopped for a night at Clark Air Force Base in the Philippines where his wife Mouza and their two daughters, Ann and Mouzetta, were living.

Bud's son Elmo, III was there, and that night he proposed to his sweetheart

Kathy on the telephone, and he seemed happy. I can't remember if she said, "Yes" or "Maybe." I think she wanted to see him back home before making a final commitment. A few days later in Saigon, young Elmo was presented a Bronze Star for courageous actions while serving as skipper of a Fast Patrol Craft (PCF) or Swift Boat in riverine warfare, part of Bud Zumwalt's "Brown Water Navy." The medal was presented to Elmo by his father with his mother in attendance. I witnessed the event. Elmo returned home to Kathy, and they were married shortly thereafter. They settled in Fayetteville, North Carolina, where he practiced law and they reared two children, a daughter Maya and a son Russell.

Tragically, Elmo died of cancer diagnosed to have been caused by Agent Orange, a dioxin used in Vietnam as a defoliant. Elmo had been exposed to Agent Orange several times during his tour with the Brown Water Navy. Ironically, Bud Zumwalt was the commander who authorized the use of Agent Orange in those areas. Its use saved many American lives and helped clear out the Viet Cong from the Delta regions. Elmo's untimely death is unfortunately part of the tragedies of the Vietnam War and still carried by those of us who knew him and Kathy and their families.

Admiral Zumwalt permitted me to return to Washington and Boston, so I could graduate with my AMP class. I managed to get into the last week of classes. Zum and Brian joined me for the last two or three days making it that much more of a special event. Brian was not yet 12 years old and seemed nonplused about the hubbub of activity, but he thought it better than being at home and going to school. Zum, along with several other wives, actually attended a few of our final classes. The professors were geared for the occasion and got them involved. We all enjoyed it.

Our banquet dinner and finale was at one of the city's hotels. It was a black tie, formal affair with several speeches and a few skits that poked fun at Harvard, the Harvard Business School faculty and AMP 58. Convivial emotions ran high, and camaraderie was the norm. We all had the sobering realization that this was the last time we would see most of these folks with whom we had shared an intense, sometimes confining 14 weeks. It was a fitting climax to a memorable and significant time in my life. I was indeed fortunate to have been a part of AMP 58.

When I returned to Boston from Saigon, I brought along some mementos that I picked up in the multitude of flea markets for my Can Mates. I also designed and had produced by a Vietnamese artisan a plaque commemorating Can Six. It featured an image of a toilet with an arm extending from the bowl and the hand clutching a pennant emblazoned with "VI." The toilet was labeled "AMP 58." I still have mine, but Zum has relegated it to the garage for viewing.

The Harvard experience

What did I gain from the Harvard experience? Basically, I came away feeling confident that most of the corporate people, particularly those who had served in one of the Armed Forces, envied the military's ability to get things done and its organized approach to act in responsible ways. Almost overwhelmingly I was told corporations could not respond in like manner. The bigger their organizations became; the more the problems were magnified. There was extreme waste in the corporate structures, but the military normally got the majority of adverse publicity for issues related to high priced toilet seats, expensive hammers and faulty weapon systems because public funds were being abused.

Ignorance of reality fortifies proverbs such as, "The grass is always greener on the other side of the fence." I was pleased to learn that we, who wore the uniforms of the Armed Forces, were thought to be doing things right and were respected. I also sharpened my knowledge of leadership, management and decision making and gained a greater appreciation for successful businesses and why they were thriving. I developed a great respect for the eternal "Bottom Line," and increased my understanding of company annual reports and the stock market in general. Added bonuses were the lasting friendships I made and my broadened base of contacts in many fields. In my post-Harvard days, I subscribed to business publications such as Business Week, Forbes, Fortune, The Wall Street Journal and The Economist. I discovered I now enjoyed reading about happenings in the business world even more than I did about sports. Well, almost. To be sure the Harvard Business School opened new vistas for me.

Back in Washington, I made plans for my immediate return to Saigon. I learned that Cdr. Tom Bigley had been assigned to serve as an aide to Admiral Zumwalt on Zumwalt's return trip to Washington through Japan, Hong Kong, Singapore, Thailand, Iran, Germany, Belgium and England. When I first met him, Tom had been an aide to Adm. David McDonald when McDonald was the CNO. We become reacquainted over the next two weeks. We became more accustomed to one another as we traveled together and shared lodging accommodations. Coincident with Admiral Zumwalt's detachment from the Commander, Naval Forces Vietnam (COMNAVFORV) command, his chief of staff, Capt. Emmett Tidd, was returning to Washington to work with the admiral as well. He was a part of our contingent, as was the admiral's Vietnam aide, Lt. (JG) Melvin "Mel" Stevens.

Bud was relieved by Vice Adm. Jerome Henry "Jerry" King, Jr. in impressive ceremonies on a ship in Saigon and was immediately promoted to a four-star admiral, the youngest four-star in the history of the U.S. Navy. He was 48 years old, 21 months older than Capt. Thompson.

Our conveyance for the return to Washington was a C-135 operating out of a squadron based at Washington's Andrews Air Force Base. A C-135 was an adaptation of the KC-135, the Air Force's tanker aircraft. And to complete the description, the 135 was an adaptation of the Boeing 707 commercial aircraft. Ours was basically a modular, VIP configured aircraft that fit many purposes. It was complete with sleeping accommodations and a galley for serving meals. It was a versatile, reliable aircraft, and the flight crews were superb.

Our trip was a busy one, especially for the admiral. At every stop we shared in the excitement and anticipation of the locals meeting the prospective CNO. There he was—the youngest flag officer in Navy history and a hero in the Vietnam War. It was fun to watch the reactions. It also was a great adventure. For his two girls, Ann and Mouzetta as well as his wife Mouza, the shopping in Hong Kong, the "World's Best and Biggest PX," was a particular highlight. When we were in Bangkok, we got the word that Emmett Tidd had been selected for flag rank causing additional excitement in our group.

Emmett and I had dinner together that night to help celebrate the occasion. "Oh, Bill," he said almost in passing. "We received a message from Washington today saying that you are a grandfather again. It was a girl." Stevii and Randy had their second child. This one was Stefanie Alexandra, born on May 27, 1970. Stevii had predicted it would happen while I was gone, she being due to deliver and "big as a house." "Stef" holds claim to being our favorite granddaughter. Truthfully, she has no competition being the only girl among six grandchildren at least in the 20th Century. She has always been a joy and "my princess."

In Iran we stopped at Tehran. Most of us stayed at the airport while Admiral Zumwalt went into the city to make a call on the Shah. At Stuttgart, Germany, headquarters for the Commander in Chief, European Command, the admiral was able to meet with some Navy personnel, primarily enlisted, for the first time on the trip. Communicating with various groups of people at all levels was one of Bud Zumwalt's numerous fortes. It didn't matter if he was commanding ships, divisions in the Pentagon or his many contingents in Vietnam. He was good at it and not many flag or general officers were his equal. After we boarded the aircraft for the flight to England, the guys gathered at a table to relax, unwind and critique the last visit. Bud asked a question about how we thought his talk with the Navy troops went. He got the usual "great job" kudos. "Haven't heard from you, Bill," he said turning to me. "What is your reaction?"

I shrugged and replied I was disappointed in the reception he received there adding that I had seen him communicate with troops before, and today was not one of his better days. Perhaps he was tired, not feeling well or had something else on his mind. That wasn't the Bud Zumwalt I know. I didn't think it was an entire washout, but it was not his best shot nor even a good one. It grew quiet at the table. Some were squirming around; some were looking about for something presumably lost. Bud Zumwalt chuckled and said something to the effect that was why he kept me around—to keep up his morale. He then agreed with me saying he didn't feel good about it and thanked me for being candid. Fortunately, the flight attendant approached the table about that time, and we all ordered something so together we could "Drink to that!" (Tom Bigley, who went on to become a three-star flag officer, has referred to that little segment of our tour several times. He said he was looking for a parachute, no, two of them, "One for me and the other for Thompson.")

In fairness to the admiral, it should be considered that this was his first opportunity since he was nominated to talk with Navy personnel. It was a significant factor when critiquing his interactions. Importantly, he was not yet the CNO and could not speak as such, nor was it appropriate to launch off on his proposed programs. He was essentially under wraps, and I'm sure that caused restraint. He was also tired from the ordeal of meeting so many international leaders and other dignitaries, having to read diligently into the backgrounds of all the countries and their armed forces and learning specifics about the individuals he met on this 'round the world flight.

I didn't think it was even a calculated risk to say what I did. He asked for my opinion, and I gave it to him in a straightforward, courteous, candid manner. I knew Bud Zumwalt well enough to know he appreciated my honesty if not my candor. I also wanted the others to know I wasn't a "yes man," or a sycophant, nor did Zumwalt want that kind of observation or advice. I have always felt that I should offer my boss my best advice. If he didn't like it, he could fire me, and we would both suffer the consequences. To be other than honest and candid would be unfair to him and the Navy. I have never worked for a boss who did not appreciate an honest appraisal, even if it did not flatter him personally. Fortunately, adverse appraisals were not a part of my everyday menu.

We touched down at Andrews Air Force Base and headed for our respective homes. It marked the completion of an interesting six months. I now had Harvard Business School experience, Bud Zumwalt was being nominated as CNO, and we had shared an around the world tour. The advent of more excitement awaited in the Office of Information. The times couldn't have been better, but could the future portend even more activity and excitement?

Tempest in the Pentagon

As expected, there was no "cruising as before" notation in Bud Zumwalt's* logbook for his tenure as the Chief of Naval Operations. Instead, it was "full speed ahead, all boilers on the line." A couple of months into the job, he was already lamenting to me privately how his term of four years as CNO was probably not enough. He was not preparing a campaign for an extension of his four-year term. Arleigh Burke had been the only CNO since World War II to go beyond the normal four years to serve a total of six. Bud was looking at the budget cycle (the annual budget go-around requesting Congressional funding), and he realized he had a limited number of budget cycles to work with. It was clearly apparent that nudging the regular course of a large organization would take a lot of energy and time.

Bud was a dynamic person, strong of mind, spirit and body. To be physically fit, he worked out each day, if possible, at the Pentagon Officers Athletic Club usually swimming laps for a half-hour or so. He brought considerable energy to his work, concentrating long hours on his multiple tasks and was seldom without a briefcase full of papers to review. He drove himself hard, laboring intently over countless timely and service-related issues. His personal physician, Capt. Bill Narva, observed him closely, traveling with him on extensive trips and seeing him frequently when in Washington. About every six months Bill would recommend that Bud leave Washington for a week to step away from the rigorous schedule and regenerate. Dr. Narva would enlist

---

* I refer to Admiral E. R. Zumwalt, Jr. as "Bud" because he first introduced himself to me that way, and we became good friends. At no time have I ever been presumptuous regarding him. When he was the CNO, I always referred to him as "Admiral" in public and only called him Bud in private meetings or conversations. I respected the man immensely and knew he was the superior, as is the practice in all military organizations. Since he was 22 months older than me, my formality in referring to him would have pleased my mother, who encouraged her children to respect their elders.

the assistance of the Vice Chief to make this happen by suggesting a change of scenery or outright shore leave (a vacation) at a convenient Navy activity.

But the "at a distance" venue was different and more relaxing. Nevertheless, he would always find time to communicate with local commanders, Navy and civilian leaders and his favorite, the enlisted personnel. Such vacations were always beneficial to the admiral as well as to local Navy personnel. The Naval Air Station at Bermuda, Barbers Point, Hawaii and the Weapons Station at China Lake, California were sites chosen for "Z" to sequester. Bud would return to his desk in Washington full of his normal zest and quickly pick up his exhaustive pace.

Change has often been feared and then anathematized by individuals as well as organizations. The resistance causes delays in the acceptance of technical and management provisions and uncertainty in the host of people affected by the change. Within the Navy some populations (for example, specialists in a sector of warfare) were not going to welcome change or accommodation to it without a fight. History discloses many examples concerning change, its slow acceptance and resulting adjustment problems. Navy files abound with examples of resistance to change. At least one story is cited in textbooks on the subject and was even used at the Harvard Business School as a classic example of organizational resistance to change. That classic reference is the story of the Navy's plight when changing from smooth bore to rifled guns. But even preceding that was the onerous change from sail to steam driven ships. Accepting the aircraft carrier as the Navy's capital ship was oppressive to some individuals. It took years and World War II to finally relegate battleships to shore bombardment and thereafter as museum ships. They were majestic manifestations of the Navy's past but not the future of modern warfare.

Admiral Zumwalt brought with him from Vietnam a conceived outline for his tenure as CNO. On arrival in Washington, with Secretary Chafee's approval, he enlisted the assistance of Capt. Stansfield Turner, Chafee's Executive Assistant, to work with him on the plan. Rear Adm. Worth Bagley, commander of a task group in the Western Pacific was on loan from Commander, Seventh Fleet and was the plan coordinator for what was labeled, "Project 60." The title was derived from Zumwalt's promise to present within

60 days of his accession to the Navy's leadership role a document to Secretary of Defense Melvin Laird and Chafee. The plan would delineate his concept of the Navy's problems and how he planned to solve them. It was to be comprehensive covering strategy, tactics, weaponry and personnel. Turner had been selected for flag rank and was about to be relieved from the Executive Assistant to SECNAV position. To assure Project 60 was accomplished, he was delayed a couple of months before taking command of a task group in the Mediterranean as a part of the U.S. Sixth Fleet.

I realized there would not be much time to initiate and institutionalize a few projects to enhance the Navy's communication programs. Previously, Stan Turner and I had agreed I would go to Harvard for the 14-week course. As a payback to the Navy, I would serve as Deputy CHINFO for at least one year. However, I knew I would need to be persuasive to get Admiral Zumwalt to let me retire even after two years. Still, one year was my goal, and I reminded the CNO about it. I only received a condescending half smile and brief utterance from Zumwalt essentially saying, "We will cross that bridge when we come to it."

No Trumpets

Without any fanfare, I relieved Ken Wade as the Deputy Chief of Information (CHINFO). We had two days of turnover briefings, and then Ken was on his way. He was retiring with 27 years of Navy service to work for Governor Ronald Reagan and the State of California as a Washington representative or lobbyist. He was one of the best of the PAO lot, and I felt humble in relieving him but was also appreciative at being cast at his level of competency.

With slight apprehension, I assumed the duties of Deputy CHINFO for the Navy Department. My anxiety arose regarding my new boss and CHINFO, Rear Adm. Lawrence R. "Larry" Geis. An aviator who had an impressive career, he was well liked and highly regarded. I assumed that Stan Turner and Secretary Chafee had talked to him about me relieving Ken Wade after completing the Advanced Management Program at Harvard. But I didn't know if he felt the Secretary had preempted him from his personal choice.

Ken Wade had told me there would be no problem and that Larry Geis was a delightful officer to work for. In the fall of 1969 on a visit to Europe and especially the Sixth Fleet in the Mediterranean, I had the opportunity to meet Admiral Geis aboard the Sixth Fleet flagship. I knew he had been designated to become the new CHINFO, but at that time the Harvard scenario had not developed for me. Nonetheless, he had favorably impressed me at our first meeting. For various reasons, we had not connected before I departed for the Harvard Business School in January.

In a few days I knew that Ken Wade was correct in his assessment of Larry Geis. He was a pleasure to work for and to be associated with. He immediately took the time to explain how he wanted us to function. He said most of his life had been devoted to the Navy and stated he continued to be first in line to defend the Navy or lead in the prosecution of its missions. However, he averred he did not know public affairs techniques nor have those skills. He was going to rely on me to do the grunt work, namely the planning and strategizing, identification of problems and solutions and the operation of the shop.

He would be there to help me if I got in trouble or when some admiral was getting too rough or becoming an obstacle. He said he was available as a speaker and advocate, and he invited me, tongue-in-cheek, to "keep him on the road," so he wouldn't bother me. He also said he had checked me out. He claimed I was the logical choice to be the Deputy and noted I had an outstanding reputation on the E-Ring and with the Pentagon press corps. He added that the public affairs community was pleased I was in the top spot for public affairs specialists. He then smiled and said he knew about and understood the relationship I had with the new CNO. He hoped it would benefit the conduct our office's business.

I responded I was there for three reasons: (1) to close my end of an agreement with Secretary Chafee for sending me to Harvard, (2) to deliver an agenda that included creating a program to improve the Navy's internal communications, and (3) to improve the Navy's public affairs community's performance and its acceptance. I concluded by saying I would work hard to make the office function smoothly and hoped we all would be happy with the results. I indicated my relationship with the CNO was strictly professional and how Zumwalt would not have me around, if he didn't feel comfortable with my advice and counsel. Some day I might trip over my own sword, and then we would have to reassess my value to the CNO. In the interim, I considered myself to be a team player, and although I had always been the quarterback in my public affairs efforts, I would be content to be left guard or whatever he wanted me to play. He concluded the "tete a tete" saying, "You are the quarterback, and I'll be the coach or general manager."

It was the start of a good and successful relationship.

One of the first tasks was to designate a Public Affairs Officer (PAO) to be the Special Assistant to the CNO (for Public Affairs). Zumwalt and I had discussed this several times. It had crossed his mind that I should be in that seat; however, the idea was dismissed early because I was designated by the Secretary to be the next Deputy CHINFO. I made the point that by being in that position I could be of more benefit to him and the Navy. I had in mind Cdr. John R. "Jack" Davey, a PAO for whom I had great respect, who had been in Vietnam with the admiral. After Jack served his tour with Admiral Zumwalt in Saigon, he spent a year at the Naval War College at Newport. I visited Jack at Newport when I was at Harvard, and we discussed a few options for his career. He realized he was destined for Washington duty. I assured him when I served as the Deputy CHINFO, he was going to be near me.

Little did we know Zumwalt was to become the CNO and present another option for his assignment. I personally nominated Jack to Bud to be his Special Assistant for Public Affairs, but I ran it by Larry Geis first for endorsement. Another option Bud considered was keeping Cdr. Jack MacKercher in the position he had filled, working for CNO Adm. Tom Moorer. Before Bud made his decision, Tom Moorer designated Jack MacKercher to be his PAO in the Joint Chiefs of Staff, making it easy for Davey to become the Public Affairs Assistant to the CNO. For the next four years Jack did a superb job of caring for the public affairs needs of the CNO, working with me and keeping me informed. It was a good fit.

Almost immediately after signing on as the Deputy, I received a Class E(asy) message (a telegram) from Lt. Waring Partridge stating he was en route from Danang, South Vietnam, having completed his year in the War

Zone. He was destined for new duty in the CHINFO staff and was traveling for two months from Southeast Asia to Europe with a couple other adventurous souls on motorcycles. He cited mechanical difficulties, pestilence, health problems, robbery, attempted murder and poor food for delaying his arrival at Frankfurt, Germany. From there he would fly to Washington.

He requested an additional one week of leave. My response on reading the request was classifying it as the most unusual and original rationale for a leave extension I had ever encountered. He definitely deserved an affirmative reply, and I sent a message approving it to him. His message caused a stir in the office. Everyone was looking forward to meeting this new addition to the staff, who was obviously a cross between Errol Flynn and Gunga Din. They got their wish sooner than expected when Lt. Partridge reported for duty on the original date, carrying his cycle helmet under his arm and a not-too-happy expression.

He said he understood I had sent a message approving his request for an extension, but he had not received it and really busted his butt to arrive on time. Since he wasn't wearing jodhpurs or puttees, I summarized him as a legitimate young naval officer who had planned a different and exciting way to exit Vietnam. His composure and presence immediately impressed me. He was 6-3 and had the facility to immediately gain eye contact with you and lock it there during conversation. His approach was something a little different from the average person. He was also self-assured but not condescending and well poised for his age. I liked him and immediately started fitting him into one of the toughest jobs we had in the Office of Information.

Early in his tenure, the CNO responding to pressure, proclaimed the establishment of a Minority Affairs Office. He didn't want to assign it to the Bureau of Naval Personnel because it most likely would be engulfed in the milieu of other special function offices. He decided to put it in the Office of Information where, under my care, it would be more transparent. We were slowly assigning people to the billets given to us with this new responsibility. A recently recalled African American Naval Reserve lieutenant commander headed the office. He had some fine attributes, but organization was not one of them. After a few days of letting Waring get settled and indoctrinated into CHINFO, I talked to him about working in that office. He thought he would like to try it as a current and challenging arena. Within six months Lt. Partridge had replaced the incumbent and did a great job for us.

Introduction to Washington Bureaucracy

A rude introduction soon awaited me. An immediate problem was a jarring one, but in retrospect it was beneficial to have it happen early in my stint as the deputy. We faced a major Reduction in Force (RIF) of about 10 people which was a large percentage of our civilian group. We worked hard within the staff to reach those mandatory cuts. We had to gut some of our long time CHINFO force; some had been there for 10 to 15 years. It was an emotional ordeal for me to call all the staff together, particularly the civilians, to announce CHINFO's RIF and to explain how we decided what billets were to be eliminated.

It was also a revelation to observe Civil Service bureaucratic procedures. I was forewarned about the "bumping" process but was still amazed to see it in action. The senior people—who we thought would be leaving—looked around the office, and selected a job rated lower than theirs which we had cut. They bumped those incumbents, who in turn bumped someone else lower on the chain. The ultimate result was that most of our senior people stayed on while the lower ranking people departed. It was also amazing that the seniors stayed at the same pay status. The reason for the RIF was to save money, but in the end we lost a few young, lower-grade employees, and the Navy didn't experience much of a cost saving.

However, it was a good learning experience for me, and I evinced sincerity in my concern about the welfare of our people. The total staff functionality helped bring our efforts together and give them focus. Afterwards the admiral's personal secretary, Ruth Donohue, who had been in that position for about 20 years, said to me, "Well done, William." She followed by sharing her thoughts that when other staff people walked into the front office, they seemed to show more respect, pride and perhaps extra confidence in being part of the organization. Overall, it was a win.

One of the objectives I had set for my term in office was to improve the competence, vitality and viability of the Navy's public affairs community. The community comprised three entities: the officers, the enlisted journalists/photojournalists and the civilians.

To be a good Navy PAO, I thought being a good naval officer with an innate desire to contribute to the Navy in the area of public affairs was a prerequisite. Secondly, a good understanding of mass communications was needed. Being creative or articulate in the written and spoken word certainly add significantly. Character traits for those taking the role should include honesty with themselves and their superiors. They needed the courage to give tough answers to tough questions. Instinct and intuition are valuable qualities usually developed as one matures in the communications business, although it can be detected in younger officers. Certainly, a diligent work ethic is also desirable. In other words, a PAO should be both a good officer and a skilled public affairs practitioner.

Based on my public affairs career, I concluded that our officer corps (about 190 strong) was a mixed bag of varying talents. Almost all of them seemed to be likeable, convivial men who were sincere in wearing the uniform and generally sharing the same course. Some were good writers which I considered to be "the" basic skill. Others were orally articulate, and still others had a passion, perspective and talent for photography, video or motion pictures. Few had a knowledge of naval history as well as public relations as a profession. Too many had little or no experience with the seagoing Navy they were representing.

I first opinioned and soon factually realized we lacked the quantity and quality of broad gauged professionals to be assigned to demanding, senior rank jobs. We definitely needed to review our accession and training programs and concentrate more on career path development. The general goal would be that when an officer reached the commander level, he would be ready for assignment to fleet staff, joint staff or other demanding positions in Washington and elsewhere.

One weakness was our selection process for accession to the public affairs program. For instance, each year BUPERS would force upon our community Naval Academy graduates who did not qualify for unrestricted line duty. Some had problems with their eyes, either being colorblind or having vision weaknesses of other sorts; still others were banged up athletes. We had a lot of "football knees" in our group, and some were otherwise physically incapacitated. I came to refer to them as the "Halt, Lame and Blind Squad." By and large, most were good officers and exemplified their four years of education and training at the Naval Academy. I continued to be a strong supporter of the Naval Academy as a stellar educational institution, but I succeeded in changing the criteria for graduates to accede to the PAO community. We welcomed Naval Academy graduates into our program, but only after an extensive interview process that brought acumen, interest, tenacity and foresight to our officer corps.

The other officers presented a mix of Naval Reservists, former Naval Reservists, former enlisted journalists, and transfers from other programs, such as photography and the unrestricted line. Unfortunately, it seemed our program provided an escape for some officers who got into trouble driving a ship, flying an airplane or just got tired of the deployments and were looking for something easier to do. I specifically remember one officer who survived the screening process. He stated he wanted to stay in the Navy but his wife said, "No" to sea duty. So he looked around and public affairs sounded especially good because he liked to party. He thought all PAOs attended a lot of cocktail parties, so he applied. He was not accessed. We worked hard at shoring up that fallacy by promoting the excitement of our business and stressing the opportunity to contribute to the success and welfare of the Navy.

In the enlisted sector, I was slightly parochial and biased because I previously had the good fortune to be affiliated with some outstanding journalists and photographers. I had developed great respect and admiration for them and their work. They were skilled in their jobs and more focused in their area of specialization than what one would expect from an officer. An officer was thought to be more of a generalist even in our specialized field. I also experienced extraordinary dedication and loyalty from our enlisted personnel. That positive feeling has persisted and endured long after I retired from the naval service. My efforts at enhancement for our enlisted personnel were to encourage professional development, provide educational opportunities, better utilize their skills and provide leadership opportunities for them.

The civilian group was another mixed bag. Some were exceptional people, and some were not. I wondered about their motivation at times. This was my first affiliation with a large group of civilian employees. I learned they were a group of individuals with little homogeneity or leadership. Our uniformed leaders in the office did not pay much attention to them, their development, training, education or career paths. There was a quiescent undercurrent of rivalry between the uniformed and civilian personnel. The civilians were definitely in the minority in numbers. It was difficult to fault them because for various reasons there was probably not much incentive for them to be employed in the Office of Information other than it was an exciting place to be. Their drummer was not in the Navy Department but in the Office of Personnel Management (OPM) and the Civil Service Commission. Their opportunity for advancement and movement to other locations was available across a the entire spectrum of government offices and agencies. OPM was also responsible for the training and education of those public affairs personnel. However, I thought we could enhance their work performance and enjoyment by paying more attention to them and their effort and ensuring they were part of the team,

As I progressed in the public affairs discipline, I became more aware of incompetence and less tolerant of it. I drove myself hard and expected others to do the same. A comment made to me in my early days as a PIO stuck in my mind. A lieutenant commander, who was one of the original 40 Public Information Specialists, said, "You, Bill Thompson, never learned how to relax and enjoy the job." That friend, whom I had worked with on several projects, retired from the Navy as a lieutenant commander. While I thought he was passably competent, he concentrated more than I thought necessary on going to bars and relaxing.

As it worked out, I was either fortunate or unfortunate. I never worked for another PAO except during my short tour of duty in the Office of Information when I was an ensign working for Cdr. Jack Pillsbury in 1948-49. I was always the only PIO/PAO in the office or the senior. It was a disadvantage in some respects, because I didn't get to work for one of the more experienced practitioners and learn from him. So when I found myself as the lead man of our community, I wasn't enamored with its content. It was somewhat similar to that old expression that says, "I didn't know how to spell engineer, and all of a sudden I are one."

As the titular head of the public affairs community, I accepted the mantel and pledged to do my best to not only be the leader but to try to enhance production, excellence and image—essentially the staff's entire lot. I had no choice other than to accept the challenge and keep that agenda running parallel to all the other things I was trying to do. I realized to succeed; I needed to know the individuals better, not judge them entirely on their professional work and to even like them. Liking them wasn't difficult. There was plenty of talent in our community, and I tried to feature those talents. I actively encouraged utilization of an individual's strong points while fostering a better understanding of our mission, the Navy, its history and its current strategies.

My door was always open, and I made it known. While I was not the Duty Chaplain, I would hear confessions, counsel on professional matters, career paths and even listen to a joke or three. I stressed that when we were involved in a project, it was imperative to understand the objectives, study the various options available and then DO IT! Paul Nitze had a poignant, related quote in his memoirs that said, "One of the most dangerous forms of human error is forgetting what one is trying to achieve." All supervisors should be mindful of that sentiment. They should further be aware they will and should occasionally have to redirect their charges to get them back on course.

Standby to Launch

To launch my internal relations ideas, I officially requested an audience with Admiral Zumwalt when we could talk for 20 to 30 minutes. This was out of the ordinary—I requested to see him officially; he had not requested my presence. For starters, I told him he probably didn't realize it, but he was communicating with Navy personnel in a manner similar to Captain John Paul Jones. Even in the 1970s the Navy was relying extensively on two mediums for internal communications—the Plan of the Day (POD) and Quarters for Muster.

All ships, stations and commands publish a POD, the agenda for the day including notes of pertinent events and other information, to be "passed down the line." It was (and undoubtedly, still is) distributed to all offices, departments and divisions and posted on bulletin boards. Quarters for Muster is another daily event that occurs at 0800 (8:00 a.m.) aboard ships, stations and commands when all hands "fall in" with their respective divisions and departments. They are to be accounted for and learn of the developments within the Navy, the fleet, their ship or squadron. The "word" is passed down from the executive officer, through the department heads, division officers and ultimately, that important tier, the chief petty officers.

I stressed that the POD and Quarters for Muster were basic to our Navy life and should remain so. However, they should be complemented by other modern mediums and methods of communication. I stated it was important for all personnel to have some knowledge of what was happening in the Navy. They needed to know what their leadership—the Secretary of the Navy and the Chief of Naval Operations —was doing, saying and thinking. Being aware of how those initiatives and follow-on events would affect them personally and make their jobs more efficient was key. It would improve the performance of their ship or aircraft squadron and contribute towards the fulfillment of the Navy's mission. A periodic rudimentary explanation as to "Why we need a Navy" was also pertinent. I referred to it as a "Salt Water Injection" that needed to be followed by continuous booster shots. I told him the most important thing I learned in the 14-week course at the Armed Forces Information School in 1948 was a quote from General George Washington, "An informed troop is a good troop."

I further argued that the Navy's leadership must take advantage of all modern means of communication. The youngsters in our Navy had been reared with the omnipresence of a television set. When they entered the Navy, TV disappeared except for one in a bar or occasionally in a barracks lounge. They did not see television on ships, but possibly viewed it on some bases and stations. I proposed as a goal during Zumwalt's administration to have all ships equipped with a closed circuit television (CCTV) station.

Some aircraft carriers then had closed circuit TV capabilities and were being given small amounts of funds to develop that type of program. The newest carrier, the John F. Kennedy had one, and its sister ship, America, had a CCTV studio in its construction blueprints. The units could be small and would not take up an appreciable amount of space that was precious in small ships. But the potential for information, education, training, command and control was great. Among its advantages, the CCTV would give the ships' commanding officers the option of speaking directly to their officers and crew. Of course, TV monitors could be strategically placed throughout the ships. Another advantage was the equipment could be bought right off the shelf—we didn't have to invent it.

I concluded by saying the Navy put less emphasis on internal information than the other services. With a little direction from the top, we could change and our personnel would be better informed and do a better job. Morale would improve, and the chance of success of the CNO's initiatives would be enhanced considerably. I also said I had several other things in mind for the implementation of an Internal Information Program.

Bud Zumwalt interrupted me by asking how much money I needed. I replied I wasn't looking for funding at the moment. I was looking for his agreement to the general concept, and I would follow with a definitive program. In general ballpark figures, I figured eventually I would need a couple million dollars to get started and a few more billets to build the staff. He replied my thinking was good, but that kind of money would need justification. I countered that the whole internal information situation needed to be reviewed by a study group, and I could make it happen with the CNO's support.

I was confident a study group's findings and recommendations would provide ample justification for a more vigorous internal information program. He agreed with that concept and pledged his assistance to get the study authorized by Secretary Chafee. Smiling, he then said I had effectively zinged him with my statement he wasn't any better off than John Paul Jones. He added facetiously how he was learning something every day in his new job. I thanked him for his response and volunteered if he ever needed assistance in the area of public or internal affairs, to please send me a blinker or hoist a flag. We closed the meeting with a handshake and a smile.

Getting started

By the time I got back to the CHINFO office, which was farthest away from the SECNAV and CNO offices that you could possibly get within the Pentagon, I had the study team concept taking shape and a cast of characters to form it in mind. I reported to Larry Geis and gave him the CNO's response and my concept for the study group. He was elated and added a few ideas and the statement, "This could lead to something big and be beneficial to the Navy and be a big boost to the skippers of our ships and squadrons. It looks like you have developed a good head of steam. Keep going! Put your concept for the study group on a piece of paper, and we will talk about it tomorrow."

Before advancing too far with the study idea, I talked with Secretary Chafee and got his approval to proceed. He seemed to understand what I was trying to accomplish. He gave his blessing, and as I left his office he gave me a great send off by saying with a wink, "Go get 'em, Tiger!"

I couldn't have asked for a better response from the SECNAV and the CNO. Next on the priority list was to get someone to lead the study group. I had a short list of candidates headed by an old friend Capt. Vincent "Vince" Thomas, USNR (Retired). I thought about a two or even a three-star admiral to lead the group to give it more prestige. But Vince was an experienced unrestricted line officer who was recalled to active duty for the Korean War and stayed on active duty until 1969 in public affairs assignments. He was one of the best, a true journalist, who had the seniority to command good top jobs in our public affairs business and was respected by everyone. He had a good feel for communications and a solid Navy background in the fleet, Washington and joint services. He had recently signed on as the executive director of the Navy League of the United States in its national headquarters in Washington. Vince accepted my offer immediately, although it caused him to lose some sleep. He was restored to active duty for a few months and also maintained his job at Navy League Headquarters, "burning the midnight oil" as Captain John Paul Jones might have said.

Considering having made a major impact on internal relations by having the SECNAV and CNO agree to a study, we realized the process had to be done professionally. We also had to be aware of those who would criticize our efforts primarily because of that old bugaboo, CHANGE. We structured the study group to include, in addition to Vince Thomas, 10 members representing a broad spectrum of the Navy, the Atlantic and Pacific Fleets, the shore establishment in the Bureau of Naval Personnel that had a strong interest in internal communications, and the Navy Material Command with thousands of uniformed and civilian personnel on its rolls.

I did not want to appear to anyone, especially the study group membership, that I was "gun decking" this effort by having a heavy hand on the helm and steering the group to my desired conclusions. I was confident the results would be conducive to my intentions of initiating the effort. In my mind, the Navy needed this program. I briefed the group, as did Larry Geis, and we offered our assistance to work with them, counsel them and open doors for their investigations. But we generally stayed out of their way and kept a low profile. Vince Thomas briefed me periodically and assured me that he was getting outstanding support throughout the Navy. He was pleased by the professionalism and enthusiasm the study group members were bringing to the task.

The group first convened in November 1970 and delivered a written report to the CNO on February 15, 1971. The report presented well the exhaustive, comprehensive work by their dedicated 11-member team. I was proud of what they accomplished in such a short time. The report stated to the Secretary and the CNO that the group could not address all the items in the precept, but hoped that the document was " ... a beginning, an indication of the direction in which the study group feels the Navy should proceed, rather than a finalized delineation of all the challenges, problems, successes and failures in Navy internal communication."

The four primary conclusions of the study group were:

     1. The Navy does not now have (nor does it ever appear to have had) a well-considered, well-planned, well-directed program of communications with its own people.

     2. Individual commanding officers have been left to their own devices in devising and executing internal information programs.

     3. The Navy has, in general, failed dismally in its obligation to keep dependents informed.

     4. The Navy is woefully backward in its understanding of the need for modern tools of communication aboard ship and at shore stations.

The report also contained 28 recommendations which in substance advocated: the Secretary and the CNO clearly establish a policy giving internal information the highest priority by commanding officers at all levels; the

Office of Information be assigned the responsibility (with full support from the SECNAV and CNO) for the direction and implementation of an internal information program incorporating the most contemporary methods of communications and guidance as to what is to be communicated; the CHINFO's internal information staff should be augmented and patterned like that of the Air Force; All Hands magazine should be transferred from BUPERS to CHINFO; and communication with dependents should be invigorated.

Moving right along

Within three months, the CNO approved the majority of the recommendations, at least those I thought we could manage at the time. CHINFO became the director of Navy internal information, and we were provided with additional billets and funding. Naturally, we didn't get everything we requested, but we were satisfied, and "our plates were full."

While we were setting up the study group, we jump-started the internal relations program by initiating a quarterly Chief of Naval Operations Situation Report (CNO SitRep) motion picture series. CHINFO produced this half-hour show primarily featuring the CNO. We let the show directors think and encouraged them to be imaginative and utilize all available resources to get the message to "all hands" through this new medium. My challenge to the CNO SitRep team was, "Okay guys, you have always wanted to be creative and effective. This is your opportunity. For all practical purposes, I am the only one who can say 'No' to your ideas. Go to it!"

For the immediate future, the CNO SitRep was on the front burner receiving maximum priority. Jack Davey became the unofficial executive producer. We considered buying him a beret and a Hollywood director's chair. He did an excellent job of conceptualizing, writing the CNO's script and helping to direct the CNO's participation. The films were sent to all ships and stations, and we encouraged using every means to promote showing the CNO SitRep motion pictures. We were gaining an edge on using audiovisual presentations to help the CNO communicate with and inform his "troops."

Early on, Jack Davey and I had discussed the feasibly of getting a mentor, a TV expert, to help coach and advise Bud Zumwalt on his public appearances, particularly television techniques. Bud had captured the imagination of the media, and there was considerable demand for his time for interviews. Davey utilized time on Bud's heavy travel schedule to good advantage, but usually had to try to satisfy requests for getting a "sound bite" or two from the CNO. We decided to talk with Peter Hackes of NBC about spending some time with the admiral. Peter was the NBC-TV Pentagon reporter and was recognized as its expert on NASA's space program.

An agreement resulted in bringing Pete back into the Naval Reserve and restoring his commissioned status rank of commander. When he had the time, and it was convenient for him to work with the CNO, he would essentially be on active duty. I recall one of Pete's first sessions with the admiral. It was a Saturday morning, and after about an hour of the two conversing, Pete returned to my office for a debrief. His reply to my initial question of how the session went was, "Great. That guy is so handsome, so smart, so charismatic, so knowledgeable, so articulate that he will make any PAO look good."

I was already familiar with those superlatives in reference to Bud Zumwalt, but I had never put them all together in that context. I figured Pete was probably right, but I didn't relate that story to Zumwalt until after we both had retired from the Navy. I didn't want the CNO to get an inflated ego nor the strange idea he could do without us.

Introduction to Pinehurst, NC

In mid-February of 1971, Larry Geis called me into his office. He said I was looking a little run down and perhaps was pushing too hard. He recommended I take a little time off to relax. "If you want to go to Pinehurst to play some golf, let me know and I'll get you there," he said. I didn't feel like I was running low, but I talked with our executive assistant, Lcdr.Jack Garrow, about the Pinehurst possibility. After a phone call or two to Zum, I accepted the boss's offer and took Jack with me to Pinehurst, North Carolina. In those days, aviators not assigned to air squadrons or air stations were required to log proficiency time in utility aircraft. If they didn't, they lost their active flying status and flight pay. Aviators would fly on weekends or whenever they could get time off. The Naval Air Facility at Andrews Air Force Base nearby in Maryland had several aircraft designated for proficiency flying. Pilots would usually fly a couple hours away, land, gas up and return. Larry set it up so two of those pilots flying a S2F aircraft would take us to Pinehurst. After a couple days another plane would return to Pinehurst and pick us up. It worked out well.

Pinehurst is a sleepy, small town stuck away in the North Carolina dunes and completely dedicated to golf. We enjoyed two nights at the Holly Inn, played golf on the afternoon of our arrival, 36 holes the next day and 18 the following morning before being airlifted away from the grass runway at Pinehurst. At the Holly Inn we had nice rooms with comfortable beds, quality food and a good bar. Jack was a little younger (about 10 years) than me and more restless. After golf, a shower, a drink and a good dinner, he wandered up to the front desk and asked the clerk, "Hey, fella, where's the action around here?"

The young clerk thought a moment and then replied, "Sir, they are playing bingo at the other hotel tonight, and I think you can still get a few cards." We thought about it, shrugged and retired to our respective rooms.

A CHINFO Coat of Arms

Another small project I initiated had to do with a logo or imprimatur for the information community. The Office of Information did not have one. I passed the word we were searching for ideas for a CHINFO emblem. A couple of PAOs frivolously recommended one that originated in Vietnam where we had a sizable contingent of PAOs. The focal point of the piece was a pair of crossed martini glasses. That didn't impress me one bit. I am not known to be prudish, but my reaction was, "Thanks, but no thanks." I added that concept should remain in Saigon. We had enough problems with our identity without exacerbating it.

Cdr. Joseph "Bill" Stierman was the head of our News Desk. His creativity impressed me as well as his sensitivities regarding image and characterizations. I asked Bill to take on the logo project and attempt to create an emblem with dignity to make a suitable statement about our endeavors. He contacted the Institute of Army Heraldry and after discussing our mission with some of their artisans within a few weeks we got a couple of recommendations. Following a few more discussions, we had an acceptable, quality piece of artwork that made a direct, concise statement for our community.

It comprised a silver banner entitled, "Office of US Navy Information" encompassing a red background. Mounted on the background was an impressive anchor with a blue shield on its shank. A gold trident was placed vertically in the middle, and there was a gold conch shell on each side. The bottom of the banner touted the Latin words Nil Nisi Verum meaning "Nothing But the Truth." The conch shells connote the sea, the ability to listen and to broadcast and have the appearance of an ear. Many times I have heard Hawaiian warriors emitting trumpet-like sounds from conch shells. It brought back personal memories of sipping Mai Tais under "my" banyan tree on the veranda of the Moana Surfrider Hotel at Waikiki Beach. That pleasant, private remembrance perhaps contradicted with the more serious image we desired to present. But within a short time, CHINFO had a logo rapidly ascribed to plaques, patches and decals. It has remained the official imprimatur for the office and has enhanced the dignity of the community.

Stop the presses! Big news!

Sometime in March 1971 I encountered Secretary John Chafee and Cdr. Herb Hetu on the E-Ring. "Bill, we have good news for you!" the Secretary exclaimed. "I've just signed the precept for the next Flag Officer Selection Board, and the Navy is going to select a Public Affairs Specialist to be the next CHINFO. Isn't that great? That is something you have always advocated."

"Wow! That's great, Mr. Secretary," I replied. That's a significant statement for the recognition of our community's effort. Thank you for that confidence in our people."

After that exciting exchange, Herb sidled up to me and said in a staged voice, "Congratulations, Admiral Thompson."

"Hey, Herb," I replied, "This is great news, and I guess I'm a contender.

But I'm not going out to buy a new uniform yet."

I was really surprised by the revelation and had not given any thought to the flag rank business, because I was preoccupied with the exigencies of the job. I had completely forgotten about the timeline for the flag selection process. I was still living with the perception there would not be a PAO CHINFO. My short-range objective was to serve out the next year or two, retire and get in the "Unemployed, Will Work for Money" line. However, Bud Zumwalt had fulfilled his promise: there would be a Public Affairs Specialist as CHINFO. He had prevailed upon Mr. Chafee that there should be a true PAO in the CHINFO job. As he later told me, he argued that the PAO community deserved to have a crack at flag opportunity. When he needed advice about public affairs, he wanted to get it from a professional, not secondhand and filtered by an unrestricted line flag officer, who had to return to his office to consult with his experts before he could come up with an answer.

It was an oversimplification he often used. But he truly believed in the importance of public affairs and its considerations in the decision making process. He told me the remainder of the battle for me to get to be a PAO admiral was how the Selection Board would grade me. He jokingly said if I wanted to worry about the selection, I could get a copy of the list of board members to determine if I had crossed swords with any of them during my career. I scanned the list as it appeared in the Navy Times weekly newspaper and determined I had no known enemies there. In fact, I knew most of them and had a good relationship with several.

The board chairman was the Vice Chief of Naval Operations, Adm. Bernard "Chick" Clarey who was certainly no stranger. However, at the time, there was nothing more to be done, nor anything that could be done to put myself forward. All the tickets were in, and my record was on the table. I always thought if whatever job I had was not one of the best, I put forth the extra effort and made it a good job. I had been much more proactive than most. My accomplishments for the Navy, at least in my mind, were as good as the others under consideration. I had given it my best shot. So be it. And then it was back to work.

Admittedly, it was a little disconcerting to have the selection in the back of my mind. I guess I was more concerned with congratulating the selectee, and wondering if I would be acceptable as the deputy. I had made up my mind that if Pickett Lumpkin was the choice, I would volunteer to stay as his deputy because I thought I could work with him. Pickett was eminently qualified, having had the Command-in-Chief, US Pacific Fleet (CINCPACFLT), Commander, US Forces, Europe and the NATO Commander-In-Chief, Southern Europe jobs as well as being the Deputy. Being 55 years old at the time of the selection, his age was not an asset. Normal age for a flag selectee was 46 to 50. I was 48.

The Big Day

The big day arrived on April 25, 1971. In retrospect I did not know when the board would report out or how long it would take for the list to clear the CNO, SECNAV and be on its way to the White House via the Secretary of Defense. When the White House forwarded the list to the Congress, nominating the officers to be approved by the Congress, it was released to the public. Navy personnel worldwide were apprised of the nominations by an All Navy (ALNAV) message from the Secretary of the Navy to all ships and stations. This particular message read concisely, "The President has approved and sent to the Senate for confirmation the names of the following officers of the line nominated for promotion to the grade of Rear Admiral." It went on to list the 49 captains who would soon be wearing two stars.

This was a unique selection of flag officers for the Navy and it generated considerable publicity. It was a larger than usual list. There were 49 names because Secretary Nitze's program to phase out older rear admirals had taken effect, and Admiral Zumwalt invigorated the process. Also, for the first time in its history, the Navy selected an African American officer to be an admiral. He was my old friend from the Naval War College days, Sam Gravley. Another historical first was the Navy's selection of an astronaut to be an admiral. He was my old shipmate, Alan Shepard, the first man in space. (Al and I were shipmates in USS Midway for a Med Cruise in 1950. He was a pilot in the embarked air group.) And, for a real historic event, this was the first time in its history the Navy selected a Public Affairs specialist. I knew

Bill Thompson, or at least I thought I did. But seeing him in an admiral's suit would be indeed strange.

There was a lot of hubbub in the office, congratulatory phone calls, notes and letters from contemporaries and messages from flag officers and friends in and out of the Navy. I thought I was handling it well, when it caught up with me. I couldn't help but say to myself, "What in the hell are you doing here?" At first, I couldn't answer, because I didn't have the answer. I had not rationalized the situation negatively before. Here I was an average guy, but a real hick from a relatively small town in Wisconsin and an even smaller one in Michigan. I probably should have gone home many years ago to work my way up to be sports editor of the Green Bay Press Gazette. I would have been writing about the Packers and thinking I was on top of the world. I stayed in the Navy because I enjoyed it and was given interesting and increasingly more responsible jobs that were fun. But, who was I kidding? To be an Admiral? I must have slipped through the cracks somewhere along the line. After twinges of inadequacy, I began to understand I was not an impostor. I wasn't supposed to be a challenge to the Bud Zumwalts, Ike Kidds and Tom Moorers of the Navy. But the Navy thought enough of me to place me in a position where I could help them succeed in leading the Navy.

I remembered a conversation a few of us PAOs had one night a few years back over a couple of drinks when the subject got to the feasibility of having a 1650 admiral. Someone said, "Well, I wouldn't want to be the first one. Those other flag officers would eat him alive!" I rationalized that "those other flag officers" weren't so bad. They all had a job to do, and they all put their pants on one leg at a time just like I did. Actually, I had a background they didn't have, and perhaps I could help them or the Navy as a whole. What evolved from my rationalization was a personal response taking the form of, "You are one lucky SOB, Willie. What a great opportunity you have been given! Put your head down, square your shoulders and run for daylight." I never regressed to negative thoughts again.

The CNO agreed that Chafee would be the one to inform me of the selection. However, Larry Geis had told me first, not to preempt his bosses, but because he was excited about it. I was naturally sworn to secrecy until the list was published, but I had the occasion to see Bud Zumwalt on other business.

He didn't announce anything to me but said Secretary Chafee would talk to me about the selection. Had I not known from Larry Geis, I would have really worried what the Secretary was going to tell me, likely imagining he would say how sorry he was that I didn't make it. I giggled about the situation but kept a straight, serious face when John Chafee summoned me to extend his congratulations. He asked if I knew, and I replied that I had an idea. However, Bud Zumwalt had said the Secretary would talk to me about the selection, and I didn't know if he was going to offer congratulations or condolences. We laughed about the situation.

Larry Geis told me that he was asked to appear before the selection board. He had told the board, "The PAO community has matured a lot, and Thompson is way out in front of the group professionally, is innovative, proactive, a hard charger, loves what he is doing and has proposed some very productive programs. And the CNO seems to have total trust and confidence in his advice and counsel."

I thought those were strong words and nice to hear, but said I would never be able to live up to those remarks. Another flag officer, a member of the board, told me later, "We went through the process, but it was your name that kept coming to the fore. It was an easy selection. You have a great record as an unrestricted line officer as well as restricted."

I had great respect for the 55-year-old Capt.Pickett Lumpkin who I thought would be the leading admiral candidate. However, the board selected William "Bill" Kotch, 52, to head another specialty group, the Aerologists (Navy meteorologists). There was another selectee at age 53. While in the Secretary's office I had tried hard to get Captain Lumpkin promoted when an opportunity arose for a Navy flag officer to be assigned to the Department of Defense (DOD) Public Affairs Office in Saigon. I had talked with Secretary Nitze about it, recommending a Navy presence in Saigon and Lumpkin for the job.

Under Secretary Robert H. "Bob" Baldwin shot him down saying he wasn't impressed with Lumpkin who was the Deputy CHINFO at the time. In retrospect, Baldwin had been acclimated to Madison Avenue (he had been a top executive with Morgan Stanley in New York and after his stint in Washington returned to head Morgan Stanley) and thought public relations people needed to be more flashy, flamboyant and perhaps worldly. My experience has led me to believe that government, and especially Defense Public Affairs is much different than Madison Avenue. The flashy, flamboyant "Madison Avenue types" would not be effective in our environment. We missed an opportunity to put a Navy flag officer in Saigon to add credibility to our war effort and ensure that Navy and Marine Corps participation in the war would be recognized.

Enjoy it!

After the dust settled, one of the nicest and profound statements came from a three-star admiral whom I had known on the E-Ring. Vice Adm. William "Bill" Malone said, "Bill, my advice to you is twofold: (1) Don't try to change your personality just because you are suddenly an admiral—too many have tried and suffered from the ordeal; (2) Enjoy it! It is a lot of fun, and the few short years you have to wear those stars pass much too fast."

A footnote to the flag selection is that four of our group went on to wear four stars. Jim Watkins became the Chief of Naval Operations and later the Secretary of Energy. Old friend Harry Train became Commander-in-Chief, Atlantic Fleet and NATO's Supreme Allied Commander, Atlantic. Wes McDonald relieved him in those positions. Five others eventually pinned on three stars.

One of the first things our FY 72 class of selectees did was to attend a weeklong indoctrination session in the Pentagon. It was designed to update the selectees on the state of the Navy. It also offered an opportunity to interact with the Navy's leadership through presentations and receptions. Some facetiously called the week "The Charm School," and others went so far as to call it "Knife and Fork School" where we were taught table manners and other basics of social intercourse. In reality, there was no need to have even a short discussion on social graces. That skill was assumed to be assimilated as one progressed through the ranks and possibly completed a tour as an aide to a flag or general officer. In reality, it was a fast paced series of lectures and presentations by the directors and leaders of all naval disciplines.

During a schedule break I was standing in the head at a urinal beside Al

Shepard. "Hey, Al," I asked casually. "How do you do this up there in the atmosphere about 200 to 300 miles up?" I didn't realize I was going to get a half-hour dissertation. The launch of Shepard's landmark trip as the first American into space was delayed while engineers tried to decide what would happen if he urinated in his spacesuit. The subject had become a particularly more serious one with the advent of the Shuttle program. Astronauts were staying aloft for three to five days, and human waste disposal became a major consideration. I left that discussion feeling that I had benefited well from a little extracurricular discourse. It was all part of a delightful week of learning more about the Navy's evolving endeavors.

Naturally, the Chief of Information, Larry Geis, was trotted out to talk to the group about what was going on in his area. Larry used the opportunity to brief the selectees on something really new. It was the Internal Information program we had been working on. The CNO had not even been briefed on the completion of our study and research. So Larry called on me to explain the background and what we had put together thus far.

"I hope you are impressed by my perfunctory introductory statement that I am really pleased to be here to talk with you," I began. It took a little while for that "perfunctory introductory statement" to sink in to their, by that time, bombarded brains. They had received a similar perfunctory statement from nearly all the speakers who stressed how they were "glad to be here" to talk with them. It was a great opportunity to give these new flag officers a heads up on the launching of our new internal communications plan. It seemed to fit into the scheme of things Admiral Zumwalt had been urging for the past nine months. I said it was time for change in the Navy, and one change would be the manner in which we would be communicating with them as commanders and the rest of the Navy's personnel.

The response was good and generally in the vein, "It's about time we did something like that." Even Larry Geis was inspired by the response of the group. "That was fantastic!" he said. "We have a lot of work to do. You don't really need that Charm School. Should I ask that you be excused?" He was kidding of course. We had another day to go. There was a disadvantage to being a "homesteader" in the Pentagon, because after the Charm School sessions, I felt compelled to get back to the office and shuffle through some papers and keep things moving.

At mid-week of the Charm School, Admiral Bud and Mouza Zumwalt hosted a reception at "The Admiral's House," the CNO's residence at the Naval Observatory on Massachusetts Avenue in the District of Columbia. The Admiral's House was the imposing colonial mansion on top of a hill, the highest point at the Observatory. The Zumwalts were the last Navy folks to live in the house, because Congress thought the prestigious home was befitting as the residence for the Vice President and then legislated it as such.

Nelson Rockefeller was the first designated vice presidential resident. But he did not move into the house because he was comfortable in his own private home in the District. Walter Mondale was the first to reside there. The party for the flag selectees was one of many held at The Admiral's House because Bud and Mouza enjoyed entertaining. They used the home and its impressive surroundings to great advantage during his term as CNO. There was a succession of many official visitors from foreign navies to be entertained. The Zumwalts hosted a series of dinners for civilian guests from throughout the country as well as many other foreign dignitaries.

A few months after I was anointed Chief of Information, Bud and Mouza hosted a reception honoring Zum and me. Guests included media representatives, principally the Pentagon press corps and their spouses. It was typical of the social life at The Admiral's House—festive, cheerful and up beat. There was great food, music played by ensembles from the Navy Band and a good, active bar. Mouza loved to dance, and her favorite song, "Tie a Yellow Ribbon 'Round The Old Oak Tree" topped the charts for a long time. Until the day she died in 2005, we could get her to smile and perk up by humming a few bars of that song. They and we harbored many memories of happy occasions atop Observatory Hill.

This type of social activity endorsed the concept that much decision making in Washington takes place at social functions, or at least the preliminaries to decision making does. Often deep discussions are instigated at these functions and followed up later, perhaps the next morning. Many fruitful seeds are planted in such gatherings that germinate new thoughts, ideas and concepts. Paul Nitze once told me a large percentage of decisions and policy statements in Washington are not derived from conference tables or study groups but from cocktail parties, receptions and dinners.

Of course, at news conferences reporters' questions sometimes force policy statements when neither the speaker nor his or her staff is ready for it. It's all part of the government communications process, and our Navy, our country and our world is better off for it. I hasten to add the process is not unique to the Navy or the military or to Washington. It is a part of human nature, particularly in a democracy, and a vital part of our culture. Those who work hard at this skill not only thrive on the discourse but also enjoy the social process. Regardless of the glamour radiating from the social pages or style sections of local newspapers, the underlying feature is that all the activity is just the business of the day. Executive assistants on their way to the office each morning are always thinking, "I wonder what the boss may have said last evening that will keep me busy for the rest of the day?"

The next important item on my agenda was the actual act of relieving Admiral Geis and becoming CHINFO. Larry and I discussed it and decided I should take some leave and return. Then he and his wife Jimmy would take some leave going to Europe for a couple of weeks. We planned to have the turnover about the end of the summer. Bud Zumwalt would have none of that. He wanted me to take over ASAP at the beginning of the summer. As things worked out in May 1971, I was frocked as a rear admiral. I immediately took off for the Western Pacific on a two-week indoctrination tour, returned to relieve Larry and then flew to Jacksonville, Florida. I was there when Larry took command of Fleet Air, Jacksonville. I then returned to Washington to slip quietly into the CHINFO job.

A Frocking Event

The "frocking" ceremony is essentially the same as being promoted. However, the individual, who is frocked into his or her new rank, doesn't get paid at that level until a vacancy occurs to fill on that tier. In my case I wore the admiral's uniform for almost six months before I made the list officially and started to draw rear admiral's (lower half) pay and allowances. At the frocking, Secretary Chafee and Admiral Zumwalt provided a little levity. The ceremony took place in the Secretary's office with the entire Pentagon news corps present along with the Secretariat staff, flag officers from the OPNAV staff, Admiral Tom Moorer, Chairman of the Joint Chiefs of Staff, Paul Nitze, former SECNAV and Deputy Secretary of Defense, Zum, Brian,

Stevii and her Will and Stefanie. (Craig was away at college.)

Secretary Chafee was in good form. He adorned me in some ancient admiral's formal shoulder boards and then asked Zum and Stevii to pin the two-star rank insignia on my shirt collars. There were several speeches, all positive and kind. Then followed the customary receiving line and a reception with heavy hors d'oeuvres. Needless to say, I enjoyed it while fully realizing the well-wishers were eager to get back to work. The newsmen would be on my back almost immediately, and then our usual kindred adversarial relationship would continue. We adjourned to the Office of Information where we had almost identical activities involving our staff. There the happily exaggerated, ceremonial two-star shoulder boards were about two feet long. Literally, a good time was had by all. Most important to me was the obvious elation the staff felt about this significant milestone.

The next morning I showered and donned for the first time my new uniform and was pleased with what I saw in the mirror. Zum kept looking at me over breakfast. I felt a little pressure, but my thoughts were involved with my trip that day to the Western Pacific. I kissed her good-bye and as I left, she said, "Oh, Admiral on your way out will you please take out the trash."

I looked at her and laughed, returned to give her a big hug and said, "Sure, Sweetie. Anytime."

A major destination on my Western Pacific tour was at Yokosuka, Japan. There I was to attend the ceremony where Vice Adm. William P. "Bill" Mack relieved Vice Adm. Maurice "Mickey" Weisner as Commander, U.S. Seventh Fleet. I was pleased to be there because Bill Mack had been a mentor to me, starting back when we were together on the Commander, Cruisers-Destroyers Pacific Fleet (COMCRUDESPAC) staff in the early 1950s. Bill was a commander at that time. He was a role model as a naval officer and someone all the youngsters wanted to emulate. He had also been CHINFO in his first assignment as a flag officer, and he performed superbly. His wife Ruth was an attractive redhead and a kind Navy wife whom we adored. She was a class lady and a great friend. It was on this tour in Japan she first suffered from cancer. She fought it for about 25 years before finally succumbing in the mid-1990s. I was also grateful to have a chance to talk with Adm. "Mickey" Weisner. He was on his way to Washington to become the Vice

Chief of Naval Operations and another one of my bosses.

En route to Japan, I stopped in Honolulu to spend a couple days at Pearl Harbor. I did the usual call making routine visiting all the flag commands and spending the evenings with the PAOs. One night I was the guest of Capt. Bill Stierman who was the Commander-In-Chief, U.S. Pacific Fleet, Public Affairs Officer (CINCPACFLT PAO). He hosted his staff PAOs and their wives for dinner at his home. It was a wonderful evening. My most significant remembrance from that evening was that his daughters, Liz and Karen, had made me a two-star flag. Eight inches tall on a stand, it featured blue stars on a white background. They were young girls in their early teens, but they had picked up on their father's enthusiasm for a 1650 Flag Officer and spent their time assembling my flag with their mother Lynn lending guidance. I was deeply grateful for that token of congratulations.

Cdr. Sid Wright, the Seventh Fleet PAO, was my escort for the two-week tour of the Western Pacific (WESTPAC). We visited Manila, Saigon, Hong Kong and Task Force 77 in the Tonkin Gulf. I made the customary calls on the commanders and spent time with the PAOs. I made it a point to talk formally and informally with the enlisted personnel (the journalists, photographers and broadcasters) giving them an insight into what we had in mind for the next few years. I also provided a Bravo Zulu (well done) for all their efforts which we really appreciated. I got a good response from the personnel involved in Navy broadcasting, radio and television. They were enthused about our surge into modernizing communications media. Naturally, I listened to all of their gripes and complaints and recommendations on how to improve their situations. It primarily involved improving the flow of news, pictures, film and opening outlets for their work.

There was no griping at all about personal problems. I came away inspired by these youngsters who believed in what we were trying to do in the war and were working hard to tell the Navy's story. I felt a close attachment to them and rededicated myself to helping them succeed. I have repeatedly shared my ever present great respect and admiration for enlisted personnel as well as young officers. I was tougher on the senior officers, but my objective on this trip was to ensure all personnel involved in the public affairs effort knew they were a part of the team and understood we were having increased success as a result of working together. There was nothing new to that approach, but now I was in the driver's seat and in a better position to help them succeed. It was most important to me. I thoroughly enjoyed it. I was buoyed by each interface I had and encouraged by their response at talking with the "First" PAO Admiral. I was eager to get back to Washington to begin our new look in Navy Public Affairs.

The year—July 1970 to July 1971—was eventful, significant and exciting. First, and most important, was being a part of Admiral Bud Zumwalt's inner circle for the start of his four-year term as the Chief of Naval Operations. The media quickly praised Bud as an individual and the merits of his programs. He became a celebrity as well as adding excitement to that first year. Getting the Navy's Internal Information program launched was probably the most significant event in my career. Being selected for flag rank was not only startling for me but provided the opportunity to effectively move forward some of the ideas I had for better communications. Those actions touched many areas within the Navy and with the public as well as perfecting the proficiency and vitality of our functioning community of public affairs personnel. It was indeed an eventful year.

What a Ride!

Relieving Larry Geis was not exactly perfunctory, but there wasn't much fanfare. Rear Adm. Geis preferred a quiet affair, and I concurred. We had a successful reception at the Washington Navy Yard Officers Club for CHINFO personnel and spouses, some of the Washington news corps and some retired PAOs. A few other social events related to the transition were staged, hosted by those closely associated with Larry and Jimmy Geis and Zum and me. We had two "wetting down" receptions at home on a Saturday night and Sunday afternoon.

The first flight's invitation list comprised senior officers, including Admiral Zumwalt and Secretary of the Navy John Chafee. The second flight had junior officers and commensurate civilians in the Office of Information and other public affairs offices in the area. Zum and I concluded we had accomplished our mission with the two parties that were successes by Washington standards. My two stars were appropriately wetted, and a good social environment had been provided. There were ample opportunities for the full spectrum of social interactions from giggles to point-to-point discussions. Our new career was properly launched. Zum, who was and remains ever observant, shared how the junior officers didn't drink nearly as much hard liquor as their seniors but ate a lot more food. The youngsters did consume white wine as a precursor of things to come with the then growing popularity of wines of all colors and tastes.

Back at the office, I decided I would not issue a proclamation about changes I would make or goals I had set. I had provided some generalities to Admiral Geis the previous year when assuming the duties as Deputy. They included working for a strong, reliable information program for the Navy, enhancing the professionalism, productivity and viability of the public affairs community and creating a good internal information program. Because I was the first PAO CHINFO, a few in the office recommended I should make a statement or deliver a proclamation of intent for our community. That wasn't my style, and I harkened back to Vice Adm. Bill Malone's advice about not changing my personality or way of doing things just because I had become a flag officer. I preferred to slip into the job and let the results speak for our program.

Office Space And Personnel Changes

I did make some changes to the internal layout of the office. A pending work order delineated some alterations to the CHINFO's office as well as his deputy's working space. After scrutinizing the plans presented by the Pentagon carpenters, I called in Lt. Cdr. Jack Garrow, my newly assigned executive assistant, and we completely rearranged the front office with the admiral's office to be where I had been located as the deputy. The former admiral's space we divided into a room for the deputy and another for a conference room. The Office of Information needed—but had not had—a conference room. It became a good, functional addition for conducting our business. Separating the admiral and the deputy offices was a large room with desks for the executive assistant, the aide, the secretaries for the admiral and deputy and the admiral's writer, a chief yeoman. It also had a comfortable seating area for visitors.

Personnel changes were minor but significant, as they reinforced the direction I wanted for the function of the front office. Most importantly, I reassigned Jack Garrow from his administrative duties to the role of executive assistant. The change merely formalized by title what existed in most offices of the Naval Operations staff. In effect, he became the office manager, the "Chief Paper Shuffler." The billet was ultimately approved and funded requiring the assignment of a PAO specialist to fill it.

The admiral's aide had been a billet for an aviator lieutenant. He piloted the admiral on short-range, domestic business flights. He functioned as a "horse holder" for the admiral and seldom got involved in the office operations. I wanted that changed to bring in a promising public affairs youngster to be the aide and take care of public affairs duties involved in the admiral's travels. Primarily, I wanted the post to be a place to learn the front office functions and to become actively involved. I thought it would be a valuable natural environment (incubator) for a rising young public affairs officer. I stipulated the assignment should be for only one year, so others could benefit by the experience and then move on to other duties in the Office of Information. Proof of the success of the intent was embodied in my first aide, Lt. Kendell Pease. He did a superb job and subsequently became the Chief of Information. Several other aides have also become leaders in the community.

Mrs. Ruth Donohue continued as my secretary until she accepted an offer for early retirement to care for her ailing husband. Ruth was replaced by Mrs. Marie Cuccinotta, who had been my secretary when I was the Deputy. Chief Yeoman Mel Wylie was my writer and a good dependable performer.

My driver was Mr. Taylor who was another of the reliable, experienced Civil Service chauffeurs employed in Washington. I learned he had spent a lot of time in the Chauffeurs Waiting Room near the Mall Entrance to the Pentagon because my predecessors didn't have much use for the car other than as a token of their position. I used the car more because I visited many places in the area. I also made the car available to the staff (first dibs, of course, went to the admiral), and it was the aide's responsibility to coordinate its use.

Mr. Taylor was an affable man who got along with almost everybody, especially me. We had our own inside jokes and opinions mostly about the driving abilities of almost everyone else on the road. In one of the frequent traffic gridlocks in Washington, an impatient driver, who was obviously in a hurry and didn't appreciate being confronted by the traffic jam, cut us off. Mr. Taylor, who had been watching the driver, said, "Admiral, I think that guy qualifies for one of your favorite expressions. He's a Dumb Shit!" I laughed, knowing how he had heard me label other equally disagreeable people that way. Thereafter I would say to him, "Mr. Taylor, you might want to give that guy one of your DS cards."

At that time all Navy cars in Washington were black, but that was a little better than the "Battleship Gray" of previous years. There were a few with white tops. Taylor advised me the white top made a 10 degree difference in the hot, steamy, summer weather and was easier on the air conditioner. Also, they were usually assigned to senior flag officers. I asked the aide to check it out, and if it was true, to see about getting a white top on ours. He reported later that the director of the motor pool advised I wasn't senior enough to have a car with a white top, it would cost about $50 to paint it and Navy money was tight. I instructed the aide to talk with Taylor and have him decide if he would really like to have his car 10 degrees cooler. If he did, then take it to an Earl Schribe Paint Shop, have it painted and I would pay for it. So our car soon ended up 10 degrees cooler and looked even better. The car pool people didn't care, as long as the paint job didn't come out of their budget. Our financial officer found some loose change and paid for it out of our operating fund. Everyone was happy, and it was legal.

I was one of the few lower half rear admirals who had an official car, and I ensured it was used for official business only. Admittedly, it was a luxury, but it was justified. We had offices in various parts of Washington, and it was handy to facilitate parking and timeliness for meetings. It was especially helpful in the heavy social schedule for Zum and me as we were frequently invited to receptions, cocktail parties, ceremonies and formal affairs. I especially appreciated the car and driver when getting to and from airports. Taylor knew the area well, and I learned from him the shortcuts and best routes to get to various places. Years later, those shortcuts were still valuable. I would like to thank Mr. Taylor, wherever he is, for his mentorship.

Later in my tenure, we had to release Taylor because of budgetary reasons, but were able to keep the car. A system was set up for junior enlisted personnel (we had only one or two), to assume on call driver duties for the day. My first experience with this new system was unforgettable. I had been invited to lunch in Washington to meet some people who were on my list of "Those I Should Know." As I departed the Pentagon, I was assured the driver knew how to get to the restaurant since he had made a dry run earlier in the morning.

Once in the car, the youngster said I was the first admiral he had ever seen. I assumed that was part of the reason he was so nervous. I tried to calm him through conversation, learning that he was from the Middle West and Chicago specifically. He had just arrived in Washington the previous week, and it was his first time in the nation's capital. After crossing the 14th Street Bridge into Washington, we got into heavy traffic. I tried to relax and read the Pentagon Early Bird for a couple of minutes. I looked up and asked if the driver had a different route to the restaurant in mind because I would have taken the ramp we just passed. He replied that it had looked familiar.

I instructed him to get off at the next ramp where we were detained because of an accident. After working our way through, we got into an area I had not seen before, and the young driver was becoming thoroughly frustrated. By this time we were 45 minutes late, and I finally said to him, "If we can get back onto I-395, we should return to the Pentagon. I'm convinced we can't get to the restaurant from here. It probably had lousy food anyway." We did get back to I-395 and to the Pentagon. Before we got there, the youngster blurted out, "Sir, I understand you like pro football, and you are a Packers fan." I acknowledged my interest but didn't elaborate much. On returning to the office for a little heart-to-heart talk with the aide, I was informed that the last instructions to the driver were, if he wasn't communicating with the admiral very well, he should talk about pro football, particularly the Packers.

At Last, A Deputy

Our small, close knit front office staff worked well together, covered for each other and got the job done. It proved beneficial because I didn't have a deputy for about three months. Admiral Zumwalt had counseled it would be best to have an unrestricted line captain for my deputy since I was the first specialist in the top job. Also the office might become isolated from the rest of OPNAV without the presence of a "Warrior" in its structure. I thought it was good advice, and Larry Geis agreed. Before I could ask the Bureau of Naval Personnel to recommend an unrestricted line captain to me, Larry Geis called to recommend a Capt. John "Swede" Hanson, an aviator who was about to be relieved as commanding officer of the aircraft carrier USS *Franklin D. Roosevelt* (CVA-42) based in Mayport, Florida, near Jacksonville.

Larry had encouraged Hanson to seek the job because it would give him good exposure on the E-Ring and help him in forthcoming selections for flag rank. With that kind of recommendation, I agreed to have Swede come to Washington for an interview. He did, and I was elated we would have an officer with his background in the deputy slot. Hanson was a Naval Academy graduate, Class of 1947 and graduated in '46 in the Academy's accelerated three-year tract World War II demanded. He was a starting end on the football team there and then a fighter pilot. He had been given command of one of the Midway Class carriers validating his credibility. I was really pleased at our good fortune and agreed to wait the next few months, so he could be relieved of the Roosevelt command and move his family to Washington. He had a previous tour of duty in OP-06, Plans and Policy, so he was familiar with the Pentagon and the OPNAV staff. He played golf, was interested in staying fit and wanted to be a part of our CHINFO racquetball squad.

Swede was with us about 18 months, and I maintained throughout how he added to the credibility and dignity of the office. I tried hard to give him the exposure he desired, and my fitness reports on him reflected details of a "Water Walker." However, competition for the few flag spots available was always tough, and he did not prevail. So he retired. I didn't know some of the details of his relationship with the staff until after I retired. Unbeknownst to me, there was a mild resentment on the part of the senior public affairs officers in the Office of Information, based on the difficulty they had in communicating with him. Apparently, it was like teaching him Public Affairs 101 each time they were promoting or defending an initiative. Also, they were accustomed to going directly to me when I was the Deputy and in the interim before Swede arrived. It was a well-kept secret because I knew nothing of the conflict, and Swede never spoke about it in the office or when we were socializing.

Replacing Swede as the deputy wasn't difficult. I realized then the PAOs could stand on their own, and I didn't need an unrestricted line officer as my backup. We were ready as a community to march off and not stray too far from the pack supporting the Navy's leadership. There were four or five strong candidates, and I talked with each one about the prospect of the deputy job. Capt. Jack Davey was the PAO for the CNO; Capt. Herb Hetu was the PAO for the Secretary of the Navy; and Capt.Jack MacKercher was the PAO for the Chairman of the Joint Chiefs of Staff. As expected, each of those three opted to stay in his current prestigious position.

My fallback was Capt. David Cooney, head of my Plans Division and a well-seasoned PAO. He was a pedantic type, the offspring of two teachers, intelligent and a good administrator. Dave would have been at the bottom of the list of those vying for the title of Beau Brummell of the Pentagon. In that period we wore civilian clothes in the Pentagon except on Wednesdays which was "uniform day." On Wednesdays his wife Beverly, a lovely lady, pushed him out of the house looking like a naval officer. On the other days, she must have lost control, because Dave would inevitably appear wearing gray or black slacks, a burgundy colored blazer from his alma mater (USC) that was beginning to show a few years, a nondescript tie and white sweat sox. When talking to Dave about the deputy's job, I facetiously said with enough reality behind it, that the position was his provided he never again showed up in the Pentagon wearing that despicable USC blazer. I don't remember if I included the white sweat sox, but they and the blazer were not exhibited again. The message was deciphered and registered. Dave proved to be a good deputy. During the course of the next months, we chuckled about the disappearance of the "Burgundy Blazer."

An Aide Who Was A Real Asset

Initially, the concept of me having an aide was not appealing. I felt a little uneasy having someone looking out for details of my official duties and getting paid for it. In my previous experiences, some of the aides I knew could easily have been stowed as excess baggage. I had been rather independent up to that time, operating out of my back pocket, structuring myself to be on time, wearing the right uniform and planning my own schedule. However, it didn't take long to realize an aide could make my days go much better, and I could accomplish more if I had assistance with logistical details. No matter how deeply I was involved in meetings or appointments, the aide was always there to remind me when I had a commitment or another appointment. It was a definite benefit with my normally tight schedules.

A 6-4 former Naval Academy (Class of 1968) football player named

Kendell Pease arrived. (Before a knee injury ended things, he was the heir apparent to Navy quarterback legend Roger Staubach.) He would later become CHINFO and then work as a vice president of communications for General Dynamics. But then he was my aide. We got along well and did considerable traveling together around Washington, the United States and Europe. Wherever we went domestically, we usually had our golf clubs, so we could socialize on the links with whomever we thought could help the Navy and us. Most were media people, a few were in corporate public relations and others were civic leaders—Navy-oriented people such as Naval Reservists who held positions of influence. We also traveled with racquetball gear and took on all comers. Kendell was a good athlete and keen at setting up the matches. He always kept our schedule busy making maximum use of our time.

At a reception on a Friday night at the U.S. Coast Guard Academy in New London, Connecticut, Pease told me he had lined up a racquetball game with the Coast Guard's best, Capt. Otto Graham, and another individual. Graham had been in the Navy V-5 Program after a brilliant career at Northwestern University where he had been an All-American quarterback and All-Big Ten basketball player. After the war, he played pro football with the Cleveland Browns, taking the Browns to NFL championships. Ultimately, he was voted into the NFL Hall of Fame. He also played basketball in the NBA. He coached football at the Coast Guard Academy and then with the Washington Redskins, which didn't turn out well for him, and he soon returned to the Coast Guard. He was a stellar and popular individual.

I readily approved of the match, and admonished Ken to get a good night's sleep. I met Graham that evening and announced Pease and I would be ready to carry onto the court the U.S. Navy honor. The next morning at the appointed time we learned Otto had been diverted to another assignment, but he had provided a substitute. We were disappointed but played anyway. Ken and I blew our opponents off the court in the first game. In the second game we continued the onslaught getting to a 20-2 lead before our wheels came off, and we lost 22-20. What a comeback the Coast Guard had made!

Before the third game, I facetiously told Pease if he didn't do better, there would be a different lieutenant sitting at the aide's desk Monday morning. Kendell, always the diplomat, replied, "I understand, Sir. I agree that if WE don't do better, our team should be dissolved." We returned to our better game and put them away decisively. Seizing the moment, we upheld the superiority of the U.S. Navy, at least on the racquetball court. Kendell and I have reminisced about that experience many times over the years. We learned again that in sport you should play your best and always be humble, no matter how difficult it might be.

Another story we retell is when I was invited to return to Green Bay in December 1971 for the last game of the NFL regular season. The extra highlight was that the Packers were playing the Chicago Bears—the best rivalry in sport. Our host was the local commanding officer of the Naval Reserve Training Center. He hyped the occasion as a "Local Boy Becomes Navy Admiral, Returns Home." The game was coincidentally the last game in the career of one of the Packer greats, Ray Nitschke, who had been a perennial All-Pro linebacker and a mainstay on some of Vince Lombardi's Super Bowl teams.

For the pre-game ceremonies, I had been invited to take the colors and salute the U.S. flag as it was raised over the stadium while the audience sang the National Anthem. I was impressed! Not only was I back in Green Bay being honored, but Nitschke was standing next to me as another honoree. He was considerably more emotional about this occasion than I was. It was his last time in a Packer uniform ending a brilliant career. He evidenced his state of mind as large tears rolled down his cheeks.

It was a typical December day in Green Bay being about 20 degrees and overcast. Zum, Kendell and I were seated in the President's Box along with the Packer organization President Dominic Olejniczak. The box was referred to as "St. Vincent's Box," an unofficial, ethereal salute to the late Vince Lombardi. While in this football shrine, we were able to move around to other suites, including one occupied by the Bears followers. There I talked with George, Jr. "Mugs" Halas, son of George, the coach. We also met other Packer greats such as Paul Hornung and Max McGee. After the game, Zum asked our driver, a petty officer, if he got cold sitting out in the stadium. He replied, "Only when I had to sit on those aluminum seats, Ma'am." Incidentally, the Packers won.

There were 28 people at the dinner that evening given in our honor including Zum, Kendell, the Naval Reserve CO, his wife, my sister Betty and her husband Lee. When introducing me for some remarks, the Reserve skipper commented that our dinner had competition in the form of another dinner in town that evening honoring Ray Nitschke. I countered by thanking those assembled for their kindness in joining us, but suggested we all move over to the Nitschke Dinner to salute the real hero of the evening. Kendell did a good job setting up interviews. We had good coverage in the Green Bay Press Gazette and were on prime time on the local TV outlets. It was a great visit to my hometown, and I returned repeatedly to similar receptions.

The Name Of The Game Is Communicate

One of my prime objectives as CHINFO was to increase the professionalism, productivity, credibility and reliability of the public affairs community. We made a good start in that regard by having one of our own selected to be the Chief of Information. That probably did more to unify the group than anything else.

There were other areas I considered faulty. The primary one was communications. We were supposed to be communicators, but the old canards, "The cobbler has the worst looking shoes" sort of fit us. We didn't communicate well with each other, and there was not much coming out of the Washington office to help coalesce the group. We had a monthly publication for the community entitled, Direction. As the Deputy, I paid some attention to it, sprucing it up and making it a little less like a staid, perfunctory corporate newsletter. It pertained largely to trade journal type articles like "How to Take Better Pictures" or, "Lessons Learned in Operation Deep Freeze." There were also some profiles of successful individuals or programs. I didn't intend to replace Direction, but thought we needed a different spin at least on an ad hoc basis.

As another—although not new—initiative, I started and personally wrote an informal newsletter that was mailed to all Navy PAOs. I definitely did not want to make it an official periodical, or we would need to get approval and budget for it. At that time the Defense Department was reducing such publications. We kept it as a "personalized" letter to principal charges. I labeled the letter, "Shucks from the Squirrel Cage," and made it the subject line of a Memorandum for All PAOs. I led off the first letter with, "While Dorothy is busy mowing the lawn, I thought I should sit here on the patio and communicate with you about what is going on in the head shed, discuss with you some of our initiatives, pass on word about programs and accomplishments in the field and give you thoughts I might have on some issues." I got many responses about Dorothy mowing the lawn: "How do I get my wife to cut the grass? Does that go with the 1650 (public affairs) designator?"

This mimeographed one sheeter—using both sides of legal sized paper—seemed to be effective. I tried not to let it get too folksy, but did mention new births, weddings and new staff accomplishments. When I traveled, I described whom I saw and dined with and what I observed. We succeeded in mailing three or four Shucks a year, and I probably spent more time than I should have wordsmithing the letters. My editorial approach was to always be positive and never preaching nor commanding. I wanted it to be informative, sometimes reportorial and sometimes subtle. It was my signature piece: communicating that I personally cared professionally and socially about the community and its individuals.

It became apparent I would be spending a large percentage of my time as CHINFO personnel detailing, much more than I had thought. A major function of the job was trying to put the right guy into the best slot for him, the information community and the Navy. I worked closely with our detailer Cdr. Douglas "Doug" Madison who also reported to BUPERS. We had to keep continually aware of our limited resources, the development of the PAO specialty and the magnitude of the job in respect to the entire Navy.

We needed to focus on our overall mission regardless of the proclamations of some commander and how hard he was pushing to have his command look good. That view is not an indictment of the commanders. We all think we have the most important job, and we all want to look good while doing it, as well we should. Once in a while, too frequently for me, I would get a call or be confronted personally by a flag officer saying that my guy working for him just was not cutting it. "Due diligence" was the term, and I applied it in all cases. I checked out the situation, talked to the PAO, talked with others in the local area and got a good fix on the situation. In almost all cases, the admiral had good reason to be unhappy, and a change was made.

In regards to limited resources, I took a long shot gamble for the betterment of the community but definitely shortchanged our immediate situation. Overall, the Navy was cutting back on personnel and funding. We had one billet per year for our post graduate degree program and had an arrangement with the University of Wisconsin School of Journalism. In the reduction process, a few of the other communities passed on their allotments for post graduate programs.

Doug Madison, an adept "smoozer," told me he could get a few extra billets for post grad work with no damage to our budget. All we needed were the bodies. That meant taking them out of the assignment cycle for a year to 18 months. I opted for that opportunity, primarily as a show of appreciation for their year of duty in Vietnam. We offered it only to those we were confident would do exceptional work and, of course, had the credentials to do graduate level college work. The University of Wisconsin made the academic credentials determination. As a result, we had a well educated community that could stand up to any other regarding master's degrees. It benefited our program in many ways especially in the years to come.

Zum and I continued our direct communication with public affairs personnel assigned to Washington. We had a continuous stream of dinners or cocktail parties for all new arrivals. Zum put out an extra effort to welcome new arrivals, especially young brides or wives who might need some help getting situated locally. She also tried valiantly to resurrect a periodic CHINFO Wives Luncheon. That was obviously becoming more difficult because many of the wives were working, helping to finance their households. I know she was well accepted and appreciated as "Mrs. Admiral" and deserved it.

Worldwide Conference

Occasionally in the past the CHINFO would have a worldwide conference inviting all commands to send a public affairs officer to Washington. These meetings were beneficial for out-of-Washington PAOs to get to know the

CHINFO staff, learn what it was doing and why and to attend briefings on naval operations, intelligence and professional enhancement. In the fall of 1970, when I was the Deputy, we scheduled such a conference.

It was conducted at the Naval Academy amid its magnificent environment featuring a beautiful campus and spacious, attractive lecture rooms and theaters. The new CNO was a featured speaker, and his session went well. As could be expected, Admiral Zumwalt communicated well with the audience. He expressed to me later that he was impressed with their vigor and enthusiasm. The following year we scheduled another conference in the same surroundings. Bud Zumwalt again was the keynote speaker and began with, "Last year when I was with you, I was asked the silly question, 'When are we going to get a 1650 Admiral?' It has taken me a year to come up with a silly answer. There he is, Rear Admiral Bill Thompson." Pointing to me, he enjoyed the ensuing standing ovation.

That meeting started an effective conclave of my "cardinals and bishops." To finish off the first day, I scheduled a 15-minute meeting with separate groups—the senior officers, captains and commanders (my cardinals), then the middle rank and junior officers and finally the civilians (the last two groups combining to be my bishops). My message to the three groups was similar, but I thought that I could communicate better to divided groupings. I varied a little with the first group pointing out, "Our community is at a crossroads or a threshold. If things go well with the opportunity the Secretary and the CNO have given us, one of you will succeed me. In order to perpetuate the 1650 Admiral, we will need qualified professionals for the selection board to look at. I am confident there will be several. However, I think that along with that, the community must improve, work together, be synergistic and communicate.

I stressed, "It is imperative because we are by far the smallest of the restricted line communities to have a flag officer. If we do not perform well, we stand a good chance of losing that distinction. If we lose it, we may never get it back. Over the years we have worked hard for this opportunity, and I am committed 24 hours a day, seven days a week, 52 weeks a year to make this work. I also know it will only succeed with teamwork. So the onus is really on you to demonstrate your leadership capabilities and make this community function as a well-oiled team and dissolve the cliques that have developed over the years. I am holding you responsible for the success of our program. Remember we are a professional group within a profession of naval officers."

I finished by saying we didn't need a BS session at the time. If there were any questions, I would take them at the bar at our Happy Hour a little later in the evening.

I lighten up on the second cluster but stressed teamwork and communication within the group. Above all, I encouraged them to enjoy what they were doing because it shows and it is infectious. With the civilians I was a little more relaxed and pledged to try to do something to disentangle their milieu. They deserved better. I concluded saying I would work on their behalf, but I felt inadequate at the time to take on the entire Civil Service Administration. I would need their help.

I left that conference with the feeling it was a success. The groundwork had been laid for our program at least for the next couple of years. Even though I did not intend to make it an issue, I had made my proclamation, my "message of deliverance."

Introducing Admiral Rickover

A surprising, disconcerting and memorable event happened soon after I took the top job. I received a phone call one day from the formidable, "Father of the Nuclear Navy" Admiral Hyman Rickover, who immediately put me on the defensive with a question. "What makes you think that you are qualified to be in that job?" he asked.

I thought he was probably testing me, so I mumbled something to the affect that I had a strong professional background at various command levels, a good apprenticeship as a seagoing officer and personally felt confident I could handle the job. As for being qualified, the past flag officer selection board had made that decision, and it was endorsed by the full confidence of the Secretary of the Navy and the Chief of Naval Operations. I added how I hoped I did well by the Navy because I enjoyed what I was doing. Obviously, that was not the right answer.

"Don't get smart with me," he screamed back. "I'll have you fired! Do you know that you have one of the most useless jobs in the Navy? What is your budget? How many people do you have in that office?"

"One hundred ten military and civilians, sir," I replied.

"Oh, my God! How much money are we wasting on you and your office?""

"Sir, our budget for this year is $540,000."

"First you show me that you are incompetent, and now you lie to me. It must be more than that. I am going to have that line item deleted from next year's budget. You know that I can do that, don't you?"

"Well, I didn't, and I don't know why you would want to do such a thing."

"Because it is a waste of money, that's why. We don't need public relations. The only thing we need is the approval of four people in this town, and they are the Chairmen of the Senate and House Armed Services Committees and the Chairmen of the Senate and House Appropriations Committees. Nobody else! That means funding support.

"We don't need public relations," he bellowed. "Why do you think we need public relations?"

"In the first place, Admiral, we do not practice public relations per se," I returned, somewhat defensively because I was answering an irate four-star admiral. "The Congress has disallowed public relations by the Armed Forces or other government agencies. We spend most of our time reacting to queries from the public and the news media. We are in the public information business. It is our duty to keep the public informed about the Navy, its accomplishments and its readiness. The American public needs to know, demands to know ..."

"Don't you preach to me," he yelled. "I can't believe you are so stupid as to believe that rubbish."

He continued his diatribe and suddenly there was a "click." He had hung up his phone. A few days later he called again, only this time he didn't ask many questions. I was attentive until another welcomed "click." About a week later, he called again. I was able to put the receiver on my desk and had no difficulty hearing him. Then "click," and I knew I was free again ... for a while. He must have known I anticipated another call because it was his way of tormenting me. But he never called again. And he didn't have our funding deleted from the next budget, nor the next, nor forever more. About three years later, I sat next to him at a luncheon in Norfolk with the CNO and other top flag officers. Rickover did not harangue me. In fact he was passive, interacting only with Admiral Ralph Cousins, then Commander In Chief, Atlantic Fleet, sitting on his other side.

Rickover had not approached my CHINFO predecessors in such a manner, and to the best of my knowledge, he harassed no successor. Ruth Donohue flippantly said one day he had accosted me only because he liked me. I ruled that out immediately and reconciled the barrage as Rickover's way of welcoming me to flag rank, putting me in a brace that would last three or four years or forever, which it did. I also rationalized it as verification that the "old man" was indeed as arrogant and egoistic as advertised. His rationale for disrespecting public affairs was so ludicrous that I dismissed it out of hand thinking he had a warped sense of reality. I was not one to divide the world into "them" and "us" and didn't have a hate list. I tried to learn from the experience. I realized I had been reamed by a real pro, a legend in his time and given an unexpected welcome to the real flag officer world. In retrospect, I consider it an honor because not many flag officers had that experience. I marked it as a milestone in my term as CHINFO.

Four-Star Identity

Another four-star admiral was having an identity problem. Bud Zumwalt was working extremely hard to nudge the Navy onto a slightly different course. To bring about change in a large organization like the Navy was difficult. Bud had his supporters, primarily the younger Navy personnel and some out-siders, who would cheer anyone attempting to bring about change. He also had his detractors, mostly in the retired Navy community, who did not com-prehend what the CNO was trying to accomplish. There seemed to be few in the middle ground between the two camps. The retired community, especially the retired flag officers, was almost unanimous against Zumwalt's conduct and programs. At one time he spoke to a group of retired flag officers in

San Diego. After he finished his presentation, he asked if there were any questions.

"What are you doing to our Navy?" one old retired admiral got up and bellowed. That was not only a question but a statement from the retired officers, most of whom had served in two or three wars in which the Navy had acquitted itself well. Along comes a young whippersnapper who in a short time had become the most popular flag officer in the public eye since Admiral Nimitz of World War II. Time magazine had Zumwalt on its cover hailing him as the most innovative leader in Navy's history, a breath of fresh air, eons ahead of the "stogy old Navy."

Pure jealousy was one of the reasons for the distaste for Zumwalt. The charismatic admiral became the darling of the media who championed his stand on various issues but primarily for being different from the traditional flag officer. He was articulate and could speak freely about foreign affairs, especially about the Soviet Union being recognized as a competent expert on the Soviets. Bud had spent considerable time studying Russia and the Soviet Union and had the advantage of working close to Paul Nitze and in arms control. Nitze was an outstanding mentor, and Bud was his prime protégé. It seemed publicity was an anathema to flag officers unless it was a puff piece about them. Perhaps the intense competition between them for top commands and the CNO position caused the disparity.

Even Admiral Arleigh Burke mentioned to me once all the publicity Zumwalt was getting. Next to Admiral Chester Nimitz, Burke was the benefactor of more publicity than any other flag officer until Zumwalt came along. Burke's opinions were sought by the media and justifiably so. Admiral Burke was a force, a strong, effective leader, and he definitely left his mark on the Navy and the Armed Forces. He was appreciated by the media and trusted. However, the timeframe and social setting were different in the decade separating their tenures as CNO.

Another large factor was the manner in which they were selected for the CNO spot. Both were deep selected, far below the normal age and experience zone, making them susceptible to criticism from the old guard. However, compared to Zumwalt's reception as the youngest flag officer ever promoted to be the CNO, Burke's story was a mere ripple. Some critics within the Navy community accused Zumwalt of seeking publicity and grandstanding for the media. I can attest to that being a falsehood or a misconception. Capt. Jack Davey, his Special Assistant for Public Affairs who traveled with Bud for four years, also contradicted that impression.

The country was changing rapidly. Historians have described the 60s decade as a period of the most significant changes in our country's history. Our social mores were affected by social injustice, racial unrest and the enormity of the Vietnam War. Protests were not unusual in our history but such demonstrations were commonplace on college campuses, and in the streets of large cities. The burning of draft cards and U.S. flags was a common sight in newspapers and telecasts. Oddly, the protesters were primarily the "Baby Boomers," the progeny of "The Greatest Generation," those who brought home victory in World War II.

But the lesson learned was that the protesters were not always radicals, extremists or unkempt malcontents. They deserved a voice in discussions on the issues. Change is not easily digested, but protesters should not be discarded as a social nuisance or annoyance. The sometimes "Terrible 60s" have been broaden by some critics to include the first five years of the 70s and the end of the Vietnam War. It wasn't all negative. There were magnificent adventures in space, culminated by landing men on the moon, sweeping evolutions in fashion design and music. And the Green Bay Packers won the first two Super Bowls.

The media is always quick to pick up on catchy labels, and Zumwalt was tabbed as the CNO who brought "Broads, Beards and Beer in the Barracks" to the modern Navy. In some of his personnel initiatives he opened career paths for all minorities including women; introduced beer dispensing machines into barracks, so enlisted personnel didn't have to go to the bars off base, and permitted male personnel to wear beards as long as they were well kept. Allowing beards was a device to assuage enlisted personnel and some officers. They looked to their contemporaries in the civilian world who were sporting beards and longer hair as part of the ongoing social revolution of the late 1960s and early 1970s and asked, "Why not me?" Within the bounds of good order and discipline, Bud's approach was that military service did not have to be a place of deprivation, and he focused keenly on individual dignity as extremely important.

By the numbers

When Bud Zumwalt assumed the job as CNO, retention rates, particularly first term reenlistments, were as low as I had ever experienced. It was less than 10%, and in aircraft carriers it was less than 4%. The Vietnam War was unpopular, but worse were the effects it had on ship deployments, time away from home and morale. We were quickly moving into the All-Volunteer Force. The Selective Service was no more; at least, the draft boards were no longer functioning as a force for the services. All accessions to the Armed Forces forthwith were to be by individuals volunteering their services to their country.

Some of Zumwalt's initiatives provided incentives for career-minded enlisted personnel, and by 1973, first term retention rates were at the 34% level. Some of his efforts opened opportunities previously restricted. Zumalt came down hard on deliberate or subtle discrimination against all minorities, including females. There was a reductions in applications "lost in the mail or shuffle" and not to be found until after deadline.

He strengthened the enlisted infrastructure starting with the roles of the Master Chief Petty Officer of the Navy (MCPON), the Command Master Chief Petty Officers (CMCPOs), Master Chief Petty Officer (MCPO) and Senior Chief Petty Officer (SCPO). Those ratings were dignified, and he demanded that they produce, be effective leaders and role models to their subordinates. The MCPON traveled extensively with the CNO and was made integral to the decision making process at the Commander Naval Personnel Command and even the CNO's own Z-Grams.

Strengthening the infrastructure was significant. Superiors exhibited new trust and confidence in the abilities and leadership of the senior enlisteds. It was returned handsomely to better the readiness and capabilities of the Navy. Bud Zumwalt personally communicated with enlisted personnel as he had done during his entire career. He enjoyed the communication and learned from the process.

Zumwalt's initiatives were not limited to personnel matters; they included weaponry, strategy, ship construction, decommissioning older ships and all aspects of the Navy's existence. New initiatives included the Trident Fleet Ballistic Missile Submarine, the Phalanx close-in support gun, the Tomahawk cruise missile, and the FFG-7 guided missile frigate program. He had a full slate, and most of the items he began or energized.

A myth developed about the way he ran things. The lethargy of the OPNAV staff was legendary and true, but it was probably no more lethargic than the Army staff or even large corporations. Zumwalt accelerated the decision making process by doing several things. The first was to establish Rear Adm. Emmett Tidd, who was his Chief of Staff in Vietnam, as OP 09C, the decision expeditor. Emmett had created over the years a system to track staff work and expedite program development. He had a series of multi-colored tasking directives, each color signifying a different level. Staff officers had a strictly monitored allotted time to act on these directives. Presentations were made to decision makers in a precise, no nonsense, tightly scheduled format. Everyone in the OPNAV staff began marching to a new beat, and the drummer was Emmett Tidd who had the full backing of the CNO.

The system worked, but the myth developed that Zumwalt didn't rely much on the Naval Operations (OPNAV) staff but instead had a "mini-staff"—a handful of officers (including me) who were close to him—who did the work to ram his initiatives through. As rumors usually go, it was alleged the OPNAV staff was bypassed at times. This opinion really grew and took on greater proportions after Bud retired. It was Bud who coined the term "mini-staff" when he and I were planning the first of our reunions held at his manse in Pinehurst. Actually, his mini-staff wasn't similar to the White House "kitchen cabinet" that existed at times when U.S. Presidents gathered a few trusted compatriots supplanting the official Presidential Cabinet.

It could be said that certain members of Bud's group were called upon at times to assist as an extra pair of legs to help as "action officers." It was a rather disparate but small cluster of officers mostly assigned to his personal staff. They were easily directed to assist on various projects or issues. So evaporates the myth that the mini-staff was a superstar device in the decision making process. Indeed, the CNO relied on the OPNAV divisions for staff work, but he had an excellent, though at times disconcerting, system of prods to energize the process.

Great Communicators

About midway through Bud Zumwalt's four-year term in early 1973, Jim Jenkins called me from Sacramento to say he was accompanying Governor Ronald Reagan on a trip to Washington. He suggested it might be a good opportunity for Zumwalt to meet with the governor, brief him on the Navy and describe the initiatives he was pursuing. Jim was the Secretary of Welfare on Reagan's staff and had developed a close relationship with him. What followed was a luncheon in the CNO's private dinning room attended by the four of us—Reagan, Zumwalt, Jenkins and me. At that time, Reagan was a wannabe presidential candidate and was quietly but deliberately maneuvering himself into the national picture. The media had been treating him as a Class B movie actor from "fruitcake California" and wasn't giving him much credit for being an astute politician or even being intelligent.

By contrast, Zumwalt was one of the best at analyzing a problem and giving a solution. By being an excellent speaker, he was capable of making the process work. He could leave an audience with understanding, appreciation, inspiration and a desire to achieve. He communicated easily with audiences of any size from hundreds to one-on-one. He was an expert communicator. And here he was, eyeballing the man who was later dubbed by the media as being the "Great Communicator."

Reagan asked how the U.S. Navy was doing and, incidentally, inquired how the Soviet Navy was doing. Bud described the various programs he had instituted and then launched into his favorite subject, the Soviet Navy's threat. He iterated how the Soviet Navy had developed from a coastal defense organization to a "Blue Water" force of forward deployment. Their formidable ships and submarines were operating far from their shores in the Pacific, the Mediterranean Sea and in the Atlantic. They were farther advanced than we because of cruise missiles aboard their surface ships and submarines. Their surveillance equipment and use of satellites was superior to ours.

Additionally, we had a ship building crisis on our hands trying to overcome the obsolescence of World War II ships. It was not a pleasant situation. He closed with his estimation: if there were a confrontation with the Soviet Navy, a major showdown, we would have less than a 50% chance of prevailing. Governor Reagan was taken aback by that statement. "That's shocking news to me," he said. "Why haven't I known of this situation before this minute?"

"Governor," Bud replied, "I am going to let the Navy's Chief of Information answer that." Turning to me, he gave me a nod and an introduction to the stage saying, "Bill."

There had been no scenario or script prepared for this luncheon, so I was a little surprised at the finger being pointed toward me. But I had learned long ago to be on my toes whenever around Bud Zumwalt. I explained to the Governor that the naval disparity was no secret. Whenever he had the opportunity, Admiral Zumwalt spoke on the subject. He had testified to the Congress on that exact issue.

I explained the Defense Department had a process for clearing speeches and statements made by officials. That process stipulated that the Assistant Secretary of Defense for Public Affairs (ASD (PA)) must approve all public utterances. Normally when Admiral Zumwalt's speeches were sent to the ASD (PA), they came back with such references to the Soviet Navy being softened or deleted. The excuses were always "policy." If we pushed, all we could get was a "this administration does not want to upset the Soviets." I added that I had determined those guidelines came from the White House. I had to assume there were justifiable reasons for those guidelines. However, I also said if anyone was asked to assess the Soviet threat, it should be the CNO.

By relating this incident, I don't infer it ignited the future president to label the Soviets as the "Evil Empire" and cause the Berlin Wall to come crumbling down. I am convinced President Reagan's leadership accomplished that and demolished communism as practiced by the Soviet Union. If our episode was another plank in his Evil Empire platform, so be it. It remains a most interesting incident amid my memories.

Our SITE CCTV Program

One of the primary issues involved in my quest to improve the Navy's flow of information to its personnel, particularly those deployed, was to provide television programming featuring education, training, entertainment and news of the day. Adding to this dimension was the facility for live visual communication by the commanding officer to all his or her personnel. The medium was to be Closed Circuit Television (CCTV). A few of the newer large aircraft carriers had CCTV capabilities with a studio included in the design of the ship. It was a major, expensive consideration because it was entailed in the always laborious ship's design, and the Navy Supply Corps was involved in the equipment procurement.

We needed to find a cheaper approach, so all ships could benefit from the new communication system. By all ships, I mean ships smaller than an aircraft carrier that didn't have any spare space to dedicate to a CCTV studio. We took a major step toward the solution when we succeeded in getting a senior civilian billet established and filled it by hiring Lt. Colonel Jordan E. "Buzz" Rizer of the USAF. Buzz was still on active duty when I interviewed him for the position. He subsequently retired from the Air Force and immediately came to work for CHINFO as a GS-14 to be Special Assistant to the Chief of Information for Armed Forces Radio and Television Services.

He was provided an assistant, Ed Burmeister, a retired Chief Journalist who was working in the Office of Information as a GS-7. Ed was a perfect fit with Buzz. That was the beginning of Navy Broadcasting. I liked Buzz because he was fearless and had large scale vision. Another virtue was his consideration of subordinates, particularly enlisted personnel, not only those who worked for him but all Navy enlisted personnel. That positive tactic was akin to our primary goal of filling the gap existing in our structure.

Buzz designed a CCTV system that could be easily installed in all surface ships and later, with a few minor configurations, was reduced in scale to be inserted into submarines. The limiting factor for submarines was getting it through the hatch. It would have been easier if our CCTV had been rounded like a torpedo. But even though compact, it was a box-like configuration and contained the system's operating framework. We labeled it the SITE system for Shipboard Information, Training and Education. All the parts were current state-of-the-art technology and in commercial production. As the expression goes, anyone could buy the components—projectors, cameras, VCRs, distribution systems, monitors and splitters—"off the shelf."

This components issue led to problems getting the SITE system approved. During a few months span, it seemed as if I was spending an inordinate amount of time "bailing out" Buzz Rizer who was the point man and carrying the ball for our SITE program. Buzz had some experience as an aide-de-camp to a general in the Air Force and seemed to have had little difficulty associating with high-ranking officials. He once lost his cool by confronting a Navy commander, a subordinate in the pecking order of the military-civil service structure.

The commander allegedly took it upon himself to thwart the SITE system because "CHINFO was out of its cage in getting into electronics and procurement of a system that wasn't tested or even wanted by the Navy." Buzz, a bantamweight at best, invited the commander outside to settle the difficulty. The commander wisely declined but reported the incident to his senior. I had some explaining to do but smoothed it over and stroked Buzz saying, "Keep going, Buzz. Let me run interference for you so I can soften up the opposition. You still have the ball. You are doing a great job. I didn't tell you this was going to be easy. Just keep a cool stool and air speed. We'll get there."

On another occasion, at a reception in Washington attended by most of Navy's hierarchy, I was confronted by Rear Adm. Raymond J. Schneider, the commander of the Naval Electronics Systems Command (NESC) [now Space & Naval Warfare Systems Command (SPAWAR)]. He demanded to know where this civil servant named Rizer I had working for me was coming from. Did I know what he was up to, demanding this and that for some fool television program?

I told Schneider the situation was not as bad as it had obviously been reported to him. I apologized for not conferring with him before my staff people began talking with his staff, because I was unaware we had moved along so rapidly. I added that I would be delighted to come to his office to explain in detail our plans for SITE. I assured him that our project was a relatively minor one in respect to those he normally concerned himself with. Further, we were trying to work things out within the system, and perhaps we were not doing such a great job in that regard. With that said, I told him I would like to buy him a drink. Of course, this occurred at a reception with a free watering trough. But we agreed my buying him a drink was a good idea. It all resulted in a few chuckles and a promise to work out the few kinks we had in our project.

Vested interests

What we were running into was a vesting of turf. CHINFO was thought to be getting into electronics, especially shipboard electronics, and we had no business there and rightfully so. All we had was a box designed to do a job for which we were responsible. Buzz was working along at his level and had suddenly moved into the Navy Electronic Systems Command (NAVELEX) arena. Some officers who were trying to help him didn't clue him into the "land mines" surrounding the organization. We had the same problem with the Supply Systems Command. Because we could buy our SITE components in local electronics stores (we actually negotiated deals with the manufacturer), we could assemble SITE at a low cost, many hundreds of dollars cheaper than the Navy supply system could because they were compelled to put each item out on a competitive bid.

NAVELEX wanted to engineer our SITE system, design special equipment, test and then reengineer it. SITE was a minor program; a total of 400 to 500 boxes were built over several years. What finally evolved was a special situation with CHINFO having its own procurement system, warehouse and installation crews. It was one of the few CNO initiatives to come in under budget and ahead of schedule. It was totally the result of Buzz Rizer's keen management skills, initiative and frugality. The only credit I took was in hiring him and giving him the responsibility.

After I retired from the Navy, CHINFO expanded Buzz's scope by adding the responsibility of Director of Navy Broadcasting to administer about 250 Navy broadcasters stationed throughout the world. In 1984, he was selected to be the Director of Armed Forces Information Services under the Assistant Secretary of Defense (for Public Affairs). He held that job until he retired from the federal government in 1998 at the top executive level. I have always been proud of Buzz and his many accomplishments. I cherish the days when I was called to extricate him or join him in firefights along the path bringing CCTV to our ships at sea as a part of enhancing our internal information program.

CHINFO Becomes A Publisher

While focusing to include television, the medium the youngsters had always known, in our internal information program, we did not ignore using print. The Thomas Study recommended that CHINFO be responsible for All Hands Magazine, the old Navy standard monthly, edited and published by the Bureau of Naval Personnel (BUPERS). I was not prepared to put up a big fight for All Hands. But we were responsible for Navy-wide internal information emanating from Navy Headquarters. So it seemed logical that established publication should be a part of our program along with the new electronic presentations.

Again the old bugaboo about change and turf surfaced. I had to go to the mat with the Chief of Naval Personnel, Vice Adm. Dave Bagley. "Why do you think CHINFO can do better than BUPERS in editing this magazine?" he asked posing the obvious question during one of our discussions in his office, I responded that CHINFO was designated as the head of internal information. The magazine was another medium used to inform our personnel as a part of our overall program. We were primarily featuring electronic presentations (radio and TV), motion pictures and still photography. I related how I had religiously read All Hands since I came into the Navy and I respected it. But it had not changed its type face in those 30 years, and its articles read like they were edited and "chopped" (initialed) by every Navy captain in BUPERS. The writing was sterile and wasn't communicating with the magazine's audience—the 90% of Navy personnel who were enlisted.

I suggested making far greater use of photography, sprucing up the writing and composition and making more use of color. It could be made more attractive and appealing and at the same time carry the message. Making it more readable and enjoyable would more readily inform our people. They would be more cognizant and more conversant about the direction the Navy was proceeding and why we were going that way. All Hands could and should be a more vital part of the Navy's leadership. I ended by using again General George Washington's quote about informed troops being good troops. I figured Dave Bagley and his staff could argue with me at length, but they would not refute George.

I remember Dave Bagley chuckling and saying I should know it was not just captains who chopped off the articles. "There are a few admirals around here who spend time doing that, too," he said. "And I'm one of them." It wasn't easy, but BUPERS relinquished control of All Hands. An orderly change was made transferring its direction to Navy Internal Relations Activity (NIRA).

A PAO In Command

Incident to the evolution of internal information, the NIRA was established under CHINFO's direction as a part of the OPNAV staff. This differed from the Office of Information operating within the Navy's secretariat. The Chief of Information was assigned to the OPNAV staff with the Code Number 007. There were no James Bond exploits, but the 007 designation was good for a giggle or two along the way. The CHINFO was responsible to the CNO as his advisor on public affairs.

Another important consideration in keeping with NIRA being a naval activity, was its having a "commanding officer" as opposed to a director or chief. So the advent of NIRA gave our PAOs the unique opportunity to be a commanding officer, probably the only opportunity for those restricted line officers to command a unit. In a relatively short time we had come a long way. Numbers wise, CHINFO's Internal Relations Division initially comprised five or six people, including an officer who was dedicated as a liaison with the Naval Reserve. The number grew to about 200 by including the Navy Broadcast unit and continued to grow. In calendar year 2000, NIRA had 400 personnel, most in the broadcast business, positioned throughout the world.

Capt. Harold "Hal" Potter, a naval aviator on his last assignment before retiring, headed the Internal Relations Division. As the new deputy, I observed Hal was not happy and had his throttles back to almost "loiter" speed. I energized him with my spiel about internal communications, and he seemed to come alive. He needed a challenge—something to sink his teeth into, thrash around with and "advance his throttles." It was invigorating to watch him respond and become involved.

We knew Hal would need some staff support, so we assigned a young intrepid officer, Cdr. James E. (Gene) Wentz, to expressly assist him with the task of structuring the new entity and doing the bulk of the paperwork. He did an exceptional job, and I was pleased to recommend him for a Navy Commendation Medal. Significantly, it was Admiral Bud Zumwalt who presented it to him in Athens, Greece. I had sent Gene there to do some of the groundwork for establishing a base for a Navy ship to be home ported there. Bud and Jack Davey, who was integral to the situation, were on a Mediterranean area tour. It's always nice when touring areas, naval bases and ships to participate in award ceremonies. The payoff is making the recipient feel good about the event, and especially in this case to receive the award from the CNO. Acting like a relief valve, the presenter is able to concentrate, if only for a few minutes, on Navy people and reward them for their accomplishments.

Delegating Responsibility

When I was in the Secretary's office and when serving as the Deputy, it was not unusual for me to spend considerable time with newsmen working on a story about the Navy. That's part of being a PAO, and to many, the most enjoyable. However, when I became CHINFO, I was cautioned, somewhat facetiously, not to upstage the younger officers, particularly those in the newsroom. I was still there to help if a situation warranted, if some doors needed to be opened or other flag officers brought into the situation.

Normally, stories of national interest were handled by the Assistant Secretary of Defense for Public Affairs (ASPD PA). We would work together, but the ASDPA had the lead. Secretary Daniel Henkin, the top man, was excellent at handling news personnel as was his deputy Jerry Friedheim. Friedheim succeeded him during the later part of my term as CHINFO. It was a good arrangement, and they were helpful to me. They had a weekly meeting of the three service chiefs—Army, Navy and Air Force—to brief and debrief pertinent public affairs situations. The Marine Corps Director of

Information was also invited.

One latent major story the country was patiently awaiting was the release of our POWs from incarceration in the dungeons of North Vietnam. Most were Navy and Air Force aviators. Many had been there a long time—some since the early days immediately after the Tonkin Gulf incident. That event escalated the U.S. involvement in the civil war going on in Vietnam between the Communist North and the Democratic South. Lt. (JG) Everett Alvarez was the first to be shot down. It happened during his first combat flight on August 5, 1964. He was flying an attack aircraft A-4 Skyhawk with the VA-144 squadron off the aircraft carrier USS *Constellation*. "Ev" and I became good friends after his release. I came to know Cdr. James "Jim" Stockdale (the future vice presidential candidate), commanding officer of an attack squadron who was shot down shortly thereafter. Secretary Nitze and I were aboard "Connie" (USS *Constellation*) at that time.

One of the stipulations President Nixon had in ceasefire negotiations with North Vietnam was the immediate release of the POWs. This release occurred on February 12, 1973, when the American POWs landed at Clark Air Force Base in the Philippines. Naturally, it was a big story in the United States and the world. Considerable planning was necessary, especially in the area of public affairs, and we had a lot of lead time. I was strong in planning, and Dave Cooney was excellent at it. When Dave moved up to the deputy job, I moved Cdr. Brayton Harris into the plans slot. He too was an outstanding officer for that job. CHINFO's plan for the POW Homecoming Program was almost completely adopted for all the Armed Forces by the Defense Department. Among many action items, we had a Navy PAO assigned to each Navy POW to be his official escort throughout the process.

Antarctica

Since my childhood days of listening to Sunday night newscasts by Walter Winchell—"Good evening Mr. and Mrs. America and all the ships at sea," I had a fascination with Antarctica. I recall, huddling around the radio in our winters as Winchell and his crew tried, many times successfully, to contact

Rear Adm. Richard E. Byrd who was spending a summer at "Little America" at the U.S. Navy Base in McMurdo, Antarctica. Winchell would ask Admiral Byrd how he was and what the temperature was. At that time of the year, McMurdo was about the same as Green Bay being in the 10°-20° range, so the temperature wasn't so exciting. Listening to Byrd from Little America was.

For various reasons my curiosity about Antarctica was quiescent for many years. As CHINFO, I started wondering about our sailors in Antarctica, especially those who wintered-over for six months in the dark with temperatures in the -20° range. They could really benefit from a SITE system. For years I had been sending newsmen and women to Antarctica for indoctrination and look-see tours. I realized I should visit. Each news person whom I encouraged to go to Antarctica or sponsored their trip, returned excited about the experience. They marveled at what they saw—the Navy's logistic support and the scientific work sponsored by the National Science Foundation (NSF).

The U.S. Navy supported the NSF in Antarctica. I talked to our Navy Antarctic folks as well as the NSF people, and they squeezed me into their tight schedule in January 1973. One of my traveling companions was Rear Adm, George Cassell, an aviator who was interested in Antarctica Development Squadron Six (VXE-6), the squadron supporting McMurdo. The Air Force occasionally assisted logistically by providing a Military Air Command C-141 Starlifter that could carry a much larger load than the Navy's C-130 Hercules.

We flew commercially to Christchurch, New Zealand, the USN staging area for Antarctic support work. The Navy had a small base there with some housing for personnel and warehousing for equipment. The stop presented an opportunity for me to visit with old friend Chief Photographers Mate Frank Kazukaitis, who had retired in Christchurch, married an Australian girl, was raising a family and worked as a television station cameraman. Kaz worked for me on Guam in 1946 as a petty officer third class (PO3) when I was an ensign. I always referred to Kaz as the Navy's best photographer, and he was exceptional.

Cdr. John Dana, skipper of VXE-6, was our pilot for the 2,300-mile flight to McMurdo. He put the Herc's skis down solidly on the not-so-smooth ice runway, and it felt good! Never a doubt! We were met by Capt. Alfred

Fowler, Commander Task Force 43, the U.S. Navy support group. We had four exciting days as his guests. Lt. (JG) Al Shackelford, the PAO, also greeted me.

Al had served a tour "on the ice" as a Journalist, First Class and while being bivouacked at Christchurch, he met and married Rhonda, a super "Kiwi" girl, for whom Zum and I have developed great affection and respect. The same should be said about Al. He represents an excellent case study to exemplify guts, determination and, yes, gumption. Al had been a Navy aviation electronics technician, a yeoman and finally a journalist. He moved up the promotion ladder to become a senior chief and at the same time was selected for warrant officer. As the Deputy, I authorized him to attend the University of Omaha for seven months to receive a bachelor's degree. Then he returned to work in CHINFO.

With his degree in hand, he applied for a direct commission, and I was proud to swear him into commissioned officer status as a lieutenant (JG). Coincidentally, I was pondering the assignment of a PAO for the Antarctic to replace an officer who apparently wasn't a good fit. I learned Al had spent three years there as a journalist. After about a two-minute conversation and with his concurrence, I detailed him to the Antarctica PAO job. I thought it would be a good place for him to put in a little time and get "salt" on his new gold braid. He had previous duty there, so he knew the environment.

Rhonda could live comfortably and conveniently near her mother in Australia while Al was on the ice for six months of the year. It was a two-year assignment and a perfect fit for Al and the Navy. His predecessors were in the lieutenant commander or commander rank. But I was confident Al was capable of doing the job because of his background, character and demeanor. Putting Al Shackelford into the Antarctic job was not a problem for Captain Fowler or me.

We were scheduled to be at McMurdo for about four days before the next flight to Christchurch. Those days were crammed with interesting and educational things for us to do and see. The most memorable event was flying to the South Pole and spending about three hours there. Again, Commander Dana was our pilot and being an old hand in Antarctica, he took on the chore of being an extraordinary tour guide. He pointed out valleys, mountain ranges and individual mountains and with his great store of anecdotes amused and amazed us. Landing on the snow and ice runway was no problem, but we were reminded that the plane commander wanted to get out of there ASAP (as soon as practicable—or possible) because of the cold and weather.

Al Shackelford accompanied us to the Pole. Having almost five years of duty in that command, he too proved to be another outstanding reliable guide. One of the first things on my agenda was to plant a Green Bay Packers pennant at the South Pole. I had brought the pennant with me in hopes of accomplishing my mission and getting a picture for the Green Bay Press Gazette. Green Bay had the reputation of being the coldest city in the NFL, but that wasn't nearly as cold as the South Pole. (The Press Gazette did publish the picture along with a sizable story.)

Next was a visit to the area where Navy Seabees were constructing a New South Pole Station. It was a geodesic dome to cover the station's main buildings. The 164-foot diameter, 50-foot high aluminum frame would house three, two-story buildings. It was to encompass a science laboratory, living quarters, galley, post office, meeting hall, communications center, store and library. It was being built about 1,700 feet upstream of the polar drift and was expected to be over the exact pole in about eight years. At the turn of the century, a new station was built to replace the old New Station. It had been completely covered with snow and had moved out of range. Who else but the Seabees would construct such a project? I had seen them perform miracles in war and peace all over the world, in the tropics and now at the South Pole.

Another day I flew by helicopter with Al Shackelford to the Dry Valleys, a virtual desert in Antarctica with no snow. It is a patch of Antarctica about 25 miles long, four miles wide and in one place 3,000 feet deep. Naturally this phenomenon aroused the interest of the scientific community. Several scientists there each year try to get answers to questions such as: Why it is snow-free? Why do certain ponds not freeze during the dark winters? What goes on in the metabolism of aquatic ecosystems?

Our Navy pilot set his helicopter down near a small stream and invited me to roam the area at will, be sure to drink water from the stream and lug back any rock samples I desired. I did just that. I drank the water and picked up a few rocks before returning to the chopper. When I was adjusted to my seat and strapped-in, the pilot turned to me and said, "Admiral, how does it feel to have walked on a piece of ground that no human has ever traversed and drunk some water that is a couple million years old? You just did that!" My reply was something to the effect that I didn't have any tingling sensations yet, but I appreciated him bringing me to the site. It was amazing! I had removed a few pieces of slate-like rock, enough for each of my offspring and one for the top of the bar in our rec room. It has proved to be an excellent reminder of that unique experience and is always a catalyst for conversation about my Antarctic adventure.

Al Shackelford and his small crew of journalists were efficient in bringing local, U.S. and world news to the U.S. personnel in Antarctica. Their mediums were a newspaper called McMurdo Sometimes and their FM radio station. The newspaper was delivered to outlying stations by air when weather conditions permitted. I thought we could certainly help them with a CCTV and beef up their radio entertainment. In my debrief to the CNO and Secretary, I recommended we do our best to get a CCTV system quickly to McMurdo before the winter closed in on them.

My second recommendation was to assign some women to McMurdo if for no other reason than to clean up the language of the personnel. My opinion was that men usually respected the presence of females by not using four-letter adjectives and expletives in normal conversation. I had observed that to be the norm down on the ice. It got a chuckle at the morning "Lineup" back in Washinton, but female personnel were eventually assigned to McMurdo.

I felt certain there would be no objection to the CCTV station being installed there and had already called my office from Honolulu to energize the project. Buzz Rizer personally delivered a spare studio that we had available. It was larger than the SITE system box for shipboard use. He had it assembled, indoctrinated personnel on its use and was aboard the last airplane to leave McMurdo in February 1973. The runway on the Ross Ice Shelf had become unstable (soft) and unable to support any more flight operations by the Hercules C-130. Antarctica was closed-in for the next six months. Buzz's wife Norma would have been upset with me if Buzz had to winter-over at McMurdo.

Racial Problems

One of the biggest problems Bud Zumwalt faced during his CNO tenure was race relations and related sensitivities within the Navy. It wasn't on his list of major issues to be addressed, but it inevitably surfaced when confronting Navy problems in the all volunteer environment. He, like many of us, was aware of some deep-rooted differences about relationships with minority personnel, particularly African -Americans, usually related to the geographical region where the individuals were reared. Officers and leading petty officers from Southern states were often less than tolerant with black personnel.

I remembered my early days in the carrier *Midway* as the aide to the executive officer and the public information officer. I did a story for the ship's newspaper about the 1,000th landing on the flight deck. It was an event that provided for a celebration marking a maturity milestone in the ship's life. The pilot who made the landing was given a plaque and cut a cake that evening at dinner in the wardroom.

When talking with the XO, something I did frequently each day, I mentioned the event. Then I facetiously said I was thinking of doing a picture and caption for the 100,000th dinner plate washed in the wardroom scullery that was adjacent to my public information office. Naturally, all the personnel in the scullery were black. The XO, being from South Carolina, looked at me quizzically, blood rising from his neck giving him a beet-red complexion, and blared out, "Don't you ever do anything like that on this ship, or I will find something else for you to do!" I had always been on good terms with the commander, and he had not previously raised his voice to me. He didn't do it again because I didn't give him cause. Thereafter, I studiously avoided racial subjects.

President Truman decreed in 1947 that the Armed Forces would be desegregated. The Army and Air Force immediately started programs to integrate minorities in the general scheme of personnel procedures. The Navy provided for minorities to enter ratings other than mess attendants. But it was difficult to implement a plan because of personal bias of the individuals or groups monitoring those procedures. Each year the Navy would enlist about 1,500 Filipinos, most of them educated, some with college degrees, but they were inducted as mess attendants. Only a few, including blacks, worked their way into other specialties.

Otherwise, the Navy generally ignored the integration order and got away with it until Zumwalt's term as CNO. His leadership coincided with the advent of the All Volunteer Force ending the Selective Service's draft. There had been criticism, particularly in the mass media, that the primary reason for Navy's lethargy was because many senior officers, including the CNOs, were from the South. While they did not refuse to obey the order, they just ignored it. I contend that part of the blame should fall on the secretariat where policy is established. I recall no pressure from that level to ensure complete integration of all minorities. If any of the Secretaries had insisted on integrating the Navy, the CNOs would have dutifully carried out a better program than existed.

Previously, I noted that Secretary of the Navy John L. Sullivan in 1947-48 "integrated" a black officer into the regular Navy and placed Lt. Dennis Nelson into the Public Information specialist program. That particular placement was ill conceived. Dennis was one of the original 13 black officers commissioned into the Navy in World War II and was a college professor. But he had no experience at sea, in journalism or public information. He was too old to start a new field of endeavor particularly in the highly competitive Navy officer corps. I knew him well and enjoyed his company, but always felt sorry for him and his situation. He retired from naval service as a lieutenant commander. As a coincidence, his son Dennis, Jr. worked under my supervision in the Office of Information. He also retired as a lieutenant commander.

An exception to the norm, one in which I was involved, was when Secretary Paul Nitze energized a program to increase the number of black officers in the Navy and Marine Corps by installing a Naval Reserve Trianing Corps (NROTC) unit at Prairie View State College in Texas. Under Secretary Charles Baird headed the project, and I assisted him on the secretariat level. The effort indicated the leadership was aware of deficiencies and trying to make positive strides. However, they were not cognizant of the depth of the problem.

Z-Gram 66

Early in his tenure, Bud Zumwalt examined personnel statistics that revealed about 5% of Navy enlisted personnel and less than 1% of the officer corps were African-American. Twelve percent of the U.S. population was black. Comparing those numbers, he believed the soon to be implemented All Volunteer Force would increase black recruitment providing an important benefit to them and to the Navy.

Simultaneously, he had two retention study groups in progress. One was for black officers and their wives; the other involved black enlisted men and their wives. The results of those studies were shocking to him and to Secretary Chafee. It resulted in Zumwalt's famous "Z-Gram 66." It was his "most heartfelt" of the 121 Z-Grams he issued. It summarized that the service men and their wives were definite and unanimous in their view that the Navy was basically segregationist and cared little for blacks. They perceived promotions were more difficult for blacks than whites, and there was little help or even an indication of caring when it came to finding housing at a new assignment.

The Navy Exchanges carried none of the sundry items sought by African- Americans. It conveyed a disturbing situation. At the debrief of the two study groups, I observed the body language of several senior officers and flag officers exhibiting embarrassment or discomfort. A few were defiant and essentially shrugged, "So what?" The CNO knew his Z-Grams on the subject wouldn't change sensitivities immediately. In fact, in retirement, we discussed the situation many times. He shared his feeling that unfortunately it would take a generation or two to change attitudes. However, he was confident that eventually, given loyal support, training and administration, minorities would prove their worth. They would become part of a winning team to help eradicate institutionalized racism.

The Navy wasn't the only group having difficulty in race relations during that timeframe. The entire country was in turmoil. The metamorphosis ongoing in the Southern states was significant and gathering speed. It kindled in December 1955 when Rosa Parks, a seamstress in Montgomery, Alabama, refused to give up her seat on a public bus to a white man. A 381-day bus boycott by 90% of local blacks followed. The subsequent desegregation of the Montgomery bus system and the introduction of a minister, Dr. Martin Luther King, Jr., who appeared on the scene to support the boycott were significant. Landmark events took place including desegregation of schools, civil rights marches and demonstrations linked with President Lyndon Johnson's Great Society vision. Race riots erupted in Washington, D.C. (1968), Detroit, Chicago and Los Angeles. All played heavily in the national news. The Human Rights movement was maturing, adding to the culture concerns of our country. The prolonged Vietnam War was becoming increasingly unpopular.

Conjoined with the war was what it was doing to the personnel structures of the Armed Forces. Naval operations tempos were demanding increased time for deployments. Up to six aircraft carriers were "on the line" at Yankee Station in the Gulf of Tonkin. They required additional support ships such as escorts and auxiliaries. Deployments were increased from the normal six months to nearly nine, and the turnaround time between deployments was abbreviated. On-line workdays were routinely 16 to 18 hours per day for weeks on end. Spare parts were difficult to secure, and more accidents and damage to aircraft and equipment occurred. The Western Pacific has some beautiful ports of call but not for warships. The old cliché, "I joined the Navy to see the world and what did I see? I saw the sea." proved realistic.

On October 12, 1972, ironically on the eve of the Navy's 197th birthday, an incident occurred in the carrier *Kitty Hawk*. The ship was returning to the Tonkin Gulf from a short stay for repairs and upkeep at the US Naval Base, Subic Bay in the Philippine Islands. *Kitty Hawk* had been in the Western Pacific for almost eight months and had set a record for number of sorties flown. The carrier had an outstanding commanding officer as well as a black executive officer, Cdr. Benjamin Cloud, recognized as a promising senior grade officer. The ship also had a functioning, well run Minority Affairs Office. A group of black enlisted men formed to object to an inquiry about one black apprentice seaman for offensive conduct ashore. The incident occurred at Olongapo, a city adjacent to the naval base. The group beat up on several white sailors onboard the ship. In the melee 60 personnel were injured and required medical attention. Twenty-six black men were charged.

Four days later, USS *Hassayampa*, a fleet oiler, docked at Subic Bay, and a dozen blacks informed the executive officer they would not sail with the ship unless money allegedly stolen from the wallet of one of the group was returned. They also threatened to attack white sailors. Five white sailors were assaulted, given first aid and returned immediately to duty. Eleven black sailors were put ashore to be investigated, and the ship sailed a few hours late to join other Seventh Fleet ships in the Tonkin Gulf. These two cases alarmed Navy folks and provoked immediate investigations from Commander In Chief, Pacific Fleet (CINCPACFLT) headquarters at Pearl Harbor.

The *Kitty Hawk* incident received heavy news coverage for a few days. Some of the media coverage of the two outbreaks did not look favorably on Z-Grams 66 and 113 that outlined the CNO's integration program. The conjecture was that Zumwalt exacerbated the situation by giving encouragement to black personnel to protest and mutiny. It was a flawed and hasty conclusion because the other services had experienced similar incidents when they initiated integration policies. The swirling tempo of Vietnam War operations raised the level of intemperance.

To investigate further into the entire integration program, Admiral Zumwalt ordered in late October the convening of a new minority officers retention study group. The review examined the status of junior officers—ensigns, lieutenant junior grades and lieutenants. The results were dismal and again, in his words, "a shocker." The group's study indicated that the Navy had refused to accept the racial situation as a problem. Some commanding officers had refused to put emphasis on minority affairs as evidenced by the assignment of Career Counselors and Special Assistants for Minority Affairs as collateral duties. Many prejudicial practices continued to exist in the Navy and were cited. The two attention grabbing ship incidents occurred far away at sea, and the news stories were relatively short-lived. However, when things are going bad, we hope for better days, but events can take you farther down. And they did.

About a week later another incident occurred. This time it involved the carrier *Constellation* while it was working up to deployment for another tour in the Tonkin Gulf. This time the ship was only extended three months for a total of nine. The "Connie" would have only six months turnaround time back in the San Diego area. It included some time in a shipyard—a miserable time for the crew—for urgent repairs and retraining a new crew that had been assembled. The new crew included a much larger percentage of seemingly non-trainable young black enlisted men. They were considered so because their low test scores indicated they were not capable of handling service school curricula. They were disgruntled because they had been assigned to the traditional deck and engineering divisions. That meant a lot of grunt work and chipping paint.

A group of 50 to 60 unhappy black sailors began holding informal meetings in the section of the mess known as the "Sidewalk Café." As is normal in such circumstances, leaders and spokesmen arose based primarily on the loudness of their voices and crudeness of their language. Again, one of the Connie's (a ship with a complement of 5,000) problems was having its Minority Affairs Officer's duties handled by a chief petty officer, who much preferred his primary duty, as a collateral duty. Another complication was having the dental officer serve as the chairman of the ship's Human Relation Council. He was not conversant with problems of working sailors, let alone minority affairs.

The dissidents caused so much disruption that the captain put 144 of them, including a few whites, ashore, while the ship returned to sea to complete its rigorous training schedule. Eventually the entire country was made aware of the situation by television and newspaper reports. The climax came when 24 men returned to the ship, and 120 were removed from the ship's roster and investigated. The proceedings resulted in 46 discharges, 36 honorable discharges and 74 men given different assignments.

"The speech"

The worst was still to come. Some of the "Zumwalt Haters" were demanding his resignation or wanting the President to fire him. In a meeting I had with Dan Henkin, Assistant Secretary of Defense for Public Affairs, and his deputy Jerry Friedheim, we discussed the Navy's dilemma and concluded that the Navy—meaning Zumwalt—should make a statement. Preferably in a speech, he could outline the Navy's policy and programs relating to minority affairs. I checked my calendar and noted that Bud had a speech scheduled in a few days for the Washington area Navy flag officers. It would be an ideal time.

I called Bud recommending the idea and shared I had been talking with Henkin and Friedheim who concurred. We intended to ride the speech hard releasing it to all outlets. He agreed. The speech was well prepared, and Bud, as always the superb speaker, was never better. He put everything he had into the delivery. He admitted to me it was probably the most important speech of his life. My reaction to the speech was that it was well received, the oratory was outstanding and the message was clear. This was the way the Navy was going to get on top of this insidious problem.

Within an hour, Fred Hoffman of the Associate Press came out with a story from the Pentagon. He wrote that the beleaguered Zumwalt had called together his admirals and chewed them out publicly. I personally doubted if any of the admirals in the audience thought they had been chewed out until they read or heard about it on the evening news. I have always thought the story was instigated and planted but could never prove it. When rereading the speech, it seemed even anyone with a heavy guilt complex would have had to worked hard to conclude he had been castigated publicly. Bud Zumwalt was an astute leader and would never do something like that.

Congressman F. Edward Hebert, Chairman of the House Armed Services Committee, announced by news release from his home in New Orleans that he had ordered a special subcommittee to investigate "alleged racial and disciplinary problems" on Navy ships. Floyd Hicks (D-WA) was installed as chairman, W. C. Daniel (D-VA) and Alexander Pirnie, (R-NY) were other members. The objective for this investigation was a different "spin" on racism. It was the Southern congressmen making a move to show what they thought of Zumwalt's programs relative to minorities—blacks, Hispanics, Filipinos and women—and their dislike for beards on sailors and women serving as aviators aboard ship.

Hebert told Bud that he was going to give him a "good scrubbing." Among Bud's virtues was being discerning and perceptive. He was also courageous. I have always felt it was good to have a man like that on our side; certainly we would not have enjoyed him as an adversary. He decided Hicks' subcommittee action should be taken as an opportunity to state the Navy's case and aggressively sought time on its agenda. At first Hicks didn't want Bud to testify. That meant Armed Services Committee Chair Hebert didn't want his conclusions muddled by facts coming from the Navy. The resistance fortified the contention we held that this investigation was to be a quick and dirty job on Bud Zumwalt and the quicker the better.

Pressure was brought to bear, and Hebert relented. Bud Zumwalt was ready for them and did an admirable job of stating his case. It was a most impressive demonstration. Here was a leader beset by myriad problems brought about by an unpopular war amidst an upheaval ongoing in the country's social structure as well as in the Armed Forces. Overshadowing things was the struggle with the beginnings of the all volunteer personnel program. All those issues were superimposed on frugal funding, not only to fight the fight in Vietnam but to prepare for the burgeoning threat of the impressive Soviet Union naval forces. Even though we were exhausting our personnel, depleting our assets and draining our resources in Vietnam; the Cold War continued.

Ironically, the United States Civil War seemed to be continuing as well. The South did "rise again" in the form of controlling a good portion of the U.S. Congress. That contingent persisted in prolonging segregation and detouring any effort to desegregate or integrate our society. The investigation of "alleged racial and disciplinary problems in Navy ships" was pure racism in reverse. From my Washington duty vantage point and having read considerably about the history and vicissitudes of our beautiful capital city and its environs, it seems one should never underestimate the power of the U.S. Congress nor its members.

Over the years, I have come to know many congressmen and senators and had the opportunity to observe them in action and be with them socially. I found it difficult to dislike many of them. They have a tough job as elected officials, and I respected all of them except when they deviated from my perspectives on pertinent issues. They included: John Chafee, one of my favorite people, former Secretary of the Navy, my boss and a true Marine Corps hero of the Korean War and its Chosin Reservoir campaign; John Warner, former Secretary of the Navy and my boss, who rose to be the Chairman of the Senate Armed Services Committee and who has a superb staff and offices throughout the state of Virginia to take care of his constituents; Jim Lloyd, congressman from California, former Navy PAO and good friend; the delegation from the Long Beach, California area I worked with in the early days after my retirement from the Navy; and Eddie Hebert, our nemesis on the integration issue, was a fun guy to be with socially and was helpful to me, personally, in my job as CHINFO. They were typical of the congressmen and senators with whom I met and worked in my career. Because of my association with the above few, I refused to disparage the lot and came to appreciate that they were doing their best to represent this nation and their constituents. I also realize there are exceptions to any rule or my conclusions.

All about hair

Much had been said about how Zumwalt had changed the appearance of sailors by letting them wear long hair and grow moustaches and beards. The issue arose as a concern of the subcommittee members. We had an answer to that accusation. It was done in Z-Gram 70 issued in January 1971 because of a confusing statement on the haircut policy released by Admiral Tom Moorer on May 29, 1970, a month before Zumwalt succeeded him as CNO.

In a personal letter to commanders, Moorer reaffirmed the long-standing policy of allowing beards, mustaches and sideburns. However, the last paragraph caused the confusion. The text included, "It is not desired that any public announcement be made of this matter or that it be highlighted." The Moorer letter directed commanders to modify standing orders or regulations that conflicted with the contents of the letter. But by not requiring publicized standards for haircuts and facial hair, he let commanding officers and commanders pretty much interpret what they wanted. Reports were received that some commanding officers followed the letter precisely, and others used their own judgment.

Destroyers frequently "nest" while alongside a pier meaning there are two, three and even four ships alongside each other. Personnel from outboard ships have to pass over inboard ships in order to go ashore. As could be predicted, at least one commanding officer refused to permit sailors from other ships to traverse his ship, if he didn't like their haircuts or beards. Generally, there was no standard, and sailors' hairstyles differed as well as their beards and sideburns. It became a concern, and the Master Chief Petty Officer of the Navy (the Navy's senior enlisted person) included the issue in a list of recommendations he was asked to make to the CNO for consideration.

The result was that Z-Gram 70 was a carefully prepared and reviewed (by fleet commanders) document on hair styles, length of hair, beards and sideburns. Because it was a Z-Gram, it received considerable publicity, and we in the Office of Information featured it in all our internal presentations. Of course, Zumwalt was both praised and blamed for longer hair, beards, mustaches and sideburns.

Because the Hicks' subcommittee criticized beards and the rest, I thought that the subcommittee should know the background. I was told they were not interested. That incited me to call my good friend, Robert "Bob" Bateman, who headed Boeing's Washington office, to ask if he knew Floyd Hicks. I was sure Bob knew well the state of all Washington's congressional groups. That night I had dinner with Hicks and Bob at the Georgetown Club. At first Hicks was not enthusiastic, but by the time we completed dinner, he asked if I would consider testifying before his subcommittee.

He said he would have to clear it first with Chairman Hebert, and I replied that I would have to do likewise with Admiral Zumwalt and Secretary Warner. Zumwalt thought it was a great idea, and Warner agreed. I had known Eddie Hebert, been with him on several occasions and he knew me by name. I called a close friend and ally in New Orleans and briefed him on the situation. If Hebert called him asking about me, he would know the background. I added that if he didn't give me a good recommendation, I would spread the word that he cheated at golf.

Two days later I was before the subcommittee where I led off with a statement and then was asked more than a few questions. My plan was to introduce the Moorer letter, explain the consequences and then get out of there! The subcommittee members—vultures, I thought—had other ideas, and they were going to enjoy feasting on me. I had observed others in my situation, but this was my first time in the barrel. I knew I had to be cool, be patient and look toward the time I could exit back to the safe, friendly haven of my office. I realized quickly I couldn't win on the subcommittee playing field.

Assessing the event, I succeeded in my mission of introducing Admiral Moorer's letter and explaining the hair problem. But my interactions during the grilling on other subjects didn't go as well as I would have liked. I was interrogated, not so much about the hair letter, but about my part in Zumwalt's speech where he allegedly rebuked his flag officers publicly. When I admitted I was central to the event, they really went after me. I could have been more perceptive and would have done better, if I had been coached by some of the available pros. I should have been more adroit at turning some of their questions around to expound on all the good Bud Zumwalt was bringing to the Navy and its people. I punished myself with those thoughts as I returned to the Pentagon and reported to Admiral Zumwalt. It was another arc on the learning curve.

"The subcommittee finds that permissiveness ... exists in the Navy today," was the substance of the report.* It was as advertised by Eddie Hebert and as transparent as his intentions. An example of the 17 findings, 11 opinions and 16 recommendations was, "Non-military gestures such as 'passing the power' or 'dapping' (fist-on-fist greeting) are disruptive, serve to enhance racial polarization and should be discouraged." As Bud Zumwalt said, "I guess rebel yells simply prove that boys will be boys."

I added that it might be a subject to be discussed in the Navy's racial seminars but to disallow it would be counterproductive. Although tumultuous at the time—to Admiral Zumwalt and his mini-staff including me—the subcommittee's report proved to be inconsequential. It proverbially went over the dam, down the river and out to sea. If anything, it seemed to strengthen Zumwalt's name and position in the minds of the American public.

I turned our resources loose on our branch offices in New York, Chicago, Los Angeles, Dallas, Atlanta and all other command PAOs. We would provide information about the Navy's programs as well as work with Navy interest groups such as the U.S. Naval Institute, Navy League of the U.S., Fleet Reserve Association, Naval Reserve Association, Naval Historical Foundation, Naval Enlisted Reserve Association and others. Coincidental to our effort, Secretary of Defense Melvin Laird was in Kansas City to meet with the Associated Press managing editors and spoke about his support for the Navy's racial programs. Many others rallied around Bud Zumwalt and his forays. By this time, Elmo Zumwalt had become a recognizable name

---

* For a more detailed description of the racial incidents and subcommittee reports, see *On Watch* by Admiral E. R. Zumwalt, Jr., Quadrangle.

in American culture, a combination of his unusual names, both family and given, his handsome, charismatic figure and his drive and zeal manifested by his quest as TIME Magazine stated, to "… drag the tradition-bound Navy into the 20th century."

A Break—Two Weeks Of Shore Leave

In August of 1973 Zum, son Brian and I were invited to join Capt. Ed McGrath and his wife Pat to do an auto tour of Germany, Italy and a little of Switzerland. Ed had an unusual Navy career starting as a Naval Reserve officer in World War II as a submariner in the Pacific. Ed was credited with devising the code used by U.S. Navy submarines in so called "wolf pack operations." He was demobilized at the end of 1945 and worked as a journalist in the Northeast ending up at the Boston Post. He was recalled to active duty during the Korean War and because of his newspaper work was corralled into duty in public information in Washington. He completed his recall duty in the Commandant, First Naval District headquarters in Boston and then returned to work at the Post.

During the Vietnam War, I was a part of a small committee that assisted CHINFO with personnel matters. (I was in the Secretary's office at the time.) We had some assignments to fill and asked several Naval Reservists to consider active duty for an indefinite time. I thought Ed would be an excellent addition to the active duty community and lobbied on his behalf. Ed stayed on for 14 years, filling several important billets and performing superbly. He was the PAO in Naples for the NATO Supreme Allied Commander, Southern Europe Command (SACSEUR) and later moved up to Darmstadt, Germany to be the Officer in Charge, Stars and Stripes, Europe. Stars and Stripes was an Army daily newspaper, a residual from World War II. In fact, it started in World War I and went defunct until revived for World War II. It was later adopted by the Defense Department, but most of its readers were Army and Air Force personnel in Europe. During my time as CHINFO, the Navy became a part of the distribution, but delivery to ships in the Sixth Fleet in the Mediterranean Sea was difficult and rather haphazard.

We drove to the Military Airlift Command base at Dover, Delaware, and flew in a C-5, the largest cargo aircraft at that time to Europe, with a stop at the Azores. The C-5 is a cavernous airplane with a few VIP seats available and other seats along each side. It was rather Spartan, but it was a free airplane ride in an airplane doing its job of delivering cargo. The term used for such travel was Space Available (Space A). The Air Force and Navy (to a much less degree) provide space when available to active duty personnel, dependents and retirees to travel worldwide wherever these cargo planes go. It is an excellent program, if one has time to spare and is a little adventuresome. The Air Force maintained a base at the Azores, an island possession of Portugal. The next day took us to Frankfurt where Ed McGrath, our chauffeur for the next two weeks, met us.

Before heading south to Italy, Zum, Brian and I grasped the opportunity to visit Berlin which, of course, was inside East Germany and then occupied by the Soviet Union. Being on active duty, I had to get special permission to take the overnight train from Frankfurt to Berlin, and I received it in due time. It was a train ride that Brian has not forgotten and neither has Zum. The train made several stops during the night, and we could hear Soviet soldiers stomping up and down the passageways of the train. They stopped at some berthing compartments to loudly rap on the doors and go through the formalities of checking passports and credentials. We could peer out our curtains to see soldiers at the stations, carrying rifles and looking menacing.

While in Berlin, one thing I thought would be interesting for Zum and Brian would be to go through "Checkpoint Charlie," the most famous gate between Berlin and East Germany. Checkpoint Charlie was made famous by the media because several Germans residing on the communist side made attempts there to escape into West Berlin. Some were successful, but many making the valiant effort were shot. I could not venture there because of my security clearances. After the midnight ride from Frankfurt, Brian had second thoughts about Checkpoint Charlie, and Zum was relieved that he felt that way. The contrast between East and West Germany was dramatic. The Western economy was burgeoning, and the people were living in the freedom of a democratic environment. The life of the people and the environment in the East was dull, drab and dark.

The first stop on our drive south was at Stuttgart, Germany, the headquarters for Commander In Chief, US Forces, Europe (CINCEUR). Capt.

Pickett Lumpkin, the command PAO, was our host although we stayed in the Bachelor Officer's Quarters (BOQ). Stuttgart is also the headquarters and primary assembly plant location for Mercedes Benz. The two Mercedes we had at home were born there. Innsbruck, Austria, was the next stop and is famous as a ski resort and the host city for the 1976 Winter Olympics. Nothing is less exciting to me than to spend a night in a hotel. So we started staying in the "Pensions," bed and breakfast places that were not only economical but provided a good way to experience the local environment and the people. We could get a room for the three of us for $3.00 or $4.00.

Seefelt, Austria, another ski resort town with excellent cross-country skiing, was the next overnight. Ed and his wife Pat had stayed there on a skiing trip and knew the town and some of the trails that weren't meant for hiking. They proved to be fantastic guides. In Rome we stayed in a hotel near the Coliseum. For dinner that evening Ed and Pat took us to one of their favorite restaurants. The food was excellent. When walking along the street returning to the hotel, Pat was on the outside of me next to the curb. A small car came along at a good clip, and a youngster leaned out the window and ripped the purse off her shoulder. Because there was considerable traffic, I had the idea I could catch them and stupidly ran after the car. However, it was for naught, and they got away. When I returned rather sheepishly to our group, Ed lectured me to never do that again especially in Italy. Brian, in his placid, discerning way, said, "What would you have done if you caught that car, Dad?"

"I don't know, Brian," I replied. "Dogs chase cars. What do they do if they ever catch one?"

Unfortunately, the purse contained money, gas coupons and Ed and Pat's passports and ID cards. We spent an extra day in Rome primarily at the police station and the American Embassy. The Italian Carabinieres (police) were sympathetic and courteous but not much help. To see an Italian Carabinieri shrug his shoulders doesn't give one much confidence in finding the family jewels. Fortunately, the purse was found, discarded by the thieves, stripped of the money of course but the other valuables were intact. So it was on to Naples with a night at a luxury hotel on the Isle of Capri. It cost us about $14.00. Now that same hotel commands over $300 per night for the same room. Pat asked Brian what he thought about Capri, and he replied, "It's a biga rocka."

We visited Sorrento and the archeological digs at Pompeii and did a day tour of the Amalfi Drive, a spectacular roadway up into the mountains. On the return trip heading toward Darmstadt, Germany, we visited Switzerland to cap off an outstanding two weeks in the "old country." We had some difficulty getting on a manifest to return to the United States. When I decided we would return to the States commercially, we got a call to get to Frankfurt right away for a C-5 flight to Dover. We have been indebted to Ed and Pat (who died of cancer a few years later) for a great adventure.

Roiling Secretariat Seas

Life with Admiral Zumwalt was never quiescent. It was a rocky, bumpy road those working closely with him accepted. "Just routine chaos" was the way we identified a normal day. His 0730 "Lineup" each morning got us started for the day. If we were not immediately energized in the lineup to get something done ASAP, some of us would retreat to the SECNAV/CNO staff wardroom for breakfast and an impromptu caucus. It included laughing and wondering what "Crazy Elmo" would be up to next. We had other terms of endearment for the admiral, and an outsider would undoubtedly have considered us to be disloyal. But au contraire, the mini-staff was a band of loyalists totally dedicated to assist Bud Zumwalt achieve his goals.

If we disagreed with any of his initiatives, we had the opportunity to discuss it with him, and he would listen. In fact, he encouraged us to dissent because he valued our input and knew we would support him when a decision was made. However, tempus fugit or as the saying goes, "Time flies when you are having fun." Bud's four-year term was coming to an end, and the challenges continued until the end of his tour. He departed from the gates at the Naval Academy on Saturday June 29, 1974, having been relieved of the duties as CNO by Adm. James L. Holloway, III. Up to the last hours of his naval career, he was threatened with a Courts-Martial or being fired by

President Nixon. Many of the difficulties could be attributed to the paranoia and decadence existing in the short-lived second term of President Nixon. The Watergate investigation was ongoing and eventually brought about the resignation, to preclude impeachment, of Richard Milhous Nixon as the 37th President of the U.S. Nixon resigned on August 9, 1974, a little more than five weeks after Zumwalt retired.**

Just prior to Zumwalt's departure, he presented me with the Distinguished Service Medal (DSM) for the "creation of the most effective and professional public affairs program in the history of the United States Navy." This was the first award of the DSM to a Navy PAO, and I was grateful for the honor. The DSM was the highest award for administrative situations such as my job. It was also awarded to fleet commanders but normally reserved for three and four-star flag officers. The presentation was done in Bud's office with only a few invited friends present. My invitees included Zum, Joanne Crown and Morgan and Helen Fitch of Chicago. In my remarks following the presentation, I was able to thank him for the privilege to be at his side during the great service transformation that took place in a whirlwind environment.

I also took the opportunity to thank Vice Adm. Tom Hayward, who was also present, for his time and efforts to "keep me whole" and informed about what was going on behind the scenes in naval strategy. Tom was Op 090, the "Money Man," in the CNO's staff. Naturally, he knew of all expenditures as well as plans for the future, because they always hinged on money. Every other week he would brief me. It was valuable, not for immediate stories, but for background on how things were evolving from the CNO's office. The briefing constituted a half-hour to 45-minute session, and he was a busy man with a tight schedule. I was forever grateful to Tom for his help. We had become good friends when as captains in the naval secretariat, he was the Executive Assistant to the Under Secretary and my office was directly across from his. We participated in a good professional and social relationship that continued even through retirement. Tom retired from the Navy about eight years later as the Chief of Naval Operations.

**See *On Watch* for more specific details.

Our Eagle Scout

An unusual and one of the brighter events during this timeframe was an evening at St. Dunstan's Episcopal Church in our neighborhood for the presentation of Eagle Scout awards. Seven youngsters from the same troop had progressed to the top rank in the Boy Scout program. Our son Brian was one of those seven. It was especially unusual because of the large number of Eagles being so honored; it was normally one boy at a time. It was also unusual because of the number of high ranking Navy officers attending and other noteworthy military connections. Secretary of the Navy William J. Middendorf, II spoke at the function as did the Chief of Naval Operations, Admiral E. R. Zumwalt, Jr.

Mike Shepherd, son of Rear Adm. Burton Hale "Burt" Shepherd, the Navy's Inspector General and former Executive Assistant and Aide to CNO Admiral Zumwalt, was among the seven honored Eagle Scouts. Five of the seven Eagles were sons of active duty military officers. Army Col. Hank Meyer was the Scout Master, obviously a good one, and also the proud father of a new Eagle Scout. I was really pleased with Brian and his achievement. Although I wasn't much help to him on his trail to Eagle, I did try at various times to work with him and motivate him. His mother provided guidance and prodding. I have long been an advocate of the scouting program and maintain that one of the best achievements that can be displayed in a resume is Eagle Scout. It commands attention and should be at least worth an interview. That scouting rank immediately indicates the individual is intelligent, diligent, dedicated and possesses actively supportive parents.

Our other son Craig got to the level of Life Scout before disinterest in his troop prevailed. Craig completed two years at Chowan College in North Carolina and decided to take a recess from college work. The Selective Service Commission had some ideas about how he could spend the next few years, so he opted to enlist in the Naval Air Reserve. He was interested in aviation and was mechanically adept, so he thought he could find a niche in aviation mechanics work. I swore him into the Naval Reserve at a small function Zum attended with me at the Naval Air Facility, Andrews Air Force Base.

Within a few weeks he was off to recruit training at the Naval Air Station in Memphis. Near the time for his graduation, I had my aide Kendell Pease call the appropriate people in Memphis to inquire if there was an opening for a graduation speaker. He said my son was graduating soon and I would also like to visit the Navy complex at Memphis. Naturally, the answer was positive. I did it that way so there would be no extra pressure put on Craig, especially at the platoon level, if they knew his father was an admiral. The day before the graduation ceremony, Craig's chief petty officer put him in a brace and railed, "I don't like surprises. Why the hell didn't you tell me your father is an admiral?"

"Sir, I'm not that dumb," Craig answered.

Kendell and I arrived on the eve of the big event, and I asked if it would be possible or convenient for me to see Craig. A short time later, there was a knock on the door to my BOQ suite. I acknowledged by calling out, "Come in, please." A sailor stepped into the room. I looked at him trying to determine if he was a messenger or security guard, said "Hello" and then turned away for some reason. The sailor said, "Dad, it's me, Craig!" I looked at him and realized it was my son, but I hardly recognized him. He was somewhat gaunt and like all recruits, his head had been shorn of his contemporary longer tresses. So the admiral hugged the seaman. "Craig," I said, "I'm sorry but you do look different. You look great! You look like a sailor!"

"Gee, I hope so," he replied. "They have been telling me that for the past eight weeks."

We had a good time together, and I got him to laugh and relax.

The graduation was exhilarating for me, and I gave one of my better speeches reminding the graduates that just 30 years ago, I too graduated from boot camp and had enjoyed the total experience. It was exciting to be in an action-oriented organization presenting vast opportunities for increased responsibilities and exercise of leadership. The naval experience was inspiring, motivating and rewarding. I encouraged the graduates to seek out opportunities, and then they would be pleased with their personal attainments and contribute to the success of the "Navy Team."

Craig remained at Memphis to attend a Service School course in aviation structures and always finished in the top 10% of his classes. From there he was assigned to a Naval Air Reserve Patrol Squadron, stationed at Naval

Air Station, Patuxent River, Maryland. His squadron flew the venerable P-3 Orion, and he enjoyed annual two-week deployments to Norfolk, Lajes in the Azores, Bermuda, Rota in Spain and Ceuta in Morocco. He ended his six-year enlistment as a third class petty officer ready for second class. He chose not to reenlist, a decision he lamented in later years. He enjoyed the Navy experience, and I know he would have been an excellent leader and tutor.

The Ole Rockin' Chair Beckons

Life after Zumwalt, at least in the Pentagon, was rather quiet, as if everyone was trying to catch a breath. The past four years had been so electrically charged, I had almost forgotten what a normal day could be. In the fall, I took two weeks of leave just to get away from the Pentagon because I wasn't feeling excited about the job anymore or what I was doing. I returned feeling recharged and ready to go. That notion stayed with me for a day or two, and then I felt lethargic again. I began to wonder if I was suffering from burnout. I discussed it informally with a Navy doctor friend and was told I probably just needed to relax a little. He didn't even like the term "burnout." He offered to schedule a series of tests but didn't recommend it at that time. I took and cleared the tests and tried to relax more.

Sometime in October, I was in a one-on-one conference with Admiral Holloway, and somehow he uttered an old Navy expression, "I'm just a smooth-bore gunner." In layman's language that means a traditionalist who isn't looking to change the world. I recalled the last time I heard that phrase was in San Diego in the mid-1950s from Jim Holloway's father, "Lord Jim." At that time he was a vice admiral and the Chief of Navy Personnel. On the way back to my office and for a time at my desk I contemplated the situation. Being sandwiched between two behemoths of Navy lore and legend by an esoteric expression perplexed me. I never believed in fairy tales and had low tolerance for seemingly mystically significant events. I certainly didn't believe that King Neptune was interfering with my life and trying to nudge me over the side with his trident. I concluded it was a humorous coincidence, and I should feel honored to be a part of an interesting story about the Holloways II and III.

That evening I told Zum about the happening, and she registered it as a "2" on a scale of 1-10. So I stashed the experience. (This is the first time I have completely shared it.) While we talked, I indicated to Zum that I had been thinking about retirement or getting myself oriented to think about it. "Good," was her immediate response, "I think you are ready," I asked for amplification, and she came right back with, "You've worked hard for years, had some successes, had a great career and contributed a lot to the Navy. It would do you some good to get away into some other field and try something else. The Navy is wonderful in so many ways, but it has devoured you."

Well, thank you, Ma'am. I think the decision had been made for me. A couple of days later, after checking out some of the logistics involved in retirement, I approached Admiral Holloway with an "unless you disagree," I would like to retire on February 1, 1975. Although surprised, he indicated I should do what I thought was best for myself and family and how I had served the Navy well. With that commentary, I submitted my retirement request, and it was approved.

A few days later Admiral Holloway asked to see me and presented me with facts about my successor. He said the precept for the next selection board had already been done, and it naturally had no provision for the selection of a public affairs flag officer. He followed by showing me the nomination for CHINFO he received from the Chief of Naval Personnel and asked if I had any comment.

I replied I had to preface any comment with a question. I asked if he envisioned the next year's flag selection board including the opportunity for public affairs specialists to compete for selection. He shrugged and said he intended to ask the Secretary to include a PAO in the next selection. I then followed with a candid response that the nominee would add nothing to the process of supporting the CNO and the Secretary in public affairs matters. It would be more efficient to have an Acting CHINFO as a captain for a year. I added that the media reps would consider not having an admiral as a step backward for Navy public affairs.

When pressed for more input on the nominee, I said I had been acquainted with that officer since we were lieutenants. Although he was affable, I didn't think he would bring anything to the table. In order to do the job effectively and efficiently, the CHINFO assimilates a lot of information and when working with news personnel must be judicious and careful about what he says. Many times those occasions occur at cocktail parties or events where alcohol is available, and I had always limited my drinking. Reporters are always aware of loose talk and are experts at piecing together threads of information to come up with the whole cloth and a story. The nominee's reputation was not conducive to that kind of circumspection.

The CNO nodded in agreement and asked whom I would consider as the Acting CHINFO. I replied, subject to his concurrence, recommending Capt. Dave Cooney, my current deputy. Holloway was familiar with him as they had worked together in the past at the Atlantic Fleet Command. He gave it a few moments of thought and then agreed. My quest in the whole situation was to continue the presence of a public affairs officer in the role of CHINFO. Having an Acting CHINFO wasn't the best solution, but I favored it instead of me remaining on active duty for another 15 to 18 months awaiting the next year's flag selection board. I had decided to retire and for good reasons. I had accomplished a new direction for the community, and it was time for me to go home. I informed Dave Cooney upon returning to the office, and he was pleased.

Next on the retirement docket was the event itself. I had decided it would be a quiet affair, possibly done in the office, and I would walk away without bands or fanfare. I had relieved Larry Geis in a similar situation. CHINFO is not a command per se. Some were probably weary of formal changes of command and would opt to keep things quiet. I spread the word about my desires, and a few days later Capt. Jack MacKercher asked to see me. He said he represented a group of senior PAOs.

They recommended I change my mind about a low key retirement and go for broke—have a full blown official ceremony, perhaps at the Sail Loft in the Washington Navy Yard with speeches, the Navy Band and all the pomp and ceremony we could engender. They also recommended a formal dinner, principally for the community, possibly on the eve of my retirement. The rationale was that we, as a community, had broken out of a cocoon we should revel about it. He concluded it would be a good exercise for the PAO community. I told Jack my rationale was that I was tired and wanted to get the event behind me. However, I understood his recommendation and would consider it. I talked it over with my boss, Zum. She sympathized with my previous decision but backed down because of the community. The next morning I called MacKercher to thank him and then told Cooney to "make it so."

Bob Hope

One event that occurred prior to my retirement was a visit to my office by Bob Hope. Bob had pretty much curtailed his Christmas tours with the troops around the world and was publishing a coffee table-type picture album about those tours. He had called earlier to inquire if the Navy had any pictures of his previous Christmas tours. Fortunately, we did and provided them. They turned out to be a major part of his book. Hope called again later to say he had a copy of his book he would like to present to me, and we set an approximate time.

It was near the time I had a regularly scheduled weekly meeting with the Vice Chief, now Adm. Worth Bagley, my old friend from SECNAV days. I forewarned the Vice Chief's staff I might be delayed, and Bagley was informed. He grunted. I arrived for my appointment and announced I might have to leave because Bob Hope had been held up in traffic but was headed to my office. "Yeah, yeah, and the moon's full of cheese, too, " Bagley retorted.

About 10 minutes into our discussion, the Vice Chief's aide slipped quietly in and said, "Bob Hope is in your office, Admiral." I asked to be excused. Bagley asked if this was for real or just another Thompson joke. I said it was definitely for real, and if he behaved himself, I would bring the legend by, and maybe Hope would autograph his hat. I left and after introducing Bob around the CHINFO offices, I brought him to see Bagley, Admiral Zumwalt and Secretary Middendorf. It was a good day, and everyone was pleased to meet Bob Hope. When I was escorting him out of the building to his limousine, he asked if there was a "head" nearby. "Absolutely," I said and steered him into one.

"Great," he said when he emerged. "Never pass up the opportunity to visit a head. The older I get the more important that is."

The retirement ceremony was an impressive event held at the Sail Loft on February 1, 1975. I invited Vice Adm. Bill Mack, Superintendent of the

Naval Academy, a former CHINFO and my mentor for many years, to be the principal speaker. Secretary of the Navy Bill Middendorf, also spoke, and I got old friend, former Chief of Navy Chaplains, Rear Adm. Jim Kelly to be the official chaplain. He dug his uniform out of retirement mothballs and journeyed up the road from his home in Charlottesville, Virginia for the event. It was a full house with many PAOs and others attending. Former Secretary Paul Ignatius and his wife Nan were there. Bud Zumwalt was on travel, so he couldn't make it. It was a memorable occasion.

The dinner the previous night was also a success. We had to limit the number to 120, so wives were not included. I still catch an evil eye from Zum when reflecting on the event. I should have included her because she would have certainly enjoyed the evening. I did get Brian, then a high school junior, wearing a tuxedo and accoutrement to accompany me. The following morning, Dave Cooney dutifully put Brian on report telling me that he along with all others at his table had smoked a cigar. I replied Brian didn't show any ill effects in the car on the way home. I further hoped he was thoughtful enough to warn Brian to tie a line around his pant legs. Smoking cigars at Brian's age could have had a telling effect.

Surprisingly, I was literally showered with farewell and retirement gifts. Some were lighthearted, and others had special significance, and I thought too expensive. A coffee table was hand constructed by Navy cabinetmakers (and paid for by PAOs). It had an antique copper plate that had been used for printing at the mapping service inlaid on top and covered by heavy glass. The plate depicts a section of the Korean coast, a reminder of my tour in John R. Craig during the Korean War. Another was a bronze wall mounting of a sailing ship under full sail and given to Zum and me by the CHINFO staff. On one of our trips, aide Lt. Ed Darrow had observed me eyeballing such artifacts and commenting how I was impressed with that type of artwork. Ed would later tease me about carefully laid hints, but I denied all accusations. Both of those gifts are prominent in our recreation room and are treasured mementos of the culmination of our Navy career and the dedicated, supportive people with whom we worked.

I measure my time as CHINFO by the objectives I set for my tour as Deputy and later as its Chief. If I failed to score a breakaway touchdown, I still gained a lot of yardage. On top of the accomplishment list was establishing a solid internal information program for Navy personnel. Our people were becoming better informed. We had banded together some of our most experienced and brightest PAOs to structure an internal information activity utilizing state of the art technologies and contemporary techniques and skills. We gained approval from the Secretary of the Navy and the Chief of Naval Operations to fund the program including necessary additional personnel (billets) to launch our ambitious program and shared vision,

The Navy Internal Relations Agency (NIRA) was fast developing into a structure envied by the other services and examined by private corporations. It had significant potential for growth and development. About 10 years later, Admiral Jack Garrow, the CHINFO and formerly my executive assistant, transformed the CNO SitRep to a weekly half-hour, magazine styled television news show. By the turn of the 21st Century, CHINFO Rear Adm. Steve Pietropaoli included the Marine Corps and renamed the program the Navy and Marine Corps Weekly News. By satellite it was broadcast to all Navy ships and naval stations and aired several times weekly by more than 150 television stations especially in areas surrounding Navy and Marine Corps shore stations and bases. (My editorial comment—"Way to Go, Team Navy PAO!") Surely, our first Commander in Chief, General George Washington would give us a nod of approval. His guiding words, "An informed troop, is a good troop," I carried with me for about 25 years. His thought inspired the NIRA's creation. Thank you, General Washington!

As for the efficiency and productivity of our public affairs community, I was equally proud of the way it reacted in times of need or crisis. When called upon, it produced creatively. The coordinator for the return of the Vietnam War POWs was the Assistant Secretary of Defense for Public Affairs. Our group brought many ideas and concepts refined by our "Murder Board" and other critiquing techniques to the planning table. We researched and published a compendium and summary of all major news events for their missing eight years—some POWs were incarcerated for eight years—so they could quickly be brought up-to-date on what happened in the United States and the world. Our New York office asked the three major TV networks for eleven copies (one for each hospital, covering all services) of every important (or really interesting) broadcast, such as the moon landing, which were readily provided at no cost. After release from the hospital each Navy

POW had a Navy PAO on call, available for assistance, consultation, and to help with the media. It was a win-win proposition, good for the POW and good for our group. The concerned cluster was intricately involve in bringing safely home those heroes, helping them to adjust to private life and in some cases assisting their return to active duty.

Overall, I thought our community coalesced, and some of the existing cliques dissolved or were not as evident. Zum helped in this respect by communicating with the wives, and, of course, we entertained and welcomed new arrivals to the office regularly into our home

I witnessed the public affairs community definitely performing higher and being better accepted by all parts of the Navy. I was positive about our small group of people and personally knew I had given it my best effort.

Wrapping up my Navy career, I realized Vice Adm. Bill Malone was correct when he advised me four years previously to enjoy my time as a flag officer because it would go by much too fast. Indeed, it did flow by rapidly. After I retired, I took time to assess what my 32 Navy years did for me and what I gave back to the Navy. Reviewing my memories was an excellent catharsis and helped me value the worth of over three decades of service. For a washed out aviation cadet, I know I had a most unusual career in the United States Navy.

I was revived by being sent to the V-12 officer training program on the wonderful Wabash College campus. Commissioned I returned to aviation as an Air Navigator, became managing editor of a daily newspaper on the forward deployed base of Guam, did a short stint in public information, steadied on a track to be a Surface Warfare Officer and then finally settled on a career path as a public affairs specialist. Of paramount importance was the patience my leaders had while shaping my early naval officer development and then later my public affairs specialty. Fortunately, they were adept at shortening the leash when I got too frisky. Perhaps when I was with them, I didn't appreciate their thoughts and concerns for me and what I was trying to accomplish. Unknowingly, I was experiencing deep-seated leadership at its best. I benefited and prospered from their leadership.

Hoisting the flag of continued camaraderie, Bud Zumwalt and I became good friends after retiring from the Navy. We started a couple

of non-profit organizations and had adjacent offices for several years at the System Planning Corporation where we served as consultants. On weekends when we could, we played tennis together and shared a couple shakers of martinis. We became shipmates again aboard cruise ships including one that visited Vietnam. On another we celebrated the 50th anniversary of VE-Day. Many times I have remarked that when I started to work for him when he was CNO, I was seven feet tall and had dark brown hair. Now I am only six feet tall and have snow-white hair. Thank you, Sir.

Today, I can't help but think it would be nice to revisit all those leaders I was so fortunate to have known, thank them for their patience and enjoy a few chuckles at my expense. Such a reunion would be heartwarming because they were not mere bosses, they were human beings for whom I developed deep respect and shared a kindred spirit. They were given a responsibility, and they did their best to perfect their unit, ship, squadron, fleet or command in attaining its mission. Their leadership extracted the best from their subordinates to get the job done with excellence. Since 1775 the United States Navy has institutionalized that process and served the country well. I am humbled to have been accepted, to have participated as a U.S. Navy officer and in a small way contributed to the success of that force. Go Navy!

Retirement?

On Friday, February 1, 1975 I retired from active duty with the U.S. Navy. On Monday morning I was in Long Beach, California reporting for duty with the city as its Washington, D.C. representative. My immediate boss was the City Manager of Long Beach, and I had responsibilities with the Employees Association of the Long Beach Naval Shipyard. Actually, I was employed to help keep the Long Beach Naval Shipyard open. Their employees association paid half of my consulting fees. The yard had been closed just before the Korean War started. Shortly afterward it reopened because of increased Navy ship activity in San Diego and Long Beach.

In peacetime the shipyard was in a precarious situation, primarily because it did not have the capabilities to handle nuclear powered ships. Eventually, all "non-nuke" West Coast Navy yards were closed. In the interim, we worked to keep the yard open. At a meeting in Long Beach a seemingly rhetorical question was asked, "Why don't we petition for establishing the Navy Shipyard as a nuclear capable yard?" I replied I doubted if the U.S. Navy wanted another Nuke-Yard and especially there. The proverbial snowball in hell would have a better chance for survival than such a petition thrown at the environmentalists in Southern California. Whoever was conducting the meeting chuckled and shared there was obviously no need to linger on the subject.

I generally enjoyed being Long Beach's "Rep." The city was well managed, and I was curious to see how it functioned. The City Council comprised men and women who seemed to be genuinely interested in guiding the city. Long Beach had to compete with other Southern California cities for tourism, but geographically it was off the beaten path of main highways. To some extent, it had to become a "destination" city. People needed a reason to go there. I admired the city's leaders' verve to buy the world famed cruise ship, the *Queen Mary*. They brought it to the Port of Long Beach to become a museum and hotel. It was really a "sea-mark" in the realm of landmark entities. I doubt if it has ever showed much profit. It is a huge ship that requires heavy maintenance including large quantities of paint.

Another imaginative move by the city was to buy Howard Hughes' World War II vintage "Flying Boat." Because of its wooden structure, it was labeled the *Spruce Goose* by the media. They positioned this once world's largest aircraft near the *Queen Mary* as an additional tourist attraction. The Goose also called for considerable attention. It needed to be preserved out of the elements in a hangar. So it was eventually sold and moved to its present home at the Evergreen Aviation Museum in McMinnville, Oregon. Another allure the city adopted was an annual Formula One race throughout downtown.

Part of the Long Beach job I was uncomfortable with was being affiliated with the shipyard's employees association. Frustrated by having had the yard closed and then shortly afterward reopened resulted in the formation of the association. It lobbied for the economic livelihood and viability of the yard. The employees wanted to keep a steady stream of labor going at the yard and what they considered their fair share of work on the ships of the Pacific Fleet. The employees didn't trust management, namely the managers of the Long Beach yard and its overall administrator, the Commander, Naval Sea Systems Command in Washington. The commander supervised all Navy shipyards and Navy ship repair work.

Complicating my involvement was Capt. Tony Duchek, the local commander of the Long Beach Naval Shipyard. He was an old friend and neighbor from Coronado days. Topping my priority list was to call on Tony and establish myself as not being an adversary. When we got together, he wondered at the value of what I was doing for the employees association. But the concern about the rub of the association's lobbying efforts and his operation of the local yard was soon lost in our reminiscing. We remembered the good times we had in Coronado and Stevii being the baby sitter for his family.

I relished the opportunity to work and interact with Long Beach's blue collar people. My background, established in Escanaba and Green Bay was industrial based and definitely blue collar. In my humble perspective of life, I have always felt such people were the salt of the earth and the core of our American culture. I could relate to the workforce and respected them.

I enjoyed a good relationship with the City Council and the Long Beach Port Authority. As the port's governing body, the Port Authority was well managed and profitable. While the shipyard was struggling, the Port Authority was helping make Long Beach the leading West Coast port. Don Phillips was a Wabash V-12 student, a Sigma Chi brother, owner of Phillips' Chicken Pot Pie Restaurants and a Long Beach city councilman. I saw him frequently during the five years of my affiliation with the city. One of the contributions I was able to make for the city and the council's efforts was to get Adm. Tom Hayward, then Commander in Chief, US Pacific Fleet at Pearl Harbor, to be the principal speaker for the city's Navy Day Celebration.

During my preparation for retirement from the Navy, I decided not to seek employment with a defense contractor. That was the normal route for most retired flag officers and most lucrative, especially for PAOs. I had tired of weapons systems and the Defense Department and wanted to get into something different. I also decided to not work for a large corporation, having been in that environment for 32 years.

George Mason University, a fast growing large educational complex in Fairfax, Virginia inquired if I would be interested in working there as head of its Development Office. I declined because fundraising didn't appeal to me. However, in retrospect, I may have been wrong. I did plenty of fundraising for the Navy Memorial and doing development work at a university would have been ideal. It would have been an excellent environment. Being associated with young people and serving a growing institution contributing to the community, state and nation would have certainly been worthwhile. Now I think it would have been a good fit for me.

My general thoughts about large corporations led me to the opposite end of the corporate spectrum. I decided to be a sole proprietor consultant, incorporating myself. I selected Admiralty Communications as my company's name because around the office I had been referred to as "Admiral T." It had a good, nautical sound to it. Formalizing the "T" by ending with "y" made it feel legitimate and extended some dignity to my endeavors, at least on the letterhead stationery. I preferred to work out of my home and established an office in one of our bedrooms being vacated by our "fleeing the nest" offspring. Having a hole-in-the-wall office in more commercial environs was an overhead expense I just didn't need.

However, I realized it was important to be able to get away from the "home" office at times. Being a consultant provided ample opportunities to do so, because the clients provided temporary workspace. Underlying everything was a subliminal desire to get away from daily pressures. Still I knew I would miss not juggling several projects and facing deadlines. After discussions with several friends who were consultants, I set the parameters for a three or four client maximum. Aware that I was 52 years old, I knew I could change my venture if it wasn't satisfactory. But enthusiastically I set out to enjoy what I was doing.

Feature Movie Producer

In 1975 on a visit to Chicago, I spent some time with Sam Sax, a friend, former Naval Reservist and president of a Chicago owned bank of which his family had a major interest. I learned from him the dramatic story of how the Israeli Navy smuggled five embargoed patrol boats out from under the nose of the French Navy at Cherbourg, France on Christmas Eve in 1969. The Israelis had contracted for nine of these boats. Four were delivered, and the remaining five had been embargoed as a sanction against Israel for bombing the airport in Beirut, Lebanon. The bombing had been done in retaliation for atrocities committed by the Lebanese. The French government also embargoed several Mirage fighter aircraft that were manufactured in France. Both of these weapon systems had been fully funded by the Israelis who were impatiently awaiting delivery.

In Cherbourg, commissioning crews were assembled. The operation was conducted under the cloak of a Christmas Eve party for the ships' crews that never materialized. With the crews supposedly away from their ships attending a party, the five boats were stealthily slipped out of the harbor about midnight. With throttles bent forward, the vessels were headed toward the Mediterranean Sea. The five boats rendezvoused with an Israeli tanker to refuel in the Bay of Biscay off Spain, entered the Mediterranean and moved onward to another fueling near Malta, They arrived at Haifa, Israel on New

Year's Eve and received a tremendous welcome from cheering Israelis at Haifa's hill surrounded harbor giving it a Super Bowl like effect. The audacious event captured the imagination and added to the legendary daring of the Israeli armed forces. The Saar 4.5 class missle boats were well suited for the Yom Kippur War in 1973. They totally suppressed the effectiveness of the Egyptian and Syrian navies.

I saw a potential book and a feature motion picture in the story. Sam Sax and I banded together to make it happen. I told the tale to Bud Zumwalt, and he arranged a meeting in New York with Golda Meir, the female school teacher from Milwaukee, who became Israel's prime minister. Bud and I spent an hour with Mrs. Meir who was playing grandma to several grandchildren in a hotel suite. I was attempting to gain support from the Israeli government, because I wanted to use the Saar boats in Haifa and produce the movie in Israel. Mrs. Meir was understanding but was concerned about a motion picture reopening the wounds of French embarrassment.

She got word to me later that she would support our project, but I found no evidence of it when Sam and I visited Israel in May 1976. We spent 10 days visiting the Israeli Navy's top commands and even had a private dinner with Ariel Sharon, the victorious general in the 1973 Arab-Israeli war and later prime minister. It was an interesting dinner but as for the movie, he was noncommittal. I returned home to McLean for our son Brian's graduation from McLean High School but disappointed in my venture into the feature motion picture business. We made several additional attempts, but to this day the storyboard gathers dust on my bookshelf. The Israelis probably did not need the visibility afforded by a motion picture displaying their chutzpah and vitality. It remains a small nation continually facing adversaries threatening its quest for survival. Whenever I retell the story about the raid, the immediate response is, "Hey, that would make a great movie!"

Politics

During the early months of 1976, Bud Zumwalt declared himself as a Democratic Party candidate for the U.S. Senate in Virginia. His counsel with other Democrats, including Paul Nitze, was that he could not conceivably defeat the incumbent, Harry Flood Byrd, Jr., who was an independent but a strong one. Senator Byrd had followed his father into the senate, and the Byrd name was a Virginia institution. There was a highway named for the elder Byrd as well as the airport at Richmond, the state's capital. The plan was that Bud would establish himself within the state and in the next election in 1978, could win against Senator William B. Spong, Jr. Senator Spong was not doing well on the Hill and was labeled as vulnerable. *TIME* Magazine identified Senator Spong as "the dumbest man in the Senate." The joke around Washington was that Spong was so dumb he called a press conference to refute *TIME's* label making him appear even dumber. The Democratic Party was frantically looking for a candidate to run against Byrd, but there was not much interest. Bud Zumwalt appeared on the horizon and immediately became "The Man!" He was acclaimed, applauded and endorsed as the Democratic Party's candidate.

When Admiral Zumwalt retired as the Chief of Naval Operations in July 1974, it had been known, at least to a few of his close friends, that he would return to his home state of California. There, he would run against Senator John V. Tunney who was considered beatable and a poor competitor in the 1976 California senatorial campaign. All Bud had to do was to return home. Instead, he decided to write his memoirs entitled, "On Watch." It concentrated on his four years as CNO, because his term was so controversial. He definitely had something to say. To his dismay and to that of many others, there was much more effort and time involved than anticipated in writing a suitable book. Although he worked diligently with the source materials archived at the Washington Navy Yard, he missed the starting bell in California. Had he returned to California, many political pundits have said he could have won the senate seat. I agree and think he would have been an outstanding senator.

Bud included me in some of the machinations of his entrance into politics and listed me on his campaign committee. After he had been endorsed by the Virginia Democratic Party at its state convention in Norfolk, a campaign structure was organized. The headquarters was to be in Richmond and another office established in Northern Virginia at Falls Church. He asked if I could arrange my clientele work schedule, so I could head the Northern Virginia campaign. After considering it for a couple of days, I told Bud it would be educational and probably exciting for me. It would certainly be different. But I considered politics to be in variance with public relations, although some probably consider the two fields in general alignment. I questioned if I could be of help to him. He assured me that I could. He wanted a steady hand in the office, since he would be devoting most of his time campaigning in the "husting." He said a little better organization in the office might also help, and I took that as my marching orders.

Bud's campaign manager was Tim Finchem, who later served in the White House with President Jimmy Carter before becoming the Commissioner of the Professional Golf Association. He was headquartered in Richmond and did a respectable job for the candidate. He was politically savvy and knew the state's Democrat Party infrastructure. Such knowledge was essential to launching the charge of a novice politician. Tim was definitely an asset to the campaign and was helpful to Bud.

At the start of the campaign, our campaign office paid for a survey that revealed Bud Zumwalt would probably get 39% of the vote. That projection turned to be painfully accurate because Bud Zumwalt got exactly 39% of the vote. To tag Bud as a political neophyte may have been erroneous to some who knew him in the Navy. One does not get to be the Chief of Naval Operations without political acumen. Bud had plenty of that. Few were any better at organizing thoughts and articulating them orally or on paper. He remained an excellent speaker and possessed a significant stage presence on or off the podium.

However, being thrust into the role of a professional politician at the U.S. Senate level was something that did not offer immediate success. It would take time to gather experience while maturing into a different and divergent venue and lifestyle. At the start, I told Bud he didn't have to be so exactingly honest in answering questions from his audience or media representatives. He could be truthful but didn't have to ponderously cover all sides of an issue. Overall, he learned quickly and by the end of the campaign, he had adapted to his new environment and presented well the image of an intelligent, confident and articulate candidate.

About six months later, we started to get organized for the 1978 campaign. By then I was listed as Chairman of the Campaign Committee. We thought it prudent to do another survey. Those results surprised us showing that should he choose to run again, he would receive only an identical 39% of the Virginia vote. That tune we had heard before. Bud asked for some time to make a decision. He was a competitor and felt the poll indicated an uphill, tough campaign. Mouza his wife was hard set against another campaign. His children still had not recovered from the shock of their father losing. So he got little encouragement at home. His loyal Democrat friends were supportive but recognized the odds were against an "outsider" succeeding in a tradition-bound Southern state.

Bud opted out. He thanked all concerned and turned his attention to other activities. I agreed with his decision. I knew he would have been an outstanding senator. But the path leading to the elected position was precarious and exhausting. I think it was fortunate in many respects that he withdrew.

His opponent would have been Virginian John Warner. Warner was the former Secretary of the Navy during part of the time Bud was serving as the Chief of Naval Operations. It was no secret that Zumwalt and Warner had differences while leading the Navy together. The campaign would have been full of animosities and issues of the time. I thought it would have been an uncomfortable experience for the two candidates, the Navy and for me. As Secretary of the Navy John Warner too had been my boss. I felt appropriate loyalties to him as well. The media would have enjoyed it, feasting on every morsel of fact or fiction. Warner was then the husband of legendary movie actress Elizabeth Taylor. He capitalized on her notoriety to gain additional name recognition and won the election. He served well as a U.S. Senator into the next century, rising to the powerful position of Chairman of the Senate Armed Forces Committee. I am proud to have been associated with him. He has been good for Virginia, developed an excellent staff to serve his constituency and was an excellent senate committee chairman.

National Strategy

The National Strategy Information Center (NSIC) was another consulting job client I had at that time. It was headquartered in New York City. Its president wisely opened a Washington office to be near the epicenter of national strategy. The organization published books, conducted seminars and took an activist role in national strategy issues. My initial job was to help the center publicize and popularize a book on national strategy it had edited and published. The book was a collection of essays and papers done by scholars and foreign affairs professionals. Having operated deeply in the shadows of Bud Zumwalt and Paul Nitze, I relished the task and enjoyed my affiliation with the center for several months.

Coincidently, its president was a Wabash College graduate and former dean of the school. We got along well, and I seriously considered joining such an organization. It was interesting work and involved equally interesting people. I felt that I could contribute to the success of an enterprise like NSIC, and it would be a great learning experience. As time went on, the opportunity arose to join in the development of NSIC. However, it was not to be because another interesting endeavor interceded.

Building The U.S. Navy Memorial

What interceded was the Navy Memorial Foundation, and it monopolized 15 years of my post-Navy retirement. Dave Cooney, my successor at CHINFO, had kept me generally apprised of the Navy Memorial project. I passively thought it was a good idea to have a memorial to those who served in the Navy. I hadn't given it much thought because of other activities.

The longstanding idea for a Navy memorial didn't gain momentum until 1977 when Adm. Arleigh A. Burke, the retired Chief of Naval Operations, proclaimed "We have talked long enough about a Navy memorial. It's time we did something about it. Now is the time!" As was customary when Admiral Burke spoke, many tuned to his words. A few years later, I asked Admiral Burke what snapped him into action about the memorial. He laughed and said it wasn't any auspicious or intriguing feelings. As a captain, he had attended the dedication ceremony for the Marine Corps' Iwo Jima War Memorial. He said he wondered, "If the Marine Corps can have a memorial, why can't the Navy?"

Admiral Burke made his "Action Now" declaration before Adm. Thomas H. Moorer, another former CNO and Chairman of the Joint Chiefs of Staff, and others. They had gathered at a Pentagon meeting called by Secretary of the Navy J. William Middendorf, II. The meeting was held in response to remarks made by famed artist Felix de Weldon. De Weldon sculpted the American flag raising atop Mt. Surabachi at Iwo Jima during the battle for that small island in early 1945. His work replicated the photograph done by Joseph Rosenthal, a World War II combat photographer for the Associated Press. It became a celebrated and highly symbolic depiction of the battle for Iwo Jima and the war in the Pacific. De Weldon's sculpture became the Marine Corps War Memorial that stands near the U.S. National Cemetery in Arlington.

De Weldon later designed a concept for a Navy memorial and was attempting to sell it to the Navy. Witnesses told me, he talked to Adm. James L. Holloway, III, Chief of Naval Operations, aboard the aircraft carrier USS *Forrestal*. The *Forrestal* was serving as the reviewing ship for the fleet review at the U.S. Bicentennial's premiere event in New York Harbor on July 4, 1976. Admiral Holloway passed on the unofficial proposal to Secretary of the Navy Middendorf. At that meeting in the Secretary's Pentagon office, the de Weldon project was not discussed, but it was decided the time had come to move forward with building a Navy memorial. Using the Marine Corps' experience building its memorial as a guide, it was obvious that one of the first agenda items was establishing an association or foundation. Its task would be to work within the private sector to raise funds, secure a design, site, and monitor the construction work.

Admiral Holloway assigned this task to his Chief of Information, Rear Adm. Dave Cooney, an excellent organizer and planner. Cooney wrestled with the project for several months. He investigated rescuing an existing memorial, one dedicated to Navy and Merchant Marine personnel lost in World War I. It sits in Washington's Lady Bird Johnson Park on a narrow strip bordered by the Potomac River, the George Washington Parkway and the 14th Street Bridge. In a meeting with the National Park Service it was decided that memorial should not be moved to a more assessable site because it addressed the Merchant Marine as well as the Navy. Another concern involved violating the original intent of the existing memorial. I didn't know Dave had probed that possibility, because I had similar thoughts when starting to evaluate concepts and sites. The Navy-Merchant Marine Memorial continues to be one of the most graceful and masterful pieces of sculpture in the Washington area. It manifests seven superbly sculpted seagulls precariously attached in formation and superimposed over a dramatic, cresting wave. Dedicated in 1954, it was sculpted and cast by Ernesto Begni del Piatta, who was commissioned by the Navy-Merchant Marine Association.

Dave Cooney wisely corralled assistance from Naval Reservists, retired officers and other distinguished Navy alumni. They quickly organized the "U.S. Navy Memorial Foundation." He enlisted the help of Samuel W. Sax, the Chicago banker and Naval Reserve commander, and Sax's lawyer, Albert E. Jenner of the Chicago law firm Jenner and Block. Jenner was famous among lawyers for successfully leading MCI in its landmark suit against AT&T. The legal action resulted in the breakup of AT&T's control of long distance telephone service. He incorporated the Navy Memorial Foundation in Illinois as an educational organization. It was then authorized to raise funds, secure a design and site and guide construction work. The founding directors were former Secretary of the Navy William Middendorf, chairman and president; Sax, vice chairman; Jenner, secretary; Robert Ferneau, administrative assistant to Middendorf, treasurer; Admirals Burke and Moorer; former Secretary of the Navy, Senator John Warner; and James Griffin, the immediate past president of the Navy League of the United States. At a subsequent meeting, Rear Adm. John J. Bergen, USNR (Retired), was elected as the ninth member of the board of directors.

Sage advice

The Foundation announced its existence and purpose at a reception Zum and I attended in the historic manse Decatur House near the White House on October 25, 1977. (It followed the formal organizational meeting of its directors.) Appropriately, several remarks were made by dignitaries who proclaimed the U.S. Navy would soon have a memorial in the nation's capital. Driving home from the reception, I told Zum that while I didn't know anything about building memorials, I doubted if the board of directors was capable of doing the job. The key men involved were either too old or too busy to take on the onerous tasks of such a sizeable undertaking. Zum said I was probably right. "Don't you dare get involved in that project," she warned. Little did I know then that over the next 15 years, I would reflect on her words occasionally and wish that she had used a 2 X 4 to enforce them.

In April of 1978 while talking with Dave Cooney on other subjects, I asked how his memorial foundation was progressing. He replied that in the past six months he had heard of no action. In fact, he had learned the Foundation had not even paid the reception bill at the Decatur House. A couple of weeks later I called Dave to tell him I had time in my schedule to devote one day a week to getting the Foundation organized and moving, provided, of course, that Admiral Holloway concurred. After we got things started, I would bow out and cheer from the sidelines. Dave called back the same day saying everyone concerned welcomed my assistance. At the time, I didn't consider that exchange as a significant event in the development of the Navy Memorial or my life. My consulting business was doing well, and I simply reasoned I could devote some time to organizing a staff nucleus to proceed with the memorial project. Basically, I thought it was probably a good idea to have a statement about the Navy embodied in a memorial in Washington. However, memorial building was something I had not studied nor discussed with anyone knowledgeable in such matters.

Many ideas are born in early discussion. As they progress, it often becomes evident that good ideas can far exceed reality. That was true of envisioning the Navy Memorial. Grandiose plans to harness the impressive strength available within its board of directors and Navy alumni to accomplish great achievements were soon muted. There was a lack of understanding of the project's scope and more basically just how to begin. In fairness to the board, there was no lack of desire or ineptitude. Most of them were high-ranking executives who normally depended on staff members to bring forth plans, recommendations or at least some suggestions for project initiatives. I soon learned the Foundation had no plans on paper or any solid fundamental ideas about the overall concept, design, a site or scale for the memorial. Even fund-raising had ceased. Start-up funds languished at $19,000, the remainder of its initial and only contribution of $25,000 from Stroh's Brewery.

I asked each director if he had any strategy for the scale or logistics of the Navy Memorial that was to be built in "a couple of years." No one did. I thought Bill Middendorf, our founding chairman would. He was a creative type who often wrote and conducted symphonies and marches for the Navy Band. With his penchant for drawing, he was never without a sketchpad. I thought he might have some design ideas. His response was unforgettable. "Oh, just go build a statue someplace," he said, "and get this thing over with." I was flabbergasted to get such a brush off. But I knew he was the president of a prominent Washington, D.C. bank that had recently been bought by a moneyed group of Middle Easterners. He was working under a lot of pressure, and I sensed he wasn't comfortable with the transition. I forgave him because we had always gotten along well when he was Under Secretary of the Navy, then later its Secretary in my post-Navy days. I liked and respected him.

I easily concluded the Navy Memorial Foundation was at best starting out as a "fly by the seat of your pants" endeavor.

Reality collided with my naiveté. I envisioned being cast adrift in a small raft with a short paddle in a sea that was starting to get rough while illusionary sharks were circling. I had committed to what was shaping up as a most difficult task. My first thoughts were that, as usual, Zum's warning to "not get involved" was correct. If I had given it my usual "up front" due diligence, speaking first with the directors individually and then in depth with Dave Cooney and others in the Navy's hierarchy, including Admiral Holloway, I might not have volunteered to get the project started. Still I knew I enjoyed conceptualizing things, especially those involving the Navy and its image. My initial disappointment might play out to my advantage. At least I would not be saddled with mandates or edicts I didn't help formulate.

I realized I had put myself into this awkward position and had to make an effort to accomplish something. I was confident that my background and understanding of Washington would help get the foundation moving. In Washington there was a plethora of information on almost any subject waiting at the other end of a telephone line. I possessed the managerial skills and experience to get this project started. An interesting challenge loomed, and somehow participating just might eventually be fun. In order to better represent the Foundation, I was designated its executive director. Assuming that title, I was ready to take on what ultimately became the toughest job of my life.

"Set The Special Sea Detail"

The first chore I undertook was to enlarge the board of directors with younger people who could actively help. I enlisted a talented troop of three. They were enterprising former naval officers B. Waring Partridge, S. Steven "Spike" Karalekas and William S. Norman. I had been previously affiliated with each one but in different venues. Waring worked for me in the Office of Information and was then associated with the management consulting firm of McKinsey and Company, Inc. Spike Karalekas, a 1965 Naval Academy graduate, was a Navy public affairs officer and still active in the Naval Reserve.

He was rising fast to become one of Washington's most successful young lawyers. Bill Norman was a naval flight officer whom Bud Zumwalt encouraged to join Zumwalt's CNO staff as the Minority Affairs Advisor instead of returning to civilian life. Bill and I had a good active duty relationship and were deeply involved in minority affairs. He was executive vice president of Amtrak Railroad Corporation.

Waring arranged for McKinsey to do a small study on how to build the memorial. He assigned an intern graduate student to the task and ensured adequate guidance and supervision were provided. The study was completed in two weeks. It put in perspective the process's various elements and theoretically provided us with a plan of action. I later augmented the plan and charted it with milestones. The five major elements identified for the memorial program were:

Enabling Legislation: Any memorial of this scope to be constructed on public land in Washington, D.C. has to be authorized by the U.S. Congress.

Design: Three U.S. government agencies—The Commission of Fine Arts (CFA); the National Capital Planning Commission (NCPC) and the Secretary of the Interior represented by the National Park Service (NPS)—are principals in design approval for any memorial.

Site Selection: The same three agencies are the principals involved in site approval within the confines of the District of Columbia.

Fundraising: Before construction can begin on a site within the District of Columbia, a guarantee of construction funds is necessary.

Construction and Maintenance: Normally, when a memorial is built on public lands in the District of Columbia, construction is the responsibility of the sponsoring organization. Upon completion, the edifice is relinquished to government ownership and maintenance provided by the Secretary of the Interior through the National Park Service.

With our major tasks crystallized, I began charting a path through the Washington bureaucracy and called on Spike Karalekas for immediate assistance. He had worked in the White House during the Nixon Administration as the executive assistant to Charles Colson the chief counsel. He had also worked on Capitol Hill as an aide to a Massachusetts congressman. He was ideal to help get enabling legislation into and out of the Congress. We were assured by everyone we talked with, that once the memorial effort was under congressional consideration there would be no difficulty winning approval. But we were advised it would be a time consuming process. And it was.

In mid-1978 we got identical bills introduced to the Congress. Rhode Island Senator John Chafee, my boss when he was Secretary of the Navy, introduced the legislation in the Senate. A friend, Representative Bob Wilson of San Diego, the ranking minority member of the House Armed Services Committee, sponsored the bill in the House. Under Spike's guidance, we concentrated our efforts in the Senate. There were fewer members to relate with, and we anticipated the House members would align with the Senate when the measure was more finalized. Time did prove to be an important factor, and it ran out on us in 1978.

The bills were reintroduced in 1979 and carefully guided to approval. In March of 1980 President Jimmy Carter, a former Navy lieutenant, signed Public Law 96-199, an omnibus bill for the Department of the Interior. In part it authorized the Navy Memorial Foundation to proceed with construction of the Navy Memorial on public land in the District of Columbia when funds were guaranteed. The law specifically stated that no federal or District of Columbia funds could be expended on the Memorial. At the end of that day, Spike and I etched a big check mark beside that major milestone.

The third member of our youth squad, Bill Norman became my heavy-duty advisor on how to run our effort, especially the composition of our board and using and orchestrating their talents. He was my perpetual chairman of the Nominating Committee. We spent many mornings at breakfast strategizing board membership and movements through the Washington maze. He was a thorough, wizened Washington hand and an excellent mentor.

Busy agenda

Concurrently with the legislative work, I was moving ahead on the project's design and site aspects. By this time, the board of directors had elected me president and chief executive officer (CEO) as well as being a member of its board of directors. I was devoting much more time to Foundation business than I had planned, certainly much more than the one day a week I had originally thought. I flinched at accusations that my 32-year Navy career hadn't taught me not to volunteer especially for impossible tasks. But the Navy had clearly ingrained in me the ideal of mission accomplishment.

I became more and more involved and deeply intrigued with the project. I saw a national memorial as a unique opportunity to make a significant, expressed statement about the Navy and its people. While seeking out possible designs and concepts, I sought counsel from professionals and laypersons. I came to realize we were approaching the task in reverse. We weren't exactly aware of what we wanted. But by evaluating suggestions and advice, we learned what we didn't want. It wasn't the normal way to proceed, but it was shaping the concept of what we wanted the Memorial to be.

Our vision cast the Memorial as actively functioning. We didn't want just a statue or icon placed on a street corner or along Memorial Drive next to the Navy's Seabee Memorial. It should be commanding but subtle. In that regard, my thoughts clung to expressing the Navy's service through the efforts of its people who had served or were serving and those who would serve in the future. The Memorial should offer information and educational resources about the Navy's history and the rich heritage. The Navy was inseparably intertwined with our young nation's development. The Memorial should provide ceremonial space to add pomp and color to the nation's capital, and if possible, afford a place for contemplation and relaxation. Basic to all these goals was the duty to honor those who had donned the Navy uniform to serve on the sea, below or above it or in other specialized groups. Although still vague, those aspects were shaping the beginnings of a broad working concept. I felt confident we were making progress, and with time we would define a formidable vision. Interacting with many people, the images were still in my mind, not transcribed but always No. 1 on my conversation list.

I didn't realize it then, but we were breaking new ground in functionality for memorials. The Vietnam Veterans Memorial has been cited as the beginning of functional memorials in Washington but that stretches the definition. The beautifully dramatic Vietnam memorial effectively provides for individual recognition, grief and sorrow. Beneath the listed name of soldiers, Marines, sailors and airman who died during that conflict, mementos can be placed. Rubbings can be made from the chiseled names on the black wall providing personal interaction and essentially serving as the precursor of a functional memorial. As this book is being written, the Vietnam War Association is constructing an adjacent museum. It will provide space for education about the war with memorabilia displays and presentations with state-of-the-art audio-visual technology. Those enhancements will add substantially to the Vietnam Veterans Memorial being a "functional" memorial.

Our next objective was to find an appropriate site to accommodate all our goals. We knew our concept would need to be agreeable to most in order to gain approval. The basic tenet of our public relations forays was to create a mutual understanding between entities and communities I engaged in the memorial building quest. We needed to offer federal and city officials a desirable or, attractive potential return for providing a good site. Suitable locations were fast disappearing in Washington, and land costs in the private sector were intimidating if not prohibitive. Raising funds for the Memorial was difficult at that juncture. Few donors were willing to support a high-risk effort without a guaranteed site and finalized design.

Office space was not initially a problem because I was operating the memorial business out of my back pocket and reporting to Chairman Bill Middendorf occasionally. I began complaining facetiously that in retired life I was doing a lot of yeoman (clerical) duties, but I had accepted it as normal. My wheel wasn't squeaking loudly then, but apparently the message was heard by the right ears. I received a phone call from Ted Lefebvre, vice president for Washington activities with the General Dynamics Corporation, a major defense industry contractor. They offered me office space while getting the memorial project started. Bert Jenner, our Foundation secretary, had contacted him. Jenner was a General Dynamics director and a member of its executive committee. I gladly accepted and usually worked out of their offices about one day a week for three months. It was a pleasant arrangement because I knew Ted Lefebvre and many of the key consultants and lobbyists in that office. However, there wasn't room to expand or set up an office with an assistant or two.

Conveniently, about that time, I was asked by a Navy associate, retired Capt. Dominick Paolucci, to be a consultant for the Santa Fe Pacific Corporation, a Washington think tank, in return for office space. That offer was a common arrangement in the Washington area. We worked it out, so

I would be able to bring in a couple of people to help me on the memorial project. It was a fortunate arrangement, and from there we started to grow. My initial staff support came from my loyal secretary and friend Mrs. Ruth Donohue. Ruth joined me on a daily basis, and I recruited Capt. Jack Davey to help with direct mail fundraising. Jack had gained experience in direct response work during his final Navy assignment as Public Affairs Officer for the Navy Recruiting Command. Not only did he know direct mail operations, but he was acquainted with professionals in the business in New York City. Retired Capt. Walt Thomas, a naval aviator with considerable public affairs experience, later agreed to work with us for four to five hours each day.

I credit Ruth Donohue for initiating the idea of the Memorial with a concert stage to be used by all the area's military bands. That thought grew out of the many conversations we had in our small office. We called these conversations "Cerebral Popcorn Sessions." It was our brand of informal brainstorming. I became captivated by an amphitheater concept, and it developed into the basis for all future physical plans for the Memorial. I thought it might be our entrée to securing a good site in Washington. I saw music as a basic medium of communication and thought perhaps it could help us deliver our concept to government agencies and potential donors.

For some, military music connotes memories of sailors from a ship or GIs from a unit getting together with musical instruments procured from almost anywhere to have a "session." They were not professional musicians but certainly served a vital purpose. Service people liked them and enjoyed their efforts. However, the principal military service bands are professional, talented groups, and most of their members possess bachelors or master's degrees in music. When not on tour throughout the country or internationally, the Army, Navy, Marine Corps, Coast Guard and Air Force bands regularly perform in the Washington metropolitan area. Prior to 1973, the bands played on the Watergate Barge moored on the waterfront behind the Lincoln Memorial. It was a popular venue for local citizens as well as tourists. However, in the fall of 1972 Hurricane Agnes swept through the area, tore the barge from its moorings and moved it several miles down the Potomac River where it was found as a demolished hulk.

Subsequently, the bands were disbursed to the Jefferson Memorial, the Sylvan Theater near the Washington Monument, and the steps of the Capitol.

The National Park Service deemed replacing the Watergate Barge impractical largely because Washington (now Reagan) National Airport had begun using the air space above the Potomac River for flights into and out of its North-South runways. During concerts, aircraft would literally bore holes through the music so often it was disconcerting to the musicians as well as audiences. We thought providing an amphitheater for the military bands in Washington would fill a longstanding need and contribute to the community. It became central to our Foundation's strategy for site and design selections.

Site search

In my zeal to test the Washington bureaucratic waters, I succeeded in being placed on the National Park Service calendar to make a presentation to its Memorials Committee. I wanted to request a parcel of land on the Constitution Avenue side of the Mall. It was where the Old Main Navy Building had been located before it was razed during the Nixon Administration. On arriving, I learned the group appearing ahead of me was the Vietnam Veterans organization. It was campaigning for a Vietnam War Memorial in Washington. During their presentation I learned several things. The group was well organized and had a fundraising campaign underway. They also had a well-publicized national competition for a design in progress. Most importantly, they had designated their desired site as almost identical to what I coveted. "Willie, you are not only in the wrong pew but you are in the wrong church," I said to myself. "You don't want to get into a contest with this organization, because you won't win."

During a short recess after the Vietnam Memorial presentation, I told the Park Service coordinating official I wanted to pass on my scheduled presentation. I said I would contact him for an appointment at a later meeting. He seemed relieved because of the full docket for that day, and he was already running behind on his published agenda. I personally supported the Vietnam War Memorial effort and worked with its staff to help its project. Ultimately, they did an excellent job, built an extraordinary memorial and led the way in a resurgence of building memorials, especially military oriented ones in Washington. We were immediately behind them in building our Memorial, learning from them and profiting immensely from their experience.

Later, I contacted the National Capital Planning Commission (NCPC), and that proved helpful. My good friend Robert Brett, a retired Navy captain who had served his last four tours of duty as a public affairs specialist with Admiral Tom Moorer, joined me in some early calls. After retiring from the Navy, Bob Brett was with the Washington staff of LTV Corporation as a lobbyist. He had developed a lot of Washington "street smarts."

Members of the NCPC staff were cordial and courteous. They sometimes seemed bemused by the intrepid duo charging into the bureaucracy of monument building in Washington. No doubt we resembled emissaries from several other well-intentioned groups they had previously entertained. Staff members we encountered were open in their responses, but they dutifully outlined the negative aspects of undertaking such a large project. They offered available site suggestions. One included Franklin Park, a large city block in Northwest Washington bounded by I and K and 13th and 14th streets, and described as a "nice place for the bands to play." Another suggestion was Anacostia Park where we could have several acres. The Potomac River waterfront south of the Key Bridge was also offered as a place to build a "needed marina" and would be a "nautical" match befitting a Navy Memorial. A space on 14th Street that is now the Reagan Building was available. Also mentioned were two sites on Pennsylvania Avenue being redeveloped by the Pennsylvania Avenue Development Corporation (PADC). The Pennsylvania Avenue possibilities peaked our interest, and we considered them immediately.

Without hesitation, Bob and I called on PADC to meet with Charles Gueli its vice president in charge of development. Gueli recited the corporation's desire to "bring life back to the Avenue." He seemed intrigued and interested in having an amphitheater in the middle of the redevelopment parcel. PADC was a federally chartered, quasi-government corporation charged with redeveloping Pennsylvania Avenue between the Capitol and the White House.

A PADC legend relates how at the end of his inaugural parade down the "Avenue of the Presidents," President Kennedy told Assistant Secretary of Labor Patrick Moynihan something had to be done about Pennsylvania Avenue's shabby appearance. He considered it a national disgrace that "Main

Street, USA," the boulevard connecting the executive mansion with the legislative domiciles and the capitol building, was in such deplorable condition. That sparked the genesis of the PADC. Subsequent legislative action produced the congressionally funded organization to buy and sell real estate on the avenue to hasten improvement.

As the redevelopment progressed, the project gained recognition as a classic historic urban renewal program. It demonstrated what could be accomplished when government and business sectors cooperated. With Perishing Square and the majestic Willard Hotel on the western end to the new Canadian Embassy that anchors the eastern edge, "The Avenue" was transformed into a stately, prestigious, functional thoroughfare befitting its national prominence.

"Single Up All Lines!"

Some in the PADC staff weren't overly enthusiastic about having the "Navy," as the Foundation was labeled, occupying a prize site on Pennsylvania Avenue. But the concept's favor grew because its amphitheater would help restore life to the avenue. I detected a trace of anti-militarism among the younger set on the PADC staff which I attributed to the Vietnam War. I sensed that most negativism was based on the fear of having a huge, powerful organization, such as the Navy, trying to take over sacred land. I did my best to relieve them of those thoughts. I assured them we were not the Navy per se, and we had something to offer. Something that could help them succeed in their mission to redevelop Pennsylvania Avenue.

Generally, patriotism and appreciation for the military was on the rise in the early 1980s. It became particularly evident during the Reagan Administration when the President dignified the Armed Services as a principal part of his campaign against the "Evil Empire" of the Soviet Union. I let the patriotism angst subside partly because there were other issues needing my time and effort. They had to be addressed, and I was the only one available to do it. One argument was, "Outdoor concerts are fine, but what happens there during the other nine months of the year?" Andrew Barnes, PADC executive director, wondered if an ice rink could be installed for the winter months.

But his idea melted away when it was discovered two ice rinks already existed in the immediate area.

Another argument was, "Why should the Navy have a prime site? What if the other services want a memorial? Why not a memorial to the Armed Forces?" I countered that the Marine Corps already had a national memorial in the Iwo Jima monument. The Army had the Tomb of the Unknown in the Arlington National Cemetery. And the Air Force had concentrated on its museum at Wright-Patterson Air Force Base in Dayton, Ohio and also had a heavy footprint in the Smithsonian Air and Space Museum. The Coast Guard too claimed a national memorial at Arlington Cemetery. As for an Armed Forces Memorial, we dismissed the idea as not being fundable unless the government underwrote it. Individual service alumni would contribute more easily to "their" memorial, but not as readily to an all encompassing Armed Forces memorial. No substantive arguments materialized, and we succeeded in presenting our case.

Our rationale as to why there should be a Navy Memorial in Washington was that although there were many Navy-related memorials in Washington (in excess of 20), such as Farragut Square, DuPont Circle and the beautifully sculptured wave action with seven seagulls in flight at Lady Bird Johnson Park, none was dedicated exclusively to the Navy, only to individuals or units of the Navy or to specific wars. Additionally, the Navy's headquarters had always been in Washington while the Army and Air Force headquarters have been spread throughout the country. Washington was definitely the Navy's "homeport," and the Naval Academy was nearby. The history rich Washington Navy Yard has also shared the Capital City's story.

Enter Tom Regan

Thomas Regan was the PADC director of operations when the dialogue between the Foundation and PADC began. He was at all times circumspect and objective regarding the Navy Memorial proposal, even though he was a member of the graduating class of 1965 at the Naval Academy. While on active duty, he was a civil engineer and served a tour of duty in Vietnam. He definitely endorsed our proposal and was instrumental in having it adopted by the PADC board of directors. He counseled me in maneuvering the proposal around Washington and before the PADC board. His suggestions were always accompanied with, "If you really want to do this and want this site, these are my recommendations. Take them for what they are worth." I considered Regan's recommendations positive, absolute and trustworthy.

I appreciated my relationship with him. Initially bound by the simple threads of Navy "Blue and Gold," our interactions matured into mutual respect, trust and friendship. When Tom moved up to the PADC's top paid position of executive director, our relationship continued. When he left PADC, I nominated him as a director for the Foundation as well as vice president of construction. He has remained a good friend.

PADC's board of directors approved the Navy Memorial being built in Market Square, a two acre parcel on the north side of Pennsylvania Avenue between 7th and 9th streets, across from the National Archives. In the late 19th and early 20th centuries, the square had been a mainstay Washington marketplace and so derived its name. The stipulations were that PADC would hold final approval of the design and the project's financing and serve as the contracting agency for construction. In this process, the Foundation would acquire another governing agency to add to the three participating entities (Commission of Fine Arts, National Capital Planning Commission and the Secretary of the Interior [National Park Service]) prescribed by law.

I was not dismayed; I was elated! We had achieved approval of a prized site halfway between the Capitol and the White House on the nation's principal thoroughfare. Further, we would benefit from the professionalism of the PADC staff and have an ally in our quest to build the Memorial. We definitely needed an ally, and this partnership would also save us a considerable amount of precious funds. Of paramount importance was PADC serving as the general contractor. It freed us from hiring a staff to handle tasks beyond our existing expertise and capabilities. Additionally, although we were mandated to guarantee funds were available before construction began, PADC would disburse the monies to the various subcontractors and vendors.

Another bonus arose from "areas of common interest" to PADC and our Foundation where costs would be shared. For instance, we learned our partner had envisioned having fountains in the area, and if we decided to have fountains or water displays, the cost would be shared equally. I had thoughts of symbolically using water, the Navy's essential element, for creative expression in the Memorial. I had investigated possibly featuring a contemplative water fountain or garden effect park and researched existing facilities throughout the country and world. But I concluded such a theme much too subtle for our purpose and returned to something more prosaic—an amphitheater perhaps featuring a world map surrounded by water fountains. The cost sharing news was definitely an incentive to include fountains in our overall concept.

Topping a long list of items to be accomplished with PADC as our partner was selecting an architect to develop a design for the Navy Memorial and the Market Square parcel. The Foundation was allocated two seats on the PADC selection committee. Drawing from a personal list of potential outstanding resources, I enlisted the assistance of retired Rear Adm. Walter Enger, a Navy civil engineer and former Commander of the Navy Facilities Engineering Command. He was also commander of the Seabees and had led the organization that built the Seabee Memorial. It had been crafted by Felix de Weldon and placed on Memorial Drive next to Arlington Cemetery. Together we sat on the selection committee that ultimately chose Conklin Rossant Architects of New York City to be the designer for the Memorial and development of Market Square. The Market Square parcel actually included the Navy Memorial area, and it extended across Pennsylvania Avenue to include all the "back yard" of the National Archives which was to be modified and refurbished.

Concepts

An unusual situation developed at a cocktail party hosted by the Chief of Naval Operations Adm. Tom Hayward. There I became reacquainted with artist Felix de Weldon whom I had known while I was a student at the Naval War College in Newport near de Weldon's residence. At the time of the CNO's cocktail party, I didn't know de Weldon had submitted a model for the Navy Memorial and was actually the indirect originator of the project. In general conversation, Felix asked what I was doing, and I replied I was trying to build a memorial for the Navy. "Oh, you are the one," he responded. "Would you like to see what the Navy Memorial will look like?" When I responded affirmatively with some degree of wonderment, he invited me to his studio in Southeast Washington the next day to see a large, one-quarter scale model of his proposal. It was a figure of a youthful warrior (to be 24 feet in actual size, the same as the Iwo Jima figures) with a magnificent physique positioned on a shaft projecting him into space above the girded sphere of planet earth. He held a shield on one arm and a bolt of lightening in the other hand. The globe was suspended over a pool of water.

Obviously de Weldon thought the Navy had accepted his proposal, and he was patiently waiting to be paid for it. Our conversation basically went as follows.

"What are you trying to express with this piece of art, Felix?" I asked.

"The United States Navy controls the world!" he announced proudly. "The pool represents the oceans, and kids can sail little boats in it."

"Looks like you have been listening to those young hot shot officers at the Naval War College," I said with a smile.

"You don't like it?" was his surprised and defensive question.

"I don't dislike it because I have learned to respect art work as well as the artist. This is your expression. However, I doubt this is the statement we will want to make in Washington. Even if it were true (thematically)—and it isn't—yours is not the statement we can make here at our Memorial. In the first place, it wouldn't be approved by the agencies overseeing memorials, and secondly, it is in bad taste. Maybe if you had another title for it or a different interpretation on the concept we could consider it, but not such an arrogant one."

"I am going to see the CNO," he said jabbing an index finger at me as his classic Italian temper took hold. "Do you know the CNO? He is a close friend of mine. I will have you fired!"

"Come on, Felix, the CNO has many other things to worry about. I'm sure he would discuss this with me before arbitrarily asking the Foundation, that the CNO initiated, to fire me. I would welcome the CNO's input to the statement we will make with the Memorial. But I am confident he would agree about not beating our breasts and boasting that the U.S. Navy controls the world. Besides, we would have the other services publicly disagreeing … as well as the Department of Defense, the Congress and the White House. Those are tough odds to be up against, Felix."

"What do you envision as your Memorial?" What is your statement?" he demanded visibly deflated and upset.

"There is nothing firm yet. Our board of directors will eventually approve a concept and are awaiting my proposal. Right now we have the opportunity to build on one of the most prestigious sites in Washington. To use that site our concept must offer something to the city and the powers that be. They are currently warm to the idea of providing a place for all the military bands to play replacing the Watergate barge. What I envision is a living memorial. Something our veterans and the public can use and enjoy …"

"Living memorial is an illusive phrase" he interrupted. "It can mean anything."

"Well, for the time being, I like it. It is vague because at this juncture, I am vague about exactly what this memorial should express or even look like. It will be a living memorial because people can use it, enjoy it and learn from it. It will provoke and promote activity. The key is that it will be functional.

"I'm new at this game, Felix," I added, as I moved to exit the studio allowing him to escort me. "I'm even learning something in this conversation, listening to you and me discuss the project."

That evening at home I received a call from de Weldon pleading that he could make his model a "living" memorial by providing a backdrop on one side of the pool, so that the bands could play there. He reminded me it was he who created the Iwo Jima War Memorial. I replied that his comments were appreciated and I would keep them in mind.

Back To Reality

With William Conklin, a World War II naval officer, at the helm and Tom Regan, newly designated as PADC executive director, at the con, a design concept was developed which might have added a new dimension to naval history. Conklin recommended that the Navy be memorialized in our nation's capital by a massive arch, copying almost in its entirety the Arc de Triomphe of Paris. The proposed design was to be two feet shorter than the Parisian original. The center of the arch would become a concert stage with the back enclosed during concerts. I was amazed by the enormity of the suggestion particularly the size of the arch. I immediately wondered how we could give the arch a more nautical theme. I had always believed arches of that size were for armies to march through. I could just see a shipload of anchors being imported to hang from the arch, and why not throw in a few dolphins to break the monotony.

Impressed by its large scale and potential statement making impact on Pennsylvania Avenue, the Foundation's board of directors enthusiastically approved the arch. The board then pressed hard for concept approval. Typical of Navy conduct, it was full speed ahead! A decision had been made. "So get on with it, Mates, and no skylarking along the way," was the direction. By this time, President Reagan had dispatched Bill Middendorf to be Ambassador to the Organization of American States. Old friend Marvin Stone, editor of *U.S. News & World Report*, replaced him on the board. Marvin had been a V-12 student, was commissioned and served in Pacific amphibious operations before returning home to begin a successful journalism career. He worked with Hearst newspapers covering the Western Pacific and later the Pentagon. He was a serious, no fluff man. "Gentleman, if we really want to build a memorial in Washington," he admonished members of the board, "now is the time. This is the opportunity we have been waiting for. If we fail, we may never get another chance."

"Amen to that," I affirmed.

Next, we set out to select a sculptor to work with the architect on designing various aesthetic elements of the Navy Memorial arch and other statuary. A selection board was structured similar to the one used by the Navy. PADC's architectural consultant, Sasaki Associates of Boston, assisted in searching national files for eligible candidates. With additional assistance from the National Sculptor Society, a large number of sculptors was initially scrutinized by Sasaki Associates. They finally presented us with a list of 36 candidates. I assembled a panel of eight people affiliated with the arts and primarily from the Washington metropolitan area. Rear Adm. Walt Enger represented our Foundation on the panel. Five finalists were chosen including Felix de Weldon. Enger lobbied aggressively for de Weldon to be included among the finalists. Enger was well aware of de Weldon's stellar reputation within the Armed Forces and had gained first-hand experience with him as the sculptor of the Seabee Memorial for which Walt had been responsible.

Another group of panelists, including myself, reviewed elaborately prepared dossiers and portfolios, personally interviewed each of the finalists and visited their studios. We selected Stanley Bleifeld of Weston, Connecticut, ending a seven-month search for a Navy Memorial artist. After ensuing congratulations and early conversations, we discovered Bleifeld had been in the Navy as an enlisted man during World War II. That fact wasn't included in his biographical data. However, it didn't contribute much to Bleifeld's nautical background other than his having worn the uniform and having some familiarity with the Navy. He was from Brooklyn, joined the Navy to "see the world" and got as far as Bainbridge, Maryland, for boot camp. The Navy ordered him to report to New York City to spend the rest of the war illustrating training manuals while living at home. Stan served well, but his Navy career hadn't been anointed by salt water, nor had he experienced gentle or gale force winds known to sailors at sea.

The Commission of Fine Arts, the PADC and the National Park Service favorably endorsed the arch concept. The eminent Carter Brown, chairman of the Fine Arts Commission and head of the National Gallery, was excited about the arch and the amphitheater. He directed us to, "Make it sing!" The fourth and final approval was to come from the National Capital Planning Commission. But the tide of momentum came to an abrupt stop, and a fallen arch resulted from a 9-3 Planning Commission vote against the design. The commission cited the arch as potentially overpowering to surrounding buildings. The towering, powerful edifice would threaten the National Archives across the street and possibly impairing the vista from the Pennsylvania Avenue side of the Archives building, up 8th Street to the National Portrait Gallery. Entities at both ends of the view displayed architectural columns that enhanced the panorama.

Recovery

I didn't feel the entire brunt of the loss of the arch immediately because there was work to be done. We needed to quell the notion that the Navy Memorial Foundation had suffered an insurmountable defeat. For several hours that afternoon I was on the phone talking with media representatives and various directors. I assured them all that the Foundation was still alive and already working on new designs. We were applying all our talents and other available assets to the effort.

In retrospect, the loss of the arch may have been a financial blessing. Even though the Conklin Rossant architectural firm had estimated the cost to be $10 million, I was later told it would have escalated to at least $15 million. Additionally, I was becoming disenchanted with the potential of the arch and its limited usable space.

The space at the top of the span would have been good for a large events room or an exhibit area. It would have been ideal for receptions or dining overlooking Pennsylvania Avenue. However, I was cognizant of the potential criticisms for having built the "Officers Club At The Top Of The Arch." Functionally, one of the piers could have contained elevators and a few smaller rooms. For the other pier, I had visions of an I-Max theater and had Bill Conklin working on designs, but none were initially acceptable. An I-Max screen has a maximum height of 77 feet but can be reduced comfortably by 10 to 15 feet. After several tries, Bill was able to shoehorn a theater into the space, but the theatergoers would be almost sitting on the shoulders of those in front of them. The seating slope was too steep for comfort, safety or consideration for physically challenged persons. So while the mass and majesty of the proposed arch held some attractions, erecting the arch in Market Square and the structure's limited functionality presented many negatives.

In the aftermath, $300,000 of arduously acquired funds had been invested in the failed arch concept, and the Foundation's financial condition was as low as its morale. Many supporters and potential contributors wrote off the U.S. Navy Memorial as "another ship that passed in the night."

It wasn't easy to acquire that $300,000. We received our first large contribution of $50,000 from a friend and now a director, Joanne Crown of

Chicago. That sum kept our small staff operational for over a year because I didn't draw my fee but managed to keep the other staff members happy. We netted $90,000 by sponsoring the motion picture premiere of *Final Countdown* starring Kirk Douglas and showcasing the aircraft carrier USS *Nimitz* and F-14 *Tomcat* fighter aircraft. Our initial direct mail solicitation to all retired Navy Flag officers featured a personal letter signed by Admiral Tom Moorer, a member of the Foundation's board of directors. It asked for a contribution of at least $100. We received a remarkable 33% response which is phenomenal for a direct mail solicitation. Usually a 1% to 2% response is considered successful. I proudly reported our return to Admiral Moorer, who was not pleased. "That means 67% didn't answer my letter," he said.

"Let's try again, and this time even I promise to respond," I jested. We did and received another 33% response. We were in something of a response rut but with good consequences. We were also beginning to have success requesting support from defense contractors.

We held a national competition for professional fundraising assistance which the Community Counseling Service (CCS) from New York City won. It was an unpleasant arrangement primarily because of the monthly $15,000 fee and the need to provide office space for a consultant and specifically dedicated secretary. We also weren't ready for the capital campaign dictated by a feasibility study. CCS indicated the fundraising environment was good for our cause with the economy good, the anti-military (Vietnam inspired) feelings subsiding and we should proceed. That would become a major undertaking requiring a considerable amount of my time as well as some of the directors.

As it was, I was immersed in the Memorial's site negotiations and design approval. I felt strongly that without evidence of a solid design, our fundraising effort would definitely be hampered. John Connelly was the Community Counseling Service consultant. He was originally from a small town in Wisconsin. He was effective in the business of appealing for funds. We spent considerable time together as he mentored me on that task. He was at my desk for two or three hours a day, and we lunched together. We traveled to visit prospective donors and got along well. Basically, his message was that I was the fundraiser, and he was the assisting consultant.

I grew impatient because funds were not developing and terminated the contract after about four months. That wasn't easy. John called me a few weeks later saying he was still unemployed and asked if I would take him on temporarily for $300.00 to work two days a week. I agreed, and he was back with us for another few months. Then he was hired again by his former company to manage its Dublin office. He was successful there, and Zum and I visited John and his wife Sinead in their attractive home in Ireland.

I grew learning fundraising techniques from my association with John Connelly. Although I was never comfortable asking for donations, I had faith in our project, and when I retired as the CEO and president, we had raised $24 million. John taught me well. I used the fundraising framework he structured throughout my tenure, although we did not undertake a major capital campaign per se.

Going forward

Tom Regan, Conklin Rossant and I worked diligently to formulate design ideas, but nothing evolved except more frustration. Even the PADC was becoming uneasy. I was unofficially given the ultimatum to come up with a design within three months. The PADC board of directors was anxious to start construction at Market Square, the last undeveloped parcel in their domain. If we could not meet that deadline, PADC would negate its approval of the Foundation utilizing the space.

One day in the office after the arch's demise, Jack Davey asked if he could talk to me about a personal matter and proceeded to make a plea that I resign from the Foundation. He said he had talked with other Navy retired PAOs. He was asked to be their emissary, but he was primarily speaking for himself. He said there was no way this project would ever succeed, and that I would be remembered as the guy who failed to build a Navy memorial. Everything I had accomplished in the Navy would be overshadowed by the failure of the Navy Memorial Foundation. The image of the Foundation was "zilch," and it would not recover. He went on to say the "8-ball" I had been maneuvering behind for the past few years was much bigger and growing by the day. Fundraising was a disaster and would not improve. So he asked me to please think about it and resign.

I stared hard at Jack for a short time trying to frame a response. "Thanks, Jack, for sharing those thoughts," I finally said. "Those are harsh words and not easily digested. However, please know that I have given this situation considerable thought. I don't want to go into detail at this time because you will think I am arguing. Generally, you are right. We are floundering, but I don't want to advertise the fact. If I quit, I doubt if a Navy memorial will be produced, at least not in the magnitude we have been considering.

"If I quit now, the stigma, if it is as bad as you think, will be there, regardless. I don't play the hero role well, but I have to stay with it. Not to figuratively go down with the ship, but to be more positive and make another try at getting a design approved, so we can then get on with fundraising. I may sound like the village idiot, but I can't see any way out but to forge ahead. I think we can do it. And Jack, I'm going to need your help. I hope you will stay with me."

That short conversation was pivotal to my 15 years with the Navy Memorial Foundation. My mind was firm. I thought my actions and discussions with the staff and the directors had indicated the same thrust, but my statement to Jack put it in concrete. I wanted it known that going forward was our doctrine. I told everyone we were not quitting and would continue to work diligently on our plan of action. I reflected privately on the spirit of "Gumption" my grandfather extolled. In this case, I hoped that it didn't lead to being stupid.

By then I had invested almost five years with the Foundation. Although the learning curve was steep at times, I had enjoyed the experience, gleaned considerable knowledge about memorial building and handling a large project. Personally significant was the experience of working with some outstanding, intelligent, professional people in Washington. They were dedicated to making the nation's capital a better place to live and work. The daily process suffocated any effort to pursue work with my Admiralty Communications, Inc. consulting firm. My list of clients had evaporated.

My contract with the Foundation started me off at a fee of $18,000 working one day a week. The board of directors doubled that retainer six years later and promised more when funds were available. The directors acknowledged that the fee was less than one-fourth the average remuneration for similar non-profit executive directors in Washington. I didn't need a financial incentive to stay with the project; the challenge was enough enticement. It was what I originally planned, but the process consumed me. I became obsessed with making a statement for the Navy in downtown Washington. However, I remained concerned about creating a decent retirement for Zum and me. I realized I would have to move out as soon as we succeeded in completing the memorial. I estimated another two or three years on the task.

Shortly after the arch's demise, I was informed by our working space benefactor, Santa Fe Pacific Corporation that we were going to be accessed a rental fee if we wanted to remain in their offices. Although we were treated well by Santa Fe, I immediately started a search, looking hard for rent-free office spaces at the Washington Navy Yard. I was reluctant to make a move there because it would double the commuting distance and be situated in an undesirable area in Southeast Washington.

When visiting with Bud Zumwalt one day, I had the opportunity to talk with Dr. Ronald "Ron" Easley, the originator, president and CEO of System Planning Corporation (SPC). He was providing office space for Bud and Paul Nitze and employing them as consultants. I explained my project and how I needed space for three or four people. Ron was aware of my relationship with Paul Nitze and Bud Zumwalt and apparently accepted me as being legitimate. He thought for a few moments, agreed then and there and added he would like to help us.

Within a week, Walt Thomas, Jack Davey and I borrowed a truck and moved our desks, files and equipment to SPC's 1500 Wilson Boulevard offices in Rosslyn, Virginia. We moved on a Saturday and were in business on Monday morning. The transition proved a small company can be efficient and certainly agile. We occupied a corner suite on the 13th floor with a room for my office and another for Walt Thomas. Ruth Donohue had a desk in the hallway outside my office. Jack Davey decided not to join us in Rosslyn but continued doing our direct mail solicitations.

I told Ron we needed the space for a short time until I got us organized. In reality, it wasn't until nine years later we (12 of us then) moved to permanent offices in the Heritage Center at the Navy Memorial. Ron was patient and hospitable and was certainly a significant benefactor in our project's success. When we needed more space because of additional personnel, computers and files, Ron moved us to their more spacious offices on Quincy

Street in Arlington. One of the buildings was formerly a bowling alley, and we resided there with ample room to expand. We did expand, but amazingly we built the Navy Memorial with never more than 12 people; there was a maximum of seven permanent employees and five part-timers.

Fundraising became more productive primarily after I recruited for our board of directors four-star Adm. George Espy R. Kinnear, II, better known as "Gus." After retiring from the Navy in late 1982, Gus became a vice president with the Grumman Corporation in charge of its Washington office. Because of his nature and personality, Gus became a leader and activist within the Washington defense industry community. Being a friend of many years, I signed him on as a director of the Foundation. I established a fundraising committee headed by Gus. We met weekly with him holding all members accountable for what they had promised to do in the previous meeting. His broad network and innate persistence were effective as evidenced by pledges of up to $250,000 over a four or five year span being acquired. I was proud our pledges had 100% validity.

An oddity arose in our fundraising. Our consultants and others advised us to forget about direct mail appeals and to concentrate on big donors such as defense contractors. That was probably good advice, except they didn't know the breath and depth of competition we faced just within the Navy community. There were several Navy-oriented endeavors simultaneously requesting support from the same donors. The Naval Academy Alumni Association was building Alumni Hall at the Academy with a much larger requirement for funds. The Naval Under Sea Museum in Keyport, Washington, dedicated to the Navy's submarine service was being built at the same time as our project. The Naval Aviation Museum at Pensacola was a big, well organized program underway with a much higher budget than ours. Those and several more organizations such as the Navy- Marine Corps Relief Society, Naval Academy Foundation, Naval Institute Foundation, Navy History Foundation, and Fleet Reserve Association were actively requesting funds from the same donor list. And that was only the competition from Navy organizations.

I considered the "no direct mail" approach flawed. Those speaking negatively didn't know or lacked experience with the loyalty, commitment and total dedication of U.S. Navy enlisted personnel. Both those on active duty or retired were intensely dedicated to just and humane causes. I was extremely aware of the historic generosity of U.S. Navy sailors. I once read an article about the "White Knights of the Sea," the Navy enlisted personnel who performed charitable deeds and gave generously to needy folks and causes worldwide. That benevolent trait was continuously validated for me throughout my lifetime. Ultimately, it served as the bedrock for a program that directly or indirectly raised more than 50% of the funding for the Navy Memorial complex.

The Navy Log

I had vowed early on that I did not want Navy personnel to pay for the memorial honoring them. That feeling was set aside when I heard of a project executed at Ellis Island in New York City coincident to the national bicentennial commemorations. Through two friends, James Hawkins and Dennis Kless, employees of Eastman Kodak Corporation and working in its Washington office, I learned of the work Kodak had done.

The corporation compiled a listing wherein émigrés or their descendants could register emigrant names, preferably with pictures, and the dates and places where they entered the United States. It became the "Log Of Immigrants" and was displayed during the commemorations and afterward. It was a highlight of the bicentennial.

After studying that experience, we initiated the Navy Memorial Log as a fundraising program but soon learned it was much more than that. It became a primary venue of the Navy Memorial. Memorial visitors gravitated to the Log Room to see data and pictures of themselves, family or friends. We charged $25.00 for entering a name into the log and an additional $25.00 for a photograph. Basically, it centered on Navy personnel, but we accepted the names of Coast Guard, Marine Corps and even the Army veterans providing they had served with the Navy in joint operations or missions. Kodak monitored the program for us, mostly through a contribution-in-kind.

Daughter Stevii and family had returned from a year at Stanford University where Randy was a Sloan Fellow, participating in the Stanford Business School's master's degree program. They lived only a few blocks from us, and I had asked if she would mind joining me in the office to sit

in for Ruth Donohue who was on vacation. That was in 1984. At the office
we had a Xerox word processing machine that had been donated to us by
Xerox's Washington office. Stevii was computer literate and conquered the
"Xerox Beast." That feat had not been well accomplished by anyone other
than a couple of part-time employees who were no longer on the scene.

I labeled Stevii the "Matriarch of the Navy Memorial Log." She inherited
a shoebox of 3 x 5 cards containing vital individual information for the log.
Stevii stayed, and her inventory grew to two shoeboxes. Soon there were
more on her desk and then on the floor surrounding her. Stevii and I normally commuted to the office together. Naturally the conversation was on the
office and especially the log. I repeatedly got the hint that she needed a computer. As the number of shoeboxes increased, the hints lost their subtlety and
became demands.

Through Rod Brubeck, a Naval Academy graduate then working with
Unisys Corporation, we sought the donation of a few computers to modernize our office's operation. Unisys came through with eight new computer
monitors and a server that took care of all our workstations. Additionally,
Unisys provided our staff with two weeks of in-office training—five days on
word processing, two on data management and three on spreadsheets. We
were elated and immediately became more productive and efficient. Stevii
was pleased and discontinued her threats to my wellbeing.

She and Randy departed McLean again for San Diego where he, having
retired from NASA as director of the Astronautics Division, was to be employed as the CEO for a start-up computer technology company. We were
successful in having her honored with the Distinguished Public Service
Meritorious Award from the Secretary of the Navy for her contribution to
development of the Navy Memorial. When she departed, we had a farewell luncheon in her honor and then needed to hire three people to replace
her. They were retired Master Chief Dave Michael, director of the Navy
Memorial Log, Jim Fleckenstein, director of the direct mail program and
Renato Pascual, who did financial work related to the log program. Stevii's
salary was about 20% of their combined contracts.

"So much for nepotism," Stevii concluded.

We missed her intelligence, broad knowledge of the Memorial project,
her good sense of humor and positive attitude. She was always a joy to have

working with us. I especially missed the "cerebral popcorn sessions" we had while commuting to and from the office. In retrospect, I should have paid her a consulting fee for the privilege.

Additional staff members

We were suffering from expanding workloads and growth. In September 1984, I hired Capt. Bob Jones, a Navy contemporary, installing him as my executive assistant. Bob was ideal for our effort being knowledgeable about Washington and the media. He had an engaging, personable demeanor making him invaluable in handling staff problems and serving as my alter ego outside the office. His seemingly computerized memory proved valuable on many occasions.

Walt Thomas was phasing out of our staff, reducing his time in the office and authoring a novel. In 1985 we hired Capt.Tom Coldwell to continue Walt's public relations work including starting a newsletter to our growing list of constituents. Tom was another PAO, about 10 years behind me in the Navy. I was familiar with his work and pleased to have him join our staff.

In the fall of 1986, we brought aboard Paul Haley as a temporary helper to enter names into the Navy Memorial Log. Paul proved to be a part-time duty survivor and a contributor to our project. He has celebrated his 20th anniversary with the Foundation and continues to serve. His kindly manner and ease of interaction made him indispensable as the director of Planned Giving. Also in 1985 we brought aboard Jim Nemer, a retired commander PAO, who grew into the task of interfacing with the contactors about the construction of the Memorial and specifically on the design and build out of the visitor's center. He had a successful 10-year career with the Foundation and served his final years as vice president and director of operations.

At the beginning, we did most of our direct mail work in-house and largely in-house at the "Thompson House." Zum was a reluctant volunteer to assist, but characteristically, once she became involved, she more or less took over. Our home became a direct mail factory. Operations included stuffing letters and other materials into addressed envelopes, sealing them, sorting by zip codes and bundling them for deposit at the post office. Zum became a walking zip code directory and was challenged by random tests from the kids and me such as the zip code for Ottumwa, Iowa, or Dillon, Montana. She would respond with either the correct code or close to it. She also played the Tom Sawyer gig well, getting her neighbor lady friends involved in big mailings. We gradually transitioned the program to contractors when we became more active in the direct mail business. Zum was a contributor and was proud of our accomplishments.

Moving again to the problem of finalizing a design, I did something unusual in the Washington bureaucracy. I formed an ad hoc committee comprised of executive directors from all our approving agencies and others in the D.C. government to help me watch over the development of a new design. I realized their presence didn't assure design approval. But by examining as many caveats as possible, I thought we could gain a concept consensus before heading into the official approval process.

I knew if we faced another denial, not only would the approval be further delayed, but it might be fatal to our effort. Normally, the committee members were rivals and turf oriented. Their usual work charters overlapped in some areas causing friction between the organizations. Professional demeanor always prevailed among these leaders, but camaraderie was definitely not prevalent.

I was told that my ploy wouldn't work, but it did. The team performed well and was a direct credit to those individuals and their desire to help. At my retirement from the Foundation, a representative from one of the organizations gave a testimonial. He said what they would always remember about Admiral Thompson was my getting four executive directors to work together with no bloodshed.

With the help of Walt Thomas, Stanley Bleifeld, John Roach, a marine artist and Naval Reserve commander with a public affairs designator, and our architectural firm, Conklin Rossant, a basic design was created, developed and evolved to become the Navy Memorial as it exists today.

The deck of the amphitheater posed some problems. Conklin Rossant preferred a fixed square or rectangular approach with a Mercator projection of a world map. I preferred a circular presentation which would require a polar projection. It wasn't until I attended a luncheon in a downtown Washington restaurant that I discovered a polar projection of the world etched on the bottom of an ashtray. "Borrowing" the ashtray, I hurriedly returned to my office to announce my discovery of the amphitheater deck design and called Bill Conklin. From then on it was Conklin Rossant working with the Defense Mapping Agency in Washington until an acceptable polar projection could be attained. Conklin Rossant did an outstanding job on the refinement and architectural engineering work. With the informal endorsement of the ad hoc committee, the design was finally officially approved by all agencies in June of 1984.

It was Bill Conklin's idea to have Washington, D.C. at the center of the projection. We were all pleased with that focus. The projection encompassed about 90% of the world's land mass and its vast oceans, the Navy's domain, displayed. "This is great, Bill," rear admiral and astronaut Al Shepard told me as we viewed the plaza when we were filming him in a fundraising commercial. "This is exactly how Mother Earth looks from about 200 miles out in space."

The new Navy Memorial design was an abrupt change from the massive, dominating arch. Currently, the amphitheater presents a relatively low profile in a 100-foot circle surrounded by four large pools, each with moving water. The two large pools next to Pennsylvania Avenue have a series of water jet fountains that provide a vertical focus to the Memorial when they operate during the summer months.

After Tom Regan left the PADC to become a commercial real estate developer in the Washington area, he said, "Within five years, Market Square will be the Rockefeller Center of Washington and its centerpiece will be the Navy Memorial." In the broader sense, Tom was correct. While the Navy Memorial doesn't have the Rockettes, there are numerous activities at the Memorial, especially during the summer months. It provides wide ranging attractions for visitors to the nation's capital and it citizens.

"Cast Off All Lines"

Stan Bleifeld arrived on the Navy Memorial scene at the time the memorial arch was in its last months. His job was to work with the architect to design adornments to make the arch "sing" and give it a nautical look. His immediate reaction to the arch was negative. His attitude didn't change, although his demeanor was circumspect and gentlemanly. After the arch fell, he began, at my request, to draw capturing his thoughts for a Navy memorial. An early sketch he shared with me displayed a collage of Navy ships in various situations filling the amphitheater.

Overlooking the entire seascape was a lone figure, a sailor, huddled in a peacoat and braving inclement conditions. The solitary figure was obviously only an adornment to the presentation's main thrust and not intended as part of the memorial. Both Walt Thomas and I agreed that no matter what happened to the rest of the work, "the lone sailor stays." That was the genesis of the "Lone Sailor." The statue eventually brought Bleifeld additional fame and fortune and ultimately became the Navy Memorial's enduring symbol. I later realized the Lone Sailor embodied the many times when a sailor is on his own, standing his watch without the benefit of a team surrounding him. It may be a fire watch, security post, after-steering or on lookout on the wings of the bridge. A sailor grows accustomed to being alone, immersed in the duties of the watch and carried by his private thoughts.

The Lone Sailor icon was another Memorial vision that grew from vague beginnings. I realized we would need a statue and perhaps several. With relative ease I concluded that "The Statue" should resemble an enlisted man, a sailor, because 90% of those who have served in the Navy have been enlisted personnel not commissioned officers. Since this was to be a Navy Memorial, it was certainly appropriate to feature the image of a U.S. Navy sailor, a "Bluejacket" garbed in a recognizable, universally accepted and appreciated uniform. I visualized the Lone Sailor as symbolic of all who have served in the Navy. Most officers agreed, but initially, the idea wasn't readily shared or accepted by females. As the Lone Sailor took on a life of its own, it didn't need any supportive rationalization. It was a stalwart piece of statuary symbolizing both the Navy Memorial and the U.S. Navy.

In my extended plans for the Navy Memorial, I envisioned adding two or three more statues representing Navy personnel. I could see an enlisted man, perhaps a 19th Century sailor poised in the International Pool and piping visitors aboard the Memorial. Nearby in the adjacent pool across the entrance on Pennsylvania Avenue, a junior officer with his long glass (the badge of his position as Officer of the Deck, In Port) could officially welcome visitors to the Memorial with a salute.

At a Memorial reception, the wife of a retired three-star aviator admiral cornered me to ask a serious question. "Bill, aren't you going to have the officers represented in the Memorial with a statue?" she inquired. I tried to explain the situation with the Lone Sailor and my attempt to include a young officer welcoming visitors aboard the memorial. She seemed relieved, "Oh, that's nice!" she exclaimed. "Of course he will be a naval aviator won't he?"

Everyday life as the Navy Memorial Foundation's CEO was exciting and definitely not mundane. But I often wondered what it would be like to be the boss at a putty knife factory.

Bleifeld worked on the basic memorial concept and made valuable contributions. Simultaneously, he was pushed to more sharply refine the Lone Sailor that I sensed could be central to our memorial. Over a five-year timeframe, he produced five versions of the Lone Sailor—four in clay model maquette and another in a painting. Normally, when an artist is commissioned to create a work, the basic concept is discussed and the process begins. The artist completes the task and presents it to the sponsor. Minor adjustments may be made, but the work is essentially complete and the contract fulfilled.

For the evolving Lone Sailor, I did not accept Stan Bleifeld's efforts until the fifth rendering. Stan was frustrated. Perhaps I didn't communicate well, or he didn't understand my ideas. But there was always trust, respect and value for one another. I was fully aware that Stan was a brilliant, accomplished artist. I learned much from him and exerted utmost patience and tact in our dealings. At all times he treated me, the art neophyte with respect. After long sessions discussing our project, we always departed with a hug. Hugging a man was unusual for me, but I found it agreeable and more expressive than a mere handshake.

In midstream of the Lone Sailor's development, Walt Thomas and I prepared, primarily for Stan Bleifeld's benefit, a narrative description of the Lone Sailor and psyche of its characterization. That description reads:

> The "Lone Sailor" is the singular symbolic figure of the US Navy Memorial complex. He is a composite of the US Navy Bluejacket—relatively young, about 26—and a senior second-class petty officer who is fast maturing to become a seagoing

veteran. He is the kid from down the street who left to join the Navy just a few years ago. Since then, he has been to Navy schools and off to sea, shipping out in different types of ships that have crossed the equator, the Arctic Circle and the international dateline. Sea duty continues to have the aura of romance—the adventure of more ports to visit, more miles to log, more training, more duties, more experience and more responsibilities—now performed with the seasoning of a veteran sailor who has been there before and is willing to go back.

He embodies two hundred years of worldwide experience, loyalty and courage, and he is a member of the world's best navy. The seas enchant him; he is fascinated by each ocean's beauty and peacefulness, as well as its emotions and its strengths, manifested when the seas roil to awesome exhibitions of typhoon fury and savagery. His personal demeanor exudes confidence, and he has a subtle swagger in his walk. He believes firmly in himself, his ship, his leaders and his Navy.

The "Lone Sailor" is pensive but alert as he surveys the sea. As he gazes out on the ocean that surrounds him, he ponders that wide domain where his country has asked him to serve— that vast area that covers three quarters of the earth's surface and which has historically claimed many of his shipmates who have fallen to its perils. The comfort and beauty of the seas usually warm him, but his serenity is often punctured by his knowledge of the powerful turbulence of the seas in turmoil. Still, he retains a special quality of love and respect for the sea.

In the distance, far beyond the horizon, is the United States—home! At sea, home is always over the horizon, in all its meanings—his roots, his loved ones, his natural habitat, his patriotism—all more real to him than described in even the best lyrics of sea songs and chanteys.

"Home and the sea" hold the answers to all questions for the professional US Navy Bluejacket.

The third version of the Lone Sailor featured a more informal pose with one foot on a mooring cleat, an elbow resting on his knee. Supposedly he was gazing out to sea, but it was easy to conjecture other conquests in his mind. Seemingly, everyone in the staff loved the model. The SPC employees working in our area had the same reaction. He was a sailor! A fun loving sailor! Ready to take on the world! But he wasn't as serious and seaworthy as I desired in our Lone Sailor characterization. He was dubbed "Liberty Hound" and attained popularity and his own charisma within our small "bowling alley" community. A full-scale bronze of the "Liberty Hound" is the centerpiece of a Navy memorial in Jacksonville, Florida. There it has taken on a more dignified status including losing his frivolous nickname.

The final versions of the Lone Sailor were figures to which anyone who had ever been to sea, Navy or otherwise, could relate. The image was first developed in a painting. Stan had the painting done by an artist colleague and recognized illustrator, Bert Silverman. Silverman's work has often appeared in *Sports Illustrated* magazine. The fifth and final version was captured in a clay model. He truly became the Lone Sailor, the only piece of statuary placed in the amphitheater and the enduring emblem of the Navy Memorial. By this time I referred to him as "he." He had become like a son and actually took on his own life. Our constituents loved him, and I received many letters, emails and comments about how realistic he was. One letter from a widow related, "The statue is exactly like my vision when I was waiting on the pier for my husband returning from the sea." Several others wrote sharing the mutual thought, "Hey, how did you get my picture? That Lone Sailor is exactly as I looked when I was a sailor."

Zum and I traveled to Beacon, New York, to join Stan Bleifeld in the special event of casting the Lone Sailor at the Tallix Art Foundry. Coincidently, the foundry was owned by a former naval aviator, Lt. (JG) Richard Polich. The Lone Sailor was cast on August 4, 1987. Foundation public affairs leader Tom Coldwell and his wife Mary Ann joined us for the event. The firing for the statue included bronze artifacts from eight U.S. Navy ships spanning the Navy's history. Included were objects from the post-revolutionary frigates *Constellation* and *Constitution*, the Spanish-American War era steamship *Hartford* and the battleship *Maine* and the submarine *Seawolf*. One last addition was a personal decoration from the modern Navy, a National Defense Service Medal donated by our Bob Jones, my executive assistant. The Lone

Sailor embodied more than 200 years of worldwide experience, loyalty, courage and commitment. He definitely holds part of me.

Bronze Reliefs

Always the Navy PAO, I envisioned a series of bronze bas-reliefs depicting the Navy's heritage and history, commemorating crucial naval events or recognizing groups or units that contributed to the Navy's success and development of the country. Roach and Bleifeld produced what we called the "Sculpture Wall." It was to display a series of 22 bronze reliefs (each 36" x 30") and be placed at the south entrance to the plaza. Organizations or groups interested in the project or a specific naval subject eventually sponsored all of these art pieces.

The Fleet Reserve Association (FRA) Auxiliary volunteered to sponsor a bas-relief about the Navy family. It raised the $50,000 cost by sponsoring bake sales and selling Lone Sailor lapel pins for $5.00. The first contracted bas-relief was "Women in the Navy." Another was sponsored by the Destroyer Escort Sailors Association (DESA) showing World War II destroyer escorts, and it was the first to be completed. The commemorative for the Construction Battalions or "Seabees" was to be sponsored by their association. More than 60 potential subjects were considered by the Foundation's Fine Arts Commissions), all collected from a large group including the Naval War College, the Naval Academy, the Naval Curator Emeritus of the Smithsonian Institute, the Director of Naval History and the Naval Historical Foundation and our own board of directors.

The DESA was the first organization to fully fund its bas-relief, and therefore, it was the first of the 22 produced. Gilbert Franklin, the sculptor, worked with coordinators Bob Jones and Leo Irrera, as well as DESA officials including John Cosgrove, one of our Foundation directors. Gil's instructions were to stay within the limits of the definition of bas-relief being about 5/8 inch in depth. Gil's product was acceptable, depicting the drama of one of the destroyers' primary World War II duty of escorting convoys. To be sure, the feisty destroyers performed a myriad of other duties then and in the Korean War and the Vietnam War. To me the presentation seemed to lack emphasis and didn't make a strong statement. But all concerned accepted the work as our first bronze.

About that time, I went to Italy to inspect and hopefully give final approval to Stan Bleifeld's "Homecoming" statue he had worked on in his studio in Pietrasanta. The approval was accomplished almost immediately. Stan did a commendable job, completing a beautiful statue that would have held meaning for anyone who has returned home from a deployment or even to a youngster returning from a two-week camping trip.

I told Stan while I was in Italy I wanted to see some bronze reliefs, such as doors to churches or cathedrals or similar works. Stan was an outstanding guide and lecturer and had an informative schedule awaiting our arrival. We visited Florence and Pizza, and it became clear to me that such relief presentations were much more dramatic and expressive when they were done in deep carvings. I discussed my view with him and returned to Washington convinced that I should tell the coordinators, Jones and Irrera, to "go deep."

The team of sculptors was encouraged to carve deeply. We set the parameters, so if they wanted to go deeper than five inches, they were to discuss it with the coordinators. We had the destroyer escort plaque redone, and the result was exceptional and far more dramatic. The dioramic presentation obviously provided a greater opportunity for expression. Also the deeper cuts added little to the cost of the plaques. The final 22 reliefs formed a powerful statement of naval history. The diorama has been described by some art critics as the largest such presentation in the United States. Commensurate with the "go deep" evolution, we forever dropped the bas-relief nomenclature choosing instead to refer to them as bronze reliefs in keeping with the formal definition.

Our ceremonial space was designed to be highlighted by a large bronze casting of a compass rose encircled by bronze rings and white granite. John Roach created and produced this large piece, and we placed it at the entrance to the Memorial on Pennsylvania Avenue. There we envisioned wreath laying ceremonies on significant holidays or by visiting dignitaries. As the Memorial matured, the only time a wreath laying occurred at the "Compass Rose" was at the dedication ceremony. Thereafter, by popular demand, all wreath laying was done at the Lone Sailor statue.

The large southwest pool took on an international aspect. It was dedicated to navies that sailed, fought alongside and went to sea in the pursuit of common causes with the U.S. Navy. Countries that helped the Memorial by contributing to its construction have their names inscribed on the wall. Argentina was the first country to contribute to the U.S. Navy Memorial. Spain, Japan, France, the Republic of China (Taiwan), the Republic of Korea, the Republic of Germany and Australia all followed. Those contributions averaged $100,000.

I struggled for several months to compose a statement to be etched in the granite of the International Pool and symbolize the bond that exists among those who sail the seas together questing for similar ends. Almost every day on my computer I clicked up the document containing the hodgepodge of my efforts. I would rearrange words or type a few new ones trying to come up with a concise, expressive statement. A telephone call or an impending appointment reminder would necessitate saving the document for a later try. Any thoughts I had of being a wordsmith were vanished by frustration. By chance, I was talking with Capt. Chuck Smith, deputy director of the Navy Historical Center, on another subject, and I mentioned my difficulties. Chuck laughed and said he could understand my feelings, but he had a solution. He had been waiting to suggest the simple statement, "To Shipmates from other Lands, The Seas that Divide us, Unite us."

"Chuck, I can make you famous by dropping it in the Navy Memorial International Pool and etching it in granite," I replied.

And so it was etched and everyone was happy. The simple words avow all we intended. I don't know about Chuck's increased notoriety, but we were and are indebted to him.

The Granite Sea

The Navy Memorial's two-color granite world map is the world's largest. A special Laurentide Blue Granite from Canada's Laurentian Mountains represent the oceans. Deer Isle Gray Granite, from Deer Island, Maine represents the land. The granite is two inches thick, giving the map the undisputed heavyweight title and weighs in at 217,634 pounds.

Shaping the two-inch thick granite presented a problem to the stonecutting contractor, New England Stone Industries, Inc. of Smithfield, Rhode Island. An advanced technology machine was devised to cut what was essentially a jigsaw puzzle. Two cuts were necessary. One to shape the Deer Isle Gray continents and the other the Laurentide Blue water. A similar machine was already being used to cut metals and baked goods. It was modified to cut granite. With a few changes, a new machine was designed and introduced to the stone cutting industry, and it has had a lasting effect for stonecutters everywhere. The machine's computer guided, water jet cutting tool developed pressures up to 60,000 psi and significantly reduced the time and cost of cutting stone.

Special care was taken to perfect the amphitheater and concert stage so they met the criteria of all military band leaders in the Washington area. I had several meetings with them for early planning and on-site when construction started. The amphitheater was designed to have a three degree rise from the stage to the back of the area. The slope allows better visibility of the bands and performers from all sectors of the theater. The concert stage was constructed on four levels and will accommodate any of the military bands and most symphony orchestras.

Adjacent to the stage but underground is a large storage room for additional seats, sound and lighting equipment that can be brought up by an elevator. The underground area also includes an electrical room and pump room for the pools. They remind me of the engineering spaces in a ship but with more room. There are also dressing rooms, lavatories for male and female performers and a special room for the bandleader. The concealed areas have been particularly useful. As one bandsman told me, "When we are on tour we usually have to change clothes and such in the bus."

The Lone Sailor Award

With the Lone Sailor becoming the symbolic signature of the Navy Memorial, I thought we should capitalize on it. It potentially presented financial benefits as well as promotional opportunities. We instituted another instant tradition in the form of The Lone Sailor Award with a periodic formal presentation at a dinner or luncheon. I wrote the original selection criteria for the board of directors to use when selecting recipients. I deliberately tried to keep the guidelines broad so as not to encumber the selection process.

Honorees were to be Navy veterans, whose after service efforts had benefited humankind. The underlying thought was to recognize exemplar individuals from among literally thousands of Navy veterans, especially from the World War II era, who returned to make positive contributions in civilian life. Some got college educations through the GI Bill programs and became successful in varied professions, politics, education and business. They provided leadership for the nation throughout the postwar years, particularly during the Cold War era.

Later an adjunct to our award program was included to recognize individuals who were not Navy veterans but had performed deeds beneficially affecting the Navy or Navy personnel. It included individuals who served in the Navy secretariats. One such person was Paul H. Nitze who had a brilliant diplomatic career before and after serving as Secretary of the Navy. This award is called the Distinguished Service Award.

Herman Wouk, my nominee, was the first recipient, and he was the classic example of the type of person we desired to recognize. He had served in a minesweeper as a young naval officer during World War II. He later distinguished himself as a novelist, authoring *The Caine Mutiny*, *The Winds of War* and *War And Remembrance* all based on World War II experiences. He also wrote several other successful novels. His three classics were produced as motion pictures and remain benchmarks as books and films.

I had the opportunity to host Herman Wouk for lunch on June 23, 1987, the day of the awards dinner. I told him that his descriptions of naval combat were the best I had read. I reread several times his depiction of the death of Warren Henry, one of the main characters of the latter two books. Warren was the son of "Pug" Henry, the books' central character. Warren was a naval aviator who is killed in the Battle of Midway, and the reader experiences his death as if they were in the cockpit with him. Wouk seemed to appreciate my comments.

That evening, Wouk's response to receiving the Lone Sailor statuette from our Chairman Senator John Tower was lucid, concise and poignant. I was enthralled hearing it and have reread it many times with the same feeling. Quoting in part:

"The Lone Sailor is one of those self-sacrificing brave spirits. I know him well.

"I saw him on the forecastle as we approached an invasion beach in the dawn, in his kapok jacket and his steel helmet at his battle station by the number one gun ready for anything that would come.

"I saw him in the wheelhouse and in the radar shack during a typhoon, when our old minesweeper was rolling 40 or 45 degrees, standing by his station and doing his job.

"I saw the Lone Sailor, as you see him in this statue, on the forecastle as we steamed homeward for a navy yard overhaul, passing from the warm South Pacific to the cold December waters off Northern California; his hands jammed in his peacoat pockets, his eyes gazing toward the Golden Gates and towards home.

"But if I know him, and I think I do, the Lone Sailor looks beyond the shores of battle and the shores of home to a distant shore, and the quintessence of the American Dream. He looks to the day when 'the nation will not lift up sword against nation, neither will they learn war anymore.'

"Until that distant day comes, he stands at his station, ready to do his job. And, I think it is because I have spoken up for him that you give me this most moving honor; because in truth you are honoring him, the Lone Sailor."

Those words and the man who delivered them were admirable. Herman Wouk was indeed a superb choice as our first Lone Sailor awardee.

Our first Lone Sailor Dinner was unique in the brief history of the Navy Memorial Foundation and continues as a memorable, important and successful event. It was held at the new Grand Hyatt hotel in Washington and was coincident to the hotel's grand opening. Dick Nelson, a former naval officer and later the regional director of Hyatt Hotels, was a member of our board of directors. He was an enjoyable associate and supporter of the Navy and the Navy Memorial. He was also manager of the Grand Hyatt Washington. It was a fortuitous arrangement for us because the hotel underwrote the food and beverage costs. We had a near sellout attendance with the hotel guests there for its grand opening and our guests who donated up to $10,000 for a table of ten or $250.00 for a seat. We grossed more than $400,000, and the net proceeds weren't far below. It certainly proved to be a win-win agreement for the hotel and the Foundation.

The theme for the evening was the "Navy Memorial Salutes Hollywood." We recognized many actors, actresses, producers and directors of movies that featured the U.S. Navy. The Eastman Kodak Company joined the benefactors by providing us with about 50 large 36"x 36" photographs of scenes from all of the movies involved. As an added attraction, we introduced the Lone Sailor at the dinner. Stan Bleifeld delivered a full-scale plaster model of the statue that was placed at the entrance to the ballroom for all guests to admire.

Dedication

Construction was moving along satisfactorily and we decided to target our dedication ceremony for the Navy's 212th birthday on October 13, 1987. In the late winter of 1986, I discussed this with the PADC; they chortled and let me know that I was probably ready for a psychiatric check. I said the subcontractors would probably say the same thing and add a "Hell, No!" But after thinking about it for a couple of days, I believed the contractors would come around with a, "We will do our best, but don't be optimistic." With a few expletives added, that is generally how it came about.

The craftsmen laying the intricate Granite Sea and others picked up the pace with a "Can Do" attitude and cut about two weeks off the scheduled completion date. Our fallback was that the Memorial would not have to be completed by that date, but it should be presentable for the celebration. After the dedication, the Memorial itself would be closed to visitors and fenced off because construction would be starting on two buildings embracing the Memorial on the east, west and north perimeters.

At the end of September Stan Bleifeld delivered the Lone Sailor from New York. We placed him in position overlooking the Granite Sea's Pacific Ocean with the shores of the western United States on the distant horizon.

On October 12, the last piece of granite was laid. Stan and I observed the final setting from the middle of the plaza and congratulated each other on the successful completion of a five-year project. The Lone Sailor was "On Watch" on his final duty station. While in our convivial mood, Stan pulled me to the statue saying that he wanted to show me something. On the back of the Lone Sailor's seabag was a bronze replica of the traditional 2 inch, square identification patch (U.S. Navy Bluejacket seabags are officially identified in this manner.) with the initials "WT." Immediately below was the faint engraving of a stenciled "W. Thompson."

My first reaction was to laugh and say, "Hey, look at that." Then I realized this was Stan's silent tribute to me, and it was not to be taken frivolously. The result was a Bleifeld-Thompson hug expressing respect and friendship. I thanked Stanley for his superb assistance to me personally and for our combined Navy Memorial effort. I also apologized for being so arbitrary at times. We were moved aside good naturedly by the artisans intent on completing the stonework surrounding the bronze base of the Lone Sailor. In later years, I have looked at my name on the seabag as my imprimatur on the Navy Memorial. Occasionally I have shown it to family and close friends who have wondered what I did after retiring from active duty in the Navy.

John Cosgrove

Considerable planning and other work that needed to be done to set up the dedication ceremonies. First, I asked John Cosgrove, one of our directors, to be the Dedication Committee chairman. John was a Navy veteran and former news reporter. He had an office in the National Press Building and was active in Press Club events. He was a leader with the Destroyer Escort Association. He was also active in several Washington associations and groups giving him access to many doors in the capital.

I thought he was ideal for the position, and he seemed to enjoy it. I was pleased because he didn't consider the title to be honorary; he was an active participant in all aspects of the event and respected his responsibilities. I was initially a little surprised, but got used to having a true partner for doing onerous work. We blended well together, and I respected his contributions, judgment, advice and counsel.

One enjoyable venture John and I undertook was to gain a White House appointment with President Reagan to present him with a 24-inch bronze replica of the Lone Sailor. During the presentation, I said the statue was symbolic of all personnel who had served in the U.S. Navy since its inception in 1775. President Reagan nodded and thanked us. "It is always a pleasure to meet someone older than I am," the President added in his whimsical manner.

John took the Memorial dedication a notch above what I had been thinking when he recommended that we hire an event planner such as Robert F. Jani Productions. That group did Super Bowl half-time extravaganzas among other major events including the nationally acclaimed Radio City Music Hall's "Magnificent Christmas Spectacular" in New York City. After discussions and negotiations, Jani said he would do our event for a reduced rate of $100,000 because we were the Navy Memorial Foundation. Being responsible for fundraising and being involved in that process every day, I was reluctant to fund the event at that price.

I told John I needed a lot of convincing. We discussed it and concluded the dedication was a rare occasion for the Foundation and a chance for nationwide publicity. As our plans were progressing, it became clear we would have had to hire a coordinator to choreograph all the events. The bands, fireworks, flyover, balloon release and many other details had to be synchronized. My credo throughout my tenure with the Foundation was when we did something; we did it first class because we were a first class organization. I grew convinced about the major enhancement for the dedication and had little trouble getting the board of directors to agree. Robert Jani became our choreographer in residence.

National Archives authorities were eager to assist and granted the use of their building's second level portico overlooking Pennsylvania Avenue as the speaking platform for the event. Across Pennsylvania Avenue, the portico overlooked the Navy Memorial. It was an ideal setting. John and I decided the only way to accommodate our anticipated audience was to close off Pennsylvania Avenue to traffic extending the reach of the National Archives portico across the avenue to the Navy Memorial. Doing that would provide added space for four large Navy bands, marching units and other participants.

I was a little leery of requesting the city fathers to close Pennsylvania Avenue, a main thoroughfare. But John in his unobtrusive manner finessed the procedure. I was pleasantly surprised by the hospitality and cordiality of the city's committee and their expressed delight at being a part of the Navy Memorial dedication. As we worked the project, clearly evident support from all levels welcomed the Navy Memorial into the city's culture. It was gratifying and inspiring.

With the large expenditures, we were not only expecting a successful dedication, but we wanted to maximize publicity and its national scope. CHINFO helped us with a strong publicity program within the Navy. A Naval Reserve public affairs unit from Detroit was authorized and assigned to work with us for five days immediately prior to the event. Capt. Dick Becker headed the group along with Cdr. John McCandless, whom I had known for many years. During my early days with the Foundation, CHINFO assigned John to work with me for training while on his two weeks of active duty. At that time, we talked about many programs and how public affairs might help. John had kept in touch, visited us at home on several occasions and continued his interest in the memorial project. He was director of public relations for Chrysler Motors in Detroit.

The day the Navy Memorial "Came alive"

October 13th was a brisk, chilly fall day in Washington, especially in the shadows below the portico on the north side of the National Archives. However, the sun was shining, and the skies were clear. Pennsylvania Avenue was carpeted in Navy blue and was magnificent surpassed only by the ebullience of the several thousand spectators. The entire spectacle was exhilarating to me as I observed the scene from the portico where I served as the preliminary master of ceremonies.

As a warm-up to the formal agenda, I welcomed the guests, described elements of the Memorial and introduced our board of directors and staff members. I then introduced John Cosgrove, our dedication chairman. While I was talking, I noticed Adm. Arleigh Burke and his wife Bobbie sitting below me visibly shivering in their seats. When I exited the VIP seating platform, I rescued the Burkes from the cold and had them brought to a warm room with floor-to-ceiling windows overlooking the portico. There they were far more comfortable, had a vantage view and could hear the speeches. The 90-year-olds appreciated the move and reminded me of it several times thereafter.

John Cosgrove introduced former Senator John Tower, chair of our board of directors. He in turn introduced a series of speakers: Adm. Carl Trost, the Chief of Naval Operations, James Webb, Secretary of the Navy, Adm. William Crowe, Chairman of the Joint Chiefs of Staff, Henry Berliner, Pennsylvania Avenue Development Corporation chairman; and Gen. P. X. Kelley, USMC (Retired), a special assistant to Vice President George H. W. Bush. Kelley read a letter from the Vice President and Secretary of Defense Caspar W. Weinberger, the event's principal speaker. Secretary Weinberger concluded his speech stating it was time to commission the Memorial and so ordered saying, "Bring this Memorial Alive!"

With that a contingent of Navy Honor Guard sailors introduced waters from the Seven Seas into each of the four memorial pools. The four pools were energized with flowing water, and the four bands gave a tremendous rendering of the National Anthem. Fireworks erupted, and 1,000 blue and gold balloons were released. Climaxing the event, Navy aircraft filled the skies over Pennsylvania Avenue with a thunderous flyover at 1,000 feet. What a spectacular event it was! Hearts were warmed, and roaring cheers and applause erupted.

During the proceedings, Navy Secretary Webb completed his address by calling me to the podium and pinning to my chest the Navy's Distinguished Public Service Award, the highest recognition the Navy has for civilians. His aide read the citation that began, "For his unswerving dedication, tireless efforts, and superb leadership, which have enabled the United States Navy Memorial to become a reality in Washington, D.C. ..."

We followed the main event with some additional ceremonies such as dedicating the Compass Rose, the official ceremonial area, and unveiling the Lone Sailor statue. I officiated at those two events after having led a participating contingent across Pennsylvania Avenue into the Memorial grounds. Included in the group were Lone Sailor sculptor Stan Bleifeld and Master Chief Petty Officer of the Navy (MCPON) Bill Plackett whom I had chosen to unveil the statue. Bill gave a poignant, concise description of the symbolism the statue elicited. I was proud of his presentation because I knew he could do it well. I had great respect for Bill Plackett. He was an excellent choice to be the MCPON, the senior enlisted man in the Navy. Also in the small group joining me was my 10-year-old grandson Braden Graves whom I included as the symbol of the youth of America. (But the rascal didn't join the Navy.)

Secretary of the Navy James Webb conducted a swearing-in ceremony for over 80 Apprentice Seamen who were recruited as a special Navy Memorial Recruit Company and assembled on the Memorial Plaza for the dedication ceremonies. It was a special day for them. They were starting their Navy careers on the Navy's birthday at the dedication of the Navy Memorial. Could anyone ask for anything better?

We completed the ceremonies with a reception for the VIPs in the beautiful Archivist Reception Room in the National Archives. We were limited to about 120 people because of fire ordnances. There were probably a few who felt slighted at not being invited to the reception and never forgave me. But I couldn't stretch the room, and at the time couldn't have done better. Overall, the dedication was considered an outstanding success.

After the reception we held our annual meeting of the board of directors. It seemed somewhat inconsequential with the euphoria of the dedication still lingering. It had indeed been a long day bringing about a few yawns during the meeting. I had contemplated informing the board that I was tendering my resignation effective upon their finding a suitable replacement. But as the day closed, it didn't seem to be appropriate.

"Thanks"

After the board of directors meeting, Joanne Crown asked me to escort her across the street to the Memorial because she had not seen it before the dedication ceremonies. I replied I would be proud to do so. As we were departing the Archives building, I grasped her arm and said, "Joanne, this has been a big day in my life. I am pleased and proud to share it with you. I feel that right now, Bob (her late husband) is looking down on us smiling and giving us the thumbs up signal.

"I am so appreciative of your support to help make this memorial possible. It was you who gave us the first big contribution—$50,000—and that sum kept us going while we were getting organized and conceptualizing this project."

Old friends that we were, she pulled my arm next to her and said the opportunity isn't always available to see what contributions accomplish. As we walked around the Memorial, I pointed out various features and explained their significance and symbolism in the overall statement we attempted to make. I said that only the visitors to the Memorial, especially Navy veterans, could validate our intentions.

During the process of this "cook's tour" of the just dedicated U.S. Navy Memorial, I became aware of a man who was watching us and following my impromptu presentation. He was obviously a Navy veteran because he was wearing a hat of one of the veterans' organizations. I recall his hat as being emblematic of the U.S. Navy Fleet Reserve Association, a strong, dedicated group of enlisted sea services personnel (Navy, Marine Corps and Coast Guard). As he edged closer toward us, I wondered about his intentions. I wasn't fearful, although Mrs. Crown, an attractive lady, certainly was. He approached me at our last stop. He had been only about six feet away, but summoning his courage, he approached closely, faced me directly and then asked, "Admiral Thompson?"

As I acknowledged his inquiry, he drew back his shoulders and stepped forward again. He took a deep breath and tried to say something. Instead he grabbed me by the shoulders and gave me a hug while muttering in my ear, "Thank you!" As he turned to walk away, I noticed tears on his cheeks. But he seemed happy and satisfied to have thanked me for "his" memorial. Unfortunately, I never saw him again, but I will never forget him or the circumstance of our meeting.

"That's an outstanding finale to a great show, Admiral Thompson," Joanne, always the ingenious one, said. "I'm impressed."

In later years when reminiscing about the occasion, Joanne would accuse me of setting her up claiming the unknown Navy veteran was a hired hand or a staff member. I only wish I could have been so resourceful. I consider that still vivid incident to be the best compliment or compensation for my 10 years of work. It was a sincere expression of appreciation from a Navy veteran. It was a more than fitting act of gratitude for the accomplishment of an ambitious project.

Media Results

The Detroit Naval Reserve unit worked well and was effective as was the work our staff did before their arrival. At the dedication we built a large media platform in the best possible location for photographing all the events. It wasn't long after the ceremony started when we ran out of space on the platform. It wasn't because the platform was too small, but the media response was much larger than anticipated.

All the networks were there with crews, and the local affiliates were providing coverage as well. C-Span aired the entire two hours live and repeated the documentary several times. The CHINFO film crew devoted its entire half-hour weekly news show to the Memorial. That broadcast went to all ships and stations and more than 100 local cable TV stations in the vicinity of naval bases and stations. Print media reps were omnipresent, and their editors were generous in their coverage of the event. Our national media effort was definitely successful. Ample proof was provided by the number of phone calls and letters we received extending warm congratulations and describing seeing the Memorial or us on television.

Completing The Navy Memorial

With dedication of the Navy Memorial completed, its success celebrated and properly archived, our staff felt the relief of pressure and anxiety as the pace slowed for the remaining three days of the week. As had been previously announced, the Memorial plaza was fenced off and closed to visitors for six months while construction of the Market Square buildings progressed through the pile driving stages to erection of the Doric columns that embrace the Northern sectors of the plaza on the façades of the two buildings. The columns complemented those at the National Archives across the street and the National Portrait Gallery four blocks to the North up Eighth Street. Architectural, art and city planning critics praised the columns for tightening the ambience of the sector and enhancing Market Square as a unifying element of the redevelopment of Pennsylvania Avenue.

The staff returned to working the list of short and long-range objectives. Finishing the Memorial plaza, replacing flawed or broken pieces of granite and pointing up a few joints in the Granite Sea were the immediate tasks. Jim Nemer was at his best doing this type of work, joshing with the contractor employees and all the time aware of ensuring an impressive Memorial. While those tasks ensued, I was negotiating an agreement with the National Park Service concerning maintenance of the Memorial, scheduling bands and ceremonies for the coming calendar year and proceeding with Visitor Center plans with a new architect and a new landlord, Trammel Crow. We also continued our Foundation Executive Committee monthly meetings to address a multitude of problems and record decisions.

In April 1987, after staff and executive committee discussions on the subject of extension of the Memorial to include a Visitors Center located ideally in one of the Market Square buildings, I prepared a memorandum for our Chairman, Senator John Tower, to sign. It establishing an ad hoc committee of eight directors plus Rear Admiral Jimmie B. Finkelstein, the Navy's Chief of Information, as a non–voting member, to study the extension of the Foundation. The pertinent issue was to study and recommend to the Board of Directors whether the Navy Memorial Foundation should go out of business, as was the initial intent or continue to exist to schedule events at the Memorial and administer the Navy Log. Waring Partridge headed the committee.

I gave the study group and other board members ample time to consider the question because I was determined that the Board of Directors should vote on the future of the foundation at our October 1987 annual meeting. It was necessary if we were to remain in business to bid for space in one of the Market Square buildings and negotiate a contract. Some lively discussions and memoranda resulted. One of our directors, Robert Bateman, responded to the Chairman's memorandum taking the position to phase out the foundation within two years because we had advertised our existence to building the Memorial, To continue in another venue would not set well with our prime donors, especially industrial corporations that understood and expected this to be a one-shot endeavor. A lack of trust, confidence and credibility in the Foundation and unenthusiastic participation in support and fund raising efforts in the future would be a natural result. Bob added that if deemed necessary, an appropriate organization could be developed to watch over the Memorial in the future.

Bob Bateman's recommendations were poignant and tough to digest but I trusted and knew him as a straight arrow type. Bob and I were classmates at Wabash College for one semester in the V-12 Program after which he was sent up the road to nearby Purdue University where he earned a degree in aeronautical engineering and after a short time in the Navy, joined Boeing Airplane Company in his hometown, Seattle, WA. He climbed the corporate ladder to become Vice President and Director of Washington, DC operations. I invited him to join our board of directors and over the years became good friends professionally and socially. I pondered his statement at some length and discussed it with him and others. In retrospect, it may have been the best move to dissolve the foundation in view of the difficulty we had raising funds for completion of the facility and later, to maintain it. However, I thought it would be more difficult to fabricate another organization to do exactly what we had been doing. In July, I wrote a six-page memorandum for the Board of Directors (BoD), giving my thoughts based on the nine years with the Foundation and what I had learned and envisioned. I thought the loss of trust and confidence in the foundation would be just as severe for the Navy veterans who contributed an equal amount of funds through the Navy Log Program if we abandoned the Log. Waring Partridge's report to the BoD for its October 13, 1987 annual meeting recommended that we stay the course, continue the Foundation until it was feasible to turn it over to another organization, if that was considered advisable. This basically encompassed some of my recommendations as well as Bob Bateman's. The BoD approved those recommendations at its meeting following the Dedication Ceremonies. With that decision, we negotiated a 25-year contract for space on the northern corner of the 701 Pennsylvania Avenue, the eastern Market Square building

The Homecoming

When Stan Bleifeld was selected to be our official sculptor, I had him come to Washington so that we could become acquainted and then dispatched him to Norfolk and the Atlantic Fleet for a week so that he could get a little salt injected into his veins and get a feel for what we wanted him to express in his work. We arranged for him to talk with flag officers, including the Commander in Chief, US Atlantic Fleet, senior and junior officers, Chief Petty Officers and other enlisted personnel. Fortuitously, his visit coincided with an aircraft carrier's return to its homeport, Norfolk, from an extended overseas deployment so that Stan was witness to the excitement and emotion of families being reunited. This event is a poignant part of the Navy's family culture and was the genesis of the Homecoming statue. Stan sketched several reunions that assisted him when he sculpted this important and heartwarming rendition of Navy life.

The Fleet Reserve Association pledged $1,000,000 to the Memorial, concentrating initially on the "Homecoming" statue that was valued at $250,000. The FRA's plan was to focus their fund raising campaign on visible succession of Memorial segments. After Homecoming the FRA adopted the Gallery Deck, the central element of the visitors Center. A million dollar pledge for an organization that had about 70,000 members was a large undertaking but the generosity and ingenuity of the U. S. Navy Bluejacket—active duty and retired—succeeded. In return, the foundation gave the FRA on permanent loan the original life size plaster cast of the Homecoming statue and it continues to reside in the entrance to its office building in Alexandria, Virginia.

Initially, and throughout development of the Homecoming statue, we intended to place it outside either on, or adjacent to, the Memorial plaza. As we moved along, we realized that its statement, strong and compelling as it is concerning the importance of the Navy family, conflicted with the thrust of the stronger statement presented by the Lone Sailor, the Granite Sea and the fountains. When completed, we wheeled the statue around the plaza on a dolly to various positions and became increasingly disappointed to realize it did not fit. These two strong artistic elements conflicted and diminished the effectiveness of both. We tried placing it outside the plaza and to a lesser degree the same conflict persisted. We considered going to great expense of having an exterior alcove constructed in the 701 building, next to the Visitors Center entrance but gave up and settled on the Homecoming Statue being positioned on the Quarterdeck, the entrance to the Visitors Center.

It has good visibility in that position and is a constant reminder that family is important to Navy personnel. The decision was not easily made and I depended on the staff and board for advice and counsel as well as outside consultants, some paid but most friends of the Foundation. I also leaned on the Commission of Fine Arts for assistance as well as leaders of the various art galleries in Washington. Follow-on Chief Executive Officers of the foundation will undoubtedly revive the debate but I made the decision based on good advise concerning our principal statements and my intuition. I was comfortable with the decision and concluded that we were fortunate to have that problem. We had two excellent art forms in our possession.

Master Chief Hood Has His Say —

Before leaving the subject of the Homecoming Statue, I should relate an integral event in the development of the final rendering. Stan Bleifeld produced the Homecoming maquette in his studio in Pietrasanta, Italy and brought it to my office when he returned to his Connecticut home for the winter. The maquette was a 24-inch original sculpture from which, if approved, the seven-foot statue would be enlarged. I was satisfied with the work and the staff liked it. At that point, if requested, we were ready to tell Stan to proceed with the seven-foot model. I was talking with our new Navy Memorial Master Chief Petty Officer, Jay Hood, in my office and when completed I said as an aside,

"Master Chief, you haven't given me your opinion of the Homecoming statue. What do you think of it?" Jay looked at the maquette and shrugged his shoulders and said, "It's OK." and started to make his exit.

I was somewhat surprised and said,

"Jay, we brought you aboard this staff because of your reputation and you didn't develop your reputation by not be forthright. We have a relatively small unit here for the size of the task and I have to trust everybody and vice versa. I feel that you are withholding something from me. That may have sounded like a frivolous question but I have asked the same of a lot of people. I not only want but need your honest opinion. I may not agree with it but we have to make a decision soon about this figure because it is going to be around here for a long time, long after we are gone."

I was posturing a bit and being rather pedant because we did not know each other well at that juncture and I thought this was a good opportunity to let him know how I felt and how much I planned to rely on him because of his background of 30 or more years in the Navy. Master Chief Petty Officers were, and are, valuable properties and integral assets to the leadership of the Navy.

Jay studied me for a few seconds and then gave me a straight forward reply to my question that almost ruined my entire day,

"OK, Admiral. My impression of this statue is that it depicts a sailor having his first liberty in notorious Naples, Italy and he is embraced by the first hooker he has met on the street and the kid is picking his pocket."

I thanked Jay and said that I appreciated his comments and may call him back for further discussion. I was amazed and flabbergasted and somewhat deflated. The rendering was meant to show the traditional homecoming reunion of a young Navy family— a pretty young wife and six-seven year old son with a young petty officer—after an extended deployment. The boy had a baseball cap on backwards and the young lady was a knockout, right out of Hollywood or Rome and adorned in a rather short dress. My impression of the boy was that he was clamoring for attention that was being monopolized by his mother. Stanley admitted using a statuesque young Italian lady as a model. My remaining schedule for the day was delayed, put on the back burner. I had to think through the Homecoming presentation in light of what I had just been told. I was confident that Jay Hood had considerable credibility and was trustworthy. I was impressed by the fact that when he retired as the Command Master Chief at the National Naval Medical Center at Bethesda, MD, four four-star admirals attended the ceremony as testimony to his credibility and good reputation. I did not see him as a frivolous man but as a positive, serious person and 100% dedicated to the Navy. Under the circumstances, I could not believe that he was jesting with me but that he was delivering what I wanted, his honest impression of the Homecoming statue. I had to consider his comments and so I did for the next few days.

After discussions with other staff members, a few System Planning employees and Jay, I concluded that Jay had some legitimate concerns and we had to tone down the artifact so as to guide desired perceptions. I called Stan to relay our feelings that changes had to be made. The artist was not pleased but understood our concerns that perhaps this did not represent a dockside reunion of a typical family. I cited several items of concern such as the dress length; the lady should maybe wear shoes with short heels rather than sandals; something a little more conservative, more in keeping with Navy decorum, reminding Stanley that this sculpture is an enduring piece of art that will be prominently displayed at the Memorial for years to come. Any error in this presentation should be on the conservative side.

Stanley acknowledged our message and his artistic response was extraordinary. The final product has the same three figures in an embrace with one of the boy's arms entwined with one of his Dad's; the boy was sans baseball cap and a great smile on his happy face; the lady had donned a pair of shoes with 1 and 1/2 inch heels; her skirt was about two inches longer and Stanley had even shaved about a quarter inch off her derriere. To make them legitimate, our sculptor included wedding bands on the left hands of the sailor and his still attractive Navy wife. I have continued to compliment Stanley on the magnificent work he did on Homecoming and Jay Hood for all his contributions to the Navy Memorial, particularly regarding the Homecoming statue.

Skiing

I was 53 years old when I started to ski. Zum and I, being from Wisconsin, had an appreciation for winter sports and enjoyed even walking in the snow, hearing the snow creak under our feet and the cold nipping at our nose and ears. In retrospect maybe the best part of it was entering the house and sitting before a crackling fire, drinking a glass of hot mulled wine or hot chocolate and reminiscing about the great winters in Wisconsin and Michigan. I ice skated a lot in my youth, sledded and tobogganed but skiing was not popular at the time because of the lack of hills in the Escanaba and Green Bay areas. We had become good friends with Jimmie and Kay Finkelstein and their three children, Jon, Andrew and Susan and we started skiing—cross country style initially. We traveled to Bryce Mountain in western Virginia and to Catoctin National Park to ski next to the U.S. Presidential hide away Camp David in Maryland and to New Germany State Park, near Grantsville in western Maryland to find some good, groomed cross country trails. Grantsville provided a large but old hotel with a dining room, bar and lounge that including a pot bellied stove radiating heat for most of the patrons. We RONed (remain over night) several times there and concluded that if Hollywood didn't have a replica, it could probably be had for a low price and be a prime site for several movies or TV series.

I finally realized that the best part of cross-country skiing was going down hill. The other parts were hard work albeit a good healthy workout.

The next year, 1977, the Finkelsteins and Zum and I motored to Killington, VT in their Recreation Vehicle (RV) to participate in our first instruction for down hill skiing. What a gas! I was immediately hooked on the sport and have often declared it is the most exhilarating sport I had ever enjoyed. We returned to Killington and that area several times and another that proved to be a great attraction was Camelback in eastern Pennsylvania. Camelback, had a unique trail titled The Glades that wandered through the tree line bordering its housing area, through trees, gullies, a creek bed and opened onto the communal area of the ski complex. It was convenient to complete the run and go immediately to the ski lift to do it again. A great experience! We also skied other slopes in New York, Connecticut, and New England with the Finkelsteins. Zum had chosen not to do down hill. Her excuse was that one had to wait too long in ski lift lines, but she was a good sport about it and enjoyed being with us. Gray Rock ski resort, about 90 miles north of Quebec in the Mt. Tremblanc area had a ski school that I attended four years. It was total saturation instruction for six days and I enjoyed the routine. I learned that I was not to be listed as a par excellent skier. I could not bring my skis close together to "parallel" as the term goes in skidom. Mine were six to 12 inches apart and a few other things were missing. But I continued to have fun and skied several resorts in Utah, California, New Mexico and West Virginia. My skiing companions changed because the Finkelstein's duty station was in Norfolk. Jack Davy, son-in-law Randy Graves and Jim Nemer were also great on the slopes and après skiing. One Christmas, Zum and I rented a spacious condo at Snowshoe Ski Resort in West Virginia and invited the entire family. The only thing I remember about that Christmas was both Randy's and my diesel cars froze and we needed assistance to leave for home. But we did ski. Well, sort of in rain on ice. We had had better days.

I started thinking about "skiing in control of yourself" as the instructors would say. I liked to ski aggressively but not recklessly and was warned a couple of times by a smiling instructor that I was "borderline." I may have thought too much about it but I didn't want to wreck myself or hurt others. Several times I had been involved in being wiped out by others or at times witnessing wild eyed youngsters definitely out of control hurling down the hill being a danger to themselves and others. At age 70, I regretfully left the slopes. It was great fun for 15 years.

Paul N. Howell

In January 1989, President George H. W. Bush nominated our Senator John Tower to be the Secretary of Defense necessitating Senator Tower's resignation as Chairman, US Navy Memorial Foundation. This was an important time in our transition from building the Memorial to construction of the Visitors Center and needed a heavyweight in our top foundation job. I looked over of membership of the Board of Directors and kept coming back to Paul Howell who was in the midst of a significant career in the petroleum industry. He also had the credentials of a Navy background, being a Pearl Harbor Survivor as an ensign supply corps officer in the USS Neosho, a fleet tanker. Four months later, Neosho was sunk at the Battle of the Coral Sea off Australia and Paul spent 48 hours in a raft before being rescued. After WWII he returned to civilian life in the Petroleum business but stayed in the Naval Reserve, attaining the rank of rear admiral and being a principal advisor to the Navy Department on petroleum matters. By that time he had his own company, Howell Petroleum Corporation, a lovely wife, Evelyn, four stellar sons and a continuing interest in and devotion to the Navy. I had successfully recruited him as a member of our board of directors a couple of years back with the help of Charles DiBona, President of American Petroleum Institute, who recommended him. Paul was a member of API, I talked with Admiral Bud Zumwalt, another director, and we decided to invite ourselves to the Howell's Jamaica vacation house to urge Paul to take over the Chairmanship job, We also enlisted the assistance of Charlie DiBona also a director of the foundation. Without reciting the reason for the desire to be with Paul, I merely told him that the Zumwalts, DiBonas and Thompsons would like to join he and Evelyn in Jamaica whenever it was convenient so we could shake off the winter woes. A date was set for April and we had an enjoyable time playing tennis, chatting, laughing and scratching, sight seeing and even visiting with other dignitaries, including retired General P. X. Kelly, former Commandant, U. S. Marine Corps, also a visitor to Jamaica. Our host was surprised by our agenda but after a day of questioning accepted our request that he assume the position as Chairman of the US Navy Memorial Foundation. Paul proved to be an excellent choice, providing dignity and wisdom to our leadership. He brought a professional approach to our Foundation business and was helpful in stabilizing our financial affairs. I developed the highest respect and trust for our new chairman. We became good friends. Paul died in August 2001 and we have maintained contact with Evelyn and two of the boys, Brad and David. David lives in Alexandria, VA and does well in the real estate business. Brad heads his own transportation company and has an interest in the Navy, as does his son, Neil. I have enjoyed assisting them in their quests for naval knowledge.

Navy Memorial Tour/Cruise Program

While engaged in building-out the Visitors' Center, we also began considering programs to enhance our primary mission of honoring US Navy veterans and to educate our constituency as well as the American public about the heritage of the naval services. At our morning staff meeting we would jest about establishing instant tradition in keeping with our Navy's recognized traditions but commensurate with the Navy Memorial's growing presence in Washington. I continued to encourage creative thinking on the part of staff members to extend our thoughts and imagination beyond the perimeters of the memorial but with the caveat to not get too ambitious with frivolity and innocuous programs that would not benefit our image.

With several historic World War II naval anniversaries in the offing, I envisioned a tour program evolving to include the 50th anniversary of the attack on Pearl Harbor on December 7, 1991, the Battle of the Coral Sea, May 4-8, 1992, D-Day at Normandy, France, June 6, 1994, Victory in Europe and Victory in the Pacific. All these and more were significant occasions to commemorate and appreciate. We initiated the program by roaming the beaches at Normandy, France in October 1989 where we commemorated the 45th anniversary of D-Day. Headed by Ray and Christi Pfeiffer, Tours of Historic and Important Places, Inc. was our tour operator, performing the administrative chores and basic tour requirements such as lodging, meals, and transportation but the ancillary refinements in the way of visiting US Navy ships, briefings by US Navy staffs and presence of US Navy dignitaries were the foundation's responsibility. We gathered our 65 Navy Memorial guests in Washington, flew to London for two days and thence to the Normandy area in France and ended in Paris.

Our second tour was a year later revisiting the beaches of Southern France that followed the Normandy invasion in 1944. The third tour commemorated the 50th anniversary of the attack on Pearl Harbor, and the United States entering WWII. We had a large contingent of Navy veterans—162 of them— and were initially concerned about the difficulties handling that number of elderly people—ages in 70s and 80s—but aside from a few isolated cases of members wandering from the group and forgetfulness, the group was well disciplined and regimented. As an example we scheduled a breakfast at our hotel at 0530 so as to meet our schedule at the USS Arizona Memorial for colors (raising the American flag) at 0800 and asked our people to muster in the dinning room, starting at 0515. A large number gathered outside the dinning room doors at 0430 because they didn't want to miss the occasion. There were no AWOL's and not even a member being put on report for being late for muster.

The Banyan Tree

Our lodging in Honolulu was the Sheraton Moana Surfrider Hotel at Waikiki Beach, the oldest of the historic, elite hotels at Waikiki. Next door to Moana is the equally famed Royal Hawaiian, the Pink Lady, so named because of its pink stucco exterior. Moana became our hotel in Honolulu and we engaged its services eight times during the life of our tour program. Other than excellent service, it featured a gigantic Banyan Tree that provided cover for a large veranda where guests gathered, garbed in their new Luau shirts and shorts to enjoy a Mai Tai cocktail, become mesmerized by the Pacific Ocean combers sliding up the sandy beaches while keeping time with live Hawaiian music provided each evening. The Moana staff seemed to appreciate our Navy

Memorial groups as well as we enjoyed their hospitality and the environment. This tour was also our first with Adventures in Travel agency and introduced us to Commander Laurence A. Price, USNR (retired), tour leader par excellence. Larry was a Naval Reserve Public Affairs Officer, who had a good career as a public relations practitioner in the pharmaceutical industry and retired in Detroit, MI, near his alma mater, the University of Michigan and its Wolverine sport teams. During my Navy tenure as CHINFO I was aware of Larry Price as a Reserve PAO and impressed by his exuberant personality and demeanor but there was no other connection. He had invested in Adventures in Travel and made a pitch to us to coordinate our Pearl Harbor tour. That was the beginning of a long relationship in which he was our organizer and guide for about 25 of our tours. He was a natural to lead our Navy veterans. He had an affinity with them and patience to care for and lead them. In turn they liked and trusted him. Zum and I adopted him and cherished the association. We had fun and did it all over the world.

For the commemoration of the 50th anniversary of Victory in Europe—V-E Day—we had two events, one tour in Northern Ireland and immediately thereafter, a cruise to the Mediterranean Sea. Zum and I led the second but planned and did an exploratory visit to No. Ireland six months prior to the event. We invited son Brian and his wife Chris as our guests and we enjoyed a week together in beautiful Northern Ireland after which Zum and I returned to Washington and Brian and Chris stayed an additional week to tour Ireland.

On the Mediterranean cruise, we had Stevii as our guest and Bud and Mouza Zumwalt were a part of our Navy Memorial manifest. We embarked at Lisbon, Portugal and 12 days later debarked at Venice, Italy. When docking at Naples, Italy, Admiral Leighton W. Smith, Commander in Chief, US Naval Forces Europe, and Commander Allied Force, Southern Europe, was there to board our ship MS Song of Norway to welcome our group and gave us a briefing about his responsibilities which at that time included the war in Bosnia. That evening he hosted us at his quarters, Villa Nicki, for a reception at which he stunned the group when he answered a rhetorical question about why he applied for the Naval Academy. "Snuffy" as we now refer to him in retired life, replied,

"It was a matter of a bunch of Arkansas hogs. You see, I grew up on a hog farm in Arkansas and I figured that if I didn't get out of there, I would spend my life raisin' hogs."

Our group loved him. The next day, our cruise ship moved on to Messina, Sicily and then on to Corfu, Greece where we were guests of the Commanding Officer and crew of the USS Arleigh Burke (DDG-51). She had been there for a few days of R&R (rest and relaxation) before transiting north in the Adriatic Sea to participate in the ongoing war in Bosnia. I cite my letter to Admiral Smith on the incident:

May 27, 1995
Admiral Leighton W. Smith, Jr. USN Commander in Chief
US Naval Forces Europe
Box 1 PSC 813
FPO AE 09620-1030

Dear Admiral Smith:
I am pleased to report to you the success of the rendezvous ARLEIGH BURKE (DDG-51) had with our cruise ship MS SONG OF NORWAY on 21 May in the Adriatic Sea. SONG OF NORWAY had in its manifest 56 Navy veterans and spouses who, under the sponsorship of the Navy Memorial Foundation, were commemorating the 50th 'anniversary of VE Day. Admiral E. R. Zumwalt, Jr. USN (Retired) and the undersigned, with our wives, co-hosted the Navy Memorial cruise.Prior to getting underway from Corfu, Greece, BURKE hosted our group on board and treated us to an escorted tour of the ship and the opportunity for the veterans to talk with the officers and enlisted personnel. This was the first time most of our group had been aboard a Navy ship since World War II. Collectively, they were amazed at the design of the ship to not only fight but to survive in battle as well as the extant habitability and creature comforts. The genuine hospitality exhibited by the officers and crew and the evident pride they had in their ship and their Navy and their composure-confidence, competence and dedication-had

our group talking for several hours.

They were pleasantly surprised at the contrast with their WWII Navy experiences and exuded pride for the remainder of the day, at least until shortly after SONG OF NORWAY got underway and set course for Venice. As planned, about two hours later, Burke bore down on the SONG from the north at flank speed, passed to our port, turned in our wake and charged up our starboard side. When about a thousand yards abreast, Burke executed a crash back maneuver, stopping almost immediately. She then accelerated to full speed, made a 1800 hard turn to starboard, turning almost within its own diameter. This demonstrated the capabilities of gas turbine engines in modern, major warships and awed the 800 passengers and 400 crew of SONG OF NORWAY who crowded all decks on its the starboard side.

The piece de resistance occurred when BURKE again came up our starboard side, this time with the crew manning the rail. When abeam, her public address system blared the Star Spangled Banner, clearly heard by all in SONG OF NORWAY. It had started to rain and Admiral Zumwalt and I sought cover on the SONG's bridge. When he realized the crew was manning the rail, he detailed me with the words, "If they are out there in the rain, so can we be." I am proud to say that we took the salute in the rain and as we stood there, I said to Admiral Zumwalt, "Over the past 50 years, I've seen more than my share of special events, but this is the capper. In the Adriatic Sea, only a few miles away from a real war, one of the prime ships of the Sixth Fleet has been assigned to salute a group of World War II Navy veterans who are commemorating the 50th anniversary of the end of hostilities in Europe and Victory for the Allied Forces in a war that was to end all wars. And we are here to witness this event. What an exhilarating experience!"

Twice the captain of SONG OF NORWAY responded with three long blasts on the ship's horn.

Admiral Zumwalt responded by calling BURKE's Commanding Officer on the radio to express his and the Navy Memorial group's appreciation for BURKE's superb salute and demonstration. Everyone aboard was proud of her officers and men, the Sixth Fleet, Naval Forces Europe, the Atlantic Fleet and the whole Navy. Bravo Zulu!

SONG OF NORWAY was buzzing with acclaim for the rendezvous event for the next two days before the-passengers disbursed for return to the United States or other destinations. The Navy Memorial Foundation thanks you for the outstanding finale to its efforts to' commemorate WWII V-E Day-Victory in Europe. It was a significant and memorable event for the 1,200 people embarked in SONG OF NORWAY, particularly for our WWII Navy veterans.

Sincerely,

William Thompson

Rear Admiral, US Navy (Retired)

CC:

COMSIXTHFLT

CINCLANTFLT

CNO

CHINFO

Our last tour was in Sep 2005 at Honolulu for the 60th anniversary of the surrender of Japanese aboard USS MISSOURI—47 trips of which I led all but three. Zum was with me for 35 but decided to discontinue because of a distressful sinus condition resulting from long airplane flights. Recovery time for each of these occasions was about two weeks. Zum contributed immeasurably by judging the temperament of each group, taking care of gripes and unhappy guests, working with Larry and me to keep the group happy and to ensure that each guest sat with us for at least one meal during the tour or cruise. I continued to travel without Zum and substituted one, two or all of our children as travel companions and that was enjoyable but I decided to hang up the title of COMBAGPAC and retire from heading the Foundation's Tour Program. I took Craig on an exciting cruise in a small ship on the Bering Sea from Nome, AL to Vladivostok, Russia and Brian on an equally exciting cruise up the Amazon River and all three on a cruise commemorating the 60th anniversary of the Normandy landings with a side trip to London. They, and their families, joined me on the last tour to Honolulu.

We started the tour program to commemorate significant naval historic events, especially WWII, and when those dissipated, we continued the program because of popular demand. Even though not related to an historic event, we were aware of opportunities to connect with visiting USN ships in foreign ports, inviting Naval Attaches in embassies or other naval dignitaries to speak to our groups. It was an active program of interest to those with a US Navy background or the maritime services. We visited Antarctica partially because US Navy was involved in the development there in the 1930's with Rear Admiral Richard Byrd, USN, leading some early programs as well as immediately after WWII. Navy continued to support the National Science Foundation in its work there until the 1990s. The US Navy had a large footprint in Antarctica. For the 50th anniversary of D-Day friend Admiral William J. Crowe, Jr. USN (Retired), newly arrived US Ambassador to the Court of St. James (United Kingdom) to host our group of 160 at his residence. Later Admiral Crowe was our principal speaker at Slapton Sands, England on the English Cannel where the Foundation dedicated a large bronze plaque to the 639 US Navy and Army personnel who lost their lives in Exercise Tiger. Tiger was a rehearsal for the D-Day landing at Utah Beach that was intercepted by a squadron of German E-Boats (similar to our PT-Boats). Two Landing Ship-Tanks) (LSTs) were sunk and another heavily damaged. Ironically, only 160 US personnel were killed in the actual landing at Utah Beach.

Inquiries have been received concerning the Foundation's Tour/Cruise Program and several fellow travelers recommended we should do another in the way of a reunion. I'm agreeable to do one more for the road but have not found time to coordinate it. The Foundation has been reluctant to renew the program because a coordinator could not be found and it was never a profitable endeavor. I ensured that the Foundation never lost money on any of its tours but profits were meager. Normally we added $100 per person to the cost of the tour. That was to cover Foundation out-of-pocket expense for printing, advertising, and a small gift such as a Lone Sailor lapel pin, a Navy Memorial ball cap or T-shirt. On some occasions, I was able to host a Navy Memorial reception. (Wine and beer only!) On most tours and cruises our tour operator allocated one free ticket each 15 registrants. Most of the time, I rode free; half of the time I paid for Zum and I always paid for family members and happy to do so. When I retired from the Navy, I thought I had traveled enough and my wanderlust had dissipated. However, the tour program took me to places I hadn't been and depending on the travel century clubs identification of countries—there are several of these clubs and there is not a standard count of countries—I had visited 115-120 countries.

The Quarterdeck

In Navy parlance, a navy ship's Quarterdeck is its front porch, and door that welcomes personnel and visitors to its environs. It is neat, polished and official and reflects the quality and dignity of the country, the command and all its personnel. We tried to replicate that aspect in designing our Quarterdeck, the entrance to the Visitors Center. On boarding the Visitors Center, guests first see the polished brass and glass doorway followed by an equally impressive granite frieze with bold gold lettering of significant battles that punctuate our navy's history. Starting with Yorktown and on to Tripoli, Coral Sea, Midway, Guadalcanal, Okinawa, Korea and Vietnam and ending with the Gulf War, navy personnel are recognized for distinguishing themselves in United States history. We exhausted the space allotted for the frieze so implicitly made a statement that there would be no more wars. The foundation will need to recover additional frieze space to enter Iraq and Afghanistan.

The next compelling presentation is the Wave Wall that taxed our imagination and proved almost too difficult to accomplish. At times we thought it was either too expensive or impossible to fabricate but it evolved into a credible artistic presentation of naval history, done without the assistance of professional artists. We didn't look at it as a piece of art. It was just another manifestation of naval heritage that we retired Navy PAOs were trying to assemble. From the entrance 13 glass panels gracefully guide visitors down the stairway to the Gallery Deck below. The continuum of panels portray three waves rolling easily down the stairs done by fusing to the full sized 1/2" glass panel a second 1/2" panel cut to resemble a wave action at about eye level and a third smaller panel about knee high. The thickness of the glass provides a color variance of green seawater, the lower 1 and 1/2" thickness had the darkest green hue. To illustrate the progression of ship development we had etchings of 32 representations of ships from the USS Alfred, one of the first two ships in the Navy's inventory (1775) down to panel #13 that had USS Supply, the newest fast combat support ship, built in the 1990s and the USS Arleigh Burke-class guided missile destroyer. I was at Bath Shipyard in Maine to see it launched on my birthday, September 16, 1989. One of the most difficult problems was to find a manufacturer of the glass panels who could bend the panel that curved down the stairway. Our architect, Morris Architects, finally found Conti Glass Studio in Miami, Florida that would contract for the project. They did a fantastic job.

The Gallery Deck was not awash in museum-type memorabilia but did have discrete displays of some Navy historic artifacts and kiosks for presentations of a collection of ships of the Navy as well as all the aircraft the Navy has had. By the time I departed the President and CEO position, we said we had photographs of 98 percent of all the ships and aircraft. We were not in a hurry to find the other two percent because it would cost about the same as it did to gain the 98%.

The Presidents' Room was designed to be our primary function facility for the gathering of people for various purposes. We labeled it to honor the eight Presidents who were affiliated with the U. S. Navy, starting with Theodore Roosevelt and Franklin D. Roosevelt who were Assistant Secretaries of the Navy. From President John Kennedy to President George H. W. Bush, six of the seven had been naval officers. Only President Ronald Reagan was not a Navy veteran, having served in the Army Air Corps. Following John Kennedy were Lyndon B. Johnson, Richard M. Nixon, President Gerald R. Ford and President James E. Carter, Jr. I insisted that portrait paintings be done to represent each of them rather than photographs but almost had to back off of that tack because most portrait artists were charging about $25,000 for a work that I had been used to seeing in the Pentagon. I hired our artist Leo Irrera to coordinate the project and we contracted with eight college or graduate students from universities in the Washington area for $2,500 each to do the portraits. Leo and I were pleased with the process as well as the products. We got a good product, were able to recognize and encourage budding young artists and give them an opportunity to have their work displayed in a distinguished, dignified setting.

The Navy Memorial Log Room was an immediate success and became the core value of the Navy Memorial. Visitors gravitated immediately to the Log Room and were not disappointed. It became a center for the release of deep-rooted emotions, some of which I personally witnessed. The sensitivity of the scenes in the Log Room covered the scale from collapse at the sight on the computer monitor of loved ones to a grand child shouting, "Grandpa did you ever really look like that?" I was soon convinced that the concerns for the cost of the center were vindicated by the acceptance and popularity of the Log Room. It was definitely a keeper.

Big John

One of the most interesting individuals I encountered during my time with the Navy Memorial was British marine artist John Hamilton. John was a captain in the British army during World War II and was severely wounded in Burma when his infantry company was fighting for possession of a tennis court. His wounds required hospitalization for two years during which part of his therapy was painting and sketching. After the war and return to civilian life, he tried several occupational ventures, including managing a reform school for young men in Ghana, a British colony in West Africa. On return to England, he and his wife, Betty, resided in Tresco in the Scilly Isles, southwest of Lands End. He decided to get serious about painting and became Tresco's artist-in-residence, depending on tourists buying his land and seascapes. Tresco is a small island with about 200 residents, a feudal state owned by a landlord who rented or leased plots of land. There were two small hotels that catered to the tourist trade. In current language, Tresco is definitely Green. There were no automobiles except a small truck that hauled passengers' baggage to one of the hotels and each home had a garden for vegetables and flowers. John's studio was conveniently located on the touring path encircling the island.

John was 6 feet 9 inches tall and one of his first automobiles was an Austin that he made convenient for himself to drive by removing the driver's seat and he sat instead in the back seat. He was an aggressive person, pushing himself for a better life. He broadened his maritime artistry to include sailing ships and his ardent interest in WWII history. That led to completion of a 60-piece series on the Battle of the Atlantic, concentrating on the Royal Navy in WWII that is on permanent display in the retired Royal Navy cruiser Belfast, moored as a museum ship in the Thames River in London.

A natural follow-on was a series on the Battle of the Pacific, featuring the U.S. Navy. That brought John and me together. When we first met in Washington, he was looking for content for his planned 60-piece Pacific series and he had about reached that level while researching at the Naval Historical Center located in the Washington Navy Yard. Being a rank Navy historic buff, I agreed to assist John in this ambitious undertaking. The Navy Memorial Foundation sponsored an exhibit of several paintings John had done for his Pacific series. I noted the gregarious John would meet a Navy veteran or a reunion group and could be easily convinced and persuaded that he needed another "important" scene for his collection. I became concerned for him and his project when the number reached 100 paintings. I counseled John get back to his studio and "go to work" rather than seeking more interesting situations and stories to add to his series. To display his 100 paintings would necessitate a large area, possibly the size of the Pentagon. He heeded that advice and returned to Tresco where he would work on eight to ten Pacific War paintings simultaneously.

All his painting was done on a special brand of plywood, usually 36" x 24" rather than canvas. Few artists used that medium. His collection rose to 120 and he realized that he had better quit and concentrate on marketing the series. After several near misses and disappointments to raise his asking price of $400,000 I succeeded in getting $120,000 in pledges and contributions for his collection on behalf of the Navy Memorial Foundation. I called John to say that I had reached the end of my fund raising effort for him and if he would take the 120 thousand we had a deal. Otherwise I was obligated to return the funds to the donors. He returned the call shortly thereafter agreeing to accept the kind offer. We officially consummated the transaction at the Lone Sailor Award Dinner in 1988. The Foundation purchased the collection and gifted it to the Navy, which put it in the custody of the Navy Historical Center. John Hamilton made some brief remarks and Secretary of the Navy H. Lawrence Garrett, III accepted the paintings and also spoke at the occasion. A number of the paintings were displayed in the Pentagon for several years as well as at the Naval War College in Newport, RI.

Zum and I visited John and Betty at their home in Tresco for an enjoyable three days, meeting their friends, becoming acclimated to beautiful Tresco, dining on fresh lobsters that we rescued that afternoon from traps strategically placed around the island, visiting his studio and thoroughly relishing their hospitality. We had become good friends and I often had the realization that we profited from our friendship and learned much from them—a keener appreciation of British culture and history and the fact that the Brits did have appetizing cuisine. John and Betty moved from Tresco to St. Mary's, the "big island" in the Scilly Isles, where John died in December 1993.

A delightful person, John definitely possessed Gumption, with the addition of a shot of chutzpas, which proved to be a good concoction.

At Sea

There were several reasons for having a Visitors Center, if it could be located contiguous to the memorial or in the immediate vicinity. The Navy Memorial Log was becoming more popular and demanded a Log Room where names, photographs and biographies would be displayed. There was a need for function rooms where people could be gathered for various purposes. In such an environment there would be a demand for Navy related souvenirs and assorted memorabilia commemorating the visit to the Navy Memorial and the answer that would be a traditional Ship's Store. In my vision of the memorial concept a Visitors Center would be an extension of the Memorial plaza with its flag hoists, one of the largest polar projections of Planet Earth, the Lone Sailor statue, the quotations citing moments in the history of the United States and its Navy and the bronze relief wall depicting historic events or recognizing elements or units of the U. S. Navy. I was enthused about building a facility that would extend our informational reach beyond the etched in granite or cast in bronze media to encompass sophisticated, modern, state of the art audio-visual presentations. Basic to this vision would be the Navy Memorial Log Room with several touch-screen monitors where members and others could command graphic and prose presentations on all members. Other kiosks would have descriptions, primarily photographs of all ships and aircraft that had ever been in the Navy's inventory. Other kiosks would feature short video presentations of historic events, perhaps even a small theater, seating 8-12 people could be available to show films about the Navy and its people. I also envisioned a larger theater to be used for various activities such as lectures, seminars, presentations of awards, reenlistments and retirements—a place to go in event of inclement conditions on the Memorial Plaza. But the theater would exist primarily to show motion pictures.

For a feature film about the Navy, I was thinking BIG, real BIG. I was thinking Imax, the large screen, beautifully photographed on 70-millimeter film and accompanied by a superb sound system. Once we got into serious feasibility research, I realized a true Imax theater was out of the ballpark for us. The true Imax production requires a screen about 77 feet high and about 55 feet wide. To do that, we would need eight floors of our building. Even our neighbor, the Air and Space Museum, could only accommodate a 55-foot elevation in their beautiful and spacious building. Jim Nemer and I did considerable traveling— to Canada, the West Coast, to Hollywood, Disneyland, Disneyworld— anyplace that had an Imax theater. We had even advanced to the level of searching for a producer of Imax films. That was not difficult because there weren't many worldwide. There were many more wannabes, producers who wanted to move up to the Imax level and they converged on us, soliciting their backgrounds and good intentions. We focused on MacGillivray Freeman Films headquartered in South Laguna, CA because it was and still is the leading Imax film producer in the entire world. Their credits at that time included one of the first productions for the big screen To Fly a feature film about the history of flight. After a quarter of a century, it is still a popular film that continues to be shown daily at the Air and Space Museum. Greg MacGillivray heads the organization. He is a brilliant producer with whom we spent considerable time discussing the project and socializing including an enjoyable weekend skiing with him and his family. In the process of developing a story board and script, I made arrangements for Greg and a crew to visit any Navy installation he desired and cruise in any type of ship to find the most exciting venue about Navy life, especially at sea. My primary guidance to Greg was that I wanted the most exciting movie he could make, not blood and guts but a vivid display of the satisfaction gained by handling the responsibilities given to Navy personnel, some in hazardous situations such as flight deck operations. The action would be based on tenets of Courage, Pride and Commitment that are basic to Navy life. He and his associates cruised in a nuclear powered attack submarine, a destroyer, a cruiser, an aircraft carrier and spent time with elements of the amphibious force. In a week they had a good idea of the Imax film potential and came back to me with a decision, "In all due respect for all the ships we visited, they all were interesting. But for our purposes, the excitement on the aircraft carrier's flight deck 5,000 personnel and the aircraft in flight is where we should be shooting our movie." I wasn't surprised but I wanted Greg and his people to make that appraisal.

Next was the development of a storyboard, which is a summary of the story concept, and the precursor of a script. Greg hired two experienced veteran Hollywood screenplay writers, Ken Thoren and Tom DePaolo. Jim Nemer and I met with them and discussed Navy and sea-going life and were impressed with their backgrounds and professional vitas. Although we didn't fully accept their submissions, it served as the basis for our motion picture. We were initially looking at a 20-minute movie, but as we progressed and wanted to not single a carrier as typical of Navy life, enlarged the concept to 32 minutes and centered the story on a fleet exercise wherein we would bring in many other aspects of our operating forces. This moved the cost of the film from two million dollars to three. We also became intrigued with the design of a theater that would be not only unique in the Washington area but the entire East Coast, done by Iwerks Entertainment that was a part of Disney Corporation for theater format development and equipment. Shortly before we encountered Iwerks, it separated from Disney to become a stand alone leading big screen motion picture theater and ancillary equipment corporation.

Executive Producers

Greg MacGillivray designated me and Jim Nemer as Executive Producer and Assistant Executive Producer, respectively and our names appear high on the credit rolls. I asked Alec Lorimore, the producer/writer to define the role of an executive producer. After a few moments of thought, he smiled and replied, "Just don't get in the way." That wasn't difficult, especially working with the likes of MacGillivray and Lorimore. However, they listened to our comments and critiques, especially Navy radio language and miscellaneous procedures in the ships. We had a superb relationship and Jim and I felt we made a contribution to the film's success. As an example of their patience with us, we reviewed all the film shot on the cruise. MacGillivray and Lorimore were excited about their work and pleased with their footage. I was disappointed in the product because I saw the takes on a small editing screen. My thought was: "Three million bucks for that?" In my candid, but discrete, manner, I said, "Well, guys, I am definitely not a film producer but in my past, I have been responsible for the production of several motion pictures and I am sorry I can't share your enthusiasm for these 70mm takes. They aren't any different than thousands of feet of 35mm and even 8mm that I have seen." Their response was still positive, "We can appreciate that but you will have to trust us. We can envision this 70mm film on a big screen. True, on a small editing box, there isn't much difference. Trust us, Bill." I was still a little leery but I trusted them and they were correct.

Fortunately, the aircraft carrier USS Constellation was moving from its homeport San Diego around South America to the Philadelphia Navy Yard for an extended overhaul. She was too wide to transit the Panama Canal. She had a squadron of F-14s aboard and was accompanied by a fleet tanker USS Roanoke (OR-7). MacGillivray and crew embarked Connie in Valparaiso, the port city for Santiago, the capitol of Chili. They debarked two weeks later at Rio de Janeiro, Brazil having experienced an excellent variety of weather and sea conditions to meet all their expectations for the forthcoming movie. When rounding Cape Horn, the southern tip of South America, Connie plowed through heavy seas, normal for the Drake Passage but fantastic for At Sea photography.

At midpoint in the production we had to shutdown because my board of directors decreed that we could not contract for nor expend funds unless they were in the bank. This stopped everything we were doing and it took me a year to get the board to agree to continue production and construction. The cost increase for the movie delay was $200,000. (It was another $800,000 added cost for continuing construction of the Visitors Center.) I had been attempting to get defense contractors to underwrite the cost of the movie but was not successful. I turned to Charlie DiBona, President of American Petroleum Institute for help and he connected me with Mobile Corporation. After a year of negotiating and selling the movie idea to Mobile that had recently moved from its New York City headquarters to Fairfax County, a suburb of Washington, DC. My point of contact was the Vice President for communication and one of his main objections was the title At Sea. He had trouble with it because it connoted being confused. That was strictly landlubber talk and I finally convinced him that At Sea was legitimate for a movie about the Navy. He liked the theater and the movie concept and finally accepted At Sea. That $3.2 million check was an extraordinary stimulus to confidence in our legitimacy.

Two sidebar stories related to the movie involved Lieutenant Ray Turner, the catapult officer in Constellation who was chosen to be the thread that wove the narrative of the film that captured life in a US Navy ship. Turner was excellent in describing and exemplifying the leadership and teamwork that molds efficiency and readiness to successfully complete assigned missions. Normally, an actor would have done the job, dressed in a lieutenant's flight deck gear. During pre-sailing visits to the ship, MacGillivray and Lorimore were impressed by Turner and arrangements were made for him to play the lead role, including becoming a temporary member of the Screen Actor's Guild. Mrs. Turner who was very pregnant with their second child, could not play the role so was substituted by an attractive actress. Mrs. Turner's admonished her husband and the MacGillivray crew was that "there will be no kissing." When viewing the film for the first time in our theater, she saw her stand-in and Ray embracing when the ship departed and returned, feigned indignation, exclaiming, "I thought I told you, no kissing!" Incidentally, Mrs. Turner was as equally attractive and vivacious as the actress. In the movie, there is a scene of Ray Turner in his stateroom reading a letter from four-year old son Lance. Lance accompanied his parents to view the movie and when he saw that scene, he abruptly departed the theater trailed by his mother. She stopped him and asked why he left the theater. Lance was crying and replied, "That was my letter to my dad and I didn't want everybody to know what I said." I guess those are some of the intrigues of show business.

We staged a West Coast Premiere in Hollywood, California a few months later at which Jim Nemer was the Master of Ceremonies. Jim's wife, Marcia, was from Inglewood and her entire family was present and that added to our delight. At Sea won the Cine Golden Eagle award, the U.S. International Film and Video Festival (Illinois) Gold Camera Award (First Place, Best Cinematography and was nominated for Best of he Festival and the Houston International Film Festival Gold Award (First Place and the Navy League of the United States Alfred Thayer Mahan Award for the Best Naval Writing for Film's Script of the year.

Opening the Visitors Center

The official opening of our Visitors Center and premiere of our large screen motion picture At Sea was staged with considerable fanfare, but not on the scale of the dedication of the Memorial about five years previously. Without closing Pennsylvania Avenue to vehicular traffic and carpeting it in blue, four military bands, fireworks, balloons, a fly-over by Navy aircraft and a long list of dignified guests as speakers, we took two days of celebrations to open our Visitors Center. On June 10, 1992 we started with a reception and the premiere showing of At Sea for more than 200 invited guests, nearly filling the 241-

seat Arleigh and Roberta Burke Theater. For the showing, I welcomed the guests and recognized our dignitaries, including actor Tom Selleck, Secretary of the Navy Larry Garrett, former Chief of Naval Operations James L. Holloway, III, our board of directors, Greg MacGillivray, producer of At Sea, Dr. Ron Easley and his wife, Linda, owners of SPC, the organization that housed our staff for eight years prior to our moving into the Visitors Center office spaces and a sizable contingent from Mobil Corporation. The Visitors Center with its Presidents' Room, Gallery Deck, Log Room and theater were well received by all.

The following afternoon we had a ceremony to officially open the center on the Memorial plaza. The principle speaker was the Under Secretary of the Navy, the Honorable Daniel Howard, who was substituting for Larry Garrett who had departed that day for an extended business trip. I had introduced Secretary Howard and returned to my seat to relax for 10-12 minutes before we "cut the ribbon." Dan Howard, was a friend of a few years, formerly was the Assistant Secretary of Defense for Public Affairs, before being moved to the Under SECNAV position. He started reading the speech and suddenly stopped, closed his speech file, and said, "Enough of this. The reason I am here is to bring Rear Admiral Bill Thompson to the podium to present him with a second Navy Distinguished Public Service Award for what he has accomplished here at the Navy Memorial. Bill, please join me while the citation is read." I was surprised by this interruption—after all, this was my show, scripted by me who doesn't like surprises. My response was definitely unscripted. I gave credit to our wonderful Board of Directors and my dedicated, hard working, faithful staff. After that, I called Zum to the podium and gave credit to her for allowing me to work on the Navy Memorial Project and praised her contribution and support for the project. I followed all that by giving her a big hug. She definitely deserved recognition and the hug.

To complete the dedication program, we had Tom Selleck cut the ribbon (a strip of 70mm film) accompanied by Anthony R. Corso, representing Mobil Corporation, Washington, D.C. Councilwoman Charlene Drew Jarvis, Under Secretary of the Navy J. Daniel Howard and myself. The date was June 11,

1992—15 years after the Foundation's first meeting of its board of directors when Zum had admonished me not to "Get involved in that thing." It was actually only eight years since we broke ground to commence construction of the Memorial plaza. We were moving right along and I reflected at the time that with the experience we had gained we could do another memorial in less than half that time.

Tailhook

Naval aviators have an organization called Tailhook Association. The title was symbolic of Navy carrier aviation. The association published a quarterly magazine entitle The Hook that concerned itself with naval aircraft carrier aviation. It sponsored an annual two-day seminar, the latest was in Las Vegas, Nevada in September 1991. Seminars and speeches monopolized the daytime agenda and evenings were usually a little raucous. This occasion became that and perceptions were greatly expanded. It ended with the Secretary of the Navy, H. Lawrence Garrett, III, being fired (actually asked by the White House to resign) and the Chief of Naval Operations having two months shaved off of his four-year tenure. I had thought that Larry Garrett was a good, solid secretary and had a unique background. He enlisted in the Navy and became a machinist mate in submarines, transferred to flight school to become a commissioned naval officer and aviator, later transferred to the Judge Advocate General's Corps. He retired on 20 years service in the Navy and served in the White House and as General Counsel of the Defense Department, then Under Secretary of the Navy and finally Secretary. I sought out Admiral Tom Moorer Chairman Paul Howell to discus presenting Larry Garrett our Lone Sailor Award. Done deal! Two weeks later Tom did the presentation along with Paul Howell to a full house of invited guests in the Arleigh and Roberta Burke Theater followed by a reception. I introduced Larry Garrett as the man who was secretary "…for all seasons and for all reasons."

Former President Jerry Ford

We learned that former President Jerry Ford lived in the Palm Springs, California area where our Foundation director Rose Narva managed the Gene Autry Resort Hotel. Rose and her husband, Rear Admiral William M. Narva (MC) USN (Retired) suggested moving the venue of the Lone Sailor presentation to President Ford to Palm Springs. On February 15, 1992, I did that at a black-tie dinner hosted by Rose and Bill at Rose's place that she decorated in Navy Blue and Gold motif. Zum and I were seated at the head table next to Jerry and Betty Ford, two delightful Midwesterners (Grand Rapids, Michigan) and we enjoyed a superb evening. During our early conversations, I led with,

"Mr. President, I first knew you through the Green Bay Press Gazette when you were an All America center at the University of Michigan and you were either drafted or offered a contract to play for the Packers. You turned down the opportunity and that didn't set well with we struggling high school athletes."

Jerry laughed and replied. "Bill, the Packer's offered me a contract for $100.00 a game and they only played eight games a season at that time so I would get $800 a year for getting beat up for eight Sundays. That is when I decided to go to law school and become a lawyer."

"Thank you for that information. " I added, "You are forgiven."

The president was pleased to receive the Lone Sailor Award and reflected so in his response. He also followed with a warm letter to me with a check for a sizeable contribution. Jerry Ford continued to be an All America to me and Betty was a perfect partner for him.

The Commander in Chief, President George H. W. Bush

President George H. W. Bush was selected to receive the Lone Sailor Award in 1991 and we put a full-court press on the White House to have the President make an appearance at our dinner to receive the award. I remember a conversation with the Naval Aide to the President who announced that the President could not make the commitment and that we should just send the statue to the White House and consider it presented. Having been in the Washington arena for a few years, I fully realized the difficulty of having the President appear to receive an award because there were literally hundreds of such requests and there was a large storeroom full of plaques, statues and memorabilia, a few which might make it to other spaces of the White House and a few more that might find a place in the Bush Presidential Library but most discarded in various ways. I politely declined the offer to "send it over to the White House" with the hope that someday we would have the opportunity to present it to the President.

That opportunity occurred when the President accepted our invitation to speak at our observance of Pearl Harbor Day on December 7, 1992. He had been narrowly defeated in the November presidential elections by Arkansas Governor Bill Clinton. That day started to be a blustery chilly morning and as we assembled on the concert stage to begin the ceremony it was still overcast but as we progressed through the preliminaries of Presentation of the Colors, the National Anthem and an opening prayer by a Navy Chaplain from over the National Archives Building emerged the sun, poking through the clouds to brighten the area. Discarding my prepared statement to introduce honored guests and the President, I briefly stated.

"Ladies and Gentlemen, honored guests, this is what your Navy Memorial is all about—A beautiful sunny day on Main Street, USA in our Nation's Capital with the Commander-in-Chief's flag flying from our mast, we are gathered to recognize the 51st anniversary of one of the most significant events in our nation's history, the attack on Pearl Harbor that led to our official entrance into World War II. I am most pleased to present to you our speaker for this occasion, a World War II veteran, our Command-in-Chief and former Lieutenant Junior Grade, USNR, President George H. W. Bush."

After the President's remarks, we proceeded with laying a wreath at the Lone Sailor statue. When returning to the podium, the President sighted a spectator whom he thought was actor celebrity Tom Selleck and deviated from my guidance to greet him, saying it was nice to see him again. Selleck had been at the White House only a day or two earlier, only in this case, this was not the real Tom Selleck; it was our son Craig who looked like Selleck, especially when he sported a mustache. Craig was seated in the honored guest section with his mother, as her escort. Next to him was Admiral Tom Moorer whom the President also recognized. Being sought out by the President was a memorable occasion for Craig, even though it was mistaken identity.

We next went to the Admiral Arleigh and Roberta Burke theater in our Visitors Center to view our large screen motion picture "At Sea," superbly showing several aspects of Navy operational units, principally an aircraft carrier with extraordinary scenes of the F14 fighter aircraft in flight. The President, a former naval aviator, was enthused about a few scenes and nudged me with his elbow and exclaimed,

"Look at that, will you! That is fantastic photography! Wow!" It was evident that the President enjoyed being "At Sea."

I then escorted him to the President's room to see his portrait as well as his position in naval history. I told him that from John F. Kennedy's term to the present, six of the seven presidents were former naval officers. I added parenthetically that Ronald Reagan had been in so many movies about the Navy that he might have thought he was a Navy veteran. When I presented his portrait, he shook his head negatively, declaring that,

"I never looked that young."

I explained that it was indeed he at the age of 19 aboard the USS SAN JACINTO (CVL 30) in the Western Pacific Ocean in 1944. The portrait's image was taken from a Navy photograph done aboard the ship. I gathered our Chairman, Rear Admiral Paul Howell, and Director Admiral Tom Moorer to present the Lone Sailor statue to the President, the belated Lone Sailor Award.

Zum joined us as we exited the President's Room and she remarked that it would have been nice to have Mrs. Bush here with him today to which he replied with a smile that he didn't think so because if Barbara got near our Ship's Store that she would put a big dent in their financial assets. By this time the President was feeling relaxed in our environment and friendly. We were chatting as a Secret Service man whispered something to him and led him out the back door of our Gallery Deck. I scanned the area and saw no evidence of his entourage so declared that I thought the Presidential visit had terminated. I was wrong. Hurrying into the room again was the President who came back to me, putting out his right hand and said,

"Bill, I apologize. I didn't say Good Bye to you or thank you for such a wonderful visit to the Navy Memorial. I really enjoyed it. Now, I must go. Thanks again." With that, he departed leaving me with another memorable event at the Navy Memorial and utmost respect for our Commander in Chief. At the day's conclusion I checked off two memorable events—a Presidential visit and presentation of the languishing Lone Sailor Award to President Bush.

Corpsman!

During our long stay in the Washington, DC area and during our entire time with the U.S. Navy, Zum and I had the resources of Navy Medicine available to us. We seldom used the facilities, except for annual examinations until age and a few maladies increased our appearances at the National Navy Medical Center at Bethesda, Maryland, only about 30 minutes from home. In 1992 I develop a urinary tract problem and underwent surgery in part of the prostrate gland. It is called Transurethral Electro-Resection of the Prostate (TURP). The procedure was successful but a small amount of cancerous cells was found in the residue. That put me on a watch list and semi annual visits to Bethesda. The growth of the cells has remained at a low state and has not bothered me. Also, I had trouble with my right knee where the cartilage had worn out and finally had a titanium replacement done and that solved the problem. There is no more pain and I do not have the agility I once had to ski, charge the net for a kill or even broad jump (now called Long Jump) but I don't intend to go there anyway. Zum had a major problem that occurred the first part of 2008 when a malignancy was found in her lower left jaw. A team of five doctors were immediately assembled and within a couple of days performed a procedure to lay open the left side of her face, having to sever the nerves, to get to the cancer. It was a successful operation, followed by 30 sessions of radiation treatment. About 95% of her speech faculties have returned but has no feeling on the left side of her tongue and face. Other than that we have good health, eat well and enjoy ourselves with family and friends.

Retirement Again

The proverb "All good things must come to an end." descended on me with the realization that the Memorial was completed and it was time to move on to other things. I didn't know what portended for the family and me but would be definitely a different venue, physically and psychologically. I looked forward to not transiting daily to the District of Columbia to the Navy Memorial offices, either by automobile or the excellent Metro-line to the National Archives-Navy Memorial station that was adjacent to and below the Memorial. Psychologically, I would have to fill my head with thoughts other than Navy Memorial related. It was a demanding job and with a small staff confronted by many problem areas, it seemed to never allow us to slip into a parade rest stance. I convinced the board of directors that I was definitely departing and set about the business of searching for a replacement. We had several viable candidates, and the most attractive to me were retired Navy captains, however, the board of directors favored having a retired flag officer. I organized a search committee and proceeded with series of interviews. After about three months of this activity, we selected retired Rear Admiral James E. Miller who was retiring from a successful career in the Navy's Supply Corps, ending with Jim being the Commander of the Supply Corps Command. He further impressed selection committee members by submitting a financial study of the foundation.

The format of my retirement comprised three events—a reception attended by 160 invited guests, friends and family at the Visitors Center, complete with a concert by the Navy Band at the Memorial's amphitheater; the next evening I was an honoree at the Lone Sailor Awards Dinner and farewells at the Foundation's Annual Board of Directors meeting the following day. At the reception, there were several speakers including Tom Regan who spoke of my vision of the memorial, a staff member of the National Capital Planning Commission who spoke briefly about what his staff will always remember about Admiral Thompson. That was when I formed an ad hoc committee of executive directors of the NCPC, the Pennsylvania Avenue Development Corporation, the Commission on Fine Arts, the National Park Service and a representative of the District of Columbia to assist me in designing the Navy Memorial as it stands today. He said it was an audacious act, successful and remarkably no bloodshed resulted. The Navy Band was at full strength for the concert and it serenaded Zum and me with "The Sweetheart of Sigma Chi."

For the Lone Sailor Awards Dinner, I was completely taken aback a month before the event when my Development Director, B. J. Andrews and I met with the dinner Chairman, Tom Pownall, to finalize plans for the dinner. Tom became a good friend after we met when I started the Memorial project and he was then Chairman and CEO of Martin Marietta Corporation that later merged with Lockheed Corporation. He was a Naval Academy graduate and an active supporter of the Navy Memorial project. He was a member of our Board of Directors. After a few pleasantries, he asked who the awardees were. I replied that we had two—Mr. H. P. "Red" Polling, Chairman, Ford Motor Company and author James Michener. Tom was silent a few seconds, then announced that we should have another one. My immediate thought was the logistics involved in getting another awardee approved and contacting the individual to inquire as to his availability and other incidentals. I finally nodded and asked whom he had in mind. He said,

"You."

I laughed and indicated he had to be kidding. He replied that he was serious. I still chuckled and said something about maintaining a high degree of credibility of the Lone Sailor Award program and I was not at the level of Polling, Michener and other awardees. I added that we have a couple hundred more prospects for the award and I said again that I thought it would be degrading for me to be an awardee. I could see that Tom was getting a little restive and impatient with me. He indicated forcefully that he had thought about it and wasn't going to back down. He said that he watched the evolvement of the memorial over the years since we first met and that I had accomplished a feat that others would have given up on and will probably not be officially recognized. The Lone Sailor Award is very appropriate for me.

I pleaded, "Tom, I would be embarrassed to be an awardee of a program

I initiated."

Tom closed the discussion by emphatically stating that if I resist any longer, he would resign as dinner chairman. I could see repercussions if that event occurred. I asked for a day to think about it. He agreed. Despite the onerous beginning of our conference, we continued to favorable results in all other matters.

When driving back to the office, B. J. announced to me that she agreed with Tom Pownall and thought I should also. In my office, I contemplated the situation and finally called Tom Coldwell of our staff, whom I considered more of a friend than an employee and laid out my predicament. I concluded my comments with the thought that if he were uncomfortable giving me advice on this problem, I would fire him immediately with the proviso that he be reinstated after the discussion. Let's talk as friends. He agreed with B. J. adding that the entire staff would be there to applaud. I talked with Zum over dinner and she merely shook her head and said to sleep on it and go to the office in the morning and call Tom Pownall and say, "Thanks, Tom." I did.

Visiting Jim Michener

The awards dinner was well attended and successful. Red Polling and Jim Michener were gracious recipients of the Lone Sailor Award and both responded with crediting their time in the Navy and an exciting and maturing experience. I visited with Mr. Polling in Detroit prior to the dinner and did the same with Mr. Michener in his home in Austin, Texas. Marvin Stone, former foundation Chairman and at that time Deputy Director of United States Information Service, was a good friend of Jim Michener and we spend an evening and the next morning with Michener and his wife. I recall two significant pieces of information I gleaned from our visit. One, he disabused me of the notion I had that he had a staff of researchers and writers to assist him in compiling his voluminous books. I thought he undoubtedly had a cadre of his students from the University of Texas where he was an instructor doing the research and probably some of the writing. No, he explained, he never had any such assistants. Everything that appeared in his books was researched by the author and channeled through his brain and transmitted to prose through his two index fingers on his old reliable stand- up typewriter. The second thing I recall is that I saw and touched the typewriter, which should be a significant museum piece. On the morning of the Lone Sailor Dinner, Mr. Michener visited the Navy Memorial and I was leading a tour around the plaza when I saw a ceremony being conducted at the Lone Sailor statue. It was a reenlistment of a sailor by his commanding officer and a common occurrence at the Memorial. I explained the ceremony to Mr. Michener and asked if he would like to issue the oath to the sailor, swearing him into another hitch in his Navy career. Michener was excited and agreed. I excused myself to approach the Captain and his charge with the opportunity to have James Michener deliver the oath. The youngster asked who James Michener was and I explained that he was the author of the world famous book South Pacific and several other best sellers and that he was in Washington to receive the Lone Sailor Award at a formal dinner that evening. The Captain told the sailor that it would be a big plus to the occasion. So it happened and Michener spent about five minutes talking with the two and their guests. It was a nice added touch to the day for all concerned. It was all in a day's work at the Navy Memorial—not always predictable but enjoyable.

At the final board of directors meeting of my tour as president and CEO, ending 15 years of a great experience, I was given the title of President Emeritus. Also, before the meeting commenced, Paul Howell told me privately that he had canvassed board members and they agreed that they would like to contract me to four years as a consultant at $25,000 each year. I was amazed and accepted. In my final remarks to the directors, I indicated that had I been intelligent, I would not have volunteered 15 years ago to help get the foundation started but I depart possessing humility, gratification and appreciation for all that I learned, all the outstanding people I had worked with on the board and in the city and federal governments who diligently toil to make our nation's capital city the world's best and most beautiful. I was also thankful that what we accomplished in this project would in some way compensate for my good fortune to have served in the US Navy for 32 years. The Navy to me was the people who serve and provide the heartbeat of the organization. I hoped that the Navy Memorial facilities erected on this beautiful site continue to honor and recognize them and their service.

Good Harbor—Safe Haven

There were 18 years separating my retiring from the Navy Memorial Foundation and my first retirement from the U.S. Navy in 1975. I didn't feel 71 years old. But I realized that I wasn't frequenting the Appalachian Trail with Brian as I did in the 1970s, nor was I pounding racquetballs with Craig at the Pentagon Officer's Athletic Club. And I wasn't skiing—at least not as aggressively as I had been. However, I was still playing tennis with Bud Zumwalt and occasionally with his son Jim. I could always find time to squeeze in a round of golf at the Army-Navy Country Club usually with Bob Seal. He was a former Air Force fighter pilot and friend from the days when he was selling airplanes for Boeing. Was I slowing down? Perhaps I was a little but only in my body not in my mind.

I fully realized that a 71-year-old was not a prime target for an employer to launch into a new career. My primary concern was keeping busy and out of Zum's way because she had not lost any vitality or direction. She continued to operate at flank speed, and the direction didn't matter as long as she got where she was going. She doubled the size of her vegetable garden to 30'x 40' at Fairfax County's Lewinsville Park. She also had flowers and veggies at home primarily in the back yard. I took care of mowing the lawn and some of the heavy work, but my only interest in the garden work was enjoying the harvest.

I wanted to keep busy and stay involved but not to the extent of seeking compensation. Even though I was underpaid for my efforts at the Navy Memorial, my investments were doing well. Except for Zum's and my concern about having funds to take care of the proverbial catastrophic misfortune that could occur, we were in good posture. We had never had the desire to be rich, but we were comfortable and could live within our means.

The System Planning Corporation (SPC) offered me an office to hide out in. Conveniently, it was only a sand wedge shot from Bud Zumwalt's office spaces. When I was in town, I reported to him for morning muster, and we often lunched together. It was a good arrangement. I was later hired by SPC to do public communications work.

Also, Sturgeon Bay Shipbuilding Company, a subsidiary of the Manitowoc Company of Wisconsin, sought me out. I assisted the shipbuilder in getting a contract with the Federal Maritime Commission (FMC) to build two large oceangoing ships. It was unusual at that time for a Great Lakes shipyard to be competitive with shipyards on the two coasts. Their workforce rose from a normal level of 250 to 1,500. FMC's commissioner,   retired Adm. Harold E. Shear, was a friend and ally while I was on active duty. I enjoyed returning to Wisconsin's Sturgeon Bay in Door County, a few miles from Green Bay. It is a near-pristine area inhabited by folks who enjoy hunting, fishing and outdoor sports. They possess spirited patriotism and that superb Midwest work ethic—my kind of people. I also enjoyed being affiliated again with Admiral Shear, who had been a submariner. He was a direct, no nonsense type, but he would occasionally share a laugh or two with me.

United States Navy Public Affairs Alumni Association (USPAAA)

After retiring from active duty, I periodically arranged (about every four months) a social luncheon for retired Public Affairs Officers. We did this because of the bond of Navy life, and once in awhile we had a guest speaker. Arranging was relatively simple—I just asked Ruth Donohue to do it. I normally selected the restaurant based on price and the appreciation of the manager to serve us. It worked. The PAOs responded in adequate numbers of about 20 to 25, and there was no goading or pressuring to enhance the numbers. I normally gave a short review of the health of our alumni which some called Thompson's Binnacle List Report. (In the Navy, a Binnacle List is published each day comprised of those who were sick enough not be at their duty station. If a sailor was not listed or on duty, the Master-At-Arms Force would be looking for him.)

If one of our PAOs was incapacitated, we had a regular mail or Email address available to help spur his recovery with messages. Realizing we had more than 300 retired PAOs officers plus 1,000 or more enlisted journalists settled throughout the country, I addressed a letter to all of them announcing we were studying the feasibility of launching a retirees group. Response was good, but there was the usual lack of leadership and stand-up volunteers to assist. I followed with another letter requesting $100 for a life membership or $25.00 for an annual membership. We had an extraordinary response and surprisingly received more life than annual memberships.

I sought out Herb Hetu, explained what I had done and how we were looking for a president. He bought into it and did an outstanding job of incorporating the group, officially entitling it the United States Navy Public Affairs Alumni Association (USNPAAA). He set the standards for the organization as it exists today. The organization flourishes in documenting and preserving the history of the Navy's public affairs community and sponsoring national meetings or reunions every 18 months. It publishes the quarterly magazine, Sightings and sponsors a series of awards.

The first awards were presented in October 1995. The Distinguished Service Award for non-members went to Admiral Zumwalt, who is credited for prompting the Navy to select a Public Affairs specialist for flag rank with the service designation as the Chief of Information. Keeping the second award within the USSNPAAA family, the Significant Achievement Award was given to me for building the Navy Memorial.

Thirteen years later at the 2008 reunion held at the Navy Memorial, the USNPAAA honored Zum and me at its major function, the Reunion Dinner, by calling it the Special Tribute to Bill and Dorothy Thompson. Key to the occasion was a "This is Your Life" production done by Jim Finkelstein and his son Jon. Jim and Jon worked on the show for over nine months doing a lot of taping of Zum and me in Jim's home. Those sessions are memorable and cherished, probably even more humorous then the final show. Jon has superb computer skills and says his dad knows how to turn on his computer if someone has already plugged it in. They worked well together, and their effort kept the audience laughing long after the dinner. It was a wonderful evening with some of the world's finest folks and our entire family present except for the younger grandchildren and great-grandchildren. Also on the program was a roast of me by Dick Busby, my former executive assistant at CHINFO. He informed me that he had roasted me seven or eight times before. I could only remember two; the other times must have been when I was not present. I do recall that the last roast at our dinner wasn't nearly as rough as previous ones.

Dead Hand

Meanwhile at the Navy Memorial, I continued to stay relatively busy but tried to stay off new Foundation president and CEO Jim Miller's paths. I was a devout opponent of the "dead hand on the tiller" philosophy in the Navy. I had seen several instances of a previous commander retiring in the same area and too often being seen on the premises. I'm sure perceptions and rumors outplay actualities. Few former commanders deliberately return to "drive the boat." But some former incumbents may possess a small degree of paranoia, a degree of insecurity and subtly reflect negative feelings about their predecessors through body language quirks or offhand comments.

I wanted to avoid that possibility even though I had been reelected to the Foundation's board of directors and had a contract as a paid consultant. I let it be known to Jim that I did not want an office in the Visitors Center. When I thought my corporate experience or background could be helpful, I privately shared my thoughts with him and didn't expound at directors meetings. He appreciated my approach.

As a consultant, I recommended a series of seminars starting with "Was President Truman correct in ordering the deployment of nuclear weapons on Japan?" commensurate with the anniversaries of the destruction of Hiroshima and Nagasaki. Jim approved and asked me to supervise the first event. I was delighted to do so and enjoyed the assignment. I invited the Naval Institute to participate as a partner because of its considerable experience in conducting seminars. It was a successful day-long event with scholars from several of the Washington, D.C. area universities and the University of North Carolina. The principal speaker was Dr. Paul Nitze, former Secretary of the Navy. At that time he was heading the Paul H. Nitze School of Advanced International Studies at Johns Hopkins University in Baltimore.

We preceded the seminar with a dinner at the 701 Restaurant over-looking the Navy Memorial. Nitze was becoming frail but handled both the dinner and his presentation in an excellent manner. The seminar was held in the Navy Memorial's Arleigh and Roberta Burke Theater with over 200 attendees. Some high school teachers from as far away as Winchester, Va. attended. There were good supporting arguments on both sides of the question. But an impromptu consensus of the audience at day's end was about 90% affirmative for Harry Truman's decision. Jim Miller was pleased with the arrangements and had high praise for my work in a report to Foundation Chairman Paul Howell. However, due to budgetary constraints, it was the only seminar held during Rear Adm. Miller's tenure.

During Miller's term, the Visitors Center was renamed the Heritage Center for good reason. It was certainly more prestigious and worthy of the expense involved to lease the space. We originally considered using that name when planning for the space but thought having a Visitors Center commu-nicated having both an information site as well as visitor amenities. I fully endorsed the name change.

Jim served three years as president and CEO and then resigned. He was succeeded by Rear Adm. Henry C. McKinney, USN (Retired). He was a graduate of Princeton University and had an excellent career as a subma-rine officer. One of the first problems Hank McKinney faced was a "hanger on'er" idea from Jim Miller involving fundraising. It involved the idea of folding the Marine Corps, Coast Guard and Maritime Service under the Navy Memorial auspices and changing its name to the U.S. Sea Services Memorial. As an offshoot of this campaign, Adm. Paul A. Yost, a retired Coast Guard Commandant, was invited to become a member of the board of directors and to help bring about the merger with the Coast Guard.

Admiral Yost presented the Coast Guard's official initiatives for changing the Navy Memorial to include the Coast Guard. I was given a copy of Admiral Yost's letter and was also tasked by our chairman to prepare a "white paper" on the issue to be presented at the next board of directors' Executive Committee meeting. I replied there wasn't enough time to do a formal paper representing the board and staff's opinions relating to the issue. However, if they desired, I would prepare a statement representing my opinions, and the idea was accepted.

About a half hour before the Executive Committee meeting began, I was asked to read or summarize my paper, as something the committee should consider. Admiral Yost preceded me on the agenda. I had developed significant respect for him through previous meetings, and Admiral Zumwalt thought highly of him when they served together in Vietnam. His presentation followed the Coast Guard's official "requests" for a starter and sought the keystone of a Memorandum of Understanding based on "openness and cooperation."

He asked for the following additions or changes: (1) two bronze reliefs added to the existing Bronze Wall, (2) plaques and additional glass etchings in the Wave Wall depicting Coast Guard ships and aircraft, (3) a life-sized statue of Medal of Honor Awardee Douglas Munro placed on the Quarterdeck, (4) a revolving display of Coast Guard art and artifacts in the Heritage Center, (5) a short, high quality film on the Coast Guard to be shown as a companion film with At Sea, and (6) the Navy Log renamed the Sea Service Log to facilitate Coast Guard participation. Additionally, space was to be provided in the Presidents Room for a large, glass encased model of a Coast Guard cutter, the Navy Hymn on the steps of the concert stage was to be retitled the Navy/Coast Guard Hymn and many more concessions were sought. None of the requests were beyond accomplishing, but some were obviously discomforting, and a few others I thought were denigrating as obvious afterthoughts.

My presentation was a rebuttal stating the suggested concept would need considerable study and was not time critical. I specifically explained how the Memorial had been designed to represent the U.S. Navy and stressed that inside the Heritage Center there wasn't much room to expand. Placing another statue on the Quarterdeck would overcrowd the small space and defeat the thematic statement established there. The Homecoming statue's distinctive message about the value of the Navy Family would be diminished. While we admired the heroism of Douglas Munro, having his statue installed there would change the symbolic venue. It also presented another significant issue. The Coast Guard has one Medal of Honor awardee, and at that time, the Navy had 377. (We had considered many venues to honor our

Navy Medal of Honor winners. However, the Pentagon maintains an excellent exhibit for that purpose alleviating to a degree not doing so at the Navy
Memorial.)

The Wave Wall was another example of specifically designing a beautiful
and expensive entrance to our Heritage Center reflecting the legacy of Navy
tradition. Each glass panel represents the flow of ship development from
the USS Alfred to the USS Arleigh Burke, and unfortunately there was not
sufficient space to recognize more newly developed ships.

I concluded my presentation saying that 600,000 sailors had contributed
to help build the $15 million U. S. Navy Memorial. The size of the Coast
Guard was one-tenth that of the Navy. If the Coast Guard was indeed sincere
about being a full partner in the Memorial, it should begin by presenting a
check for $1.5 million and guarantee that at least that much would be avail-
able to fund the other items they wanted installed.

Silence prevailed after my words until the chairman called for a 15-minute
"break." It seemed the members needed to recover from the discomfort and
anxiety caused by my presentation. After we reassembled, the chairman suggested tabling the issue for further study. "Tabling" usually means that the
issue remains tabled and gathers dust. It was true in this case. The board
of directors did not consider it again, and it was written off as an unwork-
able idea. Admiral Yost resigned from the board shortly thereafter as did Jim
Miller. Miller became a central figure in General Dynamics' financial affairs
related to building the Arleigh Burke Class guided missile destroyers at its
shipyard in Bath, Maine. Jim had a good reputation in the accounting and
financial business. He spent extensive time at the Bath shipyard precluding
much activity in the Washington area.

In other Navy Memorial business, I continued to coordinate the
Foundation's tour/cruise program until concluding my efforts in September
2005 at Pearl Harbor with a commemoration of World War II's end. We celebrated the 60th anniversary of the September 2, 1945, signing of the peace
documents aboard USS Missouri. It was a fitting site: Pearl Harbor which was
attacked by the Imperial Japanese Navy on December 7, 1941, to usher the
United States into World War II, and the USS Missouri is now a museum ship
moored at Pearl Harbor.

Zum and I enjoyed the tour program because we got to meet so many Navy veterans including those who especially cared about the Navy Memorial. Zum and I still receive Emails from several Navy Memorial "cruisers," and our Christmas card list includes an abundance of them.

A special example of those relationships was established with Clarence and Mary Whitley of Richmond whom we met on the tour program. They traveled with us five or six times, and we lunch together every four months at some restaurant between Richmond and Washington. They are solid citizens, patriotic and fun to be with. Whit is a good cook and is always in demand to prepare meals for veterans' organizations at large functions. He is also frequently sought as a speaker. He was a third class petty officer, prowling South Pacific islands during the Big War.

National Underwater Marine Agency (NUMA)

I was introduced to author Clive Cussler at a luncheon at the Army- Navy Country Club in Arlington. Clive was a former advertising executive who tried his hand at writing adventure novels. His first success was *Raise the Titanic* that was being produced as a feature motion picture starring Jason Robards.

Clive had also been busy hunting for Captain John Paul Jones' flagship the USS Bonhomme Richard in the North Sea. The Bonhomme Richard was lost in a Revolutionary War battle with the British ship Serapis. The battle was the setting for Jones' famous quotation when answering Serapis' challenge, "Are you ready to strike your colors?" "I have not yet begun to fight!" declared Jones before he and his crew stormed aboard Serapis, took command and left the sinking Bonhomme Richard to drift off.

Cussler described his new deep sea recovery organization, the National Underwater Marine Agency (NUMA). Clive served as NUMA's chairman and was the sole source of its funding. Sensing my interest in maritime history, he asked if I would like to become a director (without compensation) and how we would be involved in some interesting projects. Before lunch was over, I was NUMA's president.

Later Clive added retired Cmdr. Don Walsh, the Navy's famed

oceanographer, who was aboard the deep-diving research bathyscaphe Trieste when it made the deepest dive ever in the Marianas Trench and MIT's Harold "Doc" Edgerton, the inventor of side scan sonar. I was with the group when it found the confederate submarine Hunley that sunk the Union sloop of war Housatonic in the harbor of Charleston, S.C. I was also onboard when we found the USS Cumberland in the James River a couple hundred yards off the Newport News shipyards. My son Craig was also involved and accompanied me on most of our searches.

Clyde Smith, a former bank executive, whom I met during the Zumwalt campaign for the U. S. Senate, became involved in NUMA and continues to participate as a director. I had to resign as president because of a conflict with the bylaws of the U. S. Navy Memorial Foundation, but I have remained as a director. In 2005, I nominated Clive to receive the Foundation's Lone Sailor Distinguished Service Award and presented it to him at our annual dinner.

More Adventures with Bud Zumwalt

I followed Bud Zumwalt onto the Navy's retired list seven months after his service departure. I was aware that he was staying in the Washington, D. C. area, but I was busy establishing my Admiralty Communications, Inc. consulting firm, so I wasn't immediately in touch with him. I soon learned I was "fair game" for some of his endeavors. I didn't resist primarily because I enjoyed being with him at work or play. He was astute, energetic, a good planner and a visionary.

Our first task together in retirement was being major functionaries in a new organization entitled Americans for Energy Independence. Bud was the president, and I was the executive director. I then worked for him in his unsuccessful campaign to become a U.S. Senator in Virginia. Then we started another non-profit organization working in the preventative medicine field. A significant success in that endeavor was having William J. Casey, the former CIA director, and Dr. Michael E. DeBakey, the world famous heart surgeon, on our board of directors. Our foray into preventive medicine was launched when that medical concept was in its infancy and definitely ahead of its time.

The Chernobyl Disaster

On April 26, 1986, the worst nuclear reactor accident in history occurred at the Chernobyl nuclear power plant near the town of Pripat, Ukraine. Its release of radioactivity produced 400 times more fallout than the Hiroshima bomb blast in August 1945. The deadly plume drifted over parts of the western Soviet Union, Eastern Europe, Northern Europe and light nuclear rain fell on Ireland. More than 336,000 people had to be evacuated.

While on a visit to the USSR in 1989, Admiral Zumwalt arranged a meeting with the Soviet Minister of Health and distinguished academician Andrei I. Vorobiev. Dr. Vorobiev had been the senior medical official in charge of the recovery operations resulting from the fire and explosion of Reactor No. 4 at Chernobyl. He was convinced that a scientific examination of the Chernobyl survivors presented a historic opportunity to assess the possible adverse health effects of low dose radiation. Meetings were convened of world recognized scientific and medical research experts in Bryansk, Russia, in November 1992 and in Houston the following spring. Subsequently, it was determined that a well designed and carefully executed epidemiological project was feasible and worthwhile.

Recognizing the national security implications of this research, and more specifically as it related to the potential hazard of radiation exposure of our nuclear submarine crews, Admiral Zumwalt was able to secure congressional funding to carry out the project. Supervised by the Office of Naval Research, Zumwalt took the lead in establishing the International Consortium for Research on the Health Effects of Radiation (ICRHER). The organization comprised well recognized medical and scientific authorities and their institutions in the United States and abroad. Highly dependable and productive research sites were established in Russia, Ukraine, Belarus and Israel.

Although Zumwalt did not live to learn the results, it was through this organizational framework that the ICRHER coordinated an 11 year-long unique and scientifically reassuring epidemiological research program. In short, the findings indicated that the damage was much less than often stated. As one member of the ICRHER team mentioned at the conclusion of the research, "It is probable that more casualties would result from panic than from the effects of radiation fallout."

Zumwalt fulfilled the organizations intent to serve humankind and rectify a grievous error with his visionary leadership. In his usual manner, he successfully corralled the interests of learned experts and dignitaries in the field of radiation and allied research. He was also successful in dealing with the government bureaucracies that were compounded in this case by the project's international scope. The organization needed behind the scene functionaries to keep things moving properly and to coordinate its actions and events. Bud Zumwalt selected two of his close Marine Corps active duty associates, Col. Michael Spiro and Col. Richard McDonald.

Both men served Admiral Zumwalt as Marine Corps aides when he was the Chief of Naval Operations. Mike became the consortium's executive director, and Dick served as the director of support activities. They were an effective team especially when Dr. William J. Shull, a world-recognized geneticist and Hiroshima/Nagasaki radiation health effects expert at the University of Texas Health Sciences Center, and Dr. Robert W. Day, head of the Fred Hutchinson Cancer Research Center, Baylor College of Medicine and the National Marrow Donor Program signed on. Both researchers became involved due to Zumwalt's outreach and credibility.

In the mid-1990s, he asked me to join the board of directors because of the consortium's growth and need for public communications. The admiral died on January 1, 2000, and later Mike Spiro encouraged me to become the chairman of the group's, Executive Committee. I immediately shrouded myself in the cloak of Forrest Gump and handled the role of giving thoughtful nods of understanding without compromising myself or the consortium. It was a significant experience, and I enjoyed the excursion into medical research.

Pentagon 9/11

September 11, 2001, cast the United States again into a warrior role but in an unusual situation. The United States was attacked for the first time in 60 years, this time by the radical Muslim terrorist group al-Qaeda in its quest for world domination as annunciated by their leader Osama bin Laden. The 9/11 atrocities killed 2,603 in New York and destroyed the iconic 110-storied Twin Towers of Manhattan's World Trade Center. Forty more were killed when the hijacked United Airlines Flight 93 crashed near Shanksville, Pa., and 184 perished when American Airlines Flight 77 crashed into the Pentagon building in Arlington, Va. less than five miles from Washington, D. C.

I was playing golf with Bob Seal at the Army-Navy Country Club about 10 miles from the Pentagon. When we started the first nine, we were told that an airplane had crashed into one of the Twin Towers in New York. Bob and I joshed about an Army Air Corps plane that accidentally hit a New York City high rise during World War II. Bob had been an Air Force fighter pilot, and we kidded about the dangers modern skyscrapers pose to flying. As we finished the ninth hole, a concerned golfer yelled to us as he hurried to the parking lot that a second plane had hit the other tower. Immediately we chorused, "This is no accident!"

As we moved on to the 10th tee, we were informed that the Pentagon had been hit by a commercial airplane. I was in the tee box swinging a driver, when I stopped and asked Bob, "What are we doing here?" We were soon heading home. On arriving I found Zum still mumbling about the situation. She had gone to the commissary, our military grocery store, at Ft. Myer, less than a half mile from the Pentagon. She said she was shopping and filling her cart when she heard the roar of a jet and thought the plane was pretty close to the ground. Then there was a loud boom. Within a minute, a stern voice blared over the public address system to evacuate the commissary immediately and depart the Ft Myer base. Zum said nobody hesitated and seemed to realize it wasn't a drill. When she left Fort Myer, state and local police were already on Washington Boulevard and other surrounding gateways directing traffic away from the Pentagon.

I called the Chief of Navy Information's office to check on their situation. No one answered my call. The office was situated on the Middle Ring in the Pentagon's West Wedge. I later learned that the West Wedge was the point of impact for American Airlines Flight 77. The crash demolished the two outside rings, and the CHINFO spaces collapsed about an hour later. Fortunately, all their personnel had been safely evacuated. I was concerned about all 26,000 people in the Pentagon. But I had close friends there in the public affairs business, especially the CHINFO, Rear Adm. Steve Pietropaoli. Steve told me later he was at his desk when he heard the explosion and rumblings. He got up to look out his large window and saw the window bulge an inch without shattering. At the time of crash, the West Wedge renovation had been almost completed, and his staff was moving back into their office spaces. The windows were newly fabricated, high technology safety glass or plastic manufactured to withstand a test equal to what had just been experienced.

I followed the development of the Pentagon 9/11 story as it unfolded and was impressed by how well groups from different sectors responded and meshed to accomplish the mission of quelling the fire, evacuating personnel (some badly injured), providing first aid and keeping a sense of relative calm with organized procedures. People from federal, state, county and local law enforcement groups including the Pentagon police force were providing care and control. Fire departments and rescue squads from surrounding areas and local hospital staff members were brought in to assist as the Pentagon's clinic organized it own triage. Heroism and acts beyond the call of duty were not restricted to military personnel. Men and women of the Armed Forces were expected to assist particularly with rescuing disabled employees and directing them to safety. Relying on their training, they acquitted themselves well.

Donald Kuney, the Pentagon Maintenance Team Supervisor, arrived at the scene after the crash and was persuasive enough to gain entrance to engineering spaces, so he could shut down valves to prevent further explosions that would have devastated the entire building.

I knew the high importance of training in the military. Exercises and drills are vital to instill what to do in emergencies, so when the real thing happens and "IT IS NOT A DRILL," valuable routines are followed. The Pentagon's 9/11 experience proved the value of police, fire and rescue elements expending effort on exercises and drills.

I was impressed by the Pentagon's disaster response but knew that much of the full story was not told. I gathered a small group of public affairs veterans, and we formed a company, Admiralty Productions, Incorporated, to produce the Pentagon 9/11 story. Joining the effort are Joel Ratner, a talented friend who has been involved in all aspects of television production and is our key person; Al Shackelford, my Navy friend and public affairs officer, who is a lawyer; and Mike Dickerson, a film writer and retired Army public affairs colonel, who teaches journalism at George Mason University and has considerable experience in Hollywood productions. It is a compatible group. We have succeeded in taping some outstanding interviews about the event and established excellent relations with the Pentagon. However, after three years we have not succeeded in finding adequate funding for the endeavor. It remains a great story and should be told.

Flying High with a Former Kamikaze Pilot

Being involved in the Navy Memorial project certainly provided numerous interesting opportunities to meet a variety of people. There were presidents, politicians, Foreign Service professionals and leaders from many sectors of our society and from other lands. I encountered many veterans because of their service affiliations and interest in the Memorial.

It was a fascinating experience to become acquainted with a former enemy, a naval veteran and aviator in the Japanese Imperial Navy who became a Kamikaze. Kaoru Hasegawa was a 1944 Japanese Naval Academy graduate and a year later completed flight training. He was promoted to Lieutenant (Junior Grade) and became the commander of the 405th Bomber Squadron. The unit was comprised of 12 new Ginga land based bombers that were code named Frances in U.S. military vernacular.

On May 25, 1945, his squadron was assigned to attack U.S. Navy ships operating off Okinawa south of Japan. Hasegawa's aircraft was the only one in the squadron to successfully reach the target area while the others turned back because of weather or other difficulties. That morning he was making a run on the battleship USS *West Virginia* and was shot down by the destroyer USS *Callaghan*. His craft crashed into the sea between the two ships. Callaghan's commanding officer, Cmdr. Charles M. Bertholf, realizing there were no other enemy contacts on the radar and seeing Japanese crewmen hanging onto the wings of the downed aircraft, ordered a boat to be put into the water to rescue them. Hasegawa was one of the struggling survivors. That evening he was transferred to the USS New Mexico and taken to Guam where he was hospitalized for two weeks. From there he was sent to Hawaii for further hospitalization and finally transferred to a prisoner of war camp.

He was returned to Japan in November 1946. Then he resumed his education, graduated and entered a family business, Rengo Co., Ltd., a manufacturer of corrugated paper packing materials. Hasegawa moved up the corporate ladder to become the firm's CEO and chair of its board of directors.

Hasegawa carried with him a concern about the destroyer that had rescued him. In the early 1990s, he contacted a retired Navy intelligence officer, Capt. William C. Horn, who readily found the follow-up information for him. Horn connected him with the Callaghan's reunion group and told him that about two weeks after the rescue, the Callaghan was sunk at Okinawa by a Kamikaze and lost 47 personnel. The survivors met biannually and invited Hasegawa to one of their meetings.

A cordial relationship resulted, and the Kamikaze pilot attended the reunions until his death in 2002. I met Hasegawa at his first reunion meeting in 1995 at the U.S. Navy Memorial, and we developed a good friendship. He enjoyed telling the story, but about his only recollection of his time in the Callaghan was lying on the destroyer's deck and passing in and out of consciousness. He remembered being guarded by a tall, blue-eyed blond sailor. He related that detail when he spoke to the group in Washington.

Two years later, at the ship's reunion in Rochester, Minn., a grey haired Dr. Romaine J. Buzzetti approached him. "Mr. Hasegawa, I am that tall blue-eyed blond sailor who guarded you 52 years ago," Buzzetti said. "I think this may be your watch that I kept as a "war prize" with the captain's permission. Do you recognize this watch?"

Hasegawa recognized his old aviator's watch. Two years later at the next reunion, he returned the favor to Dr. Buzzetti by presenting him with a new Rolex wristwatch. Unlike the pilot's, the Rolex was self-winding.

Another story the Japanese pilot liked to relate was how after several reunion meetings, he was bewildered at the number of sailors who claimed they were in the boat that rescued him. He had verified that such a boat normally had a crew of three: the coxswain, the engineer and the bow hook. So many Callaghan veterans he met at previous parties had identified themselves as being in the rescue crew, he said he was flattered by the reception he had received by the boat's immense crew. Additionally, he related that his plane must have been completely riddled by bullets, because so many sailors he had met identified themselves as the one who shot him down. He always told those stories with a delightful twinkle in his eyes. Sailors must be alike in all navies.

For the Navy Memorial Foundation, the interface with Hasegawa-san resulted in an addition to the Foundation's slate of programs. A foreign student exchange effort began, initially with had eight high school students from Japan and the United States spending two weeks together (a week in each country) learning of the cultures, histories and mores of each country. Visits were scheduled to significant museums, establishments and edifices typically identified with each country.

Each nation had its own selection process for its participants. In the U.S., the Junior Naval Reserve Officers Training Corps (JNROTC) was designated to select the best eight students nationwide. The JNROTC conducted an essay contest to get the most articulate youngsters involved. Although an official follow-up program was not instituted, it was learned that several of the U.S. youngsters had done well in post high school endeavors. The U.S. Naval Academy, Naval Reserve Officer Training Corps and enlisted programs have all benefited. The program was not designed to enhance recruiting into the naval services, but their early association with the naval forces created a heightened interest for them. Costs for the program were high for the limited number of students involved and required considerable work from our staff and volunteers. It was definitely a quality program. The Rengo Company underwrote the Japanese costs, and the Henry Crown family of Chicago contributed to help defray the U.S. participation expense. When Hasegawa retired from Rengo, so did Japanese interest in the program, which was the determining factor in discontinuing the program after four successful years.

More Instant Tradition

In late May 1994, the USS *John R. Craig* (DD885) reunion group of, which I was a member, met at the Navy Memorial, and I addressed them. I welcomed them to the memorial and introduced another alumnus of *Craig*, Adm. J. M. "Mike" Boorda, the Chief of Naval Operations. As part of my introduction, I told the audience that the CNO's flag was flying from the Memorial's mast and how it was a magnificent sight as well as a great honor. Boorda responded that the CNO's flag would always fly from the Navy Memorial, and it has from that good day until now.

Taps For "The Z"

Every weekend, whenever we were at home and weather permitting, Bud Zumwalt and I played tennis, usually at the court next to his home in North Arlington or at his son Jim's Sport's Center in Herndon, Va. At times Jim would join us, sometimes with his girl friend Karin Gufuni. On a September Sunday in 1999, Bud, Jim and I had a good work out. As the three of us were leaving the court, Bud told me that he and Mouza were leaving on the following Wednesday. They were going to Raleigh, N.C. to spend time with their daughter Mouzetta and her husband, Ron Weathers. He said he wasn't feeling well and thought maybe a change of scenery might help. He planned to be back in about a week. That was the last time I saw my good friend.

Within a few days after he departed, I was notified that Bud had been admitted to the Duke University Hospital. Another few days brought the news that he had surgery for the removal of a lung. He had been diagnosed as having mesothelioma, a cancer associated with exposure to asbestos. I also learned that few survived the disease. His post-op care became frustrating but understandable to me. He could have no visitors except immediate family, and the restriction was closely monitored. Bud had many friends, and a parade of visitors would have unacceptably taxed his energies. But I would have been there in a flash if there had been the opportunity to see him.

I assumed the watch to keep his old "Mini-Staff" and a list of other close friends apprised of Bud's condition with Email and telephone calls. I had scheduled a Navy Memorial tour to Australia for the millennium, so we could be some of the first to usher in the year 2000 but considered canceling for Zum and me because of Bud's plight. We finally opted to go to Australia. There was nothing we could do to help him, and the millennium group was depending on us to pop the first cork for the next 1,000 years from Sydney's beautiful harbor.

Robbie Robertson, who lived in Durham, took the watch to keep people informed about Bud. The Admiral died on New Year's Day, a few hours into the 21st Century. The "Warrior" was laid to rest at the Naval Academy Cemetery and Columbarium in a beautiful plot atop a hill overlooking the Academy and the Chesapeake Bay. From there he can keep his eye on the Midshipmen and the quality view of the sailboats that ply and brighten the Bay. His large memorial marker identifies him as "REFORMER." Bud did not think of himself as a reformer when he was doing it. The media gave him that title, and I guess he liked it.

The funeral service was done elegantly and eloquently in the Naval Academy Chapel. Retired Marine Corps Col. Mike Spiro was his aide again, escorting "The Admiral" from the Raleigh-Durham area to Annapolis and caring for the needs of the family. Vice Adm. Emmett Tidd was in charge. There were four eulogists: President Bill Clinton, Chief of Naval Operations Adm. Jay L. Johnson, Ambassador (United Nations Security Council) Richard Schifter and Ambassador Philip Lader (Court of St. James [United Kingdom]). From differing perspectives, each speaker eloquently described Bud Zumwalt's career and character. The rest of us in the Mini-Staff were honorary pallbearers as designated by Bud. We walked the mile from the chapel to the interment site. At the gravesite, I helped move Paul Nitze in his wheelchair forward to pay his last respects, and I sensed his grief. He pulled my arm down so that that he could tell me something, "You know, Bill, this is not the way it was supposed to be. Bud was to be my eulogist." He was depressed, and I was not communicative at the time and only muttered, "I understand."

Ambassador Lader who spoke at the service was a scholar, successful businessman and founder of Renaissance Weekends, family oriented, non-partisan retreats designed to gather innovative leaders from diverse fields for relaxation and exchange of ideas.

Bud and his family participated in several retreats and became friends with the Lader family. Dick Shifter was Deputy Ambassador to the United Nations, serving under Ambassador Jean Kirkpatrick, and Bud's principal advisor during his brief political career.

The Zumwalt family had a reception for the large group of friends and admirers who gathered from all sectors of the country at the Academy's Officers' & Faculty Club to close "Z's" career.

After Bud's death, I prepared a letter to the Secretary of the Navy, Richard Danzig to be signed by Paul Nitze recommending a Navy warship be named for Bud. My intention was to have an *Arleigh Burke* Class guided missile destroyer named for him. I had the letter hand delivered to the Pentagon and Emailed a copy to Capt. Brian Cullin, the Secretary's Special Assistant for Public Affairs. I suggested to Brian that he "birddog" the letter and in the process, when discussing it with the Secretary, mention that its signer, Burke, should also be considered to have a ship named for him as well for being the most productive Secretary in the Navy's history.

Within a day, Brian called saying, "Two homeruns. The Secretary will do the Zumwalt deed and also do a ship for Mr. Nitze. He was embarrassed that he didn't think of Nitze long ago. He agrees with your assessment." Within a couple months the SECNAV held an announcement ceremony in the Pentagon for the naming of the USS *Paul H. Nitze* (DDG 94). Then on July 4, 2000 in New York Harbor aboard the aircraft carrier USS *John F. Kennedy* (CV 67), President Bill Clinton announced a new class of ship, a large destroyer type, would be named the USS *Elmo. R. Zumwalt, Jr.* (DDG 21) to honor the former CNO and usher in the 21st Century.

About two months after the Bud's burial, I was in Annapolis on business and then went to the Academy to visit the burial site. His grave was in good order, and as I departed I thought how it was the first time I had visited Bud Zumwalt without coming away with a half dozen things to do. I shared that thought with his son Jim on my return to McLean. Jim replied, "Did you really check out everything? He's been known to leave messages all over the place."

Before we had departed for Australia millennium trip, I had sent an Email to Bud via his son Jim. A few months later at a luncheon, I was informed of what had transpired, In the Email I explained my situation with the millennium celebration, missed "whipping his ass" on the tennis court and longed for the day when I could give him a big hug because I had never done that before. With his wife Karin standing beside him, Jim read the Email to him. In his weakened condition, Bud responded by smiling, nodding affirmatively and whispering, "My best friend."

Knowing Bud Zumwalt's enormous universe of friends included dignitaries, celebrities, associates, classmates and shipmates, I have taken that accolade with a great deal of humility knowing his affections extended deeply to many. I had casually referred to Bud Zumwalt as my "best friend." The kids had even fondly referred to him as "Uncle Bud" echoing my close relationship and respect for him. Reflecting on my friendship with him, he has been gone a full decade, and I continue to miss him, his sage advice, suggested solutions, analysis of foreign news, good humor, positive outlook and appreciation of my masterfully constructed "Martillaries" (my derivative of martinis).

USS Paul H. Nitze (DDG-94)

Paul Nitze was pleased and proud to have a ship named for him and especially to have it done while he was still alive and could enjoy some of the shipbuilding process. Normally, individuals are not honored in the Navy's ship naming protocol until after their deaths. Senator Carl Vinson was one of the first living persons to receive the priviledge, followed by Admiral Arleigh Burke, President Jimmy Carter and President George H. W. Bush.

With Bud's death, I was moved into the position of being the liaison between Nitze and the Navy Department in the manner of monitoring affairs related to him and being of personal assistance. I was able to help his wife Leezee Porter, who had little understanding of the Navy or the milestones in building a ship. However, as an intelligent lady and quick study, she moved smoothly into the flow, established contacts readily and all the time took care of Paul. Zum and I were invited several times to join Paul and Leezee for dinner.

One evening we celebrated one of Paul's birthdays. A significant guest was Don Rumsfeld who declared, "I have a story to tell you, Mr. Nitze. I read that in 1947 President Truman asked James Forrestal to be the first Secretary of Defense and how he was pleased to offer him the position. Mr. Forrestal replied that he was flattered but didn't think he was qualified. "Truman stopped him and said, 'I want you there.' Forrestal insisted that he needed to consult with someone before accepting the position. Harry Truman, becoming perturbed, asked, 'Well, who would that be?' He was told, 'Paul Nitze.' Truman agreed.

"Thirty years later I was summoned by President Ford and presented with the same offer, to be the Secretary of Defense. I hesitated and then replied that I wanted to talk with someone about it before I make a decision. Jerry Ford asked, 'Well, who would that be?' The answer was 'Paul Nitze.' I did not know of the Forrestal episode until recently when I was reading his biography. Now that is a great story about the respect, trust and confidence people have had in you over the years. Not only Jim Forrestal and me but two presidents."

Rumsfield's statements were followed by applause, cheers and a big grin by the "birthday boy" Paul Nitze.

Later another dinner was held to meet the prospective commanding officer of the USS *Paul Nitze*, Cmdr. Michael Hegarty. On another occasion the prospective executive officer, Lt. Cdr. Stephan Murray was introduced. The two outstanding officers were "Mustangs," (former enlisted men) with submarine backgrounds. It was a pleasure for me to work with them throughout the pre-commissioning period and for Zum and me to get to know their families.

Paul Nitze and Leezee visited the Bath Iron Works Shipyard in Bath, Maine, for the keel laying ceremony. It is unusual for keel laying ceremonies to be staged in modern day shipbuilding. The event symbolically links new ships to those of yore. Only special occasions merit the effort. But it was done for Paul Nitze and was certainly a special occasion as evidenced by his enthusiasm. He met with yard workers, and they were delighted to meet him as one of the few individuals to have a ship named for them while they were living. During the ceremony, a piece of deck plating inscribed with his initials "PHN" and the date was welded to a main member at the ship's bottom.

Among the many things Paul Nitze brought to the Navy when he was Secretary was modular shipbuilding. He introduced it, pushed it into the building of a new shipyard at Pascagoula, Miss., and then pressured other existing shipyards to modernize by adopting modular production.

The ship's formal launching ceremony came several months later. At the observance's banquet about 15 minutes before being seated, I was told that I was to be introduced to describe what it was like working for Paul Nitze. Fortunately, Leezee Porter had told me a few weeks ahead that it might happen. But I hadn't heard from the hosting shipbuilder, so I was without prepared remarks. It undoubtedly proved to be a better approach, because I enjoyed myself more casually talking about Paul Nitze and his accomplishments as the Navy's Secretary. I congratulated the Navy for its wisdom in naming of the ship for him. I concluded by saying the country was fortunate. It would have the assurance for the next 40 years or so that the spirit of Paul H. Nitze, embodied in DDG-94, would cruise the oceans questing to make the world a better place to live.

The shipyard superintendent thanked me for my remarks and announced that everybody could go home since Bill Thompson had already said everything he planned to say. Leezee and Paul also thanked me and were pleased as were Cmdr. Hegarty, Lt. Cmdr. Murray and Zum. The next day Leezee cracked the traditional bottle of champagne on the ship's bow; whistles blew, balloons and confetti were released. The Navy Band played "Anchors Aweigh." It was a great sight, especially seeing Paul Nitze happily beaming, smiling and waving to the crowd.

Paul died on October 13, 2004, about six months short of the ship's commissioning ceremony at the Norfolk Naval Base. Memorial services for him were conducted at the Washington's beautiful National Cathedral with a large assemblage of diplomatic and national security luminaries. Symbolically, about 75 members of the *Nitze's* shipbuilding crew had traveled to Washington from Maine to pay homage to that great man, their ship's namesake, whom they had met personally. A reception followed at the

Metropolitan Club. The next Sunday, Paul was buried next to his first wife Phyllis at the Nitze Farm in Maryland on the Potomac River. It was a private interment attended by family, Zum and me. I ensured that the U.S. Navy was represented at the Cathedral ceremony and the burial site. Navy sideboys and a color guard formalized the honors held at the cathedral, and a Navy/Marine Corps color guard and bugler for "Taps" were at the farm.

The *Nitze's* concluding commissioning ceremony was done on a cold, rainy day with a swift breeze blowing from Hampton Roads. Despite the bad weather, it was a joyous occasion as Navy commissionings are pleasant, inspirational events. The ship was brought to life, formally manned by her crew and the watch that will last the lifetime of the ship was set. As a part of the ritual, I was honored to present the long glass, a 24-inch long, one barrel telescope like those used in days long prior to electronic radar. However, it remains highly symbolic as the badge of authority for the Officer Of the Deck, In Port. As I made the presentation, I said, "In the spirit of Paul Nitze, I present this long glass to you. Good hunting and good fortune."

About six months later, Zum and I were the guests of Capt. Hegarty, and we cruised in the *Nitze* to Yorktown about 30 miles from the Norfolk Naval Base. I was thrilled to observe the young officers and enlisted personnel on the bridge and other units doing their jobs with Capt. Hegarty in command. I was ready to re-up; just get me to the nearest recruiting office.

Strong, following winds carried Zum and me into the safe haven of a good harbor. We smile when we recall our first trip together in a rumble seat. It was the beginning of a most extraordinary journey. Along the way, a Midwest youngster earned flag rank and the responsibility for the Navy's internal and public information. The Navy launched us upon the seas of the world and gave us a depth of unforgettable friends and life experiences. Our family, numbering 16 and growing, is healthy and prospering—good citizens all. Our legacy is the performance of public affairs excellence as befits the U.S. Navy's proud heritage and the establishment of a proactive internal information program consistent with General George Washington's proclamation, "An informed troop is a good troop."

As for the Navy Memorial, Zum and I have proudly observed the facility being absorbed into the culture of our nation's capital. It constantly reminds all that the U.S. Navy was integral to the history and development of our still young capital city as well as our republic. It continues to fulfill its credo as one of the "Crown Jewels" of Pennsylvania Avenue.

Zum and I suggest the American automobile industry consider a revival of the rumble seat. It proved a great way to get a relationship started.

Bill

Mom and I, 1923, Escanaba MI.

Don and I, 1926.

Betty, Bill, and Don,
Escanaba 1929.

With Don, growing up, Green Bay WI
(about 1935).

Naval Aviation Cadet Bill Thompson, 1943.

Dorothy Elizabeth zum Buttel, "Zum" to me then and forever and the Sweetheart of a Sigma Chi at Wabash College 1945.

Wedding Bells, Sheboygan, July 11, 1945.

Gramp Woods and my Mother at our wedding.

Daughter Stevii and our family sedan.

A home aborning, "Thumbs" Thompson in doorway, Guam 1947.

Home Sweet Home, Zum and Stevii enjoying the view from Commander Marianas Hill, Guam 1947-48.

USS Midway
(CVA 41)
Oct 49 to Dec 51

USS John R.Craig
(DD 885)
July 52 to Apr 53

Stevii, Craig with newborn Brian, 1958, Coronado, CA.

A young Senator John F. Kennedy is standing between me and my dinner at the kick-off for filming of the movie "PT 109," San Diego, 1956.

Visiting former President Harry Truman at his library, Independence, MO 1961. From right: LT Paul Leighton, aide to Commandant Ninth Naval District; Mr. Truman; RADM John Higgins, Commandant Ninth Naval District; Bill Thompson; and, significantly, the unknown Naval Reservist from Kansas City who arranged the event.

Attending an official function at Great Lakes with RADM Ira Nunn and Zum.

Giving away my little girl, who
seems happier about this than I,
at the Navy Chapel, Washington
DC, August 20, 1966.

The Thompson clan at Stevii's
reception

Secretary of the Navy and staff, March 10, 1967. Seated, from left: CAPT Worth H. Bagley, executive assistant and aide; Honorable Paul H. Nitze, Secretary of the Navy; COL Ross T. Dwyer, Jr., Marine Corps aide. Standing, from left: CAPT Bill Thompson, special assistant for public affairs; LCDR Richard D. Nagle, assistant to admin aide; CAPT Horace B. Robertson, special counsel; CDR Harry D. Train, II, admin aide; Ms Margaret S. Martin, private secretary; CAPT Enser W. Cole, special assistant; John Rhinelander, special civilian assistant; ENS Craig R. Whitney, assistant to special civilian assistant.

VADM E. R. (Bud) Zumwalt, Commander Naval Forces Vietnam, and I cruising Mekong River near Saigon, April 1970.

CAPT Stansfield Turner bids me farewell from SECNAV's office, 1970, and departure for Harvard Business School.

My first grandson Will is the center of attention; grandchild number two, Stephanie, is swell on the way. 1970.

Saigon, May 1971 - a fresh-caught flag officer. Photo by Craig Whitney, New York Times Saigon Bureau Chief.

Zum and Stevii "Frocking" the admiral with Secretary John Chafee overseeing.

My official photo as CHINFO

In January 1973 I planted a Green Bay Packer pennant at the South Pole, Antarctica. The pennant now hangs in my office at home.

Opposite, from top: - CHINFO's outer-sanctum, 1974. From left: LT Ed Darrow, Aide; Marie Cuccinotta, my secretary; CDR Howard Matson, Executive Assistant; CAPT David Cooney, Deputy CHINFO; Janey Diamond, secretary to the Deputy; Chief Yeoman Mel Wylie . . . an effective crew.

Great day! My aide LT Kendell Pease and I flanking Seaman Craig Thompson at his completion of boot camp, Naval Training Center Memphis, TN. 1972.

Bud Zumwalt and I are honored by a visit from Bob Hope, 1974.

Yucking it up at a reception with CNO Bud Zumwalt.

Former CHINFO deputies, from left: Larry Hamilton, Tom Coldwell, Ralph Slawson, Bill Steirman, John Dewey, Bill Thompson. Assembled on the occassion of the farewell to CHINFO Jack Garrow, April 18, 1986

Sculptor Stan Bleifeld and I help unload
Lone Sailor Statue for positioning on Navy
Memorial Plaza, September 1987.

The Lone Sailor statue on watch at the US
Navy Memorial.

Former Navy Journalist Willard Scott in one of his frequent NBC "Today Show" telecasts from Navy Memorial. Umbrella provided by son Craig much to consternation of NBC directors in New York.

Balloons, flags, and a flyover by Navy aircraft were all part of the Memorial's opening ceremonies on October 13, 1987.

The Navy Memorial as it looks today.

Staff of the Navy Memorial Foundation, 1987. Bottom to top, rows left to right: First: Bob Jones, Martie Klee, Karen DuBois, Dan Aragona, Jim Nemer, Tom Coldwell. Second: Stevii Graves, Lone Sailor, Paul Haley, Renato Pascual. Third: Bill Thompson, B. J. Andrews, Hope McCloud. Fourth: Mac McCloud, unidentifed temporary. Fifth: Jay Hood.

A few "old" friends, from left: "Buck" Wilhide, Merle McBain, Bob Jones, Ruth Donohue, Bill Thompson, Bob Mereness.

With President George H. W. Bush at Navy Memorial December 7, 1992.

The CHINFO Leadership Group, January 13, 2005. From Left, Rear Admirals Greg Slavonic, Tom Jurkowsky, Kendell Pease, Bill Thompson, Craig Quigley, Terry McCreary, Bob Ravitz, Jack Garrow, Steve Pietropaoli, Jim Finkelstein.

Artist Leo Irrera and I at the dedication of Navy Memorial plaque at General MacArthur Park, Inchon, South Korea on June 22, 2000.

With former Navy corpsman Bill Cosby, at the 2010 "Lone Sailor" Awards dinner at the Navy Memorial, September 15. Cosby was an awardee.

Craig and I in Nome, AL where we embarked to cruise the Bering Sea to Petropavlovsk in Russia's Kamchatka Peninsula.

Paul Nitze and I helped Navy
Memorial present "Lone Sailor" award to
Don Rumsfeld, May, 2002.

March 5, 2005, upon commissioning
of the USS Nitze (DDG 94). I participated
in a ceremonial hand-over of the
traditional symbol of authority, a
long glass, to the ensign standing the
first watch as officer-of-the-deck.

The Thompson Clan, now numbering 20, Christmas 2009. From left: (top row) Braden Graves, Zach Thompson, Jay Thompson, Randy Graves, Pat Suave, Dorothy Thompson, Bill Thompson, Brain Thompson, Stevii Graves, Will Graves, Kathyn Graves, Alex Filmer, Melissa Suave; (middle row) Jack Thompson, Paige Graves, Connor Graves; (front row) Chris Thompson, Stefanie Graves, Kelsey Suave, and Craig Thompson.

When considering retiring, it is best to have a trophy wife to bring with you.

Appendix
Navy Ranks and Commonly Used Acronyms

ACTOV	Accelerated Turnover To Vietnam
Adm.	Admiral – ADM
ADMINO	Administrative Officer
AFIS	Armed Forces Information School
AGER	Auxiliary General Environmental Research
AIRPAC	Naval Air Forces, Pacific Fleet
ALNAV	All Navy
APIO	Assistant Public Information Officer
ASD (PA)	Assistant Secretary of Defense for Public Affairs
ATP	Advanced Tactical Publication
BM	Boatswain's Mate
BOQ	Bachelor Officer's Quarters
BuPers	Bureau of Naval Personnel – BUPERS
Capt.	Captain – CAPT
Cdr.	Commander – CDR
CHINFO	Chief Of Information
CHINFO	Chief Of Information Office
CIB	Combined Information Bureau
CIB	Command Information Bureau
CIC	Combat Information Center
CINC	Commander-in-Chief
CINCEUR	Commander-in-Chief, U.S. Forces, Europe
CINCLANTLFLT	Commander-in-Chief, Atlantic Fleet
CINCPACFLT	Commander-in-Chief, Pacific Fleet
CINCPACFLTPIO	Commander-in-Chief, Pacific Fleet, Public Information Officer
CINCUSNAVEUR	Commander-in-Chief, U.S. Naval Forces, Europe
CMCPO	Command Master Chief Petty Officer
COMNAVSEA	Commander, Naval Sea Systems Command
CNFJ	Commander, U.S. Naval Forces, Japan
CNO	Chief Of Naval Operations
CNO SitRep	Chief Of Naval Operations Situation Report
CNP	Chief, Bureau of Naval Personnel
CNP	Chief Of Navy Personnel
CNRTC	Commander, Naval Reserve Training Command
CO	Commanding Officer
COMCARDIV FOUR	Commander, Carrier Division Four
COMCRUDESPAC	Commander, Cruisers Destroyers Pacific Fleet
COMELEVENTHFLT	Commander, Eleventh Fleet
COMFIRSTFLT	Commander, First Fleet
COMFOUR	Commandant, Fourth Naval District
COMNAVAIRPAC	Commander, Naval Air Force, US Pacific Fleet
COMNAVFORV	Commander, Naval Forces, Vietnam
COMNAVMAR	Commander, Naval Forces, Marianas
COMNINE	Commandant, Ninth Naval District

COMPHIBTRALANT	Commander, Amphibious Training Command, Atlantic Fleet
COMSEVENTHFLT	Commander, Seventh Fleet
COMSIXTHFLT	Commander, Sixth Fleet
CoS	Chief Of Staff
CPO	Chief Petty Officer
CRUDESPAC	Cruiser-Destroyer Force, Pacific Fleet
CWO	Chief Warrant Officer
DACOWITS	Defense Advisory Council on Women in the Services
DCoS	Deputy Chief of Staff
DD	Destroyer
DESA	Destroyer Escort Sailors Association
DMZ	Demarcation Zone
DMZ	Demilitarized Zone
DOD	Department Of Defense
DSM	Distinguished Service Medal
EA	Executive Assistant
Ens.	Ensign
FCPO	Petty Officer First Class
FDLS	Forward Deployed Logistics Ship
FHTNC	Fleet Home Town News Center
FIRSTFLT	First Fleet
Flagsec	Flag Secretary – Flag SEC
Fleet Adm.	Fleet Admiral – FADM
FPO	Force Personnel Officer
FRA	Fleet Reserve Association
GQ	General Quarters
GQ OOD	General Quarters Officer of the Deck
ISA	International Security Affairs
JOOD	Junior Officer Of the Deck
LCI	Landing Craft, Infantry
LST	Landing Ship Tank
Lt.	Lieutenant -- LT
Lt. (JG)	Lieutenant Junior Grade – LTJG
Lt. Cdr.	Lieutenant Commander – LCDR
Lt. Gen.	Lieutenant General – LTG
MAG	Military Assistance Group
Maj. Gen.	Major General -- MG
MCPO	Master Chief Petty Officer
MCPON	Master Chief Petty Officer of the Navy
NAS	Naval Air Station
NAVSUP	Naval Supply Systems Command
NEL	Navy Electronics Laboratory
NESC	Naval Electronics System Command [Now SPAWAR]
NIRA	Navy Internal Relations Activity
NROTC	Naval Reserve Officer Training Corps
NRPAC 9-2	Naval Reserve Public Relations Unit 9-2
NRTC	Naval Reserve Training Command
NWC	Navy War College
OCS	Officer Candidate School
OGU	Outgoing Unit
OIC	Officer In Charge
OOD	Officer Of the Deck in Port and Underway

OPNAV	Two meanings: Office of the Chief of Naval Operations, or, Operational Navy
OTC	Officer In Tactical Command
PAO	Public Affairs Officer
PCF	Fast Patrol Craft
PCS	Permanent Change Of Station
PHIBPAC	Amphibious Forces, Pacific Fleet
PIO	Public Information Office or Officer
PO3	Petty Officer Third Class
POAC	Pentagon Officer's Athletic Club
POD	Plan Of the Day
PRITAC	Primary Tactical Network
Quarters For Muster	Morning Quarters [For Muster, Inspection and Instruction]
Rear Adm.	Rear Admiral – RADM
SCPO	Senior Chief Petty Officer
SECNAV	Secretary of the Navy
SITE	Shipboard Information, Training and Education [system]
SOPA	Senior Officer Present Afloat
Space A	Space Available – Space-A
SPAWAR	Space & Naval Warfare Systems Command
TAD	Temporary Additional Duty
TAR	Training and Administration of Reserves
UNREP	Underway Replenishing
USAF	United States Air Force
USMACV	United States Military Advisory Command, Vietnam
USNR	United States Naval Reserve
VCNO	Vice Chief of Naval Operations
Vice Adm.	Vice Admiral – VADM
WestPac	Western Pacific (beyond Pearl Harbor) – WESTPAC
XO	Executive Officer
YNC	Chief Yeoman

Made in the USA
Charleston, SC
13 June 2011